America's Strategy in a Changing World

International Security Readers

Strategy and Nuclear Deterrence (1984)
Military Strategy and the Origins of the First World War (1985)
Conventional Forces and American Defense Policy (1986)
The Star Wars Controversy (1986)
Naval Strategy and National Security (1988)
Military Strategy and the Origins of the First World War, rev. and exp. ed. (1991)
—published by Princeton University Press

Soviet Military Policy (1989)
Conventional Forces and American Defense Policy, rev. ed. (1989)
Nuclear Diplomacy and Crisis Management (1990)
The Cold War and After: Prospects for Peace (1991)
America's Strategy in a Changing World (1992)
—published by The MIT Press

America's Strategy in a Changing World

AN *International*
Security READER

EDITED BY
Sean M. Lynn-Jones
and Steven E. Miller

THE MIT PRESS
CAMBRIDGE, MASSACHUSETTS
LONDON, ENGLAND

The contents of this book were first published in *International Security* (ISSN 0162–2889), a publication of The MIT Press under the sponsorship of the Center for Science and International Affairs at Harvard University. Except as otherwise noted, copyright in each article is owned jointly by the President and Fellows of Harvard College and of the Massachusetts Institute of Technology.

Robert Jervis, "The Future of World Politics: Will It Resemble the Past?" *IS* 16, no. 3 (Winter 1991/92); Terry L. Deibel, "Strategies Before Containment: Patterns for the Future," *IS* 16, no. 4 (Spring 1992); Robert J. Art, "A Defensible Defense: America's Grand Strategy After the Cold War," *IS* 15, no. 4 (Spring 1991); Ted Hopf, "Managing Soviet Disintegration: A Demand for Behavioral Regimes," *IS* 17, no. 1 (Summer 1992); Charles A. Kupchan and Clifford A. Kupchan, "Concerts, Collective Security, and the Future of Europe," *IS* 16, no. 1 (Summer 1991); Richard K. Betts, "Systems for Peace or Causes of War? Collective Security, Arms Control, and the New Europe," *IS* 17, no. 1 (Summer 1992) © 1992 by Westview Press, Inc. Reprinted with permission. F. Stephen Larrabee, "Down and Out in Warsaw and Budapest: Eastern Europe and East-West Migration," *IS* 16, no. 4 (Spring 1992); I.M. Destler and Michael Nacht, "Beyond Mutual Recrimination: Building a Solid U.S.-Japan Relationship in the 1990s," *IS* 15, no. 3 (Winter 1990/91); Richard K. Herrmann, "The Middle East and the New World Order: Rethinking U.S. Political Strategy After the Gulf War," *IS* 16, no. 2 (Fall 1991); Steven R. David, "Why the Third World Still Matters," *IS* 17, no. 3 (Winter 1992/93); Steve Fetter, "Ballistic Missiles and Weapons of Mass Destruction: What Is the Threat? What Should be Done?" *IS* 16, no. 1 (Summer 1991).

Selection and preface, copyright © 1992 by the President and Fellows of Harvard College and of the Massachusetts Institute of Technology.

Library of Congress Cataloging-in-Publication Data

America's strategy in a changing world : an international security
    reader / edited by Sean M. Lynn-Jones and Steven E. Miller.
        p.   cm. — (An International security reader)
    Includes bibliographical references.
    ISBN 0-262-62085-5
    1. United States—Military policy.   2. United States—Armed
Forces.   I. Lynn-Jones, Sean M.   II. Miller, Steven E.
III. Series.
UA23.A66353   1992
355'.0335'73—dc20

92-25734
CIP

Contents

The Contributors

SEAN M. LYNN-JONES is an Adjunct Research Fellow at the Center for Science and International Affairs, Harvard University, and Consulting Editor of *International Security*. He was the journal's Managing Editor, 1987–91.

STEVEN E. MILLER is Editor of *International Security* and Director of Studies at the Center for Science and International Affairs, Harvard University.

ROBERT JERVIS is Adlai E. Stevenson Professor of International Relations at Columbia University and a member of its Institute of War and Peace Studies.

TERRY L. DEIBEL is Professor of National Strategy at the National War College.

ROBERT J. ART is Christian A. Herter Professor of International Relations at Brandeis University and a Research Associate of Harvard's Center for International Affairs.

TED HOPF is Assistant Professor of Political Science at the University of Michigan.

CHARLES A. KUPCHAN is Assistant Professor of Politics at Princeton University.

CLIFFORD A. KUPCHAN is Foreign Policy Adviser to Congressman Harry Johnston.

RICHARD K. BETTS is Professor of Political Science at Columbia University.

F. STEPHEN LARRABEE is a Senior Analyst in the International Policy Department at RAND in Santa Monica, California.

I.M. DESTLER is Professor at the School of Public Affairs, University of Maryland, and Visiting Fellow at the Institute for International Economics.

MICHAEL NACHT is Dean of the School of Public Affairs, University of Maryland, and was Acting Director of the Harvard Program on U.S.-Japan Relations.

RICHARD K. HERRMANN is an Associate Professor of Political Science and Director of the Program in Foreign Policy Analysis at the Mershon Center for National Security Research at the Ohio State University.

STEVEN R. DAVID is Professor of Political Science at the Johns Hopkins University.

STEVE FETTER is Associate Professor in the School of Public Affairs at the University of Maryland, College Park.

Acknowledgments

The editors gratefully acknowledge the assistance that has made this book possible. A deep debt is owed to all those at the Center for Science and International Affairs (CSIA), Harvard University, who have played an editorial role at *International Security*. Teresa Pelton Johnson, and Stephen J. Stillwell, jr., were indispensable to the preparation of the contents for publication. Robert Art, Michael Desch, John Mearsheimer, and Stephen Van Evera offered helpful suggestions on the selection of articles for this book. Special thanks go to Peggy Kutcher, Julia Slater, and Chandra Sriram at CSIA and to Patrice Baer and Claude Lee at MIT Press for their invaluable help in preparing the volume for publication.

Preface | Sean M. Lynn-Jones and Steven E. Miller

What are the principal threats to American interests? How can they best be defended? What combination of economic, diplomatic, and military instruments should be used to protect and advance those interests? These have always been the central questions for U.S. grand strategy. But answering these questions has become far more difficult as a result of the dramatic international developments of 1989–91. The end of the Cold War and the collapse of Soviet power compel a fundamental rethinking of America's role in the world. The old answers no longer work and the new answers are not yet clear. We hope that this volume will contribute to the debate that is required on these critical issues.

During the Cold War, U.S. grand strategy was guided by a single clear principle: containment of Soviet power. American policymakers sometimes disagreed on the level and nature of the Soviet threat, but generally they felt that it was the paramount international challenge to U.S. interests. America's choice of allies, military deployments, and interventions in the Third World all were driven by concern over the actual or potential influence of the Soviet Union, its primary geopolitical rival. Critics of U.S. policy often called for different levels of military spending or denounced U.S. involvement in particular countries or regions, but most accepted the principle of containing the Soviet Union. This principle dominated American strategy and simplified U.S. policy choices from the late 1940s to the late 1980s.

Between 1989 and 1991 this era of simplicity in American strategy came to an end. As the Berlin Wall crumbled, so too did the Cold War framework for American foreign policy; as the Soviet Union collapsed, so too did the concept of containment. Indeed, by 1992, all the established verities of post-1945 U.S. grand strategy had been called into question. To be sure, some elements of America's Cold War policy—such as NATO—remained in place, but they looked increasingly irrelevant or out of place in a fundamentally different political landscape. Clearly, new answers are necessary, more appropriate to what President Bush termed "the new world order."

In the early 1990s, the United States has begun to debate the outlines of its post–Cold War grand strategy. Following the disintegration of the Soviet Union and the spread of democracy in the former Soviet bloc, most observers and policy-makers agreed that the United States can safely reduce its defense spending, although Congress and the president have disagreed on the type and extent of such cuts. Beyond this, however, there is little agreement on how the United States should adapt to the new international environment. Some commentators have suggested that the United States return to a pre-1945 or even pre-1914 strategy of isolation and aim to stay out of international conflicts. Even those who favor a continuing major international role call for shifting U.S. resources and energy to domestic problems. Some argue for replacing the Cold War mission of containment with an expanded U.S. effort to promote democracy around the globe, while others envision a pivotal global role for the United States as the world's lone superpower and the only possible enforcer of the new international order. As the 1992 presidential election approached, there was not yet a dominant defining concept for America's role in the post–Cold War international order.

Nevertheless, the end of the Cold War has raised basic questions about all of America's international relationships. Most importantly, the United States has been forced to rethink its relations with both its major allies and its former adversaries. In Europe, preserving security may require new institutions and instruments or modifications to NATO, which has lost a principal *raison d'être* with the collapse of the Soviet threat. Some commentators have proposed various systems of collective security or pan-European organizations to ensure Europe's peace. The disintegration of the Soviet Union also requires the United States to devise a policy for relations with the successor republics of the former communist superpower. U.S. and other Western assistance may enable these countries to become stable, economically healthy democracies that will not pose a threat to Western security; if not, chaos and conflict in the eastern half of Europe is sure to command U.S. attention. In East Asia, America's relations with Japan are a critical concern. Many Americans now believe that Japan has become the most important challenger to U.S. (economic) power. Some have even predicted that a U.S.-Japan war is inevitable. With the demise of the Soviet Union, relations between the United States and Japan (which former U.S. Ambassador Mike Mansfield called, even during the Cold War, the "most important bilateral relationship in the world") have become even more significant.

Nor have America's relations with the Third World been unaffected by the passing of East-West rivalry. The U.S. role in the Third World was hotly debated during the Cold War, especially during the Vietnam conflict. With the waning of Soviet activities in the Third World, America's future interests there are much more uncertain. The Persian Gulf crisis and war during 1990 and 1991 might seem to imply an ongoing major U.S. role in the Third World; the United States then deployed more conventional forces for combat overseas than it had at any time since the Vietnam War. But while the Gulf War of 1991 decisively liberated Kuwait, it may have raised more questions than it answered about the value of an activist American policy in the Third World. Over a year after the war's end, Saddam Hussein's continuation in power and the ongoing problems in the Gulf caused Americans to wonder whether U.S.-led military action had been a success, and implied that even remarkably effective applications of force may not achieve desired political objectives in Third World settings. Some felt that the war had been a vindication of the principles of collective security, but many observers emphasized that the 1991 Gulf War offered a unique combination of political and military circumstances, making it impossible to draw broader lessons from the clash in the desert. For others, the war highlighted the dangers of the proliferation of advanced weapons, including ballistic missiles and nuclear weapons, and the vulnerability of the world economy to actual or potential disruptions of the supply of oil from the Persian Gulf. Whatever interpretation one prefers, it is impossible to extrapolate from the experience of the 1991 Gulf War a clear vision of America's future interests and role in the Third World.

This collection draws together essays that address these multiple challenges to U.S. policy in the post–Cold War world. It includes several chapters that survey the overall landscape of choice for the United States in the new era, as well as analyses of the dilemmas, opportunities, and alternatives in U.S. relations with the key countries and regions of the world. The volume thus provides a fairly comprehensive treatment of the terrain of the new U.S. debate over grand strategy. It is meant to complement an earlier *International Security* reader, *The Cold War and After: Prospects for Peace* (The MIT Press, 1991). That book examined the reasons for the relative stability of the Cold War and the likelihood of conflict in the emerging international system, applying international relations theory to questions such as the role of nuclear weapons, the influence of bipolarity, and the chances for peace in Europe. This collection, on the other hand, focuses on important dimensions of U.S security policy after the Cold War.

The first section of this book includes essays that explore the nature of the post–Cold War world and the new strategic choices that confront the United States. Robert Jervis surveys the changed setting for U.S. security policy in "The Future of World Politics: Will It Resemble the Past?" After discussing the reasons why prediction is so difficult in international politics, especially in a period marked by large discontinuities, he argues that values have shifted in the liberal democratic states of the West, making peace the normal and likely state of their relations. War between them offers no significant benefits and is no longer glorified. Traditional Realist models of anarchy and conflict may no longer explain international politics among these countries. In the former Soviet bloc, however, nationalism and economic crises still pose a threat to domestic and international stability. In the developing world the end of the Cold War will probably lead to increased conflict, as there will no longer be two antagonistic superpowers with a shared interest in preventing escalation. The United States confronts a much wider range of choice in this new world. It now has the luxury of adopting primary goals other than containing the Soviet Union, including promoting the spread of democracy and human rights. The new debate, Jervis concludes, will have to decide which values and goals to seek and how to resolve the trade-offs between them.

Terry Deibel's "Strategies Before Containment: Patterns for the Future" examines paradigms of U.S. foreign policy before the Cold War to suggest elements of statecraft that could again become useful in the post–Cold War era. He identifies three categories of U.S. national interests: physical security, economic prosperity, and the projection of American values. During the Cold War, these values were served by containment, economic hegemony, and anti-communism, respectively. Deibel points out that past and future options for ensuring U.S. physical security include a balance-of-power strategy, collective security, hemispheric defense, and isolationism. Economic prosperity may be pursued through the formation of trade blocs or protectionism instead of U.S. hegemony, which has been waning for at least two decades. Projecting American values may entail actively attempting to spread democracy, or simply serving as an example to the rest of the world. With military security less at risk, U.S. grand strategy may include greater emphasis on economic prosperity and projecting American values. The challenge confronting U.S. leaders will be to formulate a coherent strategy out of the disparate elements that have been pursued in the past.

In "A Defensible Defense: America's Grand Strategy After the Cold War," Robert Art presents a comprehensive look at American power and purposes in the 1990s. Art notes that nuclear weapons and geographic isolation make the United States remarkably secure, and recognizes that this security may feed calls for U.S. retrenchment now that the Soviet threat has collapsed. Indeed, since 1945, U.S. military forces overseas have served largely to protect U.S. allies, not the United States itself. Nevertheless, a global military presence also has helped to prevent nuclear proliferation and to underpin an open international economy. A precipitous retrenchment of U.S. power would pose risks in these areas. Although some have argued that the United States should use its power to spread democracy, protect the global environment, and impose peace through collective security, Art finds flaws in the rationales for each of these new missions. He argues that the United States should hedge its bets and adopt a global "tripwire" posture based on retaining reduced levels of forces in Europe and East Asia, and maintaining forces in the Persian Gulf indefinitely. In short, Art makes the case for a continued but reduced internationalist posture for the United States, largely on the grounds that this enhances an international stability that is conducive to U.S. values and prosperity.

These three essays provide an overview of America's options in the new international environment. The remaining contributions to this collection examine specific challenges to post–Cold War U.S. security policy.

The first essay in this section focuses on U.S. policy toward what used to be called the Soviet Union. While the disintegration of the Soviet state has ended the bipolar confrontation that was the hallmark of the Cold War, the outcome of the crisis in the former USSR remains critically important to the United States, both because Moscow still controls large nuclear forces and because the kind of order that emerges—whether peaceful and stable or not—will have tremendous ripple effects from one end of Eurasia to the other. The stakes are extremely high. Consequently, developing new relationships with the republics of the former Soviet Union and seeking ways of influencing the evolution of events within and among them should be one of the main priorities of post–Cold War American foreign policy. Ted Hopf's "Managing Soviet Disintegration: A Demand for Behavioral Regimes" tackles this set of issues. It describes Western interests in Eurasia after the disintegration of the Soviet Union and analyzes the threat that conflict and disorder within and among the former Soviet republics pose to those interests. It highlights in particular the risk that an over-armed and dangerous Russia might emerge if the post-Soviet order comes to be characterized by hostility and conflict. Hopf argues that the West should seek to influence the behavior of the fifteen former Soviet republics by linking its policies toward them to codes of domestic and international conduct. He proposes that Western policymakers create and enforce a framework that rewards those republics who adhere to these codes and sanction those who do not. The aim would be to encourage policies and behavior in the former USSR that would produce a benign international environment in which arms-racing and conflict would be less likely to arise. Hopf concludes that while this approach is not certain to work, it offers the best prospect of advancing the Western interest in a peaceful and democratic order in the former Soviet Union.

The three essays that follow Hopf's have to do with the evolving security order in Europe. This part of the world has occupied center stage in American foreign and security policy in the twentieth century, and it is also the region that has been most directly and dramatically affected by the end of the Cold War. With the end of the NATO–Warsaw Pact confrontation, the substantial demilitarization of the center of the continent, the unification of Germany, and the disintegration of the Soviet Union, Europe's features have been altered to an extraordinary extent in a remarkably short time. This has led to intense interest in proposals for arrangements for the future security of Europe, and many have high hopes that a more cooperative framework, building on international institutions, can become the core of a new security system in Europe. In "Concerts, Collective Security, and the Future of Europe," Charles and Clifford Kupchan suggest the feasibility of one such cooperative approach. They argue that the level of agreement among Europe's major powers has created the conditions for a concert-based collective security system, which would avoid the pitfalls of earlier attempts at collective security such as the League of Nations. The Kupchans explain how collective security could overcome the uncertainties that plague attempts to balance power in an anarchic international system. The essence of collective security is universal agreement to oppose any aggressor. Different types of collective security systems exist, but the Kupchans argue that a concert-based system is most likely to be effective. By institutionalizing cooperative behavior to oppose aggressors and entrusting the responsibilities of leadership to a small group of powerful states, a concert-based collective security system can deter or counter aggression. A concert-based system in post–Cold War Europe would build upon the existing structures of the Conference on Security and Cooperation in Europe (CSCE). Like the nineteenth-century Concert of Europe, they argue, it would rely on coordination among the great powers to prevent major wars.

In contrast, Richard Betts argues that collective security is not the answer to Europe's post–Cold War security problems, and indeed that it may be more dangerous and less reliable than more traditional approaches to providing security. In "Systems for Peace or Causes of War? Collective Security, Arms Control, and the New Europe," he contends that collective security systems should be evaluated not in the context of the peaceful environments that might allow their creation, but in terms of the harsher environments in which they would need to function. The key question, Betts suggests, is whether the system will reliably protect individual states threatened by aggression. He believes that there are a number of reasons to doubt that collective security systems will be reliable guarantors of the security of individual states: for example, it is hard to build an automatic element into the universal commitment to engage in war on behalf of states that have been attacked; history suggests that states may choose not to honor their collective security commitments; the identity of the aggressor may often be disputed. Hence, states will always have to weigh the risk that the collective security system will not work. On the other hand, Betts notes, if the collective security system does work, it has the effect of universalizing conflict, of drawing states into war whatever their interests or preferences. Moreover, the existence of a collective security system may have the effect of undermining traditional security preparations and arrangements that might be more effective against serious challenges to peace.

F. Stephen Larrabee's "Down and Out in Warsaw and Budapest: Eastern Europe and East-West Migration" addresses a new issue that is pressing on the security agendas of European states: large-scale migration flows, a problem brought to prominence by the collapse of communism in Eastern Europe. Larrabee describes the substantial increase in migration from East to West in Europe over the past several years, caused by acute social and economic difficulties combined with relaxation or elimination of travel restrictions in former Soviet bloc countries; he notes the potential for an even larger flood of migration if disorder and privation intensify or large-scale violence erupts in the eastern half of Europe. Already, he contends, migration has become a major political issue in some European countries, especially Germany, and is causing substantial social problems. The difficulties European states will have in dealing with this problem raise the potential for hostility and conflict.

We turn next to two places of particular importance to American policy: Japan and the Middle East. In "Beyond Mutual Recrimination: Building a Solid U.S.-Japan Relationship in the 1990s," I.M. Destler and Michael Nacht explore the rise in U.S.-Japan tensions that accompanied the end of the Cold War. They regard the collapse of Soviet power, the rise of Japan, and the relative economic decline of the United States as the underlying causes of friction between Washington and Tokyo. Destler and Nacht argue that a healthy "competitive interdependence" can be attained by maintaining the U.S.-Japan security treaty, increasing savings and reducing consumption in the United States, continuing the pressure to open up Japan's relatively closed economy, and deepening U.S.-Japan interdependence instead of mobilizing for economic warfare.

Richard Herrmann's "The Middle East and the New World Order: Rethinking U.S. Political Strategy After the Gulf War" assesses America's policies before, during, and after the Gulf War. He explores the events that led to the war, arguing that the Bush administration failed to understand the changing dynamics of the Arab world, was excessively preoccupied with deterrence thinking, and never realized that Saddam Hussein was undeterrable. After offering an overview of how fundamentalist movements and populist pressures are changing Arab domestic and international politics, he calls for a U.S. Middle East strategy that emphasizes democratization and multilateralism, instead of relying, as in the past, on military force and support for repressive regimes.

The final two essays in this collection deal with the challenges that the Third World poses to American policy. In "Why the Third World Still Matters," Steven David argues that even after the end of the Cold War the United States has important interests in the Third World. He suggests that without the U.S.-Soviet rivalry that moderated many Third World conflicts, the chronic weakness of many Third World states will ensure continuing instability in Africa, Latin America, and much of Asia. Factors that have reduced the risk of war in the developed world—the spread of democracy and information-based economies—do not constrain Third World tyrants who may be tempted to use force. According to David, the Third World threatens U.S. interests in two ways: first, Third World conflicts can disrupt the West's oil supplies; second, Third World countries may acquire ballistic missiles as well as nuclear, chemical, or biological weapons, thereby becoming able to attack the United States directly. Because the Third World is likely to remain unstable and dangerous, David concludes, the United States must retain the capability to intervene there.

During the 1991 Gulf War, Iraq's attacks with Scud missiles against Israel and Saudi Arabia focused attention on the problem of ballistic missile proliferation in the Third World. The war showed that missiles carrying small conventional warheads do little damage and cause relatively few casualties, but that they may have political and psychological effects. Steve Fetter, in "Ballistic Missiles and Weapons of Mass Destruction: What Is the Threat? What Should be Done?" argues that ballistic missiles can be militarily significant, combining speed of delivery and destructiveness, if they carry nuclear, biological, or chemical warheads. Based on detailed calculations of the likely damage and death rates from these types of warheads on ballistic missiles, Fetter finds that chemical warheads would be 50–500 times more deadly than conventional warheads, while biological warheads might be 10,000 times more deadly, comparable in their lethality to small nuclear weapons. He argues that defenses against ballistic missiles are unlikely to reduce the threat posed by such warheads significantly. To respond to the potentially destabilizing spread of ballistic missiles and weapons of mass destruction in the Third World, he calls for a combination of security guarantees, multilateral arms control, and export controls, backed up by sanctions.

The essays collected here do not cover everything, but they do provide thought-provoking treatments of most of the major issues that will figure in the debate over U.S. strategy in the post–Cold War world. Our hope is that by exploring the broad outlines of U.S. strategy as well as U.S. options in vital regions and on critical issues, this volume will contribute to the important national debate that has only just begun.

Part I:
America's Strategic Options in
a Changing Security Environment

The Future of World Politics

Robert Jervis

Will It Resemble the Past?

History usually makes a mockery of our hopes or our expectations. The events of 1989, perhaps more welcomed than those of any year since 1945, were unforeseen. Much of what analysts anticipate for the 1990s is unpleasant. Nevertheless, it is clear that we are entering a new world, and I present three lines of argument about it. First, I discuss why prediction is so difficult in world politics. Among the reasons: multiple factors are usually at work, actors learn, small events can affect the course of history and, most importantly in this context, many well-established generalizations about world politics may no longer hold. This leads to the second question of the ways and areas in which the future is likely to resemble the past and the sources, areas, and implications of change. It appears that while international politics in much of the world will follow patterns that are familiar in outline although unpredictable in detail, among the developed states we are likely to see new forms of relations. In this new context, my third argument goes, the United States will face an extraordinarily wide range of policy choices and must therefore address fundamental questions that were submerged during the Cold War. Freed from previous constraints, the United States has many goals it can seek, but there are more conflicts among them than are sometimes realized.

Why Prediction Is So Difficult

We all know that it is difficult to predict the course of international politics.[1] Nevertheless, it is useful to note eight reasons why this is so.[2] First, social

Robert Jervis is Adlai E. Stevenson Professor of International Relations at Columbia University and a member of its Institute of War and Peace Studies. His most recent book is The Meaning of the Nuclear Revolution *(Cornell University Press, 1989), for which he received the Grawemeyer Award.*

A preliminary version of this paper was delivered as the Grawemeyer Award Lecture at the University of Louisville. I would like to thank students and colleagues there, at the University of Pittsburgh, and at MIT for suggestions and John Mueller for extensive comments.

1. The literature on this subject is very large. See the summary in Nazli Choucri and Thomas Robinson, eds., *Forecasting in International Relations* (San Francisco: Freeman, 1978).
2. This is not to imply that prediction rather than understanding is the goal of social science: see Stephen Toulmin, *Foresight and Understanding: An Inquiry Into the Aims of Science* (Bloomington: Indiana University Press, 1961).

scientists have only a limited stock of knowledge to rely on and there are few laws whose validity is uncontested. Take, for example, the polarity of the international system, which different scholars define differently (for some, pre–World War I Europe was bipolar, in the eyes of others it was multipolar). Following Kenneth Waltz, John Mearsheimer argues that bipolar systems are more stable than multipolar ones; this provides the foundation for his pessimistic predictions about the future of Europe.[3] But the logic of Waltz's position is open to dispute (indeed, it suffers from internal contradictions).[4] Furthermore, even if the arguments for or against this position were more compelling, they might not be true. Politics has the nasty habit of not always behaving as even the most plausible and rigorous theories suggest it should.

Second, only rarely does a single factor determine the way politics will work out. Even the best propositions are couched in terms of conditions and probabilities. Thus, I doubt that we would ever learn that either bipolarity or multipolarity is always more stable than the other. So even if multipolar systems usually are less stable than bipolar ones, this does not mean that the future will be less stable than the past. Other factors could cancel out this effect or interact with polarity in a way that makes an overall judgment about the influence of the latter impossible. The most obvious factor, as Mearsheimer and Waltz note, is the presence of nuclear weapons: perhaps in the non-nuclear era multipolar systems were less stable than bipolar ones, but today the reverse could be true.

Third, learning about international politics can act as a self-denying prophecy. Although we should not exaggerate the influence of scholarship on world politics, actors may pay attention to academic theories and alter their behavior in ways that render them incorrect. For example, if scholars find that actors who make their threats in public rather than in private are rarely bluffing, then bluffers can choose to make public threats. Or, if theorists convince statesmen that regional integration is characterized by spill-over processes in which small steps toward economic coordination lead to much greater integration than was originally envisioned, then those who do not want to reach this end may refuse to take the initial steps. Furthermore,

3. Kenneth Waltz, *Theory of International Politics* (Reading, Mass.: Addison-Wesley, 1979); John Mearsheimer, "Back to the Future: Instability in Europe After the Cold War," *International Security*, Vol. 15, No. 1 (Summer 1990), pp. 5–56.
4. These are discussed in Jervis, *Systems and Interactions* (unpublished manuscript), chapter 2.

when actors are seeking advantage over others, generalizations may be particularly short-lived as each uses any new knowledge to estimate how others
will behave and to outwit them.[5]

Fourth, unless national behavior and international outcomes are entirely
determined by the external environment, there is significant room for choice
by publics and statesmen. Since the United States is the most influential
power in the world, to predict the future of world politics requires us to
predict the future of American foreign policy. To the extent that the latter
will be strongly influenced by the values, preferences, and beliefs of particular presidents, the enterprise is particularly questionable. To the extent that
broader but still changeable domestic sources shape American foreign policy,
the task is not much easier.

Even if the external environment is dominant, there now is a fifth obstacle
to prediction: the current world situation is unprecedented. While each era
appears unique to those living through it, my guess is that even later generations will view the 1990s as unique. World politics has rarely been re-
ordered without a major war. In fact, from looking at the behavior and
condition of the Soviet Union, one could infer that it had just lost a war.
And the enormous domestic failure is the equivalent of a major military
defeat. But this is a war without another country or coalition that acts like a
winner, ready to move into the power vacuum and structure a new set of
rules to guide international behavior. Although the United States remains
the most powerful country in the world, its mood—and perhaps its economy—do not fit this position, even after the triumph of the Gulf War.

The future is also unprecedented because while the Soviet Union is economically and politically weak, it remains the only country that could destroy
the United States. Other states that are America's economic rivals (as well
as its economic partners) are its close allies (and even its friends). This
configuration is so odd that we cannot easily determine the system's polarity.
Is it unipolar because the United States is so much stronger than the nearest
competitor, bipolar because of the distribution of military resources, tripolar
because of an emerging united Europe, or multipolar because of the general

---

5. Many Realist scholars develop arguments that are both descriptive and prescriptive. They
claim not only to analyze the way the world works, but also to guide statesmen. However, they
often pay insufficient attention to the question of whether their theories will be accurate if
statesmen do not accept them (and if statesmen do, then prescription is unnecessary) and the
possibility that if their truths were generally believed, the patterns of behavior would be altered.

dispersion of power? Thus even if polarity were a major determinant of world politics, it would be hard to tell what we should expect.

To the extent that external forces are not only important, but truly constitute a system, there is a sixth difficulty in making predictions. When elements are tightly inter-connected, as they are in international politics, changes in one part of the system produce ramifications in other elements and feedback loops. Thus international politics is characterized by unintended consequences, interaction effects, and patterns that cannot be understood by breaking the system into bilateral relations. For example, a stable (if bloody) balance of power can be produced by a system in which all the major actors want to dominate or in which the relations among many pairs of countries are very bad.[6] With complex interaction and feedback, not only can small causes have large effects, but prediction is inherently problematic as the multiple pathways through which the system will respond to a stimulus are difficult to trace after the fact, let alone estimate ahead of time.[7]

It is tempting but a mistake to imagine that world politics will continue on its current trajectory, with the obvious and large exception of the drastic diminution of Soviet-American tensions. This way of proceeding is tempting because, although still very difficult, it is relatively manageable. It is an error, however, because in a system the alteration of one element will lead to multiple changes as states react. If some of the anticipated consequences of the end of the Cold War are undesired, actors will try to counteract them, although of course such efforts may produce results that are very different from the intentions. For example, it is possible that the developed countries, believing that the end of the Soviet threat will increase tensions among them, will redouble their efforts to work together and minimize frictions. But, of course, if any one state realizes that this is what the others are doing, it can seek to turn their reasonableness to unilateral advantage.

The final two arguments as to why prediction is so difficult are more controversial. The flow of international politics is, in significant measure, contingent or path-dependent.[8] History matters. Particular events can send world politics down quite different paths.[9] Stephen Jay Gould makes a similar

6. Inis Claude, *Power and International Relations* (New York: Random House, 1962), pp. 40–51; Waltz, *Theory of International Politics*, pp. 102–128.
7. For a further discussion, see Robert Jervis, "Systems Effects," in Richard Zeckhauser, ed., *Strategy and Choice* (Cambridge, Mass.: MIT Press, forthcoming).
8. Path-dependence is one of the themes of the new institutionalism. See, for example, James March and Johan Olsen, *Rediscovering Institutions* (New York: Free Press, 1989).
9. This argument has a hopeful side to it: the possibility of contingent predictions. That is, we

argument for evolution. The operation of natural selection does not preclude a large role for chance and accidents. Had certain life forms been destroyed or others survived eons ago—and there are no general principles or scientific laws that precluded this—life would have evolved very differently.[10]

If international politics fits this pattern, then in order to know what the world will be like twenty years from now, we would have to know what will happen next year, an extremely difficult requirement. While proof is of course impossible, several actual or hypothetical events can illustrate the plausibility of this claim. For example, the history of the world after 1918 was crucially affected not only by the fact that World War I occurred, but that it was a war that took place at a particular time with certain countries on each side. Even if some sort of world war was inevitable during that decade, it is hard to argue that there had to be a war in the summer of 1914. And had it occurred earlier or later, much else about it could have been different in a way that would have produced a different postwar world. The aftermath of the war was also influenced by accidents. The United States might have joined the League of Nations had Wilson's personality been different or had his judgment not been impaired by his stroke.[11] Without the Korean War, many of the characteristics we associate with the Cold War—high defense budgets, a militarized NATO, great Sino-American hostility, and American security commitments throughout the world—probably would not have developed.[12]

Looking to the future, the war in the Persian Gulf may similarly influence aspects of the post–Cold War era. Turning the clock back to August 1990, or even to October 1990 or January 1991, one can imagine a variety of policies and outcomes, each of which would have produced a quite different world. A world in which Iraq's aggression was allowed to stand would have been quite different from one in which economic sanctions forced a retraction,

---

can and should focus on saying what we expect to happen, *given various conditions*. This is worthwhile, especially for the intellectual discipline that it imposes. But if there are a large number of important variables that many states can assume and if the variables build on each other as time passes, then we cannot expect the exercise to produce many practical benefits.

10. Stephen Jay Gould, *Wonderful Life: The Burgess Shale and the Nature of History* (New York: Norton, 1989).

11. For the more extreme argument that Wilson would have taken a different position had a bizarre incident involving a low-level British diplomat not led him to refuse to hear the advice of Sir Edward Gray, the British special ambassador, see Charles Mechling, Jr., "Scandal in Wartime Washington: The Craufurd-Stuart Affair of 1918," *International Journal of Intelligence and Counterintelligence*, Vol. 4, No. 3 (Fall 1990), pp. 357–370.

12. For further discussion see Robert Jervis, "The Impact of the Korean War on the Cold War," *Journal of Conflict Resolution*, Vol. 24, No. 4 (December 1980), pp. 563–592.

which in turn would have been different from the world that emerged in the aftermath of the Gulf War. Even more clearly, the future of world politics will be shaped by whether the Soviet Union manages to stay together, whether it dissolves peacefully, or whether it is shattered by a civil war. This, in turn, may be influenced by what happens in Yugoslavia: perhaps if that country's civil war intensifies before events in the Soviet Union are determined, the object-lesson may decrease the chance of large-scale violence among the successor republics.[13] Less dramatically, the long-run state of U.S.-Japanese relations may be permanently influenced by the way in which the next trade crisis arises and is worked out. Furthermore, the way in which the U.S.-Japan trading relationship develops will strongly influence the world-wide international economic system.

It can be argued that these claims exaggerate the role of contingency because they underestimate the power of the structure of the international system and other deeply imbedded influences. While events like the Gulf War cannot be predicted, neither do they send the world along radically different paths. Instead, politics resembles roads that intersect rather than diverge.[14] Shocks may push the world in one direction or another, but eventually the underlying factors will exert themselves and return the world to something like what it would have been without the earlier "deviant" events. In international politics, however, such an argument seems plausible only if the international structure determines most behavior. One can perhaps claim that this was the case during the more competitive years of the Cold War; it is not likely to be true for many aspects of world politics in the current era.

The final reason why prediction is difficult brings us closer to the question of how different the new world will be. Even if we knew what generalizations held in the past and even if they were not sensitive to details and idiosyncracies, this knowledge would not provide a sure guide for the future if the generalizations themselves are no longer valid. In *Time's Arrow, Time's Cycle*, Stephen Jay Gould discusses schools of thought about geology in terms of their basic orienting metaphors. One school sees the large-scale history of

---

13. A KGB study reportedly examined recent developments in Yugoslavia and warned against similar disintegration in the Soviet Union. Serge Schmemann, "Report by Soviets Expresses Fears of Following the Path of Yugoslavia," *New York Times*, October 4, 1991, p. A4.
14. See Jon Elster, *Logic and Society: Contradictions and Possible Worlds* (New York: Wiley, 1978), pp. 177–178; John Gaddis, "Nuclear Weapons and International Systemic Stability," Occasional Paper No. 2, International Security Studies Program, American Academy of Arts and Sciences, January 1990; and Philip Nash, "The Use of Counterfactuals in History: A Look at the Literature," *SHAFR Newsletter*, Vol. 22 (March 1991), pp. 2–12.

the earth in terms of cycles in which there is change from one phase to another but the phases themselves recur through regular cycles; the other sees geology as revealing constant unidirectional change.[15] Each perspective can have an element of truth, as Gould argues is the case for the earth's history, and we should be suspicious of any unqualified answer. But the question of the extent to which and the ways in which international history resembles a cycle or an arrow is a useful one.

If our laws are not timeless—if history resembles an arrow—some of what we have learned will not help us understand the future. For example, many commentators have pointed out that alliances last only as long as there is a common enemy and so they have concluded that NATO will soon dissolve. But even if the historical generalization is correct, the projection of it into the future may not be, if the roles and motivations for alliances have changed. Similarly, even if previous eras of multipolarity were characterized by instability, a future multipolar world might not be. We need to understand why certain generalizations held true in the past and see whether basic impulses of international politics may work themselves out differently in a changed environment.

In some cases generalizations will no longer hold even though the basic laws that generated them remain valid. Statesmen presumably will continue to be guided primarily by considerations of national security, but their behavior will be different if there are changes in the problems they face and the solutions they see. It probably is still true that states are more likely to be pushed into war by the expectation that they will suffer grave losses unless they fight than they are pulled into war by the attraction of opportunity and expected gains.[16] But this law will work itself out differently if there are changes in the magnitude and kinds of threats that states confront. It is also possible that the import of a pattern may change as conditions do: for example, it may always have been the case that liberal democracies did not fight each other, but now this generalization yields a much more peaceful world than was true in the past because so many of the powerful states are democratic. More extreme changes are also possible, although less likely: that is, the nature of the basic connections between variables—i.e., the laws

---

15. Stephen Jay Gould, *Time's Arrow, Time's Cycle* (Cambridge: Harvard University Press, 1987).
16. See Robert Jervis, "Loss Aversion in International Politics," *Political Psychology* (forthcoming); Daniel Kahneman and Amos Tversky, "Choices, Values, and Frames," *American Psychologist*, Vol. 39, No. 3 (April 1984), pp. 341–350; Richard Ned Lebow and Janice Stein, "Beyond Deterrence," *Journal of Social Issues*, Vol. 43, No. 4 (Winter 1987), pp. 5–17.

themselves—could change. Thus statesmen might no longer place as high a priority on security as they did in the past. Of course if we make our theories sufficiently general—e.g., people seek to maximize their expected utilities— we may find they have not changed, but this will not be particularly signif- icant if the utilities and beliefs about how to reach them have changed.

What Is Constant; What Has Changed

Cyclical thinking suggests that, freed from the constraints of the Cold War, world politics will return to earlier patterns.[17] Many of the basic generaliza- tions of international politics remain unaltered: it is still anarchic in the sense that there is no international sovereign that can make and enforce laws and agreements.[18] The security dilemma remains as well, with the problems it creates for states who would like to cooperate but whose security require- ments do not mesh. Many specific causes of conflict also remain, including desires for greater prestige, economic rivalries, hostile nationalisms, diver- gent perspectives on and incompatible standards of legitimacy, religious animosities, and territorial ambitions. To put it more generally, both aggres- sion and spirals of insecurity and tension can still disturb the peace. But are the conditions that call these forces into being as prevalent as they were in the past? Are the forces that restrain violence now as strong, or stronger, than they were?

The answers may be different for different regions of the world. Even where fundamental changes have not occurred, the first seven impediments to prediction remain in place; but there we can at least say that the variables and relationships that acted in the past should continue. Where time's arrow predominates, on the other hand, our first task may be negative: to argue that some familiar patterns are not likely to re-appear. On some questions we may be able to discern at least the outlines of the new arrangements; on others, what will emerge may not yet be determined.

THE DEVELOPED WORLD

Time's arrow is most strikingly at work in the developed world: it is hard to see how a war could occur among the United States, Western Europe, and

---

17. A good example is Mearsheimer, "Back to the Future."
18. The best critique of the utility of theorizing based on the assumption of anarchy is Helen Milner, "The Assumption of Anarchy in International Relations Theory: A Critique," *Review of International Studies*, Vol. 17, No. 1 (January 1991), pp. 67–85.

Japan, at least in the absence of revolutionary domestic changes, presumably linked to severe economic depression. Indeed, peace among these countries is over-determined: there are many reasons, each of which is probably sufficient, why they should remain at peace.[19] One indication of the profound change is that although Britain's primary aim always was to prevent any power from dominating the continent of Europe, even those Britons who opposed joining the European Community or who remain opposed to seeing it develop political sovereignty would laugh at the idea of going to war to prevent its formation. The United States, too, fought to prevent Germany from dominating Europe, but sponsored European integration during the Cold War and still looks on it with favor, even though Germany is its leader.[20] Similarly, if international politics in the West had not changed, in the absence of bipolarity it would be hard to understand how the United States would not now fear the French and British nuclear forces which, after all, could obliterate it. A test of whether the standard logic of international politics will continue to apply among the developed states will be whether this fear will emerge. A parallel—and more disturbing—test will be whether Germany and Japan, freed from the security and constraints of the Cold War, will seek nuclear weapons, following the previous rule that great powers seek the most prestigious and powerful military weapons available even in the absense of a clear threat. (A decision to "go nuclear" would not prove the point, however, if it was motivated by fear of the Soviet Union or China.)

These dramatic breaks from the past and the general peacefulness of the West are to be explained by increases in the costs of war, decreases in its benefits and, linked to this, changes in domestic regimes and values. Earlier I argued that specific events sometimes send history into a different path. But these changes in the developed world are so deep, powerful, and interlocked that they cannot readily be reversed by any foreseeable event.

THE INCREASED COSTS OF WAR. The costs of war among developed states probably would be enormous even if there were no nuclear weapons.[21] But

19. See Stephen Van Evera, "Primed for Peace: Europe After the Cold War," *International Security*, Vol. 15, No. 3 (Winter 1990/91), pp. 7–57; and Richard H. Ullman, *Securing Europe* (Princeton, N.J.: Princeton University Press, 1991).

20. George Bush states that the "United States has deemed it a vital interest to prevent any hostile power or group of powers from dominating the Eurasian land mass," but in fact neither the United States nor Britain was willing to trust the benign intentions of any state that seemed likely to control the continent. George Bush, *The National Security Strategy of the United States, 1990–1991* (Washington, D.C.: Brassey's, 1990), p. 5.

21. This point is stressed in John Mueller, *Retreat from Doomsday: The Obsolescence of Major War* (New York: Basic Books, 1989).

such weapons do exist, and by increasing still more the costs of war, they also increase the chances of peace. This much is generally agreed upon. Many analysts believe that mutual deterrence means not only that each nuclear power can deter a direct attack, but also that nothing else can be deterred—i.e., that allies cannot be sheltered under the nuclear umbrella and that "extended deterrence" is a fiction. As I have argued elsewhere, however, both logic and the historical record indicates that this position is not true.[22] Because inadvertent escalation is always a possibility, a conventional war that involves a nuclear power—or that could draw in a nuclear power—could lead to nuclear devastation.

During the Cold War the risks of escalation meant that the United States could protect Western Europe even if the West had neither a first-strike capability nor an adequate conventional defense; in the current era it means that the European states gain some of the deterrent advantages of nuclear weapons even if they do not own them. Because statesmen realize that any European war could lead to a nuclear conflagration, aggression and even crises will be discouraged. This sharply decreases the incentives for proliferation: nuclear weapons are not necessary to ensure the security of European states like Germany that lack them, and would not greatly help such countries realize expansionist aims if they should develop them. Because the French and British nuclear forces increase the chance that any fighting in Europe could escalate, they decrease the likelihood of war and so, far from threatening the United States, should continue to be welcomed by it.

THE DECLINING BENEFITS OF WAR. Because the expected costs of armed conflict among the developed countries are so high, only the strongest pressures for war could produce such an outcome. Yet it is hard to conjure up any significant impulses toward war. The high level of economic interdependence among the developed states increases not only the costs of war, but the benefits of peace as well. Even in the case that shows the greatest strain—U.S.-Japan relations—no one has explained how a war could serve either country's interests.[23] The claim that a high degree of integration prevents war by making it prohibitively costly for states to fight each other has often been incorrectly attributed to Norman Angell's *The Great Illusion*, and

---

22. Robert Jervis, *The Illogic of American Nuclear Strategy* (Ithaca: Cornell University Press, 1984), chapters 5 and 6; Jervis, *The Meaning of the Nuclear Revolution* (Ithaca: Cornell University Press, 1989), chapter 3.
23. For an unconvincing attempt, see George Friedman and Meredith LeBard, *The Coming War with Japan* (New York: St. Martin's, 1990).

the outbreak of World War I a few years after this book was published is cited as proof of the error of the position. But the title of Angell's book gives its actual argument: it is an illusion to believe that war will provide economic gain.[24] The argument was as much prescription as description, and the former would not have been necessary had the latter been self-evident. The implications for today are obvious: while the objective facts of interdependence are important, one must also ask how they are viewed by the general public, elites, and statesmen.

Not only the degree but also the kinds of interdependence matter. If statesmen examine the situation with any sophistication, they will be concerned not about the size of the flows of trade and capital, but rather with what will happen to their states' welfare if these flows are halted.[25] Thus the fact that levels of trade are higher among the developed countries today than they were in 1914 may be less significant than the fact that direct foreign investment is greater and that many firms, even if they are not formally multinational, have important international ties.[26] It would be harder for states and firms to arrange for substitutes if conflict or war severed these financial ties than would be the case if it were only goods that were being exchanged.

The other side of this coin is that continued high levels of economic intercourse may significantly increase each state's wealth. This, of course, is the foundation of the argument for the advantage of open international economic systems, and the postwar history of the developed world is strongly consistent with it. Even those who call for some protection do not doubt that trade is necessary for prosperity. Most importantly for a consideration of the political relations among the developed countries, no one in any of these states believes that his or her country can grow richer by conquering any of the others than it can by trading with it, in part because the techniques of controlling an occupied country are not compatible with

---

24. See the discussion in J.D.B. Miller, *Norman Angell and the Futility of War* (New York: St. Martin's, 1986).
25. See the discussion of vulnerability and sensitivity interdependence in Richard Cooper, *The Economics of Interdependence* (New York: McGraw-Hill, 1968); and Robert Keohane and Joseph S. Nye, Jr., *Power and Interdependence* (Boston: Little Brown, 1977); as well as the pathbreaking study by Albert Hirschman, *National Power and the Structure of International Trade* (Berkeley: University of California Press, 1980 [originally published in 1945]).
26. Richard Rosecrance, *The Rise of the Trading State* (New York: Basic Books, 1986), chapter 7; Helen Milner, *Resisting Protectionism* (Princeton, N.J.: Princeton University Press, 1988).

making a post-industrial economy function well.[27] People in each country can believe, sometime with good reason, that their own fortunes would improve more if others do less well or may attribute their difficulties to extreme—and unfair—economic competition, but this does not mean that they believe that they are likely to thrive if their partners suffer significant economic misfortune.

The belief that one's economic well-being is linked to that of others is not sufficient to bring peace, however. Many values are more important to people than wealth. High levels of economic interdependence have not prevented civil wars, although it may have inhibited them; perhaps more internal conflicts would have occurred had countries not been fairly well integrated. This could help explain why modern countries rarely experience these bloody disturbances. Alternative explanations are possible, however, and the Spanish Civil War and current unrest in Yugoslavia, Czechoslovakia, and the Soviet Union at minimum show that a higher level of economic integration than that which characterizes the current international system does not prevent armed conflict.

In international politics it is particularly true that wealth is not the primary national goal. Not only will states pay a high price to maintain their security, autonomy, and the spread of their values, but the calculus of economic benefit is affected by the international context. While economic theory argues that the actor should care only about how the outcome of an economic choice affects him, those who fear that they may have to fight need to worry about relative advantage as well as absolute gains.[28] Furthermore, states that be-

---

27. Stephen Van Evera, "Why Europe Matters, Why the Third World Doesn't: America's Grand Strategy After the Cold War," *Journal of Strategic Studies*, Vol. 13, No. 2 (June 1990), p. 5; Van Evera, "Primed for Peace," pp. 14–16; Carl Kaysen, "Is War Obsolete? A Review Essay," *International Security*, Vol. 14, No. 4 (Spring 1990), pp. 53–57.
28. Waltz, *Theory of International Politics*; Arthur Stein, "The Hegemon's Dilemma: Great Britain, the United States, and the International Economic Order," *International Organization*, Vol. 38, No. 2 (Spring 1984), pp. 355–386; Robert Jervis, "Realism, Game Theory, and Cooperation," *World Politics*, Vol. 40, No. 3 (April 1988), pp. 334–336; Joseph Grieco, "Anarchy and the Limits of Cooperation: A Realist Critique of the Newest Liberal Institutionalism," *International Organization*, Vol. 42, No. 3 (Summer 1988), pp. 485–507; Michael Mastanduno, "Do Relative Gains Matter? America's Response to Japanese Industrial Policy," *International Security*, Vol. 16, No. 1 (Summer 1991), pp. 73–113. Of course even in purely economic exchanges, actors must be concerned about relative gain if getting a smaller share now means that their absolute as well as relative gains will be less in the future. This is one of the concerns of strategic trade theory. For an exposition and application see Helen Milner and David Yoffie, "Between Free Trade and Protectionism: Strategic Trade Policy and a Theory of Corporate Trade Demands," *International Organization*, Vol. 43, No. 2 (Spring 1989), pp. 237–272; and J. David Richardson, "The Political Economy of Strategic Trade Theory," *International Organization*, Vol. 44, No. 1 (Winter 1990),

come more dependent on others than others are on them will be vulnerable to pressure, as the Balkan states discovered before World War II.[29]

Both the fear of dependence and concern about relative gains are less when states expect to remain at peace with each other. Indeed, expectations of peaceful relations were a necessary condition for the formation of the European Common Market; the growth of interdependence in the developed world is as much a symptom as a cause of the basic change in international politics. Had the Europeans thought there was a significant chance that they would come to blows, they would not have permitted their economies to grow so interdependent. The price of greater wealth would have been excessive if they felt their security would be endangered, and so it is not surprising that other regions have not imitated the successful European experience.

When states fear each other, interdependence can increase conflict.[30] Thus there is at least an element of reinforcing feedback in the current situation: interdependence has developed in part because of the expectations of peace, and the economic benefits of close economic relations in turn make peace more likely. The political implications of the economic situation were very different in the early twentieth century when Britain and Germany, although trading heavily with each other, each feared that economic endeavors that strengthened the other would eventually weaken its own security. As one British observer put it after an extended tour of Germany: "Every one of these new factory chimneys is a gun pointed at England."[31] The growth of another state's political and economic power now is worrisome only if it causes harm to the first in some direct way; it is no longer automatically seen as decreasing the first state's ability to protect its interests in the next war. Samuel Huntington argues that the answer to the question of why Americans are so concerned about the Japanese challenge is straightforward: "The United States is obsessed with Japan for the same reason that it was once obsessed with the Soviet Union. It sees that country as a major threat to its

---

pp. 107–135. The broader dynamic in which a small relative advantage leads to much greater absolute (and relative) gains later is the heart of the argument in E.J. Hobsbawm, *Industry and Empire* (New York: Pantheon, 1968); and Immanuel Wallerstein, *The Modern World-System*, 3 vols. (New York: Academic Press, 1974–88).

29. Hirschman, *National Power*.
30. Waltz, *Theory of International Politics*, pp. 151–160.
31. Quoted in Paul Kennedy, *The Rise of the Anglo-German Antagonism, 1860–1914* (Boston: George Allen and Unwin, 1980), p. 315.

primacy in a crucial arena of power."[32] But it is far from clear that one state's economic progress constitutes a threat to another unless the two are likely to fight, the former's relative advantage will diminish the other's absolute wealth, or the former will gain leverage it can use in important political disputes. The first condition does not hold in the U.S.-Japan case, and it is certainly debatable whether either of the other two do. Rivalry is different in its meaning and implications when it is conducted with an eye to future fighting than when the interactions are expected to be peaceful.

CHANGES IN DOMESTIC REGIMES AND VALUES. The change in relations among the developed states is partly a result of a shift in basic outlook and values. As John Mueller has noted, war is no longer seen as good, or even as honorable, in anything less than desperate circumstances.[33] No Western leader would speak—or even think—in terms like those expressed by Chief of the German General Staff Helmuth von Moltke in a letter to his wife during the 1911 Moroccan Crisis:

If we again slip away from the affair with our tail between our legs and if we cannot bring ourselves to put forward a determined claim which we are prepared to force through with the sword, I shall despair of the future of the German Empire. I shall then resign. But before handing in my resignation, I shall move to abolish the Army and to place ourselves under Japanese protectorate; we shall then be in a position to make money without interference and to develop into ninnies.[34]

These sentiments seem archaic: we may now be seeing, among developed states, the triumph of interests over passions, as Angell and Joseph Schumpeter foresaw.[35]

As the Gulf War reminds us, it is not as though developed states do not feel a sense of pride, or even self-identity, in asserting themselves abroad.

---

32. Samuel Huntington, "America's Changing Strategic Interests," *Survival*, Vol. 23, No. 1 (January/February 1991), p. 8.
33. Mueller, *Retreat From Doomsday*. For a discussion of changes in values among Europeans on matters of domestic society and ways of life, see Ronald Inglehart, *The Silent Revolution* (Princeton, N.J.: Princeton University Press, 1977); and Inglehart, *Culture Shift in Advanced Industrial Society* (Princeton, N.J.: Princeton University Press, 1990). For a rebuttal, see Harold Clarke and Nitish Dutt, "Measuring Value Change in Western Industrialized Societies," *American Political Science Review*, Vol. 85, No. 3 (September 1991), pp. 905–920.
34. Quoted in V.R. Berghahn, *Germany and the Approach of War in 1914* (New York; St. Martin's, 1973), p. 97.
35. Norman Angell, *The Great Illusion*, 4th ed. (New York: Putnam's, 1913); Joseph Schumpeter, "The Sociology of Imperialisms," in *Imperialism and Social Classes* (New York: Kelley, 1951). The phrase is borrowed from Albert Hirschman (although the story Hirschman tells is much more complex), in *The Passions and the Interests* (Princeton, N.J.: Princeton University Press, 1977).

But the impulse is more episodic than it once was, is not directed against other democracies, and is more often exercised in the service of economic values than counterposed to them. Part of the explanation for this change is the waning of nationalism, perhaps in the sense of pride in the achievements of one's nation, and certainly in the sense of a belief that one's country is superior to others and should dominate them. The progress toward West European unification both facilitated and is made possible by a weakening of the attachment to one's nation as a source of identity and personal satisfaction. The residual feelings may be sufficient to prevent Europe from completely unifying, but the process never could have moved this far had nationalism remained even at the level of the fairly benign late 1920s, let alone of any other era. I doubt if we will see a return to these periods: reduced nationalism is now closely associated with economic and political gains and has been embodied in institutions that have become the focus of power and perhaps loyalty. Nationalism was discredited in some European states (although not Germany) after 1918, but this was because it had brought failure, not because being less nationalistic had produced success.

Change in values is also evident from the absence of territorial disputes. Germans no longer seem to care that Alsace and Lorraine are French: The French, who permitted the Saar to return to Germany in a plebiscite, are not bothered by this loss, and indeed do not see it as a loss at all. The Germans did feel sufficient Germanness to seek the unification of their country, but the desire to regain the "lost territories" to the east seems extremely low. Furthermore, unification was not accomplished against the will of any other country and, unlike manifestations of more disturbing nationalism, did not involve the assertion of the rightful domination of one country over another.

Equally important, the developed states are now democratic and it appears that liberal democracies rarely, if ever, fight each other.[36] Here too values play a large role. What would one democracy gain by conquering another? The United States could conquer Canada, for example, but why would it want to do so when much of what it would want to see there is already in place? Neither security considerations nor the desire to improve the world would impel one liberal democracy to attack another.

IMPLICATIONS OF CHANGED RELATIONS AMONG THE DEVELOPED STATES. In summary, war among the developed states is extremely unlikely because its

---

36. Michael Doyle, "Kant, Liberal Legacies and Foreign Affairs," Part 1, *Philosophy and Public Affairs,* Vol. 12, No. 3 (Summer 1983), pp. 205–235; and Part 2, ibid., No. 4 (Fall 1983), pp. 323–353.

costs have greatly increased, the gains it could bring have decreased, espe-cially compared to the alternative routes to those goals, and the values states seek have altered. Four qualities of these changes are particularly important. First, they are powerful determinants of behavior: compared to these factors, the influence of the polarity of the international system is slight. Even if multipolar systems are less stable than bipolar ones and even if the future world will be multipolar, it is hard to see how the overall result could be dangerous. The forces for peace among the developed countries are so over-whelming that impulses which under other circumstances would be desta-bilizing will not lead to violence.

Second, the three kinds of changes interact and reinforce each other. The high costs of war permit economic interdependence by reducing each state's fear of armed conflict with others. The joining of economic fates reciprocally gives each state a positive stake in the others' well-being, thus limiting political conflict. But these developments would not have had the same impact were it not for the spread of democracy and the shift of values. These changes in turn support the perceived advantages of peace. If hyper-nation-alism and the belief that one's country was destined to rule over others were rampant, then violence would be the only way to reach state goals. If states-men thought expansion brought national honor, they might risk the high costs of war as an instrument of coercion. So focusing on any one of these elements in isolation from the others misunderstands how and why the world has changed.

Third, many of the changes in West European politics and values were caused in part by the Cold War. The conflict with the Soviet Union generated an unprecedented sense of unity and gave each state an important stake in the welfare of the others. To the extent that each was contributing to the anti-Soviet coalition, each reaped political benefit from the others' economic growth and strength.[37] Since the coalition could be undermined by social unrest or political instability, each country also sought to see that the others were well-off, that social problems were adequately managed, and that sources of discontent were minimized. It would then have been costly for any country have tried to solve its own domestic problems by exporting them to its neighbors. Indeed, since the coalition would have been disrupted if any country had developed strong grievances against others in the coalition,

---

37. Joanne Gowa, "Bipolarity, Multipolarity, and Free Trade," *American Political Science Review*, Vol. 83, No. 4 (December 1989), pp. 1245–1256.

each had incentives to moderate its own potentially disturbing demands and to mediate if conflicts developed between others.

But the end of the Cold War will not bring a return to the older patterns. Rather, the changes are irreversible, especially if the developed countries remain democratic, which is likely. The ties of mutual interest and identification, the altered psychology, whereby individuals identify less deeply with their nations and more with broader entities, values, and causes, the new supra-national institutions, and the general sense that there is no reason for the developed countries to fight each other will remain.

Finally, these changes represent time's arrow: international politics among the developed nations will be qualitatively different from what history has made familiar. War and the fear of war have been the dominant motor of politics among nations. The end of war does not mean the end of conflict, of course. Developed states will continue to be rivals in some respects, to jockey for position, and to bargain with each other. Disputes and frictions are likely to be considerable; indeed the shared expectation that they will not lead to fighting will remove some restraints on vituperation. But with no disputes meriting the use of force and with such instruments being inappropriate to the issues at hand, we are in unmapped territory: statesmen and publics will require new perspectives if not new concepts; scholars will have to develop new variables and new theories. Although Karl Deutsch and his colleagues explored some of the paths that could lead to the formation of what they called a pluralistic security community—a group of states among whom war was unthinkable[38]—there are few systematic treatments of how countries in such a configuration might conduct themselves.[39]

EASTERN EUROPE

In other areas of the world, however, we are likely to see time's cycle. The resurgent ethnic disputes in Eastern Europe and the Soviet Union appear much as they were when they were suppressed by Soviet power 45 and 70 years ago. It is almost as though we had simply turned back the clock or, to

---

38. Karl Deutsch, et al., *Political Community and the North Atlantic Area: International Organization in the Light of Historical Experience* (Princeton, N.J.: Princeton University Press, 1957).

39. Keohane and Nye, *Power and Interdependence*, developed a model of complex interdependence that applies when force is not central, but much of the subsequent debate concerned whether the conditions for it were met, rather than elaborating and testing theories of how relations within a pluralistic security community would be conducted. Furthermore, the previous behavior was strongly influenced by the Cold War setting and so may be different, although still peaceful, in the future.

change the analogy, as though they were the patients described by Oliver Sacks who came back to life after medication had released them from the strange disease that had frozen them.[40] The prospects for international politics in this region are worrisome at best.

Most of the arguments made in the preceding section about the prospects for peace in Western Europe do not apply to the Eastern part of the continent. The latter is not filled with stable, democratic governments that have learned to cooperate and have developed a stake in each other's well-being. Nationalism and militarism are dangerous and grievances abound, especially those rooted in ethnic and border disputes. Even if Stephen Van Evera is correct to argue that the decrease in social stratification will remove one of the causes of hyper-nationalism,[41] the traditional sources of international strife are sufficient to lead the relations among these states to be permeated by the fear of war.

War is not inevitable, however. Statesmen realize that the costs of fighting are likely to be high, even if the likelihood of Soviet intervention has diminished. Also powerful will be the new factor of the East Europeans' knowledge that economic prosperity depends on access to the markets of the European Community and that such access is not likely to be granted to unstable, authoritarian, or aggressive regimes. Thus the very existence of the EC should encourage peace and stability in the East.[42] The West can also support democracy and moderation in Eastern Europe and the Soviet Union by seeking to build appropriate institutions, habits, and processes, although the extent of this influence is difficult to determine.[43]

Much is likely to depend on internal developments within each East European country (and the way one country develops may influence what

---

40. Oliver Sacks, *Awakenings* (New York: Dutton, 1983). The analogy should not be carried too far, however. The history of the intervening years has left strong, damaging marks: see George Kennan, "Communism in Russian History," *Foreign Affairs*, Vol. 69, No. 5 (Winter 1990/91), pp. 168–186. Alexander Motyl argues that *perestroika* has not merely permitted the rise of ethnic nationalism in the USSR, but has made it a necessity for economic survival: Motyl, "Empire or Stability? The Case for Soviet Dissolution," *World Policy Journal*, Vol. 8, No. 3 (Summer 1991), pp. 499–524.
41. Van Evera, "Primed for Peace," pp. 9–10, 43–44.
42. The incentives of ties to the rest of Europe, in conjunction with the active assistance of European politicians, facilitated Spain's transition to democracy: see Edward Malefakis, "Spain and Its Francoist Heritage," in John Herz, ed., *From Dictatorship to Democracy* (Westport, Conn: Greenwood, 1982), pp. 217–219; and Mary Barker, "International Influences in the Transition to Democracy in Spain" (unpublished ms., Columbia University, Spring 1988).
43. Jack Snyder, "Avoiding Anarchy in the New Europe," *International Security*, Vol. 14, No. 4 (Spring 1990), pp. 5–41.

happens in others as well). If the forces of nationalism and militarism are kept under control, the chances for peace will be increased.[44] This, in turn, depends in part on the success of the countries' economic programs. But whether the results are peaceful or violent, the general determinants of international politics in this region are likely to be fairly traditional ones, such as the presence or absence of aggressive regimes, the offense/defense balance in military strategy and technology, and the level of political and diplomatic skill of the national leaders. Our inability to predict the results stems from the fact that we cannot be certain about the values of a number of the key variables. But, with the exception of the pacifying influence of the hope for acceptance by West Europe, the variables at work and the ways they relate to each other should be quite familiar.

Because Eastern Europe is not alone on its continent, the optimism I stated earlier about the developed countries needs to be qualified. Probably the greatest danger—but still slight—to the peace and stability of Western Europe, and by extension to the United States, is large-scale violence—either international or civil—in Eastern Europe and the Soviet Union. The power, location, and history of Germany mean that the most disturbing scenarios involve that country, which could easily be drawn into the East by strife, generating fears that the result if not the intention would be German dominance of the continent.

This chain of events seems unlikely, however. Offensive motivations are not strong: neither the West in general nor Germany in particular is likely to see a great deal to be gained by using force in the East. More troublesome would be the threat that unrest in the East could pose to established Western interests. This problem would be greater if and when the West has extensive economic ties to the East, but even under these conditions the costs of using force probably would outweigh the expected benefits. Security could be a more potent motivator in the face of extensive violence. But quarantine probably would be a more effective response than intervention. Violence in the East could also set in motion large flows of refugees that would create an economic and political menace,[45] but here too military force would not be

---

44. This is central to Snyder's policy prescriptions in "Avoiding Anarchy." Mearsheimer also sees hyper-nationalism as "the most important domestic cause of war," but exaggerates the extent to which "its causes lie . . . in the international system"; Mearsheimer, "Back to the Future," p. 21.

45. For an excellent discussion of the links between migration and security, see Myron Weiner, "Security, Stability, and International Migration," MIT Center for International Studies Occasional Paper, December 1990.

the most appropriate remedy. Ideology might pull the West in: the urge to protect a newly-democratic regime could be a strong one. But while active diplomacy would certainly be expected in this situation, force would only be a last resort. In all of these possible cases what would be crucial for the West would be the extent of its solidarity. The danger would be least if any intervention were joint, greater if any one country—especially Germany—proceeded on its own, and greatest if different Western states were linked to opposing factions or countries in the East. To a large extent, then, the West can contain the consequences of violence in Eastern Europe even if it fails to prevent it. Indeed, maintaining Western unity is perhaps the most important function of NATO, and 1991 discussions of a joint NATO force for potential use in Eastern Europe seem to have been motivated largely by the shared desire to avoid unilateral interventions.

THE THIRD WORLD

To include all of Africa, Asia, and Latin America under one rubric is to wield an even broader brush than I have employed so far. The crudeness of this residual category is indicated by the name "Third World," which is surely a confession of intellectual failure. That being neither economically developed nor communist gives countries much in common is to be doubted; the patterns of politics are likely to be different in different regions.[46] Also, perhaps, for better and for worse, international politics in Central and South America will continue to be strongly influenced by the United States. International politics among the states of sub-Saharan Africa are likely to continue to show at least some restraint because the lack of legitimacy of borders makes them all vulnerable and thus gives them powerful incentives to avoid fighting each other.[47] Furthermore, most African countries have quite weak states, a characteristic that will continue to influence both their domestic and foreign policies by limiting both the resources that leaders can extract and the extent to which national as opposed to personal and societal interests can be expected to prevail.[48]

---

46. For general overviews of Third World security, see Yezid Sayigh, *Confronting the 1990s: Security in the Developing Countries*, Adelphi Paper No. 251 (London: International Institute of Strategic Studies, Summer 1990); and Mohammed Ayoob, "The Security Problematic of the Third World," *World Politics*, Vol. 43, No. 2 (January 1991), pp. 257–283.

47. See, for example, Jeffrey Herbst, "The Creation and Maintenance of National Boundaries in Africa," *International Organization*, Vol. 43, No. 4 (Fall 1989), pp. 673–692.

48. Robert Jackson and Carl Rosberg, "Why Africa's Weak States Persist: The Empirical and the Juridical in Statehood," *World Politics*, Vol. 35, No. 1 (October 1982), pp. 1–24; Jeffrey Herbst,

The question I want to ask here may not require much detail: is the end of the Cold War likely to increase or decrease international conflict in the Third World? To put this another way, did the Cold War dampen or exacerbate conflict? It probably did both: dampened it in some respects, exacerbated it in others; dampened it in some areas of the globe, exacerbated it in others; dampened it under some circumstances, exacerbated it under others. In the net, however, it generally dampened conflict and we can therefore expect more rather than less conflict in the future.[49]

Many analysts argued that superpower competition spread conflict to the Third World. On some occasions, strife might not have developed at all had not a superpower sought out or been receptive to the pleas of a local actor to undermine or at least to preoccupy the other superpower's client. In other cases, conflict would have been less bloody and prolonged had the states or factions not expected that they could compensate for local weakness by garnering increased aid from abroad. Furthermore, the aid itself, especially financial and military, made these conflicts more intense and destructive. The civil war in Angola epitomizes these processes, although traces can be found in many other countries as well.

This is only the most visible part of the story, however. The extent to which superpower involvement dampened Third World conflicts is more difficult to discern because it resulted in non-events. But it is at least as important. Each superpower had an interest in seeing that the other did not make significant gains in the Third World, and also realized that the other had a parallel interest. Each knew that under most circumstances to succeed too well, or to permit its clients to do so, would invite a forceful response. Of course the Soviet Union in its desire to change the status quo welcomed and assisted disruptive movements and sought clients who, in part because of the nature of their domestic regimes, challenged their neighbors. But often it was indigenous forces that created violence and were restrained from abroad. The civil strife in Sri Lanka and the Punjab shows that even without

---

"War and the State in Africa," *International Security*, Vol. 14, No. 4 (Spring 1990), pp. 117–139. As these articles note, more wars might lead to stronger states. See also Robert H. Jackson, *Quasi States: Sovereignty, International Relations, and the Third World* (Cambridge and New York: Cambridge University Press, 1990).
49. It should be noted, however, that the conclusion about the future follows from the judgment of the past only if all other things remain equal. This ignores the possibility that the end of the Cold War will trigger processes that could compensate for the removal of the superpower restraint or, on the other hand, that would alter politics in the Third World in ways that are difficult to foresee. For reasoning of this type, see Jervis, "Systems Effects."

superpower involvement, internal conflict can be prolonged and bloody. Furthermore, it is no accident that the only protracted armed conflicts in the Middle East were those that did not engage the Soviet-American rivalry (the Iran-Iraq War and Egypt's intervention in Yemen). The Arab-Israeli wars were short because they were dangerous not only to the local actors, but also to the superpowers who therefore had an interest in seeing that they did not get out of hand. In some cases, such as Angola and Afghanistan, extensive superpower involvement was compatible with a lengthy conflict, and indeed may have prolonged it. But when the superpower stakes were great, the area volatile, and the Third World actors not completely under control, the superpowers could not be content to fuel the conflict by indiscriminate assistance but also had to see that it did not lead them to a dangerous confrontation.

The 1991 Gulf War, the first case of major post–Cold War violence, might not have taken place in the earlier era. The United States could not have afforded to act as it did had the Soviet Union been Iraq's ally and a threat in Europe. The latter factor would have made the United States unable to deploy such a large military force; the former would have made it fear that a military response could call in the Soviet Union. On the other hand, aggression by a client of the Soviet Union would have been more of a threat than was Iraq's action in the actual event. So the United States would have been more strongly motivated to respond. Indeed, the Soviet Union would have realized this and might have restrained its client. Iraq's behavior also would have been different. With Soviet assistance, its need for Kuwait's wealth would have been slightly diminished. Furthermore, to the extent that it acted out of fear of isolation or the hope that the new international constellation provided it with a "window of opportunity," a continuation of the Cold War would have made the aggression less likely.[50]

The superpowers offered security to their Third World clients as well as restraining them. Unless other forces and mechanisms that would serve these functions develop, aggression will be less difficult and, partly for this reason, status quo states in the Third World will worry more about self-protection. Even absent aggressive motives, conflict will often result through the security dilemma: states' efforts to make themselves more secure will threaten others. These traditional sources of international conflict will work themselves out

---

50. See Milton Viorst, "Report from Baghdad," *New Yorker*, June 24, 1991, pp. 67–68; Saddam Hussein's speech to the Arab Summit Meeting on February 24, 1990, *Foreign Broadcast Information Service: Near East and South Asia*, February 27, 1990, pp. 1–5.

in a context that for at least several years will be changing rapidly as the states seek to adjust to the decreased superpower presence. Indeed, in some cases weak clients will collapse or be overthrown (e.g., Ethiopia), heightening the possibilities for regional disturbances.

The Third World may not necessarily recapitulate the international history of developed states. What Alexander Gerschenkron showed about domestic politics is true for international relations as well—the countries that go first change the environment so that the paths of late-comers are different.[51] Even without their Cold War hyper-involvement, the superpowers and European states will continue to exert some influence. Third World leaders may also seek to emulate the First, in part in the hope of thereby earning greater aid, investment, and access to markets. Nevertheless, as in Eastern Europe, a decrease in superpower influence will permit more of the display of aggression and mutual insecurity that constitute the standard patterns of international conflict. Nationalism, ethnic disputes, and regional rivalries are likely to be prominent. Undoubtedly there will be surprises in the details, and specific predictions are beyond reach, but there is no reason to think that the basic contours of international politics will be unfamiliar.

The Increased Range of Choice for the United States

Whether or not the new era turns out to be more violent than the Cold War, it will present the United States with a wider range of choices. While the Soviet-American rivalry did not entirely dictate American policy—witness the past 45 years of vigorous political and academic debates—Americans agreed on crucial questions most of the time: American security needs were the core of its national interest; the Soviet Union was the greatest threat; the United States had no choice but to be actively engaged in the world to protect itself. Even when the answers differed sharply, for example over whether the Third World mattered to the United States, almost everyone agreed that the question was what policy would bolster American national security.[52]

---

51. Alexander Gerschenkron, *Economic Backwardness in Historical Perspective* (Cambridge: Belknap Press/Harvard University Press, 1962). Also see Charles Tilly, *Coercion, Capital, and European States, AD 990–1990* (London: Blackwell, 1990), chapter 7.
52. See, for example, the articles by Stephen Walt, "The Case for Finite Containment: Analyzing U.S. Grand Strategy," Steven David, "Why the Third World Matters," Michael Desch, "The Keys that Lock Up the World: Identifying American Interests in the Periphery," and Robert Johnson, "The Persian Gulf in U.S. Strategy: A Skeptical View," in *International Security*, Vol. 14, No. 1 (Summer 1989), pp. 5–160; and Van Evera, "Why Europe Matters, Why the Third World Doesn't." It can also be argued that America had fewer valid security concerns during

This is no longer the case: the realm of compulsion has contracted and that of freedom of choice has expanded. The reason is not only the collapse of the Soviet Union but also the changes in world politics among the developed countries discussed earlier. If the standard rules of international relations were still to apply, the Soviet Union would be replaced as an American adversary by one of the other most powerful states in the system. But I do not believe this will occur.

REMAINING THREATS TO AMERICAN SECURITY
Some threats to American security remain: nuclear weapons in the hands of the Soviet Union and other states, scarcity of economic resources, and non-traditional menaces such as migration and pollution. While they call for serious attention, however, they are not likely to narrow the range of American choice nearly as severely as the Cold War did.

Even if the Soviet Union or the successor republics are benign, it or they will still have a nuclear stockpile that could destroy the United States. Nevertheless, the threat is much reduced even if one concentrates on capabilities and puts aside the enormous change in intentions (which, some argue, can easily revert to hostility, especially as Soviet or Russian domestic politics changes).[53] With the Soviet withdrawal from Eastern Europe, not only is there little threat to Western Europe, but it is difficult to see how a Soviet-American nuclear confrontation could develop. During the Cold War most analysts did not doubt the American ability to deter a direct attack; they feared a nuclear war resulting from NATO's inability to stop an invasion of Western Europe.

A second threat is the spread of nuclear weapons. Americans used to take comfort in the fact that most potential proliferators were enemies of the Soviet Union—e.g., Taiwan, Pakistan. But with the diminution of the Soviet threat and the increasing awareness that countries like Iraq and North Korea

---

the Cold War than was generally believed: see, for example, Robert Art, "A Defensible Defense: America's Grand Strategy After the Cold War," *International Security*, Vol. 15, No. 4 (Spring 1991), pp. 18–22; Eric Nordlinger "Prospects and Policies for Soviet-American Reconciliation," *Political Science Quarterly*, Vol. 103, No. 2 (Summer 1988), pp. 197–222; Nordlinger, "America's Strategic Immunity," in Robert Jervis and Seweryn Bialer, eds., *Soviet-American Relations After the Cold War* (Durham, N.C.: Duke University Press, 1990), pp. 239–261; Jervis, *Meaning of the Nuclear Revolution*, chapter 1; Jervis, *The Logic of Images in International Relations*, 2nd ed. (New York: Columbia University Press, 1989), pp. 244–250.
53. See, for example, Colin Gray, "Do the Changes Within the Soviet Union Provide a Basis for Eased Soviet-American Relations? A Skeptical View," in Jervis and Bialer, eds., *Soviet-American Relations*, pp. 61–75.

could acquire nuclear weapons, the menace to the United States has increased, at least relative to other threats. Former Soviet clients may at once be more desperate (lacking a powerful superpower patron) and more autonomous (lacking a superpower to restrain them). Even though they are many years away from being able to threaten the United States directly, the day is much nearer when they could menace American allies or present a potent deterrent to American intervention in their region.[54] If Iraq had possessed nuclear weapons, for example, U.S. policy in the 1991 Persian Gulf crisis and War would have been more complicated, to say the least.

The heightened danger of proliferation still provides a great deal of room for freedom of choice, however. The United States can seek to minimize the risk of having to fight a regional nuclear power by minimizing its involvement with that country and its neighbors. Alternatively, it can pursue an active foreign policy aimed at discouraging proliferation and deterring the outbreak of dangerous regional conflicts. During the Cold War, the first option was seen as unacceptable because it would permit unhindered (at least by the United States) Soviet access to the region, a concern that is no longer relevant. The Cold War also inhibited a vigorous non-proliferation policy because the United States felt it could not afford to alienate its regional allies, a consideration that is also now less constraining.

Is access to raw materials a central security concern? With the possible exception of oil, it is hard to see how a hostile power could deny any raw materials to the United States. Even oil is dispersed thoughout many areas of the world and the ability of a cartel to drive the price up—let alone withhold sales to the West—is limited by the potential availability of alternative energy sources. Thus, even if Saddam Hussein had retained control of Kuwait and gained great influence over Saudi Arabia, the United States would not have been at his mercy. To the extent that dependence on Middle Eastern oil is worrisome, conservation and the development of alternative energy sources would probably be cheaper than maintaining and using military force. During the Cold War one could reply that America's strong position was simply irrelevant because Europe and Japan were very vulnerable. Now, even if this is true, there are no immediate security reasons for

---

54. See Stephen Peter Rosen, "Regional Nuclear War: Problems for Theory and Practice," unpublished paper. For a general discussion of the danger of proliferation and possible American responses in the post–Cold War world, see Art, "Defensible Defense," pp. 24–30; and Eric Arnett, "Choosing Nuclear Arsenals," *Journal of Strategic Studies*, Vol. 13, No. 3 (September 1990), pp. 166–171.

oil to be an American concern, although a major price increase would still be economically disruptive. Furthermore, Western oil exploitation techniques applied to the Soviet Union should greatly increase the global supply, barring a prolonged civil war in that country or among the successor republics.

New threats to American security may emerge. A revolution or widespread civil unrest in Mexico could send large numbers of refugees across the border. Although this event represents the highest combination of likelihood and danger if it did occur, it is doubtful whether traditional security policies can have much influence on whether this will occur or how the United States could cope with it. Thus this menace cannot be the premise for many of the guidelines for general foreign policy.

Non-traditional security threats such as global warming, ozone depletion, and other forms of environmental degradation are also of concern. But the dangers are too far off, the scientific evidence is too ambiguous, the domestic interests involved are too conflicting, and the alternative approaches are too many for these issues to dominate American foreign policy and provide an agreed-upon basis for action as containment did previously.

THE RANGE OF CHOICE. Even with the new dangers, the United States is now free—and indeed is required—to think much more seriously about how to define its interests. Old questions of both ends and means which the Cold War answered or put in abeyance have returned. What does the United States want? What does it value, what does it seek, what costs is it willing to pay, and what methods are likely to be efficacious? If possible, Americans would like to see the world resemble them—or, to put it slightly differently, embody their values. Thus the United States seeks a world composed of states that are liberal, democratic, prosperous, and peaceful both internally and in their foreign policies. In such a world the United States would probably prosper as well and would have little cause for concern if others grew even richer, since this would threaten neither its security nor its self-image. Indeed, Americans desire such a world less for the direct benefits it would bring to the United States than because they believe that it would serve the best interests of all people.[55]

---

55. Whether this is the case is an interesting question that can be dealt with only briefly here. America's vision of the good society is not universally shared either domestically or internationally. Some people, especially those who see political and social development as unidirectional, may believe that with sufficient education and exposure to the Western world all people will want to be like Americans. Perhaps this will be true in the long run, but it appears that for the foreseeable future many in the Third World will find western liberal individualism repellant.

But these generalities do not tell us how active a foreign policy the United States should adopt. Should the United States attempt to influence others by intervention (not limiting this to the military sense) or by example? The latter tradition, overwhelmed and abandoned by the exigencies of the Cold War, has deep roots in American institutions, values, and politics. The desire to be "like a city upon the Hill" is a strong one, having been embraced by liberals and conservatives in different periods of our history. That complete isolation is impossible does not rule out a significant retraction of American involvement abroad.[56]

With security concerns no longer pressing, other values must determine how deeply and in what ways the United States should pursue an activist foreign policy. Human rights is a prime example. When the House of Representatives voted to renew China's most-favored-nation status for tariffs in the fall of 1990, it not only said that this concession would not be granted unless China eliminated major human rights violations within six months, but also permitted the president to waive this requirement if doing so would further encourage China to improve human rights.[57] Compare the Cold War, when it was routine for Congress to attach various conditions to foreign aid bills with the proviso that they could be waived if doing so was in the American national *security* interest. At least some Americans would like to elevate human rights to this privileged status. Although enhancing its status is not presently national policy, during the Cold War would the American ambassador to Kenya have so publicly criticized that government for its

---

This presents the United States with an intellectual—and emotional—conundrum as well as a policy dilemma. Americans want to see their values realized throughout the world, and one of these values is self-determination in the broadest sense of the term. But should Americans rejoice or despair if others then define themselves in ways that are antithetical to Americans' values and hostile to their interests? For an argument that if America is to have a benign effect on the world and realize its deepest values, it must "recast . . . its self-conception, its place in the West, and its relation to the former Leninist and 'third' worlds," see Kenneth Jowitt, "The Leninist Extinction," in Daniel Chirot, ed., *The Crisis of Leninism and the Decline of the Left: The Revolutions of 1989* (Seattle: University of Washington Press, 1991), p. 94. Also see Louis Hartz's seminal *The Liberal Tradition in America* (New York: Harcourt Brace, 1955), chapter 11.

56. Public opinion polls on the attitudes of the American people toward isolationism yield sharply conflicting results. According to one, 74 percent of the people want to reduce involvement abroad in order to concentrate on problems at home; *Time*, October 7, 1991, p. 15. According to another, 63 percent believe that the United States should assert itself in international politics as much as or more than it does now; R.W. Apple, Jr., "Majority in Poll Fault Focus by Bush on Global Policy But Back New Order," *New York Times*, October 11, 1991, p. 8.

57. Clifford Krauss, "Democratic Leaders Divided on China Trade," *New York Times*, October 9, 1990, p. 5.

human rights abuses?[58] Even more strikingly, the United States temporarily halted aid to Yugoslavia in May 1991 because of the "pattern of systematic gross violations of human rights" in that country, which in the past had a privileged position as a crucial bulwark against Soviet expansionism.[59]

The United States could also use its new flexibility to promote democracy abroad. To some extent it did this during the Cold War; the "Reagan Doctrine" included support for guerrillas in Afghanistan, Angola, and Nicaragua. But for Reagan the promotion of democracy meant supporting any noncommunist forces. More often, seeking democracy was seen as too dangerous: the fear of communism meant that the United States supported rightwing dictatorships out of the fear that if they were undermined, the victors would be not democratic reformers but the hard-core left wing.[60] As President Kennedy said after the assassination of the Dominican Republic's dictator, Rafael Trujillo: "There are three possibilities in descending order of preference; a decent democratic regime, a continuation of the Trujillo regime, or a Castro regime. We ought to aim at the first, but we really can't renounce the second until we are sure that we can avoid the third."[61] Although the third possibility is still disturbing because it would oppress the people in the country involved, the demise of the Cold War has sapped much of the force of the dilemma Kennedy articulated and allows American presidents to support democratic movements if they so choose.[62]

The United States could also seek to protect—or more accurately, minimize the damage to—the environment. This would have high economic costs, at least as measured by the standard—and perhaps misleading—indicators of well-being. Most obviously, curbing the emission of greenhouse gases would slow economic growth. The effort would have to be an international one,

---

58. Raymond Bonner, "A Reporter at Large: African Democracy," *New Yorker,* September 3, 1990, pp. 93–105. Also see Jane Perez, "Kenyan Magazine Editor Held After Articles on Opposition Party," *New York Times,* March 3, 1991. For reports of an American attack on human and political rights violations in Pakistan, see J. Michael Luhan, "Bhutto and Her Party Languish After Defeat," *New York Times,* May 6, 1991, p. 5.
59. David Binder, "U.S., Citing Human Rights, Halts Aid to Yugoslavia," *New York Times,* May 19, 1991, p. 10. Also see the stories in the *Times* over the succeeding week.
60. The best discussion is Douglas Macdonald, *Adventures in Chaos* (Cambridge: Harvard University Press, forthcoming).
61. Quoted in Arthur Schlesinger, Jr., *A Thousand Days* (Boston: Houghton Mifflin, 1965), p. 769.
62. For the case for making the spread of democracy the pivot of American foreign policy, see Gregory Fossedal, *The Democratic Imperative: Exporting the American Revolution* (New York: Basic Books, 1989). For balanced discussions, see Snyder, "Averting Anarchy"; Art, "Defensible Defense," pp. 42–43; Van Evera, "Why Europe Matters," pp. 25–30.

and American leadership could strain relations with other developed states and require economic concessions to developing ones. But the end of the Cold War makes it possible to give more consideration to such policies. Not only have some resources been liberated by the decline in military spending that the end of the Soviet threat permits, but part of the previous necessity for high economic growth was security in the form of staying ahead of the Soviet Union. Diplomatic capital that was previously required for anti-Soviet policies could also now be employed for environmental issues.

Encouraging domestic economic growth remains an important goal. Foreign policy may need to play an even larger role here than in the past as the pressures on the open international economic system increase due to the diminution of the shared Western interest in maintaining common strength against the Soviet Union. There is now a greater danger of the world breaking into trading blocs, damaging the American economy and increasing political frictions.[63] To prevent this, foreign political involvement and even security guarantees may be called for, as Robert Art and Stephen Van Evera argue.[64] But these measures may be neither necessary nor sufficient for the objective. Protectionist impulses have proved weaker than many analysts expected and may not be able to dominate even though proponents of free trade now lack the Cold War rationale. An activist foreign policy in the form of support for and close ties to trading partners would not reduce domestic pressures for protection unless it produced significant concessions from them, a bargain these countries might reject. Furthermore, concessions to the United States granted in return for security support might contradict the non-discriminatory principles of an open system. Thus while supporting the American (and the world) economy will continue to be an important objective, it is not likely to provide agreed-upon guidelines for U.S. foreign policy or to readily gain pride of place over other values.

An additional continuing American goal could be the prevention of the spread of nuclear weapons, less for narrow concerns about U.S. security than for the desire to spare other countries the horrors of nuclear war. If the former were all that were at stake, the United States could react to Pakistan's nuclear program by disengaging from the subcontinent. A nuclear war between India and Pakistan would not menace America. Indeed, if it turned

---

63. Robert Gilpin, *The Political Economy of International Relations* (Princeton: Princeton University Press, 1987), pp. 397–401.
64. Art, "Defensible Defense," pp. 30–41; and Van Evera, "Why Europe Matters," pp. 10–11.

out badly for both countries—which probably would be the case—it might discourage proliferation in areas of more direct concern to the United States. But security is not the only value at stake; nuclear war is an evil that is worth a significant price to suppress.

Perhaps the most ambitious goal the United States could seek is curbing if not eliminating war. However much this might have accorded with America's deepest hopes, it was out of the question during the Cold War: the intrinsic evil of war had to yield to a consideration of how the American stance toward a particular conflict would affect the world-wide rivalry with the Soviet Union.[65] As the conflict in the Gulf reminds us, the decline in Soviet power means that the United States need not fear that military interventions could trigger undesired Soviet responses, and it vastly increases the possibilities for collective security. Even before Iraq's invasion of Kuwait, President Bush called for the United States to build such a system: "As the world's most powerful democracy, we are inescapably the leader, the connecting link in a global alliance of democracies. The pivotal responsibility for ensuring the stability of the international balance remains ours."[66]

If collective security is desirable and even feasible, how much should the United States contribute to it? To the extent that the United States takes the lead, it is likely to demand primacy in setting the policy, as it did in the Persian Gulf. But it is far from clear whether other states would tolerate having as little influence as they did in that case. The alternative is a smaller American contribution and truly multilateral decision-making. But how often has the United States been willing to take a very active part in an international venture without playing the leading role? Little of the talk of a new world order asks the United States to bend its conception of the common good to that of other members of the international community. Furthermore, the collective goods problem would be harder to surmount if the American

---

65. As Arnold Wolfers put it, collective defense had primacy over collective security; Arnold Wolfers, *Discord and Collaboration: Essays on International Politics* (Baltimore: Johns Hopkins University Press, 1962), chapter 12.
66. Bush, *National Security Strategy of the United States*, p. 7. This is part of Bush's "new world order." For a good exposition of this slippery concept, see Stanley Sloan, "The U.S. role in a New World Order: Prospects for George Bush's Global Vision," Congressional Research Service Report, March 28, 1991. Slightly less ambitiously, the United States might seek a concert system. This would require extensive cooperation among the great powers but would not try to prevent all aggression. For the concert as a model for the future, see Charles Kupchan and Clifford Kupchan, "Concerts, Collective Security, and the Future of Europe," *International Security*, Vol. 16, No. 1 (Summer 1991), pp. 114–161; and Gregory Gause, "Postwar Gulf Security: Hegemony, Balance, or Concert?" unpublished paper.

contribution was less than dominant. If a sizeable number of states are asked to take relatively equal shares in the venture, each will feel that it can shirk and pass more of the burden to its partners, thereby increasing both frictions and the chance that the enterprise will collapse.

The Necessity for Choice

The Cold War has freed America from the overriding concern with security and has presented the United States with a wide range of possibilities. This poses a "necessity for choice"—to borrow the title of a book written in an era when there was actually little room for choice[67]—because the goals and values discussed in the previous section are not entirely consistent with each other. Some can be pursued only by slighting others: when foreign regimes engage in many practices of which the United States disapproves, it will have to choose which of them to most vigorously oppose. For example, if a country seeks nuclear weapons, violates civil rights, and tolerates aggression, the United States—and others—will have to order its priorities and decide which is the greatest evil. Perhaps in some cases the United States can help a new regime come to power that will cease all these practices. But this is not to be counted on. Indeed, free elections can produce a regime that follows unfriendly foreign policy and distasteful domestic practices.[68] The problem is illustrated by President Bush's recent proposal on foreign aid which sets forth "five objectives: promoting democratic values, strengthening United States competitiveness, promoting peace, protecting against transnational threats, and meeting humanitarian needs."[69] But the proposed legislation does not weight these objectives or explain how to make trade-offs among them.

Many specific conflicts between American goals are possible. The United States may have to choose between protecting some parts of the environment and maintaining good relations with Japan. Continuing frictions over fishing, whaling, and the importation of ivory may be followed by the need for the United States to decide whether to spend its political capital opposing the extensive Japanese logging of the rain forests of Southeast Asia. In the

---

67. Henry Kissinger, *The Necessity for Choice* (New York: Harper and Row, 1961).
68. This would probably be true in Algeria. See Youssef Ibrahim, "Algeria Imposes a Curfew and Promises to Use Force," *New York Times*, June 7, 1991, p. 6.
69. Janet Battaile, "Bush Seeks Expanded Powers on Foreign Aid," *New York Times*, April 14, 1991, p. 7.

security area, encouraging European unity probably would further the chances of peace as well as more deeply embed Germany in a supra-national structure. But a united Europe would be a more effective competitor for global influence and economic advantage. The goal of non-proliferation could be furthered at the cost of offering political support to authoritarian and oppressive regimes.[70] Security guarantees could be a potent tool against proliferation, but they would also bolster undesirable regimes and unjust borders as well as increasing the danger that America would be drawn into any war that did break out. In other cases, such as North Korea, the United States might emulate Israel and destroy the nuclear facilities of a would-be proliferator. But acting in this way could undermine a collective security system by convincing others that their participation was not necessary, or that the United States was too reckless to provide acceptable leadership. A collective security system, in turn, would freeze the status quo and protect tyrants unless it were supplemented by a method for producing peaceful change and curbing outrageous internal practices.

Collective security was represented and perhaps furthered by the war against Iraq. Maintaining an inclusive coalition displayed great American skill; however, it also came at the price of other American values. Thus the United States had to alter its stance toward Iran and, even more, Syria, regimes that do not fully abide by the norms of proper international—let alone domestic—behavior. Furthermore, Syria took the opportunity to consolidate its control over Lebanon, an act of aggression that the United States could not in those circumstances oppose or even protest. Other states with less direct interests in opposing Iraq also may have required significant inducements. Thus, apparently to gain Chinese cooperation in the Security Council, the United States reduced its pressure on the human rights issue.

The Gulf War has also elevated overall expectations of what the United States can and should do. As Bush himself said: "Never before has the world looked more to the American example. What makes us American is our allegiance to an idea that all people everywhere must be free."[71] Such rhetoric may lay a trap for policy. Just as twenty years ago people asked, "if the United States can put a man on the moon, why can it not end poverty,

---

70. See Richard Betts, "Paranoids, Pygmies, Pariahs, and Nonproliferation," *Foreign Policy*, No. 26 (Spring 1977), pp. 167–168, 179–183.
71. Quoted in Maureen Dowd, "Bush Stands Firm on Military Policy in Iraqi Civil War," *New York Times*, April 14, 1991, p. 1.

produce racial harmony, etc.," so now others—and American public opinion as well—expect the United States to protect the Kurds, democratize Kuwait, and perhaps bring peace and security to much of the globe. Dashing these expectations may create disappointment and bitterness that will be obstacles to a more modest policy; trying to live up to them would lead the United States to overreach itself.

The costs of leading this coalition will be particularly high if the war—and the way it was conducted—increases anti-Americanism in the Third World, especially in Muslim countries. Such a reaction would destabilize friendly regimes, set back moderate political movements, and decrease support for other American interventions in the Third World.[72] Indeed, if this proves to be the case, this exercise of collective security, far from deterring future aggressors and laying the foundations for a moderate world order, will have increased instability and violence.

During the Cold War, American security policy was marked by what was sometimes known as "the great trade-off": a deterrence policy that relied on the threat of all-out war increased the probability of peace, but at the price of risking total destruction if it failed. In the current era, the great trade-off is between America's security and non-security interests. The reduced urgency of the former allow greater attention to the latter. Moreover, while the pursuit of many values would require U.S. foreign policy to be as active as it was during the Cold War, American security could be well-served by minimizing military and even political involvement abroad. It is hard to see how the American homeland could be threatened except through commitments and entangling alliances. Furthering the other values discussed above requires promises, threats, and a variety of close political ties abroad, and these may come at some cost to American security.

More specifically, policies that seek to keep the peace in various areas of the world (especially Eastern Europe, but in the Third World as well) incur the cost of increasing the chance that the United States will be drawn into these conflicts if they occur. If the United States cared only about promoting democracy and peaceful intercourse in Eastern Europe, it would become deeply involved in that region, offering aid and investment, seeking to build liberal domestic and international institutions, and even offering security

---

72. For a related discussion, see Richard K. Herrmann, "The Middle East and the New World Order: Rethinking U.S. Political Strategy after the Gulf War," *International Security*, Vol. 16, No. 2 (Fall 1991), pp. 42–75.

guarantees. But if these policies were to fail and violence to break out in the region, there would be greater pressure on the United States to intervene, with force if necessary. This would be costly and dangerous. Indeed, the only plausible path to Soviet-American nuclear war is through the United States resisting the re-imposition of Soviet rule over Eastern Europe or break-away republics of the Soviet Union. Such Soviet actions can hardly be seen as threats to American security, however; this war would depend on a drastic extension of American interests.[73] In fact NATO recently declared that "coercion or intimidation" of states in Eastern and Central Europe would be a "direct and material concern" to the alliance, although officials also announced that this was not intended as a challenge to the Soviet Union.[74] Whether the United States and its European partners will make this a real commitment is not yet clear. Of course, the United States could get the worst of both possible worlds: it could fail to involve itself in efforts that might prevent strife and yet be unable to remain aloof when conflict broke out.[75] After all, President Bush announced that the United States would not intervene to protect the Kurds, but political (and perhaps personal) pressures overcame this stance of self-control.[76]

Conclusion

The end of the Cold War bears witness both to time's cycle and to time's arrow. Politics among the developed countries will not return to what it was before 1939. The costs of war have drastically increased while the benefits, especially compared with those available from alternative means, have decreased. Part of the reason for the latter change, in turn, is that the values of states and the individuals that compose them have changed. Although such constant factors as rivalry, the security dilemma, and the desire for advantage over others will continue, they are not likely to produce violence. And without the recurring threat of war, the patterns of international politics in the developed world cannot be the same. This is not true elsewhere on

---

73. For the advocacy of this position, see Huntington, "America's Changing Strategic Interest," p. 13. Walter Slocombe, "The Continued Need for Extended Deterrence," *Washington Quarterly*, Vol. 14, No. 4 (Autumn 1991), pp. 160–167.
74. Thomas Friedman, "NATO Tries to Ease Security Concerns in Eastern Europe," *New York Times*, June 7, 1991, p. 1.
75. I am indebted to Stephen Van Evera for discussion on this point.
76. Secretary of State Baker apparently came to support intervention only after he visited the Kurdish refugee camps.

the globe. While Eastern Europe and the Third World are not likely to simply recapitulate the West's history from which so many of our theories of international politics are derived, neither should we expect a basic change from the familiar ways in which nations relate to each other.

The combination of the end of traditional threats to American security and the continuation of violence in many parts of the world confronts the United States with a wide range of choice. Without the clear framework that constituted the Cold War, there will be conflicts between security interests and other interests. New possibilities arise but not all of them can be pursued simultaneously. While the new era will be a less constrained one for the developed states in general and the United States in particular, by the same token the intellectual and political tasks are considerably increased. How involved America should be in world politics and what values it should seek to foster—and at what cost and risk—are questions that remain open, unanswered, and largely unaddressed.

Strategies Before Containment

Terry L. Deibel

Patterns for the Future

The end of the Cold War and the disintegration of the Soviet Union demand that American foreign policy analysts rethink their most basic assumptions. This article is intended to contribute to that effort by comparing past strategic patterns with future strategic possibilities. Specifically, it examines U.S. foreign affairs strategies before the Cold War, in three areas of the national interest, for clues about the likely contours of American strategy in the post–Cold War era. Its purpose is to broaden the range of possibilities under consideration, on the premise that strategies designed to serve U.S. interests before the Soviet threat dominated American statecraft may well prove suggestive for strategists attempting to further those interests after the Soviet threat has disappeared.

Few would disagree with the proposition that the demise of the Soviet Union marks a decisive change in the circumstances of American foreign policy. Not only does it mean the definitive end of the Cold War; it also may mean the end of some eighty years of hegemonic enterprises[1]—of efforts by major industrialized nation-states to overturn the global balance of power— that have given world politics in the twentieth century its peculiar, apocalyptic character.[2] What is different today is not simply that the Soviet empire, ideology, economy, and even military power have all collapsed; after all, the Kaiser's Germany, the Third Reich, and imperial Japan also came to an end.

Terry L. Deibel is Professor of National Strategy at the National War College. He wishes to thank John Gaddis, Alan Henrikson, and David Trask for reading and offering helpful comments on this paper. Of course, the views expressed here are solely those of the author and do not reflect the official policy of the National Defense University, the Department of Defense, or the U.S. Government.

---

1. I am indebted to historian David Trask for the term "hegemonic enterprises" as used here; it follows the definition of hegemonic war in Robert Gilpin, *War and Change in World Politics* (Cambridge: Cambridge University Press, 1981), p. 15.
2. Americans in particular have difficulty comprehending just how different the twentieth century was from those that preceded it. It has been, in Raymond Aron's apt phrase, a century of total war, a period that began in the tangled alliance systems leading into World War I, continued through the fascist militarism of Japan and Germany and a second horrific global conflict, and then, under the numbing threat of nuclear annihilation, settled into over forty years of struggle against Soviet hegemony, punctuated by major wars in Korea and Vietnam. Each war, hot or cold, created conditions which spawned the next; the major industrialized powers lived in constant fear of threats to their very existence; and all, for offense or defense, spent unprecedented sums on arms. Raymond Aron, *The Century of Total War* (Garden City, N.Y.: Doubleday, 1954).

The possibilities opened by the new era stem rather from the way Soviet power disintegrated:[3] particularly because no hot war was fought, there is apparently no aspirant to forceful global domination waiting in the wings, no aggrieved nation-state with sufficient power to threaten the balance at the global level.

As a result, we may be witnessing not only the end of the Cold War, but also the end (in historical if not chronological terms) of the twentieth century. For the first time in virtually anyone's memory, Americans may be entering a period of world politics when none of the most powerful states harbors aggressive intent, and all are thereby freed of critical threats to their physical security. Of course, the great powers will continue to compete: for political influence over issues that concern their interests, for market share and technological leadership that affect their power and prosperity, and to set the rules for (and push onto each other the burdens of) their cooperative endeavors. Nor will the post–Cold War world be free of violence; too many signs in the formerly socialist and Third Worlds point in the opposite direction, and some of these conflicts (as the Gulf crisis warned) may well threaten the West's vital interests.[4] But the fear of forceful domination on a global scale does seem to have ended for the foreseeable future, and with it the distinguishing feature of international politics in the twentieth century.[5]

Along with great possibilities, however, the post–Cold War period will also pose its share of predicaments. Considered purely as a problem in foreign affairs strategy—that approach to foreign policy which attempts to orchestrate all the instruments of state power into coherent and purposeful statecraft—the next era will almost certainly be more complicated than the Cold

---

3. See Charles William Maynes, "America Without the Cold War," *Foreign Policy,* No. 78 (Spring 1990), p. 4.

4. Nor will the destructiveness of weaponry be reduced, although the turn away from tactical nuclear arms spurred by the linked revolutions in precision and conventional firepower may well contribute to a reduced sense of threat.

5. The most useful historical reference point for our times is not, then, the creative turmoil that beset American statecraft in the late 1940s as it shifted from alliance with the Soviet Union to Cold War. The last comparable turning point was rather the beginning of the twentieth century, when the world gradually slipped away from the hundred years' peace that followed the Napoleonic era, or even the second decade of the nineteenth, when European statesmen were able to establish a new world order that brought an earlier century of wars to a close. And the place to look for historical analogies may thus be not the 1940s but the nineteenth century and times in the twentieth, like the early interwar years, when the world scene seemed free of aspirants to global domination.

War. For the essence of strategy is choice, its most difficult aspect the setting of priorities. By providing a widely perceived threat of overwhelming proportions, the Cold War made the most important strategic choices for us. Although the single-minded policy coherence of the early Cold War years has been progressively undermined during the last two decades by competing demands unrelated to containment,[6] only the Carter administration publicly called for refocusing American national security strategy away from the Soviet threat,[7] and its experience provided ample if perverse evidence of the power of that threat as a central organizing principle.

Faced with this challenge, post–Cold War strategists can draw little comfort from the record of past American adaptations to massive historical change. Indeed, the twentieth century was nearly half over before the American people learned to recognize the challenges posed by its hegemonic enterprises and mustered the political will to take them on. Resistance to change was profound because Americans had enjoyed a hundred years of free security, made possible by the happy coincidence of geographic insularity with the then-primitive state of the technology of warfare. The merely fortuitous came to be seen as permanent, and when conditions changed at the turn of the century, policies did not.

Similarly, today's Americans have lived in a period distorted in its own way, by its own peculiar hegemonic threat. Will we be better able to adapt to the changes we face than were our predecessors? How shall we "disenthrall ourselves" from the dogmas of our immediate past so that we can "think anew and act anew,"[8] so that we in our time do not spend half of the twenty-first century figuring out its distinctive policy challenges and struggling to define an effective strategy for dealing with them?

---

6. Indeed, one can divide the history of American foreign policy since World War II into three distinct periods partly on the basis of just this criterion. The *post–World War II* era (up to about 1968) can be seen as one in which containment was the overriding policy goal (in that all other goals were both subordinate to and shaped by it); the *post-Vietnam* period (1968–1988) was a time in which containment still predominated, but other interests and issues unrelated to containment asserted themselves, sometimes at crisis levels (e.g., OPEC and the energy crisis, environmental concerns); while the *post–Cold War* era is one in which containment becomes at most a subsidiary policy goal.

7. See Carter's 1977 Notre Dame speech, cited in Seyom Brown, *The Faces of Power* (New York: Columbia University Press, 1983), p. 452; Cyrus Vance, *Hard Choices* (New York: Simon and Schuster, 1983), pp. 24, 27; and Zbigniew Brzezinski, *Power and Principle* (New York: Farrar, Straus, Giroux, 1983), p. 48.

8. The words are Abraham Lincoln's, from the Second Annual Message to Congress, December 1, 1862.

Three Categories of the National Interest

One way to envision a foreign affairs strategy without a Soviet threat is to look at the contours of American policy before the era of containment. This is not at all to imply that an old policy approach can be brought out of mothballs, like the World War II battleships recommissioned in the 1980s, to serve the needs of a very different historical era. But looking at foreign affairs strategies from a time when the Soviet threat was not the dominating force in American policy can be very suggestive for those accustomed to Cold War patterns of thought.

Despite the revolutionary times in which we live, the broad categories of the national interest under which these strategic patterns fall are unlikely to change.[9] The United States will continue to concern itself, first, with threats to its *physical security:* with the protection from attack of its territory, people, and their property, and with the preservation against all external threats of its domestic political system and structure of civic values. This was the dominant area of the national interest during the Cold War, the one served by various strategies of containment. Its primacy was underlined by unprecedented spending on a wide variety of policy tools, including foreign economic and security assistance, nuclear weaponry, intelligence and covert action, and conventional military forces.

Second, Americans will expect their government to see to their nation's and their own *economic prosperity,* to promote the domestic welfare. During the Cold War period this interest was safeguarded by American hegemony in the world economic system, a position enshrined in the Bretton Woods institutions (the World Bank and International Monetary Fund) and in the role of the dollar as reserve currency and source of global financial liquidity.

---

9. The national interest is defined here as the conceptual element that justifies policy; one's interests determine, in large part, the desirability of a course of action, answering the question "why are we doing this?" Although the three categories used here generally follow those found among writers on the subject (including the official *National Security Strategy of the United States,* most recently issued from the White House under the date August 1991, pp. 3–4), it leaves out such supposed interests as "good relations with allies and friends," or "a favorable world order"—the latter a category used in Donald E. Nuechterlein, *America Overcommitted: United States National Interests in the 1980s* (Lexington, Ky.: University Press of Kentucky, 1985), p. 8. The reason I exclude it is to reserve the term "national interest" at the highest level of strategy for items that are ends, not means to ends. The categories in this article are limited to security, prosperity, and value projection because these three alone have no higher justification than the values of the individual or the country espousing them; in the end, we want them because we want them.

Economic prosperity required less attention from decisionmakers than did physical security because of the overwhelming preponderance of American economic power after World War II, a state of affairs that was underlined by the country's willingness to sacrifice economic advantage to support its security interests.[10]

Third, Americans will probably continue to insist, as they have since revolutionary times, that their government attune its foreign policies to the values for which they believe their country stands. During the Cold War, the *projection of American values* abroad was accomplished under the negative rubric of anti-communism, a strategy that occasionally assumed the dimensions of a moralistic crusade. As such, anti-communism sometimes overwhelmed the mere containment of Soviet state power, with very different consequences for U.S. strategy.

Today, with no new hegemonic threat on the horizon, with the American economy slipping from control at home and under challenge from Europe and Japan abroad, and with communism utterly bankrupt as an ideology, it seems obvious that containment, economic hegemony, and anti-communism can no longer serve the nation's interests as they did in the Cold War. But American statesmen have always had to fashion strategies to deal with physical security, economic prosperity, and value projection (see Table 1), and many of their earlier approaches relate in interesting ways to the contemporary policy environment. What follows is an effort to review those past strategies in bold strokes, seeking in them some perspective on the future of American statecraft.

Protecting the Nation's Security

BALANCE OF POWER

Perhaps the oldest method by which nation-states have sought to protect their physical security in a hostile world is that of the balance of power. Although condemned in theory by Americans since before Woodrow Wilson's time as immoral and war-prone, balance of power policies have been honored in practice when the nation has felt weak or vulnerable. In the early

---

10. Joseph S. Nye, Jr., *Bound to Lead* (New York: Basic Books, 1990), argues convincingly that American preponderance in the early postwar decades was essentially economic in nature, and that the United States used that economic strength to balance some formidable Soviet military advantages. See esp. pp. 94–95.

Table 1. American Strategies in Three Areas of the National Interest.

	Cold War		Pre–Cold War	
	Global		Regional	Inward-Looking
PHYSICAL SECURITY	Containment	Balance of power Collective security	Hemispheric defense	Isolationism
VALUE PROJECTION	Anti-communism	Human rights Democratic and market systems		Great Exemplar
ECONOMIC PROSPERITY	Hegemony	Free trade	Trade blocs	Protectionism

days of the Republic, when the new United States was a small nation surrounded by the territorial outposts of hostile and much more powerful countries, the founding fathers used balance of power statecraft to protect and expand American independence.[11] Even that supposed moralist Woodrow Wilson, and after him Franklin D. Roosevelt, considered it a vital interest—over which they led the United States into war—to prevent the land mass of Eurasia from being dominated by a single power which would thereby have sufficient industrial capacity to bring war across the oceans to American shores.

After World War II, such thinking was applied beyond Eurasia to the entire world. Indeed, containment was essentially the application of balance-of-power thinking to the particular configuration of the state system that emerged after 1945.[12] George Kennan's original view was that only three contested areas were of sufficient economic importance that they had to be kept out of Soviet hands: the United Kingdom, the Ruhr Valley in Europe, and Japan. Later, under the influence of the domino theory and other dubious views of how power might shift in the international system,[13] others ex-

11. Gordon A. Craig, "The United States and the European Balance," *Foreign Affairs*, Vol. 55, No. 1 (October 1976), pp. 187–198.
12. John Lewis Gaddis, "Introduction: The Evolution of Containment," in Terry L. Deibel and John Lewis Gaddis, eds., *Containing the Soviet Union* (Washington: Pergamon-Brassey's, 1987), p. 1.
13. Stephen M. Walt, "Alliance Formation and the World Balance of Power," *International Security*, Vol. 9, No. 4 (Spring 1985), pp. 3–43.

panded the idea to argue that if the Soviet Union acquired too many allies anywhere—even poor, unstable Third World allies—it could irrevocably tip the global balance against the United States.[14] But however applied, the concept learned by the earliest American statesmen from their European forebears[15] remained essentially the same: that some combinations of power overseas might be so critical as to pose a military threat to U.S. physical security, and that American statecraft had to be engaged, the sooner the better, to thwart any such eventuality.

The question suggested by balance-of-power thinking for the post-containment era is whether, with the collapse of Soviet power, any nation is likely in the foreseeable future to pose a similar threat. Among the current great power candidates, Japan seems too anti-military, China too weak, Germany too enveloped by Europe, Europe (at the same time) too disunited, Brazil or India too young, and recovery by any of the larger Soviet republics or the new Commonwealth of Independent States too far in the future to worry about. Although some degree of nuclear threat will continue in spite of accelerated arms reductions, and occasional terrorist attacks will remain a feature of the international landscape, catastrophic military dangers to American physical security seem hard to imagine for at least the next 15–25 years.

Nevertheless, it is difficult to believe that the United States will dismiss balance of power thinking altogether. Certainly the characteristics of equilibrium in the emerging post–Cold War international system will concern the United States, as will balances in various regions.[16] Moreover, the possibilities for applying a flexible balance-of-power policy will increase in the post–Cold War era for two reasons: first, because the emerging multi-polar system offers as potential allies more states of relatively equal power; and second, because

---

14. See, for example, the text of NSC 68, in *Naval War College Review*, Vol. 27, No. 6 (May–June 1975), pp. 51–108; or more recently the thinking of the Committee on the Present Danger (CPD), in "How the Committee on the Present Danger Will Operate—What It Will Do, and What It Will Not Do" (Washington, D.C.: CPD, November 11, 1976); CPD, "Common Sense and the Common Danger" (Washington, D.C.: CPD, n.d.); CPD, "What Is The Soviet Union Up To?" (Washington, D.C.: CPD, April 4, 1977); and CPD, "Countering the Soviet Threat" (Washington, D.C.: CPD, May 9, 1980).

15. Both Felix Gilbert, *To the Farewell Address* (Princeton, N.J.: Princeton University Press, 1961), pp. 19–43, and James H. Hutson, "Intellectual Foundations of Early American Diplomacy," *Diplomatic History*, Vol. 1, No. 1 (Winter 1977), pp. 1–19, are clear about the impact of European thinking on early American statesmen, though they come to opposite conclusions as to its significance.

16. For a persuasive argument in favor of a post–Cold War balance-of-power strategy, both globally and regionally, see Samuel P. Huntington, "America's Changing Strategic Interests," *Survival*, Vol. 33, No. 1 (January/February 1991), pp. 3–17.

ideological differences that constrain realignments have declined in importance. Ultimately, unless states are able to create some other system to manage a new world order, the balance of power will remain the only game in town.[17] Although its relative power may seem less overwhelming than in the early Cold War years,[18] the United States remains—and is welcomed by a surprising array of states across the globe as—the indispensable balancer.[19]

Still, with a vastly reduced threat, the balance-of-power game will be played for far lower stakes in the future, freeing the system's major actors

17. "For the balance of power system is not one which exists only if instituted by deliberate choice; rather, it is the system which exists unless and until superseded by a consciously erected alternative." Inis L. Claude, Jr., *Power and International Relations* (New York: Random House, 1962), p. 93.

18. The debate between those who argue that the international system is unipolar—like Charles Krauthammer, "The Unipolar Moment," *Foreign Affairs* Vol. 70, No. 1 (America and the World 1990/91), pp. 23–33—and those who continue to stress the United States' relative decline depends a lot on with whom the comparison is being made and in what currency of power. Analysts who focused on the Soviet threat and therefore consider power as ultimately military in nature naturally see a triumphant United States, but those who compare the United States with Japan or Germany and think in economic terms see the country as less powerful, certainly when compared to the 1950s. Joseph Nye looks at both economic and military power and concludes that the U.S. relative decline really took place in the first two decades of the Cold War rather than in the last two, but his sophisticated argument does not really refute the contention that the *effects* of relative decline were felt more strongly after the actual decline ended than while it was taking place, nor that they may intensify in the 1990s.

First, besides the natural lag of perceptions behind reality, the political impacts of economic shifts had to await a certain maturity on the part of challenger states, as well as egregious American political and military failures (like Vietnam, Watergate, and Desert One) that exacerbated them. (OPEC, for example, acted against the West's interests in the 1970s, but it could not have done so except for changes that took place in the 1950s and 1960s, and the effects of its actions persisted throughout the 1980s.) Moreover, the impact of earlier shifts in economic power has also been postponed—and magnified—by profligate U.S. government economic policies (e.g., current budgetary stringencies may have their roots in policies of the 1970s and 1980s, but they will constrain the instruments of foreign policy most in the 1990s).

Second, Nye himself sensibly qualifies his argument by stating that as the leading power the United States will still "have to cope with unprecedented problems of interdependence that no great power can solve by itself" and that, unless it corrects certain adverse domestic trends, its current predominance "does not mean the distribution of power will continue in America's favor." Nye, *Bound to Lead*, pp. 20, 112. This leaves Nye not all that far from Paul Kennedy, who points both to "the considerable array of strengths still possessed by the United States" and "its success in 'internationalizing' American capitalism and culture" as he pleads for a policy that will "preserve the technological and economic bases of its power from relative erosion." Paul Kennedy, *The Rise and Fall of the Great Powers* (New York: Vintage, 1987), pp. 514, 533–534.

19. Whether a balancer is needed at the global level is an issue not settled by the theoretical literature on the subject. But the United States is increasingly seen as the "least undesirable" outside power in many regions (especially Southeast Asia and the Persian Gulf) by states who fear intra- or extra-regional challengers and are too weak to defend themselves even against local hegemons. See, e.g., David B. Ottaway, "U.S., Saudis to Study Long-Term Defense Needs of Gulf Region," *Washington Post*, April 21, 1991, p. A26; Barton Gellman, "U.S., Kuwait Initial Security Accord," *Washington Post*, September 6, 1991, p. A24.

to experiment with other security strategies. One of these is collective security.

COLLECTIVE SECURITY

Although not labelled as collective security until the 1930s,[20] the ideas elaborated by Woodrow Wilson stood on a long tradition of American interest in anti-war schemes that can be traced from Thomas Paine and Benjamin Franklin, through the American Peace Society in the 1820s and 30s, and into the movement for international law and arbitration that culminated in the Hague conferences of 1899 and 1907.[21] Wilson's own contribution was less to jettison or deny the balance of power than to envision its regulation by a community of power, based on mutual, reciprocal norms of conduct and managed through a multilateral organization. The heart of his proposal for a League of Nations was to guarantee the political independence and territorial integrity of all states while, at the same time, providing machinery (including a council of the world's foreign ministers and an international court) that could negotiate changes in the status quo and settle disputes without armed conflict. The genius of the League Covenant was to link these two aspects legally, pledging members to apply sanctions against any state that used force across established international boundaries before it had exhausted the full range of available settlement procedures.[22]

It was the extraordinary bad luck of this first great experiment in collective security, and of the United Nations after it, to be attempted amidst the twentieth century's hegemonic enterprises. However stunning their improvisations in economic and social affairs, decolonization, and peacekeeping, the failure of these organizations' original collective security machinery was so complete that very term "collective security" was appropriated for defensive alliances, like the North Atlantic Treaty Organization (NATO), the South East Asia Treaty Organization (SEATO), the Central Treaty Organization

---

20. Richard N. Current, "Collective Security: Notes on the History of an Idea," in Alexander deConde, ed., *Isolation and Security* (Durham, N.C.: Duke University Press, 1957), p. 44.
21. Merle Eugene Curti, *The American Peace Crusade, 1815–1860* (New York: Octagon Books, 1965).
22. Article 10 was the territorial guarantee; Articles 12, 13, and 15 dealt with pacific settlement procedures and pledged members not to resort to war until such measures were exhausted; and Article 16 provided for sanctions against any member resorting to war "in disregard of its covenants under Articles 12, 13, or 15." Louis B. Sohn, ed., *Basic Documents of the United Nations*, 2nd. ed. (Brooklyn, N.Y.: Foundation Press, 1968), pp. 298–300.

(CENTO), and other artifacts of containment.[23] But today there is a multiplicity of signs that the broad tradition of collective security, adapted in less formulaic and more flexible forms, may be applicable to the post–Cold War world on a variety of levels.

Regionally, for example, it is almost impossible to envision a Europe comprising the former Soviet republics in various states of association, a united Germany, and a free Eastern Europe without some kind of collective security arrangement. A transformed NATO, an expanded European Community (EC), a revamped Western European Union (WEU) and, especially after its November 1990 Paris meeting, the Conference on Security and Cooperation in Europe (CSCE) could all perform this role or parts of it. Some kinds of regional collective security structures might still emerge from the Gulf War and the Middle East peace process, or might supplement reduced American forward deployments in the Pacific. On the global level, the last few years have seen a dramatic evolution in both superpowers' approaches to the United Nations. The complete change of attitude by the Soviets since Mikhail Gorbachev's September 1987 *Pravda* article—including payment of long-due arrearages for peacekeeping, endorsement of the International Court of Justice, and cooperation in the General Assembly and Security Council on a wide range of issues that for decades had been Cold War battlegrounds— has been mirrored on the American side by the no less marked shift from Ronald Reagan's initial hostility to President Bush's very positive attitude towards the organization in which he once served as U.S. ambassador.[24]

The most dramatic development bearing on the prospects for a working peace system, however, was the Persian Gulf crisis occasioned by Iraq's invasion of Kuwait, in the course of which President Bush explicitly linked U.S. action to a "new world order." Here, in marked contrast to League experience in the 1930s, the great powers acted with virtual unanimity through the Security Council to legitimize collective action; economic sanctions were effectively imposed and enforced; a broad coalition was assembled and held together to carry out UN directives despite the pain of economic

---

23. Such alliances were aimed at *outside* non-member states, the very antithesis of an arrangement providing for security *among* a collective of states.
24. M.S. Gorbachev, "The Reality and Guarantees of a Secure World," *Foreign Broadcast Information Service,* SOV-87-180 (September 17, 1987), pp. 23, 25–28. Bush's interest is further indicated by his invitation to the Secretary General of the United Nations to be his first dinner guest at the White House, and his interest at least on a rhetorical level in issues like environmental pollution and climate change that demand a significant role for multilateral bodies. "Bush Commitment to U.N. Expressed at Private Dinner," *Washington Post,* February 2, 1989, p. A23.

dislocation and war; and although political and economic pressures failed to reverse aggression, armed force succeeded in doing so, at costs acceptable to the coalition.

On the other hand, the Gulf experience also included some disquieting signs and unfortunate characteristics from a collective security viewpoint. For all the talk of the new world order, the UN's role was limited to providing global legitimacy for a U.S.-managed crisis; not even the fig leaf of a UN command was allowed by Washington. Moreover, although the Gulf crisis underlined the importance of great power leadership to successful collective action, one is hard pressed to imagine another post–Cold War conflict that would so clearly engage the vital interests, not only of the United States, but of nearly the entire world community.[25] Nor was the world as united as might first appear. Germany and Japan, the economic powerhouses of the post–Cold War world, were less than enthusiastic in their support of the coalition's action.[26] Equally ominous, substantial majorities in most Arab states seemed to feel that the international delict of Iraq's armed attack across an international boundary was somehow neutralized by the sins of the rich sheiks of Kuwait. This, too, suggests the limits of consensus on the central maxims of collective security and raises doubts about whether any such scheme can be broadly enforced.

Thus, although in their summer 1991 summit the leaders of the Group of Seven announced their intention to push towards a "stronger" UN "to maintain peace and security for all and to deter aggression,"[27] it remains to be seen how willing they and other states will be to yield to the UN the power necessary to be effective, or to back it up when crisis strikes. Still, the future is likely to be plagued by many local conflicts, no one of which is sufficient to engage American interests in a major way, but which together have the potential to endanger Americans' physical security around the world and to disrupt the trade and manufacturing links so vital to economic prosperity.

---

25. Certainly the far more typical post–Cold War conflicts in Liberia, Somalia, Haiti, and Yugoslavia have not led to swift, decisive, or united action by the great powers.

26. Neither nation, of course, enjoys status in the UN commensurate with its power; and although this problem may have had little to do with their attitudes in the Gulf crisis, it is one that will have to be rectified in any functioning collective security arrangement. Robert Gilpin has discussed what can happen when the hierarchies of power and prestige in the international system are allowed to get too far out of line with one another. See Gilpin, *War and Change in International Politics*, especially chap. 1.

27. Glenn Frankel and Jim Hoagland, "Leaders Seek to Bolster U.N.'s Security Role," *Washington Post*, July 17, 1991, pp. A1, A19.

Collective bodies can share the costs of attending to conflicts like these, whose outcomes may be largely immaterial to the major powers but whose continuance is detrimental to their interests.

HEMISPHERIC DEFENSE

While balance of power and collective security are globalist strategies for physical security, a third historical American approach with resonance for the future, hemispheric defense, is decidedly regionalist.[28] It dates back at least to the Monroe Doctrine of 1823 and Henry Clay's "American system," both of which were based on the vague idea that the new world was fundamentally different from the old and therefore destined to have a cohesive future (notwithstanding the great social, cultural, and geographic distances between North and South). Although the enormous power of the United States relative to its southern neighbors (and the uses it has chosen to make of that power) have given the Monroe Doctrine a stormy history, there is an equally impressive tradition of cooperative schemes, including the Pan-American Union, the Organization of American States, the Alliance for Progress, and the Caribbean Basin Initiative.

What distinguishes hemispheric defense from a balance-of-power or even collective security strategy is the notion that the physical security of the United States still depends materially on protecting the borders of the United States. Whereas both balance of power and collective security assume the indivisibility of the peace on a worldwide basis, hemispheric defense gives much more prominence to geographic contiguity, arguing that—even in the missile age—being close enables a country to pose a greater threat to the United States than if it were far away. This perspective gains additional credibility if one focuses on immediate, concrete dangers like illegal and uncontrolled immigration or narcotics trafficking, rather than on global threats like a massive ballistic missile attack, against which no defense (SDI notwithstanding)[29] seems feasible anyway.

28. I am indebted for this argument, as well as for the thought that balance of power, collective security, and collective defense were elements of containment, to Professor Alan K. Henrikson of the Fletcher School of Law and Diplomacy. See Henrikson, "The North American Perspective: A Continent Apart or a Continent Joined?" in Lawrence S. Kaplan, S. Victor Papacosma, Mark R. Rubin, and Ruth V. Young, eds., NATO After Forty Years (Wilmington, Del.: Scholarly Resources, 1990), pp. 3–32; and Henrikson, "East-West Rivalry in Latin America: 'Between the Eagle and the Bear'," in Robert W. Clausen, ed., East-West Rivalry in the Third World: Security Issues and Regional Perspectives (Wilmington, Del.: Scholarly Resources, 1986), pp. 261–290.
29. David Trask has pointed out to the author that Ronald Reagan's original image of the

Of course, being close—and the sense of closeness—may be somewhat different in today's world than they were decades ago. Before and during World War II, the hemisphere's borders in the minds of American strategists were extended ever farther as the technology of air transport brought more distant contiguous areas closer.[30] Today it is neither an exaggeration nor an affront to logic to include the Atlantic community (and thus much of Europe), as well as the so-called Pacific Basin or Pacific rim countries, within the conceptual hemisphere. Whereas doing so surely includes vast reaches of the globe in the focus deemed appropriate for American strategy, it also discounts large areas of the world (South Asia, the Middle East, Africa, even lower South America) purely on grounds of their geographic location.

Will hemispheric defense become a more important source of American strategic thought in the post-containment era? Certainly we have seen more of this kind of thinking by American statesmen in the 1980s than in earlier decades, as illustrated by the Reagan administration's policies on Nicaragua and El Salvador, and its invasion of Grenada. Since those concerns were fueled by anti-communism and containment in a Cold War atmosphere, it is quite possible that they will disappear along with Soviet hostility. But the Bush administration's attention to Mexico,[31] its Enterprise for the Americas initiative,[32] and its 1989 invasion of Panama all attest to the post–Cold war salience of the region. With the more-distant world an increasingly friendly or at worst irrelevant place, and with their attention focused more on non-

---

Strategic Defense Initiative as a total shield against missile attack is perhaps the most modern version of hemispheric defense. I consider it more isolationist, in that it does not rely on cooperation with any foreign nation (let alone nearby countries); the threats it sees as significant and against which it protects are decidedly global and not regional in nature; and it would obviate the need for any kind of forward defense, including that in the hemisphere.

30. In particular, the demands of war supply to America's allies during World War II (across the Alaskan land bridge to the Soviet Union, and the Atlantic sea and air routes to the United Kingdom and Europe) made it common for decisionmakers to think of the hemisphere in rather broad terms. On the elasticity of the hemisphere concept, see Alan K. Henrikson, "The Map as an 'Idea': The Role of Cartographic Imagery During the Second World War," *The American Cartographer*, Vol. 2, No. 1 (April 1975), pp. 19–53, esp. pp. 28–31.

31. One thinks especially of repeated Bush-Salinas summits and the ongoing U.S.-Mexico free trade area negotiations.

32. Announced by President Bush on June 27, 1990, in response to a promise made at the Cartagena summit in February 1990, the Enterprise for the Americas initiative includes four elements: movement towards a hemisphere-wide trade zone, incentives to encourage investment reforms within and new capital flows into the region, measures to reduce commercial and official debt burdens, and action to strengthen hemispheric environmental policies. President Bush, "Enterprise for the Americas Initiative," *U.S. Department of State Dispatch*, Vol. 1, No. 1 (September 3, 1990), pp. 48–50.

traditional security threats, perhaps American strategists will decide that nearby interests supersede all others.

ISOLATIONISM

One might, however, take such logic a step further. The oldest approach devised by Americans to serve their physical security seems hardly worthy of being called a strategy at all. It is isolationism, a tradition neither global nor regional but profoundly inward-looking. Given the fact that this once-honored tradition in American foreign policy has become a loaded term for the present generation, it is important to be clear at the outset about what isolationism was and was not in American history.

First, isolationism never meant total isolation from the world. Quite will-ing—even eager—to promote overseas economic relations as long as they did not threaten the nation's security, isolationists urged only political de-tachment.[33] In contrast to collective security or the alliances demanded by a balance of power strategy, isolationism especially meant a determined non-commitment, a refusal to make advance promises in security matters that might detract from the nation's absolute freedom of action. Non-commitment in turn was reinforced by a strong pacifist element, and by the view that the casualties resulting from foreign wars could accomplish nothing of real value for U.S. interests.[34]

Second, it is important to remember that, in spite of its contemporary notoriety, isolationism was long popular with Americans because it worked. Staying out of other nations' troubles and taking advantage of what George Washington called "our detached and distant situation" was a realistic strat-egy when risks from overseas threats were slight and foreign affairs costs had to be kept low while the nation invested its growing resources in do-mestic development. What gave isolationism a bad name was not that it failed to provide security to the country for over a century, but that Americans

---

33. See Warren I. Cohen, *Empire without Tears* (Philadelphia: Temple University Press, 1987), pp. 16–17; Foster Rhea Dulles, *America's Rise to World Power, 1898–1954* (New York: Harper, 1955), pp. 144–145.
34. See Manfred Jonas, *Isolationism in America, 1935–1941* (Ithaca: Cornell University Press, 1966). The persistence of isolationist non-commitment can be seen even in the language of U.S. postwar alliance treaties, which leaves to U.S. decision the character of any U.S. response. Even NATO's Article 5 promises only that each party will respond to an attack "as it deems necessary." Ruhl J. Bartlett, *The Record of American Diplomacy*, 4th ed. (New York: Knopf, 1964), p. 734.

failed to abandon it when the conditions required for its success disappeared at the beginning of the twentieth century.[35]

Thus, the issue for post–Cold War U.S. policy is whether the future will be more like the nineteenth century, a time in which a kind of isolationism might be a realistic and workable strategy; or more like the early twentieth century, in which various domestic pressures sustained isolationism in spite of conditions which made it a dangerous illusion. Ever since the Vietnam War, a substantial group of Americans has believed that the nation's commitments are far out of line with its power, that resources available for either foreign or domestic concerns are increasingly limited, and that problems at home need priority attention.[36] Many other Americans may always have agreed with them, but felt until recently that the Soviet threat could not be ignored. Today, with international dangers vastly diminished, with the federal budget deficit and stagnant personal incomes daily emphasizing the limits on American resources, and with critical domestic needs demanding attention, multiple pressures combine toward a policy of self-interest that some label "neo-isolationist."[37]

---

35. The clumsy American policy towards Japan in the years before Pearl Harbor represented more the continuation of isolationist policies by other means than their abandonment. First, U.S. coercion against Japan was undertaken without any sort of American commitment, either to a collective security system or even to the British (whose Prime Minister was desperately seeking an American pledge to defend the Empire's supply lines in the Far East). In this sense the policy was a perfect example of involvement without commitment, its futility, and its dangers. Second, the United States was involved in a shooting war in the Atlantic well before December 1941 and certainly would have become a belligerent within a few months anyway; the Axis alliance and three decades of U.S.-Japanese hostility made a two-front war very likely. One can, therefore, only endorse isolationism in the context of the late 1930s if one believes, both that such policies would have kept the United States out of war, and that keeping the country out was more important to the national interest than foiling German and Japanese aggression. See Herbert Feis, *The Road to Pearl Harbor* (New York: Atheneum, 1965); and Paul W. Schroeder, *The Axis Alliance and Japanese-American Relations, 1941* (Ithaca, N.Y.: Cornell University Press for the American Historical Association, 1958).
36. See, e.g., Ole R. Holsti and James Rosenau, *American Leadership in World Affairs* (Boston: Allen and Unwin, 1984), chap. 4.
37. See, for example, Don Oberdorfer, "Opinion Builds for Smaller U.S. Role Abroad," *Washington Post*, October 27, 1991, pp. A20–21. A *Time*/CNN poll on September 19, 1991, found that only 19 percent of respondents thought the United States should use its leadership to help settle international disputes and promote democracy in the 1990s, while 74 percent thought the United States should reduce its involvement in world politics to concentrate on problems at home. "Vox Pop," *Time*, October 7, 1991, p. 15. Among those now prominently pushing for neo-isolationist strategies are a variety of Democratic presidential candidates, as well as Patrick J. Buchanan, "America First—and Second, and Third," *The National Interest*, No. 19 (Spring 1990), pp. 77–82; Alan Tonelson, "What is the National Interest?" *Atlantic Monthly*, No. 268 (July 1991), pp. 35–39, 42, 44–46, 48–52; Ted Galen Carpenter, "America Can't Police the Planet," *Washington Post*, August 30, 1990, p. A23; and Earl C. Ravenal, "The Case for Adjustment," *Foreign Policy*,

Globalizing American Values

Great nations are rarely satisfied protecting their own territory, people, and property. They want to stand for something, to believe that they are contributing to a better as well as a safer world. Some statesmen may support strategies of value projection in the belief that a world remade in the nation's image can also help promote physical security and economic prosperity, and that programs to project national values overseas are thus important strategic "software."[38] But ordinary Americans mainly seem uncomfortable with the idea that their nation might throw its weight around in the world simply to protect their own security. They want their country to use its power for good, too.

As a result, statesmen know how difficult it is to sustain public support for any policy—especially one demanding sacrifice—without an element of idealism. Whatever he might believe, no president ever told the American people that he was leading them to war to preserve the balance of power; Americans rather have fought "in the cause of humanity" (1898),[39] to make the world "safe for democracy" (1917),[40] to revenge "an unprovoked and dastardly attack" (1941),[41] "to prevent a third world war" (1950),[42] to defend "the value of an American commitment" (1965),[43] or "to forge . . . a new world order" (1991).[44] And from the time when Harry Truman was told to "scare hell out of" the Congress in order to get aid for Greece and Turkey,[45]

No. 81 (Winter 1990–91), pp. 3–19. Nor is the academic argument limited to a few libertarians and neo-conservatives; even the leaders of so thoroughly an internationalist organization as the Council on Foreign Relations have made similar pleas to concentrate on domestic affairs. See Don Oberdorfer, "Shift to Domestic Concerns Urged," *Washington Post,* July 19, 1991, p. A19.
38. Nye, *Bound to Lead,* p. 188.
39. President William McKinley's war message to Congress, April 11, 1898, in Bartlett, *The Record of American Diplomacy,* p. 380.
40. Wilson's war message, April 2, 1917, cited in Samuel F. Wells, Jr., *The Challenges of Power* (Lanham, Md.: University Press of America, 1990), p. 97.
41. President Franklin D. Roosevelt's war message, December 8, 1941, in Thomas G. Patterson, ed., *Major Problems in American Foreign Policy,* Vol. II (Lexington, Mass.: D.C. Heath, 1978), p. 175.
42. Harry S. Truman speech of April 11, 1951, in Patterson, ed., *Major Problems in American Foreign Policy,* p. 331.
43. Speech by Lyndon B. Johnson at Johns Hopkins University, April 7, 1965, in Patterson, ed., *Major Problems in American Foreign Policy,* p. 447.
44. President George Bush address to the nation, January 16, 1991, "President Bush Assures American People: 'We Will Not Fail'," *Washington Post,* January 17, 1991, p. A27.
45. Walter LaFeber, *America, Russia, and the Cold War, 1945–1975,* 3rd ed. (New York: John Wiley, 1976), p. 54.

anti-communism was closely associated with the physical containment of the Soviet Union in American Cold War strategies.

Projecting national values overseas usually involves direct interference in another nation's internal affairs, and because it springs from moralistic roots it is difficult to limit on grounds of realism or feasibility. Some would argue, for example, that American Cold War policies led to serious trouble precisely when decisionmakers forgot that their objective was to contain the expansion of Soviet state power and instead made global anti-communism their primary motive.[46] On the other hand, as demonstrated dramatically by the changes during the late 1980s in the Soviet Union and Eastern Europe, how powerful states organize their internal affairs unquestionably affects their international conduct in ways vital to other states' security. And there remains the fact that, whatever its policies, no country possessing the United States' power in today's highly permeable international system can avoid making a profound impact on the internal affairs of many other nations all around the world. If value projection is inevitable, one might argue, we may as well be intentional about it.

President Carter was the first modern president to make value projection his signature in foreign affairs.[47] The Carter human rights policy was highly intrusive, attempting to protect individuals in other nations against the arbitrary exercise of power by their own governments. In effect, Carter demanded that rulers worldwide, whatever their societies' traditions or their own philosophies of government, adopt the protections of free speech and assembly written into the U.S. Bill of Rights as well as its prohibitions against deprivation of life, liberty, or property without due process. And Carter tried to give effect to his policy in spite of its cost to security ties with allies thought important to containment (e.g., South Korea or the Philippines) and regardless of its effect on other major objectives of his administration, as when he chastised Soviet rights violations at the same time as he urged the Kremlin to make major cuts in strategic forces.

---

46. How else to explain two decades of American hostility to a state as non-threatening and as strategically useful as China, or U.S. failure to attempt to detach nationalist communist regimes in places like Vietnam or Cuba from the Soviet orbit, rather than waging costly struggles against them? See John Lewis Gaddis, *Strategies of Containment* (New York: Oxford University Press, 1982), pp. 141–145, 175–182.
47. See for example Seyom Brown, *The Faces of Power* (New York: Columbia University Press, 1983), pp. 466–472; Sandra Vogelgesang, *American Dream, Global Nightmare: The Dilemma of U.S. Human Rights Policy* (New York: Norton, 1980); and Joshua Muravchik, *The Uncertain Crusade: Jimmy Carter and the Dilemmas of Human Rights Policy* (Lanham, Md.: Hamilton Press, 1986).

Despite good intentions, though, the Carter administration could not maintain the unalloyed emphasis on human rights with which it had begun. U.S. security interests in places from Seoul to Moscow forced compromises, and compromises were hard to defend in a policy based on absolute moral standards. As Soviet adventurism and the "loss" of Iran, Nicaragua, and Afghanistan dominated the headlines, Ronald Reagan was able to argue that a policy promoting individual human rights in foreign countries was a luxury Americans could ill afford.

But today, given the reduction in the Soviet threat to U.S. security interests, the United States has at least as much freedom as in 1977 to make human rights overseas a top priority in its foreign affairs strategy. A Carter-like policy, focusing on individual rights with all other foreign policy considerations in second place, is certainly one option for post–Cold War American statecraft. As in the 1970s, such an objective would pose major questions regarding its implementation, but at least strategists would not have to worry about shunned allies turning to the Soviet Union for support. Public rhetoric and aid flows could thus be tied to rights considerations in ways that might have been unrealistic during the Cold War years.

Another human rights-based approach is, ironically, offered by the same Ronald Reagan who so excoriated the Carter policy. For not only did Reagan come to realize the great popularity of value projection with the American people, but his administration also eventually understood the long-run danger to American security interests of corrupt and authoritarian regimes in allied states. The Reagan team ushered Ferdinand Marcos out of power, for example, not primarily because it wanted individual liberties restored to the Philippine people; it did so because it was persuaded that the Marcos government had become so riddled with cronyism and so detached from popular sentiment that it was ineffectual in protecting either its own or American interests.

But in embracing human rights, Reagan also transformed them, changing the focus of value projection from protecting individuals against arbitrary state power to promoting American-style systems of economics and government. This too was a highly pragmatic development, beginning as early as the Cancun conference,[48] when the president told Third World nations that

---

48. The International Meeting for Cooperation and Development was held in Cancun, Mexico, on October 22–23, 1981, with 22 heads of state (including President Ronald Reagan) in attendance. It was the first major North-South gathering of the Reagan years. See Robert Solomon,

their only hope of sustained development lay in moving to market-based economic systems. Although the Reagan administration remained quite willing to work with authoritarian dictators around the world from Chun Doo Hwan to Augusto Pinochet, it was also increasingly willing to put pressure on them to move toward democratizing their countries, again on the theory that repression and resulting societal instability were as bad for U.S. security as they were for individual liberties. By the middle of his second term, Reagan had abandoned his preference for dictatorships of the right as bulwarks against communism and had declared U.S. opposition to all forms of tyranny, whether of the left or right.[49]

Following the wave of conversions to democracy and capitalism in the late 1980s, a Reaganesque approach to value projection has become perhaps the most often suggested strategy for post–Cold War American foreign policy. Many neo-conservatives, who chafed against the negative nature of containment and championed the Reagan Doctrine, now want to see a crusade for democracy become the nation's central goal.[50] But support for this approach is much broader. In a March 1990 speech in Texas, Secretary of State James Baker called for "promotion and consolidation of democracy" worldwide as the basis of American diplomacy, and Representative Les Aspin (D-Wis.) has said that "you might actually organize American foreign policy behind a rigorous and internally consistent policy of supporting democracy."[51]

However, another much less aggressive manner of projecting American values overseas might also appeal to Americans in the post–Cold War era. It is certainly the oldest form of national value projection, captured first in the eighteenth century evocation by John Winthrop of the United States as a "Citty upon a Hill." In this approach, rather than engaging in a strident

---

"'The Elephant in the Boat?': The United States and the World Economy," and Elaine P. Adam, "Chronology 1981," *Foreign Affairs*, Vol. 60, No. 3 (America and the World 1981, 1982), pp. 587, 723.

49. The preference for dictatorships was argued in Jeane J. Kirkpatrick, "Dictatorships and Double Standards," *Commentary*, Vol. 68, No. 5 (November 1979), pp. 34–45, which Reagan liked so well that he offered her the UN ambassadorship. Lou Cannon, *President Reagan: The Role of a Lifetime* (New York: Simon and Schuster, 1991), p. 85. Reagan 1986 statement cited by Robert W. Tucker, "Reagan's Foreign Policy," *Foreign Affairs*, Vol. 68, No. 1 (America and the World 1988/89), p. 21.

50. Perhaps the leading proponent is Ben Wattenberg of the American Enterprise Institute; see Wattenberg, "Our Mission: Waging Democracy," Newspaper Enterprise Association, New York (March 9, 1989). See also Carl Gershman, "Freedom Remains the Touchstone," *The National Interest*, No. 19 (Spring 1990), pp. 83–86.

51. Al Kamen, "Baker Outlines New U.S. Foreign Policy Approach," *Washington Post*, March 31, 1990, p. A7.

effort to promote American values overseas or applying American power to affect the government of those who have no voice in or control over it, the United States would merely endeavor to be the Great Exemplar of political and economic freedom in the world, showing by example the way others might follow in accordance with their own abilities, will, and traditions. Favored by George Kennan all along,[52] this approach assumes that the United States is—or can become—a society so attractive that it need not impose its principles on others. The force of its example would be the only persuasion it must or should apply. As John Quincy Adams put it in 1821: America is "the well-wisher to the freedom and independence of all. She is the champion and vindicator only of her own."[53]

A strategy of leadership-by-example might well appeal to internationalists who harbor doubts regarding the applicability of democratic forms of government and market economic systems in foreign societies, or who question the skill of Americans confronted by exotic cultures in attempting such delicate transplants. It might also commend itself to those who worry about the expense involved in making the world democratic and who, in any case, are at present more focused on the competing needs to be met here at home. Moreover, such an inward-looking strategy might avoid the excesses of another moralistic crusade in U.S. foreign policy and the disillusionment that seems so often to follow. Its distinction from a more active promotional effort would be not only in the relative paucity of policy instruments employed but also in the indeterminacy of its goals. Let others decide what is of value in our culture, politics, and economic life, it would argue; we will concentrate on making them worthy of emulation and on helping others adopt what they wish.[54]

Promoting the General Welfare

The recent emphasis on value projection as a central organizing principle for American foreign policy may be seen as part of a much larger shift, cutting across all areas of the national interest, from a threat-based to an interest-based strategy. As historian John Lewis Gaddis has pointed out, American

---

52. See, for example, Kennan, "Democracy as a World Cause," *Washington Post*, July 11, 1977, p. A23.
53. Quoted in Craig, "The United States and the European Balance," p. 193.
54. Alan Henrikson offered a similar idea in a different context in Henrikson, "The Emanation of Power," *International Security*, Vol. 6, No. 1 (Summer 1981), pp. 152–164.

policymakers during the Cold War years were often so frightened by the Soviet Union that they fell into the posture of assuming that whatever the Soviets or their clients threatened—from South Vietnam to Angola to Chad—was automatically "of interest" to the United States. Such an approach, Gaddis argues, yielded the initiative to the Soviet Union and dramatically escalated the costs of security policy.[55] Future policymakers, lacking such a threat and with costs an ever more critical factor, may find it easier to focus on promoting interests rather than on defending against threats.

The result may well be that no strategy centered on politico-military concerns will appeal to Americans in the post–Cold War era. Since late 1988, in fact, the American people have named economic competitors like Japan as greater threats to our national security than military adversaries such as the Soviet Union,[56] and public opinion polls over the last two years have added a rapid deterioration of confidence in the health of the economy to long-standing concerns regarding American competitiveness.[57] If the economic slowdown of 1990–92 turns into an extended period of sluggish growth, stagnant real incomes, and significant unemployment, economic welfare can be expected to take priority over both physical security and value projection in the 1990s.

In this area of the national interest, U.S. hegemony has been in relative decline for at least two decades. Today it is under severe stress from the twin pressures, first of others' economic vibrancy, particularly that of Japan and the European Community's 1992 single-market project; and second of Americans' own economic self-gratification, a seeming inability to defer consumption in order to save and invest, symbolized by the mounting federal (and increasingly state and local) budget deficits. International economists worry, and with good reason, whether any economic system can operate successfully without a single national hegemon to set the rules authoritatively and make the sacrifice-for-privilege trades it requires.[58] A post-hegemonic system

---

55. See Gaddis's conclusions in *Strategies of Containment* regarding NSC 68 (pp. 118–124) and flexible response (pp. 204–205 and 261), as well as his summary of the liabilities of symmetrical strategies on p. 353.
56. John Marttila, "American Public Opinion: Evolving Definitions of National Security," in Edward K. Hamilton, ed., *America's Global Interests* (New York: Norton, 1989), p. 268.
57. Richard Morin, "Majority Say U.S. Is on Wrong Track," *Washington Post*, May 23, 1990, p. A4; Dan Balz and Richard Morin, "Poll Finds Public Pessimistic on Economy," *Washington Post*, July 26, 1990, p. A10; Leslie H. Gelb, "Throw the Bums Out," *New York Times*, October 23, 1991, p. A23.
58. See Robert Gilpin, *The Political Economy of International Relations* (Princeton: Princeton Uni-

would require unprecedented levels of cooperation between the major industrialized countries; whether the United States will be willing and able to lead or even to cooperate with such a grouping will depend on the kind of strategy for economic prosperity it adopts.

To be sure, the practical end of American hegemony does not necessarily mean the end of its underlying philosophy, the belief in free trade and equality of economic opportunity for all nations, large and small. Historically, that philosophy is deeply rooted in the American psyche. It stretches right back to the revolution, when in the Treaty Plan of 1776 the United States offered access to its market and products in the naive hope that Europe would rush to join it in the war against England.[59] Once the United States was independent, an end to the restrictive trade arrangements of the British Navigation Acts and the Spanish colonial monopoly in the West Indies became major policy goals of the new nation, a small power shut out of large states' mercantilist schemes with no hope of creating similar arrangements to benefit itself.[60]

Similarly, throughout the nineteenth century the whole of American policy towards the Far East was shaped by the concept of the Open Door, the idea of free access to markets in the region for all comers on conditions of complete equality. It was a sensible approach for a country without military power in Asia and faced by active European efforts to divide China into exclusive spheres of influence. Using it, the United States opened Japan in the 1850s by suggesting that an American-led free trade regime would help forestall China-like depredations by the Europeans and would allow Japan to become a great trading nation, "the England of the Orient."[61] Free trade ultimately became orthodoxy across all American economic policy in the late 1930s under the reciprocal tariff policy of Cordell Hull, cementing itself firmly into the global economic system after World War II as progressive rounds of multilateral trade negotiations under the General Agreement on Tariffs and Trade (GATT) extended its beneficial effects worldwide.

---

versity Press, 1987); and Joan Edelman Spero, *The Politics of International Economic Relations*, 4th ed. (New York: St. Martins, 1990) for representative examples.

59. Bartlett, *The Record of American Diplomacy*, pp. 17–19. See also Paul A. Varg, *Foreign Policies of the Founding Fathers* (Lansing: Michigan State University Press, 1963).

60. Lloyd C. Gardner, Walter F. LaFeber, and Thomas J. McCormick, *Creation of the American Empire*, Vol. 1 (Chicago: Rand-McNally, 1973), pp. 1–30.

61. The phrase was used by the American minister resident, Townsend Harris, in his negotiations with the Japanese for the United States–Japan Treaty of 1858. Samuel Flagg Bemis, *A Diplomatic History of the United States*, 5th ed. (New York: Holt, Rinehart and Winston, 1965), p. 360.

The principle of equality of economic opportunity has exerted a powerful influence on American security policies as well. Although at the deepest strategic level the causes of the United States involvement in European wars had to do with preserving the balance of power, the immediate circumstances of the U.S. decisions for war in 1812 and 1917 involved protecting the country's right as a neutral to trade with all belligerents in any conflict. Until the isolationist neutrality legislation of the 1930s, in fact, Americans insisted on commercial equality of opportunity in war as well as in peace, and they proved themselves quite willing to fight for it.

American presidents still talk the language of free trade. But whether trade liberalization will continue past the GATT's current Uruguay round[62] will depend first on whether the United States continues its half-century adherence to a free trade strategy in reality as well as in rhetoric, then on whether it has the willingness and skill to shift from a solo hegemonic role to a cooperative leadership stance. Unfortunately, the burgeoning budget deficit, growing dependence on foreign oil, and the nation's seeming inability to rebuild American competitiveness all make it virtually impossible to reduce the trade deficit significantly. As Americans become increasingly convinced that free trade policies will not work with countries like Japan,[63] sustaining vetoes of protectionist legislation will be more and more difficult. At some point, if the political pressure becomes too great, the executive branch may join the Congress in espousing a different strategy for economic prosperity.

One candidate will be regional trading blocs, the idea captured by Margaret Thatcher at the 1990 Economic Summit in Houston when she spoke of "three great groups" of nations, "one based on the dollar, one based on the yen, and one based on the deutschmark."[64] Evidence for this kind of world is

---

62. The Uruguay Round, launched in Punta del Este in September 1986 with a planned completion date of 1990, is the eighth in the series of marathon multilateral trade negotiations that began with the Geneva Round in 1947. At this writing the talks are deadlocked, primarily over the fate of agricultural subsidies in the European Community Common Agricultural Policy (CAP). For a brief history of GATT negotiating rounds, see Spero, *The Politics of International Economic Relations*, pp. 73–93.

63. Of course, free trade does not work for nations that are not competitive; in Japan's case there are also factors that unfairly shut out American products, although these probably account for only 10–12 percent of the overall trade deficit. Whatever its causes, the recent *Times-Mirror* survey indicated a dramatic shift toward anti-Japanese sentiment in the United States, with favorable opinion dropping from 70 percent to 56 percent during the years 1987 to 1990 and unfavorable opinion rising from 27 to 39 percent. Donald S. Kellerman and Andrew Kohut, *The People, the Press and Politics 1990* (Washington, D.C.: Times-Mirror Center for The People and the Press, September 19, 1990), p. 9.

64. David Hoffmann, "Summit Dynamics Reflect Shift to Multipolar World," *Washington Post*, July 15, 1990, pp. A12–13.

provided by the rapid expansion of Japanese economic penetration in Asia, the U.S. free trade pact with Canada (and parallel negotiations with Mexico), and most obviously by EC-92. Although trade data from the middle to late 1980s seem to relegate regional blocs to the future,[65] Americans reeling from an increasingly non-competitive position in the world economy may see a hemispheric bloc as a way to retain some of the prosperity and control associated with America's former global hegemony, rendering the country's loss of economic primacy less painful in the short term.

If European, U.S., and Japanese-led trading blocs do emerge, there exists the danger pointed out by Robert Gilpin of a highly unstable tripolar system in which each bloc leader would fear a combination of the other two against its interests.[66] Without the Soviet threat to hold the great powers together, there is no question that serious trade-based geostrategic conflict is a real possibility. Given the historical relationship between economic deterioration, trade wars, and military conflict, one can hardly dismiss as fantasy a complete rupture of the Japanese-American alliance over economic issues, or ignore the dangers that an estranged yet technologically-advanced Japan could pose to world peace. The controversy surrounding President Bush's January 1992 trip to Japan can be seen as one illustration of how difficult trade issues are to manage during recessionary times.[67]

Some authorities argue that the emergence of trade blocs should be seen as a benign development, since they can push the frontier of liberalization beyond what is possible in a global context and thereby act as pathbreakers for later worldwide trade agreements.[68] But whether reasonable liberality could be maintained between blocs while preferential areas are nurtured within them seems problematic, given that no inward preference is possible

---

65. Peter M. Ludlow, "The Future of the International Trading System," *Washington Quarterly*, Vol. 12, No. 4 (Autumn 1989), p. 158. But see the January 1992 ASEAN decision to create a Southeast Asian regional free trade zone. William Branigan, "Southeast Asians Sign Accords on Free-trade Zone," *Washington Post*, January 29, 1992, p. A27.
66. Gilpin, *War and Change in World Politics*, p. 235.
67. After suddenly postponing the trip in response to the surprise defeat of his former attorney general in a Pennsylvania Senate race by a Democrat who campaigned on domestic issues, the president recast the trip, away from its original emphasis on reaffirming the importance of the U.S.–Japanese alliance in the post–Cold War era, to a focus on trade issues and their impact on jobs in the United States. The result was a predictable increase in friction with Japan—hardly an outcome that would contribute to any strategy for long-term improvement of the situation. Paul Blustein, "Tensions Rise in Tokyo as Bush's Visit Nears," *Washington Post*, December 25, 1991, pp. A1, A25.
68. See Ludlow, "The Future of the International Trading System."

without a concomitant outward discrimination. Such a system seems fragile at best, likely to slide under the cover of so-called "fair trade" towards increasingly managed and illiberal forms.

There waits, moreover, an alternative and inward-looking strategy that has purported to serve economic welfare for substantial stretches of American history. High-tariff protectionist policies reigned, in fact, from the Civil War to the Great Depression, except for Woodrow Wilson's Underwood tariff of 1913. Whereas tariff rates on dutiable non-agricultural products in the post-war liberal system run in the 8–10 percent range, the comparable average *ad valorem* rate from the 1860s through the 1930s lay in the 40–50 percent range, peaking in the 1930–33 Smoot-Hawley rate on dutiable imports of 52.8 percent.[69]

Those who believe that such protectionist policies were forever discredited by the Great Depression should take note of how successfully the practice of protectionism has spread under the rhetoric of free trade. The Reagan administration presided over a 23 percent increase in non-tariff barriers, one of the worst performances among nations in the Organization of Economic Cooperation and Development (OECD). Forty percent of Japanese exports to the United States currently enter under some form of protection; over $6 billion worth of Japanese cars are shut out each year.[70] Moreover, the 1988 Trade Act established adjustment machinery that is at best strongly biased in retaliatory directions, enshrining in legislation the debatable premise that protectionist measures are likely to lead to a freer system. And all of this, it should be pointed out, happened in an era of sustained domestic prosperity.

Protectionism may not make economic sense, but its history indicates that it is a highly appealing strategy. It will be all the harder to resist in the future since it will either be invoked as a means to the goal of free or fair trade in an imperfect world, or applied gradually and unannounced by those purporting to believe in the most liberal policies.

Strategic Coherence After Containment

None of these strategies, to be sure, will simply reappear in their earlier forms to replace containment, anti-communism, and economic hegemony.

---

69. Sidney Ratner, *The Tariff in American History* (New York: Anvil/ Van Nostrand, 1972), pp. 28–54; Spero, *Politics of International Economic Relations*, p. 73.
70. Editorial, "The Myth of Managed Trade," *Economist*, May 6, 1990, pp. 11–12; "Trade: Mote and Beam," ibid., pp. 22–23.

But it is a fair guess that whatever does emerge will draw on many of the traditions outlined above, combining their features in new ways that respond to new conditions. At present it seems clear only that, with the threat of Soviet expansion gone, strategies other than containment will have to be devised to serve the American interest in physical security. And as physical security itself seems less at risk, economic prosperity and value projection will probably become bigger parts of future foreign affairs strategies.

As these shifts take place, there is no intrinsic reason that the globalist, regionalist, or inward-looking strategies discussed above need necessarily group together; no reason, for example, that globalist strategies for physical security would necessarily accompany globalist strategies for economic welfare and value projection. Nor would a security focus on the northern hemisphere have to go with a North American trading bloc, or politico-military isolationism with value preservation at home and protectionist economic policies. Surely the United States could be the Great Exemplar of democratic government while leading a return to collective security, or practice balance-of-power strategies while adopting protectionist economic measures. But it is an uncomfortable fact that there has generally been a kind of macro-coincidence in American policies; that for whatever reason, strategies in one area of the national interest do seem in the past to have accompanied similar strategies in other areas.

If the process of strategic choice is cohesive in this way, which level American foreign affairs strategy settles on in the post–Cold War era will perhaps be determined most of all by perceptions among American political leaders of the nation's power. For in the short run, at least, a globalist role demands much greater resources, more optimism and activism—more of what might be called "policy energy"—than a regionalist one, and a regionalist one more than an inward-looking one, irrespective of their costs over the long run. Policymakers who do not believe that the nation can spare resources for foreign policy goals are unlikely to set objectives that require their commitment.[71]

---

71. Historically, the relationship between perceptions of power and goal-setting is eccentric, with the expansiveness of goals swinging far more dramatically than actual power shifts would seem to require. Thus, many historians argue that President Roosevelt underestimated what the United States could do to resist aggression during the Great Depression, while the steady real growth rates of the 1950s and 1960s led to the arrogance of power manifest by Lyndon Johnson in Vietnam: "We are the richest nation in the history of the world. We can afford to spend whatever is needed to keep this country safe and to keep our freedom secure." Gaddis, *Strategies of Containment,* p. 205. Politicians living through good or bad times cannot tell how

Any attempt to predict the future of U.S. foreign affairs strategy must begin, then, with the issue of whether the United States will be able to overcome its present fiscal and economic disabilities and rebuild the domestic power base on which any sound strategy must rest. If the nation fails to do so, one can anticipate a period of increasing domestic divisions and political cynicism as various groups struggle to increase or maintain their shares of a shrinking economic pie; the likely outward expression of such a state of affairs would be the most destructive kind of inward-looking policies, a non-strategy comprising actions taken or not taken because of domestic strife rather than from any sense of foreign affairs purpose. If, on the other hand, the nation does attempt to rebuild its power for foreign affairs as well as domestic reasons, a certain refocusing on internal affairs will also be necessary, but as a purposive and cohesive strategic response to the post–Cold War era rather than as the reflection of strategic abdication.[72] The outcome might be a foreign affairs strategy less globalist in the area of physical security but both more idealistic and self-interested than would have been wise, either during the Cold War years, or in response to the challenges posed by Germany and Japan earlier in the century.[73]

Until a new hegemonic threat appears, for example, the nation can well afford to worry less about its physical security. In this area, a kind of layered

---

typical their experiences will prove to be; denied the benefits of hindsight, they are more impressed than they should be with current trends, either good or bad, and act accordingly.

72. The contemporary debate about post–Cold War foreign affairs strategy reflects this basic choice nicely. On the one side are those searching for a new mission that can sustain U.S. global involvement in the post–Cold War era, arguing about such goals as spreading democracy, maintaining stability, or building a new world order. On the other side are those insisting that the country can and must set aside its foreign policy preoccupations to refocus on the home front—but their rather similar sounding pleas mask a far more fundamental division. Some want policymakers to concentrate on domestic problems strictly for their own sake; to these people, foreign policy is an unwanted, unnecessary distraction. Others in this group see solutions to problems at home as essential precisely so that the nation can operate effectively overseas, because a rebuilding of American power is necessary if the nation is to secure its interests, even its domestic interests, in an increasingly internationalized world.

73. That a refocusing on domestic issues will occur in either case seems evident from recent public opinion polls showing an enormous preference for domestic over foreign policy concerns. Even in the immediate aftermath of the Gulf War, more than two-thirds of those asked agreed that the country faced "problems at home that require greater attention to domestic, rather than foreign and military needs." Nearly the same number said that the United States should spend more on social and domestic programs, and three-fourths urged more spending on programs to create jobs and economic growth (while only a fifth wanted more spending on military and national security). "The New World Order—What the Peace Should Be," *Americans Talk Issues*, Survey No. 15, March 19–24, 1991, p. 12. See also David S. Broder and E.J. Dionne, Jr., "Voters See Big Needs at Home," *Washington Post*, November 4, 1991, pp. A1, A12.

strategy can be envisioned, one that could be conducted with a much lower level of resources than the nation spent during the Cold War. While maintaining a capacity for intervention in isolated incidents that threaten its vital interests,[74] the United States would progressively work to fashion collective mechanisms for dealing with routine instability that poses a threat to American lives and economic activity; such arrangements could rely on the military power of its European and possibly Japanese associates as well as its own, and could be based in the UN or outside it.[75] The United States will probably never recover its geo-technological isolation, so defensive measures against the more manageable threats of the post–Cold War era will commend themselves, including the post-SDI Global Protection Against Limited Strikes (GPALS) program, and anti-proliferation regimes directed against the spread of sophisticated conventional arms, nuclear weapons, and delivery systems.[76] Hemispheric defense would find a prominent place in this strategy, using primarily economic and cooperative law enforcement tools in a more systematic approach to the control of illegal immigration and drug trafficking.[77]

Strategists are realists when necessary, idealists when possible. The relative lack of post–Cold War concern for physical security would seem to free the nation to indulge its idealistic instincts; yet, ironically, it comes at a time when resource constraints would seem to demand idealism on the cheap. This consideration alone will be a formidable restraint on crusades for democracy or human rights abroad, even on the kind of large-scale humanitarian assistance undertaken in Operation Provide Comfort after the Gulf War, or envisioned for the Soviet successor states as they endure the agony of post-communist economic transformations. The inward focusing needed for economic rebirth (or forced by economic stagnation) will also work against globalist value projection strategies, as would any substantial reversal of

---

74. Don Oberdorfer, "Strategy for a Solo Superpower: Pentagon Looks to 'Regional Contingencies'," *Washington Post*, May 19, 1991, pp. A1, A14.

75. Some practical suggestions for strengthening the UN for these purposes are found in Bruce Russett and James S. Sutterlin, "The U.N. in a New World Order," *Foreign Affairs*, Vol. 70, No. 2 (Spring 1991), pp. 69–83.

76. Some programs along these lines are described in Dick Cheney, Secretary of Defense, *Annual Report to the President and the Congress* (Washington, D.C.: U.S. Government Printing Office, January 1991). On GPALS see particularly pp. 58–60.

77. The increased use of economic tools (like the Mexico–United States Free Trade Area) for hemispheric defense would be an interesting parallel with George Kennan's original strategy of containment, which relied primarily on instruments like the Marshall Plan to deter Soviet subversion. Gaddis, *Strategies of Containment*, pp. 37, 61–65.

recent democratic trends overseas.[78] Freed of the necessity of making alliances with unsavory regimes in order to protect its physical security, the United States should find the costs of a moralistic policy less obvious than they were during the twentieth century.[79] Still, although the American government can be expected to continue doing what it can to promote American values overseas, this area of foreign affairs strategy is likely to remain overwhelmingly an outcome of the American private sector's influence via the communications and transportation revolutions of our time.

Although economic conditions seem destined to push the United States towards inward-looking foreign affairs strategies, economic prosperity is, ironically, the one area of the national interest in which an inward focus might be extraordinarily destructive. As noted above, everything depends upon the way such a strategy is constructed, on whether indeed it is a strategy at all or simply a reflexive response to hard times. The internationalization of the domestic economy would certainly make a return to protectionist or mercantilist policies very damaging over the long run, and the financial and commercial elites of the U.S. economy may now be so interdependent with the outside world as to make such a policy turn unlikely. What is needed is rather an inward-looking economic strategy that is simultaneously regionalist if not globalist in nature, a strategy that undertakes domestic renewal while maintaining and strengthening overseas connections. Such a strategy would require both an adroit and committed national leadership[80] and a shift in the popular mood from consumption to investment, from self-gratification to sacrifice. Neither, at present, seems much in evidence.[81]

---

78. The combination of spreading dictatorship abroad and economic disaster at home was, of course, a powerful force for the most destructive kind of American isolationism during the 1930s.

79. American idealism played a major role in the country's rejection of the Treaty of Versailles and made Americans very uncomfortable about their alliances with Stalin during World War II and with various Third World dictators during the Cold War. Any necessity for such compromises may now largely have passed, but the unease occasioned by the sacrifice of American lives in support of the Kuwaiti autocracy was a timely reminder that the traditional rules of collective security ignore the internal character of regimes.

80. My own view of the Bush administration's strategy in this area is set forth in Terry L. Deibel, "Bush's Foreign Policy: Mastery and Inaction," *Foreign Policy*, No. 84 (Fall 1991), pp. 3–23.

81. The current pessimistic mood of the electorate, though probably a product of the extended recession, also seems to reflect a deeper understanding that the nation is in long-term economic trouble, that fundamental changes and not short-term quick fixes are needed—an encouraging sign. Whether that mood and President Bush's recent concern with domestic economic matters

So today's ultimate strategic question returns to the question of power, to whether in these difficult times the American body politic can summon the will and hence the means to capitalize on the end, not only of the Cold War, but of this century's hegemonic wars. Can the nation manage the paradox of victory in relative decline so as to take advantage of its post–Cold War opportunities? If not, given the lack of hegemonic threats, it may well be that no great harm will come, just a gradual deterioration of the nation's prosperity and position in a progressively less manageable (if for a time less consequential) international environment. But if Americans can disenthrall themselves from Cold War thinking, understand the character of the revolutionary changes they face, and create purposeful strategies to deal with them, we may be poised on the edge of the most hopeful season in international affairs since the Congress of Vienna initiated a century of hegemonic peace.

---

can be translated into meaningful action during an economic downturn, or whether alternatively the pressure to do something can be sustained if the economy improves, are at this writing unanswered questions.

A Defensible Defense | Robert J. Art

America's Grand Strategy After the Cold War

The Cold War is over and the United States won it. Now, after its forty-five year battle with the Soviet Union, what should the United States do with its power?[1]

Should it promote a new era of world politics in which collective security really works? Should it use every means at its disposal, including military force, to spread democracy around the globe, now that communism is dead as an ideological alternative? Should it continue to combat the growing forces of economic nationalism and guard against the ever-present potential for the spread of nuclear weapons? Or should it instead forget about all those goals, retreat into an isolationist posture, bring all its troops home from overseas and, safe behind its nuclear shield, enjoy the benefits of the huge North American market and concentrate on its own pressing domestic problems and social ills? Exactly where on the continuum between the two grand alternatives—unbridled internationalism and constricted isolationism—should the United States draw the line?[2]

Robert J. Art is Christian A. Herter Professor of International Relations at Brandeis University and a Research Associate of Harvard's Center for International Affairs.

For their insightful comments, I am especially grateful to John J. Mearsheimer and Stephen Van Evera. I am also indebted to the participants at the conference on "America's Foreign Policy Towards the Year 2000," April 28–29, 1990, sponsored by Brandeis University's Center for International and Comparative Studies, where an early version of this paper was presented; and to the National Security Seminar of the Olin Institute for Strategic Studies, Center for International Affairs, Harvard University, which provided much food for thought about American grand strategy. For research support, I thank the United States Institute of Peace.

1. One can date the formal end of the Cold War in the fall of 1990, when Germany was unified on October 3 and when, on November 18, the NATO Alliance and the Warsaw Pact signed the Treaty on Conventional Armed Forces in Europe at a meeting of the thirty-four–member Conference on Security and Cooperation in Europe (CSCE). See Craig R. Whitney, "The Legacy of Helsinki," *New York Times*, November 19, 1990, p. A6, for the terms of the treaty. The arguments I make in this article are predicated on the assumptions that the Cold War is over and that Soviet troops will completely withdraw from Germany and Eastern Europe in the next few years. My arguments will not be undercut if the Soviet Union becomes a right-wing military or civilian dictatorship that treats its citizens harshly or that brutally uses its army to hold the Soviet Union together, so long as such a dictatorship does not return to an aggressive, ideologically-driven, expansionist foreign policy. However, even though such harsh internal policies would not bring a return to the Cold War, they would certainly produce a marked deterioration in U.S.-Soviet relations.
2. For a short statement of the traditional isolationist position, see Patrick J. Buchanan,

The Realm of Grand Strategy

The best way to deal with all these questions is to decide what foreign policy goals the United States should pursue in the post–Cold War era; and then to determine the instruments best suited to attain them. In this article, I lay out a broad range of potential U.S. goals, but do not deal with all the instruments of statecraft. Instead, I concentrate solely on how America's military power, and especially a continuing U.S. military presence overseas, can facilitate the attainment of its goals. I thus take an internationalist, not an isolationist, posture.[3]

By analyzing the relation between American goals and U.S. military power, I enter the realm of what has properly been called "grand strategy"; but I do so in a way different from some other analysts. Some employ a restrictive definition of grand strategy that specifies only the threats to a state and the military means to deal with them.[4] Others use a broader definition that specifies the threats to a nation's security and then details the military, political and economic means to meet them.[5] In this article, I employ the term grand strategy in neither of these senses. Rather I use it, first, to specify

---

"America First—and Second, and Third," *The National Interest*, No. 19 (Spring 1990), pp. 77–82. For a carefully argued, comprehensive statement why the United States can now safely revert to isolationism, see Eric A. Nordlinger, *Masterly Inactivity: A "National" Security Strategy* (forthcoming). For a statement of the liberal internationalist position, see Charles William Maynes, "America without the Cold War," *Foreign Policy*, No. 78 (Spring 1990), pp. 3–25. A most eloquent argument for a significantly diminished world role for the United States is Robert W. Tucker, "1989 and All That," in Nicholas X. Rizopoulos, ed., *Sea-Changes: American Foreign Policy in a World Transformed* (New York: Council on Foreign Relations, 1990), pp. 204–238. For a well-reasoned and balanced statement why the United States must continue to provide world leadership, see Joseph S. Nye, Jr., *Bound to Lead: The Changing Nature of American Power* (New York: Basic Books, 1990).

3. In this essay, I use the term "isolationism" to define a situation in which the United States has no *peacetime* binding military alliances with other powers and has withdrawn its army and air power to its own territory. The U.S. navy would continue to show some presence around the world, although it would not maintain a constant presence in any given place. I do not, therefore, suggest by the term that the United States is uninvolved politically with the rest of the world, nor that it pursues economic autarky. This is consistent with the traditional use of the term: a military, not a political or economic, withdrawal to the nation's borders. It is in this sense that Robert W. Tucker employs the term for what remains the best published treatment of the pros and cons of an isolationist posture for the United States. See Tucker, *A New Isolationism: Threat or Promise?* (New York: Universe Books, 1972).

4. This is the definition employed by John J. Mearsheimer in *Liddell Hart and the Weight of History* (Ithaca: Cornell University Press, 1988), p. 17.

5. This is the meaning employed by Barry R. Posen in *The Sources of Military Doctrine: France, Britain, and Germany between the World Wars* (Ithaca: Cornell University Press, 1984), p. 13.

the goals that a state should pursue, including both security and non-security goals, and, second, to delineate how military power can serve these goals.[6] Unlike the first definition, mine includes goals other than simply security; unlike the second, my purview is restricted to military means. Non-military instruments are as important to statecraft as the military one, but I do not treat them as part of grand strategy, because I wish to preserve the useful distinction between grand strategy and foreign policy, which includes all of the goals and all of the instruments of statecraft.

Important questions have been raised about the role that military power can play in America's peacetime foreign policy (regardless of the recent U.S. and allied use of force against Iraq). More than a decade before the Cold War ended, many analysts held that U.S. military power had lost a great deal of its utility in America's relations with Western Europe and Japan.[7] The end of the Cold War, many argued, will devalue the role of U.S. military power even more, not only in America's relations with these nations, but with most other nations as well. With a severely diminished (or perhaps non-existent) Soviet military threat, states will have little need for American protection; consequently, the United States will no longer have the capacity to extract political leverage from its provision of security to others. This type of analysis leads to a compelling case for America's military retrenchment. But does it also lead to a compelling case for isolationism?

The proper way to answer this question and to set forth America's grand strategy after the Cold War is to answer four questions: (1) What interests does the United States have, now that its major adversary is defeated? (2) What threats to those interests can we now foresee? (3) What military strategies are best suited to counter the foreseeable threats? and (4) What military

---

6. Throughout this article, I use the word "security" to refer to the ability of the United States to protect its homeland from attack, invasion, conquest, or destruction. I use the term to mean the physical protection of a nation's homeland, and primarily in reference to those military capabilities sufficient for deterrence of an attack, or defense against one should it occur. Some may argue that this definition of security is too narrow and that it should include items such as the economic health of the nation, its access to raw materials, the flowering of its ideological predispositions abroad, and so on. The problem with this usage, however, is that it empties the concept of security of any meaning. To say that practically everything is related to making a nation feel secure is to say that security includes practically anything. Restricting the term to the meaning I suggest gives it analytical clarity and policy utility.

7. See, for example, Richard Rosecrance, *The Rise of the Trading State: Commerce and Conquest in the Modern World* (New York: Basic Books, 1986); and Robert O. Keohane and Joseph S. Nye, Jr., *Power and Interdependence* (Boston: Little, Brown, 1977), chap. 2.

forces are required to execute these strategies?[8] In this article, I deal primarily with the first two questions and only secondarily with the third and fourth. Although I argue against an isolationist policy, I do prescribe retrenchment, because I call for a residual, not a warfighting, U.S. overseas military presence. Once America's broad interests and the threats to them are defined, the general outlines of the proper military strategy and the requisite forces will become clear.

Table 1. Interests, Threats, and a U.S. Presence Overseas.

U.S. Interest	Prime Threat to U.S. Interest	Major Purpose of Overseas Forces	Nature of the Argument for U.S. Forces Overseas
1. Protect U.S. homeland from destruction	Spread of nuclear weapons	Selectively extend deterrence to retard spread	Based on high cost of low-probability events
2. Preserve prosperity based on international economic openness	Economic nationalism	Reduce others' relative gains worries to preserve stability	Hedge bets because of indeterminate arguments about today's interdependence
3. Assure access to Persian gulf oil	Near-monopoly control by regional hegemon	Deter attack and/or conquest of others	Simple deterrence
4. Prevent certain wars	Great-power wars in Europe and Far East; conquest of Israel and South Korea	Deter attack and/or conquest of others	Added insurance for low-probability events
5. Where feasible, promote democratic institutions and certain humanitarian values abroad	Other governments mass-murdering their citizens	Intervention in other states' internal affairs	Humanitarian motives

8. Steven E. Miller suggested this framework to me some time ago, and I continue to find it useful.

I make six arguments in this article:

First: For the indefinite future, the United States has five specific interests, summarized in Table 1. They are: (1) protection of the U.S. homeland from attack; (2) continued prosperity based in part on preservation of an open world economy; (3) assured access to Persian Gulf oil; (4) prevention of war among the great powers of Europe and the Far East, and preservation of the independence of Israel and South Korea; and (5) where feasible, the promotion of democratic governments and the overthrow of governments engaged in the mass murder of their citizenry.[9]

Second: As a general rule, the United States does not have an interest in spreading democracy by intervening militarily in the internal affairs of states; nor should it seek to impose peace among all states in every region. Spreading democracy by forceful means can too easily become a blank check for unbridled military interventionism. Imposing peace, either through a global collective security system or through unilateral American action, is a surefire recipe for assumption of the global policeman role.

Third: Nuclear weapons have severed the connection between America's security and the balance of power on the Eurasian land mass and have thereby invalidated traditional geopolitical logic. The only serious threat to U.S. security, as I have defined the term, is the spread of nuclear weapons to crazy Third World statesmen or fanatical terrorists.[10] To help retard their

---

9. There is a sixth interest: protection of the global environment, particularly by slowing the rate of global warming (the "enhanced greenhouse effect") and by stopping the destruction of the ozone layer. I do not deal with the global environment in this article, because there is little that American military power or an overseas U.S. military presence can do to deal with either threat to the environment. But I do agree with those who hold that the projected effects of ozone depletion and global warming are severe. The most important thing the United States can do to stop the destruction of the ozone layer is to see that the 1987 Montreal Protocol on Substances that Deplete the Ozone Layer, and the 1990 amendments to it, are fully implemented. The most important things the United States can do to slow global warming are to increase energy efficiency, reduce reliance on fossil fuels that pour carbon dioxide into the atmosphere, and foster international measures that will enable and encourage other states to do likewise. The best source on the current state of scientific knowledge about global warming is the Intergovernmental Panel on Climate Change (IPCC), World Meterological Organization and United Nations Environment Programme (J.T. Houghton, G.J. Jenkins, and J.J. Ephraums, eds.), *Climate Change—The IPCC Scientific Assessment* (Cambridge: Cambridge University Press, 1990).

10. Throughout this discussion, I use the term "spread" rather than "proliferation" to avoid the latter's implication of rapid or quick multiplication. Because the number of states that could quickly go nuclear is not large, and because so few states have gone nuclear, "spread" is a more accurate description of what has happened and what could happen. In this choice of terms, I follow the convention set by Kenneth N. Waltz, *The Spread of Nuclear Weapons: More May Be Better*, Adelphi Paper No. 171 (London: International Institute of Strategic Studies [IISS], 1981), p. 1.

spread, the United States should maintain a selective overseas military presence.

Fourth: There is a case for a U.S. military presence in the Far East and Europe to help preserve the open economic order among the rich industrialized nations. The rationale for this presence, however, rests more on a general argument for insurance and reassurance than on any definitive theory about the utility of military power for the preservation of international economic openness, or on any definitive conclusions about the resiliency of this era's economic interdependence.

Fifth: Assured access to Persian Gulf oil, the long-term protection of Israel, and the historical commitment to South Korea call for some type of American military presence in those areas. The nature of the American presence in the Gulf will depend on the postwar constellation of political-military forces in the region, but it should occur within a multinational United Nations format. To assure the security of South Korea from its northern counterpart, a much smaller U.S. military presence is all that is required. To provide better protection of Israel, the United States should sign a military treaty with Israel, station a residual American force there, and then cause Israel to disgorge the West Bank and Gaza.

Sixth: Overall, the United States needs a much smaller peacetime overseas military presence than it has had. With the Cold War's demise, the United States will be providing to others primarily insurance, reassurance, and stability, not large amounts of security. But it must retain the capability to reinforce those forces rapidly should the need arise.

In the first part of this article, I analyze the security threats to the United States and how to deal with them; in the second part, I show how a continuing overseas U.S. presence can help preserve an open international economic order; in the third part, I define the limits that should be put on any future American military interventions; and in the conclusion, I lay out the general principles of the post–Cold War strategy.

Ensuring America's Security in Three Eras

To assess how the United States should ensure its security in the future, it is important to analyze what threats it has faced and what actions it has taken in the past. Prior to 1990, the United States passed through two security eras. The first was the geopolitical era, which lasted from 1789 to 1945; the second, the Cold War era, lasted from 1945 to 1990. In the geopolitical era, the United States faced two potential threats: invasion and conquest by a Eurasian hegemon; or slow strangulation caused by a hegemon's imposition of a global blockade. After about 1900, the first geopolitical threat was highly improbable, and the second problematical. During the Cold War era, America's possession of nuclear weapons invalidated both these geopolitical threats, although many argued the contrary.[11] The only possible threat was nuclear attack from the Soviet Union, but this was never very likely.

After the formal ending of the Cold War in 1990, the United States entered its third security era. As in the Cold War period, the geopolitical threats remain insignificant, and the Soviet threat is markedly diminished. The only potential threats to U.S. security will come from "crazy" nuclear states or nuclear-armed terrorist groups. Although neither threat seems likely, some hedging against them is wise. These conclusions are summarized in Table 2.

THREATS IN THE GEOPOLITICAL ERA

EXTERNAL FACTORS AND INTERNAL EFFORTS. During the entire geopolitical era, five factors contributed to the security of the United States against

Table 2. Threats to U.S. Security During Three Eras.

Type of Threat	The Geopolitical Era (Pre-1945)	The Cold War Era (1945–90)	The Post–Cold War Era (Post-1990)
1. Invasion and conquest	Quite difficult after 1900	Practically zero probability	Practically zero probability
2. Slow strangulation through a global blockade	Of indeterminate feasibility	Practically zero probability	Practically zero probability
3. Nuclear attack			
From the Soviet Union		Not probable	Highly improbable
From other nations or subnational groups		Highly improbable	Not probable

11. George Kennan's writings in the late 1940s were excellent examples of the (mis-)application of geopolitical logic to the nuclear era. For Kennan's argument at the time, see John Lewis Gaddis, *Strategies of Containment: A Critical Appraisal of Postwar American National Security Policy* (New York: Oxford University Press, 1982), chap. 2.

invasion and slow strangulation: (1) geographical separation from the Eurasian land mass; (2) the balance of power on the European continent; (3) the availability of allies to absorb the initial onslaughts of potential hegemons; (4) time, bought by allies and by distance, to convert U.S. peacetime industrial strength into disposable military power; and (5) a huge industrial base that, when harnessed to war, yielded vast military forces.[12] The first four factors were external to the United States, accidents of geography and political circumstances; the fifth, internal to the United States, was a product of an abundance of natural resources and skill in utilizing them.

To provide for its security in the early geopolitical era (the years before 1900), the United States relied more on external factors than on internal resources. After the War of 1812, the United States enjoyed nearly eighty years of relative security because of the benevolence of British seapower and the dictates of Britain's imperial strategy in the New World. Britain used its maritime dominance in the nineteenth century to keep other European great powers from establishing or reestablishing footholds in the western hemisphere. Britain's goal was to dominate the foreign trade of both the Americas, first by preventing its European competitors from setting up mercantile trading centers in the western hemisphere, and second by using its industrial supremacy to undersell all others, including the Americans. In the heyday of their economic power, the British feared economic competition from no one and preferred to capture the lion's share of the world's commerce through what Robinson and Gallagher have called the "imperialism of free trade."[13] Eschewing conquest and rule in the western hemisphere, they used their seapower to protect their commerce and extend their informal political control. Thus, the one European power with a significant presence in the

---

12. The best analysis of the bases of American security in the geopolitical era is still to be found in Nicholas J. Spykman, *America's Strategy in World Politics: The United States and the Balance of Power* (New York: Harcourt, Brace, and Company, 1942), esp. chaps. 2, 3, 14, and 15. For a recent statement of the importance of the balance of power on the Eurasian land mass to America's security, see Stephen M. Walt, "The Case for Finite Containment: Analyzing U.S. Grand Strategy," *International Security*, Vol. 14, No. 1 (Summer 1989), pp. 5–50.
13. See John Gallagher and Ronald Robinson, "The Imperialism of Free Trade," *The Economic History Review*, 2d ser., Vol. 6, No. 1 (1953), pp. 1–15; and Gallagher and Robinson, *Africa and the Victorians: The Official Mind of Imperialism* (London: Macmillan, 1961). For more on the nature of British imperialism in the nineteenth century, see D.K. Fieldhouse, "Imperialism: An Historiographical Revision," *The Economic History Review*, 2d ser., Vol. 14, No. 2 (1961), pp. 187–209; and C.J. Lowe, *The Reluctant Imperialists: British Foreign Policy, 1878–1902* (New York: Macmillan, 1969). For how British seapower protected the United States, see Spykman, *America's Strategy in World Politics*, pp. 68–89; and Edward H. Buehrig, *Woodrow Wilson and the Balance of Power* (Gloucester, Mass.: Peter Smith, 1968), pp. 3–11.

western hemisphere was no military threat to the United States. Because British seapower served America's security, the United States was able to free-ride on the British, and remained largely disarmed throughout most of the nineteenth century.[14]

These fortuitous circumstances began to change in the 1890s, when Britain's naval dominance ebbed and its imperial position became overextended.[15] Facing naval challenges first from the Russians and the French, and then more severely from the Germans, the British began to curtail their naval presence in some regions overseas and to reach political agreements with the most powerful regional actors. They settled first with the Americans in the Caribbean and then with the Japanese in the western Pacific. Britain's imperial retrenchment helped prompt America's military rearmament and geographical expansion. No longer able to count on the protection of British seapower, and fearing that the Germans might establish bases in Cuba, Puerto Rico or the Central American states, or the Japanese in Hawaii, the United States enhanced its security by naval rearmament and by occupying the power vacuums into which these states might otherwise move. America's imperialism during 1894–1904 had a definite defensive component: the expansion of America's defensive perimeter outward in order to establish political, economic, and military dominance in the Caribbean, Atlantic, and Pacific approaches to the United States. The United States removed the last vestiges of European influence in the western hemisphere and preemptively occupied those points that could serve as foreign military bases close to America's shores.[16]

Invasion of the United States, but not conquest, would have been easier for a European continental hegemon before America's naval rearmament

---

14. In this period, the U.S. army was geared more to fighting Indians in the west than to repelling non-existent foreign invaders. Harold and Margaret Sprout, *The Rise of American Naval Power, 1776–1918* (Princeton: Princeton University Press, 1967), describe how low the American navy had sunk after the Civil War: "A virulent attack of politics, graft, and corruption . . . ate at the vitals of the establishment. . . . The Navy Department spent millions of dollars . . . with little in the end to show for it, save a collection of worthless antiquated ships, an army of enriched contractors, a host of political retainers, and partisan strength at the polls in the favored constituencies" (p. 180).
15. On British strategy at the end of the nineteenth century, see George Monger, *The End of Isolation: British Foreign Policy, 1900–1907* (London: T. Nelson, 1963); and John A.S. Grenville, *Lord Salisbury and Foreign Policy: The Close of the Nineteenth Century* (London: Athlone Press, 1964).
16. The best book on the defensive aspect of America's expansion during this period is John A.S. Grenville and George Berkeley Young, *Politics, Strategy, and American Diplomacy: Studies in Foreign Policy, 1873–1917* (New Haven: Yale University Press, 1966), esp. chaps. 3, 4, 7, and 8.

than after. Throughout the nineteenth century, however, there was no European hegemon. There were also no significant European imperial outposts in the western hemisphere, save Spain's Cuba and Britain's Canada; but Spain was no military threat, and Britain—the one nation that could project military power into the New World—preferred economic penetration to military conquest. As a consequence, the western hemisphere was spared the formal imperial annexations that Africa suffered after 1870 and the spheres-of-influence arrangements that China labored under at the turn of the twentieth century. With its naval rearmament and its imperial expansion, the United States had broken free from a Britain that could no longer protect it. After the United States had erected a more forward and secure defensive perimeter, largely completed by the early 1900s, invasion and conquest by a Eurasian hegemon became much more difficult.

GEOPOLITICAL NIGHTMARES. From 1900 to 1941, the United States continued to build up its naval power, but retained only a small peacetime army. With the exception of World War I, there were few threats to its security that its navy could not handle. The United States faced its first serious possibility of invasion during World War I, but the threat was contingent, not immediate. President Woodrow Wilson worried not about a direct military attack, but about the internal subversion of American democracy that a German hegemony could produce. His concern stemmed from the huge economic and industrial resources that a hegemonic Germany could have aggregated, converted to military power, and then projected against the western hemisphere. To dissuade those forces from attacking, the United States in turn would have to maintain huge peacetime armed forces indefinitely. Wilson feared the political toll on America's institutions: such forces would mean the militarization of American society and the subversion of democracy.[17] For Wilson, the only way out was the League of Nations: it would tie American power to Europe, nip in the bud any future German bid for continental

---

17. This is how Wilson stated his fear during a speech on September 5, 1919, in St. Louis, when he was campaigning for the League of Nations: "We must be physically ready for anything to come. We must have a great standing army. . . . You have got to think of the President . . . as the man meant constantly and everyday to be the Commander in Chief of the Army and the Navy. . . . And you know what the effect of a military government is upon social questions. You know how impossible it is to effect social reform if everybody must be under orders from the Government. *You know how impossible it is,* in short, *to have a free nation if it is a military nation*" (emphasis added). Quoted in Daniel Patrick Moynihan, "The Peace Dividend," *New York Review of Books,* Vol. 37, No. 11 (June 28, 1990), p. 4.

hegemony, and thereby obviate the need for a massive peacetime military force.[18]

It was not until World War II that the United States had to face the ultimate geopolitical nightmare: two hegemons—Germany and Japan—dominant on either end of the Eurasian land mass and united against the United States. These two hegemons could have controlled enormous resources and, combined, they could have projected formidable military power against the western hemisphere. The United States would have been encircled on a global scale. This encirclement, initially loose, would not have brought immediate attack against America. But would not a Germany ascendant on the European continent and a Japan dominant in the Far East at some point have brought their overwhelmingly superior resources to bear against the United States in its isolated redoubt, ultimately attacked, and perhaps defeated it?[19]

The question may seem academic, but it is of great import for our purposes because of the light that it sheds on how much of an invasion threat Eurasian hegemons could have posed to the United States. German and Japanese hegemony would have been dangerous, but their invasion and conquest of the United States would not have been easy.[20]

This was the conclusion reached by Nicholas Spykman, one of the most rigorous of the American foreign policy analysts at the time, and a follower of the Mackinder geopolitical school.[21] Writing in 1941–42, during some of

18. For a good analysis of the evolution of Wilson's thinking on the League, see Buehrig, *Woodrow Wilson and the Balance of Power*, chaps. 6 and 9.

19. Roosevelt took seriously the possibility of a German attack in South America in the early phases of World War II. "Few issues gave Roosevelt more concern in the summer of 1940 than the threat to Latin America. . . . By late May, Roosevelt had concluded that continued Nazi victories would lead Berlin to attempt the overthrow of existing Latin American governments and the transfer of Dutch and French possessions in the Western hemisphere to its control. He also saw Germany's likely acquisition of France's fleet and West African bases as a prelude to an attack on Brazil and the rest of South America." Robert Dallek, *Franklin D. Roosevelt and American Foreign Policy, 1932–1945* (New York: Oxford University Press, 1979), p. 233. For a full analysis of Hitler's plans towards the western hemisphere, see Alton Frye, *Nazi Germany and the American Hemisphere, 1933–1941* (New Haven: Yale University Press, 1967), pp. 168–186.

20. Bruce Russett argues that had the United States not intervened, Germany would not have won the war; but neither would it have been conquered. There could have been a uneasy stalemate in Europe, and the hegemonic invasion threat would never have materialized. See Bruce M. Russett, *No Clear and Present Danger: A Skeptical View of the United States Entry into World War II* (New York: Harper and Row, 1972), chap. 2.

21. Mackinder was an English geographer who wrote about the rise and fall of empires by analyzing the permanent strategic factors that flowed from a state's geographic position and natural endowments. For Mackinder's views, see Halford J. Mackinder, "The Geographical Pivot of History," *The Geographical Journal*, Vol. 23, No. 4 (April 1904), pp. 421–437; Mackinder, *Britain and the British Seas*, 2d ed. (Oxford: Clarendon Press, 1907); and Mackinder, *Democratic Ideals and Reality* (New York: W.W. Norton, 1962).

the darkest days of World War II, Spykman did not think that the United States could easily be defeated in its own hemisphere, though he did see a bleak future if the Eurasian land mass fell under the domination of Germany and Japan. In his masterful *America's Strategy in World Politics*, Spykman looked at the possibilities of invasion from across the Atlantic and the Pacific and found the task facing Germany and Japan to be daunting.[22] He argued that even when these two adversaries acquired long-range bombers, "the bombers will still have to come over without the protection of accompanying fighter planes"; and if the United States prepared well-defended air bases along the routes of attack, then "the air defense of the hemisphere can be made fairly secure."[23] In other words, the enemy's bombers could easily be shot down.

Spykman reasoned that, until air attack was perfected, a combined German-Japanese invasion would still need a naval armada. But, he argued, "invasion by water is . . . no longer as easy as it used to be." An invading naval force would require even more air protection than bombers needed, but the amount of air power that the United States could direct from its territory against any armada would have made such an effort suicidal.[24] Spykman concluded that if the western hemisphere was encircled globally, the United States could still defend continental North America, although it might lose its outposts in the Aleutians, Alaska, Greenland, and Iceland.[25]

Even though Spykman thought a defense against invasion feasible, he concluded that global encirclement would ultimately bring defeat, because "invasion is not the only form of coercion." The United States "would be surrounded by enemy territory and submitted to economic strangulation by the simple process of blockade through embargo."[26]

Here, then, was the ultimate nightmare of geopolitics: in a global test of resources, the United States could not hold out indefinitely against the two Eurasian hegemons because in time their superiority in economic-industrial resources would prevail. Although the United States could mount a defense of the continental United States for a time, it could not do so indefinitely

---

22. The crux of Spykman's military analysis is to be found in chaps. 14 and 15 of *America's Strategy in World Politics*.
23. Ibid., p. 392.
24. Ibid., pp. 392–393.
25. Ibid., pp. 412 and 453.
26. Ibid. Spykman's analysis of the ability of the United States to exploit the western hemisphere economically in order to hold out against a global blockade is found in ibid., chaps. 10–12.

because it would lack critical raw materials necessary for its war industry.[27] German and Japanese control of the Eurasian land mass would deny the United States the resources of Europe and Asia; German economic and political warfare against Latin America would deny those of the South American states.[28] Slowly strangled, the United States would be unable to launch a military counteroffensive to break the stranglehold because, without allies, it could not open a front on the European continent. Spykman had thus carried to its endpoint Wilson's fear of an America armed to the teeth, encircled, and bereft of allies. Wilson's America was militarized and its system subverted at home; Spykman's, slowly but inexorably strangled. In order to forestall this end, his conclusion was clear: "Allies across the oceans are as indispensable to us as allies across the Channel have been to Great Britain."[29]

Whether Spykman's pessimistic conclusion was correct, that blockade could bring about slow strangulation, is not clear. During World War II, Nazi Germany held out in a total war through nearly five years of blockade, subject to several years of strategic bombing, all the while engaging in a massive military effort on the eastern front. Germany was contiguous to one enemy— the Soviet Union—and therefore easy to invade, and within short air distance of another—Britain—and therefore easy to bomb. It controlled most of Europe, but possessed neither the vast spaces nor the abundance of natural resources, especially oil, that the United States had. In a global blockade, the United States would have had an ocean between it and a Eurasian hegemon, together with the resources of an entire continent and some fraction of another. If Germany was able to hold out for four years under the adverse conditions of total war and geographic propinquity to its adversaries, the

---

27. As Spykman put it: "From the purely military point of view, quarter-sphere defense [from southern Canada to the temperate zone of South America] is a feasible policy, but from an economic point of view, the restricted area is even less viable than the hemisphere as a whole. . . . The quarter-sphere does not contain the power potential necessary for an adequate system of defense against the complete encirclement which would then prevail." Ibid., p. 456.
28. Spykman's conclusion that the United States could not hold out indefinitely against a global siege resulted from his belief that the United States could not indefinitely command the political allegiance of the South American states. After exhaustive economic analysis, he concluded that hemispheric self-sufficiency was possible if the United States could maintain access to all the resources of South America. But he reasoned that this was not possible because the southern hemispheric states would succumb to Germany's economic and political pressure and would ultimately be militarily occupied by it. Hence, although a defense of the western hemisphere over the long haul was militarily and economically feasible, it was not politically possible. See ibid., pp. 314–315.
29. Ibid., p. 454.

United States might have held out indefinitely in a global blockade against geographically distant neighbors. This comparison, admittedly inexact, suggests that a global blockade would not easily have brought America to her knees. Thus, the magnitude of the one serious geopolitical threat during the first half of the twentieth century remains indeterminate.[30]

THREATS IN THE COLD WAR ERA

During the Cold War era, the United States faced no geopolitical threats from resource aggregation or slow strangulation, but it acted as if it did. It constructed military forces more suitable for geopolitical threats than for nuclear threats.

From 1950 to 1990, the United States maintained a huge military establishment with: (1) a large intercontinental strategic nuclear force having significant counterforce capabilities; (2) thousands of tactical nuclear weapons deployed in Eurasia; (3) a huge navy, far superior to anything that the Soviets ever deployed, that dominated the world's seas; (4) a standing army of over 750,000 troops, with a significant number of heavily armored divisions stationed in the heart of Central Europe to counter any possible Soviet thrust westward; (5) a formidable and versatile air force, much of it stationed overseas, capable of intercontinental bombing, deep interdiction, close air support on the battlefield, and preservation of air superiority; and (6) a sea and air power projection capability that enabled the United States to move its conventional forces with relative ease around the globe. The strategic nuclear forces provided significant counterforce capabilities to bolster the credibility of extended deterrence of Soviet conventional attacks on U.S. allies. The tactical nuclear forces were intended to counter the Soviet Union's perceived huge advantage in conventional forces. The large navy, air force, and army were deployed to fight a long conventional war in Central Europe to stalemate and thereby dissuade a Soviet conventional attack there. In constructing its forces during the Cold War era, the United States acted as if geopolitical logic was still at work.

---

30. The literature on the effectiveness of economic sanctions does not make Spykman's slow strangulation scenario look highly plausible, although he was projecting a global blockade, not partial blockades by specific nations against another nation. For differing assessments of the effectiveness of economic sanctions, see David A. Baldwin, *Economic Statecraft* (Princeton: Princeton University Press, 1985), esp. chap. 8; Gary Clyde Hufbauer and Jeffrey J. Schott, *Economic Sanctions in Support of Foreign Policy Goals* (Washington, D.C.: Institute for International Economics, 1983); and Henry Bienen and Robert Gilpin, "Economic Sanctions as a Response to Terrorism," *Journal of Strategic Studies*, Vol. 3, No. 1 (May 1980), pp. 89–98.

Had the United States been concerned only with its own security, and not that of Western Europe and Japan, it would have needed only: (1) a relatively small strategic nuclear force, a reasonable portion of it invulnerable to destruction by a Soviet first strike; (2) a modest air force and navy able to sink any Soviet surface ships that attacked across the Pacific; and (3) a small army to deal with any minor border incursions from hemispheric neighbors or other states. The nuclear forces would deter attack and could defend against a large one; the conventional forces could defend against small-scale attacks if they materialized.

Because the United States fought the Cold War to preserve the political independence of Western Europe and Japan, not its own, it chose the first rather than the second posture. Even if the United States had permitted the Soviet Union to dominate Eurasia, it could have remained secure. Its standard of living, however, would probably have been lower, because there would have been less trade with Europe and Japan; and its psychological comfort would have been less, because far fewer great power democracies would have existed. But in fact, America's security would not have suffered with isolationism, because it had nuclear weapons.

THE ABSENCE OF GEOPOLITICAL THREATS. Two traditional arguments have been offered for why the United States could not have pursued isolationism and why, therefore, it still had to balance power in Eurasia. Both are restatements of Spykman's 1942 analysis. The first involves power projection; the second, resource aggregation.[31]

Some have argued that in the early postwar period, because the United States lacked long-range bombers, it needed Western Europe and Japan: they provided the bases from which to threaten the Soviets with nuclear retaliation. A modified form of geopolitical logic still obtained because the United States did not yet have a viable intercontinental capability. Others have argued that for its own long-term interests, the United States could not permit Europe and Japan to come under the domination of the Soviet Union, because then the Soviets would have had much of the world's industrial resources and, as a consequence, could have brought the United States ultimately to heel.

---

31. For an analysis of the power-projection argument, see Melvin P. Leffler, "The American Conception of National Security and the Beginnings of the Cold War, 1945–1948," *American Historical Review*, Vol. 89, No. 2 (April 1984), pp. 346–381. For the resource aggregation argument, see Gaddis, *Strategies of Containment*, chap. 2; and Walt, "The Case for Finite Containment."

Both of these arguments are suspect. With regard to the basing argument: if, in the early postwar era, the United States lacked an adequate long-range retaliatory capability against the Soviet Union, so, too, did the Soviet Union against the United States. Neither could easily threaten the other with nuclear bombardment. Each had rudimentary intercontinental capabilities against the other only by launching suicidal, one-way nuclear bombing missions. The United States could have done so in 1945, four years earlier than the Soviet Union.[32] But mutual nuclear deterrence would work with suicidal bombing missions, no less than with round-trip bombing missions. Before the United States acquired an intercontinental bombing capability, the bases in Europe made it easier for the United States to attack the Soviet Union and thereby gave it a relative advantage. But the advantage was not essential to America's security and was of import, in the final analysis, only because it was used to protect the Europeans and the Japanese from a potential Soviet conventional attack. In short, until the mid-1950s, when the United States finally began to deploy a reasonably reliable intercontinental retaliatory force, America's European bomber bases were for the Europeans, not the Americans.

With regard to the resource aggregation argument: Soviet domination of the Eurasian land mass would not have posed an immediate or even a medium-term security threat to the United States. U.S. forces could fairly easily have interdicted any Soviet conventional naval armada or bomber force directed against the American homeland. Spykman's argument that a combined German-Japanese invasion of the United States would have been quite difficult applies with even greater force to a potential Soviet invasion. An American nuclear attack could have wiped out any Soviet invasion armada in one fell swoop, and it would have carried little risk of Soviet nuclear retaliation, because it would have been an attack on maritime forces on the high seas, not military forces or population centers on Soviet territory. This type of nuclear defense would have been highly credible, devastatingly effective, and difficult to retaliate against. In short, during the early years of the Cold War, the United States could easily have deterred or defeated any attempted Soviet nuclear or conventional attack.

---

32. As early as January 1950, the Joint Intelligence Committee (JIC) of the Joint Chiefs of Staff (JCS) estimated that "without refueling, the Tu-4s [Soviet bombers] can reach every important industrial, urban, and governmental control center in the United States on a one-way mission basis," and that "the Soviets would not hesitate to expend airplanes and crews as necessary to deliver atomic bombs on selected targets in the United States." Quoted in *Appendix B, JIC 5-2, 20 January 1950*, JCS Files, 1948–50, pp. 26–27, National Security Archive, Washington, D.C. See also Robert J. Art, *Nuclear Weapons and U.S. Grand Strategy* (manuscript), chap. 3.

The only arguable geopolitical threat to America's security in both the early and late phases of the Cold War was strangulation, not invasion. But here, too, nuclear weapons made slow strangulation nearly impossible. Nuclear weapons make the cost of defense and deterrence easy and cheap, enabling states that have them to turn their energies to tasks more economically productive than building military forces. When the low costs of nuclear defense and deterrence are combined with the flexibility of a modern economy in finding substitutes for critical goods and raw materials (as the Germans dramatically demonstrated in World War II), the staying power of modern economies becomes formidable.[33] Two more factors—America's abundance of natural resources and the combined oil resources of the western hemisphere (in Venezuela, Mexico, the United States, and Canada)—make Spykman's ultimate nightmare, of a Eurasian hegemon slowly strangling the United States by a global embargo, even more of a chimera. This does not mean that matters would have been rosy for the United States had the Soviet Union become a Eurasian hegemon after World War II, only that they would not likely have been catastrophic.

THE EFFICACY OF NUCLEAR DETERRENCE. From the outset of the nuclear age, the logic of nuclear deterrence gripped statesmen even if their military services, due to vested interests, were slow to follow suit. Truman viewed nuclear weapons as terror weapons of last resort, and there is no reason to believe that Stalin thought differently.[34] The United States has been secure since 1945 because nuclear deterrence reduced the frequency of crises and de-escalated them when they occurred. It has been the fear that crises could get out of control and escalate to total nuclear war that has prevented them from doing so. Nuclear statesmen can have no illusions about what a general nuclear war would mean for their nation. As a consequence, they run scared, not safe.[35]

---

33. For analyses of how the German economy fared in World War II, see Alan S. Milward, *The German Economy at War* (London: Athlone, 1965); and Burton Klein, *Germany's Economic Preparations for War* (Cambridge: Harvard University Press, 1959).
34. In a letter of January 19, 1953, Truman stated to then Atomic Energy Commissioner Thomas Murray: "[The atomic bomb] is far worse than gas and biological warfare because it affects the civilian population and murders them by wholesale." See David Alan Rosenberg, "The Origins of Overkill: Nuclear Weapons and American Strategy, 1945–1960," *International Security*, Vol. 7, No. 4 (Spring 1983), pp. 26–27.
35. For more on this point, see Robert J. Art, "Between Assured Destruction and Nuclear Victory," *Ethics*, Vol. 95, No. 3 (April 1985), pp. 497–516; Robert Jervis, *The Meaning of the Nuclear Revolution: Statecraft and the Prospects for Armageddon* (Ithaca: Cornell University Press, 1989), chap. 1; Richard K. Betts, *Nuclear Blackmail and Nuclear Balance* (Washington, D.C.: Brookings,

Even if one rejects this argument for the first ten to fifteen years of the Cold War, when geopolitical logic and nuclear logic coexisted uneasily and ambiguously, it is a much stronger argument for the period after 1960. By then, the United States no longer relied on overseas bases for retaliation, because it had deployed ballistic missile submarines and land-based intercontinental ballistic missiles. The overseas bases it retained served primarily as symbols of the American commitment to deter attack on others. They were hostages for America's allies, not the first line of defense for the United States.

A retrospective look at the Cold War era thus yields two important reconsiderations. First, the United States enjoyed a greater degree of security than is often thought. There were no real geopolitical threats. The period of perceived maximum danger (1947–62), when crises were more frequent between the Americans and the Soviets, coincided with a period of American nuclear superiority. The years of relative calm (1963–90) were free of severe direct U.S.-Soviet confrontation, except for a few days during the October 1973 Middle East war.

Second, the United States continued to provide security to the Germans and the Japanese long after their economic recovery had made it feasible for them to supply their own. The United States did so partly for historical reasons (to prevent the World War II aggressors from rearming without constraints); partly for stability reasons (to provide an American presence in Europe and the Far East to assuage the fears of Germany's and Japan's neighbors, and to help foster economic openness); and partly for nonproliferation reasons (to extend the American nuclear umbrella to Germany and Japan so they would not feel impelled to acquire their own nuclear weapons). All three reasons were important, but the third is the only one with any direct bearing on America's security. The American concern was that if Germany and Japan went nuclear, the precedent thereby set would dramatically enhance the likelihood of nuclear spread elsewhere. A nuclear-armed West Germany or Japan by itself would not have threatened the United States, especially if they remained allied with the United States; but the prospect that this might speed the spread of nuclear weapons to other states, which might not act responsibly, was unsettling. This spread, although al-

1987); and Kenneth N. Waltz, "Nuclear Myths and Political Realities," *American Political Science Review*, Vol. 84, No. 3 (September 1990), pp. 731–745.

ways a possibility, did not proceed very far, and did so only to states that were viewed as responsible citizens, not crazy aggressors.

Thus, throughout the Cold War era, the United States could have deterred or defended against any assault on its own territory; it did not need the Germans, the Japanese, or anyone else to do this. It did not have to protect others out of geopolitical logic, even though it may have thought so at the time. It offered protection partly out of a misconception about the continuing relevance of geopolitical logic, but also out of historical memories, concerns for stability and economic openness, and worries about nuclear spread. If there is a case to be made for isolationism in the nuclear era, it is one that becomes valid nearly immediately after World War II, certainly by the mid-1950s, and definitely by the very early 1960s.[36]

THREATS IN THE POST–COLD WAR ERA

Throughout the Cold War, geopolitical threats were absent; nuclear deterrence worked; and nuclear spread was minimal. As a consequence, the United States remained quite secure. For the post–Cold War era, the nightmares of geopolitics remain irrelevant. America's nuclear deterrent cannot be threatened through conventional means, and no nation would launch a conventional attack on a nuclear-armed United States. The notion of a global blockade by a successful Eurasian hegemon is fanciful because there is no

---

36. President Eisenhower, in private, was one of those who from the early 1950s took a quasi-isolationist position, believing that a withdrawal of American forces from Europe should occur after Western Europe had recovered economically. In a conference between Secretary Dulles and Eisenhower on December 12, 1958, Eisenhower's views were recorded as follows: "The President stated that he has worked hard for NATO himself, but that he becomes discouraged at the continuing pressure for the retention of sizeable U. S. forces. He pointed out that other countries are withdrawing forces, in spite of the fact that they are doing better financially than we at the moment; and yet, when we mention withdrawing any portion of our forces, they protest vehemently. . . . He stated that in 1951 as SACEUR he . . . had traveled through Europe insisting to the various European governments that the maintenance of the equivalent of six U.S. divisions was an emergency measure only, and would be maintained only until the effects of the Marshall Plan could take hold, allowing the European economies to take over this responsibility. He added that he had thought at that time that five years would be a maximum." *Memorandum of Conference with the President, 12 December 1958*, pp. 1–3, quoted in Robert J. Art, "Nuclear Weapons in U.S. Grand Strategy: External Necessity and Internal Choice," in Regina Cowen Karp, ed., *Security with Nuclear Weapons?* (Oxford: Oxford University Press, 1991), p. 34. There is also evidence that Eisenhower favored giving the West Europeans the nuclear wherewithal to deter a Soviet attack. He appears to have had a rather relaxed definition of what he considered to be nuclear sharing with the NATO allies. See Marc Trachtenberg, "The Nuclearization of NATO and U.S.–West European Relations" (manuscript, October 1989).

likely candidate for this role. Geopolitical imbalances therefore pose no threat to the United States.

Nuclear threats, however, could imperil America's security. The nuclear menace from the Soviet Union will remain low: if nuclear deterrence worked when U.S.-Soviet tension was high, it will continue to work whether the tension rises again or declines. In the post–Cold War era, therefore, the United States has only to worry about the spread of nuclear weapons to crazy statesmen and ruthless terrorists. How worrisome is either threat?

THE DANGERS OF NUCLEAR SPREAD. If more states acquire nuclear weapons, goes the conventional argument, then the probability of a nuclear war increases and so, too, will the opportunities for terrorists to steal and use them. The chances of things going awry does increase as more people get into the act. In more sophisticated form, the conventional argument stresses five important points about the dangers of nuclear spread.[37] The first two points, associated with the early stages of developing nuclear forces, are viewed as transitional problems that could, in theory, be managed; the third and fourth, dealing with the nature of the Third-World governments that might acquire them, are thought to be more intractable; the fifth, dealing with nuclear terrorism, appears downright frightening.

First, new nuclear forces are not likely to be as secure from preemptive attack as those of the mature nuclear states. Consequently, there will be windows of danger in which states might be tempted to launch preemptive first strikes against an adversary's nuclear forces in order to destroy them. Second, command and control arrangements in new nuclear states are not likely to be state-of-the-art. Consequently, the chances for unauthorized and accidental use will be greater. Third, many would-be Third World nuclear states do not have governments as stable as those of the more mature nuclear powers. Consequently, this increases the risk that their nuclear weapons could fall into the hands of sub-national groups waging civil war, or terrorist groups taking advantage of political chaos. Fourth, many Third World would-be nuclear states are involved in implacable regional confrontations in which reason and restraint have been far less prevalent than they have in U.S.-

---

37. For more on these arguments, see Lewis A. Dunn, *Controlling the Bomb: Nuclear Proliferation in the 1980s* (New Haven: Yale University Press, 1982), pp. 69–95; Thomas C. Schelling, "Thinking about Nuclear Terrorism," *International Security*, Vol. 6, No. 4 (Spring 1982), pp. 61–77; and Yair Evron, *Israel's Nuclear Dilemma* (Ithaca: Cornell University Press, forthcoming), chap. 5. Evron gives the best analysis I have read of the reasons not to be confident that the lessons of the Soviet-American experience with deterrence can be applied to the Middle East.

Soviet relations. Consequently, the politically restraining effects that nuclear ownership has imposed on the superpowers might not be strong enough to offset the ambitions, insecurities, hatreds, and fanaticisms that characterize many Third World conflicts. These dangers all add up to a greater likelihood that nuclear weapons will be used in interstate wars if more states get them.

Fifth, for the case of nuclear terrorism, the argument is both simple and terrifying: terrorists are not "deterrable," only suicidal. They have become terrorists precisely because they have given up all other avenues of influencing the behavior of their adversaries. They consider their own lives and those of their adversaries to be cheap. Even if they do value life, terrorists are hard to identify and difficult to locate. If they cannot be struck, then the threat to retaliate against them becomes empty.

THE SAFETY OF NUCLEAR SPREAD. To this gloomy picture of nuclear spread, three counterarguments can be offered. First is that of Kenneth Waltz: the ownership of nuclear weapons changes the psychology of their possessors and makes them more careful, because they are unable to come up with a way to use the weapons for any benefit. Second is the argument advanced by Robert W. Tucker: even if nuclear wars are more likely, the United States would not necessarily be drawn into them.[38] To these arguments I add a third: to make an effective nuclear threat, terrorists must reveal their identities; and when they do, they can be targeted and therefore deterred. If nuclear spread makes new members of the nuclear club more careful, if the United States can remain outside of any nuclear wars that may occur, and if terrorists can, indeed, be targeted, then the further spread of nuclear weapons presents no additional threat to America's security. The United States can remain indifferent to how many states acquire nuclear weapons, and it has few, if any, security reasons to retain its military alliances and keep its troops overseas.

Waltz has argued that nuclear weapons make both nuclear and conventional war less probable. He asserts that nuclear states are less likely to go to war with one another than conventionally-armed states, because nuclear statesmen clearly understand that any conflict or war might get out of control and go nuclear.[39] Thus, the political caution induced by nuclear ownership operates powerfully, irrespective of the ideology, personal temperament, and

---

38. See Waltz, *The Spread of Nuclear Weapons*, pp. 10–25; and Tucker, *A New Isolationism*, pp. 39–54.
39. Waltz, *The Spread of Nuclear Weapons*, p. 12.

political circumstances of a political leader. The fear of known results, if matters were to get out of hand, overwhelms all other factors. The ownership of nuclear weapons makes *all* possessors cautious. As more states acquire nuclear weapons, "they will feel the constraints that present nuclear states have experienced," and the zone of peace will enlarge. Consequently, says Waltz, "the measured spread of nuclear weapons is more to be welcomed than feared."[40]

Even if Waltz is wrong and the spread of nuclear weapons brought nuclear wars, Tucker is skeptical that the United States would be drawn into them. The crux of his argument is that "the effects of these weapons have been to make peace more divisible today than it has been in a very long time."[41] To say that peace is divisible is to say that a war threatens different states in different degrees, and some states not at all. Nuclear weapons are the ultimate divider of peace because they bring nearly absolute security to states that own them. Nuclear states can stay out of wars if they choose because, "in a system governed by balance of deterrent nuclear power . . . isolation and vulnerability to attack are no longer synonymous."[42] If Tucker's position is accepted, then the United States has little to fear about being dragged into other country's nuclear wars.

Finally, it is not self-evident that an increase in the states possessing nuclear weapons will increase terrorists' chances to steal those weapons; or that if terrorists somehow obtained nuclear bombs, they would succeed in nuclear blackmail or nuclear use. Governments that have nuclear weapons have taken great pains to make certain that they are well protected.[43] Certainly there have been lapses; but the record to date is clear: nuclear bombs have not made their way into unauthorized hands.[44] There is no reason to expect

---

40. Ibid., p. 30. For another statement about the peaceful effects of nuclear spread, see Bruce Bueno de Mesquita and William H. Riker, "An Assessment of the Merits of Selective Nuclear Proliferation," *Journal of Conflict Resolution*, Vol. 26, No. 2 (June 1982), pp. 283–306.
41. Tucker, *A New Isolationism*, pp. 55.
42. Ibid., p. 55.
43. If the United States drastically reduces the numbers of tactical nuclear weapons it has deployed abroad, as I argue below, they should be easier to protect and there will be far fewer for terrorists to steal.
44. Lewis Dunn cites a case to illustrate the dangers of nuclear theft that, to me, shows just the opposite: governments will go to extraordinary lengths to protect their nuclear weapons. "In April 1961, French army forces stationed in Algiers rebelled, demanding that the government in Paris reverse its decision to grant independence to Algeria. At the time, French scientists were preparing to test a nuclear weapon at the French Saharan test site in Reganne, Algeria, not too far from Algiers. Noting the proximity of the rebellion, the scientists called on the general in charge at Reganne to authorize an immediate test and thus avoid the possibility that

that new nuclear states would be so cavalier about their weapons that terrorists could easily capture them. Rather, we should expect precisely the opposite. New nuclear states will not have many bombs at the outset. Those they do have are likely to have been produced in great secrecy and under very tight control. Their delivery systems are likely at first to be vulnerable to preemptive strikes, prompting these governments take even more extraordinary methods to protect them. It is therefore more probable that new nuclear states will exercise tight control over their nuclear forces.[45]

Even if terrorists somehow arm themselves with nuclear weapons, however, they could not blackmail nuclear states as easily as has been imagined. If a threat to blow up New York City came to the U.S. president as an a unsigned message, with a deadline but with no demands to be met, it would hardly be credible. It would look like a crank note. To have credibility, a threat must state the group's political demands, spell out how it expects the demands to be met, and indicate a timetable for meeting the demands. But if a message does all this, would not the identity of the terrorist group—and more importantly the civilians whom it purports to represent—be immediately apparent? The president could make a credible counterthreat: "If New York City is destroyed, I shall destroy the entire group of people whom you claim to represent." Ruthless and coldblooded though it might sound, this threat is no different from what the Americans and the Russians have been saying to one another for forty years. If innocent civilians are not held hostage to nuclear retaliation, then nuclear deterrence will not work against either governments or terrorists. Because terrorists would have to identify themselves by the very act of making the terrorist threat, they make the groups they represent known and targetable, and the threat of retaliation credible.[46]

---

the nuclear device would be seized by the rebel troops and used for bargaining leverage. Three days after the outbreak of the revolt, the order to detonate the device came directly from French President de Gaulle; there was no attempt to undertake precise experiments, only to use up all the available fissionable material." Lewis Dunn, "What Difference Will It Make?" in Robert J. Art and Kenneth N. Waltz, eds., *The Use of Force*, third ed. (Lanham, Md.: University Press of America, 1988), p. 724.

45. Nuclear-armed states need to protect their nuclear forces against terrorist or other unauthorized seizure, against unauthorized use, and against preemptive attack. All three are components of the command and control of nuclear forces. We can have confidence that new nuclear states will do as well at the first and second tasks as do mature nuclear states, even though they may not do as well at the third task.

46. The counter to this argument is that the people represented by the terrorists could be so intermingled with others that they could not be discriminately targeted. Or they might live

dents for other would-be nuclear powers. Taking out additional insurance against nuclear weapons spread, then, is the prime, indeed the only, security rationale for a continuing military global role for the United States. It is to the non-security reasons that I now turn.

Preserving An Open World Economy

If the first essential goal for the United States in the post–Cold War era is to ensure its security, the second is to preserve the industrialized world's open international economic order. After World War II, American power helped to create and sustain an economic system that allowed the factors of production (raw materials, labor, capital, and technology) to move more easily among the rich industrialized nations. As a consequence, they developed a high degree of economic interdependence.[50] By enabling the factors of production to move freely among states, openness led to greater efficiency in their use and thereby increased the wealth of all nations that participated in the system. Because it enhances American prosperity, therefore, openness and the interdependence that results from it remain vital U.S. interests to be protected.

Must America stay abroad militarily to help preserve this order? Would economic closure accompany a complete American military withdrawal from

---

50. I use the term "interdependence" in roughly the same sense that Kenneth N. Waltz employs it. Waltz says that interdependence refers to the losses and gains that states experience through their interactions, and to the equality with which the losses and gains are distributed among them. See Waltz, *Theory of International Politics* (Reading, Mass.: Addison-Wesley, 1979), pp. 143–144. Waltz, however, emphasizes the costs of breaking ties; I emphasize the benefits of having ties. My emphasis is therefore the obverse of his: interdependence is the size of the stake that a state believes it has in seeing other states' economies prosper, so as to help its own economy flourish too. Interdependence can be high or low. The higher the perceived interdependence, the larger a state's stake in the economic well-being of the countries with which it heavily interacts, and hence the greater the incentives to cooperate for mutual gain. In a condition of low interdependence, there is little incentive for states to cooperate because there is little perceived benefit in doing so; and so concerns about relative gains overwhelm those about absolute gains. Even in a situation of high interdependence, however, where the incentives to cooperate are strong, the opportunity for absolute gain does not entirely supplant the concern for relative gain because, in a condition of anarchy, a state never forgets about how it is doing relative to others. Instead, in such situations, a state will sacrifice some of the benefits of cooperation in order to protect its relative position. In situations of high interdependence, exactly how a state balances out its considerations about relative versus absolute gains depends both on the merits of the particular issue and on how that issue is thought to be linked to other issues that the state considers vital. For an empirical demonstration that concerns about relative gains never go away, even among close allies, see Joseph M. Grieco, *Cooperation Among Nations: Europe, America, and Non-Tariff Barriers to Trade* (Ithaca: Cornell University Press, 1990).

its overseas outposts? To answer these questions, I look first at how the Cold War helped produce economic openness; second, at how resilient today's interdependence is by comparing it with the interdependence of the pre-1914 era; and, third, at how a residual military presence abroad can help maintain openness.

THE COLD WAR AND ECONOMIC OPENNESS

OPENNESS VERSUS CONTAINMENT. America's provision of security to its major postwar allies helped bring about the present relatively open economic order.[51] This order developed and matured under the American security umbrella because the Cold War facilitated economic integration within Western Europe and economic openness among Western Europe, North America, and Japan.[52] American military power was neither the sole nor perhaps even the most important factor responsible for the present international economic regime. Also crucial were the conversion of many governments to Keynesian

---

51. In analyzing the relation between military power and economic orders, I do not argue that force is the most important instrument, only that it has some role to play. It can be of greatest use only when employed with other tools of statecraft. Force is a blunt instrument, better held at the ready than readily used. Precisely because it works best when kept in the background but primed for use, its exact influence on outcomes is never easy to trace. The political effect of military power is akin to a gravitational field: it is constantly present; it affects all action, but does not predetermine it; and its effects are hard to perceive precisely because it is ever-present. Apart from waging war, playing chicken, or using force overtly to blackmail, military power's best role is to back up a nation's political and economic instruments. They are the tools most appropriate to most of the issues with which most governments most of the time deal. I therefore take the position that military power is versatile, to a degree; it can yield some leverage in non-military areas (this is what other analysts refer to as the "fungibility" of military power). But for two good arguments against this view, see David A. Baldwin, "Power Analysis and World Politics: New Trends versus Old Tendencies," *World Politics*, Vol. 31, No. 2 (January 1979), pp. 161–195; and Robert O. Keohane, "The Theory of Hegemonic Stability and Changes in International Economic Regimes, 1967–1977," in Keohane, *International Institutions and State Power* (Boulder, Colo.: Westview, 1989), pp. 74–101. For an argument that supports my view, see Nye, *Bound to Lead*, pp. 189–190.
52. For the basic argument about the links between security and economics during this period, I have relied heavily on the best statement on the subject, Robert Gilpin's *U.S. Power and the Multinational Corporation: The Political Economy of Direct Investment* (New York: Basic Books, 1975), esp. chap. 4. For arguments that a bipolar international system is more conducive to free trade among states than a multipolar one, see Joanne Gowa, "Bipolarity, Multipolarity, and Free Trade," *American Political Science Review*, Vol. 83, No. 4 (December 1989), pp. 1245–1257. For a good analysis of the links between economic and security factors in the first few years of the Cold War, see Robert Pollard, *Economic Security and the Origins of the Cold War, 1945–1950* (New York: Columbia University Press, 1985). In spite of these excellent sources, however, little work has been done on the links between American military power and the flowering of interdependence. This is a fruitful area for research because it cuts across the national security and political economy subfields of international relations.

economics; their overwhelming desire to avoid the catastrophic experience of the great depression of the 1930s and the global war that came in its wake; the lessons of the 1930s about how non-cooperative, beggar-thy-neighbor policies ultimately redound to the disadvantage of all; the willingness of the United States to underwrite the economic costs of setting up the system and of sustaining it; and the acceptance of the legitimacy of American leadership by its allies. But even though all these factors were important, where economic openness began and subsequently flourished most was among the countries that were most closely allied with the United States against the Soviet Union, that were considered most vital to American interests, and over which the United States most visibly extended its security umbrella.

Shortly before the end of World War II, the United States, in conjunction with the British, began to implement its plans for an open economic order. These included fixed exchange rates and freely convertible currencies to foster world trade; a World Bank to aid in postwar reconstruction; and an international agency (ultimately GATT, the General Agreement on Tariffs and Trade) to bring about reductions in tariffs on manufactured goods. By early 1947, however, the United States had shelved these plans at about the same time that the hard-line policy towards the Soviet Union had triumphed in Washington. By early 1947, the American government in general and President Truman in particular had concluded that only a hard line would limit Soviet aggressiveness, that long-term containment of Soviet power would be necessary, and that strong allies would be needed to assist the nation in these tasks. By early 1947, in addition, the United States had recognized that its allies were still too debilitated by the effects of World War II to proceed with the open economic order.[53]

The decision to contain the Soviets made it imperative to lay aside the postwar economic plans. Once the United States realized that openness would weaken its allies, it instead permitted them to adopt economically nationalist policies. Their need for economic recovery was overriding if they were to fend off internal communist challenges. By the early spring of 1947, then, openness had become one of the first casualties of the Cold War. Furthermore, after the the United States began its massive rearmament in

---

53. See Richard N. Gardner, *Sterling-Dollar Diplomacy in Current Perspective* (New York: Columbia University Press, 1980), chap. 15, for the details on the retreat from the open economic system; and Deborah Welch Larson, *Origins of Containment: A Psychological Explanation* (Princeton: Princeton University Press, 1985), chap. 7, on Truman's final conversion to the hard-line policy towards the Soviet Union.

the wake of the attack on South Korea in 1950, it also concluded that an economically strong Western Europe and Japan were necessary to relieve the United States of part of the military burden of containing the Soviet Union. What had started out as a plan to foster world economic growth through freer trade was scrapped for a policy of economic nationalism to rebuild allies for the long struggle against the Soviet Union. Openness and containment became inextricably entangled at the outset of the Cold War and remained so throughout its duration.

In the late 1950s, the United States began once again to implement its plans for an open world order, only after the risk of fatally weakening its European and Japanese allies had passed. It started first with the Western Europeans, after the emergence of the European Economic Community in 1958 signaled their full recovery from World War II. It began to force openness on the Japanese, with mixed success, beginning in the 1970s, after Japan's neo-mercantilist strategy began to wreak its destructive effects on selected American industries. And after openness was put into practice, it was maintained, not simply because of the economic benefits it would yield in its own right, but also because of the military benefits that strong allies would yield for the United States. In short, the primary goal of the United States was the creation and maintenance of strong allies. When openness threatened that goal, the United States scrapped it; when openness facilitated the goal, the United States resurrected it. During the Cold War, containment, not openness, was America's overriding obsession.

THE SOVIET THREAT AND THE U.S. NIGHT WATCHMAN. Once the foundations for economic openness were put into place, the Soviet threat, and the measures taken to counter it, including the presence of American forces overseas, helped foster interdependence among America's great power allies. It did so, as E.H. Carr reminds us, because markets do not exist in political vacuums: "the science of economics presupposes a given political order and cannot be profitably studied in isolation from politics."[54] The political framework that the United States provided, partly by its economic resources and its political leadership, but also by its provision of security to its major economic trading partners abroad—the West Europeans and the Japanese— facilitated the flowering of trade amongst them.

The overseas U.S. military presence facilitated economic openness in four ways. First, the security provided by the United States created the political

54. E.H. Carr, *The Twenty Years' Crisis, 1919–1939,* 2d ed. (London: Macmillan, 1961), p. 117.

stability that was crucial to the orderly development of trading relations. Markets work best when embedded in political frameworks that yield predictable expectations.[55] U.S. military power deployed in the Far East and in Europe brought these stable expectations by providing the Europeans and the Japanese with the necessary psychological reassurance to rebuild after World War II and then to grow during the Cold War. The prime reason NATO was formed was psychological, not military: to make the Europeans feel secure enough against the Soviets so that they would have the political will to rebuild themselves economically.[56] Just like the American-Japanese defense treaty, NATO created a politically stable island in a turbulent international sea.

Second, America's provision of security to its allies in Europe and in the Far East dampened their respective concerns about the German and Japanese military rearmament that the United States favored in order to help contain the Soviets. The U.S. presence protected its allies not only from the Soviets, but also from the Germans and the Japanese.[57] The military power of Germany and Japan was contained in U.S.-dominated alliances, and American troops were deployed in each nation, so, although their neighbors did not forget the horrors they had suffered at the hands of Germany and Japan during World War II, they were not paralyzed from cooperating with them. The success of the European Economic Community owes as much to the presence of American military power on the continent of Europe as it does to the vision of its founders. The same can be said for the Far East, where America's military presence helped smooth the way for Japan's economic dominance.

Third, the U.S. military presence helped to dampen concerns about disparities in relative economic growth and about the vulnerabilities inherent

---

55. Stephen D. Krasner and Janice E. Thomson argue that "the more stable the pattern of property rights the higher the level of economic transactions." See Krasner and Thomson, "Global Transactions and the Consolidation of Sovereignty," in Ernst-Otto Czempiel and James N. Rosenau, eds., *Global Changes and Theoretical Challenges* (Lexington, Mass: Lexington Books, 1989), p. 198.
56. For an excellent analysis of the psychological function of NATO in its earliest phase, see Robert E. Osgood, *NATO—The Entangling Alliance* (Chicago: University of Chicago Press, 1962), chap. 2.
57. These concerns were never far below the surface. For how they affected the very form NATO took, see Timothy P. Ireland, *Creating the Entangling Alliance* (Westport, Conn.: Greenwood, 1981). See also Josef Joffe, "Europe's American Pacifier," *Foreign Policy*, No. 54 (Spring 1984), pp. 64–82.

in interdependence, both of which are heightened in an open economic order. Freer trade benefits all nations, but not all equally. The most efficient nations benefit the most; and economic efficiencies can be turned to military advantage.[58] Interdependence brings mutual dependency that is all the greater, the more states specialize economically. In turn, dependency can mean vulnerability.[59] Through its provision of military protection to its allies, the United States mitigated these security externalities of interdependence. It also enabled the neighbors of Germany and Japan to be brought into their economic orbits without fearing that military conquest or political domination would follow.

Fourth, America's overseas military presence helped maintain the sense of allied solidarity, which, in turn, had "spill-over effects" on allied economic relations.[60] The overseas presence did not create the solidarity; fear of the Soviets did that. But U.S. forces overseas were the crucial intervening variable between the Soviet threat and alliance solidarity; they were the cement holding the anti-Soviet alliance together. U.S. troops enhanced allied solidarity because they provided visible reassurance that the United States was a reliable protector, and this prevented defection from the alliance. In turn, the heightened sense of solidarity strengthened economic openness: the need to cooperate militarily against the Soviet Union strengthened the political goodwill to overcome the inevitable economic disputes that interdependence brought. The need to preserve a united front against the common enemy put limits on how far the United States and its allies would permit their economic disputes to go, and prevented the inherent frictions among close trading partners from deteriorating into economic nationalism. In short, by strengthening solidarity, the U.S. overseas presence helped circumscribe economic disputes.

---

58. This is what Joanne Gowa means when she refers to the security externalities of free trade. See Gowa, "Bipolarity, Multipolarity, and Free Trade."

59. The classic statement on the vulnerabilities that trade can bring is Albert O. Hirschman, *National Power and the Structure of Foreign Trade*, expanded ed. (Berkeley: University of California Press, 1980).

60. The phrase "spill-over effects" was coined by Ernst Haas. He used it to describe a situation whereby the cooperation achieved on economic matters among the Western European states could be transferred to political matters, leading ultimately to the political integration of Western Europe. I use the phrase in the sense that I believe that cooperation on military issues has facilitated cooperation on economic matters. See Haas, *Beyond the Nation State: Functionalism and International Organization* (Stanford: Stanford University Press, 1964), p. 48.

INTERDEPENDENCE BEFORE 1914 AND NOW
America's overseas military presence fostered an open economic order among its rich industrial allies. Once the order was in place, goods, capital, and technology flowed more freely among the allies; as a consequence, their economic interdependence began to grow and reached a moderately high level by the early 1980s. How broad, deep, and resilient is this order now, and can it survive without the American overseas military presence that helped foster it?

One way to assess whether openness can continue without its military underpinning is to gauge the resiliency of the interdependence that openness produced. Openness *per se* means little unless it gives states a big stake in the economic well-being of their trading partners. The best measure of that stake is the level of economic interdependence among states. If interdependence is high, then the stake should be large and presumably so, too, will be a state's willingness to engage in cooperative behavior to keep its trading partners prosperous. One means to appraise the interdependence of 1958–90 is to compare it to that of 1870–1914. Although the two eras differ significantly, the comparison will reveal unique features of today's interdependence.[61]

SIMILARITIES. By one set of statistics, the current interdependence looks little different from the earlier one. If measured by exports plus imports as a percentage of gross national product (GNP), the industrialized nations since 1960 have about the same stake in foreign economic activity as they did in the forty years before World War II. Kenneth Waltz and Stephen Krasner have both shown that from 1870 to 1914, the European great powers and Japan had ratios of exports plus imports to gross national product of 33 to 50 percent, which is about the same as for 1960–90.[62] The ratios for the United States ranged from 11 to 14 percent from 1870 to 1914, and 7 to 17 percent from 1945 through the 1980s.[63] Stephen Krasner and Janice Thomson dem-

61. For useful analyses of economic interdependence, see Richard Rosecrance and Arthur Stein, "Interdependence: Myth or Reality?" *World Politics*, Vol. 26, No. 1 (October 1973), pp. 1–28; Robert Gilpin, "Economic Interdependence and National Security in Historical Perspective," in Klaus Knorr and Frank N. Trager, eds., *Economic Issues and National Security* (Lawrence, Kans.: Allen Press, 1977), pp. 19–67; and Michael Stewart, *The Age of Interdependence: Economic Policy in a Shrinking World* (Cambridge, Mass.: MIT Press, 1986).
62. See Kenneth N. Waltz, *Theory of International Politics* (Reading, Mass.: Addison-Wesley, 1979), p. 212; and Stephen D. Krasner, "State Power and the Structure of International Trade," *World Politics*, Vol. 28, No. 3 (April 1976), pp. 327 and 328.
63. Waltz, *Theory of International Politics*, p. 212; Krasner, "State Power and the Structure of International Trade," p. 328; Nye, *Bound to Lead*, p. 163.

onstrate that the recent rapid growth in world trade is not unique. In the years 1830 to 1913, just as in 1950 to 1980, the growth in world trade outstripped the growth in world GNP by roughly a factor of two. In addition, international capital movements of today, when measured as a percentage of capital flowing out of and into economies, are not dramatically different from those of the pre-1914 era.[64] What has increased is the absolute amount of capital moving abroad, largely because the GNPs of today's rich nations are so much larger than they were in the earlier era.

Thus, whether we are measuring exports and imports, rates of growth of world trade, or capital flows, the percentages do not appear dramatically different now from the decades before 1914. The industrially rich nations today apparently have no greater stake in foreign economic activity than those before 1914. If that is the case, then today's interdependence could be shattered as easily as that before 1914, this time not because of a great power war, but because of the destructive forces of economic nationalism.

DIFFERENCES. Other statistics, however, make a credible case that today's interdependence is more resilient than the pre-1914 case. First, more nations today participate in a system of lowered barriers to trade among manufactured goods than in the period before 1914. In 1990, there were over 100 members of GATT, which has been the principal mechanism since 1945 for lowering tariff and non-tariff barriers to trade in manufactured goods. By contrast, the much-heralded nineteenth-century era of free trade was not all that free, did not last all that long, and involved not all that many states. Neither the United States, Russia, nor Japan participated much, if at all, when tariff duties began to be lowered in 1860. The era of free trade was largely over by the late 1870s, when the Germans and then the French raised their tariffs again.[65] Moreover, before 1914, much of the trade by the rich nations was vertical: the industrial nations imported raw materials from the non-industrialized nations, selling them manufactured goods in exchange. By contrast, today's rich nations engage in a high level of intra-industry trade, selling to one another goods that are similar, such as automobiles, consumer electronics, and other finished goods.[66]

64. Krasner and Thomson, "Global Transactions," pp. 198–206.
65. See Fieldhouse, "Imperialism: An Historiographical Revision"; and Timothy J. McKeown, "Tariffs and Hegemonic Stability Theory," *International Organization*, Vol. 37, No. 1 (Winter 1983), pp. 80–89.
66. Rosecrance, *The Rise of the Trading State*, pp. 145–146.

Second, as Richard Rosecrance argues, the international investments of today's interdependence look different from those of the previous era. Before 1914, most investment was of the portfolio type—holdings of foreign shares easily sold on stock exchanges. Direct investment—the actual majority ownership of a plant, mine, or piece of real estate—was only ten percent of total foreign investment. Today, direct investment represents a much larger percentage of total foreign investment among the industrialized rich nations; it is less liquid than the traditional portfolio investment of the nineteenth century, and therefore reflects "the greater stake that countries have in each other's well-being."[67] Direct investment has created stronger ties than indirect investment ever could. This stake is increased by the interpenetration of investment among Western Europe, the United States, and Japan, which had become relatively balanced by the end of the 1970s after having been dominated by America's direct investment overseas in earlier decades. The large size of direct foreign investment has given the industrial economies a stake in one another's economic health that did not exist in the nineteenth century.[68] Finally, because each government is committed to full employment without inflation, they must work together to ensure one another's success.

Third, daily capital movements, not trade flows, dominate currency exchange rates and dwarf, by a large factor, the daily trade in goods. As Peter Drucker points out, "the London Eurodollar market, in which the world's financial institutions borrow from and lend to each other, turns over $300 billion each working day, or $75 trillion a year, a volume at least 25 times that of world trade."[69] With these huge flows of monies across their borders, "the capacity of national monetary authorities to influence their national money supplies, to affect their national exchange rates, or even to supervise their banking systems has been reduced to new low levels."[70] This is a far cry from the pre-1914 era, when the Bank of London and the City of London

---

67. Ibid., pp. 146–147.
68. Ibid., p. 148. Helen V. Milner has pointed out that the forces for openness have become quite strong in the United States because of the growth in the number of firms, across a wide number of industries, that have a sizeable stake in exports. As industries have become more export oriented, their stakes in economic openness have risen. See Milner, *Resisting Protectionism: Global Industries and the Politics of International Trade* (Princeton: Princeton University Press, 1988).
69. Peter F. Drucker, "The Changed World Economy," *Foreign Affairs*, Vol. 64, No. 4 (Spring 1986), p. 782.
70. Raymond Vernon and Debora L. Spar, *Beyond Globalism: Remaking American Foreign Economic Policy* (New York: Free Press, 1989), p. 100.

could exercise a great deal of centralized control over the flow of international funds.[71]

The interdependence of today, though not unique in all respects, is different from what the world experienced before 1914. It involves a larger number of states, immediately engages the livelihoods of larger numbers of people, has tighter, more extensive and more direct interlinkages, and more deeply enmeshes the economic fate of a country in how other countries are faring. States today act as if their stakes in economic openness are deep, broad, and wide.[72] But it is by no means obvious that today's economic interdependence is so resilient and so deeply rooted that it could not be shattered as the earlier one was in 1914.

If history cannot tell us the answer, perhaps logic can. The pre-1914 era of interdependence among the great powers ended in total war. War and conquest were then thought easy and legitimate. Today, the presence of nuclear weapons makes war and conquest among the great powers improbable. But they do not make economic nationalism less probable, and it could shatter interdependence as thoroughly as World War I did. Interdependence is a tricky affair, because, as Robert Gilpin reminds us, it requires that governments manage the "clash between domestic autonomy and international norms" by reconciling "Keynes at home and Smith abroad."[73] Participating in the international economy in order to reap its benefits, while at the same time trying to insulate the domestic economy from its inevitably disruptive effects, makes the management of interdependence delicate, if not downright shaky.

The retreat from openness in the waning days of the Cold War should make us cautious about how robust the open system is.[74] The fact is that we

---

71. See Robert Gilpin, *The Political Economy of International Relations* (Princeton: Princeton University Press, 1987), pp. 122–127, for a description of how the Bank of England and the City of London managed the world's flow of capital in the 1870–1914 period.
72. The extent to which states actually cooperate in economic matters is an important issue for investigation, but that they feel the need to cooperate should not be in doubt. For a careful analysis of how the countries of Western Europe, North America, and Japan perceived the need to collaborate if their own economic policies were to succeed, see Robert D. Putnam and Nicholas Bayne, *Hanging Together: Cooperation and Conflict in the Seven-Power Summits*, rev. and enl. ed. (Cambridge: Harvard University Press, 1987).
73. Gilpin, *The Political Economy of International Relations*, p. 363.
74. Gilpin concludes *The Political Economy of International Relations* with this observation: "The

simply do not know whether the world's political economy would experience even greater movement towards economic closure and managed trade if the United States were to withdraw totally into "Fortress America." Our theories about the relation between economic openness and military power are not well developed. What we do know is that the current openness was forged during the waging of the Cold War and is a partial by-product of it; that America's provision of security helped bind Western Europe, Japan, and the United States together; and that today's economic openness has been associated with a global American military presence.

As the rich nations enter the 1990s, momentous economic changes are taking place. Europe is poised to deepen its common market and may even move toward political unity.[75] Japan is seeking to bring the nations of East Asia into an even tighter link with its economy than before. The United States is doing the same with Canada and Mexico. A united Germany's economic power already dominates western Europe and will, in due course, dominate Eastern Europe as well. Japan's economic power will similarly continue to dominate East Asia and the western Pacific. The neighbors of Germany and Japan, increasingly drawn into their respective economic orbits, will inevitably develop the same love-hate relationship with German and Japanese economic power that the Western Europeans and the Japanese earlier had towards American economic power: the power is needed, respected, and admired, but not liked, and is certainly potentially feared for the loss of autonomy it brings.

A greater American economic presence in Eastern Europe, and the considerable U.S. economic presence in the Far East, could help contain fears, resentments, and unease about German and Japanese dominance, should they arise. But it is not prudent to count on the U.S. economic presence alone to assuage these concerns. A precipitate American military withdrawal could cause these concerns to grow all the greater; a residual U.S. military

---

postwar age of multilateral liberalization is over and the world's best hope for economic stability is some form of benign mercantilism" (p. 408). For his evidence to support this conclusion, see ibid., pp. 204–209 and 381–406. See also Gilpin, "The Economic Dimension of International Security," discussion paper for the Working Group on International Economic Change, Institute for East-West Security Studies, September 1988.
75. For excellent short analyses of Europe 1992, see Stanley Hoffmann, "The European Community and 1992," *Foreign Affairs*, Vol. 68, No. 4 (Fall 1989), pp. 27–47; Alberta Sbragia, "Asymmetrical Integration in the European Community: The Single European Act and Institutional Development," in Dale L. Smith and James Lee Ray, eds., *The 1992 Project and the Future of Integration in Europe* (forthcoming); and William Wallace, *The Transformation of Western Europe* (London: The Royal Institute of International Affairs, 1990).

presence can help dampen them, as it has done in the past.[76] Why, then, complicate the advancing economic integration of the Far East under Japanese leadership with a Japanese military power no longer counterchecked by the American military presence? Why, similarly, burden the considerable economic task that confronts Eastern Europe or the European Community on its march toward economic and political unification with potential fears about unchecked German military power? Political institutionalization of the magnitude planned by the European Community takes time. Political instability disrupts the process of institutionalization; stability fosters it. Stability is in turn fostered by the maintenance of an American military presence in Europe and the Far East.

There are no good reasons why the Germans and the Japanese should want the Americans to take their troops home. The presence of U.S. troops in both the Far East and Europe should help to keep those two fields fertile for Japanese and German economic dynamism. With the Soviet Union imploding, Germany and Japan no longer face a significant security threat. But they still must contend with other states' historical memories about them, and the resentments caused by their economic power. Hence, Germany and Japan should want to retain a residual American military presence in their respective regions in order to allay whatever concerns their trading partners will have about their growing power. This can also help preserve the benefits of openness for the United States and give it political leverage to affect, to its advantage, the course of regional political and economic developments.

In sum, how much of a risk does the United States want to take that a complete American military withdrawal would exacerbate the movement towards economic nationalism currently in progress? Removing the cement

---

76. Some reports indicate that the Europeans and the Far Easterners want the United States to remain. After Defense Secretary Dick Cheney announced cuts of 10 percent in American forces in the Far East on February 23, 1990, the *New York Times* reported: "Japanese officials say privately that they are worried that an overall reduction of the American presence in Asia would reawaken fears in other parts of the region about the growing influence of Japan. They say the United States is a healthy influence that reassures Asian countries that they need not fear the possibility of a Japanese military threat that would follow its expanding economic influence down the road." See Steven R. Weisman, "Japan Backs Cheney's Troop-Cut Plan," *New York Times*, February 23, 1990, p. A8. *New York Times* columnist Flora Lewis reported that: "The Europeans want NATO to continue and they want Americans in Europe. . . . There is strong evidence supporting Britain's Foreign Minister, Douglas Hurd, when he said in a newspaper interview: 'I've never known a time when there was less anti-Americanism in Europe, whether in Britain or on the Continent.' His judgment that 'American engagement is absolutely fundamental to stability' is widely shared." Flora Lewis, "U.S. Takes the Lead," *New York Times*, July 10, 1990, p. A19.

of American military power might risk causing the entire edifice to crumble. The risk may only marginally increase, but that might be enough. Much like the nuclear spread issue, then, the case for a continuing overseas U.S. military presence to shore up economic interdependence is not iron-clad, only suggestive, and is based on the principle of hedging bets.

Restraining America's Interventionist Impulses

Besides retarding nuclear spread and preserving economic openness, there are two other goals for which an overseas presence can be of help: spreading democracy and imposing peace. The United States should, however, be restrained about using military power for either objective.

SPREADING DEMOCRACY: U.S. POWER AND HUMAN RIGHTS

The spread of democracy should not be one of the prime goals to be served by American military power. I favor the spread of democracy, but I am dubious about the efficacy of military power to produce it. The aim of spreading democracy around the globe, moreover, can too easily become a license for indiscriminate and unending U.S. military interventions in the internal affairs of others. Democracies are best produced, rather, by stalemating aggressor states, by providing a stable international framework that facilitates economic development and the emergence of a middle class within states, and by using economic and other types of leverage to encourage internal liberalization.[77] As a rule, military force is of little use.

The most successful forceful conversions to democracy since 1945 clearly show the costs and limits of military power. The conversion of Germany and Japan in 1945–50 required a total war, total defeat, and extensive occupation. They show that extensive force is required for coerced conversion. The Eastern European revolutions of 1989–90, on which the evidence is not yet all in, required the withdrawal of Soviet support for repressive regimes. These transformations illustrate that stalemating imperial powers and bringing

---

77. For the classic arguments about the requisites of democracy, see Robert A. Dahl, *Polyarchy: Participation and Opposition* (New Haven: Yale University Press, 1971); and Seymour Martin Lipset, *Political Man: The Social Bases of Politics*, exp. ed. (Baltimore: Johns Hopkins Press, 1981). For an argument that the United States should aggressively spread democracy, see Gregory A. Fossedal, *The Democratic Imperative: Exporting the American Revolution* (New York: Basic Books, 1989).

about their retreat is a long, expensive process. Swift transformation requires military conquest, always a bloody matter. Stalemate takes a long time and requires a great expenditure of resources, although it is preferable to a big war. With the collapse of the Soviet empire in Eastern Europe, stalemate is no longer an option, because there are no formal empires left to stalemate.

The cases of Nicaragua, Chile, Grenada, and Panama offer a different model of the transition to democracy. America did not directly employ its military forces against Nicaragua on a sustained basis; however, it did help field and supply an extensive rebel force whose pressure helped bring about free elections in 1990. But the cost in Nicaraguan lives and economic misery was high. Chile's 1989 return to the democratic fold took much longer because of American backing for the reprehensible Pinochet regime, but once the United States began to redirect its considerable political and economic resources, the combination of international pressure and internal demand for change produced results. Chile's long-standing democratic traditions made its return to democracy easier than in other cases, but it still serves as a useful model for what the proper combination of external and internal pressure can produce. Grenada and Panama both show how swift military interventions can be effective when four special conditions are present: the nation invaded is small and militarily weak, the intervention is welcomed by the bulk of the populace, the costs in American casualties are relatively low, and the probability of success is high. But these conditions are not easily found or duplicated outside of the Caribbean and Central America.

Therefore, the United States should restrain itself from intervening militarily in the internal affairs of states to make them democratic, unless the four conditions described above are present. The United States should consider other military interventions only when a government is engaged in the mass murder of its citizens, and again only when the above four conditions obtain.[78] This second type of intervention, then, becomes a matter of human rights, not democracy; and the two are not the same thing.[79]

---

78. Stephen Van Evera makes this argument. See Van Evera, "Why Europe Matters, Why the Third World Doesn't: American Grand Strategy After the Cold War," *Journal of Strategic Studies,* Vol. 13, No. 2 (June 1990), pp. 30 and 32.

79. The two best recent candidates for this type of intervention would have been Uganda under Idi Amin and Cambodia under Pol Pot. Some may argue that humanitarian interventions of a sort did take place in each case: Tanzania ultimately invaded Uganda to depose Amin, and Vietnam intervened in Cambodia, forcing Pol Pot into hiding.

IMPOSING PEACE: EVERYWHERE OR SELECTIVELY?
If, as a rule, the United States should not intervene militarily to make other states democratic, should it interpose itself between states to keep them at peace, or go to war to punish aggressor states, as it has against Iraq? And if it should, then where and when? To answer these questions, I first look at the argument for preventing all wars and reject it, and second, outline why the United States should confine its war-prevention efforts to the Middle East, Europe, and the Far East in a highly selective fashion.

GLOBAL COLLECTIVE SECURITY? The Iraqi aggression against Kuwait demonstrated the potential of collective security, and has helped resurrect the United Nations. The U.S. government justified its intervention partly on the basis of creating the "new world order" that President Bush hopes will succeed the Cold War. We should, however, be skeptical about whether the UN action against Iraq foreshadows a bright future for UN peacekeeping efforts.

Three special conditions, unlikely to be repeated, allowed much of the world to support economic and military measures against Iraq: (1) Iraq sat quite close to the largest proven reserves of the world's oil, upon which the industrialized economies depend to a critical extent, and this led to a uniquely strong shared interest; (2) Iraq's imports and exports were easy to blockade by sea because it has only one port and only three oil pipelines to the oceans; and (3) Iraq's leader, Saddam Hussein, was widely disliked and feared because of his grandiose ambitions and because of his ability, unless stopped, to use his oil earnings to acquire even larger military capabilities, even more chemical and biological weapons, and ultimately nuclear weapons. Combined with America's military mobility, which let it quickly set up a defensive barrier along the northern border of Saudi Arabia, these three factors explain the relative ease with which a collective security response initially was engineered by the United States in the United Nations.[80] Because these special

---

80. These three factors pertain only to the nature of the Iraqi regime and the character of its aggression. There was a fourth factor vital to UN action: the cooperation of the Soviet Union. I do not believe that the first three factors are sufficient to account for the Soviet Union's cooperative behavior. In light of the fact that Iraq has been an ally of the Soviet Union for almost twenty years and has received massive military assistance from it, Soviet cooperation in the UN has been remarkable. Gorbachev's efforts at internal reform have required that he seek good relations with the United States and its allies in order to reduce his government's military expenditures and receive economic and technical assistance from the West. Gorbachev put cooperation with the West above support for Saddam Hussein. We cannot count on the fact that in the future, a Soviet government, even if headed by Gorbachev, will value military

conditions will rarely be present, the UN action against Iraq in 1990–91 is not likely to be the model for future UN peacekeeping.

Any future collective United Nations actions will require: (1) the marshalling of overwhelming majorities in favor of sanctions, including the threat or actual use of military power; and (2) an effective military force operating in the name of the United Nations. Collective security systems can dissuade aggression only if all the member states pledge in advance to punish any aggressor state for its aggression regardless of its identity. Should dissuasion fail, the UN could attack the aggressor and roll it back. But if either the dissuasion or punishment of aggression is to be global in nature, then the United Nations must have at its disposal a military force of global reach; and, of necessity, in such a force America's military power will have to be a key ingredient. Today and for the foreseeable future, only the United States can operate globally, because it is the world's only true conventional superpower. But such an American commitment would bind the United States to fight potentially everywhere. It is difficult to imagine Congress agreeing to this police role for the United States, or the American public marching off to wherever the United Nations has voted it should go, especially if other states seek to pass the buck and allow the United States to do the fighting for them.

SELECTIVE WAR PREVENTION. The key question thus becomes: in which regions and under what circumstances should the United States use it military forces to deter or punish aggression? Given its historic ties and major interests, the United States should concentrate its military efforts in Europe, the Far East, and the Middle East.

In Europe and the Far East, only a war among the great powers should concern the United States. Such a war would wreak havoc on economic openness and would dramatically enhance the incentives for nuclear spread. In contrast, wars among lesser powers in either region (for example, a war between Hungary and Romania over Transylvania) would not require American involvement. Such wars may be tragic for the peoples involved, but their stakes for the United States are small, unless they would cause a great power war.

The one exception to this rule is a North Korean attack on South Korea. Through formal alliance, the United States has guaranteed the independence of South Korea for forty years. To scuttle that commitment now would

---

reductions and Western aid enough to produce the U.S.-Soviet cooperation that makes UN peacekeeping actions possible.

significantly diminish the credibility of America's other political-military commitments and would likely prompt the South Koreans to acquire nuclear weapons. To dissuade a North Korean attack, the United States must retain a military presence in South Korea, but at a much lower level than the 44,000 American troops currently there.[81] If the two Koreas unify peacefully, then the United States can withdraw its protection.

Fortunately, small wars will not cause a great power war in either Europe or the Far East; and a great power war in either region is unlikely, even in the absence of smaller wars. The Europe of today is not the Europe of 1914 or 1939.[82] Neither drives for territorial hegemony (as with Germany in 1939) nor fears of political isolation (as with Germany in 1914) are causes for concern. In 1914, ethnic rivalry and border disputes in Eastern Europe became the cause of war only because they threatened one great power with destruction (Austria-Hungary) and another with political isolation (Germany). Today, similar rivalries and disputes may cause civil or foreign wars in Eastern Europe, but it is hard to see how any of these wars could escalate to a great power war. The two great powers who would most likely be involved, Germany and the Soviet Union, are militarily secure and currently preoccupied with their respective internal problems. Their internal preoccupations may eventually decrease, but they will continue to remain secure. The Soviet Union, like France and Britain, never need fear an attack by Germany or anyone else, because it has nuclear weapons. And if Germany continues to host a residual American presence on its soil, the Germans also do not need to fear attack.[83]

---

81. Secretary of Defense Dick Cheney, *Annual Report to the President, January 1990* (Washington, D.C.: U.S. Government Printing Office [U.S. GPO], 1990), p. 74. In late February 1990, Secretary Cheney announced plans to reduce American forces in East Asia and the western Pacific by ten percent, which would reduce American forces to about 40,000 in South Korea. See Weisman, "Japan Backs Cheney's Troop-Cut Plan." I see no reason to keep more than 10,000 American troops in South Korea.

82. Stephen Van Evera has thoroughly laid out the reasons why the likelihood of war in Europe is quite low. Much of what he says about Europe can also be said for the Far East. See Van Evera, "Primed for Peace: Europe After the Cold War," *International Security*, Vol. 15, No. 3 (Winter 1990/91), pp. 7–57.

83. Figuring out the exact political formula that will make a residual American presence in Europe politically saleable is by no means easy. For an excellent discussion of the various institutional formulas and a persuasive recommendation for a modern-day Concert of Europe housed in the Conference on European Security and Cooperation (CSCE), see Charles A. Kupchan and Clifford A. Kupchan, "Concerts, Collective Security, and the Future of Europe" (manuscript). See also Malcolm Chalmers, "Beyond the Alliance System: The Case for a European Security Organization," *World Policy Journal*, Vol. 12, No. 2 (Spring 1990), pp. 215–251.

Similarly, in the Far East, no great power seeks territorial hegemony. With the exception of the two Koreas and Taiwan, borders are well defined and accepted. China has nuclear weapons and is secure; Japan can still count on the United States for whatever residual protection it may require. Its interest, moreover, lies in taking a low military profile so as not to engender political resistance to its ever-growing economic power in the region.[84]

Because the probability of a great power war in Europe and the Far East is so low, the American presence in either region need not be large. Nuclear deterrence alone has not produced this condition of peace, but it will guarantee peace among the great powers if other peace-promoting factors disappear. A residual American presence in both regions adds insurance to two stable situations at a small price in order to hedge against a highly unlikely but terribly costly possibility.

In the Middle East, matters are not quite so simple. The United States has two clear interests: preservation of secure access to Persian Gulf oil, and protection of Israel. The first may require a semi-permanent American presence in the Persian Gulf area to deter a future Iraqi government, or any other self-aggrandizing power in the region, from trying to control access to a large share of Persian Gulf oil. It is not simply the price of oil that concerns the United States; it is also who controls access to the oil, and the ways in which that access could be manipulated. Those who control the access will have to sell the oil, but it is a mistake to underestimate the bargaining and blackmail leverage that control over oil reserves could give an ambitious aggressor like Saddam Hussein. Those who earlier argued that it was not important to have a military capability to intervene in the Gulf have had their arguments punctured.[85] Control of access to Persian Gulf oil is a matter of power, pure and simple. Aggressive, erratic, and otherwise ill-disposed states that threaten to grab a large measure of control over the world's most economically vital raw material must be stopped, with military force if necessary. The United States must continue to act to prevent any potential regional hegemon, be it Iraq,

---

84. For good analyses of Japan's military and economic interests in the Far East, see I.M. Destler and Michael Nacht, "Beyond Mutual Recrimination: Building a Solid U.S.-Japan Relationship in the 1990s," *International Security*, Vol. 15, No. 3 (Winter 1990/91), pp. 92–120; and Kenneth Hunt, "Japan's Security Policy," *Survival*, Vol. 31, No. 3 (May/June 1989), pp. 201–209.
85. See, for example, Robert H. Johnson, "The Persian Gulf in U.S. Strategy: A Skeptical View," *International Security*, Vol. 14, No. 1 (Summer 1989), pp. 122–161. Most of Johnson's other recommendations are excellent, especially about the need of the United States to conserve oil in order to lessen its dependence on oil imports.

Iran, or a Saudi Arabia turned unfriendly, from dominating access to Gulf oil.

Through extensive economic and military aid, the United States has underwritten Israel's security for over twenty-five years. To cease assistance now would have the same damaging effects on perceptions of U.S. reliability as cancellation of the treaty with South Korea. Additional reasons to maintain these ties include preservation of a democracy, the long-standing moral commitment to statehood for the survivors of the Holocaust, and the preservation of Israel's current ambiguous nuclear status. But U.S. protection of Israel will be made easier if a lasting settlement of the Palestinian issue can be achieved. There are only three possible solutions: (1) Israel annexes the West Bank and Gaza and forcibly expels the Arab populations from them; (2) Israel annexes the West Bank and Gaza and either permanently rules over, or makes equal citizens of, the Arab populations; or (3) Israel withdraws from the West Bank and Gaza, with adequate security arrangements.

The first course would bring Israel even greater political isolation than it now experiences and most likely also economic collapse, because the United States would probably withdraw the economic and military aid without which Israel cannot survive. The second course either would destroy Israel's democratic character through permanent rule over Arabs who have been made second-class citizens, or would destroy the Jewish character of the state if it remains a democracy and enfranchises all the Arabs annexed. The reason is that the birth rates of the Arabs far exceed those of the Jews. Even the immigration of huge numbers of Russian Jews will not change the ultimate result, only defer for a brief time its arrival.[86] Thus, after a number of years,

---

86. The demographic facts are stark. In Israel proper, together with the West Bank and Gaza, there are currently about 4 million Jews and 2.4 million Arabs (650,000 Arabs in Israel proper, 800,000 in Gaza, and 1,000,000 in the West Bank). The Jewish birth rate is 65 percent of that of the Arabs living in Israel, and 50 percent of that of the Arabs living in the West Bank and Gaza. Today, a majority of the children in all three areas combined are Arab. The best estimate of Israeli demographers is that every 100,000 Russian immigrants coming to Israel (of whom it is estimated that up to 30 percent are not Jewish) postpone by only one year the day of demographic reckoning when Jews become a minority in their own "greater state." Assuming a total of 500,000 Russian Jewish immigrants over the next 3–4 years, Jews will constitute 58 percent of the population in ten years, 54 percent in twenty years, and 50 percent in thirty years. (Today, 60 percent of the population between the Jordan river and the sea is Jewish.) I am indebted to Professor Ian Lustick of Dartmouth College for providing me with these figures, which come from a symposium held at the Van Leer Institute in Jerusalem, May 24, 1990, entitled "The Demographic Problems in Israel in the Wake of Soviet Jewish Immigration." For additional population figures, see Central Bureau of Statistics, *Statistical Abstract of Israel* (Jerusalem: Hamakor Press, 1987), pp. 3 and 702.

Jews in a "greater Israel" will find themselves a minority in their expanded state. But before that happens, the state would be corrupted from within. The signs are already apparent. Thus, if Israel retains the West Bank and Gaza and all the Arabs in them, demographic realities will force Israel to make a harsh choice between remaining democratic or remaining Jewish.

The third alternative is the only chance for Israel to have a durable peace and normal relations with its neighbors and to remain both democratic and Jewish. In return for Israel's agreement to release the bulk of the occupied territories, therefore, the United States should sign a military alliance with Israel and station a residual American force there, either a ground-force division or tactical air power.[87] This course of action would test Arab and Palestinian proclamations that they would accept peace if Israel returned the lands captured in the 1967 war, and it would allow Israel to feel secure enough to trade land for peace.[88] If the Arabs and the Palestinians did not then make peace, Israel would have gained the political high ground, and would have the added security that a clear-cut U.S. presence would provide. In the last analysis, this third course carries miminal risk for Israel because she has the ultimate guarantor of her security in her own hands—nuclear weapons.[89]

Wars elsewhere among smaller nations in Africa, Asia, Central America, or Latin America, though tragic for the peoples involved, do not threaten the core interests of the United States and certainly would not decrease its

---

87. I do not underestimate the difficulty of getting Israel to trade land for peace even once it has an alliance with the United States and some American military presence. Even after the United States dispatched Patriot anti-missile batteries with American crews to Israel to defend it from Iraq's Scud missile attacks in the early days of the Gulf war, Ze'ev Schiff, military editor of Israel's *Ha'aretz* newspaper and one of Israel's most prominent military columnists, cautioned: "I don't think America's action in recent days can ever be a substitute for territory. Yes, it shows the friendship of the United States and that it can be relied on. But we remember quite well how we were pushed aside during the last five months of this operation, and we still believe that when it comes to political issues Americans might be sometimes very naive about events in the Middle East. We remember your policy toward Iraq before August 2. You can make a big mistake and absorb it. We can't. So it's good to know that they can protect us sometimes, but don't look for any revolution in Israeli strategic thinking overnight." See Thomas L. Friedman, "Hard Times, Better Allies," *New York Times*, January 21, 1991, p. A9.
88. I have sidestepped two thorny issues: the political status of the West Bank and Gaza once freed from Israeli rule, and the status of Jerusalem. Neither issue will be easy to resolve politically, but no start on either can be made unless Israel is prepared to trade land for peace. My point is only to argue that an American presence in Israel is the best way to bring Israel to the point where it will make the trade.
89. See Evron, *Israel's Nuclear Dilemma*, chap. 3, for details on the nuclear force. Some estimate that Israel has nearly 100 nuclear warheads.

security.[90] Should the United States for some reason find it difficult to stay out, the cardinal principle should be: "Never go in alone." It is precisely because the temptation for the one nation that has a global military reach to employ it is so great that the United States generally should refrain from doing so. Capability should not father policy. Because it is impossible to foresee all contingencies, there may be other cases in the future that will require an American military presence in these regions, but the burden must lie on those who favor it to demonstrate how such cases would adversely affect American interests and why other nations in the region are not better placed to deal with them.

America's Post–Cold War Strategy

In sum, the United States should retain some type of peacetime military presence abroad to prevent five adverse situations: (1) an acceleration of nuclear weapons spread that could increase the likelihood of nuclear wars into which the United States could be drawn, or that could bring terrorist nuclear threats against it; (2) a serious decline in economic cooperation among the rich industrialized nations, due to a growth of economic nationalism, such that world trade, and thus American prosperity, would suffer significantly; (3) a great power war in Europe or the Far East that could wreck economic openness and hasten nuclear weapons spread; (4) control by a regional hegemon over Persian Gulf oil reserves that could threaten access to them; and (5) the conquest or destruction of either Israel or South Korea, which could fatally weaken other states' belief in the reliability of the United States.

For the era we are just now entering, the ultimate case for some type of American overseas military presence is a preventive one. It is a case that calls for buying insurance and for proceeding gradually, out of the judgment that matters could unravel if America entirely cast off its global military presence. It is a realist position because it assumes that international cooperation proceeds best if some nation or group of nations is willing to stabilize the international political and military environment. It is a defensive position

---

90. Given the long-standing U.S. commitment to the independence of South Korea, an exception for it must be made. The United States should continue to maintain some residual presence there as long as it is wanted by the South Koreans in order to deter any residual North Korean threat, until a political solution can be found for the division of Korea.

because it assumes that prevention is cheaper, easier, and ultimately more effective than cure. The purpose of a residual overseas American presence is, thus, insurance and reassurance.

How much insurance, then, should the United States buy and how much reassurance need it give? The functions that the overseas forces are to serve should dictate the type of forces that need to be retained. The forces should be for signaling, not warfighting, purposes; but the United States must retain the ability to deploy forces capable of fighting major wars. The forces that remain abroad are to show the flag, not to destroy "the enemy." Their function is to demonstrate America's commitment tangibly and to engage the United States politically by a presence that is more than merely token, but not so large that it becomes burdensome to the American public that pays for it or offensive to the nations that accept it. Above all else, the overseas presence must be politically sustainable and financially affordable.[91] Both considerations dictate drastic cuts from the current size of the U.S. overseas force.[92]

The largest of the permanent reductions should come in Europe, where the bulk of overseas U.S. forces are stationed. It is hard to find reasons for keeping more than 30,000–50,000 American troops on the European continent, once the Soviets take their troops out of what used to be East Germany and send them back to the Soviet Union. The smaller the American presence, the less offense it will give to the Germans, and the greater the likelihood that it will be politically acceptable over the long term. In addition, in order to counter the residual Soviet threat and thereby keep Germany's appetite for nuclear weapons at its present low level, some tactical nuclear presence on the continent is desirable, but there is no reason for these forces to exceed

---

91. Considerations of affordability dictate that those states with adequate resources should help defer a large percentage of the costs of American forces overseas: Germany and Japan for Europe and the Far East, Kuwait and Saudi Arabia for the Gulf if there is a sizeable American presence there.

92. At the end of fiscal year (FY) 1989 (September 30, 1989), the United States had 510,000 troops stationed abroad as follows: Germany, 249,000; other Europe, 71,000; Europe afloat, 21,000; South Korea, 44,000; Japan, 50,000; other Pacific, 16,000; Pacific afloat, 25,000; Latin America/Caribbean, 21,000; and miscellaneous foreign, 13,000. These sum to 341,000 for Europe; 135,000 for East Asia and the Pacific; and 34,000 other. Figures are taken from Secretary of Defense Cheney, *Annual Report to the President and Congress, January 1990*, p. 74. I have used FY 1989 as the peacetime base for comparison because this is likely to have been the high point of America's permanent peacetime overseas presence. The figures for 1990 and 1991 are affected by the permanent projected withdrawals from Europe and the deployment of substantial forces to the Persian Gulf, some of which came from Europe.

a few hundred. Since the early 1970s, the main rationale for having tactical nuclear weapons in Europe has been to maintain a capability for limited use to send a political signal to the Soviets that escalation to a big nuclear war was at hand, not for waging a tactical nuclear war against Soviet forces.[93] Especially now that NATO has declared its nuclear forces to be "weapons of last resort," this purpose is better served with the smallest tactical nuclear force (primarily gravity bombs and air-to-ground missiles) that legitimate military considerations about survivability will permit. All other U.S. tactical nuclear weapons should be taken out of Europe.

Given the uncertainties about the future constellation of power in the Persian Gulf, it is difficult to prescribe what types and amounts of U.S. forces should be stationed in the region. Two considerations will need to be balanced: U.S. forces must be large enough to deter future aggressions, yet small enough to minimize the political disruptions that the forces might cause within those states that agree to host them. Had Kuwait agreed to some American military presence before August 2, 1990, Saddam Hussein would probably not have attacked, knowing beyond a doubt that if he did, he would have killed American troops and thereby directly engaged and enraged the United States. The smaller the military capability that Iraq has after the war is over, the smaller the American presence needs to be. It is vital that the U.S. forces that remain in the Gulf be part of a multinational presence under UN auspices, so that the political responsiblity for the military presence will be shared with many states.

The stationing of some American forces in Israel, of whatever the type and mix, will not sit well with the Israeli government, which prefers to have American aid and backing, but not American advice and restraints. An American military presence in Israel would inevitably constrain Israel's political and military freedom of action. But the Israeli government is kidding itself if it thinks that it is now or can be completely free of such restraints. The United States possesses this power by virtue of the economic and military aid it gives to Israel, without which the state could not survive; but U.S. governments have chosen not to exploit it fully. Israel should recognize that it is better to be constrained and secure than constrained and insecure.

In the Far East, the case for large cuts in overall U.S. forces is not compelling yet because the Soviet Union has not begun to drawn down its forces

---

93. See J. Michael Legge, *Theater Nuclear Weapons and the NATO Strategy of Flexible Response,* R-2964-FF (Santa Monica, Calif.: RAND, April 1983), pp. 17–28.

there as it has in Europe. But the Soviets inevitably will do so, and it is in America's interest to match their cuts. The case for large cuts in U.S. troops in South Korea, however, is already strong because the South Koreans are not weak. Once mutual U.S.-Soviet reductions have been agreed to, the American presence in the Far East, apart from some ground forces in South Korea and Japan, should be largely a maritime and air power presence.[94]

In this article, my purpose has been to present the merits of the case for retaining an American military presence abroad, not to describe in detail what that presence should look like.[95] The details of policy are important, because the details *are* the policy. But to determine the details requires direction from an organizing strategy. Without the vision of where to go and how to get there, policy will be made by the drift of events and by the exigencies of budgetary politics. The world and the United States both still need some residual U.S. global military presence. The guiding principles for that presence are that it should be politically acceptable to the nations who will continue to host the forces, that it should be financially affordable to the American people who will continue to pay for it, and that it should be capable of rapid reinforcement from the United States should the forces be attacked.

For the current era, the duration of which no one can be certain, circumstances dictate retrenchment, but not withdrawal.

---

94. If the United States cuts its European force to 50,000–70,000, including the forces afloat; reduces, when appropriate, its western Pacific and East Asian contingent to 50,000; and stations 5,000–10,000 forces in Israel, it would have an overseas force, exclusive of what may be needed in the Persian Gulf, of 150,000–175,000, compared to 510,000 at the end of FY 1989. The Bush administration is formally committed to reducing the European force to 200,000–225,000, and cutting the East Asian and Pacific force by 10,000–13,000 over the next few years.

95. Two excellent comprehensive statements of what a reduced presence should look like are William W. Kaufmann, *Glasnost, Perestroika, and U. S. Defense Spending* (Washington, D.C.: Brookings, 1990); and Senator Sam Nunn, *Nunn 1990: A New Military Strategy* (Washington, D.C.: The Center for Strategic and International Studies, 1990).

Part II:
Dimensions of U.S. Strategy
After the Cold War

Managing Soviet Disintegration

A Demand for Behavioral Regimes

One could easily believe that the collapse of the Soviet Union is all to the good. The military threat that emanated from Moscow throughout the Cold War has been all but eliminated. Peoples whose identities were suppressed for three-quarters of a century under Communist rule, and as long as 250 years under Russian rule, can now exercise their right to national self-determination. Socialist economic practices are being consigned to the dustbin of history.

Unfortunately, these welcome consequences of Soviet disunion have a dark and dangerous side as well. While Western security is not threatened by the prospect of Soviet hegemony over Eurasia, it is affected by the proliferation of weapons of mass destruction to the new non-Russian republics. The exercise of national self-determination has led to nationalistic excesses against other national minorities within these new independent states. These excesses are not only morally repugnant, but they also have security implications, in that an aggrieved minority may effectively appeal for aid to its motherland—in most cases, Russia. The prospect of wars among the post-Soviet republics is discouraging enough, but far worse are the spirals of hostility and arms racing that they are likely to set off. The result could easily be the resuscitation of the threat from Russia: a paranoid, insecure state, surrounded by hostile republics, that over-arms against all of them in response. An over-armed Russia would once again raise the specter of a threat to Western security that the collapse of the Soviet Union was to have forever buried.

Russian security is a *Western* security interest. The West should adopt policies now that minimize the chances that this specter will reappear. The West should try to ensure that Russia's security environment remains as

Ted Hopf is an assistant professor of political science at the University of Michigan. He is the author of the forthcoming book, Peripheral Visions: Deterrence Theory and Soviet Foreign Policy in the Third World.

The author would like especially to thank Mike Desch, Sue Peterson, and Jon Mercer for criticizing several drafts of this paper. He also wishes to thank Charlie Glaser, Bob Axelrod, Karl Mueller, Matt Evangelista, and Nick Westcott for useful and timely comments. Anne Sartori and Nina Beebe provided research assistance. The Ford Foundation's Consensus Project furnished financial support. The John M. Olin Institute for Strategic Studies provided a stimulating forum for an early presentation of the author's arguments.

International Security, Summer 1992 (Vol. 17, No. 1)
© 1992 by the President and Fellows of Harvard College and of the Massachusetts Institute of Technology.

benign as possible. This probability can be increased by helping post-Soviet republics avoid setting off spirals of hostility amongst themselves. The West should establish standards of conduct on domestic and military policy for all of the new post-Soviet states, including Russia. The West should reward adherence to these rules with political, economic, and security advantages. Failure to adhere should have clear costs for the violators.

In sum, the West should establish behavioral regimes for the new post-Soviet republics. The rules of the regimes, if observed, would address Western security concerns by establishing a benign security environment for Russia and its new sovereign neighbors. The failure to attempt such regime-creation is likely to allow the gains from Soviet disintegration to go unreaped.

Current Western policy is not adequate to the task of advancing Western security interests even though, at first blush, it may look as if the West, or at least the United States, is already setting standards of behavior for post-Soviet republics. For example, during Secretary of State Baker's recent tour of the Soviet Union, he told the leadership of each republic he visited that Washington would not recognize them unless they fulfilled four conditions: 1) adhere to all treaties concerning nuclear and conventional weapons that the former Soviet Union had signed; 2) treat national minorities properly; 3) respect human rights; and 4) undertake economic liberalization.[1]

Unfortunately, however, the administration apparently bowed to criticism from Democrats that Bush and Baker were not recognizing the post-Soviet republics rapidly enough. Instead of resisting this partisan attack, and developing a strategically sound policy, the administration acted hastily. The United States now has diplomatic relations with each of the fifteen former Soviet republics, even though only Russia has signed and ratified the various arms control treaties, and respect for human and civil rights in the former Soviet republics is not commonplace.

This premature granting of diplomatic recognition is symptomatic of the more fundamental error being made by the West. It is giving away rewards without receiving iron-clad concessions in return. Diplomatic recognition,

---

1. Moreover, reporters who accompanied Baker on this tour of eight republics recounted how the leaders of these republics were willing to sign any piece of paper Baker's aides put before them in order to win diplomatic recognition from Washington. Such perfunctory commitments should not take the place of membership in comprehensive regimes. Not only are they unlikely to bind those who profess them, but their neighbors also receive no comfort from these kinds of assurances. See Thomas L. Friedman, "Baker Opens Tour of the Caucasus," *New York Times*, February 12, 1992, p. 6; and Friedman, "Republics Promise to Protect Rights," *New York Times*, February 13, 1992, p. 5.

normal commercial relations, and membership in international and regional institutions should not be given away so lightly.[2] Moreover, Baker's list is neither comprehensive in the kinds of behaviors it covers, nor part of a coherent policy for handling post-Soviet Eurasia. Instead, it looks like an *ad hoc* list of American preferences without any guiding strategic hand behind it. It lacks any enforcement mechanisms. It lacks any explicit commitment to particular rewards and punishments directly linked to various kinds of compliance or deviance on the part of the republics. Instead, "diplomatic recognition" appears to be the only encouragement offered to these new states. Finally, and not least important, it lacks any kind of framework for cooperation with either Europe or Japan in establishing and enforcing the standards.[3] Even the January 1992 meeting of 47 donor states in Washington, hailed by the administration as an effort to forge such coordination, focused almost exclusively on the tactical question of how to provide emergency economic aid to the Commonwealth. In sum, while there is definitely a U.S. policy toward the former Soviet Union, there is no Western or even U.S. strategy forming a foundation for it.

Below, I identify what Western security interests are in the region, and both the presumed benefits and the real risks that Soviet disintegration poses to those interests. I then elaborate on how behavioral regimes may be a solution to the dangers posed by Soviet disunion. I end by assessing the probability that these behavioral regimes will yield the promised rewards, concluding that despite several objections to their feasibility, behavioral regimes are necessary to preserve the Western security bonanza brought by the Soviet collapse.

Western Interests in Eurasia and the Benefits of Soviet Disintegration

There has traditionally been a hierarchy of Western interests in Eurasia.[4] First and foremost is the protection of Western security against military threats

---

2. For example, Russian membership in the International Monetary Fund (IMF) has been awarded solely on the basis of economic criteria. The United States failed to insist that Russia meet other Western concerns about Russia's military and domestic behavior before receiving IMF membership. This is a serious failure to use Western leverage effectively. On the criteria for IMF membership met by Russia, see Steven Greenhouse, "Buying Time for Yeltsin," *New York Times*, April 2, 1992, pp. A1, A7; and Andrew Rosenthal, "$4 Billion From U.S.," *New York Times*, April 2, 1992, pp. A1, A6.
3. Indeed, Stephen Kinzer reported that European leaders had no idea what kind of criteria they should be applying when recognizing the republics. Kinzer, "Europe, Backing Germans, Accepts Yugoslav Breakup," January 16, 1992, *New York Times*, p. A6.
4. The Realist and Neorealist schools of thought are the most consistent exponents of a hier-

from the East. This conventionally has been understood as requiring prevention of any single power from dominating Eurasia.[5] A necessary part of that mission is securing the West against any military adventures launched from the East. It is obvious that this Western security interest has been greatly enhanced with the collapse of the Warsaw Pact and the massive unilateral arms cuts initiated by former Soviet President Gorbachev.

A secondary Western concern is economic prosperity. It is hard to argue that Western economic interests are affected significantly by any outcome in the Soviet Union. The Soviet Union played so small a role in Western trade and investment figures that if its economy disappeared, the rest of the world would hardly miss it.[6]

A tertiary concern is the advancement of human and civil rights abroad. I argue that the advancement of this lesser interest in the former Soviet republics is, paradoxically, critical to attaining the primary Western interest in making durable the dramatic reduction of the military threat arising from Moscow.

---

archical ordering of the interests of Great Powers. See, for example, George F. Kennan, as described and quoted by John Lewis Gaddis, *Strategies of Containment: A Critical Appraisal of Postwar American National Security Policy* (New York: Oxford University Press, 1982), pp. 37–43. Bernard Brodie, despite his eloquently stated normative concerns, also acknowledges the existence of a hierarchy of interests, with security at the top, and morality at the bottom. Brodie, *War and Politics* (New York: Macmillan, 1973), chap. 8. See also Kenneth N. Waltz, *Theory of International Politics* (Reading, Massachusetts: Addison-Wesley, 1979), esp. chap. 7; and Michael Desch, *When the Third World Matters: Latin America and U.S. Grand Strategy* (Baltimore: Johns Hopkins University Press, forthcoming), chap. 1.

5. For example, see Kennan's analysis cited in Gaddis, *Strategies of Containment*, p. 30.

6. To put matters in perspective: Total U.S., EC, and Japanese foreign trade for 1990 was $3.8 trillion; of this total, only $44 billion (or all of 1.1 percent) was with the Soviet Union. Similarly, combined Organization of Economic Cooperation and Development (OECD) GNP (gross national product) for 1989 was $13.6 trillion, while Soviet GNP for the same year is very generously estimated at $2.7 trillion. These figures are from: International Monetary Fund, *International Financial Statistics*, November 1991; *OECD Economic Outlook: Historical Statistics, 1960–1989* (Paris: OECD, 1991); CIA National Foreign Assessment Handbook of Economic Statistics (Washington, D.C.: CIA, 1990); and *External Trade Statistical Yearbook 1990* (Luxembourg: Office of Official Publications of the European Community, 1990). Some argue that while the West itself gains little from economic intercourse with the former Soviet Union, this misses the point. Since former COMECON members are heavily dependent on trade with Moscow, they argue, a Soviet economic collapse will set dominoes tumbling in Eastern Europe, which will affect Western Europe, if only through refugee flows. But this argument rests on old data. In fact, since 1989, Poland, Hungary, and Czechoslovakia have effected a dramatic reversal in the direction of their trade flows. They have sundered ties with the former Soviet Union and forged new links with the West. Bulgaria and Romania remain far more closely tied to the former Soviet Union, but for all five countries, the trend is toward deepening economic interdependence with the West and a distancing from the East. See, for example, the figures in *The Economist*, February 1, 1992, p. 117.

In sum, the collapse of the Soviet Union has greatly advanced the paramount Western interest in its own physical security, as the Soviet hegemonic threat to Eurasia has disappeared. But this interest remains at risk so long as the former Soviet republics can adopt domestic and military policies that threaten stability in the region. If Russia rearms, the West will be faced with yet another round of containment in Eurasia.

It is important to distinguish the real from the supposed benefits for the West. For example, one could argue that the threat of hegemonic control over Eurasia declines as the number of post-Soviet entities increases. A single Soviet Union is able to amass a far larger military machine than one that is broken up. The coordination problems required to forge an alliance capable of threatening the West increase as the number of post-Soviet states increases.[7] Hence, one might argue, it is in Western interests to continue the process of Soviet disintegration past the point of fifteen republics. But matters are not so simple.

Even the benefits from the disintegration of *Russia* do not appear so great if we remember that the West very successfully coped with the much larger *Soviet* threat over the past 45 years. Why take any risks now to reduce only marginally a threat with which the West dealt handily when that threat was much more serious? Moreover, consider the effects that a Western policy of furthering Russian disintegration would have on future Russian decision-makers' attitudes toward the West. These policymakers, and indeed the Russian people, are most likely to draw the lesson that the West harbors hostile intentions toward their country. Such Russian paranoia plus Western overreaching would yield a security dilemma, a spiral of hostilities, and a real rather than simply a potential Russian threat to Western security.[8] In other words, a Western policy aimed at achieving the best possible security environment would kill the very good, and yield the worst.

---

7. See Mancur Olson, *The Logic of Collective Action* (Cambridge, Mass.: Harvard University Press, 1965)

8. On the security dilemma and the closely related topic of spiral dynamics, see Robert Jervis, "Cooperation Under the Security Dilemma," *World Politics*, Vol. 30, No. 2 (January 1978), pp. 186–214; and Jervis, *Perception and Misperception in International Politics* (Princeton, N.J.: Princeton University Press, 1976), chap. 3. On the effects of the external environment on decisionmaker's attitudes toward potential adversaries, see Charles L. Glaser and Ted Hopf, "Models of Competition and Cooperation in U.S.-Soviet Relations," in William Zimmerman, ed., *The Changing Soviet Union and New Directions in Western Security Policy* (Ann Arbor: University of Michigan Press, 1992). On how Western behavior designed to avert a Russian threat may in fact provoke it, see Jack Snyder, "The Transformation of the Soviet Empire: Consequences for International Peace," in Kenneth A. Oye, Robert J. Lieber, and Donald Rothchild, eds., *Eagle in a New World* (New York: HarperCollins, 1992), pp. 259–280.

Another corollary of Soviet dissolution that is not an unadulterated good is national self-determination. Of course, it is marvelous that people are being allowed to decide their fates. However, execrable excesses are also committed in the name of this value. Moreover, there is the question of how to limit the scope of this principle in practice: while there appears to be unanimity in the West, and indeed even overwhelming support in Russia, for the creation of fifteen sovereign republics out of the old Soviet Union, should the West support also the creation of new states within Russia and the other republics?[9] (See map, p. 155.) Should the West withhold economic and political rewards from the Russian government in Moscow until it lets these people leave? What would be left of the Russian state besides ancient Muscovy and parts of Siberia? Vindication of the principle of self-determination would require that the West support any and all calls for independence by any nationality, no matter how small.

A universal principle of national self-determination resonates far beyond Russia: Crimea has voted for independence from Ukraine, and Poles have declared independence on the territory of Lithuania.[10] And it does so not just in the former Soviet Union. The mixed West European reaction to events in Yugoslavia is revealing: Germany was keenest to support Slovene and Croat independence, while Spain, France, and Britain were not as enthusiastic. It is not merely coincidental that Spanish Prime Minister Gonzalez must worry about Basques and Catalans; French President Mitterrand the Bretons; and British Prime Minister Major Ulster, Scotland, and Wales. What happens if this principle is applied to Africa, many of whose borders are far more recent than those in either Russia or Europe? What about India's ethnically divided federation? Native Americans in the United States in many places have no less legitimate a claim than various peoples in Russia to national statehood. In short, unless the West wants to live in a world of virtually continual eruptions of nationalist warfare, it should resist giving national self-determination the status of a universal "principle" or "right." Perhaps national self-determination should be treated as a rare occurrence,

---

9. In Russia alone, Tatarstan, Chechen-Ingushetia, Mordovia, Mari-el, Chuvashia, and Komi-Permyak have all declared independence. Abkhazia and South Ossetia in Georgia have done likewise, as have the Dnestr Republic and Gagauzia in Moldova. And within Chechen-Ingushetia, Ingushetia has itself expressed a desire for independence.
10. The Crimean parliament voted in September 1991 for status as an independent and autonomous republic within Ukraine; "Crimea Declares Independence," *New York Times*, September 6, 1991, p. A12. On Poles in Lithuania, see Stephen R. Burant, "Polish-Lithuanian Relations: Past, Present, and Future," *Problems of Communism*, Vol. 40, No. 3 (May–June 1991), pp. 67–84.

whose vindication should only occur in very restricted circumstances. Unfortunately, establishing these limits will inevitably be arbitrary.[11]

In sum, the West should center its policy on the preservation of the real gain from Soviet disintegration: enhanced Western security. And the West should resist chasing illusory goals such as promoting the further disintegration of Russia or unreservedly supporting national self-determination.

The Real Risks from Soviet Disintegration

Soviet disintegration may trigger four developments that seriously increase the risk of major war in Europe: nuclear proliferation, security dilemmas, the abuse of minorities, and the denial of civil and human rights. The latter two are not security threats in themselves, but they greatly increase the probability that security dilemmas may lead to armed clashes and proliferation.

MANAGING THE POST-SOVIET NUCLEAR ARSENAL

If nuclear proliferation were a perfect process, perhaps we would not need to worry about any of the post-Soviet republics having its own nuclear weapons.[12] If each Soviet republic could, *simultaneously* and *instantaneously*, be given a secure second-strike capability, then we could be somewhat confident that mutual deterrent relationships had been created without the risks of preventive strikes by any side against another, or pre-emptive strikes in times of crisis. But of course this is not how nuclear proliferation has ever

---

11. Establishing such boundaries is beyond the scope of this paper. For a view that there is no logical endpoint to "national liberation" on the globe, see David D. Laitin, "The National Uprisings in the Soviet Union," *World Politics,* Vol. 44, No. 1 (October 1991), p. 142.
12. For an optimistic view about the effects of well-managed proliferation, see Kenneth Waltz, *The Spread of Nuclear Weapons: More May Be Better,* Adelphi Paper No. 171 (London: International Institute for Strategic Studies, 1981). For a similar sanguine attitude about nuclear proliferation in post–Cold War Europe, see John J. Mearsheimer, "Back to the Future: Instability in Europe After the Cold War," *International Security,* Vol. 15, No. 1 (Summer 1990), pp. 5–56. Eighty-five percent of the former Soviet nuclear arsenal is in Russia. The rest of the strategic forces are in Ukraine, Kazakhstan, and Belarus. Reginald Bartholomew, U.S. under-secretary of state for international security affairs, has testified that all tactical nuclear weapons have been withdrawn from the fifteen republics and are concentrated in Russia, Ukraine, and Belarus. And the latter two republics have announced they will transfer those weapons to Russia by July 1, 1992. David Binder, "4 New Republics Provide Details on Dismantling Ex-Soviet Arsenal," *New York Times,* February 7, 1992, p. A4. For an excellent overview of the problems associated with the nuclear arsenal in the former Soviet Union, see Kurt M. Campbell, Ashton B. Carter, Steven E. Miller, and Charles A. Zraket, *Soviet Nuclear Fission: Control of the Nuclear Arsenal in a Disintegrating Soviet Union,* CSIA Studies in International Security, No. 1 (Cambridge, Mass.: Harvard University, Center for Science and International Affairs, November 1991).

occurred, or is likely to occur in the future. Moreover, arguments about the salutary effects of perfect proliferation may be wrong. Thus the most prudent course is to stop the process before it gets started. After all, even if the probability of a nuclear exchange between one of these new republics, Russia, and/or a West European country is negligible, the product of that probability, when multiplied by catastrophic costs, looks very scary indeed.

Another outcome would be even more desirable than perfect proliferation, but its likelihood is quite low: It would be extremely stabilizing if the Russian nuclear button required multiple fingers.[13] If several different national governments' consent were necessary to launch any nuclear weapons, this would be a very favorable outcome from the standpoint of Western security, because any single country could veto any launch. But this happy circumstance is not probable, because no state, and especially not Russia, will want to cede control over its deterrent to any other.[14]

The bottom line is that Soviet disintegration increases the autonomous risk of a nuclear launch from former Soviet territory.[15] With imperfect prolifera-

---

13. This seems to be an outcome that non-Russian republics have preferred. Kazakhstan's President Nazarbayev, for example, told British Prime Minister John Major that, "control over Soviet nuclear weapons should not be a monopoly of the old center, but of a general staff consisting of the defense ministers of the eight republics who have signed the treaty on economic cooperation." Reported in *Kommersant*, October 28–November 4, 1991, p. 21. (All transactions from Russian are the author's, except where otherwise noted.) The Ukrainian Parliament has also asked for a veto over the nuclear weapons in its republic. "Ukraine Wants Voice in Use of Atomic Arms," *New York Times*, October 25, 1991, p. A8. Ukraine's President Kravchuk has expressed a desire for "collective control" over the weaponry. Francis X. Clines, "Change is 'Natural', Ukrainian Says," *New York Times*, November 30, 1991, p. 5. And in declarations accompanying the formation of the Commonwealth of Independent States, the leaders of Russia, Ukraine, and Belarus committed themselves to the "joint command" of nuclear arms. Serge Schmemann, "Declaring Death of Soviet Union, Russia and Two Republics Form New Commonwealth," *New York Times*, December 9, 1991, p. 1. Yeltsin told the Russian parliament in December 1991 that the leaders of all four nuclear republics (Russia, Ukraine, Kazakhstan, and Belarus) had to agree before he could launch CIS strategic forces. Serge Schmemann, "Union Put to Rest," *New York Times*, December 26, 1991, p. A1.
14. For example, Gennadi Burbulis, a senior Yeltsin aide, has reiterated Russia's claim to a "greater responsibility" for nuclear weapons located anywhere on former Soviet territory. Serge Schmemann, "Soviets Hail U.S. Arms Plan," *New York Times*, September 29, 1991, p. A1. And Kazakhstan has manifested a reluctance to disarm if that leaves Russia the sole nuclear power. See Helen Womack, "Yeltsin in Defence Squabble," *The Independent*, December 27, 1991.
15. "Autonomous risk" refers to the probability that crises will escalate to the nuclear level *independent* of decisionmakers' intentions, as a consequence of weapons characteristics, the exigencies of crisis bargaining, the misinterpretation of intelligence, etc. Thomas Schelling wrote that autonomous risk arises from "reactions that are not fully predictable, from decisions that are not wholly deliberate, from events that are not fully under control." The multiplication of nuclear republics increases the chances for such unpredictable processes to occur. Thomas C. Schelling, *Arms and Influence* (New Haven: Yale University Press, 1966), pp. 94–95.

tion, this risk increases substantially. Hence, we should seek the second-best solution, one finger on the Russian trigger, with far lower levels of weaponry.

SECURITY DILEMMAS AND SPIRAL DYNAMICS

The major reason to be concerned about nuclear issues in the former Soviet Union is the chance, even if small, that a nuclear conflagration could occur. The major reason to be concerned about security dilemmas is twofold. First, they are powerful stimulants for states to acquire weapons of mass destruction, and so they make preventing proliferation much harder. Second, they cause states to arm themselves beyond objective security needs. An over-armed Russia would create precisely the threat of Eurasian hegemony that the collapse of the Soviet Union has removed.[16] The probability of such security dilemmas must be reduced to the lowest possible level.[17]

A security dilemma arises when a state, while arming itself for purely defensive reasons, unintentionally makes its neighbors feel more insecure. The neighboring states in response increase their own arsenals, believing they have redressed a serious imbalance in forces. The original state, seeing this activity by its neighbors, *and* believing that nothing it did caused its neighbors to arm, infers that its neighbors must have offensive intentions— otherwise they never would have armed—and consequently increases its own arsenal in response. A spiral of mutual armament and increasing levels of suspicion about each other's intentions is thus set into motion.[18]

The security dilemma has particular implications for the non-Russian republics. Given their size relative to Russia, and their consequent lack of confidence in their ability to defend themselves with conventional forces, security dilemmas are more likely to make them want to acquire nuclear, chemical, and biological weapons. This has two unpleasant consequences. First is the direct effect of an increased autonomous risk of nuclear war, sketched out above. Second is the equally troubling effect of making probable

---

16. Soviets themselves have recognized this problem. See, for example, Gorbachev's speech in Murmansk, *Pravda*, October 2, 1987, and Evgenii Primakov (now head of the foreign intelligence directorate of the successor to the KGB), "U Poroga Tretevo Tysyacheletiya" (On the Threshold of the Third Millenium), *Literaturnaya Gazeta*, February 5, 1986, p. 14.
17. Analysts in the former Soviet Union have begun writing about the dangerous effects of a military competition among the new republics. Describing the problem in terms of security dilemma dynamics is Alexander Orlov, "The Army: Financial Cross-Section," *Moscow News*, No. 52/1991 (December 29, 1991–January 5, 1992), p. 8.
18. See Robert Jervis, "Cooperation Under the Security Dilemma," *World Politics*, Vol. 30, No. 2 (January 1978), pp. 186–214; and Glaser and Hopf, "Models of Competition and Cooperation," in Zimmerman, ed., *The Changing Soviet Union*.

the otherwise very improbable, that is, the resurrection of a Russian military threat to Eurasia.

The dynamics are simple, and can begin even if no republic tries to acquire nuclear weapons. Suppose that the Ukrainian government in Kiev decides it needs an army of 400,000.[19] The Russian government, certain it harbors no malign intentions toward Ukraine, wonders how this army could possibly be intended to enhance Ukrainian security, since Ukraine faces no threats to its security.[20] Russia decides that it had better be safe, and deploys perhaps three times that number of men against Ukraine. Russia has other defense commitments as well, so that its total military forces might be double or triple the forces designated for the theatre against the Ukraine. The Kiev government is faced with several considerations.

First, since the Ukrainian leadership sees nothing at all offensive about its 400,000-man army, it finds it hard to understand why the Russians are amassing forces in southern Russia.[21] Second, it realizes that its population of 52 million does not have a chance in a conventional arms race against Russia, with 147 million people. The Ukrainian leadership therefore decides that nuclear or chemical deterrence is the only way out of the security dilemma. This presents Russia with a choice: acquiesce as Ukraine develops such a capability, or fight a preventive war or launch a preventive strike against nascent Ukrainian weapons of mass destruction.[22]

---

19. This is not just hypothetical. On October 21, 1991, the Ukrainian parliament authorized the creation of a 400,000-man army. But shortly before his election as president of an independent Ukraine in December 1991, Leonid Kravchuk scaled back these plans to a standing force of 90,000, with the higher figure to be used only for "planning purposes." Ukraine is the most appropriate example because it is the republic with far and away the most potential to be a security threat to Russia. Its population is over two and one-half times that of the next most populous republic, Uzbekistan. Moreover, it has by a large margin the largest non-Russian share of the military industrial base of the former Soviet Union.

20. Russian decisionmakers probably would ignore, for example, both the historical enmity between Poland and Ukraine, and Ukrainian suspicions about their former Russian rulers' intentions. Russians already are writing about the security threat a Ukrainian army poses to Russia. See Pavel Felgengauer, "Raznoglasiya v SNG po Voprosam Oborony" (Differences in the CIS on Questions of Defense), *Nezavisimaya Gazeta*, January 3, 1992, p. 1.

21. Personal conversations with several scholars from the University of Lviv bear out this point. They simply dismissed as ludicrous any possibility that Russia could ever feel threatened by Ukraine, no matter how large an army Kiev decided to deploy.

22. On the incentives for preventive war in situations where one party is faced with another state whose military power is going to grow over time, see Stephen Van Evera, "The Cult of the Offensive and the Origins of the First World War," *International Security*, Vol. 9, No. 1 (Summer 1984), pp. 58–107; and Jack Levy, "Declining Power and the Preventive Motivation for War," *World Politics*, Vol. 40, No. 1 (October 1987).

Whether or not Russia launched a preventive strike, Western security would be adversely affected. If Russia were to attack Ukraine successfully and withdraw, it would raise grave suspicions in the West about future Russian intentions.[23] If the Russians were to attack Ukraine and remain there as occupiers, the West would see a clear Russian threat; security dilemmas would become much worse between Russian and each Western country. Even if Russia did not launch a preventive war or strike, it would still be likely to compensate for Ukrainian actions by building up its military, which would be likely to evoke Western anxieties and countermeasures. This dangerous outcome occurs even if both states want to maintain the *status quo*. It is not necessary to conjure up aggressive states to foresee violent behavior in the post-Soviet world.

Uncontrolled military competition between Russia and other former Soviet republics is very likely to cause eventual threats to Western security through the operation of security dilemmas and the spirals of hostility they spawn. Hence, Western policy must be aimed, first and foremost, at the prevention of these dilemmas and spirals before they occur, and at their mitigation or elimination once underway.

THE ABUSE OF ETHNIC MINORITIES

Discrimination against minority peoples by republic governments has generally been regarded as merely a human rights issue, but this is too narrow a perspective. Republican governments who mistreat their ethnic minorities can set off dynamics that will negatively affect Western security. Nuclear proliferation and security dilemmas are givens in international politics, but various factors can mitigate or exacerbate their severity;[24] one factor that can greatly enhance their danger is the abuse of minorities who have protectors in other republics. A glance at Table 1 shows where those protectors and their proteges live in the former Soviet Union.

---

23. It cannot be excluded, however, that a new international norm may be developing that allows the "selective and surgical" destruction of weapons of mass destruction and of the ability to produce them. Iraq is a recent example, and the fate of North Korea's facilities will probably be the same if Pyongyang does not voluntarily open them to inspection. If such a norm evolves, then Russian preventive elimination of Ukraine's nascent capabilities might be tolerated by the West and not interpreted as a sign of broader aggressiveness.

24. See Jervis, "Cooperation Under the Security Dilemma"; Stephen Van Evera, "Why Cooperation Failed in 1914," in Kenneth A. Oye, ed., *Cooperation Under Anarchy* (Princeton: Princeton University Press, 1986); and Glaser and Hopf, "Models of Competition and Cooperation."

Table 1.   Where Are Minorities in the Former Soviet Union?

	Population total (in millions)	Titular nationality as % of total	Main minorities as % of total
Russia	147	82	
Ukraine	52	73	22% Russian
Uzbekistan	20	71	8% Russian
Kazakhstan	17	40	38% Russian
Belarus	10	78	13% Russian
Azerbaijan	7	83	6% Russian, 6% Armenian
Georgia	5	70	8% Armenian, 6% Russian, and 6% Azeri
Tadjikistan	5	62	23% Uzbek, 7% Russian
Moldova	4	65	14% Ukrainian, 13% Russian
Kirghizia	4	52	22% Russian, 12% Uzbek
Lithuania	4	80	9% Russian, 7% Polish
Turkmenistan	4	72	9% Russian, 9% Uzbek
Armenia	3	93	2% Azeri
Latvia	3	52	35% Russian
Estonia	2	62	30% Russian

SOURCE: Adapted from *The Economist,* August 31, 1991, p. 38.

Map: Potential New States Within Russia.

Russians, for example, constitute around a third of the total populations of Kazakhstan, Latvia, and Estonia. They are nearly a quarter of the population of Ukraine and Kirghizia, and are significantly represented in Belarus and Moldova. If any of these governments adopt legislation discriminating against Russians, then these aggrieved people might call for help from their mother republic of Russia. There is no reason to believe that the Russian government would manifest restraint in responding to these pleas. Russian Information Minister Mikhail Poltoranin, asked how Russians in other republics should be taken care of by Moscow, replied that, "anti-Russian feelings will not be silently swallowed by the Russian leadership. One must borrow an example from the USA. Do you remember the reaction of America when they began to abuse its citizens in Grenada?"[25] Moreover, democracy itself is likely to *increase* the rewards for any politician in Russia who follows public opinion polls on the issue of foreign treatment of expatriate Russians. There are likely to be electoral gains for a Russian politician who takes a tough stand against any republic that is abusing Russians living or working there.[26]

Indeed, abuse of minority rights is the match that could light the fuse of security dilemma and spiral dynamics. This is so because the critical boundary between peace and war under the security dilemma is determined by how each side perceives the other's *intentions*.[27] A Ukrainian government

---

25. *Moskovski Novosti*, November 3, 1991, p. 7. Non-Russians are extremely sensitive to Moscow throwing its weight around within the Commonwealth. The vice-president of an association of Caucasian peoples, history professor Hadji Murat Ibragimbeili, related that as a consequence of Yeltsin's threatened intervention in Chechen-Ingushetia, his colleagues from the region were convinced that "the Russian empire is alive and it is not getting ready to give freedom to its 'colonies'." See Natalya Pachegina, "'Terpenie Liudei Nelzya Ispytyvat Beskonechno'" (You Cannot Try the Patience of People Forever), *Nezavisimaya Gazeta*, January 3, 1992, p. 3.
26. An aide to the chairman of the international affairs committee of the Russian Supreme Soviet, Vladimir Averchev, recently told a reporter that "many in the Parliament are dissatisfied with the Russian Ministry of Foreign Affairs," because it is not looking after the rights of the Russian minority in Estonia with sufficient care. See Dmitrii Panaev, "Luchshe Pozdno, no Navsegda" (Better Later, but Forever), *Kommersant*, December 23–30, 1991. The mayor of Moscow, Gavriil Popov, widely acclaimed in the West as a "liberal," is also one of those who has most strongly urged Yeltsin to defend the interests of Russians living outside of the homeland. See Mark R. Beissinger, "The Deconstruction of the USSR and the Search for a Post-Soviet Community," *Problems of Communism*, Vol. 40, No. 6 (November–December 1991), p. 3, note 33. In the Caucusus, Azerbaijan President Ayaz Mutalibov was forced to resign for not escalating the military defense of Nagorno-Karabakh against Armenia. See, "Three Peace Missions Are Seeking To Quell Ethnic War in Caucasus," *New York Times*, March 10, 1992, p. A6.
27. After all, if a government believes that the forces of its potential adversary are meant for purely defensive purposes, there is little incentive to respond with military deployments of its own.

that builds a 400,000-man army with protestations of good faith is one thing. A Ukrainian government that fields such an army while it simultaneously passes legislation barring Russians from educational and employment opportunites is quite another. In the latter case, Russian leaders are more likely to infer malign Ukrainian intentions.

Moreover, Ukrainian abuse would provoke public calls in Russia for intervention to save fellow Russians from mistreatment.[28] Ukrainian leaders, hearing this kind of debate in Russia, might well take military precautions against Russian intervention. These precautions will only exacerbate the dangerous dynamics between the two states, and lead both sides to actions that ultimately threaten Western security.

In sum, the West has a *security* interest in how post-Soviet governments treat their minorities. The West should insist on certain standards of behavior for these governments, the content of which I discuss below.

THE DENIAL OF CIVIL AND HUMAN RIGHTS

As in the case of minority rights, how governments behave domestically is rarely considered an issue of international security. But there is reason to treat the failure to allow democratic liberties as an ultimate threat to Western security. If citizens of the new republics do not have ready access to competing sources of information about the conduct of their government, they are not likely to be able to mount any opposition to policies that can exacerbate security dilemmas and spirals.

For example, if the Ukrainian government were to propose creation of a 400,000-man army, there should be a free and open debate as to the need for such a force. But such a debate depends on competing sources of infor-

---

28. Insofar as Russia is democratic, not heeding this public outcry would have high political costs to the regime in power. Shortly after the August 1991 coup attempt, Yeltsin's press secretary Pavel Voshchanov made an alarming declaration that Russia did not consider its borders to be immutable. Celestine Bohlen, "Russian Vice President Wants to Redraw Borders," *New York Times*, January 31, 1992, p. A9. Yeltsin, in a speech before the Congress of People's Deputies after Ukrainian and Kazakh political leaders objected to the spokesperson's comments, asserted that: "Russia is going to be loyal to its treaty obligations, and in this respect, will defend the interests of Russians outside the Russian Republic." Francis X. Clines, "Soviet Congress Resists Reshaped Union," *New York Times*, September 5, 1991, pp. A1, A6. And even if the Russian government does not heed the call directly or immediately, Russian "volunteers" might go to the aid of the aggrieved party and then draw Moscow in to protect them. In the Trans-Dniester area of Moldova, where fighting broke out between the Moldovan army and Russian and Ukrainian rebels, 4000 Ukrainian and Russian Cossacks reportedly crossed into Moldova from Ukraine to help the rebels. See "Moldova Imposes Emergency Rule and Orders Disarming of Militias," *New York Times*, March 29, 1992, p. 11.

mation from different newspapers, journals, universities, interest groups, and political parties.[29] Without them, if the Kiev leadership began to exaggerate the Russian threat in such conditions, it would be difficult or impossible for any social or political force to present the contrary brief. And if Russia countered this build-up because of percieved abuses of the Russian minority, Ukrainians would have no way of determining the validity of their government's denials and countercharges against Moscow.

Thus, the West has a security interest in ensuring that the policies of each of the post-Soviet republics can be openly scrutinized by the citizenry. The absence of such freedom increases the probability that republic governments could adopt risky foreign and military policies that could ultimately threaten Western security.

SUMMARY OF SECURITY THREATS

The collapse of the Warsaw Pact followed by that of the Soviet Union has made the West more secure than at any time since the destruction of Hitler's bid for Eurasian hegemony. Such an invaluable position requires careful maintenance, and intelligent maintenance necessitates discerning what the possible threats to that position might be. There are two serious sources of alarm for the West. The first is nuclear proliferation and loss of Russian control over the former Soviet nuclear arsenal. The second threat is the resurrection of Russian military power. The most likely cause of the latter is Russian insecurity that leads it to over-arm against its potential adversaries. Russian insecurity might be a product of a security dilemma with Ukraine that would be exacerbated and fueled by governmental abuses of ethnic minorities and denial of democratic and civil liberties. The West, therefore,

---

29. Other scholars have stressed the importance of free and open domestic debate to increase the probability that benign security policies will be selected. See, for example, Van Evera, "Primed for Peace"; Jack Snyder, "Averting Anarchy in the New Europe," *International Security,* Vol. 14, No. 4 (Spring 1990), pp. 5–41; and Charles A. Kupchan and Clifford A. Kupchan, "Concerts, Collective Security, and the Future of Europe," *International Security,* Vol. 16, No. 1 (Summer 1991), pp. 159–160. It should be acknowledged that confidence in a democratic prophylaxis against pernicious policies and ideas, while having some empirical validity (see, for example, Michael Doyle, "Liberalism and World Politics," *American Political Science Review,* Vol. 80, No. 4 [December 1986]), is primarily a philosophical assumption of Liberalism that awaits more decisive and rigorous empirical testing. This argument is most eloquently and convincingly articulated in Karl Popper, *The Logic of Scientific Discovery* (New York: Basic Books, 1959). In Popper's "evolutionary theory of knowledge," he argues that truth and knowledge are advanced only through the rigorous testing of competing theories. Only democracies provide the unfettered arenas necessary for such a competition. See also Karl Popper, *Objective Knowledge: An Evolutionary Approach* (New York: Oxford University Press, 1972).

must develop policies that minimize the possibility of Russian insecurity. These include the development of codes of conduct for the former Soviet republics in the areas of military, foreign, and domestic policy. I turn to these standards of behavior now.

Managing Soviet Disintegration: Creating Behavioral Regimes

The West should try to do what clearly is *necessary* to avert a renewed security threat from Russia. The West should establish a set of standards for each republic's armed forces, security policy, foreign conduct, and domestic behavior. Inducements and penalties from the West should be allocated according to how faithfully individual republics adhere to these standards. The carrots and sticks of a behavioral regime consist of economic, political, and informational elements.[30]

STANDARDS OF MILITARY POLICY

The objective in creating restraints on former Soviet military and foreign policy is to alleviate the effects of the security dilemma as much as possible. This means preventing the proliferation of weapons of mass destruction, and establishing limits on the acquisition and deployment of conventional weapons and the doctrines that govern their use.

First, every post-Soviet republic, including Russia, should be required to sign the Non-Proliferation Treaty on nuclear weapons, thereby accepting intrusive international inspections of their civilian nuclear energy programs.[31]

---

30. By choosing the word "regime" I do not mean to imply that I am adhering strictly to regime theory. Instead, I am primarily talking about institutions created by parties who do not themselves participate in the regime that the institutions are designed to monitor. I use the word regime, however, because many of the benefits and characteristics of regimes are associated also with the institutions I discuss. The version of regimes I recommend is perhaps closest to the notion of an "imposed regime" raised by Oran Young, in "Regime Dynamics: The Rise and Fall of International Regimes," in Stephen D. Krasner, ed., *International Regimes* (Ithaca, N.Y.: Cornell University Press, 1983), p. 100. For a useful introduction to regime theory in general, see Stephen D. Krasner, "Structural Causes and Regime Consequences: Regimes as Intervening Variables," in Krasner, ed., *International Regimes.*

31. For an excellent analysis of how and why the non-proliferation regime functioned effectively during the Cold War, see Joseph S. Nye, Jr., "Maintaining a Non-Proliferation Regime," *International Organization,* Vol. 35, No. 1 (Winter 1981), pp. 15–38. As recent experience with Iraq has suggested, the guidelines and restrictions enforced by the International Atomic Energy Association (IAEA) must be made far more stringent, with much more intrusive inspection procedures. The strictest version possible should be part of the behavioral regime I am proposing for the former Soviet republics.

These new republics should also be required to sign international conventions renouncing the right to produce, acquire, or possess chemical and biological agents. Since the international institutional machinery for ensuring compliance with these conventions is mostly ad hoc, monitoring mechanisms will have to be established on a permanent basis.[32]

Signing on to these non-proliferation treaties has positive effects beyond making it much harder to acquire these weapons. Just as important is the information that these regimes provide to each republic government about what other potential adversaries are doing.[33] Since one of the most powerful forces behind the security dilemma is uncertainty about intentions, a disinterested institution providing trusted information about capabilities (which are very often used to infer intentions) can go a long way to undermine these suspicions.[34] Moreover, this information can provide political leverage for domestic resistance against republic governments that are trying to garner public support through diversionary militarism.[35]

In the area of conventional weapons, each new government should sign the Conventional Forces in Europe (CFE) treaty, which would severely limit

32. Explaining that the Biological and Toxin Weapons Convention "regime" is ad hoc and underfunded is Nicholas A. Sims, *The Diplomacy of Biological Disarmament: Vicissitudes of a Treaty in Force, 1975–85* (New York: St. Martin's, 1988).

33. My argument here goes beyond Keohane's position that the "demand for regimes" in international politics is, in part, explained by the fact that they reduce the costs of obtaining information, and lower transaction costs in general. Instead, I am suggesting that the regime is the *only* feasible source of the information necessary to allow its members to reach a cooperative (and Pareto-optimal) outcome. Consequently, high "issue density" is not a necessary condition for a high demand for regime creation. See Robert O. Keohane, "The Demand for International Regimes," in Krasner, ed., *International Regimes*, pp. 150–167; and Keohane, *After Hegemony* (Princeton, N.J.: Princeton University Press, 1984), chap. 6, esp. pp. 92–98. See also Stephen D. Krasner, "Global Communications and National Power: Life on the Pareto Frontier," *World Politics*, Vol. 43, No. 3 (April 1991), p. 342. One regime whose primary product is information about its members is the International Monetary Fund (IMF). See the discussion in Charles Lipson, "The International Organization of Third World Debt," *International Organization*, Vol. 35, No. 1 (Autumn 1981), pp. 603–631. For example, Ukraine announced it would no longer transfer battlefield nuclear weapons back to Russia, until it was assured that they were being destroyed. A security institution could fill the role of providing the necessary information. Eric Schmitt, "Russia is Said to Plan for a Small Armed Force," *New York Times*, April 2, 1992, p. A6.

34. The most recent opportunity for establishing a security regime is the Open Skies Treaty. On March 24, 1992, the 24 members of the CSCE agreed to extensive overflights of their territories. This treaty should be incorporated into the security regime proposed here.

35. It has been argued, for instance, that GATT membership has been used by government officials as a weapon in internal debates over trade policy. See Jock A. Finlayson and Mark W. Zacher, "GATT and the Regulation of Trade Barriers: Regime Dynamics and Functions," *International Organization*, Vol. 35, No. 4 (Autumn 1981), p. 600. For the effects of institutions on governmental debt and development policy, see Barbara B. Crane, "Policy Coordination by the Major Western Powers in Bargaining with the Third World: Debt Relief and the Common Fund," *International Organization*, Vol. 38, No. 3 (Summer 1984), pp. 399–427.

the level of conventional forces each republic can deploy. The tricky, but essential, task is to set these limits low enough so that each republic can feel as secure as possible against its neighbor, but high enough so that each new state can credibly defend its territory against at least one of its neighbors without assistance from another republic.[36] Numerical limits are only one part of the set of constraints to be imposed on post-Soviet forces. The republics should also accept limitations on the types of weaponry they deploy, what kind of units are deployed, their geographic location, the nature of their training exercises, and the military doctrines that govern their use in battle. The objective is to address the balance between offensive and defensive military advantage, one of the central issues of the security dilemma.[37]

Fortunately, these issues have been part of the East-West arms control agenda for the last five years, so Western and Soviet defense establishments and foreign policy officials have been thinking seriously about these problems over a sustained period of time. Moreover, the CFE agreement already recognizes the principle that some weapons are more offensive than others, and the former must be severely limited in quantity as a result of their inherently more dangerous qualities.[38] The treaty has also established the principle of geographical restrictions on deployments. By establishing where weaponry is to be located, the treaty necessarily establishes where it is forbidden. This makes monitoring compliance with the agreement much easier, as you need find only one violation of the provisions, rather than count up all the weapons, to discover if a party is in violation. Moreover, movement of stipulated weaponry off the reservation provides an instant warning about the presumably malign intentions of the violator. This warning receives even greater weight because it is delivered by monitors attached to an international institution whose integrity and disinterest are manifest. Such arrangements can help defuse possible security dilemmas among Russia and the other post-Soviet republics.

The other standards of military behavior that should be enforced concern confidence-building measures (CBMs) and constraints on military doctrine

---

36. No republic will be able to defend itself singlehandedly against Russia, and no republic other than Russia will be able to go it alone against Ukraine.
37. On how offense and defense affect the security dilemma, see Jervis, "Cooperation Under the Security Dilemma."
38. Weapons that are more strictly controlled include heavy armor, long-range fighter-bombers, and long-range mobile artillery. For an effort to establish a conventional balance favoring the defense in Central Europe, see Jack Snyder, "Limiting Conventional Forces: Soviet Proposals and Western Options," *International Security*, Vol. 12, No. 4 (Spring 1988), pp. 48–77.

and training. The task of implementing CBMs is eased by the fact that the Conference on Security and Cooperation in Europe (CSCE) has already created a lengthy list of such measures to which the Soviet Union and the West have agreed.[39] These include advance notification of any movement of troops and weaponry above a certain numerical level; the invitation of international observers to all training exercises above a certain size; geographical restrictions on exercises; and the prohibition of various kinds of possibly provocative exercises. Additional limits that should be included are a prohibition against deployment of forces abroad and the disallowance of any foreign troops on any republic's soil. The cumulative effect of such measures should be to increase certainty among potential adversaries that others' military forces are not likely to be directed against them.

Finally, each former Soviet republic should be required to participate in international discussion of its military doctrine. This process was begun between the United States and the Soviet Union. Each side accepted the principle of "defensive defense," the development of a military doctrine oriented away from offensive warfare.[40] The former Soviet republics should be persuaded to adopt military doctrines that are clearly defensive in orientation. Again, this goes right to the heart of security dilemma concerns. The new republics are likely to feel far more secure if they can be certain that their neighbors' military doctrines are inappropriate for offense. This certainty would be maximized if information about military doctrines is provided by an institution whose only interest is to provide accurate data about this question.

The standards of military conduct outlined above are designed to minimize both the possibility of proliferating weapons of mass destruction and the possibility that security dilemmas will spiral into destabilizing arms races among Russia and its neighbors. The ultimate objective is to keep proliferation and arms races from resuscitating a Russian military threat to the West. I argue that requiring the republics to join the nuclear non-proliferation regime, to forswear the acquisition of chemical and biological weapons, and to permit intrusive methods of inspection is the best way to prevent both

---

39. See Ralph A. Hallenbeck and David E. Shaver, *On Disarmament: The Role of Conventional Arms Control in National Security Strategy* (New York: Praeger, 1991), chap. 8.
40. One of the first Soviet efforts to deal with the question of "defensive defense" was Andrei Kokoshin and V.V. Larionov, "Kurskaya Bitva v Svete Sovremennoi Oboronitelnoi Doktriny" (The Battle of Kursk in Light of Contemporary Defense Doctrine), *Mirovaya Ekonomika i Mezhdunarodnye Otnosheniya (MEiMO)*, August 1987.

proliferation and security dilemma dynamics between these new states and their neighbors. To further reduce the possibility of Russian re- and over-armament, new republics must accept further restrictions on the numbers, types, locations, and doctrinal guidance of their conventional forces.[41]

STANDARDS OF DOMESTIC CONDUCT

The West should create a set of general rules for how the new republic governments treat their citizens. These standards should apply both to national minorities and to the general population. It is necessary to convince these governments that a good reason that they should not abuse minorities is that such repression could trigger an intervention by the mother republic of the aggrieved citizens. If the new governments are required to protect the civil liberties of their citizens, they are less likely to be removed by their people. The information that would be provided by the international institutions monitoring military affairs would be almost useless if it could not be used for free discussion and debate in each republic.

The first set of standards would discourage governments from acting against minorities in ways that would be likely to provoke the suspicions of the minorities' mother republics.[42] First and foremost, there must be a clear prohibition against official use of violence against any ethnic minority.[43] Other forms of suppression probably are less likely to cause a foreign republic's response, but still may indirectly have security consequences. The West, therefore, must also erect barriers against governmental suppression of a minority's language, culture, or religion. Nor should the West tolerate official discrimination against minorities that prevents them from pursuing their

---

41. One might well argue that the best solution to the problem of security dilemmas at the conventional level is to have a single "Russian" or Commonwealth army. While this would be ideal, I cannot imagine any post-Soviet republic, at least for the foreseeable future, renouncing its right to defend itself by conventional means. Insisting on such an outcome might result in the loss of the good in a quest for the best.

42. The types of provocative actions that should be discouraged would include the Moldavian government's August 1991 arrest of the leader of that republic's Russian and Ukrainian minority, Igor Smirnov.

43. Georgian repression of its South Ossetian minority is an ugly example, as are Uzbeki attacks on Meshketian Turks. This does not imply that the West should condone acts of violence against non-minority citizens, or minorities who do not have the advantage of mother republics to protect them. I only mean to stress here the *security* implications of acts against minorities and the need to sanction it on that basis. One might want to discourage the less discriminate violence on moral grounds, but this essay does not speak to that source of Western interests.

chosen careers or professions.[44] In sum, the first set of standards should prohibit behavior by the republics with respect to their minority populations that is likely to invite foreign intervention on behalf of the aggrieved peoples. The second set of standards in the domestic arena has a different objective. This list is designed to create circumstances most likely to ensure that governments are accountable for their actions to their citizenry. As I argued above, republic governments are far more likely to build up their militaries, inflate foreign threats, and threaten military action themselves if there are no competing parties or organizations arguing against the actions and statements of the government. The government, therefore, should be required to maintain an open arena for this war of ideas and policies.[45] The ownership of, and access to, the media—newspapers, journals, radio, and television— should be widely distributed among groups with different political viewpoints.[46] Such groups must also be free to organize and to run in free and fair elections. Foreign correspondents' rights to report freely from these republics should also be guaranteed.[47] Finally, the national history that is

---

44. An example of actionable conduct would be former Georgian President Zviad Gamsakhurdia's declaration that only residents who could trace their ancestry back over 200 years could be eligible for citizenship or property rights in Georgia. James Brooke, "4 Die in Georgia as Military Units Clash," *New York Times,* September 26, 1991, p. A8. Similarly, Estonia has imposed three-year residency requirements for non-Estonians living there, which effectively deprives most Russians of citizenship so that they cannot vote in upcoming local and parliamentary elections. Latvia's recently enacted citizenship laws are more draconian, requiring a sixteen-year term of residence and a qualifying language examination. For a description of these laws, and the Russian reaction to them, see Andranik Migranyan, "'Russkie Pribaltiki'," (Russian Balts), *Nezavisimaya Gazeta,* January 3, 1992. Migranyan warns the Baltic republics that their actions against local Russians only encourage "fascist, nationalistic" sentiments in Russia itself. The Moldovan government has passed legislation requiring proficiency in Romanian for many jobs, which harms that republic's large Russian and Ukrainian minorities. The latter have taken up arms in the Trans-Dniester region, in part because of these discriminatory laws. Celestine Bohlen, "Russia Takes Over Command of Army in Moldova," *New York Times,* April 2, 1992, p. A7.
45. A troubling example is Uzbekistan, where President Islam A. Karimov has arrested the leadership of the main opposition Birlik party, including its chair, Abdulrakhim Pulatov. In Kazakhstan, Nazarbayev has incarcerated the leaders of the Islamic party Alash. "Vegas of the East," *The Economist,* March 7, 1992, p. 52.
46. This is meant to guard against actions such as those taken by Gamsakhurdia. Shortly after the August 1991 coup attempt, his government seized control over all TV and radio stations, and closed all newspapers until "suitable" replacements could be established. He also ended the airing of Moscow television and the distribution of any newspapers from outside Georgia. (For a remarkable, and unique, effort to defend Gamsakhurdia's actions across the full range of anti-democratic and illiberal behavior, see Darrell Slider, "The Politics of Georgia's Independence," *Problems of Communism,* Vol. 40, No. 6 [November–December 1991], pp. 63–79.) Similar actions against independent media have been taken in Uzbekistan.
47. In September 1991, foreign reporters were expelled from both Georgia and Uzbekistan; in

taught in schools should be the subject of scrutiny, both by groups within the republic, and also by the international institution charged with responsibility for monitoring domestic standards of conduct (see below).[48] This measure is aimed at preventing the government from presenting a view of its nation that is likely to inspire nationalistic excesses against local minorities and foreign nations.

Unlike the security realm above, where there are already international institutions operating rather effectively in each of the major areas I have identified,[49] new organizations will have to be created to ensure adherence to the political code of conduct envisioned here.[50] The most important task of an "Organization for Democratic and Civil Rights" will be its monitoring capacity. It must become a source of information about the political practices of the signatory nations. The credibility of this organization must be such that the information it supplies will be regarded as accurate by the West, by the nations being monitored, and by the citizens of each of the republics.[51]

This organization must provide "transparency" for all republics.[52] Each must be able to see inside its neighbors and be convinced that potential adversaries are neither mistreating minorities, nor engaging in other behaviors that might reasonably evoke suspicions about their intentions abroad. This institution also can be a critical source of informational ammunition for political opposition within a republic that is trying to resist a particularly

---

the case of Uzbekistan, even Russian journalists were ejected. Edward A. Gargan, "Some Changes in Soviet Asia," *New York Times*, September 18, 1991, pp. A1, A7.

48. On this idea, see Stephen Van Evera, "Why Cooperation Failed in 1914," in Kenneth A. Oye, ed., *Cooperation Under Anarchy* (Princeton: Princeton University Press, 1986); and Van Evera, "Primed for Peace." See also the suggestions of Kupchan and Kupchan. An encouraging counterexample to the tendency to whitewash one's own history and demonize the neighbors' is found in Lithuania, where it is precisely the nationalist organizations that are revealing the history of Lithuanian participation in the Nazi genocide against 200,000 Jews in the 1940s. See Michael Ignatieff, "In the New Republics," *New York Review of Books*, November 21, 1991, pp. 30–32. On the importance of accurate history to healthy societal development, see David Remnick, "Dead Souls," *New York Review of Books*, December 19, 1991, pp. 72–81.

49. Each of those institutions would, however, have to be greatly expanded in size, scope, technological and technical capacity, and membership.

50. While the actions of Helsinki Watch groups, Charter 77, Solidarity, and other human rights monitors have been admirable, the proposal here foresees a more systematic and intrusive monitoring institution that has international backing and receives its authority in part from the host government's agreement to its activities.

51. Kupchan and Kupchan propose a Commission on Political Development and a Commission on Democracy, both of which aim at addressing some similar problems in Eastern Europe. See Kupchan and Kupcahn, "Concerts, Collective Security, and the Future of Europe," pp. 159–160.

52. This function is very similar to the proposed security institution's role of providing trusted information about each republic's military activities.

dangerous course by that government. If the government tries to whip up a nationalistic frenzy over the alleged abuses occurring next door against kinspeople, credible information provided by the disinterested institution can be used by the political opposition to counter governmental charges. Nongovernmental media outlets can publicize this contrary position, further undermining the government's efforts to mobilize the populace.

WILL THESE STANDARDS STICK?
Below I sketch out why there is some hope that behavioral regimes may prevent misguided military and domestic policies.[53] I also discuss some of the more powerful objections to my prescriptions, and why these objections need not be crippling to my argument.

REASONS FOR OPTIMISM. Republics which sign on to these behavioral regimes can expect both immediate benefits and long-term gains. The former are straightforward exchange relationships: if your government behaves in this manner, here is what the West is prepared to do for you. The long-term gains are the benefits supplied by the institutions.

The immediate gains are political and economic. Adherence to the prescribed norms should be rewarded by official recognition of that state as a sovereign member of the international community with all the diplomatic privileges attached to that status, including membership in any and all international organizations and institutions that the republic wishes to enter. Another immediate benefit is less tangible. Many citizens of the republics, especially members of the political class and intelligentsia, are desperate to become members of "Europe," not the European Community with its economic benefits, but rather the civilization and political culture of Europe. Very many believe that they have been denied access to Europe by a skein of repressive tsarist and communist governments. Now they want to participate in a legacy and culture previously refused them. Faithful adherence to the norms described above should be regarded as a guarantee of the right to participate in the European civilization.[54]

---

53. The regimes are necessary in order to prevent threats to Western security that arise through security dilemma dynamics and the proliferation of weapons of mass destruction. But neither they, nor any other imaginable policy, are sufficient to prevent the emergence of a Russian threat, for any state's proclivity for an aggressive foreign policy can develop out of many different causal roots. The proposed regimes, while they address a large part of the universe of possible causes, are not exhaustive.
54. I am speaking particularly of the Baltic republics, Belarus, Moldova, Ukraine, Russia, and Armenia. Michael Ignatieff reports, for example, that although Latvia and Estonia would very

The second set of direct rewards to the new republics for observing constraints on their military and domestic behavior is economic. I am not proposing handouts of large quantities of economic aid. Instead, I am suggesting that the behavior of republics be taken into account when making decisions about economic relations that are, for the most part, grounded wholly in economic considerations. For example, governments must choose whether or not to extend most-favored nation (MFN) status to a given republic. While this choice is primarily based on economic considerations, e.g., whether the party will grant reciprocal concessions,[55] Western countries should consider also a prospective recipient's military and domestic activities in their evaluation.

Other discretionary economic rewards should include membership in the General Agreement on Trade and Tariffs (GATT), the International Monetary Fund (IMF), and the European Bank for Reconstruction and Development (EBRD). There are significant benefits to membership in each of these institutions. GATT facilitates trade relations among its members. The IMF helps finance short-term balance of payments deficits. The European Bank has been created to help identify and finance development projects in Eastern Europe and the former Soviet Union; it has an official bias toward financing private enterprise, and provides training programs for would-be entrepreneurs. A deviant republic would lose access to all these advantages. Moreover, there are bilateral economic relationships that would also be put in jeopardy in the event of excessive militarization and domestic repression. These include direct government assistance (say, from Washington to Kiev), as well as private corporate relationships. Government assistance includes both discretionary financial and material aid, and technical training and education programs. Private corporations promise not just direct foreign investment, but also the transfer of manufacturing technology, training of a skilled work force, and a marketing and distribution network abroad that no republic business could hope to cultivate even in the medium term. All these economic relationships should be presented to the republics as benefits of

---

much like to expel as many Russians as possible from their countries, in retaliation for the years of repressive Soviet rule, their desire to be "good Europeans" stays their hands. See Ignatieff, "In the New Republics," p. 30. I have not seen any evidence, however, that the idea of Europe has the same allure for Central Asians, Georgians, or Azeris.

55. Throughout the Cold War, American policymakers treated MFN status as a political lever on the Soviet Union and other socialist countries. For a fascinating discussion of the politics of the Nixon administration's efforts to grant MFN status to the Soviet Union, see Paula Stern, *At the Water's Edge* (Westport, Conn.: Greenwood, 1979)

adherence to the prescribed rules, and their denial as a cost of disregarding these constraints.

In other words, conformist republics should be offered normal economic relations with the West based on economic opportunities created by the domestic economic policies of the republic government, supplemented at the margins by official aid. Republics that flout domestic and military norms should be denied the benefits of both normal economic relations and official aid.

While the economic and political incentives for the republics are largely direct exchange relationships—the West reciprocates good conduct with economic and political rewards—in the case of security incentives, the main reward the West provides is institutionalized information and monitoring. The West, through the expanded operation of already extant international organizations, essentially promises to provide each new republic with the kinds of data about its potential adversaries that only an intrusive inspection system could provide. No individual republic could ever hope to know as much, with such high confidence, about the military capabilities of its neighbors as it can as a consumer of information provided by these security institutions.[56]

These security institutions have effects very similar to regimes: they have the potential to turn Prisoners' Dilemma relationships toward cooperative solutions.[57] Let us take the example of the suggested constraint on nuclear, chemical, and biological proliferation. In the absence of institutions, the following dynamic is probable: both Russia and Ukraine want chemical weapons and each would feel most secure if it had them, but the other side did not. But each would prefer that neither had them, rather than both. This is the typical preference structure for a game of Prisoners' Dilemma. The security institution, however, intervenes in the game and manipulates the preferences so that the probability of a cooperative outcome is significantly

---

56. Unlike the economic and political benefits described above, the West has an interest in providing even a deviant republic with military information about its neighbors. Objective data about its security environment may encourage a deviant republic not to arm as much.

57. On the difficulty of creating security regimes, see Robert Jervis, "Security Regimes," in Krasner, ed., *International Regimes*. There is one crucial difference between usual discussions of security regimes and the situation I describe. Security regimes are expected to emerge under conditions of anarchy, i.e., in the absence of any kind of final arbiter above the regime participants (or states). But the circumstances I am describing include a set of referees who impose a regime of sorts on the participant republics. This alters the player's calculations considerably, as each now has "perfect" information about the others, and any suspicions it might have will be investigated by the security institution's directors.

enhanced. By assuring each side that the other is not arming, the institution allows each side to gain more security, at lower cost. Not only is the security dilemma mitigated, with its attendant risk of war, but the costs of fielding an effective military force are reduced, and relations with a potential adversary are improved. This is no small gain from adhering to a code of conduct.[58] In the absence of this institution, Prisoner's Dilemma dynamics imply that both Russia and Ukraine would try to deploy chemical weapons.[59]

The rest of the security institutions' activities are designed to reinforce these gains. The intrusive on-site inspection, permanent stationing of observers on each republic's territory, challenge inspection and overflight rights, restrictions on training exercises, deployment points, and weapons characteristics, and confidence-building measures among republics are all aimed at convincing each republic that it can be certain that its potential adversary simply cannot gain any unilateral military advantage.

In sum, there is an impressive bundle of benefits available to republic governments who choose to abide by the suggested behavioral norms. There are political gains from being sovereign members of the international community and European civilization. There are economic gains from establishing normal economic relations with the rest of the world and receiving capital, technology, advice, and aid from Western governments and corporations. Finally, and perhaps most important, there are gains from a reliably secure environment, devoid of unnecessary arms races and malignant security dilemmas.

REASONS FOR PESSIMISM? There are reasons, however, to be skeptical about the effectiveness of the suggested behavioral regimes, although I argue that

---

58. For ways to solve Prisoners' Dilemmas in international relations and the obstacles that often preclude such solutions, see the contributions in Oye, ed., *Cooperation Under Anarchy*. The policies outlined here also manipulate the republic payoffs by increasing their gains from pursuing a cooperative strategy. Providing information allows a republic to choose cooperation with confidence that it will not receive the "sucker's" payoff, but the array of political and economic incentives additionally increases the gains that can be expected by not defecting from the regime. In a way, the regime is pushing the republics into a game of Stag Hunt, rather than Prisoners' Dilemma, by increasing the gains from cooperation and the costs of defection. However, this regime will produce no cooperative solution if one of the players is a "Bully," i.e., if one of the players prefers unilateral deployment of a weapon system to mutual restraint. On games of Bully, see Glenn Snyder and Paul Diesing, *Conflict Among Nations* (Princeton, N.J.: Princeton University Press, 1977), pp. 122–124.

59. The security institution may work effectively even if one of the states does deploy. Instead of immediately retaliating through a counterdeployment, the institution may provide sufficient assurances to the aggrieved party that the latter will stay its hand until the institution has an opportunity to try to reverse the behavior of the deploying republic. Of course, such restraint will not hold for long. But in the absence of the organization, it might never have been attempted.

on balance, it appears that the promised rewards of compliance with the regimes can overcome these obstacles. There are four sets of problems: republics might not accept infringements on their sovereignty; the Western alliance might not be able to cooperate in imposing sanctions and rewards; the West might not be able to afford the packages of incentives; or the very operation of the regime's sanction mechanism might undermine the regime's relevance.

The most serious objection is the argument that it is absurd to expect these republics, which have just gained their sovereignty in the face of such terrible odds, to allow the West unilaterally to place such demanding restrictions on the exercise of their sovereign rights. They might argue that the West is attempting to impose second-class citizenship on them or to consign them to some kind of perpetual international purgatory, a half-way house to full membership that no other state has had to endure. But several factors constitute powerful evidence that these new republics would not reject the constraints on their behavior recommended in this article.

The first consideration for the republics has to be the cost of noncompliance with the West's demands. They risk severing political and economic ties with the West that are essential to their full development as sovereign states. They also risk entering completely unregulated security environments that are likely to spawn security dilemmas, conflicts, and wars. While the costs of deviance are high, the benefits of compliance described above are quite substantial, including both direct economic and political rewards and a much more benign security environment.

Moreover, there is ample precedent of sovereign states accepting infringements on their autonomy by other states and international institutions. One need only consider the dozens of IMF adjustment packages that are in current operation in many Third World countries.[60] Lest we think sovereignty is ceded only by the weaker members of the international community, one must remember that both the United States and the former Soviet Union, and indeed all members of NATO and former members of the Warsaw Pact, have accepted numerous restrictions on their military behavior, including

---

60. On the very intrusive prescriptions and inspections required by IMF adjustment packages, see Benjamin J. Cohen, "Balance-of-Payments Financing: Evolution of a Regime," in Krasner, ed., *International Regimes*. Oran Young writes that consensual knowledge gives rise to "social conventions" that lead regime participants to consider constraints on their behavior as "legitimate or proper." See Young, "Regime Dynamics: The Rise and Fall of International Regimes," in Krasner, ed., *International Regimes*, pp. 94–95.

intrusive on-site inspection regimes. The new republics, therefore, will not have to feel as if they are singled out for discriminatory treatment.

There are also examples of governments changing the treatment of their citizenry in response to international demands. For example, it is widely acknowledged that the Spanish government was able to resist neo-Franco forces in the late 1970s and early 1980s, in part at least by pointing to the conditions laid down by the European Community (EC) for ultimate membership. The EC also affected the domestic behavior of Greece and Portugal. Indeed, governments sometimes *need* international demands to provide domestic political cover for taking unpopular or controversial measures. Third World regimes, for example, quite often excoriate the IMF before their domestic audiences, while complying with its adjustment packages. Moreover, some political leaders in the Commonwealth of Independent States (CIS) have already expressed a desire to be subject to international constraints on their domestic behavior. President Nursultan Nazarbayev of Kazakhstan, for example, has invited international monitors to his republic to inspect and report on how human and civil rights are being protected there.[61] Finally, international pressure has already worked in a former Soviet republic. The Lithuanian government decided to reverse its decision to exonerate several hundred war criminals convicted by Stalinist courts after the United States and Israel protested that many of those being exculpated had in fact participated in Nazi killing of Lithuanian Jews in the 1940s.[62]

In sum, the costs of deviance, the benefits of compliance, examples of other states' tolerance of limits on their sovereignty, and explicit expressions of a willingness to accept these constraints combine to give cause for optimism that these new republics will accept effective international participation in their domestic and military affairs. The evidence certainly does not support an argument that the West should not make the effort.

The second objection to the construction of standards of conduct concerns the West's inability to maintain a united front on these issues. It is argued

---

61. Nazarbayev made this plea in a speech before the Supreme Soviet shortly after the August 1991 coup attempt. See Celestine Bohlen, "Gorbachev Threatens to Quit Unless Republics Find a Way to Preserve a Modified Union," *New York Times*, August 28, 1991, pp. A1, A6. Gorbachev called for international monitoring of the entire former Soviet Union in his speech at the CSCE human rights meeting in Moscow in September 1991. Craig R. Whitney, "Moscow Rights Conference Sees Danger in Nationalism," *New York Times*, September 11, 1991, p. A10.
62. Stephen Kinzer, "Lithuania Starts to Wipe Out Convictions for War Crimes," *New York Times*, September 5, 1991, pp. A1, A7; and Marvine Howe, "Lithuanian Vows Inquiry on Nazis," *New York Times*, November 17, 1991, p. A8.

that members of the Western alliance may not be able to agree on the content of the regimes, and thus they will not develop common policies on sanctions and rewards. The effectiveness of the regimes would be greatly weakened if some Western governments continue to provide aid or maintain economic relations in the face of a republic's clear violation of some norm.[63]

Two points counter this argument. First, the level of dissension among members of the Western community is probably exaggerated by many because they rely on the Cold War record for their historical lessons. Second, this risk of Western incoherence would be minimized if the leader of the Western alliance, i.e., the United States, would abandon its current ad hoc approach to the former Soviet Union, identify its strategic objectives, and then develop and implement the policy of behavioral regimes in close coordination with its allies.

Throughout the Cold War, there was a running battle among the United States, its NATO allies, and Japan over developing a common understanding of what kinds of commercial relations should prevail with the Soviet Union and its allies. Preferences were at variance because Washington consistently held a more alarmist view of the Soviet threat to Europe than did the Europeans themselves. This fundamental difference no longer exists. In fact, if anything, the kinds of threats discussed in this article are feared more by Europeans than by the United States.[64] Once sanctions against deviant republics are adopted, there should be much less "leakage" than occurred during the Cold War. The Europeans, far closer to the potential instability, conflict, and refugee flows, are likely to be very quick to enforce the penalties prescribed by the regime. And the United States, although unaffected by the proximate threats in Eastern Europe, would still be very concerned by the long-term threat of Russian military recrudescence.

---

63. There are signs of differences already. When NATO issued a declaration strongly suggesting that each republic return its nuclear arsenal to the center's control, French President Mitterrand demurred, criticizing the alliance for interfering in the internal affairs of that region. President Bush similarly announced the rapid recognition of Ukraine without consulting, or even informing, any European allies. Germany is alone in pressing Ukraine on such issues as the size of its army. Meanwhile, Canada has unilaterally extended credits to Kiev, and the United States has granted diplomatic recognition to Ukraine. Such lapses must be avoided if behavioral regimes are to operate effectively. See "Message to Kiev," *The Economist*, February 8, 1992, p. 15; Clyde H. Farnsworth, "Ukraine is Getting Canadian Credits," *New York Times*, February 23, 1992, p. 14.
64. Indeed, German Foreign Minister Hans-Dietrich Genscher has suggested that the CSCE should create a new mechanism whereby its members could send human rights observers to countries suspected of abuses without the consent of the accused country. Craig R. Whitney, "Moscow Rights Conference," *New York Times*, September 11, 1991, p. A10.

Bush administration policy in the wake of Soviet disintegration, in which the United States has acted unilaterally toward the former Soviet republics, asked them to adhere to a set of ad hoc standards of conduct in exchange for diplomatic recognition, and then, long after the fact, invited Europe to discuss coordination of policy toward the CIS is very likely to lead to just the kind of incoherence that will ensure that any former Soviet republic can safely ignore the demands of any single Western power. Effective coordination could occur if the Western countries could agree on what kind of strategic landscape they would all like to see in Eurasia: a demilitarized and secure Russia, having sole possession of the former Soviet nuclear arsenal, surrounded by independent states that adopt domestic and military policies that will not trigger security dilemma dynamics with Russia. Coordination in the West is more feasible than during the Cold War, but requires the first step of reaching agreement on the strategic future of Eurasia.

It is also possible to object to the construction of these regimes on the basis of cost. The straitened budgets of the United States and Germany, in particular, simply do not contain the resources to reward compliant republics. But the economic rewards for compliance consist of normal economic relations and membership in international economic institutions, not piles of free money. The financial cost of institution-building is quite low, given the fact that the security and economic institutions already exist, and require only expansion and rule-creation. Finally, and most important, one must measure the costs of these behavioral regimes against the costs of not creating them. The costs of nuclear conflict are incalculable, and the costs of another round of even a conventional military competition with Russia are certainly far higher than the five to ten billion dollars per annum that can reasonably be estimated for regime maintenance costs.

Finally, it may be argued that if the West imposes sanctions because a republic violates the rules of a regime, the West thereby loses influence over that government at the very time when such influence is most necessary. In other words, these regimes may make effective deterrents, but if deterrence fails, they will be impotent to affect deviant republics' behavior. However, regimes can be constructed in such a way as to minimize this problem by ensuring that there is a stream of rewards whose flow can be regulated according to the behavior of the member. By calibrating sanctions to behavior, the regime retains a reserve of rewards not yet denied. Moreover, every sanction that is imposed is simultaneously a reward waiting to be granted. IMF adjustment packages work precisely in this fashion. If a country is granted a total of one billion dollars, for example, this money is allocated on a schedule corresponding to required reforms by the recipient government. In this way, the IMF maximizes the leverage it can exert on the recipient's behavior.

If, however, a republic engages in a dramatic violation of a regime, such as invading a neighboring republic, the above objection is apt. All rewards will be withdrawn and sanctions will be imposed. But short of a military response by the West, there is no alternative policy and I oppose the Western use of force to ensure compliance. First, the security threat does not warrant the use of military force by the West. The very worst possible case is the resuscitation of an over-armed Russian Empire of some kind. And this kind of threat was dealt with effectively, albeit at great cost, during the Cold War without a preventive war. Second, military intervention by the West, regardless of its protestations of good faith, is very likely to set off precisely the security dilemma dynamics that will cause the outcome the intervention was slated to prevent: Russian insecurity.

In sum, while it is sensible to be skeptical about the feasibility of establishing behavioral regimes and then gaining adherence to their rules, this skepticism should not overwhelm the reasons for optimism. New republics can be confronted with a choice: either join these regimes and gain the benefits that accrue therefrom, or refuse to join and risk the costs of that choice. Virtually all states accept some limitations on their sovereignty, so these republics are not being singled out for lesser status in the international community. Finally, the creators of the regime are likely to act more coherently than they did during the Cold War, the costs of the regime are reasonable, and their enforcement mechanisms can be effective.

Conclusion: Soviet Disintegration and Western Security

The disappearance of the Soviet Union greatly enhances Western security. But continued enjoyment of this situation requires a consideration of how a Russian military threat might re-arise. Maintaining Russian security is the key to averting a rearmed and over-armed Russia from emerging. Reassuring Russia requires establishing limits on the sovereign activities of the republics, including Russia itself. The West must establish codes of military and domestic conduct, and international institutions designed to monitor these behavioral regimes. The United States, Europe, and Japan must be prepared to act in concert against any violators and for regime adherents. The Bush administration's current ad hoc policy, while having elements that point in the right direction, is without strategic foundation, and so risks incoherence and lack of allied cooperation. Moreover, with each passing day, an increasing number of rewards are simply given away by the West in exchange for promises about *economic* behavior, but not about political or military behavior. IMF membership, for example, is being granted without any attention to the strategic concerns of this article. The United States has granted diplomatic recognition to all fifteen new republics without any concern for the more fundamental strategic landscape of Eurasia or how to make that landscape one that promotes Western security interests. U.S. leadership is essential, but sorely lacking.

In sum, the risks of Soviet disintegration require united Western efforts to establish behavioral regimes that will channel former Soviet republics in the direction of pacific relations among themselves and with their own peoples. While this may not be sufficient to prevent unpleasant outcomes, it is preferable to disjointed policies unconnected by any strategic thread.

Concerts, Collective Security, and the Future of Europe

Charles A. Kupchan
and
Clifford A. Kupchan

Europe's strategic landscape has been transformed. Whether we like it or not, the architecture of the postwar order is outmoded. The Warsaw Pact has been disbanded. NATO is struggling to define a role for itself; the threat it was built to resist may soon be nonexistent. Profound and probably irreversible change in the Soviet Union and Eastern Europe means that we must confront the difficult task of erecting new security structures for a new era.

A debate rages over how to respond to these changes in Europe's landscape. Two broad schools of thought have emerged. The pessimists, pointing to the waning of the Cold War and the end of bipolarity, fear a return to a more fractious multipolar Europe.[1] The optimists, on the other hand, welcome the end of the East-West struggle and do not fear a return to multipolarity. They argue that many of the causes of war that produced conflict during the first half of the twentieth century have either been eliminated or substantially moderated. While these optimists recognize that the political and economic future of the Soviet Union and Eastern Europe remains uncertain, many argue that some form of collective security—a pan-European

Charles A. Kupchan is Assistant Professor of Politics at Princeton University. Clifford A. Kupchan is a Ph.D. candidate in Political Science at Columbia University.

The authors would like to than the following individuals for their assistance: Robert Art, Henry Bienen, James Chace, Cherrie Daniels, Joanne Gowa, Robert Jervis, Thomas Risse-Kappen, Nicholas Rizopoulos, Jack Snyder, Patricia Weitsman, and the participants of the International Relations Study Group at Princeton University, the Olin National Security Seminar at Harvard's Center for International Affairs, and the Foreign Policy Roundtable at the Council on Foreign Relations. Research support was provided by the Center of International Studies, Princeton University, and a German Marshall Fund grant to the Dulles Program on Leadership in International Affairs.

1. The most prominent proponent of this view is John Mearsheimer, "Back to the Future: Instability in Europe After the Cold War," *International Security*, Vol. 15, No. 1 (Summer 1990), pp. 1–56. Mearsheimer's main concerns stem from his assertion that multipolar worlds are inherently more unstable than bipolar ones.

Other analysts, some of whom fall into the optimist camp, voice different concerns about the end of the Cold War: that Germany might again seek to dominate Europe; that failed attempts at political and economic reform in the Soviet Union and Eastern Europe might produce aggressive autocratic regimes; that ethnic hatreds might trigger border conflicts. For a review of these arguments and documentation, see Stephen Van Evera, "Primed for Peace: Europe After the Cold War," *International Security*, Vol. 15, No. 3 (Winter 1990/91), pp. 7–9.

order predicated on the notion of all against one—can best preserve peace in the post–Cold War era.[2]

Whether collective security can work in the new Europe is thus a critical issue underlying much contemporary debate over how to respond to the waning of the Cold War. A thorough analysis of collective security is also needed because, even though the concept has been invoked with increasing frequency by scholars and politicians alike, the debate has been muddied by differing interpretations of what collective security is and how it would operate to preserve peace in Europe. In addition, skeptics of collective security derive considerable ammunition from the apparent failure of the League of Nations to prevent aggression during the 1930s and the marginal significance of the United Nations during the Cold War. Unless this historical legacy can be proved inaccurate, collective security is not likely to win widespread acceptance.

This article will clarify what collective security is, and make the case that erecting a collective security structure in Europe is both viable and desirable. The conditions necessary for a collective security structure to form and function successfully are now present. Such a transition is not only possible, but also desirable; it would provide a more stable—that is, less war-prone—international environment. In designing a new collective security structure for Europe, we draw on the nineteenth-century Concert of Europe. The Concert kept the peace for forty years in the absence of bipolarity and nuclear weapons, the two factors that conventional wisdom credits with preserving stability since 1945.[3] We propose that a new concert-based collective security

---

2. See Malcolm Chalmers, "Beyond the Alliance System: The Case for a European Security Organization," *World Policy Journal*, Vol. 7, No. 2 (Spring 1990), pp. 215–250; Gregory Flynn and David Scheffer, "Limited Collective Security," *Foreign Policy*, No. 80 (Fall 1990), pp. 77–101; James Goodby, "A New European Concert: Settling Disputes in CSCE," *Arms Control Today*, Vol. 21, No. 1 (January/February 1991), pp. 3–6; Clifford Kupchan and Charles Kupchan, "After NATO: Concert of Europe" (Op-Ed), *New York Times*, July 6, 1990; Harald Mueller, "A United Nations of Europe and North America," *Arms Control Today*, Vol. 21, No. 1 (January/February 1991), pp. 3–8; John Mueller, "A New Concert of Europe," *Foreign Policy*, No. 77 (Winter 1989–90), pp. 3–16; Alice Rivlin, David Jones, and Edward Myer, "Beyond Alliances: Global Security Through Focused Partnerships," October 2, 1990, available from the Brookings Institution, Washington, D.C.; Jack Snyder, "Averting Anarchy in the New Europe," *International Security*, Vol. 14, No. 4 (Spring 1990), pp. 5–41; Richard Ullman, "Enlarging the Zone of Peace," *Foreign Policy*, No. 80 (Fall 1990), pp. 102–120; and Van Evera, "Primed for Peace."

3. See Kenneth Waltz, *Theory of International Politics* (Reading, Mass.: Addison-Wesley, 1979); John Lewis Gaddis, "The Long Peace: Elements of Stability in the Postwar International System," *International Security*, Vol. 10, No. 4 (Spring 1986), pp. 99–142; and Mearsheimer, "Back to the Future," pp. 6–7. For arguments challenging the notion that bipolarity is more stable than multipolarity, see Van Evera, "Primed for Peace," pp. 33–40.

organization for Europe be erected. Concert-based collective security relies on a small group of major powers to guide the operation of a region-wide security structure. This design reflects power realities—an essential condition for a workable structure—while capturing the advantages offered by collective security.

We present our design for a new European security order in the following manner. The first section makes the argument that collective security provides an alternative to the Realist, Hobbesian view of international relations in which self-help and the competitive pursuit of power are the only means through which nation-states can cope with an anarchic and conflict-prone system. We then define collective security, discuss the different types of structures that fall within the collective security family, and identify the conditions that allow such structures to take shape and preserve peace. Next, we explain why collective security is desirable, and how it would promote stability. We argue that adequate and timely balancing against aggressors is more likely to emerge under collective security than in a world in which each state is left to fend for itself; balancing under collective security more effectively deters and resists aggression than balancing under anarchy. Collective security also enhances stability by institutionalizing, and thereby promoting, cooperative behavior, and by ameliorating the security dilemma. In the section that follows, we argue that a concert-based structure provides the most practicable and effective form of collective security under current international conditions. We show that a concert is attainable today by demonstrating that the underlying features of the nineteenth-century international system that gave rise to the Concert of Europe are once again present. Moreover, we contend that the current international setting is even more suited than that of 1815 to a concert-based security structure. The concluding section describes how a new concert of Europe would work today. We argue that the Conference on Security and Cooperation in Europe (CSCE) should be recast to function as a concert-based collective security organization. A security group of Europe's major powers would guide the operation of a pan-European security structure. We spell out the essential architecture of such a system and point to new mechanisms that could be introduced to enhance the ability of a collective security organization to preserve peace in Europe.

Defining Collective Security

Realism has deeply influenced both the study and practice of international relations during the postwar era. Realism provides a stark vision of an anarchic, competitive international system in which states, in order to ensure survival, must be preoccupied with augmenting their economic and military power.[4] Cooperation is very difficult to achieve and sustain because states do not trust each other and because a competitive setting makes them concerned with relative as opposed to absolute gains.[5] States therefore rely on their own resources to provide security, unless forced to do otherwise. When unable to marshal sufficient resources to resist an external threat, states seek alliances to aggregate military capability. According to Realists, states therefore have two principal means of providing security in an anarchic setting—balancing against others through domestic mobilization (self-help) or, when necessary, balancing through the formation of temporary alliances. Even though states cannot escape from the Hobbesian world, balancing behavior, at least in theory, allows states to keep pace with each other, thereby maintaining a balance of power that deters aggression. Deterrence operates because states confront each other with relatively equal military capability.[6] Stability is thus the product of antagonism and confrontation.

In practice, however, balancing behavior in an anarchic world often fails to prevent wars. In some cases, deterrence fails because states balance belatedly or not at all; aggression meets little resistance and conquest augments the aggressor's power capabilities.[7] In other cases, states engage in excessive military preparations, setting off a spiral of reciprocal threats that may contribute to mounting hostility and quicken the onset of war.[8] Even if balancing

---

4. For classical statements of the Realist position see Hans Morgenthau, *Politics Among Nations: The Struggle for Power and Peace*, 5th ed. (New York: Knopf, 1973); Waltz, *Theory of International Politics*; and Stanley Hoffmann, *The State of War: Essays in the Theory and Practice of International Politics* (New York: Praeger, 1965). For a more recent and concise statement of the Realist vision see Mearsheimer, "Back to the Future."
5. See Joseph Grieco, "Anarchy and the Limits of Cooperation: A Realist Critique of the Newest Liberal Institutionalism," *International Organization*, Vol. 42, No. 3 (Summer 1988), pp. 485–508.
6. Many analysts of balance-of-power theory contend that balancing under anarchy, when it works properly, produces a roughly equal distribution of power. The underlying logic of this proposition is that states turn to internal mobilization and alliance formation to respond in kind to each other's actions, thereby producing a rough equilibrium of power. See, for example, Inis Claude, *Power and International Relations* (New York: Random House, 1962), p. 42.
7. The events of the 1930s represent a case in point. France, Britain, and the United States did little to stop Japan's initial bouts of aggression in the Far East or Germany's growing predominance in central Europe. French and British rearmament proceeded at a far slower pace than that of Germany. The United States remained relatively isolationist. As argued below, the absence of more timely and adequate balancing should not be blamed on the League of Nations, but was a product of political and economic conditions in France, Britain, and the United States.
8. Prior to World War I, the Anglo-German naval race and the competition for ground superiority between the Triple Alliance and the Triple Entente pushed the two blocs toward war. For a general discussion of spirals and deterrence failures see Robert Jervis, *Perception and Misperception in International Politics* (Princeton, N.J.: Princeton University Press, 1976), pp. 58–113.

works in accordance with the Realist vision, it tends to produce relatively equal balances, which lack the deterrent effect and the robust defensive capability of preponderant opposing force.[9]

Students of international politics have long pointed to two ways of mitigating the anarchy, competitiveness, and war-proneness of the Hobbesian world: world government and collective security. World government involves centralized management of international politics. States devolve control over their foreign policy to a central authority. Because it compromises national sovereignty, however, world government enjoys few proponents.[10]

Collective security rests on the notion of all against one. While states retain considerable autonomy over the conduct of their foreign policy, participation in a collective security organization entails a commitment by each member to join a coalition to confront any aggressor with opposing preponderant strength. The underlying logic of collective security is two-fold. First, the balancing mechanisms that operate under collective security should prevent war and stop aggression far more effectively than the balancing mechanisms that operate in an anarchic setting. At least in theory, collective security makes for more robust deterrence by ensuring that aggressors will be met with an opposing coalition that has preponderant rather than merely equivalent power. Second, a collective security organization, by institutionalizing the notion of all against one, contributes to the creation of an international setting in which stability emerges through cooperation rather than through competition. Because states believe that they will be met with overwhelming force if they aggress, and because they believe that other states will cooperate with them in resisting aggression, collective security mitigates the rivalry and hostility of a self-help world.[11]

---

9. Prior to the outbreak of hostilities in World War I, the Germans believed that the military balance between the Triple Alliance and the Triple Entente was roughly equal. The Germans believed they had a chance of attaining victory, but were by no means confident that they would prevail. Had the Germans faced an opposing force of overwhelming capability, they might well have been deterred. On German assessments of the balance, see Volker Berghahn, *Germany and the Approach of War in 1914* (New York: St. Martin's Press, 1973), pp. 167, 173; Fritz Fischer, *World Power or Decline: The Controversy over Germany's Aims in the First World War*, trans. Lancelot Farrar, et al. (New York: W.W. Norton, 1974), p. 26; Jack Snyder, *The Ideology of the Offensive: Military Decision Making and the Disasters of 1914* (Ithaca: Cornell University Press, 1984), pp. 112, 115, 148.

10. Works on world government include Grenville Clark and Louis Sohn, *World Peace through World Law*, 2nd ed. (Cambridge: Harvard University Press, 1960); Robert Hutchins, et al., *Preliminary Draft of a World Constitution* (Chicago: University of Chicago Press, 1947); and Wesley Wooley, *Alternatives to Anarchy: American Supranationalism since World War II* (Bloomington: Indiana University Press, 1988).

11. A considerable body of literature exists on collective security, much of it written during the

Collective security organizations can take many different institutional forms along a continuum ranging from ideal collective security to concerts.[12] These organizations vary as to number of members, geographic scope, and the nature of the commitment to collective action. What Inis Claude calls ideal collective security entails participation of all states of the world, covers all regions of the world, and involves a legally binding and codified commitment on the part of all members to respond to aggression whenever and wherever it might occur:

The scheme is collective in the fullest sense; it purports to provide security *for* all states, *by* the action of all states, *against* all states which might challenge the existing order by the arbitrary unleashing of their power. . . . Ideal collective security . . . offer[s] the certainty, backed by legal obligation, that any aggressor would be confronted with collective sanctions.[13]

---

first fifteen years of the post–World War II era. It falls into three broad categories. First, analysts sought to provide a historical account of the League of Nations and the United Nations. Research focused both on the formation of these bodies and on how they dealt—or failed to deal—with international aggression. See Richard Current, "The United States and Collective Security— Notes on the History of an Idea," in Alexander DeConde, ed., *Isolation and Security* (Durham, N.C.: Duke University Press, 1957); Gilbert Murray, *From the League to the UN* (London: Oxford University Press, 1948); F.S. Northedge, *The League of Nations: Its Life and Times, 1920–1946* (New York: Holmes and Meier, 1986); Charles Webster, *The League of Nations in Theory and Practice* (Boston: Houghton Mifflin, 1933); and Roland Stromberg, *Collective Security and American Foreign Policy: From the League of Nations to NATO* (New York: Praeger, 1963). Second, scholars attempted to address some of the underlying theoretical issues concerning how collective security operates, its relationship to the notion of balance of power, and the conditions under which it can preserve peace. See E.H. Carr, *The Twenty Years' Crisis, 1919–1939* (New York: Harper and Row, 1964); Inis Claude, *Power and International Relations*; Claude, *Swords into Plowshares* (New York: Random House, 1956); Morgenthau, *Politics Among Nations*; Roland Stromberg, "The Idea of Collective Security," *Journal of the History of Ideas*, Vol. 17 (April 1956), pp. 250–263; Kenneth Thompson, "Collective Security Re-examined," *American Political Science Review*, Vol. 47, No. 3 (September 1953), pp. 753–772; Arnold Wolfers, "Collective Defense versus Collective Security," in Arnold Wolfers, ed., *Discord and Collaboration* (Baltimore: Johns Hopkins Press, 1962); and Quincy Wright, *The Study of International Relations* (New York: Appleton-Century-Crofts, 1955). Third, research focused on evaluating collective security, and determining whether it should be pursued as a means of preserving peace or abandoned as a fundamentally flawed concept. See John Herz, *International Politics in the Atomic Age* (New York: Columbia University Press, 1959); Morgenthau, *Politics Among Nations*; Robert Osgood, "Woodrow Wilson, Collective Security, and the Lessons of History," *Confluence*, Vol. 5, No. 4 (Winter 1957), pp. 341–354; and Roland Stromberg, "The Riddle of Collective Security," in George Anderson, ed., *Issues and Conflicts: Studies in 20th Century American Diplomacy* (Lawrence: University of Kansas Press, 1959), pp. 147–167. An excellent anthology containing excerpts from many of these works is Marina Finkelstein and Lawrence Finkelstein, eds., *Collective Security* (San Francisco: Chandler Publishing Co., 1966).

12. Because a concert operates on the notion of all against one and relies on collective action to resist aggression, it falls into the collective security family. Robert Jervis refers to a concert as a "nascent collective security system." Jervis, "From Balance to Concert: A Study of International Security Cooperation," *World Politics*, Vol. 38, No. 1 (October 1985), pp. 58–59, 78.

13. Claude, *Power and International Relations*, pp. 110, 168.

An ideal collective security organization assumes a very high degree of congruent interest among its members. Inter-state rivalry and power politics are effectively eliminated. Balancing behavior occurs only in response to aggression.

A concert lies at the other end of the continuum; it represents the most attenuated form of collective security. Though predicated on the notion of all against one, membership in a concert is restricted to the great powers of the day. A small group of major powers agrees to work together to resist aggression; they meet on a regular basis to monitor events and, if necessary, to orchestrate collective initiatives. A concert's geographic scope is flexible. Members can choose to focus on a specific region or regions, or to combat aggression on a global basis. Finally, a concert entails no binding or codified commitments to collective action. Rather, decisions are taken through informal negotiations, through the emergence of a consensus. The flexibility and informality of a concert allow the structure to retain an ongoing undercurrent of balancing behavior among the major powers. Though a concert is predicated upon the assumption that its members share compatible views of a stable international order, it allows for subtle jockeying and competition to take place among them. Power politics is not completely eliminated; members may turn to internal mobilization and coalition formation to pursue divergent interests. But the cooperative framework of a concert, and its members' concern about preserving peace, prevent such balancing from escalating to overt hostility and conflict.

THE LEAGUE OF NATIONS, THE UNITED NATIONS, AND THE CONCERT OF EUROPE
In theory, the family of collective security organizations runs from those that are universal in membership, global in scope, and legally binding in terms of commitment to collective action, to those that are limited in membership, regional in scope, and non-binding as to the nature of commitments to collection action. In practice, however, none of the organizations that have been erected to date meet the requirements of ideal collective security. The League of Nations and the United Nations came closest, but both fell far short.

The League, formally established in 1920 when the Versailles Treaty came into force, was meant to include all countries and to resist aggression in all parts of the globe.[14] While all members participated in the General Assembly,

---

14. Thirty-two Allied and Associated powers attended the meeting convened to set up the

the League Council—an inner body that was to consist of five permanent members (the United States, Britain, France, Japan, and Italy) and four smaller powers serving on a rotating basis—was established to guide the operation of the organization.[15] Article 16 of the League Covenant stipulated that a state engaging in aggression "shall *ipso facto* be deemed to have committed an act of war against all other Members of the League."[16] Members would then automatically impose collective economic and diplomatic sanctions. The League Covenant was far more ambiguous on the question of joint military action. Article 10 did not bind members to respond automatically to aggression with military force.[17] Rather, the Council was to decide when the use of force was warranted and to recommend how much military capability each member should contribute to uphold the Covenant (Article 16 [2]). The Covenant also stipulated that the Council's recommendations would be authoritative only when reached unanimously.[18] This provision effectively gave each member of the Council—whether permanent or rotating—the power to exercise a veto.[19]

The United Nations, like the League, emerged in the wake of a devastating war.[20] The UN was also to be global in terms of both its membership and its geographic scope. And the UN Charter, similarly to the League Covenant, established a General Assembly while giving the major powers—the United

---

League and became its original members. Thirteen neutral states were also invited to join. By 1938, the League had grown to fifty-seven members. See Northedge, *The League of Nations*, pp. 46–47, Appendix B.

15. During the 1920s, the composition of the Council was changed. Germany was given a permanent seat and the number of rotating members was increased. See Webster, *The League of Nations*, pp. 82, 87.

16. The complete text of the League Covenant, embodying amendments in force as of February 1, 1938, can be found in Northedge, *The League of Nations*, Appendix A, pp. 317–327.

17. Article 10 of the Covenant committed members to "undertake to respect and preserve as against external aggression the territorial integrity and existing political independence of all Members of the League," but left open "the means by which this obligation shall be fulfilled."

18. The unanimity rule did not apply to members who were party to the dispute that the Council was seeking to address. See Article 15 (7). Decisions within the General Assembly, for the most part, also required unanimity, though certain issues such as membership and procedure required only a simple or a two-thirds majority. See Northedge, *The League of Nations*, p. 53.

19. Despite the fact that all Council members had this veto power, there was an implicit understanding—at least in the United States—that participation in the League involved a tacit, moral commitment to meet aggression with collective force. This view was fostered by President Wilson's own interpretation of the Covenant. See Stromberg, *Collective Security and American Foreign Policy*, p. 28; and Claude, *Power and International Relations*, pp. 173–174. The League suffered an early setback when the United States Congress refused to approve U.S. participation in the organization, in large part because of concern about entering into an obligation to engage in collective action.

20. The UN was founded in 1945 with fifty-one original members.

States, Great Britain, France, the Soviet Union, and China—considerable control over the body by making them permanent members of the Security Council, the inner body which was to guide the operation of the UN. Unlike the League Covenant, the UN Charter did not provide for automatic economic and diplomatic sanctions in response to aggression. The Charter did, however, go further than the League Covenant in establishing a mechanism through which collective military action would take place. Article 42 granted the Security Council the power to decide if and when a military response to aggressive action was warranted. Article 43 obligated member states "to make available to the Security Council, on its call and in accordance with a special agreement or agreements, armed forces, assistance, and facilities . . . necessary for the purpose of maintaining international peace and security."[21] At the same time, the Charter also granted veto power to the permanent members of the Security Council. The veto ensured that the UN's provisions for collective action could not be directed against any of the major powers, and they prevented the UN from being able to address the most serious threats to peace, disputes between the great powers.[22]

Like the League and the UN, the Concert of Europe emerged from the midst of a postwar settlement.[23] The Concert was established by Great Brit-

---

21. Efforts to negotiate agreements as to the size and nature of the contingent that each member was to keep ready and to contribute to collective action failed to produce concrete results. In this sense, Article 43 did not constitute a legally binding commitment on behalf of members to engage in collective action when requested to do so by the Security Council. See Mumullah Venkat Rao Naidu, *Collective Security and the United Nations: A Definition of the UN Security System* (New York: St. Martin's Press, 1974), p. 36. For a text of the UN Charter see Claude, *Swords into Plowshares*, pp. 463–489.

22. The UN veto provision is even more constraining than the League's unanimity rule in that all permanent members of the Security Council retain veto power regardless of whether they are party to the dispute under consideration. See Claude, *Power and International Relations*, pp. 159–165; and Naidu, *Collective Security and the United Nations*, pp. 36–41.

23. Historians differ as to the period during which the Concert operated. The Concert is commonly dated from the Congress of Vienna (1815) to the Crimean War (1854), though the Concert did exist in name until 1914. Historians also differ as to whether the 1815–54 period should be characterized as a concert or as an example of balancing under anarchy. Edward Gulick, for example, views this period as a classic example of power balancing under multipolarity. See Edward Gulick, *Europe's Classic Balance of Power* (Ithaca: Cornell University Press, 1955). Many historians and almost all political scientists, however, view the years from 1815–54 as one during which a concert clearly operated. See, for example, Paul Schroeder, "The 19th-Century International System: Changes in the Structure," *World Politics*, Vol. 39, No. 1 (October 1986), pp. 1–26; Richard Elrod, "The Concert of Europe: A Fresh Look at an International System," *World Politics*, Vol. 28, No. 2 (January 1976), pp. 159–174; Robert Jervis, "Security Regimes," *International Organization*, Vol. 36, No. 2 (Spring 1982), pp. 173–194; Robert Jervis, "From Balance to Concert"; Paul Gordon Lauren, "Crisis Prevention in Nineteenth-Century Diplomacy," in Alexander George, ed., *Managing U.S.-Soviet Rivalry: Problems of Crisis Prevention*

ain, Prussia, Russia, and Austria at the close of the Napoleonic Wars (1815). France was admitted in 1818. In contrast to the League and the UN, membership in the Concert of Europe was restricted to Europe's major powers. Nor was the Concert intended to be global in its geographic scope. Members focused on regulating relations among each other and preserving peace in Europe; they dealt with disputes in other areas only when colonial conflicts threatened to spill over into Europe. The Concert was predicated upon an understanding that each of the five powers would honor the territorial settlement reached at the Congress of Vienna in 1815. Members agreed to defend the territorial status quo, or to allow change only when they reached a consensus to do so. Collective action emerged through informal negotiations, not through formal mechanisms of the type spelled out in the League Covenant or UN Charter. Decisions were reached through consensus; there was no unanimity rule or veto. Furthermore, mechanisms for implementing collective action were left unstipulated. A British memo of 1818 captured the informality and flexibility of the understanding reached by the powers:

There is no doubt that a breach of the covenant [of the territorial system of Europe] by any one State is an injury which all the other States may, if they shall think fit, either separately or collectively resent, but the treaties do not impose, by express stipulation, the doing so as matter of positive obligation. . . . The execution of this duty [of enforcement] seems to have been deliberately left to arise out of the circumstances of the time and of the case, and the offending State to be brought to reason by such of the injured States as might at the moment think fit to charge themselves with the task of defending their own rights thus invaded.[24]

Despite or, as we will argue, *because* of its informality, the Concert of Europe was able to preserve peace in Europe for almost four decades. The Concert's impressive record is one reason why we base our model for a new collective security organization in Europe on the notion of a concert. But our preference for a concert-based organization also rests on the similarities between the

(Boulder: Westview Press, 1983), pp. 31–64; Stephen Garrett, "Nixonian Foreign Policy: A New Balance of Power—or a Revived Concert?" *Polity*, Vol. 8, No. 3 (Spring 1976), pp. 389–421. For diplomatic histories of the period see Carsten Holbraad, *The Concert of Europe: A Study in German and British International Theory, 1815–1914* (New York: Barnes and Noble, 1970), pp. 2–4; W.N. Medlicott, *Bismarck, Gladstone, and the Concert of Europe* (New York: Greenwood Press, 1969); Charles Webster, *The Foreign Policy of Castlereagh, 1812–1822* (London: G. Bell, 1963); Paul Schroeder, *Metternich's Diplomacy at Its Zenith* (New York: Greenwood Press, 1968); Alan Sked, ed., *Europe's Balance of Power, 1815–1848* (London: Macmillan, 1979).
24. British Memorandum submitted at the Conference of Aix-la-Chapelle, October 1818, cited in René Albrecht-Carrié, *The Concert of Europe* (New York: Walker, 1968), p. 37.

international conditions that gave rise to the nineteenth-century Concert and today's international setting, and on several deductive arguments about how concerts capture the peace-causing effects of collective security. Before making our case for a concert, then, we first examine the conditions that allow collective security to function, and analyze why collective security is preferable to balancing under anarchy.

THE PRECONDITIONS OF COLLECTIVE SECURITY
Three conditions must be present if a collective security organization is to take shape and function effectively.[25] One of these is a structural condition; it has to do with the international distribution of power. The other two are ideational; they have to do with the content of elite beliefs about the international environment. The first condition is that no single state can be so powerful that even the most robust opposing coalition would be unable to marshal preponderant force against it. Put differently, all states in the system must be vulnerable to collective sanctions.[26]

The second condition is that the major powers of the day must have fundamentally compatible views of what constitutes a stable and acceptable international order. There can be no revisionist power, no state intent on overturning the international order for either ideological or power-related reasons. Whether they refer to "a status quo . . . on which the nations with predominant strength agree," or to "a firm nucleus of great power agreement," virtually all students of collective security recognize that it can work only when the major powers share similar visions of international order.[27]

The third condition is that the major powers must "enjoy a minimum of political solidarity and moral community."[28] More specifically, elites must share an awareness of an international community, the preservation of which furthers long-term national interests. It is not sufficient for the major powers simply to share compatible views of a desirable international order; they must also believe that efforts to protect and promote political solidarity are needed to bring this vision of order to fruition. In this sense, national self-

---

25. These conditions are concisely enumerated by Kenneth Thompson in "Collective Security Reexamined," pp. 758–762. Although other studies of collective security often point to other preconditions, they are generally reducible to these three.
26. See Claude, *Power and International Relations*, p. 195.
27. Thompson, "Collective Security Reexamined," p. 758; Marina Finkelstein and Lawrence Finkelstein, "The Future of Collective Security," in Finkelstein and Finkelstein, *Collective Security*, p. 255.
28. Thompson, "Collective Security Reexamined," p. 761.

interest becomes equated with, but not subjugated to, the welfare and stability of that international community. In addition, elites in one state must believe that elites in other states share appreciation of this community. As Robert Jervis puts it, "the actors must also believe that the others share the value they place on mutual security and cooperation."[29] It is this minimum level of trust that allows states to pass up opportunities for short-term gain and to exercise restraint under the assumption that others will do the same. In the words of Hans Morgenthau, "collective security expects the policies of individual nations to be inspired by the ideal of mutual assistance and a spirit of self-sacrifice."[30] Before examining whether these conditions are now present in Europe—that is, whether collective security is feasible—we first examine whether it is desirable.

The Advantages of Collective Security

In this section, we present three reasons why collective security provides a more stable—that is, less war-prone—international environment than balancing under anarchy. First, collective security more effectively deters and resists aggressor states. It does so by making more likely the formation of an opposing coalition and by confronting aggressors with preponderant, as opposed to roughly equal, force. Second, collective security organizations institutionalize, and therefore promote, cooperative relations among states.[31] Third, collective security ameliorates the security dilemma and therefore reduces the likelihood that unintended spirals will lead to hostility and conflict.

MORE EFFECTIVE BALANCING AGAINST AGGRESSORS

In terms of providing for effective balancing against aggressors, collective security has two main advantages over balancing under anarchy. First, it strengthens deterrence by reducing the uncertainties of coalition formation associated with balancing under anarchy. Under anarchy, a state contemplating aggression would be uncertain about whether a balancing coalition

---

29. Jervis, "Security Regimes," pp. 176–178.
30. Morgenthau, *Politics Among Nations*, excerpted in Finkelstein and Finkelstein, *Collective Security*, pp. 222–223.
31. We use the terms collective security and collective security organization interchangeably. The notion of collective security becomes operational only when embodied in formal agreements, conferences, or other institutional mechanisms.

alliance will certainly emerge.

will take shape and about the military strength of that coalition. Collective security both increases the likelihood that a balancing coalition will form and confronts aggressors with the prospect of preponderant, rather than roughly equal, opposing force. Preponderance provides a more robust deterrent than equality and eliminates the possibility that war might result from an aggressor's misperception of the strength of the opposing coalition. Collective security by no means guarantees that a robust opposing coalition will take shape. But it does make it more likely that states will join a balancing coalition by establishing pre-existing commitments to do so. *Ceteris paribus*, a state is more likely to join an opposing coalition if it has made a commitment to do so than if no such commitment exists; states have at least some incentives to fulfill international obligations.[32] Even if the currency of international obligation fails to elicit participation, collective security would still produce a more robust opposing coalition than balancing under anarchy. Under anarchy, only those states directly threatened by the aggressor and states with vital interests in the threatened areas will band together to resist aggression. Under collective security, because states have clear interests in protecting an international order that they see as beneficial to their individual security, they will contribute to the coalition even if they have no vital interests at stake in the actual theater of aggression. As we discuss below, collective security also leads to the formation of a preponderant coalition by providing mechanisms which facilitate and reduce the transaction costs involved in collective action. By increasing both the likelihood that a balancing coalition will emerge and the likelihood that this coalition will possess preponderant military strength, collective security more effectively deters and resists aggression than balancing under anarchy.

Second, collective security facilitates identification of aggressor states. As we argue below, collective security organizations enhance transparency and encourage states to maintain relatively low levels of military—especially offensive—capability. Because of these features, it would be very difficult for a state to develop robust offensive capability without being detected.[33] Fur-

---

32. These incentives stem from two sources. First, a state may face direct economic or diplomatic sanctions for failing to fulfill its commitment to collective security. Second, a state's reputation for cooperation could be damaged, impairing its future relations with other states on a wide range of issues. For further discussion of reputational considerations, see Robert Keohane, *After Hegemony: Cooperation and Discord in the World Political Economy* (Princeton, N.J.: Princeton University Press, 1984), p. 105.

33. This discussion focuses on major aggressor states—powers with sufficient military capability

thermore, a significant military buildup would automatically be interpreted as a sign of aggressive intent, triggering a response. Identification of an aggressor would be more difficult in an anarchic setting: a military buildup undertaken to prepare for war might be interpreted by other powers as an unexceptional manifestation of arms racing and rivalry.[34] An inadequate response could result.[35] Easier identification of aggressor states makes for more timely and effective deterrence.

Critics offer two main rebuttals to the claim that collective security can provide effective deterrence against aggressors. First, they assert that nuclear weapons undermine collective security's deterrent effect because they make it impossible to marshal preponderant force against a nuclear-capable aggressor.[36] Indeed, nuclear weapons would alter the calculus of both the coalition powers defending the status quo and the aggressor state; both would be more reluctant to use force. But deterrence under collective security in a nuclear world would operate much more strongly than in a non-nuclear world. The logic of all against one would mean that an aggressor would face an opposing coalition not only of preponderant conventional force but also of preponderant nuclear capability. Nuclear weapons could embolden an aggressor in its efforts to play a game of brinkmanship; its bargaining stance would be stronger than if it did not have nuclear weapons. But an aggressor

---

to engage in significant and sustained offensive operations. We are not concerned with narrower questions, e.g., identifying which party is responsible for firing the first shot.

34. Britain's reaction to Germany's burgeoning naval program at the turn of the century is a case in point. With the First Naval Law of 1898, Germany embarked on an ambitious program to build a battleship fleet. Although the British Admiralty indeed took note of these developments in calculating naval requirements, it was not until 1904–05 that British war plans began to be reoriented to focus on the possibility of a conflict with Germany. In a collective security setting, a naval program of the size embarked upon by Germany might well have triggered far earlier a reorientation of British war plans. See Paul Kennedy, *The Rise of the Anglo-German Antagonism, 1860–1914* (London: Allen and Unwin, 1982), pp. 251–288; and Paul Kennedy, *The Rise and Fall of British Naval Mastery* (London: Macmillan, 1983), pp. 205–237.

35. Although identification of an aggressor would be easier under collective security, the initial response might be slower than under balancing under anarchy. As argued below, one of the ways in which collective security ameliorates the security dilemma is by encouraging states to tolerate initial acts of defection. In the presence of an emerging aggressor, such tolerance could prove costly: it might lead to a time lag between initial identification of aggressive behavior and an effective response. The wariness associated with balancing under anarchy would, *ceteris paribus*, reduce this lag. However, given high levels of transparency and low initial levels of offensive capability, the lag associated with collective security is not likely to be consequential. Aggressors would enjoy only a quite limited head-start. On the question of time lags and identification of aggressors, see Wolfers, "Collective Defense versus Collective Security," pp. 184, 188 (reprinted in Finkelstein and Finkelstein, *Collective Security*, pp. 128–140).

36. See, for example, Herz, *International Politics in the Atomic Age*, excerpted in Finkelstein and Finkelstein, *Collective Security*, p. 251.

in a nuclear world would be less likely to follow through with military attack than in a non-nuclear world because it would face not only conventional defeat, but also nuclear devastation. Far from undermining deterrence based on preponderant force, nuclear weapons, by raising the potential costs of aggression, should enhance the stabilizing effects of collective security.

The second argument that critics use to challenge collective security's ability to provide robust deterrence stems from the tarnished histories of the League of Nations and the United Nations. The League's failure to respond to successive bouts of aggression during the 1930s, and the UN's marginal significance during the postwar era, it is argued, provide adequate proof that collective security organizations are unable to prevent or even to respond adequately to aggression.[37]

This line of argument is unfounded; the League and the UN might have failed to preserve peace, but the historical record suggests that military, economic, and political conditions at the national level, not collective security itself, were the root of the problem. Without question, the League of Nations failed to organize an effective response to repeated Japanese and German violations of international treaty commitments. It is unjustified, however, to blame the absence of a more timely response on the League or on collective security more generally. The core of the problem was the unwillingness of the major powers to act decisively, not the existence of the League itself.[38] Particular, historically-contingent circumstances—American isolationism, economic and military weakness in Britain and France, British revulsion against involvement in another continental war—were key in delaying a more timely and activist response.[39] It is hard to imagine that had the League not existed, these powers would have been any more inclined to take preemptive

---

37. See, for example, Raymond Aron's comments on the experiences of the United Nations in "Limits to the Powers of the United Nations," *Annals of the American Academy of Political and Social Sciences*, Vol. 296 (November 1954), pp. 20–26 (reprinted in Finkelstein and Finkelstein, *Collective Security*, pp. 239–241).

38. We do admit that the League may have fostered free riding. The mere existence of the League, by enabling the British and French to delude themselves into believing that others would provide for their security, may have contributed to the absence of a more timely and effective response to German and Japanese aggression. This dynamic, however, certainly played a minor role in inhibiting a more appropriate response to rising threats.

39. On the causes of the failure of Britain and France to respond in a more timely fashion see R.P. Shay, *British Rearmament in the 1930s* (Princeton, N.J.: Princeton University Press, 1977); Michael Howard, *The Continental Commitment* (London: Temple Smith, 1972); and Jean Doise and Maurice Vaïsse, *Diplomatie et Outil Militaire, 1871–1969* (Paris: Imprimerie Nationale, 1987).

action against either Japan or Germany. As Roland Stromberg has argued, the failure of the status quo powers to preserve peace during the 1930s "can be explained wholly without reference to the League. . . . The lamentable weakness of the powers opposed to Germany and Japan is of course the key to the period, but it has nothing to do with an abstraction called collective security."[40]

As far as the United Nations is concerned, the core of the problem was that U.S.-Soviet wartime cooperation almost immediately gave way to peacetime discord. The United Nations was formed under the assumption that the two countries emerging from World War II with predominant military capabilities could cooperate in forging a postwar order.[41] But even as the UN was coming into being, the United States and the Soviet Union were pursuing conflicting goals, making collective security untenable. The Cold War era does not represent a legitimate test of collective security because one of the key preconditions was missing: American and Soviet visions of an acceptable international order were simply incompatible.[42] Commitments to collective security were repeatedly challenged—and superseded—by the rivalry and hostility associated with the Cold War.[43] The histories of the League and the UN demonstrate only that collective security does not always work, not that it cannot work.

In addition, the history of the Concert of Europe demonstrates that timely and adequate balancing can in fact occur under collective security. As we illustrate below, Concert members repeatedly resorted to joint diplomatic initiatives, military threats and military action to preserve peace in Europe. The historical record thus tells us that it would be unwarranted to dismiss collective security on the claim that it cannot provide adequate balancing against aggression. We have no reason to doubt the deductive case for the claim that balancing under collective security more effectively deters and stops aggression than balancing under anarchy.

---

40. Stromberg, "The Idea of Collective Security," excerpted in Finkelstein and Finkelstein, *Collective Security,* pp. 233–234.
41. On the views of the Roosevelt administration toward the UN and cooperation with the Soviet Union, see Daniel Yergin, *Shattered Peace: The Origins of the Cold War and the National Security State* (Boston: Houghton Mifflin, 1977), pp. 47–48; and John Lewis Gaddis, *The United States and the Origins of the Cold War, 1941–1947* (New York: Columbia University Press, 1972), pp. 28–31.
42. Inis Claude, "The UN and the Use of Force," *International Conciliation,* No. 532 (March 1961), pp. 325–384 (reprinted in Finkelstein and Finkelstein, *Collective Security,* p. 100).
43. See Wolfers, "Collective Defense versus Collective Security."

INSTITUTIONALIZING AND PROMOTING COOPERATION

A popular criticism of collective security is that it works only when it is not needed. If the conditions for collective security—great power compatibility, a shared sense of international community—are present, critics charge, then a security structure is not needed to preserve peace.[44] Our second argument about the advantages of collective security directly challenges this criticism. We claim that a collective security organization can strengthen and deepen the foundation of cooperative behavior that makes collective security feasible to begin with. We base this claim on the neo-liberal assertion that regimes promote cooperation. Regimes are "sets of implicit or explicit principles, norms, rules, and decision-making procedures around which actors' expectations converge in a given area of international relations."[45] Institutions and organizations are formalized regimes, usually embodied in more explicit and rigorous rules and decision-making procedures. If the neo-liberal argument holds, then a collective security organization, by building on and promoting the political compatibility that makes such an institution possible, may perpetuate and make more durable a peaceful and desirable international setting. As Robert Keohane notes, regimes arise from, but also produce, cooperation: "Although regimes themselves depend on conditions that are conducive to interstate agreements, they may also facilitate further efforts to coordinate policies."[46]

Realists challenge the notion that institutions markedly increase the likelihood of inter-state cooperation. Under anarchy, they claim, "international institutions affect the prospects for cooperation only marginally."[47] The difficulties involved in obtaining security in a self-help environment tend to override the potential cooperation-inducing effects of international institutions. As Joseph Grieco has convincingly argued, because states are fearful that others will exploit their cooperative behavior, and because they are concerned primarily with relative as opposed to absolute gains, cooperation under anarchy is difficult to achieve even in the presence of robust institutions.[48]

---

44. See, for example, Stromberg, "The Riddle of Collective Security," pp. 165–167.
45. See Stephen Krasner, *International Regimes* (Ithaca, N.Y.: Cornell University Press, 1983), p. 2.
46. Keohane, *After Hegemony*, p. 57.
47. Grieco, "Anarchy and the Limits of Cooperation," p. 488.
48. Ibid., pp. 485–507.

While the Realist critique of regime theory indeed has some validity, its claims weaken markedly as anarchy is mitigated. We contend that the ability of institutions to promote cooperation increases substantially as consensual beliefs among the major powers dampen the rivalries and insecurities of a Hobbesian setting. When inter-state cooperation has already begun to emerge because of shifts in elite beliefs, and the Realist assumptions of a competitive, self-help world are thus relaxed, a fertile ground exists for institutions to play a much more prominent role in shaping state behavior. States are less concerned about being exploited. They are more free to pursue absolute as opposed to relative gains.[49] Under these conditions, neo-liberal arguments about the cooperation-inducing effects of institutions become all the more compelling.

In general terms, institutions promote cooperation by clarifying and operationalizing a set of norms, rules, principles, and procedures that guide state behavior and allow for increased coordination of policy. Rules and procedures create a road-map; they define a range of behavior associated with the notion of cooperation and provide states with a set of instructions for preserving a cooperative setting. Institutions also alter a state's expectations about how other states will behave in the future and about how its own behavior will affect the future behavior of other states. States become more willing to cooperate because they assume others will do the same.[50]

In more specific terms, institutions can promote and deepen cooperation through several discrete mechanisms. First, they increase the level of information available to all parties. Even if states have compatible interests, peace may not be stable under anarchy because of the difficulties and costs involved in gathering complete information.[51] Incomplete and asymmetrical information increases uncertainty about the intentions and capabilities of other states, thus heightening fear of exploitation. A collective security organization could disseminate information on force levels and force postures to reassure mem-

---

49. We admit that uncertainty about the future will always make states somewhat concerned about gaps in payoffs that affect their relative position in the international system. But, as Grieco notes, sensitivity to these gaps declines as inter-state relations become more cooperative. See ibid., p. 501.

50. Robert Axelrod and Robert Keohane, "Achieving Cooperation Under Anarchy: Strategies and Institutions," *World Politics*, Vol. 38, No. 1 (October 1985), p. 234; and Krasner, *International Regimes*.

51. For discussion of how uncertainty and incomplete information affect cooperation, see Keohane, *After Hegemony*, pp. 92–97, 100–103.

bers that no party is preparing to engage in aggressive action. Similarly, institutions increase the effectiveness and lower the costs of monitoring and verifying inter-state agreements. In short, institutionalization increases transparency—the sharing of information—and in so doing promotes cooperation. Second, institutions increase the costs of defection—and help define what constitutes defection—by formalizing punishment regimes and making them more effective.[52] By creating mechanisms for punishing defectors, institutions increase the likelihood that states will incur considerable costs if they ue non-cooperative behavior. As a result, states contemplating defection will be more likely to be dissuaded from doing so, and states defending the status quo will be less fearful of exploitation and thus more willing to pursue cooperative strategies.[53] An institution would thus enhance collective security's deterrent effect and reinforce its ability to encourage states to practice restraint and self-sacrifice.

Third, institutions can promote cooperation by increasing the likelihood that issue-linkage will lead to international agreements. Institutions bring many different issues into one negotiating forum. Even if states disagree on a specific issue, they may be able to resolve the dispute through reciprocal concessions: one side gives ground on the issue under consideration in return for concessions on some other issue. Institutions also facilitate such arrangements by reducing the transaction costs associated with the negotiation of international agreements. As Robert Keohane puts it, "insofar as their [regimes'] principles and rules can be applied to a wide variety of particular issues, they are efficient: establishing the rules and principles at the outset makes it unnecessary to renegotiate them each time a specific question arises."[54]

Fourth, institutions hold the potential to promote inter-state socialization, to transform a "minimum of political solidarity" into an international community in which states share similar values and normative orientations.[55] Regular meetings and conferences allow ideas and values to cross national boundaries and circulate among different communities of elites. Similarity of

---

52. Defection can take two forms under collective security. First, states might engage in acts of aggression. Second, states might renege on their commitment to resist aggression through collective action. A formalized punishment regime increases the costs of both types of defection.
53. In Keohane's words, "regimes make it more sensible to cooperate by lowering the likelihood of being double-crossed"; *After Hegemony*, p. 97.
54. See Keohane, *After Hegemony*, pp. 90–91; see also pp. 89–92.
55. See G. John Ikenberry and Charles Kupchan, "Socialization and Hegemonic Power," *International Organization*, Vol. 44, No. 3 (Summer 1990), pp. 283–316.

values is conducive to compatible policy preferences.[56] In the early post–World War II years, the network of institutions erected to coordinate policies within the Western alliance played an important role in spreading among the allies the norms associated with liberal multilateralism. The spread of these norms in turn facilitated coordination of national policies.[57] Institutions operating under conditions of mitigated anarchy can thus promote cooperation by deepening the normative and ideational basis of an international community of nations.

These four mechanisms through which institutions promote cooperation counter the charge that a collective security organization is not needed if the conditions that make it possible are present. On the contrary, a peaceful international setting only increases the role that institutions can play in shaping state behavior. Taking concrete steps to perpetuate a peaceful international environment makes far more sense than simply hoping that such an environment will persist of its own accord.

AMELIORATING THE SECURITY DILEMMA

The third major advantage of collective security over balancing under anarchy is its ability to ameliorate the security dilemma. The security dilemma refers to the notion that a state's efforts to increase its security, by threatening another state which then responds with steps to increase its own security, paradoxically erodes the first state's security.[58] The two states, without intending to do so, thus find themselves in a spiral of mounting hostility and arms buildup. The intensity with which the security dilemma operates depends upon a number of conditions: the degree of trust between states, the extent to which uncertainty and incomplete information produce misperception of intentions, whether offensive or defensive forces would have the advantage, and whether states can distinguish between others' offensive and

---

56. There are two related arguments within the literature as to how the dissemination of ideas and beliefs promotes international cooperation. One tradition holds that institutions spread certain beliefs and normative ideals that guide states toward the pursuit of common goals. See, for example, John Ruggie, "International Regimes, Transaction, and Change: Embedded Liberalism in the Postwar Economic Order," in Krasner, *International Regimes*, pp. 193–231. The other tradition suggests that institutions spread "consensual knowledge," which facilitates cooperation. See, for example, Ernst Haas, "Why Collaborate? Issue-Linkage and International Regimes," *World Politics*, Vol. 32, No. 3 (April 1980), pp. 357–405.
57. Ikenberry and Kupchan, "Socialization and Hegemonic Power," pp. 299–303.
58. See Robert Jervis, "Cooperation Under the Security Dilemma," *World Politics*, Vol. 30, No. 2 (January 1978), pp. 167–214.

defensive armaments.[59] The operation of the security dilemma is one of the key reasons that peace under anarchy may not be stable. Even if no states have explicitly aggressive intentions, anarchy fuels the security dilemma and can produce spirals that lead to growing hostility and, ultimately, to conflict.

As Jervis notes, it is impossible to eliminate the security dilemma, but it can be ameliorated: "The ideal solution for a status quo power would be to escape from the state of nature. But escape is impossible. The security dilemma cannot be abolished, it can only be ameliorated. Bonds of shared values and interests can be developed. If actors care about what happens to others and believe that others care about them, they will develop trust and can cooperate for mutual benefit."[60] The conditions that make collective security possible indeed ameliorate the security dilemma to a certain extent. When the major powers hold compatible views of an acceptable international order and share a minimum sense of political community, ideational change has already mitigated the suspicion and competitiveness that fuel the security dilemma. But capitalizing on the presence of these conditions to create a collective security organization is to take further important steps to dampen the sources of unintended spirals.

Collective security ameliorates the security dilemma in four important ways. First, a collective security organization, through the mechanisms outlined in the previous section, promotes and deepens cooperation. Over time, repeated acts of cooperation alter expectations and foster trust and confidence. As states come to expect each other to reciprocate concessions, rather than to exploit them, the wariness that fuels the security dilemma gradually subsides. Fear of exploitation gives way to increasing willingness to practice self-restraint and mutual assistance. Furthermore, an institution promotes the dissemination of values and normative orientations. Collective security thus helps as Jervis writes, to build the "bonds of shared values and interests" that play a key role in ameliorating the security dilemma.

Second, collective security ameliorates the security dilemma by dampening concern about demonstrating resolve. One of the sources of instability associated with balancing under anarchy stems from the tendency of states to seek to strengthen deterrence by engaging in actions intended primarily to bolster a reputation for resolve. Deterrence under anarchy is weakened by a

---

59. Jervis, "Cooperation Under the Security Dilemma"; and Jervis, *Perception and Misperception in International Politics*, pp. 58–113.
60. Jervis, *Perception and Misperception*, pp. 82–83.

potential aggressor's uncertainty about the likelihood of coalition formation. States, even if not faced with imminent threats, therefore have incentives to strengthen deterrence by behaving in ways that demonstrate to potential adversaries that adequate balancing will take place.[61] Such behavior fuels the security dilemma. Actions which one side takes to demonstrate resolve are interpreted by the other side as aggressive acts challenging its own resolve and therefore potentially threatening its core security interests. Collective security, by reducing the uncertainties associated with balancing under anarchy, dampens the need to bolster resolve to make deterrence more credible.[62] Moreover, deterrence under collective security will be most credible when a potential aggressor believes that other states will honor the commitment to collective action and participate in the formation of a cohesive and robust opposing coalition. Given that reassurance and mutual assistance are the key instruments that foster cohesion under collective security, states worried about strengthening deterrence will seek to develop a reputation for cooperation and self-sacrifice, not intransigence.[63]

This logic suggests that, under collective security, states will less frequently engage in actions intended to bolster a reputation for resolve. In addition, even when states do engage in such actions, they are less likely to elicit a response in kind. Because status quo powers are not preoccupied with protecting their own reputations for resolve, relatively minor shifts in the military balance, in the tenor of diplomatic relations, and even in territorial boundaries are less likely to be seen as threats to core security.[64] Collective security allows states to develop a certain degree of immunity toward isolated devel-

---

61. American involvement in Third World conflicts during the Cold War was in large part motivated by a perceived need to demonstrate resolve in the periphery, lest the Soviets be encouraged by U.S. inaction to challenge core American interests. See Robert Johnson, "Exaggerating America's Stakes in Third World Conflicts," *International Security*, Vol. 10, No. 1 (Winter 1984/85), pp. 32–68; and John Lewis Gaddis, *Strategies of Containment: A Critical Appraisal of Postwar American National Security Policy* (Oxford: Oxford University Press, 1982), esp. pp. 198–273.

62. This assumes, of course, that no aggression has taken place. Collective security organizations as a unit must indeed be concerned about their own reputation for action. Failure to respond to major acts of aggression would weaken deterrence by indicating that future acts of aggression might also go unanswered.

63. As Keohane notes, states wanting to promote collective activity want to develop a reputation for keeping their commitments: "Governments will decide whom to make agreements with, and on what terms, largely on the basis of their expectations about their partners' willingness and ability to keep their commitments. A good reputation makes it easier for a government to enter into advantageous international agreements; tarnishing that reputation imposes costs by making agreements more difficult to reach." Keohane, *After Hegemony*, pp. 105–106.

64. On this point, see Jervis, *Perception and Misperception*, pp. 102–107.

opments and changes in the strategic setting that would, under anarchy, have far greater reverberations. Collective security thus ameliorates the security dilemma by making demonstrations of resolve less likely and by decreasing the chances that such demonstrations, when they occur, snowball into major confrontations.

Third, collective security, by increasing transparency and thereby reducing uncertainty and the chances of misperception, decreases the likelihood of unintended spirals. Uncertainty is one of the key factors fueling the security dilemma. When faced with incomplete information about the intentions and capabilities of others, states are forced to remain on guard, to prepare for the worst case. The difficulties involved in interpreting the behavior of others leaves much room for misperception. Uncertainty and incomplete information thus provide fertile ground for unintended spirals.[65] Collective security increases transparency and therefore reduces the likelihood of misperception. Provided with more complete information, states would also have higher confidence in their assessment of others' intentions and capabilities. Accidents and garbled communication would therefore be less likely to trigger an escalation of hostility.[66]

Fourth, collective security ameliorates the security dilemma by enabling states to adopt predominantly defensive military postures. Under collective security, states would need to maintain some level of offensive capability to make credible the threat to counter aggression through collective action. But they would not need offensive capabilities robust enough to carry out major acts of aggression.[67] States do not need robust offense because deterrence is easier under collective security. States are less worried about demonstrating resolve through projecting force to protect third parties, nor do they need to deter through the threat of offensive retaliation. Anarchy, on the other hand, tends to produce robust offensive capabilities.[68] In an anarchic setting, states believe that they need offense to deter potential adversaries through the

---

65. See Jervis, *Perception and Misperception*, pp. 67–82.
66. See Jervis, "From Balance to Concert," pp. 73–76.
67. See Chalmers, "Beyond the Alliance System," p. 240. As Chalmers notes, the offensive capability that the major powers would maintain as a matter of course would be sufficient to invade smaller states. But they would not need sufficient capability to invade each other.
68. In an anarchic setting, all states could conceivably adopt exclusively defensive military postures. If they believed that they could build impenetrable defenses, states might simply barricade themselves in to cope with a threatening and unpredictable international setting. But the competitive environment associated with an anarchic setting is, in reality, likely to produce far more robust offensive capabilities than the more cooperative setting associated with collective security.

prospect of retaliation and to bolster reputations for resolve. Settings in which forces are more offensive in nature are more war-prone than those in which forces are predominantly defensive in nature.[69] States that acquire offensive capability, even if for defensive purposes, threaten their neighbors and thereby induce spirals. The existence of offensively postured forces also creates incentives for preemption; each side wants to take advantage of its offensive orientation. Offensive doctrinal and tactical considerations serve to shorten the fuse.[70] It follows that collective security would ameliorate the security dilemma and enhance stability by reducing the level of offensive capability that states find it prudent to sustain.[71]

To summarize, the advantages of collective security over balancing under anarchy are three-fold. First, collective security more effectively deters and resists aggressor states by making more likely the formation of a balancing coalition and by confronting aggressors with the prospect of preponderant, as opposed to roughly equal, force. Second, collective security institutionalizes, and therefore promotes, cooperation. Third, collective security ameliorates the security dilemma, thereby enhancing stability and reducing the likelihood of unintended spirals of hostility.

The Case for Concert-Based Collective Security

The preceding section showed why collective security can provide a more stable international environment than balancing under anarchy. The analysis was not meant to suggest, however, that collective security has no shortcomings that could jeopardize its ability to foster a peaceful international order. On the contrary, collective security, when operationalized, can fall prey to several types of problems that could impair its ability to preserve peace. We begin this section by considering some of the critical weaknesses associated with ideal collective security. We then argue that a concert-based structure

69. See Snyder, *The Ideology of the Offensive;* and Stephen Van Evera, "The Cult of the Offensive and the Origins of the First World War," *International Security,* Vol. 9, No. 1 (Summer 1984), pp. 58–107.
70. For a succinct review of the reasons why offense-dominance makes more war likely, see Van Evera, "Primed for Peace," pp. 11–12.
71. A collective security organization, by increasing transparency, would also make it easier to distinguish between the offensive and defensive capabilities sustained by other states. While it is sometimes impossible to determine whether a given weapon is offensive or defensive (or both) in nature, transparency can provide information on force postures, logistics, bridging equipment, and other indicators of offensive capability. Assurances that others have only moderate offensive capability allows states to limit their own offensive capability.

offers many of the advantages outlined above without falling prey to these weaknesses. Finally, we argue that a concert can function successfully in today's international conditions because the features of the nineteenth-century international setting that gave rise to the Concert of Europe are again present. We also show why a contemporary concert is likely to be even more durable and effective in preserving peace than the nineteenth-century Concert.

WEAKNESSES OF IDEAL COLLECTIVE SECURITY

Ideal collective security organizations are distinguished by two features: their inclusivity and the automatic, codified, and binding nature of the commitment their members make to resist collectively acts of aggression. Both features impair the successful functioning of collective security. Inclusivity is problematic because it leads to a large membership and therefore makes political cohesion more difficult to sustain. The greater the number of states in a collective security organization, the greater the probability that disagreements will emerge over what constitutes aggression and when to engage in collective action. Political cohesion would be especially difficult to maintain if the body included states that occupy radically different positions within the international hierarchy of power. Minor powers and major powers may well have differing views of what constitutes an acceptable, just status quo. Even when members reach agreement on these matters, the logistical problems involved in coordinating policies among states can hamper timely, effective action. Large organizations are also more likely to fall prey to what Mancur Olson has called the collective action problem.[72] In large groups that form to provide a collective good, each member has incentives to free-ride rather than contribute to the provision of the good in question. A collective security organization provides a public good, stopping aggression. Each state benefits from deterring or defeating an aggressor regardless of the amount of resources that it commits to the opposing coalition. Because of free-riding, an organization with many members is likely to under-produce the public good in question. The sheer size of ideal collective security organizations

---

72. See Mancur Olson, *The Logic of Collective Action* (Cambridge: Harvard University Press, 1965); Mancur Olson and Richard Zeckhauser, "An Economic Theory of Alliances," *Review of Economics and Statistics*, Vol. 48, No. 3 (August 1966), pp. 266–279; Keohane, *After Hegemony*, pp. 75–79; and Charles Kupchan, "NATO and the Persian Gulf: Examining Intra-Alliance Behavior," *International Organization*, Vol. 42, No. 2 (Spring 1988), pp. 317–346.

thus militates against political cohesion and exacerbates the collective action problem.

Automatic and binding commitments to collective action have several problematic implications. First, fear of being dragged into a war whenever and wherever aggression occurs makes it less likely that states will be willing to participate in a collective security organization. A commitment viewed as automatic and legally binding constitutes too severe a loss of national autonomy. Second, codified stipulations that bind members automatically to undertake collective action potentially open the organization to obsolescence when conflicts of members' interests emerge. If acts of aggression go unanswered or if some members opt out of collective action, the credibility of the organization is jeopardized.[73] Third, codified and binding commitments to stop aggression explicitly stipulate when collective action can and should take place, but also implicitly stipulate when it should not. Ideal collective security would delay balancing against a rising aggressor state by effectively allowing collective action to take place only after a legally defined act of aggression has occurred.[74] While an ideal collective security organization could authorize diplomatic steps to warn a potential aggressor to desist from making war preparations, preemptive military action would not be allowed. This attribute prevents states from taking timely action to stop aggression before it occurs, a serious shortcoming given that it is often less costly to prevent aggression than it is to undo it.

Codified stipulations that delay directed balancing have one final important implication. One of the drawbacks associated with all forms of collective security is that member states, because they rely on *collective* action to resist aggression, individually risk being unprepared to meet an aggressor should a balancing coalition fail to form. States maintain a lower level of preparedness than they would in a self-help environment. Ideal collective security, because it delays directed balancing, means that member states find out only after aggression has already occurred how robust the opposing coalition will

---

73. Deterrence may be undermined as potential aggressors begin to doubt the efficacy of collective security arrangements. Status quo powers may begin to defect from the organization, fearful that it will not meet their security needs. The League of Nations, for example, suffered a serious setback when it failed to block Japanese aggression in Northeast Asia in the early 1930s. According to Northedge, "the League's failure to halt Japan's annexation of Manchuria in 1931–33 and to restore to China what was hers by right was by every test a grave, almost fatal blow . . . to the League." Northedge, *The League of Nations*, p. 161.

74. In Naidu's words, "aggression has to be determined first before releasing the mechanism of sanctions." Naidu, *Collective Security and the United Nations*, p. 20.

actually be. At that point, it may be too late for threatened states to marshal the resources necessary to protect themselves. The later the test of commitments to collective action, the greater the risk that states will find themselves dangerously exposed if a collective security organization unravels.

ADVANTAGES OF A CONCERT

The design of a concert circumvents the flaws of ideal collective security. A concert's small membership facilitates timely joint decision making. A concert is open only to major powers; disagreements are less likely when fewer states interact.[75] A concert's small membership also ameliorates the collective action problem. In small groups, a few powers jointly provide the good in question because it is in their interests to do so. They behave as an oligopoly: they provide the public good while monitoring and reacting strategically to each other's behavior. As Keohane puts it, regimes "are often most useful when relatively few like-minded countries are responsible for both making the essential rules and maintaining them."[76]

Though predicated on the notion of all against one, a concert does not entail codified and automatic commitments to collective action. In addition, a concert functions through an informal decision-making process in which collective action emerges from consensus. A concert's informal decision structure and lack of codification enhance the body's flexibility and resilience. Members do not expect that all instances of aggression will necessarily elicit a collective response. In instances in which one or more states prefer not to engage in collective action, they may be able to justify their abstention and refrain from participation without alienating other members or undermining the foundation of the concert.[77] Acts of aggression can go unanswered with-

---

75. While disagreements can certainly occur in small groups, they are likely to occur less frequently than in large groups.

76. Keohane, *After Hegemony*, pp. 246, 76. For further discussion of why small groups can overcome the collective action problem, see Duncan Snidal, "The Limits of Hegemonic Stability Theory," *International Organization*, Vol. 39, No. 1 (Autumn 1985), pp. 579–614; and Kenneth Oye, "Explaining Cooperation Under Anarchy: Hypotheses and Strategies," *World Politics*, Vol. 38, No. 1 (October 1985), pp. 18–20.

77. Consider the following example from the nineteenth-century Concert. In 1820, rebels calling for political liberalization staged an uprising in Naples. King Ferdinand I responded by granting a constitution. Austria, Prussia, and Russia saw these developments as a threat to conservative regimes in Europe and called a series of conferences. Metternich urged the British to participate in suppressing the revolt, but Castlereagh declined. But, although he initially stood in Metternich's way, Castlereagh eventually came to recognize that Austria had special interests in the area and he pledged to support the actions of Austria, Prussia, and Russia "provided only that they were ready to give every reasonable assurance that their views were not directed to

out eroding the credibility of the organization. In fact, concerts play as important a role in orchestrating inaction as in coordinating collective initiatives. By serving as a forum in which the major powers can make mutual pledges of self-restraint, the body can moderate competition for influence in strategic areas and defuse or, in some cases, prevent great power intervention and conflict.[78]

A concert also retains a subtle undercurrent of competitive balancing and jockeying among its members. This attribute means that divergences of opinion and conflicts of interest not resolved through negotiation will trigger a set of balancing mechanisms, rather than paralyzing and undermining the body, as they would if a veto or unanimity rule existed. Sometimes such balancing occurs simply through applying diplomatic pressure. Other times, temporary coalitions may form. In more extreme circumstances, an offending power may even be temporarily excluded from the concert until its behavior conforms to what is considered acceptable by the other members.[79] The

purposes of aggrandisement subversive of the Territorial System of Europe." Circular Despatch to British Missions at Foreign Courts, January 19, 1821, cited in Albrecht-Carrié, *The Concert of Europe*, p. 50. See also Jervis, "Security Regimes," pp. 180–181. Austria, with the authorization of Russia and Prussia, proceeded to send troops to Naples, where they promptly put down the uprising. See Lauren, "Crisis Prevention," p. 47.

78. During the nineteenth-century Concert, members established special intermediary bodies to avoid conflict in contested areas. Buffer zones were used to separate rival powers physically. Neutral zones were established in areas of particular strategic importance in order to preempt competition for their control. Demilitarized zones were used to reduce the likelihood of armed conflict in other potentially contested areas. See Lauren, "Crisis Prevention," pp. 37, 39; and Schroeder, "The 19th-Century International System," pp. 18–20.

79. In 1833–34, for example, an informal alliance of Britain and France lined up against Russia, Prussia, and Austria over the question of Unkiar-Skelessi and Russian predominance at Constantinople. See Paul Schroeder, "Alliances, 1815–1945: Weapons of Power and Tools of Management," in Klaus Knorr, ed., *Historical Dimensions of National Security Problems* (Lawrence: University of Kansas Press, 1976), p. 234. The Concert's handling of the Egyptian Crisis of 1839–41 is another case in point. The crisis revolved around a struggle between Mehemet Ali, the Viceroy of Egypt, and the Sultan, ruler of the Ottoman Empire, for control over Egypt. France, hoping to enhance its position in the Middle East, stood behind Mehemet Ali. The four other Concert members, fearful that the disintegration of the Ottoman Empire would have destabilizing consequences in Europe, backed the Sultan. The four powers banded together against France, excluded the French from the meeting convened in London to deal with the crisis, and authorized the dispatch of British troops to the Middle East. The revolt was soon suppressed. France had little choice but to accept the outcome. Soon after the defeat of Mehemet Ali, Louis Philippe sent a note to the four powers declaring that "the spontaneous actions of several of the signatory Powers [of the Concert] . . . are evidence to us that we should not find them in disagreement with our view. . . . France wishes to maintain the European equilibrium, the care of which is the responsibility of all the Great Powers. Its preservation must be their glory and their main ambition." Cited in Albrecht-Carrié, *The Concert of Europe*, p. 142. For a summary of the crisis see ibid., pp. 129–151.

cooperative framework of a concert and members' interests in preserving peace ensure that subtle balancing does not turn into deliberate exploitation or unintended spirals.[80]

This undercurrent of balancing also combats three other shortcomings of ideal collective security. First, it allows, and in fact encourages, pre-aggression deterrence. Subtle jockeying among members, in combination with the absence of codified agreements stipulating aggression as a necessary condition for collective action, allow a balancing coalition to form as soon as aggressive intent becomes manifest, not only after aggression has already occurred. A concert thus enables members to deter potential aggressors not only through the prospect of countervailing force, but also by taking concrete steps—emergency meetings, sanctions, mobilization of forces, even preemptive action—to deter and resist aggression. Second, this undercurrent of competitive balancing ameliorates the problems of buck-passing and free-riding. Subtle and ongoing balancing among concert members induces them to sustain a prudent degree of watchfulness and readiness. Concerts by no means eliminate free-riding. But by edging a step closer to a self-help environment, they make it less attractive than under ideal collective security for states to depend heavily on others to meet their defense needs. Third, this same watchfulness means that states are less likely to find themselves dangerously exposed if others forgo their commitment to collective security. Because pre-aggression measures are likely to be implemented, the fracture of an opposing coalition, if it is to occur, is likely to happen earlier, not only after aggression has occurred. Individual states will have a better sense of who their ultimate allies will be and how much they will contribute to collective action. This attribute decreases the likelihood that states, when they eventually confront imminent threats, will find themselves unprepared with few allies to come to their aid.[81]

---

80. During the nineteenth-century Concert, members developed several mechanisms to dampen spirals. They sought to fence off regional conflict. Members undertook efforts to resolve colonial disputes and to ensure that heated disputes in the periphery, when unavoidable, not be allowed to spill over into Europe. See Schroeder, "The 19th-Century International System," pp. 14–15. Concert members also established spheres of influence, recognizing that each of the major powers, for historic and geographic reasons, had special prerogatives in certain areas. See Garrett, "Nixonian Foreign Policy," p. 415; and Lauren, "Crisis Prevention," pp. 43–44.

81. The outbreak of the Crimean War in 1854 raises questions about the Concert's ability to prevent conflict among its members. On the surface, it appears that the threat of collective action was insufficient to deter Russia from demanding a degree of influence over the Ottoman Empire that was unacceptable to the other Concert members. France and Britain thus had to intervene to protect the Sultan. A closer historical reading, however, suggests that the series of

A concert indeed has its own set of drawbacks. Because concerts are an attenuated form of collective security—one which retains an undercurrent of ongoing balancing—some of the advantages associated with ideal collective security are less pronounced. The absence of a binding commitment to collective action may weaken deterrence. Potential aggressors may be more uncertain about the likelihood that a balancing coalition will emerge.[82] But a concert would still pose a considerably stronger deterrent than balancing under anarchy; a commitment to collective action—albeit an informal one— would be in place. A concert would also be less effective than ideal collective security in ameliorating the security dilemma. Because a concert retains subtle balancing and an undercurrent of competitive behavior, member states may be more concerned with preserving reputations of resolve. States might maintain more robust offensive capabilities. Unintended spirals might be more likely than under ideal collective security. But concerts still substantially moderate the security dilemma when compared to balancing under anarchy. In these respects, a concert is thus a compromise, but one well worth making, given that it provides an attractive alternative to balancing under anarchy without falling prey to the shortcomings of ideal collective security.

---

revolutions that swept Europe in 1848 effectively brought the Concert to an end and played a key role in precipitating the outbreak of the Crimean War. These revolutions had a devastating effect upon the Concert system for three main reasons. First, they installed a new generation of leaders, many of whom had not been socialized into the norms upon which the Concert was predicated. Second, upheaval politicized the public and fostered a domestic political milieu in which elites increasingly resorted to external success as a means of securing internal cohesion and order. Third, revolution jolted the international status quo in Europe and precipitated a revival of the nationalistic competition and power politics that characterized the pre-1815 era. For a concise review of these events see Anthony Wood, *Europe, 1815–1960* (Harlow: Longman, 1984), pp. 118–152. From this perspective, the cause of the Crimean War was not Russian aggression. On the contrary, the core of the problem was that, despite Austria's earnest efforts to arbitrate the dispute and Russia's willingness to make concessions, Britain and France were predisposed toward going to war, largely for domestic reasons. See Paul Schroeder, *Austria, Great Britain, and the Crimean War: The Destruction of the European Concert* (Ithaca, N.Y.: Cornell University Press, 1972), pp. xii, 136; Norman Rich, *Why the Crimean War? A Cautionary Tale* (Hanover, N.H.: University Press of New England, 1985), pp. 36, 48ff, 57ff, 63–64, 226; John Shelton Curtiss, *Russia's Crimean War* (Durham, N.C.: Duke University Press, 1979), pp. 50, 236. In essence, then, the Crimean War confirmed, rather than caused, the end of the Concert. Europe's major powers confronted each other on the battlefield for the first time since the Napoleonic Wars because the revolutions of 1848 had effectively undermined the conditions necessary for the Concert to function successfully.

82. Deductive analysis of the impact of ideal collective security and concerts on free riding is indeterminate. Ideal collective security, by creating binding commitments and sanctioning defectors, decreases the likelihood of free-riding. However, the expectations of each state that others will uphold their commitment creates added incentives for free-riding. In a concert, the absence of codified commitments reduces the sanction-related costs associated with free-riding, but the undercurrent of balancing and the concert's small size minimize free-riding.

One final disadvantage of a concert is its exclusivity. As it operated during the nineteenth century, the Concert acted as a great power club, effectively ignoring, and at times violating, the concerns of Europe's smaller powers. In a normative sense, this attribute compromises the collective nature of the enterprise of collective security. While a concert's exclusivity may have been politically acceptable in the nineteenth century, it would not be so today. While major powers still have more influence than minor powers in shaping events, international relations have, at least to some extent, been democratized.

Our solution to this political obstacle is to create a hybrid structure that combines the representative breadth of ideal collective security with the effectiveness and practicality of a concert. We call such a structure a concert-based collective security organization. An inner group of Europe's major powers would guide the operation of a region-wide security structure. A concert-based collective security organization would capitalize upon the co-operative potential of today's international setting without violating power realities or entailing undue risks. Such an organization falls far short of ideal collective security, but we believe it represents the highest practicable form of collective security, one that captures its principal advantages without falling prey to its main weaknesses.

WHY A CONCERT IS POSSIBLE TODAY
There is one final and critical reason for basing a new security order on the concept of a concert: a remarkable degree of correspondence exists between the features of the international environment that gave rise to the Concert of Europe in 1815 and the features of today's international environment. Indeed, the post–Cold War era provides an international setting that is even more conducive to the establishment of a concert-based structure than the post–Napoleonic Wars era. Four key features of the nineteenth century setting made possible the formation of a concert and are again present today: (1) common satisfaction with the status quo; (2) common appreciation that war between major powers is of little utility; (3) the practice of reciprocity; (4) a high degree of transparency. It is important to note that these four features encompass two of the three necessary conditions for collective security outlined in the first section: that the major powers share compatible views of an acceptable international order and that a minimum sense of political community exist among them. The third condition—that no state be so powerful that it is immune to collective sanction—we take to be self-

evident. Our analysis here shows not only that the general conditions necessary for collective security are present, but also that the same features that gave rise to the Concert of Europe are again present in today's Europe. We now examine these features in more detail, pairing each nineteenth-century feature with its contemporary analogue.

COMMON SATISFACTION WITH THE STATUS QUO. The nineteenth-century Concert was predicated upon the assumption that none of its members desired to alter the international order in a fundamental way, and that the status quo, though subject to peaceful change through consensus, was acceptable. As Paul Lauren notes, "there could be no power so dissatisfied that it questioned the legitimacy of the entire international order."[83] At its core, the Concert revolved around a territorial settlement and the willingness of the major powers to agree to Europe's existing borders. The idea was not that these borders were immutably fixed, but that they could be altered only through the agreement of Concert members. As Richard Elrod put it, the system could thus "accommodate the forces of change and yet preserve peace and stability."[84]

The radical change in Soviet foreign policy orchestrated by Mikhail Gorbachev means that all major powers are again coming to hold a common view of what constitutes an acceptable status quo. Despite recent backsliding, the broad contours of Soviet foreign policy remain compatible with the Western vision of a stable international order. The Soviets have unilaterally withdrawn troops from Eastern Europe, agreed to allow a unified Germany to enter NATO, effectively renounced their support for "liberation movements" in the Third World, and stood firmly behind the international coalition that drove Iraq from Kuwait. They have strongly endorsed international institutions: the Soviets have become firm supporters of the UN, obtained observer status in the General Agreement on Trade and Tariffs, and expressed interest in participating in the World Bank and the International Monetary Fund.[85]

---

83. Lauren, "Crisis Prevention," p. 47.
84. Elrod, "The Concert of Europe," p. 163.
85. This reformulation of policy has been accompanied by a dramatic shift in Soviet thinking about the role that ideology should play in Soviet foreign policy. Prominent analysts are placing increasing focus on national economic interests and have directly attacked ideology as a motive force behind foreign policy. See, for example, Igor Malashenko, "Interesi strani: mnimie i real'nie" (Interests of the Country: Imaginary and Real), *Kommunist*, September 1989, pp. 114–123; and A. Bogaturov, M. Nocov, and K. Pleshakov, "Kto oni, nashi soyuzniki" (Who Are They, Our Allies?), *Kommunist*, January 1990, pp. 105–114.

Change in Soviet thinking about an acceptable international order is not only profound, but also unlikely to be reversed. Market reform and stabilization of the economy require a peaceful international environment: the Soviet economic crisis is so dire that the commitment to lowering defense spending and attracting foreign capital is unlikely to change regardless of the fate of Gorbachev.[86] The range of policy options before the Soviet leadership makes highly unlikely, at least in the near term, a return to an aggressive and ideologically driven foreign policy.[87] While the Soviets and the Western powers still need to resolve outstanding issues, profound change in the Soviet Union suggests that the major powers now agree on the essential features of a desirable international order.

COMMON APPRECIATION THAT WAR BETWEEN MAJOR POWERS IS OF LITTLE UTILITY. At the Congress of Vienna, the victorious powers, just beginning the process of recovering from a series of destructive wars, recognized the need to erect a new system that would reduce the likelihood of armed conflict between major states and allow disputes to be resolved through negotiation. While force would still be effective in dealing with lesser powers, war between major powers was simply too costly.[88] A British official, in negotiations with Russia that paved the way for the Concert, spelled this out: "It seems necessary . . . to form a Treaty to which all principal Powers of Europe should be parties . . . above all, for restraining any projects of aggrandisement and ambition similar to those which have produced all the calamities inflicted on Europe since the disastrous era of the French Revolution."[89] In short, the powers agreed that major war was no longer a useful instrument of policy.

Much stronger beliefs about the dangers of war prevail today. In the nuclear age, the major powers agree that they must avoid war among each other; they believe that force is of declining utility in regulating great power relations. A consensus exists that it would be difficult to contain general war to the conventional level and that even a limited nuclear war would have devastating consequences.[90] Even though there have been no recent conflicts

---

86. Even leading right-wing politicians such as Yegor Ligachev support integration of the Soviet Union into the world economy.
87. See Allen Lynch, "Does Gorbachev Matter Any More?" *Foreign Affairs*, Vol. 69, No. 3 (Summer 1990), pp. 19–29.
88. Garrett, "Nixonian Foreign Policy," p. 395.
89. Official communication to the Russian Ambassador in London, January 19, 1805, cited in Albrecht-Carrié, *The Concert of Europe*, p. 28.
90. The evolution of Soviet thinking about the declining role of military force in international politics has been particularly profound. See, for example, A. Arbatov, "Skol'ko oboroni dostatochno" (How Much Defense Is Enough?), *Mezhdunarodnaya Zhizn'*, No. 3 (March 1989).

between the major powers, World Wars I and II, like the Napoleonic Wars, left vivid memories of the horrors of war. In addition, all the powers are coming to realize that economic capability is an increasingly important determinant of international influence.[91] Some scholars also argue that the experiences of the two World Wars have led to shifts in international standards of what constitutes culturally and morally acceptable behavior. War, according to John Mueller, is becoming obsolete among the major powers.[92]

PRACTICE OF RECIPROCITY. Another feature of the nineteenth century system that facilitated the operation of the Concert was the practice of reciprocity. Reciprocity means that powers makes concessions in the belief that they will be repaid later, either through concessions on the same issue or on some other matter of mutual interest.[93] Concert members frequently entered into mutually self-denying arrangements based on shared appreciation of a broad, long-term understanding of self-interest. For example, in settling the dispute over Greek independence from the Ottoman Empire that broke out in the 1820s, Concert members agreed that they would "not seek, in these arrangements, any augmentation of territory, any exclusive influence, or any commerical advantage for their Subjects, which those of every other Nation may not equally obtain."[94] The practice of reciprocity built up an important degree of trust among the statesmen engaging in Concert diplomacy.

Reciprocity is increasingly coming to characterize relations among the major powers. Mutual concessions have emerged on a broad range of issues. The Soviets have made deep cuts in conventional forces and begun to withdraw troops from Eastern Europe. Although these actions initially occurred on a unilateral basis, the Western powers eventually reciprocated by proposing further mutual cuts in force levels and exercising restraint in reacting to ethnic crises within the Soviet Union. Washington and European capitals have deliberately avoided pressuring Moscow over its treatment of ethnic uprisings in the Baltic republics, Azerbaijan, and Georgia. Soviet approval of NATO membership for a unified Germany was clearly linked to Western offers of economic aid to the Soviet Union. In December 1990, the United States approved a billion dollars in loans to the Soviet Union, explicitly

---

91. See Richard Rosecrance, *The Rise of the Trading State* (New York: Basic Books, 1986).
92. John Mueller, *Retreat from Doomsday: The Obsolescence of Major War* (New York: Basic Books, 1989). See also Carl Kaysen, "Is War Obsolete? A Review Essay," *International Security*, Vol. 14, No. 4 (Spring 1990), pp. 42–64.
93. Jervis, "Security Regimes," p. 180.
94. Cited in Albrecht-Carrié, *The Concert of Europe*, p. 109.

linking U.S. assistance to a relaxation in Moscow's emigration policy.[95] Increasing reciprocity has indeed furthered the process of ending the Cold War.

HIGH DEGREE OF TRANSPARENCY. The era following the Napoleonic Wars
was characterized by a high level of transparency, or sharing of information.
France's adversaries had been cooperating and sharing information through
the coalition that formed to block Napoleonic ambition. This coalition improved the regularized channels of consultation and the highly developed
diplomatic system that already existed among the major powers. Shortly
after the Congress of Vienna, Castlereagh instructed British diplomats "to
adopt an open and direct mode of intercourse in the conduct of business,
and to repress on all sides, as much as possible, the spirit of local intrigue
in which diplomatic policy is so falsely considered to consist, and which so
frequently creates the very evil which it is intended to avert."[96] Frequent and
open contact established a level of transparency that eased mutual suspicions
and bolstered confidence, thereby facilitating the formation and functioning
of the Concert.[97]

An extremely high level of transparency characterizes relations among
today's major powers. The NATO allies have for decades been sharing strategic information. Openness between the Western allies and the Soviet Union
has also increased in recent years. Summits, confidence building measures,
military doctrine seminars, on-site verification, and consultation on the war
against Iraq have all served to enhance the flow of information among the
major powers. Satellite reconnaissance has also vastly increased the information available to decision makers.[98] Sharing information is coming to be
seen as a way of facilitating cooperation, rather than as a potential risk to
national security.

NEW CONDITIONS IN TODAY'S EUROPE
During the past two centuries, so much change has taken place in state
structures and inter-state relations that comparisons between the post–
Napoleonic Wars era and post–Cold War era must be treated with caution.

---

95. "Bush Lifting 15-Year-Old Ban," *New York Times*, December 13, 1990. The lifting of the ban
also appears to have been linked to Soviet cooperation in dealing with the Persian Gulf crisis.
96. Jervis, "Security Regimes," p. 179.
97. Jervis, "From Balance to Concert," pp. 73–76.
98. John Lewis Gaddis, "The Evolution of a Reconnaissance Satellite Regime," in Alexander
George, et al., eds., *U.S.-Soviet Security Cooperation: Achievements, Failures, Lessons* (New York:
Oxford University Press, 1988), pp. 353–372.

We have particular confidence in drawing this analogy, however, because four key changes that have occurred since 1815 make the current international setting even more conducive than the nineteenth century to the successful operation of a concert.

THE SPREAD OF DEMOCRACY. Of Europe's major powers, four of the five have enjoyed at least forty years of stable democratic rule. The Soviet Union has also been moving—although haltingly—toward political and economic liberalization. A contemporary concert would not be split ideologically between liberals and monarchists, as was the original Concert.[99] Disputes over how to react to domestic political changes among Europe's smaller states would therefore be less likely to emerge than during the nineteenth century. Furthermore, democracies tend not to go to war against each other. The spread of democracy in Europe should therefore facilitate the formation of a stronger concert.[100]

THE INFORMATION REVOLUTION. The expanding network of telecommunications systems, computers, and copy machines has radically altered the availability of information. The increased flow of ideas and data should strengthen cooperation in Europe through several mechanisms. First, the information revolution furthers the spread of democracy by making impossible the hermetic sealing of society that facilitates totalitarian control. The

99. Britain and France were developing parliamentary institutions, while Prussia, Russia, and Austria were staunch defenders of monarchy.

100. Although the historical record offers no cases in which liberal democracies have gone to war against each other, John Mearsheimer justifiably argues that the empirical evidence is too scanty to draw firm conclusions. In Mearsheimer's words, "democracies have been few in number over the past two centuries, and thus there have not been many cases where two democracies were in a position to fight each other." For those cases that do exist, the presence of a common external threat provides at least as compelling an explanation for harmony as does common domestic structure. See Mearsheimer, "Back to the Future," pp. 50–51. The deductive case for the claim that the spread of democracy should lead to a more peaceful international setting is, however, quite compelling. The literature contains six main points. First, leaders that are democratically elected do not need to turn to external ambition as a means of legitimating their rule. Van Evera, "Primed for Peace," p. 27. Second, the common public—the sector which stands to suffer most from war—can use the electoral process to prevent elites from engaging the state in war. Third, citizens in one democratic state will respect the political structure of other democratic states, and therefore be hesitant to engage in hostilities against them. Michael Doyle, "Liberalism and World Politics," *American Political Science Review*, Vol. 80, No. 4 (December 1986), pp. 1160–1161. Fourth, the electoral process tends to produce elites that are risk-averse and policies that are centrist. Both attributes militate against decisions for war. Snyder, "Averting Anarchy in the New Europe," pp. 18–19. Fifth, states willing to submit to the rule of law and civil society at the domestic level are more likely to submit to their analogues at the international level. Flynn and Scheffer, "Limited Collective Security," p. 83. Sixth, democratic debate exposes policy to the marketplace of ideas, thereby allowing unsound ideas to be critically evaluated and challenged. Van Evera, "Primed for Peace," pp. 27.

contagion of political change that altered the face of Eastern Europe in 1989 was unquestionably related to the increasing flow of information and ideas.[101] Second, increased inter-state communication opens societies to the spread of pan-European values and norms. Ideological sources of aggression, such as hyper-nationalism and ethnic hatred, should therefore find less fertile ground in which to take root. Third, the information revolution enhances transparency. Even if states do not enter into arrangements which facilitate the sharing of information, new technologies make data collection and monitoring of arms control agreements far easier.[102] As argued above, enhanced transparency facilitates cooperative behavior.

THE FOUNDATION OF ECONOMIC ACTIVITY. Because of changes in the nature of economic activity and sources of wealth, territorial expansion is today less valued than it was during the nineteenth century. As the orientation of national economies has shifted from agricultural to industrial to post-industrial, territorial conquest has declined in importance as a source of state power.[103] Many of the incentives that drove states to expand during the nineteenth and earlier twentieth centuries are now far less compelling. While Europe's major powers will no doubt compete for influence in Eastern Europe, such competition is likely to focus on economic advantage, as opposed to territorial conquest.

ECONOMIC INTERDEPENDENCE. Europe is now far more economically integrated than it was during the nineteenth century. Interdependence can promote cooperation by creating incentives for states to work together to produce shared gains. Interdependence, however, does not necessarily enhance cooperation. Because states accord higher priority to security than to prosperity, preoccupation with relative, as opposed to absolute, gains means that interdependence promotes cooperation only when gains are shared proportionally. Even if two states both stand to gain from a given economic activity, a state will prevent that gain from being attained if it believes that its partner will obtain a relative advantage that could eventually manifest itself in terms of an increased military threat.[104] Interdependence can also serve as a proximate cause of war. If states believe that their dependence on others is a

---

101. Michael Howard, "The Remaking of Europe," *Survival*, Vol. 32, No. 2 (March/April 1990), pp. 99–106.
102. See, for example, Gaddis, "The Evolution of a Satellite Reconnaissance Regime."
103. Rosecrance, *The Rise of the Trading State;* Kaysen, "Is War Obsolete?" pp. 48–58; Van Evera, "Primed for Peace," pp. 14–16.
104. See Grieco, "Anarchy and the Limits of Cooperation."

source of vulnerability, they may resort to hostility to end such dependence.[105]

But both of these arguments supporting the proposition that interdependence does not promote peace assume a competitive, anarchic international
setting. We maintain that in a European setting characterized by the four
features enumerated above, interdependence is more likely to promote than
to impede cooperative behavior. States are relatively free to pursue prosperity
and absolute gains. A Europe in which security concerns have been minimized should bring out the cooperation-inducing effects of interdependence.
As Mearsheimer himself notes, "cooperation is much easier to achieve if
states worry only about absolute gains, as they are more likely to do when
security is not so scarce. The goal then is simply to insure that the overall
economic pie is expanding and each state is getting at least some part of the
resulting benefits."[106] In today's Europe, economic interdependence should
therefore allow a concert to function even more successfully than during the
nineteenth century.

A New Concert for Europe

Four criteria shape our proposal for a new European collective security organization. First, the structure of the organization should allow effective
leadership and reflect current power realities. Effectively, this means that the
body should be guided by Europe's major powers. Second, the body should
develop mechanisms based on the notion of all against one for deterring and
resisting aggression. It should also develop long-term prophylactic measures
for dampening the domestic sources of expansionist behavior. Militarism,
autocratic rule, and hyper-nationalism have played key roles in leading states
to pursue policies of forceful expansion.[107] Third, the body should avoid

---

105. Japan's decision to advance into Southeast Asia to obtain access to oil is a case in point.
See Michael Barnhart, *Japan Prepares for Total War: The Search for Economic Security, 1919–1941*
(Ithaca, N.Y.: Cornell University Press, 1987). See also Mearsheimer, "Back to the Future,"
pp. 42–48.
106. Mearsheimer, "Back to the Future," pp. 44–45.
107. Military organizations, when they achieve too much political power, may propagate ideas
that persuade the state to pursue aggressive foreign policies. The services support external
ambition in order to further their narrow professional interests. Autocracy gives rise to external
ambition because elites do not face the critical evaluation and the network of moderating checks
and balances associated with democratic systems. In addition, because autocrats lack the legitimacy associated with representative government, they often seek foreign success to sustain
domestic support. Hyper-nationalism refers to belligerent and aggressive ideologies, not those

codified commitments to collective action and allow members the flexibility to tailor their responses to specific challenges as they arise. Fourth, the body should include all European states and thus serve as a vehicle for building a pan-European consensus and promoting cooperation.

What might a new collective security structure for Europe look like? A framework for this structure already exists: the Conference on Security and Cooperation in Europe (CSCE). Founded in 1975 with all European countries (except Albania, but including the Soviet Union) plus Turkey, the United States, and Canada as members, CSCE has dealt with a host of issues: political-military confidence building measures; human rights; and scientific, cultural, and educational cooperation.[108] CSCE played an important role in moderating repression and expanding civil liberties in the Soviet Union and Eastern Europe during the 1980s. Many European leaders have come to look to CSCE as a vehicle for welcome change. That CSCE enjoys legitimacy and popularity, especially in Eastern Europe and the Soviet Union where a new institution is most needed, makes the Conference the ideal venue for a new security structure.[109] In its present form, however, CSCE is too unwieldy to serve as an effective security structure.[110] Each of its thirty-four members has

that focus on autonomy or self-determination for specific ethnic or national groups. Hyper-nationalism contributes to the emergence of aggressor states by infecting the populace with expansionist ideologies. Public clamor for expansion comes to shape elite decision making, pushing the state to pursue more ambitious external policies. For discussion of these domestic sources of aggression see Van Evera, "Primed for Peace," pp. 18–28; Jack Snyder, *Myths of Empire: Domestic Politics and Strategic Ideology,* (Ithaca, N.Y.: Cornell University Press, forthcoming 1991); and Charles Kupchan, *The Vulnerability of Empire,* unpublished manuscript.

108. The first CSCE conference took place in Helsinki and lasted from 1972 to 1975. The meeting produced the "Final Act," which mandated CSCE to focus on three "baskets" of activity: political-military, economic and scientific, and humanitarian issues. For a definitive account of these negotiations, see John Maresca, *To Helsinki: The Conference on Security and Cooperation in Europe* (Durham, N.C.: Duke University Press, 1985).

109. Many scholars have noted that regimes and institutions are harder to create than they are to maintain. It therefore makes sense to house a new security organization in an existing body. See, for example, Keohane, *After Hegemony,* p. 244; and Snyder, "Averting Anarchy in the New Europe," p. 30. The primary reason for housing a new security structure in CSCE is that the body took shape during the Cold War but nevertheless bridged the East-West gap. Jack Snyder (ibid., p. 32) argues that a pan-European institution should emerge from the European Community (EC). Yet the EC does not and, for the foreseeable future, will not include Eastern Europe or the Soviet Union. The military, political, and economic trajectories of the former Eastern Bloc countries are critical variables shaping the prospects for stability in Europe; despite the EC's proven strength, these countries cannot await the day of its hypothetical expansion.

110. In order to enhance its role in shaping a post–Cold War order, CSCE's members took steps to strengthen the body's institutional structure at the Paris Summit in November 1990. See CSCE, "Charter of Paris for a New Europe," Paris, 1990, available from the U.S. Department of State. The new structure revolves around annual summit meetings at the head-of-state level. In

an equal vote and any action requires unanimity. It is wholly unrealistic to assume that the major powers would devolve to such a body responsibility for managing a new European security order. To adhere to the unanimity rule would ensure CSCE only a marginal role in shaping a new Europe. By recasting CSCE along the lines of a concert, however, the body can be turned into a viable collective security structure.[111]

A new security system must find a way of balancing the need to reflect power realities with the need to foster consensus among the states of Europe. We therefore propose a two-tiered design for CSCE: a security group consisting principally of Europe's major powers, with jurisdiction over core-level security issues; and the full thirty-four member body, with jurisdiction over a host of other security-relevant matters. The security group would deal with issues that have direct and immediate bearing on national security, such as arms control, territorial boundaries, and peacekeeping. The strong, efficient leadership that only a small group can provide is essential in these core areas if the efforts to build a collective security organization for Europe are to come to fruition. In dealing with these core-level issues, the security group would take into consideration, but not be bound by, the interests expressed by each of CSCE's members. The full body, while it would indeed have input into core-level security matters, would have exclusive jurisdiction over the following types of issues: enhancing confidence and security building measures (CSBMs), suppressing hyper-nationalism, promoting democratic institutions, and monitoring human rights. On these matters, CSCE would retain its unanimity rule; CSCE's traditional role as a consensus builder would continue.

THE SECURITY GROUP

The new organization should evolve around a concert of Europe's five major powers: the United States, the Soviet Union, Britain, France, and Germany.

---

addition, a Council of Foreign Ministers is to meet periodically, and a Committee of Senior Officials is to gather on a regular basis to support the work of the Council. A secretariat located in Prague will provide administrative services to these three bodies. The Charter also created two new centers with substantive tasks. The Conflict Prevention Center (CPC) will serve to increase military transparency and develop mechanisms for conflict resolution. The Office of Free Elections (OFE) will work to ensure that national elections are open to foreign observers, disseminate election results, and sponsor seminars on the creation of democratic institutions.

111. Others also argue that CSCE should drop its unanimity rule. See, for example, Flynn and Scheffer, "Limited Collective Security"; Goodby, "A New European Concert"; and Mueller, "A United Nations of Europe and North America."

The big five would serve as a core security group within CSCE, bringing the body more into line with current power realities and facilitating its ability to act in a timely and coordinated fashion. A limited number of other CSCE members should join the security group on a rotating basis to ensure input from Europe's smaller countries. We envisage three such members, selection occurring on a regional basis so that the concerns of countries in northern, eastern, and southern Europe are represented. As in any concert, the security group would have no explicit decision-making rules or binding contracts of collective action to enforce commitments to the notion of all against one. Decisions for action would not require unanimity—as they did in the League Council—nor would members have a paralyzing veto, as they do in the UN Security Council. The powers would pledge to respect Europe's existing boundaries and allow alterations only through joint decision. Members acting against the collective will would face censure, temporary exclusion from the group, and, if need be, sanctions. The absence of more formal security guarantees and decision rules provides a flexibility that would be essential to the efficacy of a collective security organization.[112]

During its initial phase of five to ten years, the security group should coexist with NATO. NATO has certainly served well and should remain in place until a workable alternative exists. The near-term strategy would thus be two-track: relying on NATO while nurturing a new pan-European institution. Should all go well and the Soviet Union maintain non-threatening and cooperative foreign policies, NATO would cede increasing responsibility to the security group. The Warsaw Pact already having disappeared, the security group would become the natural forum to oversee continent-wide security issues. This arrangement presents minimal risk to NATO members because if this new security structure fails to develop, NATO can reassert control over European security; the NATO command structure would remain ready to provide collective defense to its members.[113] Furthermore, because

---

112. The security group should meet regularly at each level of the CSCE structure—summit meetings, gatherings of the Council of Foreign Ministers and Committee of Senior Officials, and the Secretariat. Regular conferences among the governmental elites of Europe's major powers are the *sine qua non* of a durable and effective collective security system. The nineteenth-century Concert's lack of institutionalization left it extremely vulnerable to changes in political leadership in member countries.

113. In this respect, the United States must retain the capability to bring significant force to bear on the European continent. Light and heavy divisions, and the lift needed to transport them to Europe, should be readily available. Leaving a sizable U.S. presence of troops and equipment on the continent even after the devolution of NATO's functions to CSCE is also crucial to the successful operation of a new collective security structure. Members must remain

the security group would operate as a concert, retaining an undercurrent of balancing behavior, NATO members would remain watchful for signs of renewed aggressive intent in the Soviet Union. Weapons procurement and operational planning would remain tied, to an appropriate extent, to Soviet behavior and capabilities; concerts do not breed naivete. The security group should develop the following mechanisms to preserve stability in Europe:

ARMS CONTROL NEGOTIATION AND VERIFICATION. Given the demise of the Warsaw Pact, the security group would serve as a natural body to oversee the process of arms control in Europe. Its concert-like structure would allow the United States and the Soviet Union to remain the central parties in negotiations on both nuclear and conventional reductions, but the process would be more open to other European powers. The security group should also establish a permanent verification center. The Treaty on Conventional Armed Forces in Europe (CFE) agreement provides for the creation of a Joint Consultative Group (JCG) to serve as a forum in which participating nations could file complaints regarding compliance. The JCG could be turned into a permanent verification and monitoring center for Europe, pooling information that would be available to all CSCE members.[114] Devolving responsibility for verification and monitoring of arms control agreements to a multinational body would depoliticize the process and make it far less susceptible to the vicissitudes of domestic political change.

PREVENTION OF NUCLEAR PROLIFERATION. The security group should strengthen mechanisms for preventing nuclear proliferation. The presence of nuclear weapons in Europe, provided they continue to be based in an invulnerable manner, would serve to increase the peaceful effects of a concert. These weapons work with, not against, the underlying logic of a concert: they induce caution, minimize the chance that misperception of military capability will lead to deterrence failures, and reinforce the deterrent effects associated with the notion of all against one. A concert-based structure would not, however, rely on nuclear weapons to preserve peace in Europe. It would preserve stability primarily through the stabilizing effects of collective security. Furthermore, a collective security structure, by dampening the insecurity

---

willing and able to uphold their commitment to resist aggression. Britain, as well, should maintain a firm continental commitment, in terms of both capability and resolve, and not allow itself to slip into the illusory belief of the 1930s that its security can best be preserved by avoiding the engagement of its troops on the European continent.

114. For a related idea, see Stanley Sloan, "Conflict to Cooperation: On Building a New Berlin," *International Herald Tribune*, December 9–10, 1988.

that many non-nuclear states may feel in the new Europe, would diminish the incentives of these states to acquire nuclear weapons. The reduced demand for nuclear weapons, current political opposition to proliferation, and the extreme dangers inherent in the spread of nuclear capability make the prevention of proliferation an important task for the security group.[115]

PEACEKEEPING AND JOINT ACTION. Under a peacekeeping mandate, the security group would undertake joint diplomatic and military initiatives. Such actions could range from joint declarations of policy, to joint recognition of newly independent states, to coordinated peacekeeping activities.[116] The demand for peacekeeping in Europe is likely to be related to border conflicts arising from national and ethnic rivalries. Forces might be needed to prevent hostilities, to circumscribe fighting, or to enforce a ceasefire.[117] As during the nineteenth-century Concert, one or more powers could be authorized to act on behalf of all. The security group could also consider the establishment of a permanent multinational peacekeeping unit for rapid deployment in the event of crisis.[118]

AREAS OF SPECIAL INTEREST. Despite the waning of the Cold War, the major powers continue to view certain regions, for geopolitical and historical reasons, as of special importance. The security group should recognize that certain powers will retain areas of special interest and it should delineate each state's rights and obligations in contested areas. Such rights and obligations will exist whether explicitly recognized or not; explicit recognition

---

115. The main dangers involved in proliferation are as follows. First, especially in Europe's less well-developed countries, economic, geographic, and technological factors could hamper efforts to build secure, invulnerable nuclear forces. Vulnerable forces undermine crisis stability. Second, proliferation increases the chances that nuclear weapons might be used as a result of accident or terrorist seizure. Third, emerging nuclear powers, who have thus far been bystanders in the nuclear revolution, may face difficulties integrating nuclear weapons into their military doctrines. Fourth, proliferation in Europe is most likely to occur precisely when it would be most dangerous—when international tensions have forced non-nuclear states to seek the protection of nuclear deterrence. On the advantages and disadvantages of proliferation, see Mearsheimer, "Back to the Future," pp. 37–40.
116. The establishment of joint criteria for diplomatic recognition of new states could be crucial given the growing momentum of independence movements in the Soviet Union and Yugoslavia.
117. A peacekeeping force could be very useful if, for example, Slovenia and Croatia decided to secede from Yugoslavia. Bulgaria and Yugoslavia might come into conflict over the status of Macedonia, as might the Soviet Union and Romania over Moldavia.
118. The organization and dispatch of a peacekeeping unit are often hampered by issues of nation participation, burden-sharing, and force sizing. See Brian Urquhart, "Beyond the 'Sheriff's Posse,'" *Survival*, Vol. 32, No. 3 (May/June 1990), pp. 196–205. A standing, multinational force under the direction of the security group would minimize these problems and increase the likelihood of timely deployment.

decreases the chances of misunderstanding.[119] Michael Howard, for example, has argued that the Western powers must accept that the Soviet Union has "a certain *droit de regard* in Eastern Europe."[120] The major powers should similarly recognize Germany's prominent interests in Central Europe.

FENCING OFF REGIONAL CONFLICT. The end of the Cold War will by no means lead to the end of conflict in the Third World. The security group should ensure that peripheral conflicts are fenced off or resolved and not allowed to jeopardize cooperative efforts in Europe. The United States and the Soviet Union already have taken steps in this direction. In Nicaragua, the superpowers cooperated to encourage free elections, and similar arrangements may soon be extended to other areas in Central America.[121] The powers could further dampen rivalry in the periphery by agreeing to strict "rules of the game" governing engagement in third areas.

THE FULL BODY

While the security group would be able to act on core-level security issues without the approval of each CSCE member, it would continuously consult with the full body in reaching decisions.[122] Matters other than core-level security issues would fall under the jurisdiction of the full body. CSCE's traditional mandate would remain fully intact. The thirty-four would continue to strengthen CSBMs through the Conflict Prevention Center (CPC)

---

119. Others agree that spheres of influence should be made explicit. See Van Evera, "Primed for Peace," p. 45; and Mearsheimer, "Back to the Future," p. 34.

120. Howard, "The Remaking of Europe," p. 103.

121. See Michael Kramer, "Anger, Bluff—and Cooperation," *Time Magazine*, June 4, 1990, pp. 38–45. In areas where the legacy of the Cold War remains more prominent—such as Angola, Ethiopia, and Afghanistan—tensions are more fenced off than they were during the 1980s.

122. Some may object that a concert-based structure tramples on the rights of Europe's smaller powers. Establishing a CSCE security group that functions as a concert indeed endows the major powers with predominant influence in Europe. Yet these states have such influence *de facto* from their dominant economic and military capability. In effect, concert-like behavior has characterized European diplomacy for much of the postwar era. Germany, France, and Britain dominate the European Community. The United States, Germany, and Britain effectively call the shots in NATO. A concert structure only formalizes these relationships. Furthermore, the creation of a security group would in fact broaden European input into the formation of policy; the two countries that have dominated the shaping of Europe's strategic landscape—the United States and the Soviet Union—would have to make more room for France, Britain, and Germany. Our proposal leaves to the full body jurisdiction over all security-relevant issues covered by CSCE's current mandate. It also gives the thirty-four member countries input into the full range of core-level security issues that now lie outside CSCE's purview. In addition, by transforming CSCE into an effective pan-European security organization, a concert-based structure strengthens the voices of East European countries, which are currently unattached to any meaningful security organization.

and would protect human rights in member states. In addition, the full body should oversee the task of developing and implementing prophylactic measures to prevent the emergence of aggressor states.[123] In dealing with these matters, CSCE would maintain its current unanimity rule. The full body should fulfill its tasks through the following mechanisms:

CONFLICT MANAGEMENT. CSCE should continue to develop two procedures for conflict management: examination of unusual military activity and arbitration through third parties.[124] Current procedures within the CPC give all CSCE members the right to request explanation of unusual military activities within forty-eight hours of observation. If the party is unsatisfied with the response, it can refer the matter to a meeting of concerned states. Current proposals for third party arbitration call for a group of experts to serve as fact finders and to make recommendations for resolving disputes. Many CSCE members also favor the identification of a typology of disputes, certain classes of which would be subject to mandatory, binding arbitration.[125]

SHARING OF MILITARY INFORMATION. The full body should oversee and expand the CPC's efforts to increase transparency and encourage contact between national military establishments. The widespread and symmetrical provision of military information is crucial to the operation of a collective security organization and underlies many of its advantages. The CPC is

---

123. Some analysts argue that newly emerging problems such as migration and the environment should be placed on CSCE's security agenda. For example, Flynn and Scheffer "Limited Collective Security," suggests that CSCE should establish a council for environmental cooperation. The traditional notion of national security is indeed being challenged by new threats to national well-being. The potential for massive migrations across Europe could pose formidable problems of border control and place severe strains on national economies. Degradation of the environment could threaten the quality of life in all states. While these are indeed matters that warrant considerable attention, they do not obviate the need to address traditional military concerns. While CSCE's security organs would want to monitor the military implications, if any, of population movements and environmental problems, it would be unwise to widen the already broad mandate outlined above. Differences of opinion over how to deal with migration might spill over into negotiations on military matters. The critical focus of CSCE's security organs on avoiding war in Europe should not be diluted by diverting attention to issues only tangentially related to conflict. See Daniel Deudney, "The Case Against Linking Environmental Degradation to National Security," *Millennium*, Vol. 19, No. 3 (Winter 1990), pp. 461–476; Jessica Tuchman Matthews, "Redefining Security," *Foreign Affairs*, Vol. 68, No. 2 (Spring 1989), pp. 162–177; and Norman Myers, "Environmental Security," *Foreign Policy*, No. 74 (Spring 1989), pp. 23–41.
124. The following discussion draws heavily on interviews with U.S. government officials familiar with the CSCE negotiations.
125. For a comprehensive discussion of third party arbitration, see Goodby, "A New European Concert," pp. 3–6. See also "Report of the CSCE Meeting of Experts on Peaceful Settlement of Disputes" (Valletta, Malta, February 8, 1991), available from the U.S. Department of State; and *CSCE Vienna Follow-Up Meeting: A Framework for Europe's Future*, Selected Documents, No. 35 (Washington: D.C.: U.S. Department of State, Bureau of Public Affairs, January 1989), pp. 7–8.

currently working on improving the dissemination of information on forces-in-being, new weapons deployments, and defense budgets. It is also constructing a new communications network, strengthening provisions for foreign observers to be present at national military maneuvers, and developing plans for new exchanges between military establishments.[126]

SUPPRESSION OF HYPER-NATIONALISM AND PROMOTION OF DEMOCRACY. The full body should establish two permanent commissions to oversee the task of developing and implementing prophylactic measures to prevent aggression. The Commission on Political Development (CPD) would focus on the suppression of hyper-nationalism. History provides ample demonstration of the potentially disastrous consequences of unchecked nationalism.[127] The Commission on Democracy (COD) would concentrate on promoting democratic institutions and values. As we have argued, the spread of democracy will contribute to the preservation of peace in Europe. It is no coincidence that the three principal aggressor states of the twentieth century were ruled by essentially autocratic governments.[128]

The Commission on Political Development can contribute to the suppression of hyper-nationalism through three principal mechanisms. First, the CPD can watch carefully to ensure that national elites do not use hyper-nationalist propaganda as a domestic tool. It should expose those caught doing so, single them out for censure, and pressure them to cease by widely circulating a "blacklist" of irresponsible leaders. Second, efforts to protect the rights of foreign journalists would play an important role in making local elites more accountable for their actions and rhetoric.[129] At the same time, the CPD should take steps to ensure that a free domestic press thrives in all

---

126. See Stanley Sloan, "CSCE: A Start on a Structure," *Arms Control Today*, Vol. 20, No. 10 (December 1990), pp. 4–5. A military doctrine seminar has been scheduled for 1991. These military doctrine seminars enhance transparency by promoting extensive military-to-military contacts. The seminars could serve as an important vehicle for promoting defensive force postures and doctrines of defensive defense.

127. See, for example, Boyd Shafer, *Nationalism: Myth and Reality* (New York: Harcourt, Brace, 1955); Louis L. Snyder, *German Nationalism* (Harrisburg, Pa.: Stackpole, 1952); Berghahn, *Germany and the Approach of War in 1914*; Van Evera, "Primed for Peace," pp. 23–25; and Louis L. Snyder, *Encyclopedia of Nationalism* (New York: Paragon House, 1990).

128. The Reichstag did maintain a marginal degree of political power throughout the pre–World War I era. But the government largely succeeded in emasculating the legislature and investing the kaiser and his advisers with enormous autonomy in formulating policy. The system was, in Hans-Ulrich Wehler's words, "a semi-absolutist, pseudo-constitutional military monarchy." Wehler, *The German Empire, 1871–1918*, trans. Kim Traynor (Leamington Spa, U.K.: Berg Publishers, 1985), p. 60.

129. See *CSCE Vienna Follow-Up Meeting*, p. 33.

member states. The CPD should also become involved in local radio and television programming, in terms of both monitoring broadcasts and countering nationalistic propaganda through its own broadcasts. Third, the CPD can monitor the education system in member states. It is critical that the textbooks used in primary and secondary education present accurate accounts of national history.[130] CSCE should also continue to encourage freedom of access to national archives for all scholars, both foreign and national.[131] CSCE should set forth guidelines in each of these three areas, and access to European development funds should be made contingent upon compliance with these guidelines.

The Commission on Democracy, which would incorporate the existing Office of Free Elections (OFE), can take several steps to promote the spread of democracy. In addition to fulfilling the OFE's current tasks, the COD could open branches in all member countries to support representative institutions and democratic values. Based on the notion that the free flow of ideas undermines authoritarian regimes, the COD should fan the spread of the information revolution. It should help to ensure that all political groups have access to photocopiers, fax machines, and computers. The College of Europe in Bruges would be a natural location for COD activities in the education field. Students from leading national universities could come to Bruges to study democratic theory and pan-European political processes.[132]

Conclusions

We have developed four main arguments in this essay to show that collective security can best preserve peace in post–Cold War Europe. First, we have shown that collective security has clear advantages over balancing under anarchy in promoting international stability. Collective security promises to deter and to resist aggressors more effectively should they emerge. At the same time, it offers to deepen and perpetuate a cooperative and peaceful international environment. Second, we have shown that concert-based col-

---

130. See Van Evera, "Primed for Peace," pp. 52–53.
131. See *CSCE Vienna Follow-Up Meeting*, p. 36.
132. An inter-parliamentary body could serve as a forum for political elites to exchange ideas about democratic procedures. See Joseph Biden, "Helsinki II, Road Map for Revolution," *New York Times*, January 28, 1990. This idea is amplified in "The Support for East European Democracy Act of 1990," U.S. Senate, 102nd Cong., 1st sess., bill before the Committee on Foreign Relations, unpublished, 1990.

lective security is the most appropriate and practicable form of collective security for today's Europe. A concert-based structure, by retaining an ongoing undercurrent of subtle balancing, allows the major powers to keep on guard in a Europe that is still in flux. Third, we have shown that the conditions necessary for a concert-based structure to form and function successfully are present today. Finally, we have argued that CSCE should be recast to function as a concert-based collective security organization. We have laid out mechanisms through which this body can preserve peace in Europe.

In order to minimize the risk that our proposal presents to the Western alliance, we recommend that NATO and a recast CSCE coexist until political and economic conditions in the Soviet Union stabilize. Should the Soviet Union again pursue an aggressive foreign policy, collective security would become unfeasible and NATO would reassert control over European security. On the other hand, if Soviet foreign policy continues on its current trajectory, NATO would gradually cede more security functions to CSCE.[133] The eventual endpoint would involve the dismantling of NATO and the transformation of CSCE into an effective and viable collective security structure built around a small and workable concert of the big five.

This proposal is grounded in historical precedent, would succeed in bringing the European order more into line with the changing strategic landscape, and would provide a more stable and peaceful international environment. Because the world is at a unique historical juncture, it is necessary to rely on the past to think creatively about the future, and to take the initiative in forging a new European order.

---

133. The implementation of a collective security system in Europe might even increase the chances that Soviet reform will continue to move forward. CSCE's efforts to promote democracy could further political reform. Soviet participation in the security group and the broader network of all-European institutions that are likely to emerge would facilitate the process through which Soviet elites come to embrace the norms underpinning a new European security order. On the potential effects of the international environment on Soviet domestic change, see Jack Snyder, "International Leverage on Soviet Domestic Change," *World Politics*, Vol. 42, No. 1 (October 1989), pp. 1–30.

Systems for Peace or Causes of War?

Collective Security, Arms Control, and the New Europe

Richard K. Betts

Promotion of the idea of collective security has created a psychological situation in which the United States cannot turn its back on the concept, not because of what collective security can accomplish . . . but because of what millions of people . . . believe it may accomplish in time. Collective security has come to be the chief symbol of hope that . . . a community of nations will develop in which there will be no more war.

Arnold Wolfers[1]

The achievement of orthodox status is very often fatal to the integrity of a concept. When it becomes popular and respectable . . . men are strongly tempted to proclaim their belief in it whether or not they genuinely understand its meaning or fully accept its implications. If the tension between their urge to believe in it and their disinclination to believe that it is valid becomes too strong, they tend to resolve the difficulty by altering its meaning, packing into the terminological box a content that they can more readily accept.

Inis L. Claude, Jr.[2]

Collective security is an old idea whose time keeps coming.[3] The term has been resurrected and revised in three generations of this century, once after each World War—the First, the Second, and the Cold War—and has been

The author is grateful to Bruce Cronin, Will Daugherty, Robert Gilpin, Stanley Hoffmann, Charles Kupchan, Deborah Larson, John Mueller, Joseph Nye, Paul Schroeder, Paul Stares, Richard Ullman, and Kenneth Waltz for criticism of earlier drafts, and the Pew Charitable Trusts for support. This draft still does not do justice to all the criticisms, especially those of Kupchan and Ullman. A similar version of this article will appear in Jack Snyder and Robert Jervis, eds., *Coping with Complexity in the International System* (Westview Press, forthcoming).

Richard K. Betts is Professor of Political Science at Columbia University.

1. Arnold Wolfers, *Discord and Collaboration* (Baltimore: Johns Hopkins University Press, 1962), p. 197.
2. Inis L. Claude, Jr., *Swords Into Plowshares*, 4th ed. (New York: Random House, 1971), p. 246.
3. The concept can be traced at least as far back as the last millennium, when French bishops in a council at Poitiers and a synod at Limoges declared war on war, decided to excommunicate princes who broke the peace, and planned to deploy troops under a religious bannner to use force against violators. Stefan T. Possony, "Peace Enforcement," *Yale Law Journal*, Vol. 55, No. 5 (1946).

used to refer to: (1) the Wilsonian or ideal concept associated with the Fourteen Points and League of Nations; (2) the Rio Pact, the United Nations, and anti-communist alliances including the UN Command in Korea, NATO, the U.S.-Japan Mutual Security Treaty, SEATO, the Baghdad Pact, and CENTO;[4] and (3) current proposals for organizations to codify peace in Europe.[5]

The protean character of collective security reflects the fact that many who endorse it squirm when the terms are specified or applied to awkward cases. This has occurred with all incarnations of the idea.[6] The main problem is the gap between the instinctive appeal of the idea in liberal cultures as they settle epochal conflicts, and its inherent defects in relations among independent states as they move from peace toward war. When particular cases make the defects obtrusive the idea is revised rather than jettisoned. When revisions vitiate what essentially distinguishes the idea from traditional concepts it is supposed to replace, the urge to salvage the idea confuses strategic judgment. That is harmless only as long as strategy is not needed.

---

4. This was prevalent in official thinking in the first half of the Cold War. For example, see John Foster Dulles, *War or Peace* (New York: Macmillan, 1950), pp. 89–95, 204–207; and Dean Rusk, as told to Richard Rusk, and Daniel Papp, ed., *As I Saw It* (New York: Norton, 1990), pp. 503–505.

5. For example, Richard Ullman, *Securing Europe* (Princeton: Princeton University Press, 1991); Gregory Flynn and David J. Scheffer, "Limited Collective Security," *Foreign Policy*, No. 80 (Fall 1990), pp. 77–101; Charles A. Kupchan and Clifford A. Kupchan, "Concerts, Collective Security, and the Future of Europe," *International Security*, Vol. 16, No. 1 (Summer 1991), pp. 114–161; Malcolm Chalmers, "Beyond the Alliance System," *World Policy Journal*, Vol. 7, No. 2 (Spring 1990), pp. 215–250; John Mueller, "A New Concert of Europe," *Foreign Policy*, No. 77 (Winter 1989–90), pp. 3–16; James E. Goodby, "A New European Concert" and Harald Mueller, "A United Nations of Europe and North America," *Arms Control Today*, Vol. 21, No. 1 (January/February 1991); John D. Steinbruner, "Revolution in Foreign Policy," in Henry J. Aaron, ed., *Setting National Priorities: Policy for the Nineties* (Washington, D.C.: Brookings, 1990). Steinbruner terms his overall vision "cooperative" rather than "collective" security, but the description is similar to the Wilsonian conception: "a global alliance. . . . all countries are on the same side and their forces are not directed against each other. . . . there are no neutrals." Ibid., pp. 68, 74, 109. For a mixed view of prospects, see Stephen F. Szabo, "The New Europeans: Beyond the Balance of Power," in Nils H. Wessell, ed., *The New Europe: Revolution in East-West Relations*, Proceedings of the Academy of Political Science, Vol. 38, No. 1 (New York: Academy of Political Science, 1991).

6. "For while the transmutation of lead into gold would be no nearer if everyone in the world passionately desired it, it is undeniable that if everyone really desired . . .'collective security' (and meant the same thing by those terms), it would be easily attained; and the student of international politics may be forgiven if he begins by supposing that his task is to make everyone desire it. It takes him some time to understand. . . . the fact that few people do desire . . .'collective security,' and that those who think they desire it mean different and incompatible things by it." E.H. Carr, *The Twenty Years Crisis, 1919–1939*, 2d ed. (London: Macmillan, 1946), pp. 9–10.

Among those who like the idea of collective security, negotiation of arms limitations among states is also popular. Many proponents of the League of Nations linked it closely to plans for general disarmament. That contributed to the association of Wilsonian collective security with utopian visions. In the second half of the Cold War, the shift from pursuit of complete disarmament to limitations aimed at fixing the distribution of military power in stable configurations made the enterprise more serious; indeed it became institutionalized over the past twenty years.

Arms control treaties designed to stabilize military relationships, however, are vestiges of the Cold War. They make sense between adversaries, not friends, and the Russians are on our side now. This may not last, but the size and identity of coalitions that would be arrayed in a new strategic competition—information essential for prescribing the regulation of military balances—cannot yet be known. Bureaucracies and peace strategists nevertheless continue to lobby for arms control as a means to reinforce the current amity. Although constituencies for collective security and arms control overlap, there is at best little connection between the logic of the two goals, and at worst a contradiction.

The main argument in this article is that reborn enthusiasm for collective security is fueled by confusion about which is the cause and which is the effect in the relation between collective security and peace, and by conflation of *present* security *conditions* (absence of a threat) with *future* security *functions* (coping with a threat). This conceptual confusion raises doubts about the congruence of form and function in a collective security system. Is the system designed in a form that will work in conditions where it is needed, or does the form reflect conditions where it is not needed? If changes in conditions prevent the system from functioning according to its design, it will not make war less likely, and will thus make coping with threats harder than if alternate security mechanisms had been developed.

The second possible danger is that instead of failing to perform according to design, collective security or arms control, in succeeding, would *worsen* military instability. Implementing collective commitments could turn minor wars into major ones, and equalizing military power of individual states through arms control without reference to their prospective alignment in war might yield unequal forces when alignments congeal. The usual criticism of collective security and arms control is that they will not work; the other criticism is that if they do work, we may wish they hadn't.

Yes, these are opposite arguments. Moreover, not all of the other criticisms I make of collective security or arms control proposals are mutually consistent. This would be dirty pool if the aim were to discredit the ideas with a contrary prediction of my own. My own view of the future, however, is agnostic. Various potential defects in ambitious proposals for systemic reform are listed not because they will go together, and not to stack the deck of argument, but simply to make the case that a wide range of possibilities is not foreclosed. That simple point precludes confidence in predicting whether or how institutions of collective security or arms control would work.

Granted, nothing important in politics is predictable in detail. Indeed, systems of all sorts, whether simple or complex, often produce unanticipated results,[7] and even enthusiasts for collective security and arms control admit that they will not assure the permanence of sweetness and light in Europe. The least we should try to do when prescribing a system, however, is to make the assumed sequences of cause and effect clear, and to identify dysfunctions or counterproductive effects that *can* be anticipated. The following section frames the issues in terms of some considerations of systems theory. Subsequent sections etch the specific critiques of collective security and arms control; those not interested in systems theory may wish to skip ahead.

Security Systems

The function of a security system is to produce security, and the system should be judged by how it does so rather than by other things associated with it. This also means that a system designed in good times to cope with bad times should be judged in terms of the bad times rather the good times. By my reading, many current proposals for collective security do not fully share these assumptions. To judge the efficacy of the idea and the potential for perverse effects, we need to clarify what the system is supposed to do, how it is supposed to do it, and when.

For reasons argued below, the definition of collective security that we should use as a reference point is the classic Wilsonian ideal. Some charge that criticizing the ideal type prevents appreciation of more limited and realistic variants. We find on closer consideration, however, that most of the qualifications applied in current proposals make collective security more

---

7. See the chapter by Robert Jervis in Jack Snyder and Robert Jervis, eds. *Coping with Complexity in the International System* (Boulder, Colo.: Westview Press, forthcoming).

realistic by making it less collective and less automatic—and thus hard to differentiate from the traditional balance of power standards it is supposed to replace. Unless collective security *does* mean something significantly different from traditional forms of combination by states against common enemies, in alliances based on specific interests, the term confuses the actual choices.

The essential element in the Wilsonian concept is the *rejection of alliances*, expressed in the commitment of all members of the system to oppose any attack against another: "all for one, and one for all." Peace is indivisible. Alliances for defense are mandated only if collective security fails (on the same principle that a threatened citizen may rely on her own gun if the police fail to answer her call). Instead of planning against an identified adversary, security policy consists of the guarantee of united reaction against whoever might transgress. No grievance warrants resort to force to overturn the status quo; military force is legitimate only to resist attack, not to initiate it. States are to be legally accountable for starting wars. In contrast to traditional international relations, protection comes not from balance of power, but from preponderance of power against any renegade, guaranteed by universal treaty obligation to enforce peace whether doing so happens to be in a state's immediate interest or not. Community of power replaces balance of power.[8] The penalty for aggression is to be automatic economic or military sanctions. (Some collective security schemes rely primarily on economic punishment.[9] To keep discussion manageable within space constraints, my ar-

---

8. G.F. Hudson, "Collective Security and Military Alliances," in Herbert Butterfield and Martin Wight, eds., *Diplomatic Investigations* (Cambridge, Mass.: Harvard University Press, 1966), pp. 175–176; Kenneth W. Thompson, "Collective Security," *International Encyclopedia of the Social Sciences* (New York: Free Press, 1968), pp. 565–566; Kenneth W. Thompson, "Collective Security Reexamined," *American Political Science Review*, Vol. 47, No. 3 (September 1953), pp. 753–756; Wolfers, *Discord and Collaboration*, chaps. 11–12; Inis L. Claude, Jr., *Power and International Relations* (New York: Random House, 1962), chap. 4; Claude, *Swords Into Plowshares*, chap. 12; Roland M. Stromberg, "The Idea of Collective Security," *Journal of the History of Ideas*, Vol. 17, No. 2 (April 1956); Robert E. Osgood, "Woodrow Wilson, Collective Security, and the Lesson of History," *Confluence*, Vol. 5, No. 4 (Winter 1957), p. 344; M.V. Naidu, *Collective Security and the United Nations* (Delhi: Macmillan, 1974), chap. 2; Frederick H. Hartmann, *The Conservation of Enemies* (Westport, Conn.: Greenwood, 1982), chap. 13; Erich Hula, "Fundamentals of Collective Security," *Social Research*, Vol. 24, No. 1 (Spring 1957). Some have argued that collective security is really just an extension of the balance of power system (e.g., Edward Vose Gulick, *Europe's Classical Balance of Power* [New York: Norton, 1967], pp. 307–308), but this makes little sense unless one is defining it empirically rather than normatively.
9. This helps to sell the idea to those skeptical of military entanglement. See, for example, James T. Shotwell, *War as an Instrument of National Policy and Its Renunciation in the Pact of Paris* (New York: Harcourt, Brace, 1929), p. 221.

gument addresses the stronger form of the idea, which assumes military obligations.)

The Wilsonian ideal involves a strong analogy to domestic law enforcement, as in the principle that anyone who takes another's property by force will be arrested and punished, no matter whether the particular seizure seems to threaten other taxpayers or not, and no matter whether the assailant claims legitimate grounds for the attack (for example, saying that he was repossessing funds swindled from him). In domestic society, such claims are permitted to be argued in a court suit, but not by violence. To the extent that this domestic analogy is accepted, it poses severe problems for the logic of collective security in the international system where there is no authority to adjudicate suits (and thus to obviate individual claims to the right of self-enforcement of self-determined legitimate claims). To the extent that this problem is recognized, on the other hand, and the idea of collective security is qualified to allow exceptions to the general rule according to case-by-case judgment on the merits of interests and claims, the distinction of the concept from a regular alliance becomes hopelessly blurred.

WHAT KIND OF SYSTEM?

A collective security system is a mechanism to guard the sovereignty of its members, one designed to function according to certain norms.[10] Since it is not oriented to deterring a specific adversary, it does not function continuously in peacetime. It is an emergency safety mechanism, sitting on the shelf unless activated by emergence of a challenger to the status quo, in a sense comparable to the emergency back-up system in a nuclear power plant, which functions only in the highly unlikely event that normal operation goes awry.

To judge the effectiveness of an emergency system, it is useful to distinguish whether its most essential elements are automatic or volitional. That is, are the safety switches tripped by the alarm, or does the machine depend on *ad hoc* human choices to start it up and keep it going? If a set of conscious choices is required to run the machine, how many are real choices? Are there good reasons that those responsible might decide deliberately not to flip the

---

10. To purists like Kenneth Waltz, defining a system normatively, in terms of a product expected from it, may be illegitimate. Nor might collective security or arms control be considered systems in themselves. Together, however, they come closer, since collective security is an "ordering principle" of sorts, and arms control affects "the distribution of capabilities across the system's units." See Kenneth N. Waltz, *Theory of International Politics* (Reading: Addison-Wesley, 1979), pp. 82, 97, and passim. I will recklessly use the term "system" anyway.

switches necessary to keep the machine performing according to design? Are the "rules" for how the system works primarily empirical or normative? That is, do they describe how the linked components *do* work, in terms of laws of physics or evidence from experience; or prescribe how they *should* work; or how they would work *if* the operators make the choices stipulated by the designers?

As Charles Perrow makes clear, the interactions in a complex system based on automatic switches may not be fully predictable.[11] They should be far more predictable, however, than the outputs of a system that depends on a combination of deliberate choices. In the latter, the probability of unanticipated interactions of components is potentially doubled, as mechanical uncertainties are compounded by decisional ones. The problem of predictability is further complicated by the strategic quality of decisions in a security system—statesmen trying not just to second-guess machines, but to outwit each other. These differences are of course what makes action in any system of politics harder to predict than in one of physics.

Realist theories of balance of power systems are both empirical and normative, but primarily the former. Just as automobiles in most countries should drive on the right side of the road because they must do so to avoid a crash, states *should* seek power because they *must*.[12] The starkest versions of realism imply that precious little real choice is even available. The deterministic aspect of realism emphasizes automatic qualities of power-balancing

---

11. Charles Perrow, *Normal Accidents* (New York: Basic Books, 1984), chap. 3.
12. Since this article rests more on realist theory than its alternatives, I should admit the troublesome circularity involved here (even though it evokes questions far too large to handle satisfactorily without changing the focus of the article). Idealist statesmen are criticized because failure to bow to necessity and obey the rules of balance of power threatens the security of their nations. Why? Because other states follow the rules and will run over them. But if *some* states do not do what they "must," then in principle there can be no iron law that others will, no strictly logical reason for denying that all states could act according to another norm. In theory, all states could decide to drive on the left. The realist answer would be that empirical evidence shows that most do not do that, so a decision to drive on the left will probably get you killed. (More rigorously developed "neo" realist formulations avoid some of these problems in traditional realist thinking. See Kenneth N. Waltz, "Realist Thought and Neorealist Theory," *Journal of International Affairs*, Vol. 44, No. 1 [Spring/Summer 1990], pp. 21–37.) Thorough-going realism is an insufficient guide to life after the Cold War, however, if only because it offers little to explain why the Cold War ended. Just before the Soviet surrender of Eastern Europe the reigning dean of neorealism could still write (as almost anyone would have): "The Cold War continues. It is firmly rooted in the structure of postwar international politics, and will last as long as that structure endures." Kenneth N. Waltz, "The Origins of War in Neorealist Theory," in Robert J. Rotberg and Theodore K. Rabb, eds., *The Origin and Prevention of Major Wars* (New York: Cambridge University Press, 1989), p. 52.

in the international system more than do idealists who focus on cooperation or moral choices. Extreme realists see the rules of balance of power as almost a cybernetic process of constant adjustment to maintain equilibrium. If one state or coalition begins to dominate the system, the others, like thermostats, move to coalesce and right the balance.

A collective security system depends more on volition and normative rules. The design of collective security rests on the norm that states must subordinate their own immediate interests to general or remote ones. While there is disagreement about how thoroughly the theory and practice of balance of power systems have coincided in history, few claim that the case for collective security has yet been confirmed by experience. (As I argue below, the Concert of Europe is not a good example.) Indeed, the main theoretical argument against collective security is that its normative rules have been discredited by the empirically validated rules of balance of power.[13]

All of this highlights the question of congruence between form and function. Will the system's performance correspond to the rules in its design? If not, will the design be just superfluous, or counterproductive? Or will it ever have to perform at all? The test of a security system is how it functions when a challenge to security arises. If it is never tested, its function is only symbolic, not substantive.

Testing, however, poses two problems. One is that the first test may kill the system if the design is flawed—if empirical rules contradict normative ones, and form does not govern function. There are no simulations or dry runs in international conflict comparable to what can be done with real machines. Another is that we may not know when a test occurs. As with deterrence in general, if the design is so good that a would-be challenger does not even dare to try, the system has worked, but no one can prove that it has because there is no certainty that the challenge would have been made otherwise.

FORECASTING AND SYSTEM ASSESSMENT

Since an emergency system functions only when the normal environment or operating condition breaks down, its design depends on assumptions about

---

13. Collective security can be defined empirically. Ernst B. Haas does so in terms of patterns of UN peacekeeping actions. Haas, "Types of Collective Security: An Examination of Operational Concepts," *American Political Science Review*, Vol. 49, No. 1 (March 1955). See also John Gerard Ruggie, "Contingencies, Constraints, and Collective Security: Perspectives on U.N. Involvement in International Disputes," *International Organization*, Vol. 28, No. 3 (Summer 1974). To evaluate the concept as a model for the more important aim of preserving peace in Europe, however, it is more useful to address it in terms of the aim.

hypothetical and improbable futures. The implication of this point is not quite so obvious that spelling it out should insult a reader's intelligence.

First, many people naturally do think of a security system as one that functions from day to day, in normal times. This is true when normal times are conflictual, as they were in Europe during most of the lifetimes of anyone contemplating the question. Cooperation modified the East-West competition occasionally, but the term "Cold *War*" meant that reliable peace did not exist. Clarity of alignments enabled contingency planning and targeting of strategy against identified threats to develop as ongoing activities. NATO and the Warsaw Pact, high defense budgets and peacetime military readiness, episodic combat in the so-called Third World, and arms control negotiations all went with a security system for an insecure world. Under collective security, in contrast, threats to security remain abstract and everyone is supposed to be willing to act against anyone, so highly developed strategic preparation is circumscribed.

Enthusiasm for collective security emerges from the end of the Cold War, as it did for a while after 1918 and 1945, because the end of an epochal conflict makes peace appear normal. After four decades of Cold War, however, it should not be surprising if people remain psychologically disposed to think of any security system as they thought of NATO, as a machine whirring along from day to day, keeping threats under control. The renewed *appeal* of the idea of collective security flows directly from the present: the happy shock of liberalism's transcontinental triumph shows that radical optimism is not naive after all. The *relevance* of the idea, in contrast, lies in a less happy future where other surprising, rather than likely, changes have occurred.

Second, while the design of an emergency system depends on forecasting the emergencies with which it might have to cope, there are no practical grounds for faith in political forecasts. While everyone will accept the bromide that no one knows what the future will bring, what does one do when asked to predict? The most common approach (and the one that evokes less skepticism than others) is to extrapolate—to project the future as a trajectory from present trends. This reinforces any disposition to think of a collective security system as a constantly functioning one like an alliance. It is also conducive to relaxed specifications for the system's design, because interest in the solution is highest when worry that it might have to be implemented is lowest.

Basing plans for a security system on extrapolation from current trends makes the problem easy. All the great powers are on the same side now, and all the discernible sources of violence are internal score-settling between national groups within states, or between states that are minor powers. To base plans on anything *other* than extrapolation seems arbitrary. Unless one of the great powers goes bad, or the small scraps in Eastern Europe metastacize, the nature of the international mechanism for preserving security is not terribly important. For either of the malign developments to occur, we have to imagine a sequence of changes in the present trend creating a nasty scenario, but discussion in terms of scenarios has an air of unreality. It is as easy for optimists to reject such approaches as "worst-case" alarmism as it is for pessimists to warn of the complacency in projecting the future from the present.

The problem for security policy is to predict threats and to devise means for coping with them, yet it is especially reckless at the moment to invest confidence in any particular estimate of why, how, and when things will go wrong. Major discontinuities in international relations are seldom predicted. Who would not have been derided and dismissed in 1988 for predicting that within a mere three years Eastern Europe would be liberated, the Communist Party of the Soviet Union deposed, and the Union itself on the ash heap of history? Yet it is hard to believe that the probability of equally revolutionary negative developments, of economic crisis and ideological disillusionment with democracy, of scapegoating and instability leading to miscalculation, escalation, and war several years from now is lower than the probability of the current peace seemed several years ago.

With unusually low confidence in the identity of future threats, flexibility and adaptability to unforeseen contingencies are unusually important. This is not a truism. To increase flexibility for various contingencies precludes optimizing preparations for any particular contingency.[14] Flexibility and power are traded off against each other. Flexibility aims to maximize freedom of choice, which varies inversely with the number of independent actors who must concur with a decision to act. Power, on the other hand, varies directly with the number of actors deciding to join forces.

What does this imply for mechanisms to produce security? *Unilateral* measures (or what Kenneth Waltz calls "internal balancing") are the most flexible; they can be directed against any country and depend least on the cooperation of others. The price of maximal flexibility is a lower limit on the maximum

---

14. Perrow, *Normal Accidents*, pp. 86–94.

amount of deployable power. *Alliances* combine reduced flexibility with increased power; any member's policy choices are more circumscribed than if it operates independently, but the grouping pools resources for agreed purposes. *Collective security* (if it is to function according to design) is the least flexible because it requires the most extensive cooperation among independent states, according to the most rigid rules, but it offers the greatest potential power (everyone else in the system against any defector).

Alliances should offer the best compromise between unilateralism's weakness and collective action's rigidity. An alliance without a respectable adversary to give it life, however, is bound for dessication. NATO will endure, because popular organizations can survive for a long time from inertia. The longer peace lasts, however, the more NATO will become a shell—not quite hollow, and replete with parades, committee meetings, and rhetorical affirmations—but bereft of serious strategic activity. Shells are far from useless—they can keep the base from which to coordinate remobilization in a shorter time than if it had to be done from scratch—but they do not provide the animating originality that revolutionary political changes seem to mandate. So collective security generates interest more by default than by its own merits: unilateralism seems ineffective or illegitimate, and alliance without an adversary seems anachronistic and empty.

Collective Security as a Norm

If we cannot test the mechanism before putting it into use, as we might test a nuclear power plant safety system, a heavier burden necessarily falls on deduction, and on comparison with cases where security systems have indeed been tested, to validate the logic in the design. Therefore it is not pedantic to take current discussions of collective security to task for imprecision or ambivalence in defining the concept and prescribing functions.

Those who identified the concept with the regional anti-communist alliance organizations spawned in the first decade of the Cold War were stretching the idea to cover arrangements really more consistent with traditional strategy. Dignifying regional coalitions like NATO by calling them collective security organs helped to brand communist states as outlaws and confirm the moralism in American policy, but the fact remained that they were alliances playing the power-balancing game. Many current proponents of collective security, in contrast, trim the concept to cover less than either the Wilsonian or Cold War variants, by allowing big exemptions from the obligation to discipline countries who resort to force. These variants evade what distinguished collective security from either traditional alliances or military isolation. If a collective institution is really to function as a security system rather than a slogan, the elements that are conceptually unique rather than those that are shared with other constructs should set the standard for assessing the idea. The principles of automaticity and universality are what most differentiate collective security from balance of power.

Many who now claim to endorse collective security demur on the ironclad obligation to join in countering any and all aggression. This vitiates the concept. Unless collective security requires states to act on the basis of the legal principle rather than their specific interests in the case at issue, and unless it forbids neutrality in the face of aggression, the concept adds nothing to traditional conventions of collective defense based on alliances and balance of power. Collective security, wrote Arnold Wolfers, "presumably would add nothing to the protection that victims of aggression would have enjoyed under the old system unless such victims could now expect more military assistance than they would have received otherwise." To add to the strength of defense and deterrence, nations must be willing to fight in situations where,

> if they had not been devoted to the principle of collective security, they would have remained neutral or fought on the side of the aggressor. Instead of being allowed to reserve their military strength for the exclusive task of balancing the power of countries considered a threat to themselves or their allies, nations committed to a policy of collective security must divert their strength to struggle in remote places or, worse still, take action against friends and allies.[15]

Nevertheless, in the generations after Wilson many felt the need to endorse collective security while defining it in ways that overlapped significantly with traditional arrangements. They did so because they recognized that the weakness of the League of Nations and the UN had embarrassed the pure concept as naive, yet they still resisted the argument that balance of power politics cannot be transcended.

---

15. In the 1935 crisis over Ethiopia, "when faced with the choice of losing the support of Italy or else defaulting on collective security, France chose the latter course." Wolfers, *Discord and Collaboration*, pp. 167–169, 187.

WHAT'S WRONG WITH COLLECTIVE SECURITY?

Before confronting attempts to salvage the principle by softening it, we should note the reasons that so many have rejected it altogether. The main criticism has been that collective security does not work because states fail to honor commitments to automatic action. In the background of the many reasons that they renege is the problem that the animating motive for *constructing* a collective security system ("No More War") is in tension with the imperative required to make the system function when challenged ("No More Aggression"). The former reflects abhorrence of war, but the latter requires going to war where immediate self-interest might not. This reduces the odds that parties to the system will feel the same way about the principle when it comes to cases.

A second objection is that the collective security principle's legalism is too rigidly conservative, since it requires honoring the *status quo ante* irrespective of its merits.[16] Elihu Root complained about Article 10 of the League Covenant:

If perpetual, it would be an attempt to preserve for all time unchanged the distribution of power and territory made in accordance with the views and exigencies of the Allies in this present juncture of affairs. . . . It would not only be futile; it would be mischievous. Change and growth are the law of life, and no generation can impose its will in regard to the growth of nations and the distribution of power, upon succeeding generations.[17]

This is especially problematic because third parties often do not agree about which side in a war is the aggressor. The closest thing to a criterion that is both general and neutral would be "whoever strikes first across a national border," but this would never be universally accepted. For example, it would have required members of a collective security system to act against the British and Russians in World War II for occupying Iran, against Israel for preempting in June 1967, and against the United States in the 1980s for invading Grenada and Panama. Once we admit that justifications may exist for initial resorts to force, any standard for "aggression" becomes too slippery

16. John H. Herz, *International Politics in the Atomic Age* (New York: Columbia University Press, 1959), pp. 85, 90–91.
17. Quoted in Arthur S. Link, *Wilson the Diplomatist* (Baltimore: Johns Hopkins Press, 1957), p. 136. "The dilemma of collective security has been that its major proponents have been driven to oppose social change in the name of the sanctity of treaties." Thompson, "Collective Security Reexamined," p. 770.

to serve consistently. "The problem is not, as the Wilsonians imagined, one of suppressing an infrequent case of diabolism. . . . To determine the aggressor is really to decide which is a bad nation. And a general law can never do this."[18]

Insensitivity to this ambiguity arose in part because, from the establishment of the League of Nations through the war in Korea, "aggressors" were ideologically repugnant states; for democracies "it was natural . . . to assume that committing themselves to deter or punish 'any aggressor anywhere' meant in fact committing themselves to oppose nondemocratic aggressors who were their national enemies anyway." Not until the Suez expedition of 1956 did assigning guilt become awkward.[19]

A third standard objection is that, in practice, organizing according to the principle of collective responsibility undermines preparations to balance the power of troublesome states. Potent alliances cannot be developed with a snap of the finger when innocent states suddenly lose faith in the collective guarantee. "No arrangement would be more likely to create conditions in which one nation can dominate," wrote Kissinger of the Wilsonian dream. "For if everybody is allied with everybody, nobody has a special relationship with anybody. It is the ideal situation for the most ruthless seeking to isolate potential victims."[20]

Fourth, the responsibility to counter every aggressor can endanger a threatened coalition, as when members of the League considered the obligation of resisting the Soviet attack on Finland after Britain and France were already at war with Germany.[21] The counterproductive effect of collective security came closer to actuality earlier, in the case of efforts to punish Italy for its aggression against Ethiopia. Where proponents of the norm see those efforts as feeble, conservative realists charge that they helped push Italy into the Axis alliance. This argument also cuts against current proponents of "limited" collective security as an alternative to the unrealistic demands of the ideal

---

18. Stromberg, "The Idea of Collective Security," pp. 255, 258.
19. Wolfers, *Discord and Collaboration*, pp. 185–186.
20. Henry A. Kissinger, "Germany, Neutrality and the 'Security System' Trap," *Washington Post*, April 15, 1990, p. D7.
21. "We still read that the path to Nazi aggression was made possible by the failure of the League to coerce Japan in 1931 and Italy in 1935. We have the absurdity, to which collective security is always being reduced, of saying that war in 1931 would have prevented war in 1941. It is implied that had the western states been fighting Japan in Asia they could have fought Germany better in Europe. The verdict of careful history might be that the ill-conceived effort to apply 'sanctions' against Italy in 1935 weakened, not strengthened, the front against Germany." Stromberg, "The Idea of Collective Security," p. 254.

type. The problem in the 1930s was precisely the limitation of the concept, a compromise response; either of the extremes would have been preferable. Had *pure* collective security been applied, the fascist powers could have been crushed early; or had pure balance-of-power strategy been applied, Italy might have been kept in the allied camp by ignoring its depredations in Africa. Falling between the stools, however, truncated collective security and left France and Britain with the worst of both worlds.

A fifth, more general criticism is the structural realist argument that collective security requires centralization which conflicts with independence:

States cannot entrust managerial powers to a central agency unless that agency is able to protect its client states. The more powerful the clients and the more the power of each of them appears as a threat to the others, the greater the power lodged in the center must be. The greater the power of the center, the stronger the incentive for states to engage in a struggle to control it.

States, like people, are insecure in proportion to the extent of their freedom. If freedom is wanted, insecurity must be accepted. Organizations that establish relations of authority and control may increase security as they decrease freedom. If might does not make right, whether among people or states, then some institution or agency has intervened to lift them out of nature's realm.[22]

The main reason that liberals lost interest in collective security in earlier generations was that it did not work, and the challenge to it had to be met with traditional means. The League Covenant and Kellogg-Briand Pact neither deterred nor defeated fascist aggressions in the 1930s, because the volitional elements of the system faltered; when principle came to practice, statesmen chose not to honor the commitment of the Covenant to united action; they chose not to flip the switches on the collective security machine.

Conservative realists, however, do not just fear that the principle would not work; to them it can be awful if it *does* work. Their criticism is that if abstract commitments are honored, the system inevitably turns small conflicts into big ones, by requiring states to get involved when it is not in their interest to do so. This was the main reason that realists like Hans Morgenthau and George Kennan fell out with liberal hawks over the Vietnam War. The Cold War redefinition of collective security as the global coalition against communist aggression, in rhetoric from Dean Acheson to Dean Rusk, fed

---

22. Waltz, *Theory of International Politics*, p. 112.

the domino theory: South Vietnam was important not in itself, but as a matter of principle. Fighting in Vietnam meant avoiding the mistakes of the 1930s in not fighting in Manchuria or Ethiopia. Morgenthau posed the counterproductive effect of the principle:

It is the supreme paradox of collective security that any attempt to make it work with less than ideal perfection will have the opposite effect from what it is supposed to achieve. . . . If an appreciable number of nations are opposed to the status quo. . . . the distribution of power will take on the aspects of a balance of power. . . . The attempt to put collective security into effect under such conditions . . . will not preserve peace, but will make war inevitable. . . . It will also make localized wars impossible and thus make war universal. For under the regime of collective security as it actually works under contemporary conditions, if A attacks B, then C, D, E, and F might honor their collective obligations and come to the aid of B, while G and H might try to stand aside and I, J, and K might support A's aggression. . . . By the very logic of its assumptions, the diplomacy of collective security must aim at transforming all local conflicts into world conflicts . . . since peace is supposed to be indivisible. . . . Thus a device intent on making war impossible ends by making war universal.[23]

Realist arguments against a collective security system for Europe rest on both fears—that it would not work when needed, or that it would work when it should not. If commitments falter in a crunch, defense against a rogue power will be weaker than if the regular NATO alliance had remained the guarantor of security. If it does work, however, it precludes denying protection to Eastern European countries against each other or a great power. This makes a crisis in that cauldron of instabilities more likely to erupt than to stew in its own juices. Concern with this implication of the classic scheme of collective security for involvement in the Balkans, embodied in Article 10 of the League Covenant (to "preserve as against external aggression the territorial integrity of all members"), was a specific reason for U.S. domestic opposition to joining that organization over seventy years ago.[24]

WHY DOES COLLECTIVE SECURITY KEEP COMING BACK?
The Wilsonian ideal of collective security was buffeted by history from all sides in the 1930s, and again after the anti-fascist alliance split. Redefinitions

23. Hans J. Morgenthau, *Politics Among Nations,* fifth ed. (New York: Knopf, 1973), pp. 411–412. See also Stromberg, "The Idea of Collective Security," pp. 258–259.
24. Henry L. Stimson and McGeorge Bundy, *On Active Service in Peace and War* (New York: Harper, 1948), pp. 102–103.

in the first half of the Cold War were also driven from favor—for hawks, by disappointment with the development of the UN after Korea, and for doves, by disillusionment with the crusade in Vietnam. The term's renewed popularity does not come from a change of mind about the earlier disillusionments, but from the apparent inadequacy of alternative constructs for adjusting to the outbreak of peace, and because some now define the concept in narrow ways that avoid troublesome implications. At the same time, there is no agreement on whether the most troublesome commitment would be to counter aggression by a great power or to pacify wars between Eastern European states over borders and ethnic minorities.

Many proponents of a collective security system for post–Cold War Europe are ambivalent or opposed outright to requiring intervention in a new generation of Balkan wars. Richard Ullman proclaims that "Europe's peace has become a divisible peace," yet endorses a European Security Organization (ESO) that would include "a generalized commitment to collective security. Each member state would commit itself . . . to come to the aid of any other if it is the victim of an armed attack." The obligation, however, would not extend to little victims. Eastern Europe's fate is to be excluded as "a vast buffer zone between the Soviet Union and Germany." If cross-border violence erupts over national minorities in Kosovo or Transylvania, "the major powers would be unlikely to get involved to an extent greater than through diplomacy and perhaps economic pressure." Besides "walling off" local conflicts, the benefit of the buffer zone that Ullman anticipates is to facilitate great power confidence in a shift toward defensively-oriented military doctrines.[25] Similarly, Charles Kupchan and Clifford Kupchan prescribe collective security, yet at the same time make a gargantuan concession to traditional balance of power by endorsing tacit recognition of "areas of special interest" such as a Russian *droit du regard* in Eastern Europe.[26] These notions recognize the defects in the Wilsonian ideal type, and they may reassure the great powers about their security, but they de-collectivize collective security.

Uncertainty about whether the system would cover Eastern Europe is crucial. There are two essential trends in Europe today: in the West, economic and political integration, consensus on borders, and congruence between nations and states; in the East, the reverse—disintegration and lack of con-

25. Ullman, *Securing Europe*, pp. 28, 29, 68, 73–74, 78, 147.
26. Kupchan and Kupchan, "Concerts, Collective Security, and the Future of Europe," pp. 156–157.

sensus or congruence. Will the stability of the West be protected by holding the mess in the East at arm's length? Ullman believes the new collective system would handle misbehavior by one of the great powers, but not small ones,[27] presumably because the stakes are higher. By the same token, however, the costs and risks (such as involvement of nuclear weapons) would be higher too, so the balance of costs and benefits does not obviously make pacification of small wars in Eastern Europe a less attractive objective.

It should hardly be as daunting for the system to settle a fight between Hungary and Rumania or between Ukraine and Poland as to confront one between Russia or Germany and the rest of the continent. At the same time, apparent sideshows in Eastern Europe may offer occasions for abrasions and misperceptions among the great powers if they disagree about intervention. One nightmare would be a Russian attack on Ukraine (far less fanciful than a Soviet attack on NATO ever was; Russian vice president Rutskoi has already broached the issue of recovering the Crimea for Russia).[28] Under true collective security, members of the system would have to aid Ukraine—doing what NATO would not do for Hungary in 1956—thus evoking the danger of escalation and nuclear war. Under realist norms, the West should leave Ukraine to its fate—tragic for the Ukrainians, but safer for everyone else. If we prefer the latter course, why try to dress it up by associating it with collective security?

If one is genuinely interested in collective security as something different from traditional spheres of influence and alignments based on power and national interest, it is hard to write off responsibility for dealing with wars involving *either* great or small states; but if one is primarily interested in avoiding escalation of limited wars into large ones, it is hard to accept advance commitment to engage either sort of challenge before knowing exactly what it is. Since the collective security concept cannot be copyrighted, promoters have the right to amend it to accommodate standard criticisms. Confronted with questions about how the system would handle particular worrisome scenarios, however, some of the revisionists argue not just that the system should be exempted from responsibility for that type of conflict, but that such problems will not arise.

---

27. Ullman, *Securing Europe*, p. 68.
28. Celestine Bohlen, "Russian Vice President Wants to Redraw Borders," *New York Times*, January 31, 1992, p. A9.

Conceptual Confusion and System Dysfunction

If revisions of the collective security idea are used to cover arrangements that fit better under other basic concepts like traditional alliance formation, or are used to dignify an arrangement other than a functioning security system, they make it less likely that effects of the system can be predicted from its design. Since collective security is an emergency safety system, and cannot be tested in peacetime the way a real machine can, dysfunctions due to confusions in design may not be evident until the time when the system is most needed.

CONFUSION OF CAUSES AND CONSEQUENCES
Since the collapse of communism it has not always been clear whether the invocation of collective security is meant to enforce peace or to celebrate it. Less emphasis is usually placed on how the system would restore peace in the face of war than on why war (or at least war worthy of concern) will not arise. Ullman writes:

If one were to rely on the historical record of generalized commitments to collective security, one could not be hopeful. . . . But it is arguable that the conditions now emerging in Europe make the past a poor predictor. . . . No major state has revisionist ambitions that its leaders think they could satisfy by sending troops across borders. . . . A genuine congruence of interests and goals sharply distinguishes the present from previous eras. . . . *it is unlikely that the great powers will soon find their commitments to collective security put to the test of a large, searing, and escalating crisis.*[29]

Ullman does recognize that things could go bad, and urges taking advantage of the current window of opportunity to get an ESO going, so that the regime could buttress stability in fouler weather. Why collective security should work any better in the face of the many logical and historical criticisms noted earlier, however, remains unclear, apart from the idea that it can work because it will not have to (since there will be no rampaging rogue states), or because not all aggressions will have to be countered (so statesmen and strategists can pick and choose, just as they have traditionally). Such hopes may also deflect reservations about automatic commitment to combat un-identified future aggressors, but they imply that *peace is the premise of the*

---

29. Ullman, *Securing Europe*, p. 66 (emphasis added).

system rather than the product, that peace will cause peace rather than that collective security will cause peace. If we fasten on the import of the current calm, we muddle the difference between the current need for a security organization (which we can see is low) and the future efficacy of such an organization (which we should want to be high).[30]

One can argue that even if peace may be the cause rather than the consequence at the beginning, it can become the consequence as a regime, once established, promotes cooperation and takes on a life of its own. Speaking of the Concert of Europe, Robert Jervis notes that the expectation that it "could continue to function helped maintain it through the operation of familiar self-fulfilling dynamics. . . . There were no 'runs on the bank'." Rules, reciprocity, and institutionalization reinforced opposition to attempts to change the status quo. Recently, the Kupchans argue, the norm of reciprocity is growing again, as reflected in mutual concessions such as Soviet and Western troop withdrawals from Central Europe.[31] These examples are weak reeds.

First, while the nineteenth-century Concert "influenced the behavior of states in ways that made its continuation possible even after the initial conditions had become attenuated," when the conditions eroded, the regime's efficacy did too. By 1823, a mere eight years after the Napoleonic Wars, the Concert was fraying.[32] The Concert "worked" well only as long as the great powers' disagreements were minor; when the consensus cracked over the Crimea in 1854, and again later in the century, so did the Concert.

As to the second argument, the idea that growing reciprocity characterized East-West relations in recent years misreads the end of the Cold War. The peace settlement was no compromise; it was a series of outright victories for the West. The Soviet Union surrendered in arms control negotiations, ac-

---

30. An analogous issue for nuclear power safety is suggested by the Nuclear Regulatory Commission's inability in the early 1980s to think of a way to deal with the potential problem of genetic damage from a plant accident. "If the risks of an accident are kept low enough, they said, there will be no problem with ignoring inter-generational effects. This conclusion answers the question about consequences of accidents by saying they will be trivial because there will be so few accidents." Perrow, *Normal Accidents*, p. 69, citing U.S. Nuclear Regulatory Commission (NRC), "Safety Goals for Nuclear Power Plants: A Discussion Paper," *NUREG* 0880 (Washington, D.C.: NRC, February 1982), p. 15.
31. Robert Jervis, "Security Regimes," in Stephen D. Krasner, ed., *International Regimes* (Ithaca: Cornell University Press, 1983), pp. 181–182; Richard N. Rosecrance, *Action and Reaction in World Politics* (Boston: Little, Brown, 1963), p. 56; Kupchan and Kupchan, "Concerts, Collective Security, and the Future of Europe," p. 130.
32. Jervis, "Security Regimes," p. 184.

cepting NATO's terms which required grossly asymmetrical reductions in both the treaties on Intermediate Range Nuclear Forces (INF) and Conventional Forces in Europe (CFE). Moscow gave up political control of Eastern Europe without a fight in 1989, getting nothing in return. Within a year the Warsaw Pact was defunct while NATO lived on. The West did not reciprocate Soviet concessions, it just pocketed them. There was more reciprocity during the Cold War when both sides were bargaining with each other (as in SALT I and II or the Helsinki accords) than there was in the ending, as the Russians rolled over belly-up.

Perhaps regimes can bootstrap themselves from consequences to causes, but in the realm of security systems we still lack robust and reassuring models. As to whether regimes can promote peace independent of prior peaceful conditions, why are the failures of the League of Nations or the United Nations to do so not indicative? Indeed, few who think collective security can now work in a Europe of thirty-plus nations are ready to endorse it as viable for the world as a whole. Why not? If an ESO can guard peace, why not the UN? Presumably because the rest of the world has not progressed beyond violent contests and is still "mired in history."[33] When exceptions to the applicability of collective security are pointed out, few reasons are offered for continuing to believe in the idea that do not come back to citations of peace, satisfaction with the status quo, and consensus on legitimate behavior as preconditions for their own enforcement. If Europe remains at peace, it is likely to be not because a collective security system causes it, but because the nations and states of Europe are satisfied.

Few dare propose a pure collective security system, but some argue that realistically limited versions are at least more effective than traditional "balancing under anarchy."[34] This misunderstands the choice. Collective security commitments do not obviate international anarchy any more than an alliance does; only political federation would. And if the salvage job for the concept is completed by dispensing with the unrealistic requirements of universality and automaticity, what then is really left that is not consistent with traditional "balancing under anarchy" to which collective security is ostensibly opposed?

Stripping away the rhetoric of collective security, the actual results that seem to be envisioned by the more realistic proposals that invoke the term are: (1) marginal peacekeeping functions comparable to what the UN has

---

33. Francis Fukuyama, "The End of History," *The National Interest*, No. 16 (Summer 1989), p. 15.
34. Kupchan and Kupchan, "Concerts, Collective Security, and the Future of Europe," p. 116.

attempted in the Congo, Cyprus, Sinai and Gaza (until Nasser evicted the UN force just before the 1967 war), and Lebanon; (2) a collective security cachet on what really amounts to policing by a single dominant power, comparable to the UN actions in Korea and Kuwait where many nations sent token forces but the preponderance of power was imposed by the United States; (3) a condominial system of great power tutelage modeled on the nineteenth-century Concert; or (4) a *de jure* overlay of collective security norms on a *de facto*, unorganized security system, comparable to the Rio Pact "system" in South America.

The limitations of the first of these are well recognized. Cases of UN peacekeeping have generally been modest monitoring and interposition operations,[35] not forthright defeat of aggression as supposed in the basic model of collective security (in large part because there was no international consensus on which sides were the aggressors). The UN missions intervened impartially to separate contending forces under truces which the contenders accepted. Peacekeeping is not peacemaking. Even the peacekeeping was dubious: when the contenders fell out violently again (as in the June 1967 war, the Greek Cypriot coup and Turkish invasion in 1974, or the Israeli invasion of Lebanon in 1982), the UN troops were brushed aside by the combatants. After Korea, UN forces "kept" peace only where and when local contenders did not try to break it.

U.N.-mandated action in the Korean War and against Iraq in 1991 come the closest to real collective security, and the symbolic value of the large number of nations sending combat units was indeed quite significant. In neither case, however, was the military participation of countries other than the United States vital to the outcome. In the recent war, for example, it is implausible that the anti-Iraq coalition forces could have liberated Kuwait without the Americans, or that the Americans could have failed to do so without the assistance of the other forces (although it would have needed the bases in Saudi Arabia). The principle of collective security, however, was indeed vital in motivating the American decision to attack Iraq.[36]

---

35. See *The Blue Helmets: A Review of United Nations Peace-keeping* (New York: United Nations Department of Public Information, October 1985).

36. Once Saudi oil was guarded by the Desert Shield deployment, there was no crucial material interest requiring the United States to spend blood and treasure for tiny Kuwait. Nor was enthusiasm for democracy an explanation. After booting Iraq out, Bush handed Kuwait back to the Sabah family oligarchy that had suspended the country's reasonably democratic constitution (and he then stood aside as Saddam Hussein slaughtered the Shi'ites and Kurds who rose

The third and fourth variants suggested above deserve more scrutiny. The relevance of the Concert model has been overestimated, and that of the unorganized system has been underestimated.

THE OLD CONCERT AND THE NEW EUROPE

If we had to find a reasonable hybrid version of collective security, the nineteenth-century Concert of Europe would be it. As a modification, the Concert does not go so far as to become identical with eighteenth- or late nineteenth-century balance of power models. The Concert departs from important aspects of the ideal definition, however, and it also rests on archaic ideological premises. These problems may not disable it as a model for twenty-first century collective security, but they do weaken it.

One discrepancy between ideal collective security and the Concert is that the former sanctifies the security of all nations while the latter subordinates the sovereignty of the weak to the interests of the strong. Under the Concert the great powers colluded to keep peace by keeping each other satisfied; the rights of a Poland were not in the same class as those of an Austria, Prussia, or Russia. The security nurtured by the Concert was selectively collective.[37] To be accurate rather than confusing, we should call it *condominial* rather than collective. Also, maintaining a balance of power (by cooperation rather than competition) remained an important object of the nineteenth-century Concert regime.

The moral glue of much of the Concert (at least of the Holy Alliance in the East) was monarchical conservatism and opposition to liberalism and nationalism. Yet liberalism and nationalism are precisely what most characterize the recent revolution in Europe. This weakens the proposition that the time for another Concert is ripe because the underlying conditions "are once again present," and because burgeoning democracy is conducive to it.[38] Only if the

---

against Baghdad). Opposition to aggression as a matter of principle is the primary explanation of the U.S. decision for war.

37. See Richard B. Elrod, "The Concert of Europe," *World Politics*, Vol. 28, No. 2 (January 1976), pp. 163–165. Consider that the United Nations in 1945 resembled a Concert. The role of the Security Council apart from the General Assembly accorded special rights to the great powers, and Poland's pre-war borders were changed to suit the Soviet Union.

38. Kupchan and Kupchan, "Concerts, Collective Security, and the Future of Europe," pp. 116, 149. On achievments of the regime, see Paul W. Schroeder, "The 19th-Century International System," *World Politics*, Vol. 39, No. 1 (October 1986). It is true that in the West the Concert did accommodate the new forces, as in the creation of Belgium. British and French ideological disagreements with the eastern powers, however, reduced the Concert's unity. See F.H. Hinsley, *Power and the Pursuit of Peace* (New York: Cambridge University Press, 1963), chaps. 9–10.

fact of ideological consensus *per se* were all that mattered, irrespective of its content, would this be convincing.

The liberal consensus in today's world, however, has different implications for the rights of great powers. Outside of academic hothouses, liberals are unlikely to rejoice in the pacifying effects of transcontinental democracy in one breath and endorse a two-class system of policymaking and security rights in the next. They cannot easily promote collective security for the big boys on the block, and every-man-for-himself for benighted weak states in Eastern Europe. The point was clear in the statement by Czechoslovakia's Foreign Minister Jiri Dienstbier that, "the core of any collective system of European security must be a treaty committing every party to provide assistance, including military assistance, in the event of an attack against any participant."[39]

Can we imagine the western powers giving the back of their hand to the new heroes of the liberated zones? Maybe in whispered back alley conclaves, but not in the formal conferences such as defined the Concert system at its height. Even then, as Gregory Flynn and David Scheffer note in dismissing the Concert as a form of collective security, "No one is prepared to redraw the map of Europe for balance-of-power purposes. . . . International law has evolved substantially to protect the integrity of all states."[40] A Concert today would have more trouble juggling two contradictory sets of values: national self-determination, and the sanctity of existing state borders.

Nor can a collective security regime be shorn of ideology, because the essence of the concept is an assumption of legal order and moral obligation independent of immediate national interest. To ignore this is hardly feasible when the flush of enthusiasm for collective security comes mainly from teleological liberalism.[41] The mechanics of the system and the prediction of how it would function cannot easily be separated from the values that are integral to its design.

IS AN ORGANIZED SYSTEM NECESSARY?

Collective security is popular, despite all the logical problems, because it is hard to think of what else should replace the Cold War alliance system. It

---

39. Quoted in Flynn and Scheffer, "Limited Collective Security," p. 88.
40. Flynn and Scheffer, "Limited Collective Security," p. 81.
41. For example: "There is an inherent logic to the emerging era. . . . The basis of security is being altered by a natural historical progression." Steinbruner, "Revolution in Foreign Policy," p. 66.

seems to go without saying that there must be a grand design and formal regulatory structure. If the structure is not to be designed in terms of bipolar alliances like the Cold War, or multipolar alliances like the classical balance of power, or a fully United Europe, or American dominance, then collective security becomes appealing by process of elimination. Coupled with the celebration of peace, collective security becomes a talisman, a security blanket legitimizing relaxation, rather than a serious action plan for collective war against yet unknown "aggressors." Analysts, however, should bite the bullet and ask what this means about the substance of the security order.

If what we are facing is really a durable condition of natural security in Europe, a post-Hobbesian pacific anarchy, why assume the need for an organized functioning security system of any sort? Why is strategic *laissez faire*, with *ad hoc* adaptation as we go along, unthinkable? What would be wrong if the organization of security on the European continent became like that in South America for the past half-century, where symbolic organs like the Rio Pact continue to exist without substantive import, and states dispense with significant alliance arrangements because there is little concern with the prospect of major international war?[42] Instead of an ESO, why not a UPE (Unorganized Pacified Europe)? If something goes wrong, states could look for allies or other tried and true solutions when the time comes. If this is what ambivalent fans of collective security are implicitly getting at, the two could coexist: an ESO overlay of symbolic commitment in principle to collective security, left sufficiently ambiguous to allow the evolution of traditional initiatives for self-protection in the underlying UPE. In Perrow's terms this would be a "loosely coupled" collective security system, with more potential for adapting to unforeseen circumstances,[43] but its substantive significance would be low; sensible states would not count on it in a pinch.

Unorganized need not mean chaotic and unstable. In physics, equilibrium in thermodynamic systems is called disorganization.[44] Among satisfied states

---

42. In South America as in Europe, there are exceptions to stability, such as the Beagle Channel dispute which has brought Argentina and Chile close to war (most recently at the end of the 1970s). Unlike Cyprus in 1974, however, such fault-lines have not burst open. Reasons for the impressive long peace in South America since the Chaco War of 1932–35 are not obvious, and present a significant challenge to theories on the causes of war offered by both of the major traditions of international relations theory, realism and liberalism. See the forthcoming Columbia University Ph.D. dissertation by Felix Martín-Gonzalez.
43. Perrow, *Normal Accidents*, pp. 88–97.
44. "Organization or order is lost. . . . When complete equilibrium (disorganization) has been reached it is said that the maximum *entropy* for the system has been achieved." The problem is that entropy is possible only in closed systems, which hardly ever exist. Open systems can have

that recognize each other's satisfaction, the security dilemma is not auto-matically a problem. Here the symbolic value of a collective security organi-zation might indeed take on a slight substantive function, if the rituals of meetings and consultations reinforced mutual perceptions of innocent aims. As long as genuflection to collective security forms did not impede traditional strategic adaptation to changing circumstances, it would be helpful at best and harmless at worst.

Arms Control Without Alignment

Most enthusiasts for collective security also favor negotiated limitations on armament. Collective security organizations and arms control treaties alike aim to establish legal orders that deter challenges to peace. The rationales behind them, however, are not consistent.

The two forms of regulation deal in different currencies. Collective security is based on commitments of *intent* (that states will act against aggressors). Arms control is based on constraint of *capabilities.* These could be comple-mentary, but there is still a difference between the political logic of one and the military logic of the other. Arms control relies on balance of power, aiming to construct a military balance that in itself dissuades states from thinking that they can use force effectively for attack; moral status in disputes between the parties to arms control is irrelevant to a treaty's impact on the stability of deterrence. Collective security, in contrast, relies on imbalance of power, a preponderance of the law-abiding many against the law-breaking few; moral claims of the states involved are everything.

The impact of arms limitations on military stability depends in principle on beliefs about what would happen if the forces allowed under the agree-ment were to crash into each other in battle: stability implies that neither side could win by striking first. Thus a stable agreement would be evaluated according to force ratios calculated in terms of dyads. If there is any strategic logic to an arms treaty, it must assume knowledge of who would be on whose side in event of war. It would be nonsensical for A, B, and C to agree to binding constraints of equal armament, forswearing options of unilateral military buildup, if they think that in a pinch two of them are likely to

---

steady states, but these must be maintained by negative feedback mechanisms. Floyd H. Allport, *Theories of Perception and the Concept of Structure* (New York: Wiley, 1955), pp. 474–475, 484–485 (emphasis in original).

combine against the third. There is nothing stable about a peacetime ratio of 1:1:1 if it translates into a wartime ratio of 2:1. A country expecting that it may have to fight alone will want the option to increase its power unilaterally, and will not logically settle for limits that prohibit that option.

Whereas arms control logically depends on specifying prospective alignment, however, collective security depends explicitly on *not* doing so. It *assumes* that if one breaks the peace the others must join to overwhelm it; that is the whole point of the system. And if collective security rests on the guarantee that members of the system will act together against a renegade, then the individual levels of armament among the states in the system hardly matter as long as no single one develops as much power as the others combined. On the other hand, if the system cannot rely on the universal guarantee, and collective defense has to be substituted for collective security, then the identity of alignments is crucial for judging the stability of peacetime force configurations.

MILITARY CRITERIA FOR LIMITATIONS

Few proposals address in detail what standards or formulas would mesh limits for armament with the logic of a collective security system. Those who embrace the treaty on Conventional Forces in Europe (CFE), or who endorse further reductions along its lines, would base arms control on the old Cold War framework of bipolar alliances that is already gone. The CFE Treaty itself makes no strategic sense (at least for Russia) since the dissolution of the old order. It says nothing about what forces should be allowed to the successor states of the Soviet Union, and aside from that problem the formula for military balance in the treaty is logical only as long as the former members of the Warsaw Pact are assumed to have more strategic affinity with Moscow than with the countries of western Europe.

Another proposal does attempt to supersede the old framework, but with dubious implications. It would establish a supranational "organization, to which all states belong, that regulates the conditions of military deployment for everyone."[45] What would be the benchmarks for regulation? At one point John Steinbruner suggests that "standardized criteria for setting force ceilings *would ensure that no state faced a decisive advantage against any other single state,* and the residual alliances would offer protection against the formation of

---

45. Steinbruner, "Revolution in Foreign Policy," pp. 108–109.

aggressive coalitions." In the next breath, however, it is proposed that each state be allowed force levels proportional to the length of its borders. By the author's own estimates this showed the old Soviet Union with *more than double* the "offensive potential" of Germany and a far higher margin against any other European state; Turkey with nearly four times as much as its enemy Greece; and Germany with more than twice as much as either Poland or France. All of this contradicts the prior criterion of no decisive advantage between any two states,[46] and shows that the identification of coalitions would remain absolutely essential to assessing the stability of military relationships on the continent.

If the prior criterion were to take precedence, the arms control order should be denominated in terms of force-to-force rather than force-to-space ratios, and should accord absolutely equal forces, battalion for battalion, to all states, irrespective of their size, population, or other asymmetries; Belgium's forces should equal Germany's. The proposal does not do so, because it seeks to endow the new military allotments with a technical character more favorable to defensive operations than to attack, and assumes that this is related to capacity to cover borders with satisfactory force-to-space ratios. To take that criterion seriously, however, contradicts the aim of significant reductions of forces, or for many of the countries in Europe, of any reductions at all.

Ensuring a linear defense means maximizing the density of forces covering the line, to prevent probing attacks from finding a gap or weak point that can be penetrated. Yet the Steinbruner proposal, although denominated in terms of force-to-space ratios, seeks to reduce density rather than maximize it. It aims at an allowance of one brigade per seventy-five kilometers of front,

---

46. Steinbruner, "Revolution in Foreign Policy," pp. 74–76 (emphasis added). The estimates also include figures for "defensive potential," but the bar on the graph for the Soviet Union's offensive potential is still longer than the bars for any of the other countries' defensive potentials, and Germany's offensive bar is longer than the defensive ones for any other countries in the compilation except the Soviet Union. (The United States and the United Kingdom do not appear on the chart. Also, the figures for the Soviet Union appear to include only the portions of its border west of the Urals.) A better rationale for the figures is available, ironically, if we substitute assumed coalitions for the notion of "global alliance." This can be read into Steinbruner's mention of "residual alliances," although there is only one alliance of any sort on the continent anyway, since the Warsaw Pact has dissolved and many of its former members would like to join NATO. Allotting to Russia forces that are grossly superior to any other state in the region might bring the actual situation closer to balance if we assume that solitary Russia were to face a coalition of many of the others. Moreover, as Malcolm Chalmers suggests ("Beyond the Alliance System", p. 245), an ESO would limit obligations to Europe, and thus would not guarantee Russia against security problems in Asia or challenges to its southern borders, so Moscow would have another justification for a surplus of capability.

which is a mere one-fifth of the ratio considered adequate (and only a tenth of the optimum) in tactical doctrines of modern armies.[47] This could conceivably be rationalized by compensating for thinner ground forces along the line with unusually large amounts of mobile firepower from air forces, yet the proposal seeks to reduce that dimension of capability as well, and to do so disproportionately (on grounds that airpower is an offensive capability).[48] Low density on the ground, uncompensated by other sources of firepower, opens up much larger possibilities for offensive movement. If total force levels were low enough on both sides, this would prevent penetrations from occupying much of the defender's territory, operations could degenerate into the raiding/counterraiding style of medieval warfare, and strategy would move from denial or conquest toward punishment, but it would all be hardly conducive to linear defense.[49]

Defense-dominance is easier with high force levels and low tech than with low force levels and low tech.[50] If one really wants to base operational

---

47. John J. Mearsheimer, *Conventional Deterrence* (Ithaca: Cornell University Press, 1983), pp. 181, 265 n.

48. Steinbruner, "Revolution in Foreign Policy," p. 77. He argues that because "it is generally believed that a standard brigade would have to be concentrated in less than a five-kilometer segment of front . . . in order to overcome well-prepared, competently positioned defenses," overall reduction of force levels would require an attacker to concentrate a larger proportion of its ground units, thus exposing its own defense in other sectors to greater risk of counterattack (p. 75). This, however, appears to lose sight of the relativity of requirements. If the defender's line is much thinner than the standard norm, the concentration an attacker needs to penetrate will be lower as well.

49. See Archer Jones, *The Art of War in the Western World* (Urbana: University of Illinois Press, 1987), pp. 558–560, 652–653, 666–667. At one end of the continuum of force-to-space ratios would be the western front in World War I, where density was so high that sustained penetration proved impossible for most of the war. At the other end would be guerrilla wars, where the ratios are so low that governments cannot cover all points they need to defend, while rebels can concentrate at will to raid those left vulnerable. Force-to-space ratios are certainly not all-determining, especially given big differences in equipment and tactical doctrines between forces. For the most extensive survey of the question, see Stephen D. Biddle, et al., *Defense at Low Force Levels: The Effect of Force to Space Ratios on Conventional Combat Dynamics*, IDA Paper P-2380 (Alexandria, Va.: Institute for Defense Analyses, August 1991).

50. This point must be emphasized because the Steinbruner proposal uses the counter-argument that high-tech defenses and surveillance, coupled with limits on advanced offensive weapons, allow forward defense with low force levels. This is dubious for two reasons. First, it implicitly assumes that defensive forces can move and reconcentrate instantly, in response to instant intelligence detection of concentration by the attacker. No reasons are suggested as to why the strategic initiative, and the prerogative of choosing circumstances of weather and terrain, give the attacker no significant advantage in timing. Second, the proposal is unrealistic about the strategic flexibility of combined arms operations, which blurs simple distinctions between dominantly defensive or offensive characteristics of weapons. For example, in October 1973 the Egyptians used surface-to-air missiles and precision-guided anti-tank munitions (both normally tagged as inherently defensive weapons) to screen the advance of armored forces into the Sinai;

doctrine on linear defense and force-to-space ratios, and simultaneously to reduce the mobile firepower available to defenders for quick movement to threatened sectors, the answer would be to *increase* ground forces (while limiting their mobility), not reduce them. The most effective capability for defense that posed the least capability for attack would be, in effect, heavily armed infantry, lined up shoulder-to-shoulder all along the border, with their legs cut off. To increase forces, however, is hardly a plausible response to the end of the Cold War, no matter what the military logic.

Tactical complexities aside, endorsement of technological and doctrinal "defense dominance" by proponents of collective security[51] is reasonable, but not unambiguously so. Compared with traditional strategic arrangements, which usually develop war plans, deployments, and doctrine in regard to an identified enemy, collective security is likely to *delay* reaction to attack, because the members of the system must react, mobilize, and coordinate their response *ad hoc*. Since preponderant power is not arrayed against an attacker before transgression occurs (if it were, the system would be a regular alliance, not collective security), and strategic initiative can often negate tactical advantage,[52] defeat of aggression will usually have to rely on counterattack to take back lost territory, rather than on direct defense. In that case the tactical advantage of defense passes to the original aggressor, and the counterattack has to rely on its disproportionate strength or offensive ingenuity at the strategic level to succeed. This was indeed the case in the two international actions of the past half-century that came closest to the collective security model: the responses to the North Korean attack in 1950 and to the Iraqi invasion of Kuwait in 1991.

POLITICAL CRITERIA FOR LIMITATIONS

The legalism of collective security, which establishes obligations in terms of hypothetical rather than actual enemies, is an apolitical guide to arms control.

---

similarly, the Israelis used "offensive" attack aircraft to defend against the advancing Egyptian tanks. Had both sides been limited to the "defensive" elements of force structure only, the Israelis might have held if they had manned the Suez Canal Bar-Lev Line with high force-to-space ratios, but the line was lightly manned.

51. In addition to Steinbruner see Kupchan and Kupchan, "Concerts, Collective Security and the Future of Europe," p. 136; and Ullman, *Securing Europe*, pp. 73–74.

52. See Carl von Clausewitz, *On War*, Michael Howard and Peter Paret, eds. and trans. (Princeton: Princeton University Press, 1976), pp. 363–364, 367; Richard K. Betts, *Surprise Attack* (Washington, D.C.: Brookings, 1982), p. 15; and Betts, "Conventional Deterrence," *World Politics*, Vol. 37, No. 2 (January 1985), pp. 163–172.

If no danger of war ever arose, the various potential dyadic power balances affected by treaty limits would not matter strategically, and the arms control agreements' value would depend on how much they facilitated cuts in military expenditure. Nor would limits matter much if a challenge to collective security did arise and all the members of the system honored the obligation to roll back the aggressor. If war were to break out more raggedly, however, with a great power or a set of states challenging the status quo while a number of the others stood aloof from combat, the balances established by apolitical criteria could be disastrous; having been decided without reference to the wartime lineups, it would be only fortuitous if the distribution of capabilities happened to favor the side with defensive objectives.

Worse, formal limitations, especially if they do not produce a balance of power in the relevant dyad, could have more directly dangerous effects. Accords can provide advance warning of aggression, arms controllers claim, facilitating timely countermobilization. As the Kupchans write, "a significant military buildup would *automatically* be interpreted as a sign of aggressive intent, *triggering* a response."[53] If the agreement is violated in order to prepare to commit aggression, automatic reaction would be a good thing; if the violation is motivated by anxiety about military vulnerability, on the other hand, such reaction would be destabilizing, producing the stereotypical escalation of tension that "spiral" theorists worry about. It is quite plausible that anxious states facing an unfavorable balance of forces with emerging enemies could feel compelled to abrogate limitations on their own options imposed by prior apolitically designed arms control formulas. Had legal constraints not existed, their military buildups could seem more innocent or ambiguous, and response could be determined according to the merits of the balance of power rather than the legal order of allowed armament.

This is a particular problem if we have reason to worry about a future change in Russian attitudes toward traditional security. The Soviet Union let the Warsaw Pact crumble not simply because it had no choice; there is no reason to assume that laying down the law with a little violence before November 1989 (as in East Germany in 1953, Hungary in 1956, Czechoslovakia in 1968, and as would have happened in Poland in 1981 had Jaruzelski not imposed martial law) would not have kept Communist governments in power. Instead, Gorbachev adopted a liberal foreign policy, mouthing all the

---

53. Kupchan and Kupchan, "Concerts, Collective Security, and the Future of Europe," p. 127 (emphasis added).

axioms about cooperation, trust, insanity of the arms race, and obsolescence of traditional concepts of security that we have always heard from doves in the West.[54] If we can unwind the coiled spring of mutual suspicion and tension, Gorbachev believed, we would jointly conquer not just the symptom but the cause of conflict. "New thinking" embraced collective security because the new thinkers, like many liberals in the West, believed security was an artificial problem more than a real one, that there was nothing to fear but fear itself. These were the same new thinkers, however, who believed that the Soviet Union would survive as a state if it reduced its reliance on coercion.

The concessions that happily ended the Cold War were a precipitous loss of security for Russia in the hoary terms of balance of power. The Reds may never come back, but what if the Realists do? What if economic disaster, apparent failure of western liberal models, nasty maneuvers by newly free republics, oppression of Russian minorities in those areas, and upsurge of populist and nationalist bitterness bring the principle of "Looking Out for Number One" back into favor? Will noticing that the old subservient buffer of Eastern Europe is not only gone, but aligned with the West, spur no Russian interest in rearmament? The limits in the CFE agreement, conceived in the context of the two old alliances, preclude parity between Russia and a new western coalition that could include former members of the Warsaw Pact (and even some former Soviet republics). In a meaner world, such military inferiority might seem less tolerable to Moscow than it does now, when it seems irrelevant.

Arms control could make sense in the Cold War because the relevant alignments by which stable force ratios might be estimated seemed clear and durable. By the same token, limitations on individual nations' forces could be pernicious after the Cold War because there is no logical basis by which to determine the allowed ratios before new cleavages emerge and harden. Military balances that appear neutral under one pattern of alignment or lack of it can instantly become destabilizing when countries start lining up in a different pattern. As Charles Fairbanks and Abram Shulsky argue:

---

54. "Peace is movement toward globality and universality of civilization. Never before has the idea that peace is indivisible been as true as it is now. . . . at the end of the twentieth century force and arms will have to give way as a major instrument in world politics." In the West, words like this always used to strike hardheaded types as pacifist globaloney, but they were typical Gorbachev rhetoric. "Excerpts From Gorbachev's Speech: 'The Idea That Peace Is Indivisible'," *New York Times*, June 6, 1991, p. A12.

Arms limitation agreements, which by their very nature involve precise ratios and numbers of arms permitted to each side, are far more specific than most treaties. *They thus lack the flexibility that enables most international agreements to bend with change and be infused with a new political content.* . . . When the rigid structure of an arms limitation agreement can no longer contain changed political forces, it will snap apart. The cost may be heavy: after an arms limitation treaty not renewed, as after a divorce, one cannot return to the starting point.[55]

This potential does not matter as long as there is no antagonism that could raise the danger of war, but for the same reason, neither does arms control matter in those circumstances, except to save money. That would be a big exception, and a valuable one if technical stability of military relationships is unimportant. But would arms control necessarily produce lower expenditures than *laissez faire*?

OTHER PERVERSE EFFECTS

In the present atmosphere most governments will rush to cut military budgets unilaterally, and with less attention to the effects on arcane calculations of military stability than in the past. Negotiating on prospective legal regulations, however, necessarily fixes more attention on technical calculations and nuances of disparity. This will especially be a problem if countries seeking arms control *do* worry about how it will affect stability. The goal of arms control might produce ongoing negotiations that reach no conclusion but retard unilateral cuts. The parties "will strain to be sure that all dangers and contingencies are covered," John Mueller writes. "Participants volunteer for such regulation only with extreme caution because once under regulation they are often unable to adjust subtly to unanticipated changes. . . . Arms *reduction* will proceed most expeditiously if each side feels free to reverse any reduction it later comes to regret."[56]

Cold War critics claimed that arms control stimulated military spending (or at least failed to constrain it), as when Kennedy's Limited Test Ban Treaty, Ford's Vladivostok Accord, or Carter's SALT II Treaty coincided with defense budget increases. More indicative for the post–Cold War world should be

---

55. Charles H. Fairbanks, Jr., and Abram N. Shulsky, "From 'Arms Control' to Arms Reductions: The Historical Experience," *Washington Quarterly*, Vol. 10, No. 3 (Summer 1987), p. 68. (Emphasis added.)
56. Mueller, "A New Concert of Europe," pp. 6, 9.

the 1922 Washington Naval Treaty that fixed capital ship ratios among the great powers, since it was concluded in a period of minimal international tension and was multilateral rather than bipolar in construction. Britain responded to that agreement "with greater activity in naval building than at any time since the armistice."[57] That treaty is also sometimes charged with having stimulated competition in unregulated dimensions of weaponry (for example, the "treaty race" in bigger and better cruisers, replacing the battleship race), and having channelled innovation away from defensive developments (fortifications were prohibited in the western Pacific to secure Japanese agreement to the battleship ratio) and into weaponry of more offensive, destabilizing, "first-strike" capability (aircraft carriers).[58]

Finally, contrary to conventional wisdom, arms control designed in the context of peacetime could endanger crisis management. Collective security proponents usually claim that arms control will reinforce crisis stability because treaty provisions for monitoring and verification will create "transparency" and rules of the road that will reduce chances of accidental escalation in a crisis confrontation.[59] This argument means the most to those who worry that uncontrolled interactions of military forces operating in alert conditions are a more probable cause of war than premeditated resort to force.

Positive reasons for such controls certainly exist.[60] Their relative importance after the Cold War, however, is oversold, while their potential negative consequences are overlooked. Primary concern with crisis interactions as an autonomous cause of war—the notion of "inadvertent" or "accidental" war—is inconsistent with faith in the durability of the current causes of peace. You cannot get hair-trigger alert operations like those in the crisis of October 1962, or mobilization spirals like those in the crisis of July 1914, without a crisis.

---

57. Stephen Roskill, *Naval Policy Between the Wars* (London: Collins, 1968), p. 332, quoted in Fairbanks and Shulsky, "From 'Arms Control' to Arms Reductions," p. 65.
58. Fairbanks and Shulsky, "From 'Arms Control' to Arms Reductions," pp. 66–67. See also Robert Gordon Kaufman, *Arms Control During the Pre-Nuclear Era* (New York: Columbia University Press, 1990).
59. Ullman, *Securing Europe*, pp. 141–142; Kupchan and Kupchan, "Concerts, Collective Security, and the Future of Europe," p. 131; Steinbruner, "Revolution in Foreign Policy," p. 75.
60. See Scott D. Sagan, "Nuclear Alerts and Crisis Management," *International Security*, Vol. 9, No. 4 (Spring 1985), pp. 99–139; Scott D. Sagan, "Rules of Engagement," *Security Studies*, Vol. 1, No. 1 (Autumn 1991), pp. 78–108; Bruce G. Blair, "Alerting in Crisis and Conventional War," in Ashton B. Carter, John D. Steinbruner, and Charles A. Zraket, eds., *Managing Nuclear Operations* (Washington, D.C.: Brookings, 1987); Bruce G. Blair and John D. Steinbruner, "The Effects of Warning on Strategic Stability," Brookings Occasional Paper (Washington, D.C.: Brookings, 1991); Kurt Gottfried and Bruce G. Blair, eds., *Crisis Stability and Nuclear War* (New York: Oxford University Press, 1988).

Yet crisis presupposes conflict. A crisis does not arise through a *deus ex machina*, with no prior clash of interests. A conflict serious enough to produce a military confrontation will mean that the premise of continental content-ment has been shattered, in which case *that* problem looms much larger than the technical one of crisis instability due to communication breakdowns.

As others have often noted, it is hard to think of any case of a genuinely accidental war (that is, one due to causes beyond political authorities' control, as distinct from one due to their miscalculation).[61] World War I, the favorite case for those who worry about the problem, does not qualify. Marc Trach-tenberg has shown how strategic mythology over the last several decades grossly exaggerated the political "loss of control" in the July 1914 crisis, even if one rejects the Fritz Fischer thesis that German aggression caused the war.[62] To promote arms control measures in order to limit accidental escala-tion elevates the secondary to the essential. This was reasonable in the Cold War context, when the essential problem endangering security—the ideolog-ical and power competition between East and West—was well recognized and addressed steadily through alliances and defense plans, but not now, when the principal problem is to anticipate what basic conflict of interest could arise.

It is also short-sighted to assume that treaty arrangements for verification in peacetime will help defuse crises. Inspection regimes are unlikely to be operating and "transparency" will probably have gone by the boards by the time a crisis erupts. Treaty obligations are usually abrogated before that point

---

61. Alexander George defines *inadvertent* war as one "neither side wanted or expected at the outset of the crisis." "Findings and Recommendations," in George, ed., *Avoiding War: Problems of Crisis Management* (Boulder, Colo.: Westview Press, 1991), p. 545. This is expansive enough to include deliberate decisions by political authorities to initiate combat, which are not the same as hypothetical cases where decentralization of authority could produce military operational activities that elude policymakers' control and provoke escalation autonomously. See Paul Bracken, *The Command and Control of Nuclear Forces* (New Haven: Yale University Press, 1983), pp. 48, 53, 231–232; or John D. Steinbruner, "An Assessment of Nuclear Crises," in Franklyn Griffiths and John C. Polanyi, eds., *The Dangers of Nuclear War* (Toronto: University of Toronto Press, 1980), pp. 39–40. For a study that admits the importance of the danger in principle but shows persuasively the overwhelmingly powerful restraints against it in practice, see Joseph F. Bouchard, *Command in Crisis* (New York: Columbia University Press, 1991). Geoffrey Blainey persuasively debunks the notion that accidental wars have occurred, but argues that if miscal-culation is included in the definition, virtually all wars could be considered accidental. Blainey, *The Causes of War*, 3d ed. (New York: Free Press, 1988), chap. 9, especially pp. 144–145.
62. Marc Trachtenberg, *History and Strategy* (Princeton: Princeton University Press, 1991), chap. 2, especially pp. 54–60, 77–80, 84–87, 90–92, 97–98. (A shorter version of this chapter appeared as Marc Trachtenberg, "The Meaning of Mobilization in 1914," *International Security*, Vol. 15, No. 3 (Winter 1990/91), pp. 120–150.)

is reached. There are no bolts from the blue; wars do not explode at the instant a conflict of interest develops. Germany junked the arms control provisions of the Versailles Treaty long before 1939, and Japan renounced the 1922 Naval Treaty five years before Pearl Harbor. While abrogation may provide political warning of crisis, it is misguided to count on the monitoring provisions of arms control agreements to provide strategic warning of war or tactical warning of attack.

If inspection regimes or other agreements oriented to crisis management did remain in place during the run-up to crisis, they could just as easily have a counterproductive effect as a dampening one, since the effect of abrogating *during* the crisis could seem much more threatening. It is more likely then than in normal peacetime that an anxious state would rush to revoke restraints on its options for self-defense, or intrusive inspections helpful to its adversary, and that such actions could be read by the adversary as preparations to strike first. "Transparency" can only apply to capabilities, not intentions. If the value of such greater openness depends on the assumption that actions inconsistent with arms control agreements will be presumed evidence of aggressive intent, the regime could harm crisis management as much as help it.

Conclusion

If there is any time when establishing a collective security institution should be feasible, this is it, but collective security will hardly matter unless the present peace goes bad. If there is any time when negotiated arms control should *not* matter, this is it, but agreements achieved now would leave equations of power whose significance could be utterly different, and dangerous, if peace goes bad. Conservative realism, on the other hand, is too fatalistic a guide, since it underestimates the potential grounds for pacific anarchy in Europe. Anarchy, and the competition for power that it encourages, are necessary but not sufficient causes of war. They need a *casus belli* to push conflict over the edge.[63] The "Unorganized Pacified Europe" de-

---

63. World War I is sometimes cited as caused by pure power rivalry, but without nationalist-imperialist ideologies, territorial disputes, and militarist romanticism it would have been much harder to get the war started. Blainey argues against viewing motives, grievances, or substantive aims as causes on grounds that they are only "varieties of power." Blainey, *The Causes of War*, chap. 10. That all-inclusive definition, however, makes the argument practically tautologous.

scribed above is not markedly less probable than John Mearsheimer's hyper-realist nightmare.[64] Either one, however, is more plausible than a *functioning* collective security system or a politically disembodied arms control regime. Instituting a collective security organization might be acceptable, nevertheless, for its symbolic value. Despite the negative emphasis in the rest of this article, I am not set against the idea, provided that it is not taken seriously enough in practice to bar parallel security arrangements that should be considered incompatible with it in principle. Similarly, serious and comprehensive arms regulation may never be achieved if leaders lose their sense of urgency and get wrapped up in more important problems, while their bureaucracies get bogged down in technical questions. In any event, arms control constraints that could prove destabilizing in a Europe riven by new alignments would probably be abandoned long before a crisis at the brink of war, so strategists should not fall on their swords to prevent such agreements. But beware of too much insouciance.

In another context Jack Snyder has argued that "neo-liberal institution-building will do great damage if it is attempted, but doesn't work." [65] The same is true of pressures for transforming old security institutions in Europe into a collective security organization, or concluding new arms control agreements, unless we are disingenuous or subtle enough to couple them with other initiatives that work in different directions. If collective security and arms control were important only as symbols, we could accept them as harmless or reject them as diversionary. But symbols can have substantive effects. The effects may be consistent with the symbol if it motivates statesmen to conform with the value that it enshrines; this is what regime theorists hope collective security might do. Or the effects may be antagonistic to the symbol if it obscures reality and prevents properly adaptive action; this is what Realists fear it might do.

All this implies accepting three different but partially overlapping rings of security organization.[66] One ring would be a new European Security Organization, including all the countries in the Conference on Security and Co-operation in Europe (CSCE), but without replacing the second ring, the old

---

64. John J. Mearsheimer, "Back to the Future: Instability in Europe After the Cold War," *International Security*, Vol. 15, No. 1 (Spring 1990), pp. 5–57.
65. Jack Snyder, "Averting Anarchy in the New Europe," *International Security*, Vol. 14, No. 4 (Spring 1990), p. 40.
66. A similar formulation was first suggested to me in an unpublished paper by Captain Victor Bird, USA.

NATO. This combination is accepted by many current fans of collective security, although some would turn NATO into the sole ESO by admitting Russia, which would be a mistake. The latter aim should be accomplished in the third ring, a discreet concert of the United States, Britain, France, Germany, and Russia, without highly publicized formal meetings like the economic summits (if that model were followed, membership of the concert would have to expand in response to pleas from other big states in the system). We might also want to accept arms control agreements as long as they are modest enough not to confine freedom of adaptation (e.g., alliances according to emergent threats, decisions to refrain from intervention in wars between small states).

The risk in this recommendation is that it will sound either stupid—a mindless endorsement of anything in response to uncertainty about everything—or cynical—a deliberate commitment to institutions whose rationales contradict each other. In either case the idea would prove infeasible. If governments devote themselves symbolically to collective security in a way substantial enough to have any beneficial effects, we cannot count on them to be cynical enough to pursue divergent policies in an equally substantial way. If the happily pacific order of the new post–Cold War Europe goes bad, then the process of traditional adaptation will probably be more hesitant and delayed than otherwise. That might leave us the worst of both worlds: a collective security organization that falters when the chips are down, and a hysterical scramble to establish a better balance of power that goes in such a hurry that it aggravates political tensions.

But what else should we do if not tread water by dabbling in several somewhat inconsistent solutions? While a UPE may be possible, at least for some period of time, it would be reckless to bank on it; while NATO may last, it may wither if nothing new and big and scary replaces the Marxist menace; and while a collective security commitment may capture imaginations, it could leave us in the lurch if we count on it. The problem is, we cannot prescribe a system (if we expect actual statesmen to make it work) based on a principle without reference to cases; we cannot compose a definite new solution until we confront a definite new problem. The current peace is not what makes some novel solution to security suddenly plausible, it is what makes it *harder* to settle on any formula, and what encourages the logically inconsistent policy of overlaying various schemes, regimes, or organizations on each other.

Inconsistency is reasonable if we do not yet know when and against whom we will once again need a functioning security system for Europe. Relying on any single scheme is too risky in the new world where the current threat is uncertainty. Yes, the idea that post–Cold War strategy must define itself against "uncertainty" is becoming a tiresome and suspiciously facile cliché. That is unfortunate, but cannot be helped, because it happens to be true.

Down and Out in Warsaw and Budapest

| F. Stephen Larrabee

Eastern Europe and East-West Migration

In the last few years the issue of migration flows has emerged as a significant political problem, especially in Europe.[1] In the early postwar period, the free movement of people had generally been considered to be a positive development and a spur to economic growth. But in the 1970s, this attitude began to change as economies in Western Europe began to contract and the need for cheap labor declined. At the same time, during this period Europe changed from a net emigration region to an area of net immigration. This change was largely due to two factors: (1) economic growth in Western Europe made it an attractive area for many in developing countries; and (2) traditional markets for unskilled labor began to contract.[2]

Nevertheless, immigration was largely considered a manageable problem, at least in the medium term, well into the 1980s. The collapse of communism in Eastern Europe and the Soviet Union, however, has given the question of East-West migration an entirely new dimension.[3] In the 1970s and the early 1980s, the outflows of people from Warsaw Pact states numbered only about 100,000 annually. This changed dramatically in 1989 when a total of 1.2

F. Stephen Larrabee is a Senior Analyst in the International Policy Department at RAND in Santa Monica, California.

This article is a revised version of a paper originally presented at a conference on "Prospective Migration from the USSR" in Santa Monica, November 17–19, 1991, sponsored by RAND. It is part of a larger RAND project on "Current and Emergent Migration and Emigration from the Former USSR: Domestic and International Consequences." The views expressed in the article are the author's own and do not necessarily reflect those of RAND or its sponsors.

1. See Jonas Widgren, "International Migration and Regional Stability," *International Affairs*, Vol. 66, No. 4 (October 1990), pp. 749–766. Also Hans Arnold, "The Century of the 'Refugee': A European Century?" *Aussenpolitik*, No. 3 (1991), pp. 271–280; and Peter Opitz, "Refugee and Migration Movements," ibid., pp. 261–270. For a useful survey of the literature on the subject, see Kimberly A. Hamilton and Kate Holder, "International Migration and Foreign Policy: A Survey of the Literature," *Washington Quarterly*, Vol. 14, No. 2 (Spring 1991), pp. 195–211. See also the contributions in the special silver anniversary issue, "International Migration: An Assessment for the '90s," *International Migration Review*, Vol. 23, No. 3 (Fall 1989).
2. Widgren, "International Migration and Regional Stability," pp. 753–754. The "push factor" was more powerful.
3. See François Heisbourg, "Population Movements in Post–Cold War Europe," *Survival*, Vol. 33, No. 1 (January–February 1991), pp. 31–43.

International Security, Spring 1992 (Vol. 16, No. 4)

million people left the former Warsaw Pact states.[4] With the passage of the new passport law in the former Soviet Union in May 1991, allowing freedom of travel to all Soviet citizens, this number could increase significantly.

In addition, as economic restructuring and privatization gather momentum in both the former Soviet Union and Eastern Europe, they will create further pressures for out-migration. According to recent estimates, a rapid demilitarization of the Soviet economy could put as many as 35–40 million people out of work.[5] Many might seek employment in Western Europe. Some, however, might go to Eastern Europe, especially Poland.

These migratory pressures will create major dilemmas for both Eastern and Western Europe. Western Europe has long pressed for freedom of travel for East European and Soviet citizens. Now that this has become possible, can Western Europe close its doors to these new immigrants? Having themselves fought hard to win the right to travel freely, can the East European countries now deny that right to the citizens of the former Soviet Union?

The prospective new wave of migration comes, moreover, at a time when Western Europe finds itself facing significant constraints on its ability to absorb a massive influx of new populations. In the last few years Western Europe received 800,000 regular migrants, including a record number of refugees seeking political asylum from non-European, Third World countries. In the period 1983–89 the number of asylum seekers more than tripled. A growing number of these were from Eastern Europe.

The unexpected increase in the number of asylum seekers, together with changes in U.S. and Australian policies that are slowing down admission of refugees, has aggravated the difficulties for traditional transit points, like Austria and Italy, for immigrants to the United States and Australia. These countries now find themselves host to a growing number of migrants from the East who have nowhere else to go.

Perhaps even more importantly, the motivations behind the new emigration from the East are changing. A decade ago most immigrants from the East were political refugees: they sought asylum from persecution based on their political beliefs. Today the majority of refugees and asylum seekers are

---

4. Widgren, "International Migration and Regional Stability," p. 757.
5. Jean-Claude Chesnais, "Migration from Eastern to Western Europe, Past (1946–1989) and Future (1990–2000)," paper presented at the Conference of Ministers on the Movement of Persons Coming from Central and Eastern European Countries, sponsored by the Council of Europe, Vienna, January 24–25, 1991, p. 23.

"economic refugees"; that is, the primary motivation for emigration is economic betterment, not political persecution. As a result, they are not eligible for asylum under the 1951 Geneva Convention on Refugees. This has left a large pool of refugees essentially stranded, causing major headaches for governments in Eastern and Western Europe.

At the same time, as a result of the greater freedom of travel in the East, irregular migration has increased. Many immigrants from the East arrive on tourist visas and find illegal employment. This has created new economic and social problems in Western Europe. The problem, moreover, is no longer confined to the traditional receiving countries in the north (France, Germany, and Austria); it has also begun to affect countries in southern Europe.

The problem posed by migration, however, is not limited to Western Europe. Some countries in Eastern Europe such as Poland and Hungary are already beginning to face an influx of refugees and asylum seekers from other Eastern European countries, especially Romania. Many of these eventually move on, but some stay, creating new social and economic burdens at a time when these countries face massive economic problems due to the need to restructure their economies along market lines.

These trends highlight the degree to which migration from the East is beginning to become a major security issue. Moreover, large-scale unrest in the former Soviet Union or an outbreak of ethnic tensions elsewhere in Eastern Europe could accentuate these problems. Thus there is a need for both East and West to address the question of East-West population migration more seriously, and to cooperate more closely to manage its consequences.

To date, however, little scholarly work has been devoted to the implications and policy dilemmas posed by the potential migrations from the Soviet Union and Eastern Europe.[6] In part this is due to the difficulty of obtaining data; many of the countries in Eastern Europe have not published or do not have detailed figures on immigration. Moreover, much of the migration is "irregular" or illegal; which makes its dimensions difficult to assess. But the lack of attention is also due to a slowness in appreciating the broader security implications of the issue.

This article seeks to help fill the current void in the scholarly literature. It is divided into five parts. The first section examines the pattern and possible dimensions of migration from the former Soviet Union. The second section

---

6. Two notable exceptions are Heisbourg, "Population Movements in Post–Cold War Europe," and Chesnais, "Migration from Eastern to Western Europe."

discusses the problem posed for Eastern Europe by increased migration from the former Soviet Union and the efforts undertaken by these countries to cope with this increased migration. The third section focuses on the problem of migration within Eastern Europe itself, that is, from one East European country to another. The fourth section examines the impact of migration from the East to the Federal Republic of Germany (which is the main recipient of the emigrants from the East), and the policy dilemmas that this migration poses. A final section focuses on the future policy agenda and the ways in which East and West might cooperate to control and manage the population outflows.

Migration from the Former Soviet Union: How Many? How Soon?

The disintegration of the Soviet Union has focused attention on the issue of emigration and its security implications. Many in Eastern and Western Europe fear that the collapse of the Soviet Union could lead to a massive flight of Soviet citizens to the West. How realistic are these fears? How many people are likely to leave? And what would be the consequences of any mass exodus for Eastern as well as Western Europe? To answer these questions it may be useful to view emigration from the Soviet Union in historical perspective. In the postwar period there have been four major waves or stages of Soviet emigration.[7] (See Table 1.)

The first stage (1949–70) was one of relatively low levels of emigration. The second stage (1971–80) witnessed a dramatic increase in emigration—largely due to the improvement in East-West relations—although levels began to taper off toward the end of the 1970s as détente soured. The third stage (1981–86) was a period of reduced emigration as East-West relations deteriorated.

The fourth stage (1987 through at least the end of 1991) has seen an unprecedented upsurge in the number of emigrants. During 1990 more Soviet citizens (377,200) left the Soviet Union than in any preceding 12-month period. Moreover, the pattern and motivation for emigration also began to change. In the past, emigration was limited primarily to three groups: Jews,

---

7. For a detailed discussion of the dimensions of this emigration and its causes, see Sidney Heitman, *Soviet Emigration since Gorbachev* (Cologne: Bericht des Bundesinstituts für ostwissenschaftliche und internationale Studien [BIOSt], 1989) and by the same author, "Soviet Emigration in 1990," ibid., 1991. Also Klaus Segbers, *Wanderungs-und Flüchtlingsbewegungen aus der bisherigen UdSSR* (Ebenhausen: Stiftung Wissenschaft und Politik, January 1991).

Table 1. Soviet Emigration 1948–1990.

Period	Total
1948–1970	59,600
1971–1980	347,300
1981–1986	44,000
1987–1989	308,200
1990	377,200
	1,136,300

SOURCE: Heitman, *Soviet Emigration in 1990,* p. 5.

Germans, and Armenians. But in 1990 other groups such as Pentacostal Christians and Pontian Greeks began to join the ranks of emigrants from the Soviet Union.[8]

There were three main reasons for the increased emigration. First, an increasing number of Jews and Germans were motivated to emigrate by concerns about rising ethnic conflict. Second, many Jews and Armenians feared that prospective changes in U.S. immigration regulations would foreclose their option to emigrate at a later date. Third, Soviet emigration regulations and practices were relaxed. While many previous restrictions remained on the books, they were more leniently applied and the overall emigration procedure was speeded up.

Despite the increase, however, emigration has until now remained an "ethnic privilege": 95 percent of the emigrants have come from one of four major ethnic groups: Jews, Germans, Armenians, and Greeks. Emigration, moreover, has been almost entirely to four countries: Israel, Germany, the United States, and Greece. (See Table 2.)

The passage of a new Soviet passport law in May 1991, which gave every Soviet citizen (except those dealing with military secrets) the right of free travel,[9] together with the growth of ethnic unrest in the various republics, has increased concern that the West could be faced with a massive exodus of Soviet citizens. The figures on how many people may leave vary. Some

8. Heitman, *Soviet Emigration since 1990,* p. 13.
9. For a detailed discussion of the law and its implications, see Sidney Heitman, *The Right to Leave: The New Soviet Law on Emigration* (Cologne: BIOSt, 1990); also Heitman, *Soviet Emigration since 1990,* pp. 23–31.

Table 2. Destinations of Soviet Emigrants by Country, 1948–90.

Destination	Group	1948–89	1990	Subtotals by group	Totals by destination
United States	Jews	170,800	6,500	177,300	268,500
	Armenians	63,800	6,500	70,300	
	Evan. and Pent.	14,000	4,100	18,100	
	Other	200	2,600	2,800	
Israel	Jews	191,900	181,800		373,700
Germany	Germans	266,400	148,000	414,400	420,400
	Jews	—	6,000	6,000	
France	Armenians	12,000	—		12,000
Greece	Greeks	10,000	14,300	24,300	25,800
	Armenians	1,500	—	1,500	
Other		28,500	7,400	—	35,900

*NOTE: "Others" refers to emigrants who resettled in countries other than those listed in this table. These include 14,000 Jews who went to Poland and later re-emigrated to Israel; 21,300 Jews who resettled in various Western countries; 300 Evangelical and Pentecostal Christians; and 800 Armenians.

SOURCE: Heitman, "Soviet Emigration Since Gorbachev," p. 7.

Soviet officials have claimed that the figures may be as high as seven or eight million,[10] while others such as Vladimir Scherbakov, Chairman of the State Committee on Labor and Social Services and head of the Soviet Delegation to the Conference of Ministers on the Movement of Persons from Central and Eastern European Countries (sponsored by the Council of Europe in Vienna, January 24–25, 1991) have put the figure at 1.5–2 million.[11]

At the moment it is impossible to say with certainty how great the outflow will be. This will depend on internal developments in the former Soviet Union, above all the success of the reform process in the Western republics (Russia, Ukraine, and Belorussia [Belarus]) and the degree of social unrest

10. Judith Dempsey, "Seven Million May Leave Soviet Union," *Financial Times,* January 26, 1991.
11. Celestine Bohlen, "Moscow Predicts 1.5 Million Will Move West," *New York Times,* January 27, 1991.

and ethnic violence that occurs as the former Soviet Union reconstitutes itself. Three factors in particular, however, are likely to restrict the outflow: (1) the capacity of the underdeveloped and dilapidated Soviet transportation system to transport large masses of people; (2) visa and other restrictions by the potential receiving countries; and (3) the personal and practical costs of emigrating.

The second factor is particularly important. Migratory pressures do not automatically result in massive migration. As many international migration theorists emphasize, it is the policies of the receiving countries that determine whether migration takes place, and what kind of migration occurs.[12] Thus if the countries of Western and Eastern Europe impose visa restrictions, this may act as a disincentive for many citizens from the former Soviet Union to emigrate and thus reduce the number of potential immigrants.

In addition, one needs to differentiate between a *desire to emigrate* and an actual *willingness to emigrate*. The two are by no means the same. Many Soviet citizens may contemplate emigration, but be unwilling to undergo the practical hardships—the loss of friends, cultural isolation, uprooting of family, etc.—when confronted with the choice of actually leaving. This too may constrain the outflow.

These factors have led some Western analysts to take a skeptical view about the prospects for a large wave of emigration from the Soviet Union.[13] Some analysts have argued that large-scale migration is likely to be primarily internal. They point out that with the exception of the Jews, Armenians, and Germans, Soviet citizens have little tradition of emigration. This is particularly true in the case of the Central Asians, who seldom leave their own republics in spite of low living standards and high unemployment.[14]

However, the pattern and extent of emigration could change if social and economic conditions in many areas of the former Soviet Union continue to deteriorate. In this connection, it is important to note that the pattern of internal migration has been changing since the mid 1970s. Prior to the mid-1970s the principal internal migration was from Siberia and Central Russia to the southern republics (Moldavia, Ukraine, Trans-Caucasus, and central Asia). Since the mid-1970s, however, the pattern has been in the opposite

---

12. See Aristide R. Zolberg, "The Next Waves: Migration Theory for a Changing World," *International Migration Review*, Vol. 23, No. 3 (Fall 1989), pp. 405–406.
13. Segbers, *Wanderungs-und Flüchtlingsbewegungen aus der bisherigen UdSSR*, p. 19.
14. Chesnais, "Migration from Eastern to Western Europe," p. 22.

direction, from the southern republics and districts to central and eastern Russia.[15]

In particular, there has been a trend toward "re-migration" on the part of the Russian population back to Russia. This re-migration has been caused principally by increased population growth in the southern republics, which has put growing pressures on the labor market. As a result, more and more jobs have been taken by the native population, forcing the Russian population to migrate back to Russia.[16] This trend is likely to intensify with the proclamations of sovereignty and independence in the other republics. Changes in citizenship laws and other regulations may put the Russian population at a disadvantage, causing many to leave these republics. However, if conditions continue to deteriorate in Russia, many of these Russians will be unable to find good jobs and suitable housing in Russia and they may decide to emigrate abroad.

The Impact on Eastern Europe

The prospect of large-scale emigration from the former Soviet Union has important implications not only for the West, but also for Eastern Europe. Even the lower figure of 1.5 million emigrants cited by Scherbakov would pose major problems for the countries of Central and Eastern Europe, which have a limited capacity to absorb refugees or provide gainful employment for new emigrants at a time when their economies are facing radical restructuring. Moreover, some of these countries could become transit points for former Soviet citizens trying to move on to the West.

POLAND

Poland would be particularly affected by a massive outflow of Soviet nationals. The number of Soviet tourists to Poland has grown rapidly in recent years. In 1990 nearly a quarter of all tourists to Poland (4,200,000 out of 18,000,000) came from the Soviet Union. This represents a 67 percent increase over the previous year.[17] In 1991 the number is expected to reach 6,000,000

---

15. Zhanna Zaiyontchkovskaya, "Effects of Internal Migration on Emigration from the USSR," paper presented at the RAND conference on "Prospective Migration from the USSR," Santa Monica, November 17–19, 1991, p. 6.
16. Ibid., p. 21.
17. Christopher Wellisz, "Soviet Coup Renews Fear of Exodus," Radio Free Europe/Radio Liberty (RFE/RL), *Report on Eastern Europe*, September 13, 1991, p. 19.

(out of an expected 21–22 million tourists). How many of these will stay in Poland is not known. However, according to Polish officials, Soviet citizens account for nearly 80 percent of illegal immigrants.[18]

Soviet citizens entering Poland need either a visa or an officially certified invitation letter. However, there is a large black market for false travel documents. The growing number of Soviet citizens entering Poland with false travel documents is becoming a serious problem and source of concern to Polish officials. According to an internal Polish report, around 300 Soviet citizens trying to enter Poland with false travel documents are turned back at the border daily.[19]

Poland has taken a number of measures in order to prepare for a massive wave of emigration from the Soviet Union. In January 1991 the Ministry of Internal Affairs announced a plan to tighten security along Poland's eastern frontier. The plan called for the construction of fourteen new watch towers and the modernization of border control equipment. A contingency plan for the mobilization of troops to stem a large influx of refugees was also prepared.[20]

Poland has also set up a Refugee Office within the Ministry of Internal Affairs. However, according to Colonel Zbigniew Skoczylas, advisor to the Refugee Office, Poland could afford to accept only 50,000 refugees at most, at a cost of 1.5 trillion zloty per year ($130 million). He warned that there will be a complete breakdown of the economy if Poland is forced to accept several million refugees.[21] Even 200,000–300,000 would pose enormous problems, particularly at a time of recession and rising unemployment.

Interestingly, the coup attempt in the Soviet Union in August 1991 did not lead to a massive outflow of Soviet citizens into Poland. During the three days of the coup, only fifty Soviet citizens applied for asylum in Poland. Moreover, the number of Soviet citizens entering and leaving Poland remained more or less equal.[22] This has led some Polish officials to conclude that the emigration problem may not prove as serious as they initially feared.

A more immediate problem is the large influx of Soviet citizens who enter Poland for a short stay (1–3 days). Polish authorities estimate that on any

18. Private discussions with Polish officials, October 1991.
19. Thomas Urban, "Polen verstärkt Grenzkontrolle," *Süddeutsche Zeitung*, September 28, 1991.
20. Wellisz, "Soviet Coup Renews Fear of Exodus," p. 19.
21. Mary Battiata, "Poland, Others Forecast Flood of Refugees," *Washington Post*, November 14, 1990.
22. Private discussions with Polish officials, October 1991.

given day, there are about 140,000 Soviet and Baltic citizens on Polish territory, most of whom come for short stays. Many of them engage in smuggling
and blackmarketeering in order to earn hard currency. Upon returning, they
smuggle vodka into Poland and sell it, converting their zloty into dollars.
They then convert their dollars into rubles, making a substantial profit. The
illicit vodka smuggling deprives Poland of important tax revenues at a time
when Poland badly needs hard currency. According to one estimate, $80
million leaves Poland every month through illicit vodka sales.[23]

Another problem is posed by Soviet citizens who seek to work illegally in
Poland. According to official Polish estimates, there are 20,000–30,000 illegal
Soviet workers in Poland, most of them engaged in construction and agri-
culture.[24] These workers work for about half the normal Polish wage. However, this is still 2–3 times what they would earn at home. As unemployment
increases—it reached 9.4 percent in July 1991—and more Poles find it hard
to get work, the issue of illegal Soviet workers could become a serious
problem, exacerbating social and political tensions.

A third and potentially more serious problem could be posed by the large-
scale emigration of the Polish minority living in the Soviet Union. According
to the 1989 census, there were 1,126,334 Poles residing in the Soviet Union;
the actual figure is probably somewhat higher. Eighty percent of the Soviet
Union's Polish population resided in the three republics of Belorussia
(417,720), Lithuania (257,994), and Ukraine (219,179). In addition there were
sizeable Polish populations in the Russian SFSR (94,594), Latvia (60,416), and
Kazakhstan (59,956).

In the last several years there has been a growing interest in repatriation
on the part of many of the Poles in the Ukraine. Unlike the Poles in the West
who have much-needed skills and hard currency, the Poles in the Soviet
Union are poor, old, and unskilled. Many of them are retirees. They would
pose a burden on the Polish economy if they returned. According to a recent
study by the Polish Foreign Ministry, the repatriation of one million Poles
over the next five years would cost 20–30 trillion zloty ($1.8–2.7 billion). Thus
the report recommends that Poland discourage their repatriation. Instead it
suggests that Poland should support a general improvement in the conditions
of the minority in order to help them maintain their national identity and to
provide an incentive for them not to emigrate.[25]

---

23. *Gazeta Wyborcza*, July 17, 1991.
24. Wellisz, "Soviet Coup Renews Fear of Exodus," p. 20.
25. Ibid.

There are also about 260,000 ethnic Poles in Lithuania. They make up about 7 percent of the population. The treatment of the Polish minority in Lithuania has traditionally been a source of friction between the two countries.[26] During the communist period this friction was largely kept under control. However, as Lithuania moved closer toward independence, tensions with Poland over the treatment of the Polish minority resurfaced. Relations were strained in particular by the decision of the Lithuanian government in September 1991 to disband the self-governing councils in the Salcininkai and Vilnius districts, in which Poles make up 80 and 60 percent of the population, respectively, on the grounds that the councils had allegedly supported the coup attempt in Moscow.[27]

Rising nationalist tensions or a drastic deterioration in economic conditions in the Ukraine, Belorussia, or Lithuania could result in a decision by many members of the Polish minority in these areas to emigrate to Poland. In such a case, Poland would be hard pressed, morally and politically, not to accept these refugees.[28] But a massive influx of these refugees would significantly exacerbate Poland's already serious economic problems, severely undercutting the prospects for successful reform.

Polish officials believe, however, that the likelihood of a massive emigration by the Polish minorities in the Ukraine and Belorussia is small. The minorities in both republics are highly assimilated and relatively well-treated. Moreover, Poland has made respect for minority rights an issue in its effort to improve relations with both republics. In October 1990 it signed a Declaration-of-Friendship Agreement with the Ukraine which contained a provision guaranteeing respect for the rights of minorities.[29] A similar agreement was signed with Belorussia in October of 1991.

The Friendship Declarations are part of a broader effort by Warsaw to improve relations with both republics as they move toward greater sover-

26. For a comprehensive discussion, see Stephen Burant, "Polish-Lithuanian Relations: Past, Present and Future," *Problems of Communism*, May–June 1991, pp. 67–84.
27. See Christopher Bobinski, "Lithuania Warned on Polish Minority," *Financial Times*, September 16, 1991; Edward Lucas, "Lithuania Dispute with Poles Worsens," *The Independent*, September 19, 1991; and Jan de Weydenthal, "The Polish-Lithuanian Dispute," RFE/RL, *Report on Eastern Europe*, October 11, 1991, pp. 20–23.
28. According to a recent poll by the Public Opinion Institute CBOS in Poland, 80 percent of those polled felt that members of the Polish minority in the USSR should be allowed to settle in Poland without any restrictions. See Thomas Urban, "Polen verstärkt Grenzkontrollen," *Süddeutsche Zeitung*, September 28, 1991.
29. An agreement containing similar guarantees was signed with Russia as well. For background, see Anna Sabbat-Swidlicka, "Friendship Declarations Signed with Russia and the Ukraine," RFE/RL, *Report on Eastern Europe*, November 2, 1990, pp. 25–27.

eignty or independence. One of the basic aims of Polish policy is to encourage the integration of both republics, particularly the Ukraine, into pan-European institutions and processes like the Conference on Security and Cooperation in Europe (CSCE), the negotiations on reducing Conventional Forces in Europe (CFE), and the Council of Europe. Poland views such integration as an important safeguard against the emergence of a highly nationalistic and chauvinistic regime in Kiev that would curtail the rights of the Polish minority. Polish authorities also believe that the Ukraine's need for Western assistance will act as a moderating constraint on Kiev's treatment of the minority.

The situation with Lithuania is more complicated. Unlike the Ukraine, Lithuania feels more threatened by Poland. Its nationalism also has a stronger anti-Polish edge. However, the two countries, in January 1992, signed a Declaration of Friendship similar to the Declarations signed by Poland with Ukraine and Belorussia. This should help to reduce tensions and provide important guarantees for minority rights. Moreover, the fact that the Poles in Lithuania are less educated (educational level generally has a strong impact on emigration) suggests that the rate of outmigration is likely to be modest.

HUNGARY

Hungary's problems are of a less urgent nature and magnitude. There is a small Hungarian minority (150,000–200,000) in the Trans-carpathian *oblast* of the western Ukraine. However, members of the minority have generally been well-treated and have shown little inclination to emigrate or request repatriation. Like Poland, Hungary has consciously sought to improve relations with Ukraine lately. In June 1991 the Ukraine and Hungary signed a declaration of basic principles as well as a joint statement guaranteeing the rights of national minorities.[30] This statement is regarded by Hungarian officials as an important means of ensuring that the ethnic, cultural, educational, and linguistic rights of the Hungarian minority in the Ukraine will be respected. They believe that the general improvement in the situation of the Hungarian minority in recent years reduces the likelihood of any large-scale emigration of the Hungarian minority in the Ukraine to Hungary.[31] However, if the

---

30. For details see Alfred A. Reisch, "Agreements Signed with Ukraine to Upgrade Bilateral Relations," RFE/RL, *Report on Eastern Europe*, June 21, 1991, pp. 14–17. See also Alfred Reisch, "Hungary and Ukraine Agree to Upgrade Bilateral Relations," ibid., November 2, 1990, pp. 6–12.
31. See the interview with former Foreign Minister Gyula Horn, Chairman of the Hungarian Socialist Party, *Magyar Nemzet*, April 24, 1991. Translated in Foreign Broadcast Information Service (FBIS) EEU-91-084, May 1, 1991, p. 22.

situation of the minority deteriorated and many decided to emigrate, there would be strong moral pressure on Hungary to allow them to be repatriated.

Hungary has set up an Office of Refugee Affairs within the Interior Ministry and has built several refugee camps, including one sponsored by the United Nations at Bieske (outside of Budapest) to house refugees. Hungarian officials, however, do not expect to face a major wave of immigrants from the Soviet Union. They believe they can handle any increase in immigration through measures already in force or which can be introduced quickly, such as visa and currency requirements. In October 1991 Budapest introduced stricter border controls on foreigners, including currency restrictions. While the restrictions were mainly aimed at curbing the influx of Romanians, especially gypsies, they also apply to Soviet citizens.

In addition, Hungary tightened the regulations on hiring foreigners. According to a decree passed in October 1991, foreign citizens wishing to work in Hungary will have to apply for a special "work permit visa" at Hungarian missions in their respective countries. The move is designed to reduce the influx of illegal foreign workers at a time of rising unemployment in Hungary.

CZECHOSLOVAKIA

Czechoslovakia does not seem likely to face a serious immigration problem from the Soviet Union. Unlike Poles or Hungarians, there are few Czechs or Slovaks living in the Soviet Union. About 15,000 Czechs and Slovaks live in the Volyn area of the Ukraine. Few of these, however, have expressed a desire to be repatriated. And even if many of them did seek to emigrate, the number is not so large as to prove unmanageable.

Nevertheless, the Czechoslovak government has made preparations to handle an increased flow of refugees. A Refugee Affairs Office has been set up, staffed by officials from the Defense and Interior Ministries. Czechoslovakia has also doubled the number of guards along the Soviet border. In addition, in December 1990, a law was drafted that would make it legal to use the army to contain any large-scale migration.

In November 1990, Czechoslovakia passed a new Law on Refugees, which went into effect on January 1, 1991. Under the new law, a refugee must declare his or her intention to claim refugee status at the border and is obliged to stay in a special camp until his or her application for refugee status has been accepted or rejected. The Federal Ministry of Internal Affairs is obligated to act on the application within 90 days. After five years, a refugee whose application is accepted can apply for citizenship.

To date the influx of refugees has been limited. As of January 1991, there were some 1,200 refugees in Czechoslovakia.[32] They are housed in four camps and several "emergency stations" in the Czech republic. In addition, Slovakia is setting up five refugee camps for potential Soviet refugees, which will be paid for by the Czechoslovak Red Cross. However, government spokesmen have said that the camps could not accommodate more than 12,000 people annually.[33]

ROMANIA

Romania is a major "exporter" of emigrants, rather than an importer. According to the Romanian media, more than 800,000 Romanians emigrated from Romania in the first eight months of 1990.[34] Many of these were young and highly educated. If accurate, this would represent a major hemorrhage for a country of 23 million people.

In the foreseeable future, Romania is likely to remain a migration exporter rather than an importer. Developments in Moldavia (Moldova), however, could complicate this assessment. There are 3,350,000 "Moldavians" in the area of the former Soviet Union, including 2.8 million in Moldavia and 320,000 in the Ukraine. They are ethnic Romanians. While they feel a strong sense of kinship with their brethren in Romania, they have little inclination to emigrate to Romania, in large part because of the low standard of living in Romania and the chaotic political conditions existing there. However, if Russia were to attempt to reassert control over Moldavia or if there was a serious rise of ethnic tensions between the Russian minority (about 13 percent of the population) in Moldavia and the Romanian majority, many Moldavians might decide to emigrate to Romania. A mass migration of Moldavians to Romania would exacerbate Romania's already serious economic and political problems, adding to the chaotic conditions that exist there and making any effort to establish a stable democratic system all the more difficult, if not impossible.

BULGARIA

Bulgaria is unlikely to be seriously affected by any migration from the Soviet Union. There are some 370,000 Bulgarians in the Soviet Union: 23,000 in the

---

32. Vladimir Kusin, "Refugees in Central and Eastern Europe: Problem or Threat?" RFE/RL, *Report on Eastern Europe*, January 18, 1991, p. 37.
33. Ibid.
34. See Dan Ionescu, "The Exodus," RFE/RL, *Report on Eastern Europe*, October 26, 1990, pp. 25–31, and Ionescu, "Recent Emigration Figures," ibid., pp. 21–24.

Ukraine and 90,000 in Moldavia. They have not shown any strong inclination to be repatriated or to move West, although this might change if there were to be serious unrest in Russia, the Ukraine, or Moldavia.

The main problem for Bulgaria has been the absorption of the ethnic Turkish minority. Under the Zhivkov regime, discriminatory legislation prompted some 310,000 ethnic Turks to emigrate in 1989. Zhivkov's successors reversed much of the discriminatory legislation in December 1989 and since then about 150,000 ethnic Turks have returned. The reversal of the legislation against the Turks, however, sparked large-scale demonstrations in several Bulgarian cities in January 1990. The question of minority rights for the Turks continues to be a controversial issue in Bulgarian politics.[35]

Migration Within Eastern Europe

A second problem is created by the emigration within Eastern Europe itself from one East European country to another. Here the main problem is posed by the emigration of Romanians, many of them gypsies. The goal of most of these gypsies is to reach the West—Austria or Germany—rather than settle in the East European countries through which they pass. However, many of them do not have visas or valid papers and are turned back at the German or Austrian border. They are forced to return to various East European transit countries. For the countries of Central Europe, these gypsies are becoming a growing social problem. Many of them remain in limbo, eking out a meager living and often resorting to begging or petty crime.

Poland in particular has been faced with a large influx of Romanian gypsies. It is estimated that there are today between 50,000 and 70,000 Romanian gypsies in Poland.[36] In order to stem the influx, Poland tightened its regulations for admission to the country in December 1990. Romanians now must produce an officially certified invitation for the visit as well as a return ticket and must show that they have at least 200,000 zloty in cash for each day of their expected stay.

The influx of gypsies has caused growing popular resentment and social tension. In July 1991, hundreds of gypsies fled from Poland to Sweden after

---

35. See Duncan Perry, "Ethnic Turks Face Bulgarian Nationalism," RFE/RL, *Report on Eastern Europe*, March 15, 1991, pp. 5–8.
36. Dan Ionescu, "Recent Emigration Figures," RFE/RL, *Report on Eastern Europe*, February 15, 1991, p. 21.

a mob of Poles in the town of Mlawa attacked a group of gypsies and ransacked their homes.[37] The gypsies are particularly resented because many have become wealthy through illicit deals and smuggling.

The large influx of gypsies has also led to an increase in the number of illegal border crossings.[38] Many of the gypsies enter Poland illegally and then proceed on to Germany, where they seek to cross the border illegally. Those that are caught are turned back, where they remain in legal limbo, often waiting to make another attempt to cross the border illegally. The sharp rise in the number of illegal border crossings has exceeded the capacity of the German border guards to deal with the problem and created strains in Warsaw's relations with Bonn.[39]

The vast majority of the refugees in Czechoslovakia are also from Romania. Many of them have entered illegally. In June 1991, Czechoslovakia deported a total of 226 refugees, most of them Romanians, who had tried to cross Czechoslovakia illegally on their way to Germany. Another 800 were deported in July on special aircraft, after the Hungarian government refused to allow trains carrying them out of Czechoslovakia to cross Hungary on the way back to Romania.[40]

Hungary has faced similar problems. According to the Office of Refugee Affairs, nearly 30,000–35,000 Romanian citizens entered Hungary before 1989. Most of these were ethnic Hungarians and were integrated relatively easily into Hungarian society. However, more recently the refugees have included a growing number of ethnic Romanians, many of them gypsies. In order to reduce the influx, in early October 1991 Hungary introduced stricter border controls on foreigners, including currency restrictions. This move, however, has been criticized by the Hungarian minority in Romania, who claim it complicates their situation.

The conflict in Yugoslavia has seriously exacerbated Hungary's refugee problem.[41] According to the Red Cross, there were more than 35,000 refugees

---

37. "Poles Vent Their Economic Rage on Gypsies," *New York Times,* July 25, 1991.
38. According to Jaroslaw Zukowicz, press spokesman of the headquarters of the Polish border guards, between January and June 1991, 4,406 persons sought to cross the Polish border illegally. The vast majority of these were Romanians (1,679) followed by Bulgarians (407) and Czechoslovaks (206). RFE/RL, *Daily Report No. 146,* August 2, 1991.
39. Ulrich Reitz, "Zwischenstation Polen," *Die Welt,* July 22, 1991.
40. "The Other Europeans on the Move," *Financial Times,* August 17/18, 1991.
41. See Judith Pataki, "Refugee Wave From Croatia Puts Strain on Relief Efforts," RFE/RL, *Report on Eastern Europe,* September 27, 1991, p. 12.

in Hungary as of October 1991.[42] The majority of these (some 67 percent) are ethnic Croats, who are seeking only temporary refuge and want to return home once the fighting stops. However, about 25–26 percent are ethnic Hungarians.[43]

Hungarian authorities are particularly concerned about the large Hungarian minority in Yugoslavia. There are nearly 430,000 ethnic Hungarians in Yugoslavia, most of them located in the Vojvodina region of Serbia. Along with the Albanians of Kosovo, they have had their political rights progressively restricted by the Serbs since 1989. If their rights continue to be curtailed, many of them might decide to flee or emigrate. Absorbing another major influx of refugees would impose a serious burden on the Hungarian economy, already severely strained by the need to feed and house the large number of other refugees, and could aggravate social tensions.

The growing problems posed by the increased influx of migrants and refugees have prompted the three countries of Central Europe (Hungary, Poland, and Czechoslovakia) to step up cooperation. As a first step the three countries agreed in October to coordinate their policies regarding refugees, and to work out uniform laws and regulations for handling applications for refugee status. This move is part of a general trend toward increased cooperation between the three countries since the Visegrad summit of February 1990, which could have important regional implications.

Germany and East-West Migration

The prospect of increased emigration from the East poses major dilemmas for Western Europe and especially for the Federal Republic of Germany. In the last decade West Germany has been confronted with a massive influx of foreign immigrants. This began well before the fall of the Berlin Wall in November 1989 and has increased steadily since. A growing number of these have come from Eastern Europe. In 1974, for instance, only 7,994 persons emigrated to the Federal Republic from Eastern Europe. This represented only 5.3 percent of the total inflow of foreigners. In 1988, by contrast, 133,742

---

42. Celestine Bohlen, "Refugees from Yugoslavia are Welcomed in Hungary," *New York Times*, October 18, 1991. Also Peter Maass, "Refugees from Croatia Flood into Hungary," *Washington Post*, October 7, 1991; and Carol J. Williams, "Serbian-Croatian Conflict Spills into Hungary," August 25, 1991. It is difficult to obtain accurate figures about the number of refugees because many stay with relatives and return home when the fighting in their neighborhood stops.
43. Figures provided by Office of Refugee Affairs, Budapest, November 1991.

persons from Eastern Europe emigrated to the FRG,[44] 39.7 percent of the total inflow of foreigners in that year. Of these, Poland sent nearly one-third of the immigrants, followed by Turkey (12.1 percent) and Yugoslavia (8.6 percent).[45]

ETHNIC GERMAN EMIGRATION

The influx of foreigners from Eastern Europe to the FRG has consisted mainly of two types: (1) repatriated ethnic Germans (*Aussiedler*); and (2) non-German asylum seekers (*Asylanten*).[46] The *Aussiedler*, however, have certain advantages not available to non-German refugees from Eastern Europe: they are considered Germans and thus have access to the German labor market and are entitled to certain social benefits. They have also tended to be more highly skilled and have greater proficiency in the German language, though in recent years both the language proficiency and occupational qualifications of the *Aussiedler* have declined. As a result the problems of both groups have become more similar.[47]

Since 1988 the influx of *Aussiedler* has grown steadily. (See Figure 1 and Table 3.) In 1990, 397,073 ethnic Germans emigrated to Germany.[48] This was nearly twice as many as in 1988 (202,673). Of the 1990 immigrants, the largest number (147,950) came from the Soviet Union, followed by Poland (133,872) and Romania (111,150).

The statistics reveal some interesting trends: the number of *Aussiedler* from the Soviet Union has steadily increased (See Table 4). In 1990, the number of *Aussiedler* from the Soviet Union (147,950) increased by more than a third over 1989 (98,134) and tripled over 1988 (47,572). Immigration rose in 1991 as well: in the first nine months more than 113,000 Soviet *Aussiedler* emigrated to the Federal Republic. If this trend keeps up, the German population in the Soviet Union could be nearly depleted within five to ten years.

44. Elmar Hönekopp, "Migratory Movements from Countries of Central and Eastern Europe: Causes and Characteristics, Present Situation and Possible Future Trends—The Cases of Germany and Austria," paper prepared for the Conference of Ministers on the Movement of Persons Coming from Central and East European Countries, Vienna, January 24–25, 1991, pp. 25–27.
45. Ibid., p. 27.
46. A third group, emigrants from the former German Democratic Republic GDR (*Übersiedler*), is outside the scope of this analysis and not considered here.
47. Hönekopp, "Migratory Movements from Countries of Central and Eastern Europe," p. 8.
48. "1990 mehr Aussiedler nach Deutschland als je zuvor," *Frankfurter Allgemeine Zeitung*, January 4, 1991. The statistics in the article are based on official figures released by the German Ministry of Interior.

Figure 1. Ethnic German Immigration to FRG (1950–91), Countries of Origin.

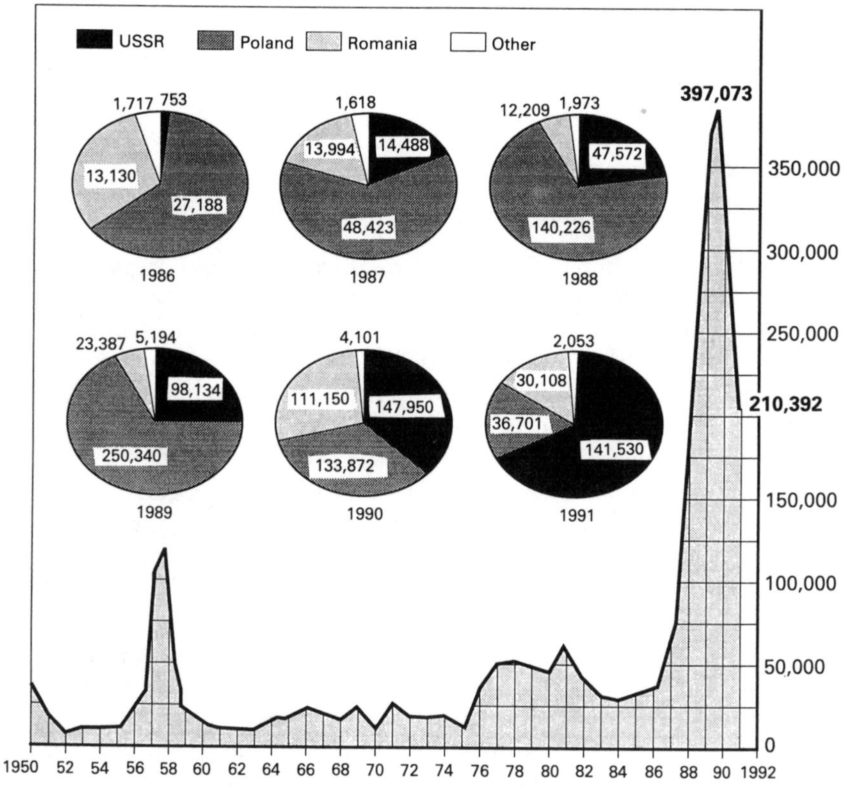

SOURCE: *Die Welt,* January 10, 1992.

In addition, the number of *Aussiedler* from Romania more than quadrupled in 1990 over 1989 (111,150 in 1990 vs. 23,387 in 1989 and 12,902 in 1988.) The 1990 emigrants represented nearly half of all the ethnic Germans in Romania.

Table 3.   Ethnic German Emigrants, Country of Origin, 1980–1990.

Year	Poland	USSR	Romania	Total
1980	26,637	6,954	15,767	51,984
1981	50,983	3,773	12,031	69,336
1982	30,355	2,071	12,972	47,992
1983	19,121	1,447	15,501	37,844
1984	17,455	913	16,553	36,386
1985	22,075	757	14,924	38,905
1986	27,188	882	13,130	42,729
1987	48,423	14,488	13,994	78,498
1988	140,226	45,572	12,902	202,645
1989	250,340	98,134	23,387	377,036
1990	133,872	148,000	111,000	397,073
1950–1990	1,372,182	403,308	353,320	2,345,229

NOTE: Only the most important source countries are shown.

SOURCE: Mirjana Morokvasic-Müller, "Beyond the Invasion Scenario: Circular Migrations from and within Eastern and Central Europe," paper presented at the RAND conference on "Prospective Migration from the USSR," Santa Monica, November 17–19, 1991, p. 19.

Table 4.   Emigration of Ethnic Germans from the Soviet Union to the FRG.

Period	Total
1948–1970	22,400
1971–1980	64,300
1981–1986	19,500
1987–1989	160,200
1990	147,950
1991	141,530

SOURCE: Heitman, *Soviet Emigration in 1990,* p. 5; 1991 figures from *Die Welt,* January 10, 1992.

If this trend continues, there will be almost no ethnic Germans remaining in Romania within a few years.[49] The main reason for the increase was the

---

49. For a detailed discussion of recent emigration trends and their implications, see Dan Ionescu, "Countdown for the German Minority," RFE/RL, *Report on Eastern Europe,* September 13, 1991, pp. 32–41.

removal of travel restrictions by Ceausescu's successors as well as the in-creased economic and political unrest in Romania itself.

The number of *Aussiedler* from Poland, on the other hand, declined by nearly half in 1990 (133,872) compared to 1989 (250,340). (See Table 3.)

However, since mid-1990 there has been a decline in the number of ethnic Germans emigrating to the FRG. The decline continued in 1991, when 221,995 *Aussiedler* emigrated to the Federal Republic. Compared to nearly 400,000 in 1990, this represents a drop of nearly half.[50]

The decline in the number of *Aussiedler* is largely due to the change in the German law regarding the emigration of ethnic Germans (*Aussiedleraufnah-megesetz*) in July 1991, which requires prospective *Aussiedler* to make their applications for emigration in their home country before emigrating. Bonn's stepped-up efforts to provide direct material assistance to areas populated by ethnic Germans (*Aussiedlergebiete*) has also played a role. This assistance has been directed particularly at the nearly two million ethnic Germans in the Soviet Union and has been designed to give prospective *Aussiedler* incen-tives to remain where they are. Bonn has pressed the Soviet—and more recently the Russian—authorities to restore to ethnic Germans the Volga republic from which Stalin deported them in 1941.[51] Gorbachev pledged to restore their homeland in a message to the Congress of Soviet Germans in October 1991. During his visit to Bonn in November 1991, Yeltsin reaffirmed this pledge.[52] However, the pledge prompted protests from many of the inhabitants of the Volga region who fear being displaced by the resettlement, and since then Yeltsin has adopted a more equivocal attitude, calling for a gradual, step-by-step resettlement of the German community.

The prospect of obtaining their own homeland, however, has not suc-ceeded in stemming the flow of *Aussiedler* from the former Soviet Union. Although the number of *Aussiedler* overall declined in 1991, the number of *Aussiedler* emigrating from the former Soviet Union remained about the same as in 1990 (141,350 in 1991, compared to 147,950 in 1990). According to some reports by ethnic German authorities in the former Soviet Union, as many

---

50. "Im vergangen Jahr fast 260,000 Asylbewerber in Deutschland," *Frankfurter Allgemeine Zei-tung*, January 4, 1992.

51. See John Tagliabue, "Bonn Wants Russia to Restore Republic for Ethnic Germans," *New York Times*, January 19, 1992.

52. "Yelzin verspricht Wolga-republik," *Die Welt*, November 22, 1991; "Deutsche Wolgarepublik nicht vorrangig—Bundregierung dringt auf konkrete Vereinbarungen," *Suddeutsche Zeitung*, No-vember 23, 1991.

as 90 percent of the ethnic German community are ready to emigrate.[53] How many of these will actually do so depends to a large extent on developments in the various republics, especially Russia. However, unless there is a significant improvement in the situation of the ethnic German community very quickly, a large number are likely to leave, adding to Bonn's already considerable immigration problems.

ASYLUM SEEKERS

In addition to the record number of *Aussiedler* who arrived in Germany in 1990, the number of applicants for asylum in 1990 more than doubled over 1989.[54] In 1990, 193,063 persons applied for asylum in the FRG, an increase of 59 percent over the previous year. This represented close to half of all asylum applications within the EC as a whole. (See Table 5.)

The largest number of applicants (35,345) came from Romania—a nearly ten-fold increase over 1989 (3,121). It was followed by Yugoslavia (22,114 in 1990 vs. 19,423 in 1989) and Turkey (22,082 vs. 20,020 in 1989). The number of applications from Bulgaria also significantly increased (8,341 in 1990 vs. only 429 in 1989). In addition, there was also a sharp increase in applications from a number of Third World countries such as Lebanon and Vietnam.[55]

Table 5.   Asylum Seekers in the FRG.

	Country of Origin				
	Romania	Yugoslavia	Turkey	Poland	Totals
1989	3,121	19,423	20,020	26,092	121,318
1990	35,345	22,114	22,082	9,155	193,063
1991	40,504	74,854	23,877	3,448	256,112

NOTE: Totals include asylum seekers from other countries also.

SOURCE: *Frankfurter Allgemeine Zeitung*, January 6, 1992.

53. "Reform des Asylrechts: Neuer Vorstoss der Union," *Deutschland Nachrichten,* January 10, 1992.

54. Figures are from "Zahl der Asylbewerber in Deutschland 1990 mehr als verdoppelt," *Frankfurter Allgemeine Zeitung,* May 5, 1991. The article is based on figures released by the German Ministry of the Interior.

55. Most of the Vietnamese had been working in the former GDR prior to unification.

The number of applicants from Poland, by contrast, dramatically declined from 26,092 in 1989 to 9,155 in 1990. This decrease is probably due to the increased freedom of travel. Many Poles travel to the West, especially Germany, seeking temporary (illegal) work and then return to Poland. There is thus less pressure to emigrate. (See Table 5.)

The number of asylum seekers shows no signs of abating. In 1991, 256,112 persons applied for asylum in Germany—32.7 percent more than in 1990.[56] The highest number of these (74,854) came from Yugoslavia, more than three times as many as in 1990. The next largest number came from Romania (40,504), followed by Turkey (23,877) and Bulgaria (12,056). Significantly, the number of asylum seekers from the republics of the former Soviet Union more than doubled (5,690 in 1991, vs. 2,337 in 1990). The number of asylum seekers from Poland, by contrast, continued to decline (3,448 in 1991, vs. 9,155 in 1990 and 26,089 in 1989).

The main reason so many refugees apply for asylum in Germany is the Federal Republic's liberal asylum laws. In contrast to other countries within the EC, Germany cannot turn refugees back at the border. Under the German constitution (Article 16), they have the right to apply for asylum. In addition, the Federal Republic is the only country in the EC in which a rejected applicant has the right to remain in the country.

The political changes in Eastern Europe and the Soviet Union since 1989 have significantly complicated the asylum problem and contributed to the increase in asylum seekers. However, many applicants from Eastern Europe who before 1989 might have qualified for asylum on grounds of political or religious persecution today are rejected. Most applicants for asylum today from Eastern Europe are not political but economic refugees. They thus do not qualify for refugee status. As a result, the number of applicants who are granted asylum has significantly declined. In 1986, for instance, 16 percent of all applicants received asylum. In 1990 the figure dropped to just below 5 percent.[57] Many prolong their stay, however, by dragging out the appeal process.

At the same time there has been a sharp increase in the number of illegal or "irregular" immigrants, who clandestinely cross the German borders from

---

56. "Im vergangen Jahr fast 260,000 Asylbewerber in Deutschland"; "Die meisten Asylbewerber kamen aus dem einstigen Jugoslavien," *Frankfurter Allgemeine Zeitung*, January 6, 1992.
57. "Der Feind des Guten ist das Gutgemeinte—Für eine Europäisierung des Asylrechts und der Einwanderungspolitik plädiert der Vize-Präsident Martin Bangemann," *Frankfurter Rundschau*, September 13, 1991.

Poland and Czechoslovakia. According to figures released by the German Ministry of the Interior, in the first half of 1991 some 42,000 people clandestinely entered Germany. The German authorities seized 5,422 "illegals" on the Czechoslovak-German border and 2,960 illegal entrants on the Polish-German border. Nearly 70 percent of these were Romanians, most of them gypsies.[58]

The sharp increase in asylum applicants has contributed to a visible growth of social tensions in Germany, and a marked increase in violence against foreigners.[59] While this hostility toward foreigners has been most acute in eastern Germany (the former GDR) where unemployment is high, it has increased significantly in the western part of Germany as well. Some polls, in fact, suggest that support for right-wing hostility against foreigners may actually be stronger in West Germany than in the former GDR.[60]

Concern about the influx of refugees has become a major issue in German domestic politics. In the local elections in Bremen at the end of September 1991, the German People's Union (DVU), a right-wing political party that campaigned to increase restrictions on foreigners seeking to take advantage of Germany's liberal asylum law, won 6.2 percent of the vote, gaining seats in the local parliament for the first time. The big loser, the Social Democrats (SPD), opposed any change in the constitution to tighten restrictions on asylum. The DVU drew much of its new-found strength from voters, especially in working-class districts, who had traditionally voted for the SPD.[61]

The asylum issue has become the focal point of an increasingly heated debate between the major parties in Germany over the last year.[62] The Chris-

58. See "Schäuble regt internationale Konferenz über illegale Einreise an," *Frankfurter Allgemeine Zeitung,* August 3, 1991.

59. In September there were more than 200 attacks against asylum seekers, immigrants, and foreign workers. See Stephen Kinzer, "German Vote Raises Foreigner's Fears," *New York Times,* October 8, 1991; Stephen Kinzer, "A Wave of Attacks on Foreigners Stirs Shock in Germany," ibid., October 1, 1991; Stephen Kinzer, "German Visits Refugees, Attacks Go On," ibid., October 5, 1991; Quentin Peel, "Racist Attacks Mar German Unity Anniversary," *Financial Times,* October 4, 1991; Marc Fisher, "Anti-Immigrant Violence Grows in Germany," *Washington Post,* September 30, 1991. For German views see, for example, Robert Leicht, "Hoyerswerda in den Köpfen," *Die Zeit,* September 26, 1991; Thorsten Schmidtz, "Die braven Burger von Hoyerswerda," ibid.; and Gunter Hoffmann, "Hilflos vor dem Fremdenhass," ibid., October 3, 1991.

60. According to a poll taken by the public opinion research institute EMNID in Bielefeld in September 1991, 21 percent of East Germans and 38 percent of West Germans expressed "understanding" for right-wing hostility aimed against foreigners. See *Der Spiegel,* No. 40, 1991, p. 30.

61. Klaus-Dieter Frankenberger, "Protest der 'Kleinen Leute'," *Frankfurter Allgemeine Zeitung,* October 11, 1991.

62. See "Tauziehen um die Asylrechtsreform in Bonn," *Neue Zürcher Zeitung,* September 29/30,

tian Democratic Union (CDU), together with its sister party the CSU, has called for changes in the German constitution that would allow border guards to turn back refugees at the border. The Social Democratic Party (SPD) and Free Democratic Party (FDP), however, oppose any changes in the constitution. Given the fact that a change in the constitution would require a two-thirds majority and thus support of the SPD, it is unlikely that the CDU's efforts will succeed. However, in order to defuse the current tensions, the three main parties agreed in October 1991 to speed up the procedures for processing asylum applications, and to increase the number of refugee centers, especially in the new *Länder* in the former GDR.

Some SPD politicians have argued that Germany should abandon special rights for ethnic Germans (*Aussiedler*) and simply set quotas for all immigrants. The Kohl government, however, has rejected any restrictions on the number of ethnic Germans—the *Aussiedler* are an important CDU constituency—while insisting that Germany is not an "immigration country."[63] Instead it has advocated a combination of policy measures to address the migration/refugee problem:

- increased financial and material assistance to the East designed to provide incentives for would-be emigrants to stay home;
- changes in the constitution restricting the right of asylum;
- a harmonization of visa and asylum policies within the EC;
- a more equitable division of refugees within Europe (not just the EC).

Bonn has called for greater cooperation within the EC to address the problem. At the Luxembourg summit in June 1991, Kohl pressed for a common EC policy toward asylum and immigration.[64] Such a policy is essential if the EC is to meet its target of scrapping all borders by the end of 1992. Once these borders are removed, all EC citizens will have unlimited freedom

---

1991; "Political Parties Draw Closer on Emotional Issue of Asylum," *German Tribune*, August 18, 1991; "Weitere starre Fronten in der Asyl-Debatte," *Die Welt*, September 25, 1991; "Asylrecht: Schäuble dämpft Erwartungen," ibid., September 27, 1991; "Bewegungen in der Asyl-Debatte," ibid., September 28/29, 1991; and "Die Bonner Parteien sehen keine Mehrheit für eine Änderung des Asyl-Grundrechts," *Frankfurter Allgemeine Zeitung*, September 28, 1991.
63. See "Schäuble: Aussiedler werden ohne Einschränkungen aufgenommen," *Frankfurter Allgemeine Zeitung*, April 13, 1991.
64. At the EC summit in Luxembourg, in June 1991, Kohl pushed the EC leaders to agree to a harmonization of individual members' policy on asylum. See "L'Allemagne propose de définit une stratégie commune européenne en matière d'immigration," *Le Monde*, June 30–July 1, 1991. Also Christopher Parkes, "Germany Calls for EC Asylum Policy," *Financial Times*, September 3, 1991.

of movement within the internal market, but also all persons legally residing within the Community, including applicants for asylum, will be able to move freely. A common EC asylum policy within the EC, however, would probably require a change in the German constitution, since few West European governments are likely to agree to the liberal rights of asylum provided under Article 16 of the German constitution.

Bonn has also intensified cooperation with the individual countries of Eastern Europe, in order to manage and control the problem of illegal entry better. Cooperation with Poland in particular has been strengthened in an effort to reduce the number of immigrants who illegally cross the Polish-German border. In December 1990 Poland introduced visa and currency restrictions on Romanians entering Poland. This has helped to diminish the number of illegal immigrants who transit Poland into Germany.

These measures alone, however, are unlikely to resolve the problem. Sooner or later it seems likely that Germany must admit that it is becoming an immigration country and must establish quotas for immigrants rather than relying on the cumbersome system of granting asylum for political refugees. While there is still considerable resistance to this idea, particularly within the CDU/CSU, over the long run this may prove the most effective way to manage what has become a major social, economic, and political problem. It would allow Germany to channel the influx of immigrants and harmonize their entry with the labor and housing market. It would also reduce the number of illegitimate asylum seekers and illegal migrants.

Toward East-West Cooperation: The Policy Agenda

The problems faced by the Federal Republic, while more acute than elsewhere in Western Europe, are part of a larger problem in Europe as a whole.[65] In the last decade, the number of asylum seekers in Europe has dramatically increased from a few thousand in the early 1970s to nearly 500,000 in 1990. The unexpected arrival of so many refugees has caught Western European countries unprepared and has overtaxed procedural systems for handling these refugees. Administrative difficulties have been further compounded by the fact that many arrive without travel documents or valid visas. Costs of

---

65. For a detailed discussion of Europe's attempts to deal with the growing refugee crisis, see Gil Loescher, "The European Community and Refugees," *International Affairs*, Vol. 65, No. 4 (Autumn 1989), pp. 617–636.

processing have also soared. In 1989 the cost for the care of asylum seekers in ten European countries plus Canada was at least $4.5 billion; by 1992 it is expected to rise to $8 billion.[66]

The process of political liberalization in the former Soviet Union and Eastern Europe since 1989 has added to these problems. Exactly how large the population outflow from the East will be in the coming decade is difficult to estimate since it is highly scenario-dependent. However, given the gulf between the two parts of Europe and the length of time needed for adaptation by the economies of Eastern Europe, it seems likely that the number of people wishing to leave will be higher in the short term than Western Europe will be able to absorb.[67]

By the early twenty-first century, however, the drop in the birth rate in Western Europe in the 1960s and 1970s should lead to a chronic labor shortage and provide new opportunities for workers from the East. Even countries like Italy, Greece, and Spain, which have traditionally been exporters of labor, will face a labor shortfall and could benefit from an influx of labor from the East over the long run.

The problem is the short term—the next decade, especially the coming 2–5 years when the former Soviet Union and Eastern Europe will face massive adjustment problems and rising unemployment. This is likely to increase the number of migrants to Western Europe and parts of Eastern Europe. Even if the worst scare scenarios do not transpire, increased cooperation between East and West will be necessary to manage the large westward flow of populations. The problem of irregular migration in particular is likely to become acute.

To date the response by many countries in Western Europe to the growing migration pressure from the East has been to tighten border controls and visa restrictions. However, such measures alone are unlikely to stem the migration because they do not deal with the root causes of the outflow, which are the "push factors" in the East. Moreover, they contravene the basic spirit and objectives of Basket Three of the Helsinki Final Act, which calls for the free flow of people, information, and ideas.

What is needed is a broad-gauged, multi-faceted long-term strategy that combines some tightening of controls with development measures that address the root causes of the outflow. However, if this strategy is to be

---

66. Robert Rice, "Europe's Need for a Common Front," *Financial Times*, July 23, 1991.
67. Chesnais, "Migration from Eastern and Western Europe," p. 24.

successful, it cannot be a purely national or even Western endeavor. It must involve cooperation with the prospective sending countries in the East.

In particular, Russia, Ukraine, and the Baltic states need to become integrated in West European efforts to control migration. These areas are likely to be the main sources of emigration from the former Soviet Union.[68] Their cooperation is therefore essential in trying to regulate and stabilize East-West migration.

At the same time, more attention must be paid to the security implications of the possible large-scale emigration of the Soviet scientific intelligentsia, especially those who have worked in sensitive areas of the military-industrial complex. As the impact of market reforms and arms control agreements begins to be felt, tens of thousands of highly skilled scientists will be forced out of work. Many may be tempted to emigrate to countries like Libya or Syria by the prospect of immediate employment and high salaries. Were these scientists to put their skills and knowledge at the disposal of such regimes, this could have a damaging impact on Western security. Thus a concerted Western policy must be worked out to ensure that such a development does not occur.

In addition, several other measures should be part of a comprehensive strategy for dealing with the consequences of possible large-scale migration:

- *Harmonization of rules and practices related to granting asylum within the EC.* In particular, the Community members must agree on criteria for refugee status and streamline the process of asylum adjudication.
- *EC cooperation with the countries of Eastern Europe and the Western republics of the former Soviet Union regarding visa policy, measures to prevent illegal immigration, and deportation agreements.* East European visa and immigration policies in many cases are very liberal for Third World nationals. Consequently, South-North immigration flows are diverted to Eastern Europe and subsequently reach Western Europe illegally. Greater cooperation could reduce this flow, as well as that of East European nationals to Western Europe.
- *Harmonization of policy within the EC on immigration from Eastern Europe and the former Soviet Union.* The goal should be a European Migration Conven-

---

68. In 1989 64 percent of all emigrants from the USSR came from Russia, the Ukraine, and Kazakhstan (which has a large Russian population). Segbers, *Wanderungs- und Fluchtlings-bewegungen aus der bisherigen UdSSR*, p. 16.

tion that establishes immigration quotas for East Europeans and former Soviet nationals, and provides for effective and orderly migration.

- *Increased financial and development assistance to the countries of Eastern Europe and the key republics of the former Soviet Union.* This assistance should be designed to help these countries and republics address the consequences of large-scale immigration as well as to create incentives to keep their own populations from migrating. Such aid can have a dual effect: it can counteract the "push factor" by improving the economic conditions in the sending countries; it can also weaken the "pull factor" by helping to narrow the gap between the sending and receiving countries.[69]

In the final analysis, the migration problem is closely linked to the larger question of the success of the reform process in the East as a whole. If the reforms are successful, the pressure on sizable numbers of citizens from the East to move West will be gradually reduced. But if the reforms fail, many in the East will "vote with their feet." This gives the West a strong incentive to support measures to help stabilize the reform processes now underway in Eastern Europe and the former Soviet Union. Without such support, these reforms could falter, increasing the prospects for instability and disorder in both parts of Europe.

---

69. The relationship between development and migration is complex. Push and pull factors are rarely the only factors determining migration flows. Other socioeconomic factors, such as kinship ties between migrants in the receiving countries, and the political relationships between sending and receiving countries also play a role. Thus migratory flows may persist even after the original economic causes have been considerably weakened.

Beyond Mutual Recrimination

Building a Solid U.S.-Japan Relationship in the 1990s

I. M. Destler and Michael Nacht

The United States and Japan entered the 1990s with both the security and the economic sides of their relationship at some risk. The *Washington Post* headlined a "low point" in bilateral dealings.[1] A *New York Times/CBS News/Tokyo Broadcasting System* poll reported that 58 percent of Americans found "the economic power of Japan" to be "a greater threat to the security of the United States these days" than "the military power of the Soviet Union," with only 26 percent believing the opposite. And citizens of each nation overwhelmingly saw the other as its "strongest competitor."[2]

At the elite level, there has been a rise of "revisionists" in both countries stressing Japan's strength and uniqueness, and the divergence of Japanese and American interests.[3] An outgoing State Department official even played

This article was prepared for a forthcoming volume on *United States Foreign Policy Towards the Year 2000*, edited by Robert Art and Seyom Brown, and presented in preliminary form at an April 1990 conference at Brandeis University. We are grateful to C. Fred Bergsten, and to participants at the Brandeis conference, for their helpful critical comments on that draft.

I.M. Destler is Professor at the School of Public Affairs, University of Maryland, and Visiting Fellow at the Institute for International Economics. Michael Nacht is Dean of the School of Public Affairs, University of Maryland, and was Acting Director of the Harvard Program on U.S.-Japan Relations.

1. See Fred Hiatt and Margaret Shapiro, "U.S.-Japanese Relations Seen At Low Point," *Washington Post*, February 12, 1990, pp. A1, A16.
2. "Japan Survey" for *New York Times/CBS News/Tokyo Broadcasting System*, June 5–8, 1990 (U.S.) and May 31, June 7, 1990 (Japan); results summarized in *New York Times*, July 10, 1990. Reciprocal popular sentiment remained predominantly favorable. The number of Americans who saw themselves as "generally friendly" to Japan dropped modestly, from 87 to 75 percent, between July 1985 and July 1990, while the percentage of "generally unfriendly" rose from 8 to 18. The parallel Japanese percentages in 1990 were 66 percent friendly and 30 percent unfriendly, little changed from past surveys. For comprehensive, balanced assessments of polling data, see William Watts (in collaboration with Seizaburo Sato), "America and Japan: How We See Each Other," Washington, D.C.: Report for the Commission on U.S.-Japan Relations for the Twenty-first Century, May 2, 1990; and Eileen M. Doherty, "American and Japanese Polls on the Bilateral Relationship: Trends and Implications," Washington, D.C.: Japan Economic Institute, Report 9A, March 2, 1990. As Doherty reports, the overall trend in American attitudes toward Japan appears to be "toward the negative," but the picture is decidedly mixed, with citizens in both nations giving major weight to the domestic roots of bilateral economic problems.
3. Prominent "revisionist" writings include James Fallows, "Containing Japan," *Atlantic Monthly*, May 1989, pp. 40–54; Karel van Wolferen, *The Enigma of Japanese Power: People and Politics in a*

on the old enemy/new enemy perception by calling for a "Team B" intelligence analysis of U.S. policy toward Japan.[4] Across the Pacific, respect for the United States has been on the wane: reporting on a survey of public and elite opinion in Japan, the April 2, 1990, cover of *Newsweek* showed an American infant with the heading: "What Japan Thinks of Us: A Nation of Crybabies?"

These negatives are difficult to justify in terms of the specifics of the relationship. In the political-military sphere, the bilateral security treaty of 1960—long a lightning rod for Japan's opposition parties—has been transformed through the seventies and eighties into the basis for a practical, working defense relationship. Over the same period, American-Japanese geopolitical cooperation has deepened. Tensions did rise over Japan's initial slowness in contributing to the American-led effort to defend Saudi Arabia against Iraq. But thereafter Tokyo increased its commitment.

Economically, the trade imbalance remains high, but important trends are in the right direction. Since 1985, the two nations have cooperated in major exchange rate adjustment, moving the yen from over 250 to the dollar to well below 150. Contrary to widespread myth, this has had a major impact on bilateral trade—in 1988 and 1989, for example, U.S. exports to Japan rose by 34 and 18 percent, while imports grew by only 6 and 5 percent.[5] In the first half of 1990, the trade deficit shrank further. Clearly, many U.S. exporters have been making sales, and many who compete with Japanese imports have gotten relief.

Stateless Nation (London: Macmillan, 1989); Clyde V. Prestowitz, *Trading Places: How We Allowed Japan to Take the Lead* (New York: Basic Books, 1988); and, across the Pacific, Akio Morita and Shintaro Ishihara, *The Japan That Can Say No* (unpublished ms., unofficial Washington translation).

4. Kevin L. Kearns, "After FSX: A New Approach to U.S.-Japan Relations," *Foreign Service Journal*, December 1989, pp. 43–48. (The "Team B" reference comes from the "Team B" assessment of the Soviet strategic threat conducted by conservative analysts under President Gerald Ford and then–CIA Director George Bush.)

5. This was more rapid than overall improvement in U.S. trade: global U.S. exports rose by 27 percent in 1988 and 13 percent in 1989, while global imports grew by 9 percent and 7 percent, respectively. And it was at least comparable to changes in U.S. trade with the European Community (EC): there U.S. exports grew by 25 percent and 14 percent, and imports by 5 percent and 0.2 percent, respectively, during the same two years. The U.S. bilateral trade deficit with Japan receded only moderately—from $56 billion in 1987 to $49 billion in 1989—whereas the U.S. balance with the European Community swung from a deficit of $21 billion to a surplus of slightly over $1 billion. But this relatively small shift in the overall balance, cited by critics as evidence of the failure of exchange rate adjustment to affect U.S. trade with Japan, was inevitable given the arithmetic involved: since Japan's sales to the United States in 1987 were triple those flowing in the other direction, a much higher rate of growth of U.S. exports was necessary just to keep the overall deficit from growing. (See Table 1 for the numbers since 1980.)

Moreover, there were, as the decade began, no important current issues upon which the two governments were in basic disagreement. Concerning the most visible source of contention—the trade imbalance—both governments agreed that it had little relationship to the Japanese trade barriers upon which it is typically blamed.[6] And in the spring and early summer, the two governments reached agreement on a broad range of issues, from trade in supercomputers and forest products to "structural" issues affecting bilateral trade relations.

Given these circumstances, the bilateral relationship ought to be in pretty good shape. Why then has the air been filled with warnings of U.S.-Japan economic conflict? Some reflect frustration about the limited nominal decline in the bilateral trade imbalance (and in the global U.S. trade imbalance, which remains around $100 billion annually). Some reflect strongly-held views on specific issues, such as friction over semiconductor competition, the controversy on how best to co-develop the FSX (Fighter Support Experimental) aircraft, and the American concern that Japan will shortly make major inroads in the U.S. domination of the global aerospace market. Some have been a product of the trade-political calendar written into the Omnibus Trade and Competitiveness Act of 1988, under which the United States named Japan in 1989 as one of three countries with a pattern of unfair barriers to U.S. imports, and which led to subsequent talks with deadlines in the first half of 1990.

But the underlying causes of this deterioration are undoubtedly to be found in two major power shifts: (1) the sudden decline of the Soviet Union, coinciding with (2) the steady rise of Japan, which has clearly become a superpower in manufacturing, finance, trade, and technology.

A further cause is the relative economic decline of the United States; without clear U.S. policies to address the roots of this decline, the result is public frustration and incentives for scapegoating. Another is the persistence of Japanese insularity, reflected economically in a level of manufactured goods imports well below what economists would expect, recent increases

---

6. As stated in the 1990 report of the Council of Economic Advisers, "removal of [Japanese] import barriers is likely to increase both Japanese imports and Japanese exports. The net effect on overall trade imbalances is unclear." Council of Economic Advisers, *Economic Report of the President*, February 1990, p. 249. Concerning the U.S. trade deficit, both governments agree that it is essentially "made in America," and that the way to attack it is to reduce the federal budget deficit and/or to increase private savings. This view was incorporated in the June 1990 agreement on structural impediments to trade, discussed below.

notwithstanding.[7] Taken together, these fuel a growing sentiment among Americans that the Japanese cannot be trusted and that their economic success will ultimately be to the detriment of the United States.

As we enter the nineties, Americans face a number of alternative futures—and Japan figures importantly in them all. Conceivable scenarios for the U.S.-Japan relationship range from maintaining—perhaps even deepening—current security and economic interdependence, on the one hand, to growing economic—and perhaps, ultimately, political-military—rivalry and conflict on the other. The preferred outcome is clearly the former. Given the severe costs to U.S. interests of the alternatives, achieving a balanced and durable interdependence is, we believe, a first-order priority for U.S. foreign-policymakers over the coming decade, equal in importance to the redefinition of the NATO/European alliance structure, and to keeping the Soviet Union headed toward political and economic reform. It could also prove very difficult.

To bring about this relatively happy outcome, the United States needs a strategy that includes:

1) A basis for retaining security cooperation under a condition of reduced threat and increased concern about technological competition;

2) Shoring up areas of weakness in the U.S. domestic economy, to strengthen the U.S. foundation for cooperation and competition with Japan;

3) Continued U.S. efforts to open up the Japanese economy through processes and substantive agreements that become progressively more two-sided in substance, as well as form;

4) An explicit strategy of reinforcing and deepening economic interdependence; and

5) Articulation of "competitive interdependence" as an explicit alternative to U.S.—and Japanese—economic nationalism.

We develop our case for such a strategy in the pages that follow.

---

7. For example, Robert Z. Lawrence finds Japanese imports of manufactured goods "about 40 percent lower than one would expect of a typical industrial economy." Lawrence, "Imports in Japan: Closed Markets or Minds?" *Brookings Papers on Economic Activity*, No. 2, 1987, p. 523. For recent comprehensive surveys, see Edward J. Lincoln, *Japan's Unequal Trade* (Washington, D.C.: Brookings, 1990); and Bela A. Balassa and Marcus Noland, *Japan in the World Economy* (Washington, D.C.: Institute for International Economics, 1988), chap. 3. For a contrary view, that "foreign penetration of the Japanese market is equivalent to the experience of other major industrial economies," see Gary R. Saxonhouse, "The Micro- and Macroeconomics of Foreign Sales to Japan," in William R. Cline, ed., *Trade Policy in the 1980s* (Washington, D.C.: Institute for International Economics, 1983), p. 285.

Policy Background

THE STRENGTHENING OF SECURITY COOPERATION

Twice since World War II, in 1951 and 1960, the United States has affirmed through formal treaties its commitment to maintain the security of Japan. This commitment made very good sense thirty years ago; Japan had emerged from World War II struggling to establish democratic institutions under close American supervision and was encouraged by Washington to focus on rebuilding its economy and society, while the United States took care of Japanese security.

The American security commitment was intimately connected to the policy of global containment, and the stationing of U.S. forces on Japanese territory was seen as the principal manifestation of this policy in the Western Pacific. Their presence not only protected Japan but facilitated the projection of American military power on the Asian mainland. U.S. naval power in the region aimed at denying the Soviet navy access to open ocean areas and countering the Soviet attack submarine fleet. American bases in Japan served as staging bases for actions taken during the Korean and Vietnam Wars.

There was persistent anti-American sentiment among leftist and extreme rightist Japanese groups in the 1950s and 1960s. These brought sporadic outbursts against the alliance and the Liberal Democratic Party (LDP) that supported it, peaking in the mass demonstrations which forced President Dwight Eisenhower to cancel his planned visit in 1960. The Vietnam War also became a rallying point for opposition to the United States, particularly in the late 1960s, just as in many other countries around the world.

But by the early 1970s, the security relationship had won broader support in Tokyo as well as in Washington, with the U.S. agreement to return Okinawa to Japan, the American (and Japanese) openings to China, and the promise of a Soviet-American détente symbolized by the signing of the Strategic Arms Limitation Treaty (SALT) in May 1972. Based on an asymmetric economic and strategic relationship between the two nations, a still-threatening international environment, and a sense of mutual respect, the U.S.-Japanese security relationship came to be seen as healthy and mutually beneficial.

This relationship survived a few rough moments in the latter 1970s. The Carter administration's nuclear nonproliferation policy threatened initially to place severe restrictions on Japanese reprocessing of spent nuclear fuel. Carter also mistakenly sought to withdraw American forces from South Korea without consulting the Japanese—fueling post-Vietnam anxieties that the United States was "leaving Asia." Finally, the Carter administration made the mistake of pressuring Japan to spend more than one percent of its gross national product on defense without concrete recommendations for how these funds should be spent.

Nonetheless, by the 1980s it was clear that the U.S.-Japan security relationship had grown much stronger. Bilateral defense cooperation had evolved to include real operational cooperation between U.S. and Japanese forces. It evolved also from U.S. military and commercial sales in the 1960s (e.g., of the F-104 fighter, Airborne Warning and Control System aircraft [AWACS], and CH-47 attack helicopters), to licensed production of American systems in Japan in the 1970s and early 1980s (e.g., F-15 aircraft and Sidewinder missiles), to co-production in the late 1980s (e.g., Aegis destroyers and the Boeing 767).[8] Major U.S. aerospace firms such as McDonnell Douglas and Raytheon became deeply entrenched in cooperative efforts with the Japanese Defense Agency. The Reagan administration eased frictions over Japan's relative contribution by shifting the debate from the level of Japan's defense budget to the "roles and missions" the Japanese Self Defense Forces should perform. Some of the concepts, such as the determination that Japanese naval forces should defend the sea lines of communication (SLOCs) out to 1000 miles from Japan's territorial waters, were of limited operational utility, but the overall health of the security relationship could not have been better. The strong personal ties between President Ronald Reagan and Prime Minister Yasuhiro Nakasone—the "Ron-Yasu" relationship—added an important stabilizing element that sustained bilateral security cooperation through the decade.

THE BROADENING OF ECONOMIC COMPETITION

As defense ties grew, so did economic interaction, but here the net impact on bilateral relations has been less salutary. The breadth of the change has been enormous. As recently as twenty years ago, the United States and Japan were enmeshed in a quarrel over textile trade, a matter central to the economy

---

8. See Stephen N. Wooley, "Defense Industrial Cooperation in the Pacific Rim: A New Approach to Policy," paper written for the University of Maryland School of Public Affairs, 1988.

of neither.[9] Today, the economic issues between them involve high-technology industries critical to the economic futures of both, and huge financial flows on which each is highly dependent. Yet while old-style issues involving the impact of Japanese exports no longer hold center stage, they have not disappeared. Instead, they share billing with four other broad and overlapping categories of economic issues (listed here in rough order of their historical emergence):

1) *Import issues* (1955–), resulting from the impact of Japanese products on U.S. producers and markets. These have moved steadily from labor-intensive to capital- and knowledge-intensive goods: from textiles, to steel and consumer electronics, to automobiles and semiconductors;

2) *Export issues* (1969–), typically initiated by U.S. officials seeking to expand trade by breaking down Japanese barriers to American products. Beginning with pressure for tariff reduction, these officials moved in the late seventies to emphasis on non-tariff barriers to U.S. sales of such products as beef and citrus, telecommunications equipment, satellites, semiconductors, supercomputers, and wood products. Increasingly, these have been punctuated with Congressional and industry demands for specific reciprocity and a "level playing field";

3) *Macroeconomic and structural issues* (1971–), raised in response to persistent Japanese trade surpluses and growing U.S. deficits, and involving efforts to influence policies that affect overall balances: monetary and fiscal policies, "structural" measures with impact on savings rates and business practices, and intervention in foreign exchange markets;

4) *Technology-related trade and investment issues* (1982–), arising particularly from Japanese success in high-tech, triggering anxieties in the defense establishment about U.S. technological leadership and security leakage, and broader concerns about overall U.S. "economic security" and leadership; and

5) *Financial, investment and related issues* (1987–), a product of now-massive capital flows from Japan to the United States, reflecting the overall shift in relative economic power.

---

9. For that full story, see I.M. Destler, Haruhiro Fukui, and Hideo Sato, *The Textile Wrangle: Conflict in Japanese-American Relations, 1969–1971* (Ithaca, Cornell University Press, 1979).

The emergence of issue types 2–5 has coincided, of course, with Japan's rise over two decades to across-the-board manufacturing pre-eminence and financial power. And over these two decades, the two governments became much more skilled in the management of economic conflict. Many specific crises have been defused through timely agreements; substantial policy changes were in fact negotiated, particularly in Japan's trade and regulatory regimes.

But as the number and diversity of conflicts grew, so did their political difficulty. It was much harder to crack Japanese import markets than to negotiate export restraints; it was a new challenge to engage in meaningful bargaining over "domestic" fiscal and monetary policies or "structural" matters such as savings incentives and land use policies. And the massive cross-border capital inflows of the eighties were without parallel in America's twentieth-century experience. They financed record U.S. trade and budget deficits, with the Japanese Ministry of Finance literally saving the dollar from collapse in 1987. But this represented a financial dependence that both constrained American freedom and multiplied American discomfort. Signaling these developments at the popular level were visible Japanese investments like the purchases of Columbia Pictures and Rockefeller Center.

The Current Situation

THE SECURITY RELATIONSHIP
As we enter the 1990s, the tangible elements of the U.S.-Japan Treaty of Mutual Cooperation and Security remain intact. U.S. Forces–Japan is maintained as one of two subordinate unified commands (the other being U.S. Forces–Korea) under the U.S. Pacific Command (USPACOM) headquartered in Hawaii. This command includes 2000 army personnel; almost 24,000 Marines; 16,500 airmen and 120 combat aircraft including 72 F-15 C/Ds and 48 F-16s; and 8300 naval personnel who operate several facilities including the naval base at Yokosuka, headquarters for the U.S. Seventh Fleet. American forces extend from Okinawa in the south of Japan to the Misawa Air Force Base in the northern part of Honshu.[10]

---

10. See International Institute for Strategic Studies (IISS), *The Military Balance 1989–1990* (London: IISS, 1989), p. 26; and Defense Agency, Japan, *Defense of Japan 1988* (Tokyo: Defense Agency, 1988), pp. 335–336.

Despite the heavy criticism that has often been leveled against Japan for not investing sufficiently in defense, the facts tell a different story. By 1989 Japan's defense budget (approximately $30 billion) was on the verge of sur-passing those of the Federal Republic of Germany, France, or Great Britain.[11] The Japanese Ground Self Defense Forces (GSDF) included more than 160 tanks, 180 artillery pieces, 170 armored personnel carriers, and a variety of surface-to-ship guided missiles, anti-tank helicopters, transport helicopters, and surface-to-air guided missiles. The Maritime Self Defense Forces (MSDF) boasted more than 60 destroyers (twice as many as are in the Pacific-based U.S. Seventh Fleet), including two equipped with the Aegis defense system. Consequently, Japan's forces in the northern Pacific are not trivial when compared to the American commitment. The MSDF have also deployed 100 P-3C anti-submarine aircraft (just 23 are in the U.S. Pacific Fleet). The Air Self Defense Forces have 200 F-15s and 100 F-4s.[12] Moreover, Japan provides roughly 40 percent of the costs of stationing U.S. forces in-country[13] and is likely to increase this contribution, in part to assuage American pressures.

The future trends in the security relationship turn on narrower issues of defense technology competition and on broader issues concerning the rapidly changing geo-strategic environment. With respect to issues of technology competition, two recent examples serve to illustrate the long-run problem: semiconductors and the FSX. It is obvious even to casual students of contemporary military affairs that sophisticated weapons systems are increasingly dependent on advanced micro-electronics. Information processing and target acquisition are especially dependent upon the capabilities of advanced semi-conductors. A major Pentagon review of the semiconductor industry pointed out that Japanese firms have become dominant across a range of crucial products and technologies. Some analysts have been relatively relaxed about this development, but the authors of the report sounded the alarm that the

---

11. Further growth in Japan's defense budget is now uncertain given the continued erosion of the Soviet threat and the increase in oil prices caused by the Iraqi invasion of Kuwait and the subsequent embargo of Iraqi and Kuwaiti oil. See "Back Under One Percent" *The Economist*, August 4–10, 1990, p. 26. Nonetheless, as summarized in the discussion that follows, Japan has deployed a significant force, far greater than is generally acknowledged, to defend its home islands against a conventional weapons attack.
12. A useful summary of these capabilities is contained in Gary K. Reynolds, "Japan's Military Buildup: Goals and Accomplishments," Congressional Research Service, *Report for Congress*, January 27, 1989.
13. See Richard Solomon, "Sustaining the Dynamic Balance in East Asia and the Pacific," Statement before the Subcommittee on Asia and Pacific, House Foreign Affairs Committee, Washington, D.C., February 22, 1990, p. 2.

United States was in danger of becoming excessively dependent on Japanese suppliers for critical elements of its national security capability and that this trend needed to be reversed.[14] This concern was underscored when Japanese Diet member Shintaro Ishihara asserted in 1989 that the provision of Japanese semiconductors to the Soviet Union could change the global balance of power.[15]

The semiconductor controversy highlights one longer-term trend in defense relations with Japan. It is likely that future military power will rely increasingly on three capabilities: sophisticated information processing techniques; the use of directed energy, such as lasers and particle beams, as weapons of precision (in target acquisition) and high-confidence command and control; and the ability to utilize space for military platforms. Besides the superpowers, only Japan is well-positioned to play a leading role in this emerging security environment. Therefore, Japan has, by definition, military potential, and this potential is increasingly seen in Washington as a threat to American predominance in this field.[16]

The FSX controversy that greeted President Bush upon his assumption of office in early 1989 illustrates a related problem. The FSX program involves the development of a new, advanced fighter aircraft that would be deployed by the Japanese Air Self Defense Forces in the mid-to-late 1990s. Tensions in U.S.-Japan relations materialized over whether the aircraft would be a modified version of the F-16 or a new aircraft developed primarily by the Japanese. In Washington, the issue triggered a struggle between the Departments of State and of Defense, on the one hand, and on the other, the Commerce Department, the Office of the U.S. Trade Representative (USTR), and the Office of Management and Budget (OMB). Representatives from State and Defense felt that the deal—in which General Dynamics would be a major subcontractor to Mitsubishi Heavy Industries—was the best the United States could get. Moreover, they had negotiated it with their Japanese counterparts over several years and were committed to defending the results. Commerce, USTR, and OMB, however, saw the FSX as a major stimulus to the establishment of a Japanese aerospace industry that would pose a long-term

---

14. See *Report of Defense Science Board Task Force on Defense Semiconductor Dependency* (Washington, D.C.: Department of Defense, February 1987).
15. Morita and Ishihara, *The Japan That Can Say No*, p. 3.
16. How this Japanese military potential fits into the broader array of contemporary U.S. national security concerns is discussed in Michael Nacht, "Cold War: The Arms Race Isn't Over Yet," *Washington Post Outlook*, April 15, 1990, pp. D1, D4.

challenge to American domination of this industrial sector. Urged on by members of Congress, they succeeded in persuading Bush to reopen the matter and win further Japanese concessions.

If in Tokyo, therefore, the controversy grew to symbolize American inconstancy and unpredictability, from the Washington perspective what the FSX came to symbolize more than anything else was the fear that defense collaboration with Japan would jeopardize the pre-eminent U.S. position in the development of military technology and the manufacturing of advanced weapon systems. Technology transfer to Japan could also, it was argued, nourish future commercial competition in the one major high-tech trade area where the United States remained dominant.

In sum, the emerging Japanese economic prowess has now clearly spilled over into the defense sector. As in other areas of economic activity, the bilateral defense technology relationship will likely be marked by complex patterns of cooperation and competition.[17]

In broader terms, the U.S.-Japan security relationship has rested on the shared sense of the threat posed by Soviet military forces to Japanese territory and to the East Asian region generally. For years both felt genuine concern about potential Soviet strikes against Japanese military targets, a "grab" of the northern island of Hokkaido, and the use of the Soviet theater nuclear forces deployed in the Soviet Far East to coerce Japan into making economic and political concessions. In the mid-to-late 1960s there were also expectations that the People's Republic of China (PRC) might mount a serious challenge to Japanese sovereignty.

By 1990 these prospects had lost virtually all credibility. The PRC has not been seen as a military threat to Japan for many years, and its economic and domestic political difficulties are likely to occupy the full attention of its leadership well into the next century. The panoply of major Soviet concessions in arms control negotiations and Gorbachev's permissive and even encouraging attitude toward the collapse of communism throughout Eastern Europe have largely stripped away the sense of Soviet threat felt in the West, including Japan.

---

17. Two useful reports on bilateral technological trends are "Science, Technology, and the Future of the U.S.-Japan Relationship," Issues Paper Prepared by the Committee on Japan, National Research Council (Washington, D.C.: National Academy Press, 1990); and "Technology and Competitiveness: New Frontiers For the United States and Japan" (New York: Japan Society; Washington: Council on Competitiveness, January 1990).

Soviet-Japanese relations have improved relatively little under Gorbachev, in part because of continued Soviet control of the four small islands north of Hokkaido and, more deeply, because of the century-old Russo-Japanese animosity symbolized by Russia's humiliating defeat by Japan in 1905. Even Gorbachev's meeting with South Korean President Roh Tae Woo in June 1990 was not wildly applauded in Tokyo, because it raised the prospect of a possible step toward Korean reunification which many Japanese find threatening. The Soviet president's planned visit to Tokyo in 1991, however, could greatly improve Soviet-Japan relations if Gorbachev's desire to rescue the Soviet economy from near-collapse were to push him to relinquish the northern islands in return for Japanese financial aid, technical assistance, management training, and investment in Siberian development. Indeed, the recent Soviet offer to return two of the islands is perhaps a harbinger of a more flexible policy toward Japan. On the other hand, the Soviet move toward Seoul has stimulated Tokyo to enhance its dialogue with *North* Korea, reflecting inherent tensions among the major powers in Northeast Asia. On balance, although the bilateral relationship between Tokyo and Moscow is not warm, the decline of the Soviet threat has unquestionably undercut the primary strategic rationale for the U.S.-Japan security relationship.

THE CURRENT ECONOMIC RELATIONSHIP

Meanwhile, the lightning rod for economic relations remains the bilateral trade imbalance. This totaled $49 billion in 1989, with U.S. imports from Japan at $93.6 billion, roughly double U.S. exports to Japan of $44.6 billion. Contrary to conventional political wisdom, this is an improvement in recent years, as Table 1 illustrates. As recently as 1987, U.S. imports of $84.6 billion from Japan were *triple* U.S. exports of $28.2 billion, and the rise of Japanese imports was much slower from 1986 to 1989 than it was from 1983 to 1986. But as Table 1 also illustrates (in its far-right columns showing the ratio of the U.S. deficit to total trade with Japan), the proportionate imbalance with Japan remains substantially greater than that with the world as a whole, as has been true since the sixties.

The bilateral imbalance rises and falls with the overall U.S. deficit, but would persist even if overall global accounts were squared. There is nothing wrong with this *per se:* there is no particular reason why U.S.-Japan trade should balance bilaterally. In fact, experts generally agree that a significant imbalance in Japan's favor is normal. Given the nation's strong comparative advantage in high-quality industrial products and its dearth of natural re-

Table 1.   U.S. Trade Balances, 1980–90.[1]

	U.S. Trade Globally				U.S. Trade with Japan			
	Exports	Imports	Balance	Deficit/Trade[2]	Exports	Imports	Balance	Deficit/Trade
1980	224.3	−249.7	−25.5	.053	20.8	−30.7	−9.9	.192
1981	237.1	−265.1	−28.0	.056	21.8	−37.6	−15.8	.266
1982	211.2	−247.6	−36.4	.079	21.0	−37.7	−16.8	.286
1983	201.8	−268.9	−67.1	.143	21.9	−41.2	−19.3	.306
1984	219.9	−332.4	−112.5	.204	23.6	−57.1	−33.6	.416
1985	215.9	−338.1	−122.1	.220	22.6	−68.7	−46.1	.505
1986	223.4	−368.4	−145.1	.245	26.9	−81.9	−55.0	.506
1987	250.3	−409.8	−159.5	.242	28.2	−84.6	−56.3	.500
1988	320.3	−447.3	−127.0	.165	37.7	−89.5	−51.8	.407
1989	360.5	−475.3	−114.9	.137	44.6	−93.6	−49.0	.355
1990[3]	193.0	−241.9	−48.9	.112	23.5	−43.1	−19.6	.294

SOURCE: U.S. Department of Commerce, Bureau of the Census and Bureau of Economic Analysis.
NOTES: 1. Figures are in billions of current dollars. Minor discrepancies are due to rounding.
2. The deficit as a proportion of total trade (exports plus imports).
3. Figures through June 1990.

sources, Japan naturally runs surpluses with major importers of manufactured goods (e.g., the United States and the European Community) and deficits with sources of food and raw materials (e.g., Australia, Canada, and Indonesia).[18] As for the overall American trade imbalance, the proper remedies remain home remedies—as the Japanese keep reminding us. Americans should cut demand by reducing the federal deficit and increasing private savings. Together with the decline of the dollar that such policies—and multilateral macroeconomic cooperation—might facilitate, this is the route to bringing overall U.S. trade into balance.

There was incremental progress in federal deficit-reduction during the second Reagan term. Domestic stalemate put major steps beyond reach for Bush's first fifteen months. Thereafter, faced with a deteriorating budget situation, the administration initiated bipartisan deficit-reduction talks with Congressional leaders. With the president's June 1990 acknowledgement that

---

18. C. Fred Bergsten and William R. Cline, *The United States–Japan Economic Problem*, Policy Analysis No. 13, 1st ed. (Washington, D.C.: Institute for International Economics, October 1985), esp. pp. 32–41.

"tax revenue increases" would be necessary, a meaningful budget package became possible. And after a tumultuous process which bloodied both the president and Congressional leaders, an October compromise was enacted that should have substantial impact on the budget deficit over the next three to five years. But trade diplomats still have to cope with the persistence of the U.S. global deficit, Japan's substantial (though recently declining) global surplus, the bilateral trade imbalance, and Japanese resistance to imports. There is surface plausibility to the claim that the first three of these are caused by the last; at the very least, it puts heat on U.S. Trade Representative Carla Hills and her associates to stand tough on trade matters.

Also exerting heat have been the provisions of the Omnibus Trade and Competitiveness Act of 1988. Designed not to assert direct Congressional control, but to force the executive branch to try harder, it institutes a series of deadlines; the most visible and controversial is a new provision of Section 301 of the Trade Act of 1974, as amended. "Super-301," as it is labelled, calls upon the administration not just to pinpoint barriers to specific American exports that are "unreasonable" or "unjustifiable," but to single out and name "priority foreign countries" for the "number and pervasiveness" of their "acts, policies, or practices" that impede U.S. exports.[19]

Since the provision was written with Japan in mind, the Bush administration had little practical choice in its first year but to declare Japan a trade "sinner." This it did in May 1989, though it limited its bill of particulars to three product cases: supercomputers, satellites, and wood products. Reaction was strong in Japan, but a way was found to negotiate on these three specific issues, and settlements were reached on all of them in the spring of 1990, before the deadline built into the Super-301 law. The two nations also joined in a new negotiation, the so-called Structural Impediments Initiative (SII). Undertaken as an alternative to overall indictment of Japan's economy under Super-301, these talks targeted deep-seated behavior patterns in Japan (and the United States) which lay behind Japanese import resistance (and U.S. non-competitiveness). Consultations continued on the yen-dollar exchange rate, bilaterally and within the "Group of Seven" (G-7) advanced industrial nations. Both the U.S. Treasury Department and the Japanese Ministry of Finance were frustrated by the rise of the dollar above 150 yen in the first half of 1990, but it fell back down to 130 yen in the early fall.

---

19. See I.M. Destler, "United States Trade Policymaking in the Eighties," forthcoming in Alberto Alesina and Geoffrey Carliner, eds., *Politics and Economics in the 1980s* (University of Chicago Press, for the National Bureau of Economic Research).

Talks on product and structural issues took place under the spotlight of a frenetic press in Tokyo, punctuated by the rhetoric of a demanding Congress in Washington. SII was the most comprehensive and difficult negotiation. The focus on structural matters was good economics, since they underlay many of the specific trade frustrations, and some of them (like incentives to save in Japan and to spend in the United States) contributed to the overall trade imbalance. But it was fractious politics, since taken to their logical extreme the SII talks attacked politically embedded institutions like Japan's land-tax system which so favors small farmers, or the U.S. mortgage tax deduction that skews investment toward housing and away from tradable goods.

While reciprocal in form, the SII talks were one-sided in fact. They followed the venerable pattern of employing *gaiatsu*, or foreign pressure, as trigger and pretext for Japanese policy change. This pattern featured U.S. initiative and Japanese deference. Exploited and refined by officials in both nations through the postwar period, it had gotten the two nations through many economic crises. And it produced results again in 1990—a preliminary agreement on SII in April, and a final agreement in June. The latter, facilitated by Bush's domestic concession on taxes, included a Japanese commitment to increase public works expenditures over a ten-year period.

Yet the *gaiatsu* pattern was based on two now-obsolete presumptions: the predominance of American power and the soundness, in Japanese eyes, of U.S. policies. It worked one more time in 1990. But neither Washington nor Tokyo can long defer the challenge of explicitly addressing Japan's emergence as an economic, technological, and financial superpower and the challenge this poses to both.[20]

In the phrase of Ezra Vogel, Japan has become "Number One" in a wide range of manufacturing industries—from automobiles to consumer electronics to semiconductors—and is clearly the world's leader in the technology and management of the production process.

---

20. On "Japan's emergence as a technological superpower" and the policy dilemmas this poses for Americans, see National Research Council, "Science, Technology, and the Future of the U.S.-Japan Relationship." For an anxious view of Japanese financial power, see R. Taggert Murphy, "Power Without Purpose: The Crisis of Japan's Global Financial Dominance," *Harvard Business Review*, Vol. 67, No. 2 (March–April 1989), pp. 71–83. For a more positive view of Japanese statesmanship, but one which also highlights Japan's rapid financial rise, see the writings of David Hale of Kemper Financial Services, for example, "Does America Really Want Japan to Pursue Rapid Financial Liberalization?" (unpublished ms., June 1989).

Even with the substantial drop in the Nikkei stock index in the first nine months of 1990, the total value of stock of companies traded on Japanese exchanges remains about equal to the total value of those traded on U.S. exchanges.[21] The current market value of all the land in Japan is several times that of the land in the United States. These assets represent enormous financial power in Japanese hands, available for use abroad as well as at home.

In recent years, annual capital outflow from Japan has approached $100 billion, far higher than any other nation. Japanese buyers have become indispensable at the auctions of Treasury bonds to finance U.S. budget deficits, and Japanese direct investment in the United States (while only a fraction of portfolio investment) has grown rapidly in recent years, with particular concentration in the banking sector.[22]

As noted above, studies by experts in both countries "share the conclusion that Japan's high technology capabilities are now on par with or ahead of the United States in many areas."[23]

Over the past two years, though Japan's economy is roughly half as large, the absolute level of Japanese capital investment has exceeded that of the United States.

Under these circumstances, there was a certain droll absurdity to the notion, prevalent in the Japanese press, that current United States demands

---

21. At the end of 1988, stock on Japanese exchanges was worth $3,815 billion (39.8 percent of the global total), compared to $2,414 billion (25.2 percent) for American exchanges. At the end of 1982, the numbers had been $417 billion (16.1 percent) for Japan, and $1,304 billion (50.5 percent) for the United States. These statistics, attributed to Goldman Sachs, are reported in David Hale, "Should Central Banks Target Share Price Multiples or How Asymmetries in Global Financial Markets Affect Exchange Rate Movements?" Paper Prepared for the U.S.-Japan Consultative Group on International Monetary Affairs, November 1989, Table 1.1. Since 1988, however, the trend has been the other way. As of early fall 1990, Japanese and American exchanges each totaled roughly one-third of global stock values.

22. In 1988, Japanese direct investment in the United States rose to 16.2 percent of total foreign investment, with Japan replacing the Netherlands as the number two ownership country. (Britain remained number one, with 31.0 percent.) In 1987, foreign-owned firms controlled "3 to 4 percent of the U.S. economy as a whole and 7 to 10 percent of the manufacturing sector; by 1988 foreign firms controlled 15 to 20 percent of the U.S. banking sector." Japanese direct investment is particularly concentrated in banking, totaling over half of all foreign investment in banking and hence nearly 10 percent of total banking assets in the United States. (Direct investment is ownership that carries with it actual control over what is owned; this aspect of control distinguishes direct investment from portfolio investment, which is simply the establishment of a claim on an asset for the purpose of realizing some return.) See Edward M. Graham and Paul R. Krugman, *Foreign Direct Investment in the United States* (Washington, D.C.: Institute for International Economics, 1989), esp. pp. 34, 2, and 20.

23. National Research Council, "Science, Technology, and the Future of the U.S.-Japan Relationship," p. 7.

in the SII talks represented the third American reshaping of Japanese society.[24] There is a similar unreality in the standard Capitol Hill rhetoric, threatening dire U.S. actions if Japan doesn't finally act on trade. Americans must stop talking as if they can reshape Japan, though pressure at the margins can reinforce trends we find promising. And Japanese advocates of domestic change must stop waiting for Americans to do their political dirty-work for them.

Alternative Futures: An American Perspective

For the U.S.-Japan alliance, both the geostrategic and the economic contexts have been transformed. The United States no longer dominates the economic relationship. Nor do the two nations still share a perception of a strong threat in the international security environment. And with persistent economic conflict, the core sense of trust between elites of the two societies has been somewhat shaken. A pessimist might conclude from these changes that the very basis for constructive U.S.-Japan relations has been undermined. But this interpretation is one-sided because it emphasizes only the centrifugal forces that are pulling us apart and does not highlight the centripetal forces that tend to keep the relationship intact and functioning.

The Lower House Japanese elections of 1990 are a case in point. The Liberal Democratic Party (LDP), in power since 1955, was rocked in 1989 by the "Recruit" scandals and other major problems that led to the resignation of two prime ministers in quick succession. The LDP was also politically vulnerable for having pushed through an unpopular tax and, in rural areas, for making agricultural trade concessions to the United States. Yet, though it suffered severely in the Upper House election of July 1989, the LDP emerged from the election of February 1990 with a healthy majority in the critical Lower House of the Diet. The dominant explanation in Japan for this result was that the electorate, though frustrated on a number of matters, was unwilling to change political horses when the horse it had been riding had produced unprecedented levels of peace and prosperity for Japanese society. This reasoning is relevant to Japanese attitudes about its bilateral relationship with the United States, and to American attitudes as well.

---

24. The first two, of course, were Commodore Perry's opening of Japan in the mid-nineteenth century, and the U.S. occupation under General Douglas MacArthur after World War II.

Despite efforts to diversify its markets, Japan remains highly dependent on access to the American market to maintain its economic health. Indeed, the rise in Japanese investments and financial interests in the United States has acted to increase Japanese dependence in important respects. Moreover, many influential Japanese remain uneasy about the potential resurgence of militarism in their society and see the continued American military presence as a stabilizing force. Indeed, the long-time support of "unarmed neutrality" by the Japan Socialist Party was predicated, in part, on the desire to constrain such militarism. In the United States, an enormous appetite has grown up for Japanese goods, not just among connoisseurs of video-cassette recorders but among sophisticated American producers who rely on Japanese inputs or Japanese capital. There are also important cultural and organizational linkages between the two societies, ranging from Japanese affection for base-ball, Kentucky Fried Chicken, and American rock stars, to the work of such organizations as the Japan Society, the Asia Society, the Japan Center for International Exchange, and others that promote positive interactions including student and university exchanges, between the two cultures. We must also not forget that we are dealing here with complex relations between two democracies. The Japanese have weathered a number of difficult political and economic storms in the post–World War II period and their democratic system has continued to flourish.

In the short run, a strong inertia and an interaction of mutual interests tend to keep the overall relationship reasonably steady and healthy, not-withstanding the storms of visible political conflict that grab the headlines. For the present, this more than offsets the forces driving the countries apart. But given this balance of centripetal and centrifugal forces, what might the future portend? Three scenarios seem plausible: across-the-board confrontation; competitive techno-nationalism; and competitive interdependence.

ACROSS-THE-BOARD CONFRONTATION
Under this scenario, the image of "Japan As Economic Rival" comes to dominate the relationship. Its underlying premise is that the strength of national economies will be, sooner or later, the determinant of future political power. Japan and the European Community are increasingly recognized as the main U.S. economic, and hence, political competitors. In this future it is also assumed that Japan's alleged uniqueness—its cultural exclusivity in particular—will limit the prospects for cooperation and will reinforce the tendency toward greater inter-state conflict. As conflict grows, so will support

in the United States for the argument that Americans must recognize the "zero-sum" nature of the relationship and mobilize for the competition, rather than wait for further gains by Japan (and perhaps by the European Community as well).

This future would pose serious economic and security problems. On the economic side, the United States would incur, at least in the short term, substantial losses as Americans consciously sought to "contain" economic interaction with Japan and to subsidize U.S.-based competition. This would cause particular difficulties for an open economy without the institutions or mechanisms geared to promote either economic insulation or an industrial policy. Sooner or later, it would appear that across-the-board confrontation would lead to the collapse of the post–World War II international economic order, including the General Agreement on Tariffs and Trade (GATT) and the liberal trade regime, the G-7, and other institutions for cooperative economic leadership.

In security terms this scenario would severely erode the U.S. geo-strategic position in East Asia. In an across-the-board economic confrontation, anti-Japanese sentiment in the United States could easily translate into severe protectionist legislation against Japanese imports that would greatly damage Japan's economy, at least in the short run. This legislation would in turn trigger enormous anti-American sentiment in Japan. It is hard to visualize support in either Washington or Tokyo for the maintenance of U.S. forces in Japan under such circumstances. The U.S. withdrawal from Japan and from the security alliance would then stimulate a new defense debate in Japan. Without American military protection or the explicit U.S. guarantees of Japanese oil deliveries from the Persian Gulf, there is a serious risk that Japan would become a major new military rival capable of equalling or even surpassing the United States in the development and deployment of high-technology weaponry. The renewed sense of threat from Japan would, in turn, stimulate an arms buildup in Korea, the People's Republic of China, Indonesia and elsewhere in East Asia.

A variant of this scenario envisages the United States and Japan sliding into confrontation without an explicit intention on the part of either to intensify the rivalry. As economic conflicts continue, over time they could undermine commitment to the broader relationship. Government leaders in Tokyo and Washington would become increasingly frustrated with trying to patch over differences and bearing the burden of the relationship in domestic politics. After a while, these differences might extend beyond economic and technological competition to fundamental disagreements over policies toward third countries in the Middle East, Europe, or elsewhere. At some point leaders in one of the countries would decide that it was in their nation's strategic interest or in their own personal political interest to visibly resist or confront the other, or perhaps even to renounce the alliance.[25]

Movement in this direction could be fueled by arguments that the U.S. geostrategic position in Asia no longer served any useful purpose. With the removal of the Soviet threat, some claim that American forces in the region are configured to counter an enemy that no longer exists and are incapable of influencing other troubles in East Asia—turmoil in China or the conflict in Cambodia, for example. But this logic is faulty. The United States retains enormous interest in the stability and prosperity of the region, with which its trade now substantially exceeds trade with Europe. And this stability depends on a continuing U.S. political-military presence.

In contrast to Europe, with its web of long-standing and substantial multilateral institutions and relationships (particularly the North Atlantic Treaty Organization and the European Community), multilateralism in Asia is very weak. The Association of Southeast Asian Nations (ASEAN), which includes Indonesia, the Philippines, Singapore, Malaysia, Thailand, and Brunei, has not moved beyond limited economic cooperation. The newly formed Asia-Pacific Economic Cooperation Council (APEC), which includes all the ASEAN members plus the United States, Canada, Japan, South Korea, Australia, and New Zealand, has yet to define its purposes. The Southeast Asia Treaty Organization (SEATO) collapsed after the American defeat in Vietnam, and it never included East Asian nations.

Instead, what has endured in U.S.–East Asian security policy has been bilateral security relationships, carefully developed and nurtured, with Japan, South Korea, and the Philippines, as well as strong bilateral ties with Australia, Thailand, and Taiwan. In Europe, it may be possible for the United States to curtail sharply its military presence and redefine its security role within a redefined set of multilateral institutions, but this option is not now available in Asia. Some trimming of U.S. forces may well prove feasible, but an American withdrawal and a U.S.-Japan confrontation would put the entire

---

25. As C. Fred Bergsten notes, such an evolution could lead to a "European-Japanese nexus" against the United States, or alternatively a U.S.-European alliance against Japan. See Bergsten, "The World Economy After The Cold War," *Foreign Affairs*, Vol. 69, No. 3 (Summer 1990), pp. 102–103.

East Asian security balance "up for grabs." Notwithstanding the receding of the Soviet threat, the U.S. political-military presence is the one broadly-accepted stabilizing force.

This stabilizing role is especially noteworthy on the Korean peninsula, where U.S. forces not only serve as a tripwire to deter a North Korean attack on the South, but discourage the development of adventurism in Seoul toward the north. While much has changed since the outbreak of the Korean War in 1950, the situation remains tense and volatile; the border is one of the most heavily militarized areas in the world. It would be foolhardy and dangerous to remove U.S. forces now.

Finally, there are no guarantees that Chinese or Soviet militarism in the region will not reemerge. The brutal force used by the Chinese leadership to put down the pro-democracy student movement in 1989 demonstrates that not all communist regimes are willing to fade quietly from the scene. The coming succession crisis in Beijing could bring about enormous instability and civil strife; the political situation in the Soviet Union is in extraordinary flux. While U.S. forces would not be directly engaged in shaping developments in either of these great nations, it is difficult to see how reduction or removal of the American presence could lend stability to East Asia.

COMPETITIVE TECHNO-NATIONALISM
Under a second scenario, the two nations might eschew the risks of confrontation and seek to maintain a general geopolitical alliance and relatively open trade, but simultaneously intensify their competition for global technological leadership. Seeing this as the key to power in the twenty-first century, they might strengthen governmental efforts both to protect and to develop technology on a national basis, with official programs supporting private firms and research and development consortia that exclude or limit participation by foreign firms.

Like mercantilism, "techno-nationalism" views development of new products and processes as a competition among nations, whereas traditional liberals see it as a competition among firms.[26] Advocates of this approach for

---

26. The techno-nationalist perspective is explicit or implicit in most of the "competitiveness" literature. Examples include: Prestowitz, *Trading Places;* Stephen S. Cohen and John Zysman, *Manufacturing Matters: The Myth of the Post-Industrial Economy* (New York: Basic Books, 1987); and Bruce R. Scott and George C. Lodge, eds., *U.S. Competitiveness in the World Economy* (New York: Harper and Row, 1985). It is also an unexamined assumption in much of the politics and journalism that addresses U.S.-Japan relations in both countries.

Americans often see it as doing unto the Japanese what they have been doing to us—or, more benignly, doing *for* ourselves what the Japanese have been doing for themselves.

In addition to its plausibility as a strategy, techno-nationalism has two sorts of domestic political appeals. It offers a rationale to mobilize Americans to change their public and private behavior: to attack the federal deficit, to save more and spend less, to invest for the future. And for Democrats, it offers an appealing marriage of nationalism and government activism.

Critics of such an approach, in turn, see it as a blend of protectionism and counterproductive government meddling in matters better left to markets. Advocates counter that some losses in short-term economic efficiency would be well worth taking if, over the longer term, the American economy can be "restored" or "rebuilt" into the unquestioned global leader it once was. Even if this is beyond reach, America (and the world) might still be a gainer if the relative U.S. position could be stabilized, and interdependence limited and managed. The managed trade likely to be part of such an approach might even serve to damp the fires of U.S.-Japan conflict.[27] After all, "good fences make good neighbors."

The techno-nationalist option responds to undeniable Japanese industrial and financial power. But is it feasible, given the internationalization of the global economy and the openness of American society? Is it desirable, given the rising share of economic and technical innovation that takes place outside our borders?

Feasibility problems begin with deciding what is "national" or "American." What economic institutions should a techno-nationalist policy support? Or to put the question in Harvard economist Robert B. Reich's words, "Who is Us?"[28] Certainly a General Motors plant in Michigan would be included, or a U.S.-owned semiconductor enterprise operating in Silicon Valley. But what about IBM/Japan, or the North American Honda Company? American multinational business would opt for including the former and excluding the latter. Labor has understandably taken the opposite view: encouraging some Japanese investment here and criticizing offshore operations by American firms.

---

27. Stephen D. Krasner, *Asymmetries in Japanese-American Trade: The Case for Specific Reciprocity*, Institute for International Studies Policy Paper No. 32 (Berkeley: University of California Press), p. 72.
28. For extended discussion of this question, ending with an argument that U.S. policy should favor enterprises operating in the United States, not those that fly the American flag, see Reich, "Who Is Us?" *Harvard Business Review*, Vol. 68, No. 1 (January–February 1990), pp. 53–64.

But from the techno-nationalist perspective, both vessels—foreign firms operating here, and American firms operating abroad—are leaky.

Even if this problem can somehow be surmounted, consider the fact that industrial process technology has a strong engineering component. How would American techno-nationalism cope with the fact that 50 percent of new U.S.-trained engineering PhDs each year are foreign-born? Given the need for capital, how would the United States "protect" its enterprises from the pull of Japanese technology or the lure of Japanese money? The U.S. Semiconductor Manufacturing Technology consortium (Sematech) may exclude Japanese firms from membership, but it cannot exclude its American members from far-reaching joint ventures with those very same Japanese firms—business interest, and financial need, are just too strong. And we have not even reached the classic problems of deciding *which* technologies government should underwrite, and at what stage in the movement from development of product and process technology to construction of specific plants the public subsidies should stop.

If feasible, is techno-nationalism desirable for the United States? Would it maintain or restore U.S. pre-eminence? By fencing U.S. technologies in, do Americans not simultaneously fence others out, cutting themselves off from the growing volume of innovation that takes place elsewhere, particularly in Japan?[29] Doesn't this risk protecting the second-rate?

Even if pursued with great intensity, a U.S.-Japan technological competition might prove hard to contain. It could well spill over into the security and political sphere, leading in time to confrontation.

COMPETITIVE INTERDEPENDENCE

A third approach would be to work consciously at building "competitive interdependence."[30] The U.S. and Japanese governments would work to mute "us-versus-them" stereotypes, by stressing the benefits that citizens of each nation are bringing to the economic welfare of both. To counter the prevalent mercantilist, zero-sum, U.S.-versus-Japan perspective, national leaders would find it in their interest to build a future on the benefits of

---

29. Clyde Prestowitz suggested at one point that Sematech should accept the offer of Nippon Electric Corporation (NEC) to join it, since NEC possessed and could contribute leading-edge technologies. NEC recently announced plans to build a major factory in Rosedale, California, to manufacture 4-megabit memory chips.
30. The phrase is from C. Fred Bergsten, *America in the World Economy: A Strategy for the 1990s* (Washington, D.C.: Institute for International Economics, 1988); see esp. chap. 8.

interdependence. Because both nations are so rich in economic assets and institutions, they gain much if these institutions become intertwined.[31] This is obviously the preferable future. It is also the choice, we believe, of most of those who weigh the alternatives carefully. In such a scenario, the maintenance of strong ties between the United States and Japan is seen as part of a broader pattern of promoting economic interdependence and of protecting the national security interests of major states. The lesson that endures is that economic growth and great-power peace have been achieved over the past forty years through security cooperation and a growing global economy, not through narrow nationalism. It is these conditions that need to be sustained for the maintenance of American welfare and power.

National governments still have a stake in increasing the returns, absolute and relative, from factors of production based within their territory; because this increases their citizens' welfare, and because it contributes to overall national power and influence. But this interest—the "competitive" concern—would be pursued in ways aimed at muting economic conflict between nations and maximizing the gains from cooperation.

Making "Competitive Interdependence" a Reality

The front page of the April 6, 1990, *Washington Post* may be a harbinger for the future: the announcement of the dates of Gorbachev's forthcoming Washington visit was upstaged by a report of the interim results of the SII talks between Japan and the United States. In the 1990s, America's place in the world may depend more on working out continuing, constructive relationships with economic allies-cum-competitors, than on our dealings with a declining strategic adversary. Some brief guidelines follow.

---

31. What follows discusses interdependence in bilateral, U.S.-Japan terms. This should not be taken as an argument for excluding consideration of other nations. In fact, a multilateral interdependence approach may be not just more rational economically, but easier to sell politically in both Washington and Tokyo. But since the two nations treated here are the largest—and in different ways the most chauvinistic—of the world's economic powers, it is particularly important to focus on ways that *they* might be "internationalized." Advocates of an interdependence strategy must bear in mind, however, the question posed by James Fallows: whether "any of Japan's . . . great power centers will ever share their power with non-Japanese." He would be, he declares, "delighted by the creation of a hybrid U.S.-Japanese state," but he considers this "impossible, because of social resistance on the Japanese side"; Fallows, "Containing Japan," pp. 53–54.

MAINTAIN THE U.S.-JAPAN SECURITY TREATY

It is hard to see any reason not to continue the mutually beneficial arrangement of the U.S.-Japan security treaty. It is easy to see large costs in breaking it off. The geostrategic changes that swept across Europe in 1989 are also being felt in Asia—Gorbachev met with South Korean President Roh Tae Woo in San Francisco in June 1990, Sino-Soviet relations have improved, and polarization in the Philippines is growing over the American military presence at Subic Bay and Clark Field—but the withdrawal of American military forces from Japan would not serve U.S. interests. Not only does the American military presence reassure our allies in that region against a possible resurgence of the Soviet military threat, it also serves to dissuade the Japanese from acquiring power-projection forces of their own. U.S. forces in Japan have a political and psychological "pin-down" effect, constraining the relatively small but potentially influential circles in Tokyo—some senior officials in the Ground Self Defense Forces, militant nationalists within the Liberal Democratic Party such as Shintaro Ishihara, some key members of the business community, a few journalists and intellectuals—who resent the American-authored Japanese constitution, believe that the days of the United States as a superpower are numbered, and argue that Japan needs to begin to acquire military and political power commensurate with its economic might.

The residual animosity toward Japan throughout Asia remains substantial,[32] and the termination of the U.S.-Japan security treaty would multiply security anxiety throughout the region. It would almost certainly trigger a fundamental reappraisal of Seoul's security position and would strengthen the arguments of those in Korea who would defend the need to acquire ballistic missiles or nuclear weapons.[33] Thus, even if Japan initially had no

---

32. This animosity is evident in periodic anti-Japanese outbursts in Korea and China over Japan's unwillingness to admit its guilty and cruel behavior in World War II, the tensions in Sino-Japanese relations that arose in the mid-1980s when Japanese textbooks were published that failed to acknowledge Japan's invasion of China in 1931, and repeated warnings about the threat of resurgent Japanese militarism conveyed to visiting Americans, including the authors of this paper, who have discussed the matter with officials in and from Seoul, Jakarta, Taipei, Singapore, and other Asian countries.

33. South Korea began to take steps toward the acquisition of a nuclear weapons capability in the mid-1970s when its leaders believed that the American defeat in Vietnam presaged a general U.S. withdrawal from Asia. It took serious diplomatic arm-twisting by U.S. officials in Seoul and the threatened termination of the U.S. security treaty with South Korea to dissuade the Koreans from pursuing their program. See Robert Gillette, "U.S. Squelched Apparent S. Korea A-Bomb Drive," *Los Angeles Times*, November 4, 1978; and Leonard Spector, *The Undeclared Bomb* (Cambridge, Mass.: Ballinger, 1988), pp. 70–72, 341–342.

plans to enhance its armed forces, the removal of the American military presence from the Japanese home islands would risk provoking a regional arms race that would be in no one's interest.

It is desirable to broaden the Japanese defense contribution through operational and technology cooperation, and through increases in Japanese financial support of U.S. defense activities based in Japan. But the United States should not pressure Japan to increase its defense spending further as a share of GNP.

There remains the genuine dilemma of U.S. defense dependence on Japanese technology. Dependence on foreign sources for critical components is obviously a problem—it would be better for American interests, certainly, if everything our military needed were "made in USA." But the globalization of defense-related industries is a fact of life, as is the position of Japanese firms in the forefront of technological and product development. The way to cope with this is not by narrow "buy-American" policies, but by encouraging multiple sources of supply, by strengthening U.S.-based technology development, and by pursuing the strategy of competitive interdependence.[34]

SHORE UP THE AMERICAN ECONOMY

Since the distribution of nationally-based productive power does matter, for the welfare of citizens as well as the place of the nation in the world, the United States needs to strengthen its capacity to hold its own in future economic growth, and to eliminate areas of obvious and unnecessary weakness. Above all, the United States should end its $100 billion per year financial dependence on Japan (and the rest of the world), by steps which increase domestic savings and reduce consumption by $150–200 billion per year (3–4 percent of current U.S. gross national product). The best way to do this is to end public "dis-saving" by moving the total federal budget (Social Security included) from deficit to surplus. This requires, however, a painful exercise in domestic political burden-sharing, with Republicans sharing responsibility for new taxes and Democrats consenting to restraints on Social Security and other programs that serve their constituencies. Any budget agreement concluded in 1990 will be, at most, a first step along a rocky road.

Such a restoration of macroeconomic sanity should be reinforced by selected microeconomic steps. Since private firms pursuing their own interests

---

34. See Theodore H. Moran, "The Globalization of America's Defense Industries: Managing the Threat of Foreign Dependence," *International Security*, Vol. 15, No. 1 (Summer 1990), pp. 57–99.

tend to underinvest in research and development, the United States should strengthen governmental support of technology development, particularly on production processes, in broad areas of present (and likely future) economic importance to U.S. and other advanced industrial economies.[35]

Also necessary are stronger public programs in such critical areas as education and infrastructure development. Concerning investment, Americans might shelve the current sterile debate about the capital gains tax and try to find out what really does move business and individuals to save and invest. This could lead to realistic incentive packages encouraging long-term business investment in productive assets, and longer-term planning and profit horizons.

CONTINUE PRESSURE FOR OPENING UP JAPAN
Americans should continue their efforts to open up and internationalize Japan's enormously productive but still relatively closed economy. This goal should be pursued, however, through processes and substantive agreements that become progressively more two-sided, involving reciprocal pressure, as appropriate to a relationship of equals (or near-equals). In this sense, the SII talks are correct in form, though insufficiently balanced in practice.

WORK EXPLICITLY TO DEEPEN INTERDEPENDENCE
Rather than mobilizing as if for economic warfare, and rather than crying with alarm at each new Japanese international economic venture, Americans should seek ways to reinforce and reward Japanese internationalists. Continuing pressure for investment access in Japan, for example, should be joined by encouragement of Japanese and other foreign direct investment here, particularly that which underwrites high-value-added economic activity within our borders. Joint ventures should be, in most instances, welcomed. They are particularly welcome in manufacturing, since the operations of Japanese firms in the United States can be a particularly effective means for the transfer of technology from Japan to the United States.[36]

Government support of research and development programs should extend to all firms, U.S.- and foreign-owned, that are carrying out important

---

35. Martin Neil Baily and Alok K. Chakrabarti, *Innovation and the Productivity Crisis* (Washington, D.C.: Brookings, 1988), ch. 6.
36. Robert Z. Lawrence finds that Japanese auto investment has had this effect in the 1980s. See Lawrence, "Foreign-Affiliated Automakers in the United States: An Appraisal" (Washington, D.C.: Automobile Importers of America, Inc., March 1990).

research and development and technology-intensive production on U.S. soil, although it might be appropriate to insist that the government-supported activity be carried on within our borders. Learning from the technological progress of Japan-based firms requires a strengthened U.S. capacity for on-going dialogue with them and the people who make them work.

SPEAK OUT FOR COMPETITIVE INTERDEPENDENCE

Finally, leaders in both nations should offer a rhetorical alternative to economic nationalism, by giving voice to the goal of competitive interdependence and developing programs in its name. To hold their own, Americans need to correct their economic policies and shore up their institutions. But to get the maximum gains from the dynamic global economy, with minimum risks of future interstate conflict, Americans should want the Japanese involved in the U.S. economy, just as Americans should be involved in Japan, and both in Europe. There should be top quality economic activity going on in all of them.

Such an approach serves to vindicate the main lesson of the last forty years: that welfare gains come not from competition in armaments, but from progress in production and in global economic integration. Leaders in Washington—and Tokyo—should keep reminding us of these lessons and adopt policies that put them into practice.

The Middle East and the New World Order

Richard K. Herrmann

Rethinking U.S. Political Strategy After the Gulf War

On March 6, 1991, President Bush declared victory; the Allied coalition had defeated Iraq in the Gulf War.[1] He spoke of a "New World Order" in which the principles of justice and fair play would protect the weak from the strong and in which the United Nations, freed from the Cold War, could fulfill its historic vision. The United States would pursue a four-part strategy to secure a political victory from the military success. It would build shared security arrangements in the Gulf, reinforce its effort to control the proliferation of weapons of mass destruction, foster economic development, and seize the new opportunities to find peace and security in an Arab-Israeli peace process.

This postwar strategy quickly ran into the complexities of Near Eastern politics. The security arrangements, based on the Gulf Cooperation Council (GCC) plus Egypt and Syria, drew uncertain support from the GCC as Saudi Arabia, evidently worried about its own domestic legitimacy, asked Egyptian and Syrian forces to withdraw. The United States was drawn into the Iraqi civil war in defense of the Kurds, which complicated the situation in eastern Turkey, while Saddam Hussein reconsolidated control and new U.S. intelligence estimates concluded that the damage to Iraq's air and missile capabilities were not as extensive as immediate postwar estimates had hoped. Iran, meantime, seeing the United States as the strong state that weak countries needed protection from, moved quickly to organize an alternative security coalition with the Islamic states of Iran, Pakistan, and Turkey. China announced new plans to sell ballistic missiles to Syria and Pakistan. Nobody with resources to spend seemed interested in regional economic development schemes, and Secretary of State James Baker quickly ran into the same Arab-Israeli stalemate over the Arabs in East Jerusalem and who would represent the Palestinians that had confounded his peace efforts in 1989 and 1990. Both the Arabs and the Israelis expected the United States to use its postwar leverage to push the peace process forward but each, in return for their

Richard K. Herrmann is an Associate Professor of political science and Director of the Program in Foreign Policy Analysis at the Mershon Center for National Security Research at the Ohio State University.

1. "President Bush's Address on End of the Gulf War," New York Times, March 7, 1991, p. 8.

International Security, Fall 1991 (Vol. 16, No. 2)

support during the war, expected the United States to compel the other to bend on fundamental issues like land-for-peace.

The purpose of this article is to take a new look at the post–Cold War and post–Gulf War Middle East and to argue for a U.S. strategy that might mitigate the hostile political trends while protecting intrinsic U.S. interests. I begin with an assessment of U.S. interests and the threats to them in the 1990s. Intrinsic interests in oil and Israel have not changed, but other concerns that derived from the Cold War need to be reevaluated. So does a political strategy that relies mostly on deterrence. "Desert Storm" reduced the likelihood of a near-term military threat, but it did not defuse the anti-American political trends that Saddam Hussein played on with some success and which still threaten the stability of American allies.

The second part of the argument turns to how U.S. policies in defense of U.S. interests failed to prevent the Gulf War. My contention is that the war cannot be properly understood as simply a failure in U.S. deterrence policy. It reflected the failure of a political strategy that relied too heavily on deterrence. Washington was preoccupied with deterring Iran and lost sight of the intra-Arab politics that were polarizing the region. It put too little emphasis on developing a sophisticated political strategy toward regional security and ultimately was forced to rely on overwhelming military superiority.

The third section of the article turns to the military and political trends in the Middle East that will define the regional context for U.S. policy in the 1990s. I emphasize the political trends because in many ways they are more disturbing than the military situation. Unless a major shift toward hostility takes place in the Soviet Union, no potential regional hegemon can compete with the potential projected military power of the United States. Regional actors can militarily threaten American interests, but only at the risk of suffering devastating consequences. Threats are more likely to come from inside Arab and Islamic societies and be targeted at the local elites that sustain the U.S. relationship and vulnerable Americans. The strategic dilemma for the United States is more political than it is military. It can protect its influence by force and coercion, as Moscow did for years in Eastern Europe, but how can it build positive relationships with Middle Eastern countries that will survive internal change and growing demands for public empowerment? If the United States is seen as an imperial enemy by large sections of the Arab nationalist and Islamic populist communities, it will face continuing challenges and be compelled to rely on superior force indefinitely.

Finally, I offer prescriptions based on skepticism about Washington's ability to engineer political change in the Near East and on unwillingness to place exclusive reliance on military force and to risk periodic wars. The hostility toward the United States that is evident in Arab and Islamic populist movements may be immutable. (There is an important academic debate about this point and I avoid strong assumptions either way.) But Washington should not put U.S. interests at risk based on hopeful expectations about democracy in the Middle East, nor should it create a self-fulfilling prophecy by showing only hostility toward populist movements and political change.

There is room to move beyond deterrence and to broaden American diplomacy to include a new place for multinational institutions, arms control, and democratic empowerment. The process of change will be frightening, as has been the traditional pattern of war and revolutions, but it may better serve U.S. interests in the 1990s than a return to the failed strategies of the past.

U.S. Interests: Intrinsic and Instrumental

The perceived Soviet threat to Washington's two main interests that are intrinsic to the region—oil and Israel's security—traditionally motivated Americans to contain communism, protect access to oil, and discourage political change.[2] The operational pursuit of these objectives led to a search for allies that over the years involved large-scale military and financial assistance, the direct projection of U.S. force, and covert political intervention. The Arab-Israeli conflict complicated matters. It drove some Arab nationalists to the Soviet Union for support, and for others made association with Washington more difficult and embarrassing. Although leaders in Washington occasionally hoped for a "strategic consensus" that would join Arabs, Israelis, Turks, and Persians in common cause against the Soviet Union, it never materialized. Instead, Washington worked to develop a unilateral force to project its military power to the Gulf regardless of political complications.[3]

The end of the Cold War did not change the U.S. interests that are intrinsic to the Middle East, but it radically changed the threat to them. The Gulf, for instance, still holds 65 percent of the world's proven oil reserves. It currently

---

2. See Seth Tillman, *The United States in the Middle East: Interests and Obstacles* (Bloomington: Indiana University Press, 1982); Alan Dowty, *Middle East Crisis: U.S. Decision-making in 1958, 1970, 1973* (Berkeley: University of California Press, 1984); James Bill, *The Eagle and the Lion: The Tragedy of American-Iranian Relations* (New Haven: Yale University Press, 1988); and Richard Cottam, *Iran and the United States: A Cold War Case Study* (Pittsburgh: University of Pittsburgh Press, 1988).
3. See Charles Kupchan, *The Persian Gulf and the West: The Dilemmas of Security* (Boston: Allen and Unwin, 1987), pp. 68–125; and Thomas McNaugher, *Arms and Oil: U.S. Military Strategy and the Persian Gulf* (Washington, D.C.: Brookings, 1985).

accounts for 25 percent of the world's oil production and as world demand increases this will climb to over 50 percent by the end of the decade. However, danger of Soviet hegemony over the Gulf came not because it could increase the price of oil, but because it could turn the flow of oil off and hold the Western economies hostage to Soviet intimidation in Europe. The same danger could not arise from any potential regional hegemon. They are heavily dependent on oil revenues for development projects and the purchase of most of their military equipment.[4] They can threaten to increase the price of oil, but the fungibility of oil and the vulnerability of regional economies to financial and trade counter-measures from the advanced industrial economies limit the range of blackmail scenarios. While these scenarios represent real threats to conservative Arab governments and to Israel, the threat to the United States is much less direct. The United States, like other strong industrial powers, does not need control of regional events or even dependent clients to secure its basic energy requirements.

The United States government has accepted the existence of Israel as a basic foreign policy interest. There are moral, emotional and political reasons for this commitment.[5] Most of them are unlikely to change in the near future. Agreement on the importance of Israel's security does not preclude heated arguments over what is necessary to achieve this security. Israel's occupation and settlement of the territories acquired in the 1967 War have become the most visible point of dispute. For some Americans any threat to Israel's occupation and permanent control of the territories is synonymous with threats to Israel's existence.[6] Many others disagree and see the occupation and creeping annexation as contributing to Israel's insecurity.[7] President Bush in his March 6 address reaffirmed his interest in Israel's basic security, but also affirmed his belief that U.S. interests rest in a compromise that trades territory for peace.

In August 1990, President Bush argued that the U.S. involvement in the Gulf War was motivated by a third basic interest, that is, a commitment to

---

4. See Alan Richards and John Waterbury, *A Political Economy of the Middle East: State, Class, and Economic Development* (Boulder, Colo.: Westview, 1990), pp. 52–80.
5. See Steven Spiegel, *The Other Arab-Israeli Conflict: Making America's Middle East Policy, from Truman to Reagan* (Chicago: University of Chicago Press, 1985); Peter Grose, *Israel in the Mind of America* (New York: Knopf, 1983); and Wolf Blitzer, *Between Washington and Jerusalem* (Oxford: Oxford University Press, 1985).
6. For the debate see Hyman Bookbinder and James Abourezk, *Through Different Eyes* (Bethesda, Md.: Adler and Adler, 1987).
7. See, for instance, Robert Art, "A Defensible Defense: America's Grand Strategy After the Cold War," *International Security*, Vol. 15, No. 4 (Spring 1991), pp. 48–49.

principle.[8] The American interest in principle may not have been an intrinsic concern that has been consistently pursued in the past, but in this case, the interest in principle was parallel to Washington's self-interest. Iraq's use of force threatened Washington's friends in Kuwait and Riyadh. Principles such as the non-use of threats and force, the sanctity of the United Nations as the arbiter of legitimate claims to territory and international disputes, and the inviolability of the postwar state system all were threatened by Iraq's action, and if respected in this case would strengthen Washington's friends.

The analogies with Munich, along with fears that Saddam Hussein would be armed with nuclear weapons by the mid-1990s, certainly convinced many Americans that resolute action was necessary. They did not, however, convince many Arabs or Moslems that Washington was motivated by a commitment to principle. Many recalled that Iraq's aggression in 1980 and the Iran-Iraq War evoked not principle, but instead balance of power politics.[9] Washington had not worked as hard to implement UN resolutions that dealt with the Arab-Israeli issue (e.g., UN 242 and UN 338) or the Iran-Iraq cease-fire (UN 598) as it was working to implement the twelve UN resolutions pertaining to Kuwait.[10] Moreover, many regional elites saw Washington's resort to war after only five months of sanctions as premature. When it was coupled with the massive and unrelenting nature of the aerial bombardment, they concluded that Washington was pursuing a "preventive war" designed to destroy the capability base of a strong Arab state, not just to liberate

---

8. See President Bush, "The Arabian Peninsula: U.S. Principles," Address to the Nation, August 8, 1990, Current Policy No. 1292 (Washington, D.C.: U.S. Department of State, 1990).

9. Many Iranians assumed the United States supported Iraq's attack or even ordered it. The war weakened Iran and Iraq and isolated Syria in its confrontation with Israel. For a balance of power view, see Alvin Rubinstein, "Perspectives on the Iran-Iraq War," *Orbis*, Vol. 29, No. 3 (Fall 1985), pp. 597–608. On the intra-Arab politics of the war, see Alan Taylor, *The Arab Balance of Power* (Syracuse, N.Y.: Syracuse University Press, 1982), pp. 73–96; Richard Cottam, "Levels of Conflict in the Middle East," in Joseph Coffey and Gianni Bonvicini, *The Atlantic Alliance and the Middle East* (Pittsburgh: University of Pittsburgh Press, 1989), pp. 17–72, 30–41; and Patrick Seale, *Asad of Syria: The Struggle for the Middle East* (Berkeley: University of California Press, 1989), pp. 312–314, 354–365.

10. UN Resolutions 242 and 338 call for Israeli withdrawal from territories occupied in 1967, respect for and acknowledgement of the sovereignty and territorial integrity of every state in the region, and a just settlement of the refugee problem. For their texts, see " 'Just and Durable' Peace: Resolutions 242 and 338," *New York Times*, July 19, 1991, p. A8; or William Quandt, *The Middle East: Ten Years After Camp David* (Washington, D.C.: Brookings, 1988), pp. 445–446. On UN 598 see Gary Sick, "Slouching toward Settlement: The Internationalization of the Iran-Iraq War, 1987–1988," in Nikki Keddie and Mark Gasiorowski, eds., *Neither East Nor West: Iran, the Soviet Union, and the United States* (New Haven, Conn.: Yale University Press, 1990), pp. 219–245.

Kuwait. Total casualties rather than civilian casualties captured their attention, while the West's failure to support the postwar Kurdish, Shi'a, and anti-Saddam anti-Ba'ath Iraqi uprisings reinforced regional assumptions that Washington had narrow economic motives and did not welcome mass-based political change.

However unfair populist regional perceptions may seem to U.S. policymakers, they represent a psychological and political situation that Washington has an interest in changing. The United States may be able to defend its intrinsic interests with military force alone, but only a more positive public image in the region will lay the foundation for a secure future. The military success of the Gulf War salvaged a failed political strategy. It defended the oil-exporting monarchies and Israel, but reinforced the imperial-enemy images of the United States that are held by Arab nationalists and Islamic fundamentalists. It enhanced Washington's credibility as a deterrent power, but did not solve its persisting security dilemmas. Before we turn to future strategic options it is important to look carefully at why the past U.S. policies failed to avoid war.

The Road to the Gulf War

U.S. POLICY IN THE GULF

In the later half of the 1980s, Iran became the primary determinant of American security policy in the Persian Gulf. The perception of Soviet threat receded as Iran became the focal point of American deterrence efforts.[11] Cold War instincts were still relevant, as the timing of the reflagging of Kuwait tankers in 1987 illustrates, but were not decisive.[12] Washington was prepared to tilt to Iraq regardless of Baghdad's association with Moscow; even analysts who typically took a hard-line position toward the Soviet Union and a very pro-Israeli stance advocated the tilt toward Iraq.[13]

---

11. See, for instance, Les Aspin, Chairman, House Armed Services Committee, "Persian Gulf Policy Should be Containment of Iran," Committee News Release, Tuesday, October 13, 1987.
12. The Reagan administration was initially reluctant to reflag the tankers. After Kuwait turned to Moscow for help, the administration engaged actively to keep the Soviet role to a minimum. See International Institute for Strategic Studies (IISS), *Strategic Survey, 1987–1988* (London: IISS, 1988), pp. 75, 127–32; and Caspar Weinberger, *Fighting for Peace: Seven Critical Years in the Pentagon* (New York: Warner Books, 1990), pp. 389–391.
13. See Daniel Pipes, "Why the U.S. Should Bolster Iraq," *New York Times*, May 31, 1987, p. 29; Daniel Pipes and Laurie Mylroie, "Back Iraq," *The New Republic*, April 27, 1987, pp. 14–15, and Laurie Mylroie, "After the Guns Fell Silent: Iraq in the Middle East," *Middle East Journal*, Vol. 43, No. 1 (Winter 1989), pp. 51–67.

The U.S. determination to contain Iran made Iraq important. Saddam Hussein was transformed into a "moderate" (i.e., someone willing to accommodate U.S. policy), defending the Eastern flank of the Arab world.[14] Iraq's abysmal human rights record, its use of chemical weapons, and its aggressiveness in the tanker war in the Gulf were not overlooked but were viewed as defensive.[15] As had happened so often in the Cold War, the political image of a Third World ally was retailored to match perceived U.S. geo-political interests.[16]

On two key issues, the Soviet Union and Israel, Saddam Hussein was "moderate." Despite the Iraqi-Soviet Friendship Treaty, Saddam was hardly a reliable Soviet ally. He executed the leaders of the Iraqi Communist Party in 1978, and condemned Moscow's behavior in Ethiopia and South Yemen.[17] In 1980, he also condemned Moscow's invasion of Afghanistan. Iraq's oil revenues allowed Saddam to diversify military suppliers, and in 1980 he needed them to prosecute the war with Iran.[18] The Soviet Union, for its part, condemned Iraq's invasion of Iran, offered arms to Tehran, and stopped shipment of military supplies to Baghdad.[19] As the tide of battle shifted in Iran's favor, Moscow was prepared to assist in forestalling Saddam's defeat, but only for cash on the barrel-head. By 1989, Moscow was actively pursuing a rapprochement with Iran, while Saddam was bankrolled by the conservative Arabs in Kuwait and Saudi Arabia. Iraq had aligned with Egypt and Jordan, Washington's most important Arab allies in the Arab Cooperation Council, signed a Non-Aggression Pact with the Saudis, and become a major

---

14. See Christine Moss Helms, *Iraq: Eastern Flank of the Arab World* (Washington, D.C.: Brookings, 1984).

15. See Frederick Axelgard, *A New Iraq? The Gulf War and Implications for U.S. Policy* (Boulder, Colo.: Westview, 1988); and Axelgard, *Iraq in Transition: A Political, Economic, and Strategic Perspective* (Boulder, Colo.: Westview, 1986). Officially the State Department continued to condemn Iraq's human rights record as abysmal. See U.S. Department of State, *Country Reports on Human Rights Practices for 1989* (Washington, D.C.: U.S. Government Printing Office [U.S. GPO], 1990), pp. 1411–1422; and U.S. Department of State, *Country Reports on Human Rights Practices for 1990* (Washington, D.C.: U.S. GPO, 1991), pp. 1457–1467.

16. For arguments advocating the coincidence of U.S.-Iraqi interests, see Laurie Mylroie, "The Baghdad Alternative," *Orbis*, Vol. 32, No. 3 (Summer 1988), pp. 339–354; and Adeed Dawisha, "Iraq: The West's Opportunity," *Foreign Policy*, No. 41 (Winter 1980/81), pp. 134–153.

17. See Richard Herrmann, *Perceptions and Behavior in Soviet Foreign Policy* (Pittsburgh: University of Pittsburgh Press, 1985), pp. 98–101, 142–54.

18. See Robert Freedman, "Soviet Policy Toward Ba'athist Iraq, 1968–1979," in Robert Donaldson, ed., *The Soviet Union in the Third World: Successes and Failures* (Boulder, Colo.: Westview, 1981), pp. 161–191.

19. See Richard Herrmann, "The Role of Iran in Soviet Perceptions and Policy," in Gasiorowski and Keddie, *Neither East Nor West*, pp. 63–99.

importer of American rice.[20] By no mere coincidence, in early 1990 the United States was importing oil from Iraq at the rate of 675,000 barrels a day. At this rate, even with Commodity Credit Corporation and Eximbank programs, the United States in 1990 would have run a $2.5 billion trade deficit with Iraq, if the war had not frozen trade and Iraqi assets.[21]

In 1989, Iraqi propaganda supported Yasir Arafat's decisions to renounce terrorism and implicitly to accept Israel's right to exist by his endorsement of a two-state solution.[22] Arafat was under serious attack from other Palestine Liberation Organization (PLO) and Palestinian hard-liners for these concessions. They saw his faith in American mediation as utterly naive and traitorous in the midst of the *intifada* (the Palestinian uprising in Gaza and the West Bank that began in December 1987). So did Syria's Hafiz Asad, whose personal animosity for Arafat was matched only by his hatred for Saddam.[23] Iraq was prepared to support whatever the PLO-Fatah would agree to—in 1989 this meant acquiescing to Baker's peace plan and Israeli-Palestinian talks in Cairo.

In hindsight it is clear that Saddam's alliance with conservative Arabs and his "moderation" were imposed by the war with Iran. At the time, however, American officials and many specialists were determined to contain Iran and to take advantage of Iraq's commercial potential. They were ready to explore cooperative relations with Iraq and to concentrate U.S. regional diplomacy on the Arab-Israeli issue. The Bush administration put high priority on reviving the Camp David process.[24] It tried to use the legitimacy of the notion of elections in the West Bank and Gaza to engineer face-to-face Israeli-Palestinian talks. The focus was on process in the hopes that, over time, a situation and relationship would emerge in which the substance of the conflict could be addressed.

The Baker Plan built on the Camp David idea that Washington would reassure Israel by enhancing Israeli leverage and hope that Israel would

---

20. See Alan Cowell, "Arabs are Forming 2 Economic Blocs," *New York Times*, February 17, 1989, p. 3.

21. The United States provided Iraq with credit guarantees to buy U.S. agricultural products. See John Kelly, Assistant Secretary of State for Near Eastern and South Asian Affairs, "U.S. Relations With Iraq," Current Policy No. 1273 (Washington, D.C.: State Department, April 26, 1990).

22. See Arafat's Speech to the UN in Geneva, *New York Times*, December 14, 1988, p. 1.

23. See Seale, *Asad*, pp. 125, 156–157, 280–288, 354–365, 386, 411, 422. Also see Richard Cottam, "Levels of Conflict in the Middle East," pp. 36–40.

24. See Secretary Baker's Speech to AIPAC (the American Israel Public Affairs Committee), *New York Times*, May 23, 1989, pp. 1, 10, and *Washington Post*, May 23, 1989, p. 1.

compromise from a position of strength.[25] It ran the risk of letting the Likud government avoid serious tradeoffs and thereby associating the United States in Arab eyes with a disingenuous process of stalling. Egyptian President Hosni Mubarak's strategy, like that of his predecessor Anwar Sadat, included attempts to reassure Israel, but relied more on the United States. It began from an assumption that Washington's leverage was critical and that the United States would guard against any Israeli inclination to pocket Arab concessions and up the ante. Mubarak gave up tactical leverage through various compromises in the hopes of engaging Washington's strategic strength. When the Baker Plan for elections faltered, the secretary of state expressed his frustration and reluctance to push the process any further. His failure to exercise meaningful leverage with Israel to obtain its positive agreement to the U.S. plan seriously weakened Mubarak.[26] The polarization in the Arab world intensified and Saddam Hussein roared into prominence with a radically different strategic vision.[27]

SADDAM HUSSEIN AND WASHINGTON'S DETERRENCE FAILURE

Saddam presented a vision of an Arab great power emerging from the demise of Soviet and American bipolar hegemony.[28] The Arab world would be independent and self-reliant; it would not apply for Western favor as a supplicant but would demand fair and just treatment from a position of strength. It was a thrilling message for millions of Arabs. They saw Saddam as their Bismarck. Saddam could eclipse Asad, as Syria continued to advertise its client status *vis-à-vis* a declining Soviet Union, and could compel Egypt and Saudi Arabia to follow him.[29] Iraq's strength and the failure of the Baker Plan

25. On Camp David see William Quandt, *Camp David: Peacemaking and Politics* (Washington, D.C.: Brookings, 1986), pp. 30–62; Jimmy Carter, *The Blood of Abraham* (Boston: Houghton Mifflin, 1985). On reassurance strategy see Harold Saunders, *The Other Walls: The Politics of the Arab-Israeli Peace Process* (Washington, D.C.: American Enterprise Institute, 1985); and Herbert Kelman, "The Political Psychology of the Israeli-Palestinian Conflict: How Can We Overcome the Barriers to a Negotiated Solution?" *Political Psychology*, Vol. 8, No. 3 (September 1987), pp. 347–364.
26. See John Goshko, "Baker Says Israel Must Compromise: Secretary Warns of Halt in Effort to Revive Middle East Peace Process," *Washington Post*, June 14, 1990, p. 1.
27. On Arab polarization compare Saddam Hussein, "Speech to Baghdad Summit," with Hosni Mubarak, "Speech to Baghdad Summit," and King Husayn, "Speech to Baghdad Summit," all on May 28, 1990, *Foreign Broadcast Information Service Daily Report, Near East and South Asia* (FBIS-NES), May 29, 1990, pp. 2–11; and *FBIS-NES*, May 30, 1990, pp. 5–9.
28. See Saddam Hussein, "Speech to ACC Summit," February 24, 1990, *FBIS-NES*, February 27, 1990, pp. 1–5; Saddam Hussein, "Speech to Arab Summit in Baghdad," May 28, 1990, *FBIS-NES*, May 29, 1990, pp. 2–7.
29. Asad continued to define the Soviet alliance as critical, while Saddam stressed his theme of regional independence. See Hafiz al-Asad, "Speech to People's Assembly Dinner," February 27,

increased Saddam's leverage over the conservative Arabs.[30] Externally he could intimidate them with vastly greater military force; internally he could constrain their efforts to seek American protection by stoking anti-Israeli, anti-American, and Arab nationalist symbols.

American policy-makers adjusted to Saddam's new course slowly. They generated plausible defensive interpretations for Saddam's moves: he feared another Israeli strike as in 1981, so his threats against Israel were deterrents; the Romanian experience of revolution and the VOA's broadcast of pro-democratic messages to Iraq unnerved him with regard to domestic stability and American intentions; and his economic problems at home led him to seek foreign policy grandeur.[31] Moreover, during the 1980s the State Department, the Pentagon, and the CIA had institutionalized the goal of containing Iran. Programs that bolstered Iraq were part of this; so was the bureaucratic resistance to deflating these programs or doing other things to weaken Iraq that would thus by default "help" Iran. Finally, beyond the bureaucratic inertia that went forward without redirection from above, the existing views were reinforced by the advice of respected Arab leaders such as Hosni Mubarak, Saudi King Fahd, and Jordan's King Husayn.

The United States failed to deter Saddam Hussein's attack on Kuwait, and while it could have done more to deter, to reduce the episode to questions of signalling is superficial and misleading.[32] A steady stream of U.S. officials visiting Baghdad in 1990 spelled out American concerns about Iraq's aggressive and hostile behavior.[33] The U.S. government, not being a party to the

1990, *FBIS-NES*, February 29, 1990, pp. 4546; and "Interview with Hafiz al-Asad," May 7, 1990, *FBIS-NES*, May 8, 1990, pp. 27–32.
30. See Stephen Pelletiere, Douglas Johnson II, and Leif Rosenberger, *Iraqi Power and U.S. Security in the Middle East* (Carlisle Barracks, Pa.: U.S. Army War College, 1990).
31. For an official statement of these views, see John Kelly, Assistant Secretary of State for Near Eastern and South Asian Affairs, "U.S. Relations With Iraq," Current Policy No. 1273 (Washington, D.C.: U.S. State Department, April 26, 1990).
32. The administration could have pushed for trade restrictions and sanctions. The Reagan administration had pursued "Operation Staunch" against Iran, even though other international actors might not follow suit. Similar action could have been taken against Iraq. Iraq was also operating outside the Paris Club norms by rescheduling debt on a bilateral basis. This too could have been restricted. UN Resolution 598, passed in July 1987 as the formula for settling the Iran-Iraq War, called for the withdrawal from territory and the return of prisoners of war (POWs). The United States stressed the return of POWs and soft-pedaled the Iraqi occupation of Iranian territory. A tougher position on Iraqi withdrawal might have deflated some of Saddam's image of victory over Iran. Washington might have also engaged the Soviet Union in direct talks about the Gulf. Talks on other regional conflicts were underway. A joint Soviet-American push to implement UN 598 might have constricted some of Saddam's options.
33. For the chronicle of trips and signals, see Don Oberdorfer, "Missed Signals in the Middle East," *Washington Post Magazine*, March 17, 1991, pp. 19–41.

territorial and economic disputes between Iraq and Kuwait, did not take a position on the exact terms of settlement. Its envoys did not, however, signal that the United States was indifferent about whether the arbitration would be peaceful. While it did not invent treaty obligations to defend Kuwait that did not exist, the administration did order the U.S. Air Force to conduct well-publicized military exercises in July 1990 out of the United Arab Emirates.[34] Even this small military signal, however, was not reinforced by Washington's Gulf allies but defused by them, which highlighted the very real obstacles to sending a credible military threat.[35]

Saddam's decision not to seize Saudi territory and his later decision to release Western hostages indicate that he may have felt that Kuwait could be absorbed without war.[36] He may have believed that American interests were not sufficiently threatened to evoke a massive military response and that Washington lacked the will to fight. It is just as likely, however, that Saddam Hussein doubted American capabilities more than he misread Washington's commitments and intentions. He began in early 1990 to spell out his collision course with the United States.[37] Describing the United States as the enemy of the Arab Nation, Saddam never failed to predict its hostility. He seemed to understand that his agenda would evoke American opposition and even military confrontation. It is not clear that sharper American warnings would have been effective.

Predictions that Saddam could be compelled to leave Kuwait with the development of a credible offensive option proved to be wrong. So were expectations that he would retreat after a few days of fighting or before a ground war. Given the magnitude of what we now know he was prepared to suffer, the necessary deterrent action may have been well beyond what the United States could have engineered in the pre-August environment. Of course, after August 2 the stakes had increased for Saddam. The United

---

34. Michael Gordon, "U.S. Deploys Air and Sea Forces After Iraq Threatens Two Neighbors," *New York Times,* July 25, 1990, p. 1.
35. "Spokesman Explains 'Routine Maneuvers' with U.S.," *Kuna* (Kuwait), July 25, 1990, *FBIS-NES,* July 26, 1990, p. 19; and "Statement Denies Joint Maneuvers," *Wakh* (Manama), July 25, 1990, *FBIS-NES,* July 26, 1990, pp. 19–20.
36. Both of these moves diminished Iraqi leverage; they made sense if Saddam's intent was to reduce the causes of war in the hopes that Washington would not fight.
37. See Saddam's Speech to the ACC February 24, and his "Speech at the Baghdad Summit." Also see Saddam Hussein, "Speech to Arab Trade Unions," April 18, 1990, *FBIS-NES,* April 19, 1990, pp. 23–25; Saddam Hussein, "Speech to Arab Parliamentary Union," April 19, 1990, *FBIS-NES,* April 20, 1990, pp. 16–18; and Saddam Hussein, "Arab Solidarity Conference," May 8, 1990, *FBIS-NES,* May 9, 1990, pp. 11–13.

States was attempting compellence, not deterrence, a much more difficult matter. Just the same, the Iraqi leader still had viable options to save face. The United States would not give him linkage on the Palestinian question (Washington was determined to discredit the Arab "peace through strength" strategy, not reward it), but the Bush administration could not stop Saddam from accepting the Soviet initiatives, the Algerian Plan, the advice of Arab Islamic leaders, or the UN option.[38] Any of these would have started a partial withdrawal and set the scene for a protracted haggle. They would also have broken Iraq's international isolation and left the Iraqi army, the *mukhabarat* (intelligence and internal security apparatus), and economic assets in place. Saddam bypassed them all. Even his February 15, 1991, agreement with the Soviet Union that was designed to forestall the ground war hardly moved beyond Iraq's August 12, 1990, proposal and gave no assurances of total withdrawal.[39]

---

38. There were many diplomatic efforts to persuade Saddam to withdraw or at least start a withdrawal process. Moscow sent Yevgeni Primakov in October and February with proposals. Numerous Jordanian and Yemeni efforts also failed to move Saddam. Algerian President Bend-jedid toured the Middle East in December 1990 and presented a comprehensive proposal to Saddam. Saddam, however, was still unwilling to begin the pullback as the first move. He continued to insist on linkage and some payoff on the Arab-Israeli issue. See Primakov, "The Inside Story of Moscow's Quest for a Deal," *Time*, March 4, 1991, pp. 40–48; and Gorbachev's message to Saddam, *FBIS-NES*, January 22, 1991, pp. 37–38. On the Algerian visit, see "Interview with Foreign Minister Sid Ahmed Ghazali," *Algiers Domestic Service*, December 24, 1990, in *FBIS-NES*, December 27, 1990, pp. 9–12. On Saddam's reaction to the World Popular Islamic Leadership see *FBIS-NES*, December 17, 1990, pp. 14–17. Also see the "Interview with Musawi, al-Ghanushi, and Shaqaqi," *Keyhan* (Tehran), December 18, 1990, *FBIS-NES*, January 2, 1991, pp. 65–68.
39. On August 12 Saddam proposed to withdraw from Kuwait if at the same time Israel would withdraw from the occupied territories, U.S. troops would withdraw from Saudi Arabia, and all boycott and sanctions decisions regarding Iraq would be lifted. Iraq stuck to these conditions throughout the crisis. On February 15, 1991, the Iraqi Revolutionary Command Council agreed to withdraw if there was a total ceasefire, all UN Security Council resolutions pertaining to the crisis were abolished, the United States would withdraw its forces from the Middle East, Israel would withdraw from Palestine and Arab territories it occupies in Golan and southern Lebanon, the al-Sabah family would not return to Kuwait but instead the nationalist and Islamic forces would control the new political arrangements, the countries that attacked Iraq would pay all the costs of Iraq's reconstruction, all Iraqi debts would be erased, and the Arabian Gulf region would be declared a zone free of all foreign military presence. On February 21, 1991, Saddam addressed his nation to tell them that the February 15 proposals were designed to "divide the enemy ranks," that the Allied coalition was afraid of ground war, and that Iraq would not retreat. See "Saddam Hussein's Initiative," *Baghdad Domestic Service*, August 12, 1990, *FBIS-NES*, August 13, 1990, pp. 48–49; "Statement by the Iraqi Revolution Command Council," *Baghdad Domestic Service*, February 15, 1991, *FBIS-NES*, February 15, 1991, pp. 17–19; and "Saddam Hussein Address to Nation," *Baghdad Domestic Service*, February 21, 1991, *FBIS-NES*, February 21, 1991, pp. 21–24.

Deterrence and compellence failed, in my view, because Saddam Hussein had drawn four conclusions about the evolving system of power in the Near East in the post–Cold War world. They were: (1) that the United States would oppose Iraqi hegemony but might not use force; (2) that if the United States did use force it would not have the interests at stake or the resolve to suffer heavy casualties; (3) that the level of Arab and Islamic populist animosity against the United states was so intense that no Arab government would dare to have U.S. troops on its soil; and (4) that if Arab governments did turn to the United States for protection, they would lose their legitimacy at home and be overthrown. Saddam was not prepared to abandon these conclusions without the final test in war. Saddam's first and third assumptions were wrong. He never figured out a way to test the second one. His short-run hopes for the fourth did not materialize, but there is little evidence that the Arab regimes in the Allied coalition feel secure from adverse domestic and regional fallout that might ensue from their Gulf War policies.

Washington's diplomacy in the 1980s had failed to shape a regional environment in which its perceived interests were secure. It had failed to contain Iraq's ambitions or the arms race in the Gulf. It had not put to rest its fears of Soviet intentions in the region, nor had it developed a cooperative superpower approach to Gulf security. It had not defused mounting anti-American populist sentiments, both nationalist and Islamic, nor had it succeeded in moving the Camp David process closer to direct Israeli-Palestinian talks. Since the days of the Iranian Revolution, the United States had been preparing the combat forces necessary to project power into the region, should the threatening trends come to a head. Washington was able to rescue its friends in Kuwait with the overwhelming application of this military force. The military victory reestablished a clear picture of the relative military balance, but did not solve Washington's persisting security problems.

Regional Trends in the Post–Gulf War Near East

There are many levels of conflict in the Middle East. Inter-state competition is complicated by intra-Arab and intra-Islamic as well as ethnic and class differences and disputes.[40] Personal rivalries within communities and across national boundaries compound the intricacy. While trends at all of these

---

40. See Cottam, "Levels of Conflict in the Middle East."

levels are fascinating, they are not all equally relevant to U.S. policy. The task of building a political strategy requires concentrated attention on the trends that most directly affect U.S. concerns. These are the military trends that provide the capability to attack U.S. interests and the political trends that affect the regional desires to do so.

REGIONAL MILITARY TRENDS

Traditionally, Washington has focused on the military threats to oil and Israel. Developments in Soviet weapon systems and projection capabilities defined the major concern, along with Soviet transfer of aerial and offensive strike power to Syria, Iraq, Libya, and potentially to Iran. The direct Soviet military threat to the Gulf receded with Moscow's withdrawal from Afghanistan and with the reduction in its transfers of military systems to Iraq and Syria.[41] During the Gulf War, there was serious disagreement over policy in Moscow. Soviet military leaders and conservative analysts complained bitterly about Foreign Minister Eduard Shevardnadze's cooperation with Washington. They returned to Cold War arguments about American imperial intentions, brutality, and threats against Soviet security.[42] But they did not divert Gorbachev's restrained course.

Saddam misread the military power trends before the war. Even with access to advanced Soviet weapons, Iraqi and Syrian arsenals were no match for Israeli airpower, much less the combined arms of the U.S. military. Although his forces were improving and they had better weapons than ever before,[43] the balance in relative terms was more important. Here Saddam was evidently poorly informed about the advanced weaponry available to potential adversaries. Just as Israel routed Syria in 1982, the U.S. Air Force

---

41. Moscow did not abandon the Kabul regime, but its withdrawal did reduce the air power it could easily put over the straits of Hormuz. See Richard Herrmann, "The Soviet Decision to Withdraw from Afghanistan: Changing Strategic and Regional Images," in Robert Jervis and Jack Snyder, eds., *Dominoes and Bandwagons: Strategic Beliefs and Great Power Competition in the Eurasian Rimland* (New York: Oxford University Press, 1991, pp. 220–249). Soviet arms transfers from 1986–89 to Syria were down 44.30 percent compared to 1982–85. See Richard Grimmett, *Trends in Conventional Arms Transfers to the Third World by Major Supplier, 1982–1989* (Washington, D.C.: Congressional Research Service, June 19, 1990), p. 60.
42. V. Afanasyev, "Bloodshed Could Have Been Avoided," *Sovetskaya Rossiya,* January 18, 1991, p. 5, *FBIS-SOV (FBIS Daily Report, Soviet Union),* January 18, 1991, pp. 11–12; Colonel Ye. Shchekatikhin, "Protracted Downpour," *Sovetskaya Rossiya,* February 2, 1991, p. 5, *FBIS-SOV,* February 6, 1991, pp. 32–33; V. Kobysh, "A Special Kind of War," *Izvestiya,* January 22, 1991, p. 5, *FBIS-SOV,* January 23, 1991, pp. 12–14.
43. See International Institute for Strategic Studies, *The Military Balance, 1990–91* (London: IISS, 1990), pp. 105–106.

demolished the Iraqi air defense and shell-shocked the Iraqi army. With Iraq's defeat the regional military trend toward any viable Arab "peace through strength" strategy was smashed. Regardless of who rules in Baghdad, Iraq's military ability to launch external aggression will be limited. The Iraqi forces have proved to be more resilient than American estimates at the close of the war predicted, but they are still far below pre-war levels.[44]

Under the terms of the cease-fire agreement, UN Resolution 687, Iraq will not be able to pursue its traditional policy of weapons acquisition and will find it harder to advance its programs in nuclear, chemical, and biological weaponry. It remains to be seen if these programs can be contained by international constraint and UN inspections, but even if these UN programs are only partially effective they will slow down Iraqi military recovery. Iraq will still have some offensive strike power—for example it may hide a few Scud missiles from UN inspection teams, and will retain tanks and aircraft—but it is likely to be preoccupied with domestic instability and reconstruction.

Although Iran has been politically strengthened by the 1991 Gulf War, it remains economically and militarily weak. Eight years of war and ten years of relative isolation have taken their toll. Since 1989, President Rafsanjani has been trying to shift attention to domestic reconstruction and economic recovery.[45] In 1990 he succeeded in pushing the most messianic Islamic leaders away from the center of power.[46] The Gulf War has revived the security debate in Tehran but has not changed Iran's material situation. To pursue an active military agenda it needs to revive its economy and obtain access to advanced industrial providers.[47] Neither task is an easy one, and

---

44. Early postwar U.S. intelligence agency estimates of Iraqi equipment destroyed or captured were quite high, although not as high as estimates made by the allied Central Command. The agencies estimated that Iraq still had 703 of 4550 tanks, while the Central Command thought there were 580 of 4280 left. The agencies estimated 1430 of 2880 armored personnel carriers survived; the Central Command estimated 1014 of 2870. The agencies reported 340 of 3257 artillery pieces still remaining while the Central Command estimated 970 of 3110. See Michael Gordon, "Much More Armor than U.S. Believed Fled Back to Iraq: Re-examining the Toll," *New York Times*, March 25, 1991, p. 1.
45. Richard Cottam, "Inside Revolutionary Iran," *Middle East Journal*, Vol. 43, No. 2 (Spring 1989), pp. 168–185; and R.K. Ramazani, "Iran's Foreign Policy: Contending Orientations," *Middle East Journal*, Vol. 43, No. 2 (Spring 1989), pp. 202–217.
46. Hashemi Rafsanjani arranged to make passing a religious competency test a precondition for candidacy in elections for the Assembly of Experts. Several of his key competitors among the religious hard-liners failed to pass this test. The device resulted in the disqualification of Sheykh Mehdi Karrubi, Ali Akbar Mohtashemi, and Sheykh Sadeq Khalkhali. See *FBIS-NES*, October 25, 1990, p. 57; and *FBIS-NES*, October 30, 1990, pp. 62–63.
47. See Patrick Clawson, "Iran After Khomeini: Weakened and Weary," *Orbis*, Vol. 34, No. 2

while Iran may become a renewed concern for the Arab Gulf, especially if the Shi'ite Iraqis who follow Iranian-supported Muhammad Baqir al-Hakim take power in Baghdad, the threat will not be a military one.[48]

Syria's military arsenal may be more impressive than ever, but it is still no match for Israel. It is also constrained by economic weakness. Moscow's willingness to bankroll Asad's military aspirations has declined substantially under Gorbachev.[49] Unless pro-Syrian voices in Moscow reverse this trend, Asad will grow increasingly dependent upon Saudi and Gulf state financial support. Whether these conservatives will underwrite Asad's desire for arms is unclear, but their experience with Saddam ought to give them pause.

During the Gulf crisis, Asad was able to enforce the terms of the 1989 Taif Accords governing the resolution of the Lebanese civil war. This involved using force both to oust the last-ditch resistance of Michel Aoun and to set the scene for the implementation of the internal Lebanese disarmament process. Syrian influence in Lebanon was preserved in the May 1991 Syrian-Lebanese Treaty, and Asad gained by stabilizing the Lebanese front. If Syria is successful in acquiring missiles from China, its ability to threaten Israeli population centers will increase.[50] This might allow Asad to inflict more damage than Saddam could, but would still leave him unable to protect Syria from the devastating defeat that would follow from any Syrian-provoked "Desert Storm II." Missiles will add to Syria's deterrent capabilities but are unlikely to strengthen Damascus's compellence options against Israel.

(Spring 1990), pp. 241–246; and Patrick Clawson, "Islamic Iran's Economic Politics and Prospects," *Middle East Journal*, Vol. 42 No. 3 (Summer 1988), pp. 371–88.

48. In 1982, Muhammad Baqir al-Hakim, son of a leading Iraqi ayatollah of the 1960s, established the Supreme Assembly for the Islamic Revolution in Iraq (SAIRI) in Tehran. In 1980, Saddam had executed Ayatollah Sayyid Muhammad Baqir as-Sadr, the leading Iraqi Shi'a religious leader at the time, and banned Ad-Dawah al-Islamiyah, the major Shi'a opposition organization. The relationships between SAIRI, Ad-Dawah, and the current leading Grand Ayatollah in Iraq, Haj Sayyid Abu-al-Qasim al-Khu'i, are complex. Al-Khu'i has religious status unmatched by any living Ayatollah in Iran and has not supported Khomeini's version of the primacy of the supreme religious authority (*velayat-e faqih*). See Hanna Batatu, "Shi'i Organizations in Iraq: al-Da'wah al-Islamiyah and al-Mujahidin," in Juan R. I. Cole and Nikki R. Keddie, eds., *Shi'ism and Social Protest* (New Haven, Conn.: Yale University Press, 1986), pp. 179–200; and Eric Hooglund, "Government and Politics," in *Iraq: A Country Study* (Washington, D.C.: U.S. GPO, 1990), pp. 177–211.

49. See Grimmet, *Trends in Conventional Arms Transfers to the Third World*; and John Hannah, *At Arms Length: Soviet-Syrian Relations in the Gorbachev Era*, Policy Paper No. 18 (Washington, D.C.: The Washington Institute for Near East Policy, 1989).

50. Nicholas Kristof, "U.S. Feels Uneasy as Beijing Moves to Sell New Arms," *New York Times*, June 10, 1991, p. 1.

The United States will try to freeze the military power disparity resulting from Iraq's defeat. With Iraq and Iran weakened and Syria in transition, Washington can promote a security arrangement that rests on Egypt and the Gulf Cooperation Council and which tries to contain the reemergence of the Iraqi or Iranian threats. "Operation Staunch" has aimed at limiting Iranian arms for years. It has not been entirely successful, but the weapons that get through from China, North Korea, and even surplus European stocks are no match for Allied technology and training, as was evident in Iran's war against Iraq. Washington has begun to pursue with its NATO allies new restrictions on military transfers to the Middle East.[51] The Gulf War has heightened sensitivity to the export of non-conventional warheads and ballistic missiles and has stimulated new American interest in slowing down the proliferation of these technologies.

U.S. POLICY AND MILITARY TRENDS

Washington can use several mechanisms to affect the post–Gulf War military situation. Promotion of regional arms control, agreements by the "Group of Seven" (major industrialized nations) on weapons export policy, and COCOM-type restrictions for transfers to Iraq, Iran, and Syria would contribute to containment.[52] So would a Group of Seven agreement to encourage Soviet and Chinese compliance with similar restrictions, pegging the trade and credit opportunities to their abstention from similar arms sales. Limiting missile technology and non-conventional weapons is more complicated. The Arab states and Iran already have signed the Non-Proliferation Treaty (NPT) and agreed to International Atomic Energy Agency (IAEA) inspection. Iraq was thought to be the Arab state most actively pursuing nuclear weapons capability; the evidence on its success before the war was mixed.[53] Postwar revelations suggest that Iraq was actively seeking a nuclear capability and had devised a way to enrich the necessary fuel. How much fuel it had actually

---

51. The most dramatic evidence of success at this point are the restrictions imposed on Iraq in the UN cease-fire resolution; Paul Lewis, "UN Votes Stern Conditions for Formally Ending War," *New York Times*, April 4, 1991, p. 1, 10.
52. The Consultative Group–Coordinating Committee (CoCom) was established in 1949 to limit economic commerce with the Soviet Union that could contribute to Moscow's military development. It includes the NATO countries plus Iceland and Japan. For other ideas on restrictions, see Michael Klare, "Fueling the Fire: How We Armed the Middle East," *Bulletin of the Atomic Scientists*, Vol. 46, No. 1 (January/February 1990), pp. 19–26.
53. See David Albright and Mark Hibbs, "Iraq and the Bomb: Were They Even Close?" *Bulletin of the Atomic Scientists*, March 1991, pp. 16–27. After the war, Iraq's progress was found to be greater than previously thought. See Jeffrey Smith, "Iraq's Secret A-Arms Effort: Grim Lessons for the World," *Washington Post*, August 11, 1991, pp. C1, C4.

produced, however, remained a controversial question. The ban imposed on Iraq by the UN cease-fire resolution will retard future developments. Washington could take up President Mubarak's pre–Gulf War proposal to ban all non-conventional weapons from the region, but Israel will have little reason to participate.[54] It has no near-term nuclear opponent and Iraq failed to mount an effective chemical deterrent during the war. Israel was not willing to link chemical and nuclear issues before the war and has no greater reason to agree to this equation now. Likewise, Arab and Islamic regimes have little incentive to legitimate, even if they must accept, Israeli superiority or international restrictions that apply disproportionately to them. The basis for a negotiated regime limiting regional non-conventional weapons may be too thin to build on, but Washington will surely try.[55]

In the past, Washington has not relied on multilateral efforts to restrict regional military developments but has instead provided unilateral security assistance. Short-term programs can try to use both multilateral constraint and unilateral transfers, but over time there will be a growing tension between these means. To achieve multinational compliance with limitations that affect Iraq, Iran, and Syria, Washington will be encouraged to employ restrictions with regard to Saudi Arabia, Egypt, and Israel. Given the modest capacities of Egypt and Saudi Arabia to threaten other regional actors, establishing mutual arms control regimes while bolstering their deterrent strength is probably possible. However, involving Israel is much more complicated.

It is much too early to predict a trend away from the militarization that characterized the Middle East in the 1980s. The most threatening military trends have been reduced, but the inclination to acquire superior arms has not been reduced in Israel; to the contrary, it has been reinforced.[56] Saudi Arabia has the money to buy a vast array of weapons, and by the end of the decade Iran and Iraq will probably have the financial strength as well. Even if messianic ambitions wane in the region, the security dilemma facing the

---

54. The Mubarak proposal, reiterated in the Damascus Declaration, calls for a ban in the Middle East on all non-conventional weapons, atomic, biological, and chemical. Egypt, Syria, Saudi Arabia, and the other GCC states are parties to the Damascus Declaration. See "Damascus Declaration," March 6, 1991, *FBIS-NES*, March 7, 1991, pp. 1–2.
55. For a pre–Gulf War proposal see Avner Cohen and Marvin Miller, "Nuclear Shadows in the Middle East: Prospects for Arms Control in the Wake of the Gulf Crisis," DACS Working Paper (Defense and Arms Control Studies [DACS], Center for International Studies, MIT, 1990).
56. See Yitzhaq Shamir, "Address to Knesset," February 4, 1991, *FBIS-NES*, February 5, 1991, pp. 30–33; "Interview with Prime Minister Shamir," March 13, 1991, *FBIS-NES*, March 14, 1991, pp. 23–27; "Interview with Foreign Minster David Levi," February 27, 1991, *FBIS-NES*, February 27, 1991, pp. 31–33, and "Interview with Chief of Staff Dan Shomron," March 3, 1991, *FBIS-NES*, March 8, 1991, pp. 30–35.

various antagonists can revive the arms race. There are real technical difficulties in establishing trade limitations when so much of the technical transfer takes place at the level of semi-finished products. Even if this problem could be mastered and potential enemies reassured by verified limits on finished weapon systems, it is not clear that any agreement could be reached on the acceptable mix of forces.

Unlike the American-Soviet case, mutual assured destruction does not pertain in the Middle East today. Given Israel's offensive options and the perceived possibilities for anti-missile defenses, it can aspire to a secure superiority. This may be an illusion based on optimistic assessments of the Patriot missile performance in the Gulf War, but when coupled with Israeli offensive options, it may convince many Israelis that unilateral deterrence and defense is preferable to arms control. Israeli leaders will want arms control regimes to preserve the one-way deterrent relationship, while Arab nationalist and Islamic leaders will see few incentives to legitimate it. Chinese, Pakistani, and North Korean nuclear programs will give Israel additional incentives to pursue unilateral options.[57]

The Gulf War has at least temporarily reduced the military threat to U.S. interests. Terrorism will continue to threaten, but direct military challenges from regional players are unlikely. At the same time, political threats remain. If Saudi Arabia or Egypt defects from the coalition, the situation could change quickly. An alliance among Syria, Iran, and an Iraq without Saddam (led by the Ba'ath Party, Shi'a and other Islamic groups, or a democratic federation of multinational and Islamic groups) could also set new trends in motion. The trends in intra-Arab and intra-Islamic politics require careful attention.

POLITICAL TRENDS

Both the Arab and Islamic worlds are very diverse, a fact often overlooked in Western analyses. Generalizations about Arab culture or Islamic conceptions of government often serve only polemical purposes. Unfortunately, in an article aimed at strategic analysis, simplification is nevertheless necessary.

---

57. Pakistan's nuclear program presented concerns in Washington before the war that led to a suspension of military aid in fall 1990. The Pakistani prime minister struck a middle ground during the war but was clearly under domestic pressure to side with Iraq. The Army chief of staff, General Mirza Aslam Beg, seemed more determined to promote self-reliance and Pakistan's long-term regional identity with Iraq and Iran. See Prime Minster Nawaz Sharif, "Address to Nation," January 20, 1991, *FBIS-NES*, January 23, 1991, pp. 55–57. On Beg's view see *FBIS-NES*, January 29, 1991, pp. 55–57. Also see Editorial, "World Bully at It Again," *The Muslim*, March 12, 1991, p. 6, *FBIS-NES*, March 13, 1991, pp. 59–60; and Bashir Ahmed, "U.S. Aid to Pakistan," *Pakistan Times*, December 9, 1990, p. 4, *FBIS-NES*, December 11, 1991, pp. 57–58.

I begin with the continuing trend toward mass participation and popular empowerment. It has many causes including the processes of urbanization, public education, and the development of a multi-dimensional middle class.[58] Maintaining political order in the face of societal change and new demands for popular sovereignty is not a new problem.[59] Arab regimes, monarchies and republics alike, have employed a series of techniques to limit the pace of mobilization, to co-opt new political participants, and to preserve authoritarian institutions. In the past, party bureaucracies, security networks, and growing economies supported effective control systems that granted regimes substantial latitude in shaping public policy. Today, the demand for popular empowerment involves more people as political attentiveness has spread, and it thus imposes increasing constraints.

Political control can be secured with four basic methods: coercion, utilitarian satisfaction, symbol manipulation, and the laissez-faire acceptance of habitual patterns.[60] Most governments rely on control systems that mix all four devices in various proportions. The first three are the most useful for regimes facing socio-economic change and the tasks of resource mobilization, while legitimacy might be thought of as a measure of the ability to exercise control and to extract human and material resources on the basis of symbol manipulation alone.[61]

The evolution of mass politics is defining a new basis for political legitimacy. Independence from imperialism has been a potent symbol since the nationalist era in the middle of the century. Both the nation and Islam have powerful emotional appeal today. Popular sovereignty also has increasing appeal, as do social welfare and cultural dignity. Governments that are not credible advocates of these symbols in the eyes of their attentive publics must depend on coercion and utilitarian co-optation, but in a period of rising mass participation and economic stagnation, these are expensive and unreliable control devices.

58. See Richards and Waterbury, *A Political Economy of the Middle East*, pp. 296, 329, 350–351, 428, 437. On the Islamic character of the populist empowerment, see Augustus Richard Norton, *Amal and the Shi'a: Struggle for the Soul of Lebanon* (Austin: University of Texas Press, 1987); Gilles Kepel, *Muslim Extremism in Egypt: The Prophet and the Pharaoh* (Berkeley: University of California Press, 1986); Shireen Hunter, *The Politics of Islamic Revivalism* (Bloomington: Indiana University Press, 1988); and John Esposito, *Islam and Politics* (Syracuse: Syracuse University Press, 1987).
59. See Samuel Huntington, *Political Order in Changing Societies* (New Haven, Conn.: Yale University Press, 1968).
60. See Amitai Etzioni, *The Active Society: A Theory of Societal and Political Processes* (New York: Free Press, 1968), pp. 313–395; and Max Weber, *The Theory of Social and Economic Organization*, trans. by A.M. Henderson and Talcott Parsons (New York: Free Press, 1947), pp. 324–386.
61. For the best discussion of legitimacy in the Arab world, see Michael Hudson, *Arab Politics: The Search for Legitimacy* (New Haven: Yale University Press, 1977).

Middle East governments have reacted to the pressures for public empowerment and changing demands of legitimacy in various ways. In Iran, the Shah tried to manipulate Islamic and National symbols but had little popular effect, relying ultimately on coercion and co-optation. A relaxation in repression along with economic inflation sparked an urban revolution.[62] The Shah's skills at Byzantine bureaucratic construction and courting foreign support were no match for the populist charisma of Ayatollah Khomeini and the talent for mass organization of Ayatollah Mohammad Beheshti (a central religious figure who led the revolution inside Iran). In Pakistan, General Zia captured populist symbols with his alliance to Islamic parties, and associated the security forces with the symbols of nation and Islam.[63] In Jordan and Algeria, two very different regimes both took the path of democracy. In November 1989, Jordan's King Husayn allowed parliamentary elections to defuse mounting economic frustration, while in April 1990 the National Liberation Front (NLF) in Algeria allowed competitive municipal elections.[64] In both cases economic decline eroded the efficacy of utilitarian co-optation and forced the regimes either to increase repression or to accommodate to public empowerment. Islam and democracy dominated both processes as the Moslem Brotherhood in Jordan and Abbassi Madani's Front for Islamic Salvation (FIS) in Algeria showed impressive electoral strength.[65] In May 1991 the FIS and the Algerian government clashed over the character of parliamentary elections as the FIS insisted on open presidential elections as well. The spring elections were postponed amidst FIS protests and civil violence. Elections later in the year were promised, but FIS leaders like Madani and Ali Belhadj were arrested, FIS offices closed down, and much of FIS's ruling council detained under the state of siege ordered by the government. In

---

62. On the politics and economics of the revolution see Richard Cottam, *Nationalism in Iran*, 2d ed. (Pittsburgh: University of Pittsburgh Press, 1979), pp. 312–364; and Homa Katouzian, *The Political Economy of Modern Iran, 1926–1979* (New York: New York University Press, 1981).
63. See Selig Harrison, "Ethnicity and the Political Stalemate in Pakistan," Stephen Cohen, "State Building in Pakistan," and John Esposito, "Islam: Ideology and Politics in Pakistan," in Ali Banuazizi and Myron Weiner, eds., *The State, Religion, and Ethnic Politics: Afghanistan, Iran, and Pakistan* (Syracuse: Syracuse University Press, 1986), pp. 267–298, 299–332, 333–369.
64. See Patrick Tyler, "Five Reported Killed in Jordan Riots," *Washington Post*, April 20, 1989, p. 29; Patrick Tyler, "Security Forces Halt Riots in Jordan," April 23, 1989, p. 25; Jonathan Randal, "Moslem Fundamentalists Hold March in Algeria," *Washington Post*, April 21, 1990, p. 16.
65. See Caryle Murphy, "Islamic Fundamentalists Win One-Fourth of Seats in Jordanian Election," *Washington Post*, November 10, 1989, p. A46; Youssef Ibrahim, "Islamic Party in Algeria Defeats Ruling Group in Local Elections," *New York Times*, June 14, 1990, p. 1; Youssef Ibrahim, "Final Count in Algeria Shows Islamic Party Sweep," June 15, 1990, p. 9.

Tunisia, Rashid Ghanushi's al-Nahda party also predicts electoral success, should Ben Ali decide to risk open elections.

The modern states of Syria, Iraq, and Egypt were founded on the symbols of Arab nationalism and independence.[66] Like the NLF in Algeria, these regimes are reluctant to give up their national and republican legacy. At the same time, their ability to rely on symbols has seriously declined. Asad uses the national symbol but has had to rely on brutal repression to contain Islamic movements.[67] He has not overcome the religious differences in Syria and has not been successful in promoting the Arab nationalist agenda in foreign policy. Saddam also used the national symbol mixed with Islam, but relied on repression to dominate the Kurds and the Iraqi Shi'a. His foreign policy record is also one of failure on a colossal scale. Mubarak inherited Sadat's attempt to revive Islamic support for the Egyptian government. He has allowed partial democratization but still relies heavily on party patronage, the security institutions, and strict limitations forbidding Islamic parties. Mubarak has the advantage of operating in a community that emotes strongly to Egyptian national symbols, but must also contend with the millions of Egyptians who also identify intensely with the Arab Nation and the Islamic *umma* (the transnational Islamic community).[68]

Because Arabs identify with multiple communities, several of which do not correspond to the state boundaries drawn at the end of the colonial period, leaders can compete with one another by using transnational symbols. Nasser challenged the legitimacy of the monarchs in Jordan, Saudi Arabia, and Yemen by appealing to Arab nationalist and republican symbols. Ayatollah Khomeini challenged the strength of the Saudi royal family's association with Islam and its independence from imperialism. Saddam Hussein more recently appealed to Arab nationalist aspirations in Egypt, Syria, and Saudi Arabia. The Gulf War did not end these efforts to delegitimate regional rivals; to the contrary, it fueled them.

Although Saddam Hussein touched a chord among many Arab nationalists, he could not rupture the control systems of rival Arab leaders. His

---

66. See William Polk, *The Arab World* (Cambridge: Harvard University Press, 1980), pp. 115–182.
67. See Raymond Hinnebusch, *Authoritarian Power and State Formation in Ba'thist Syria: Army, Party, and Peasant* (Boulder, Colo.: Westview, 1990), pp. 276–300; and Seale, *Asad*, pp. 316–338.
68. See Raymond Hinnebusch, *Egyptian Politics under Sadat: Post-Populist Development of an Authoritarian-Modernizing State* (Cambridge: Cambridge University Press, 1985), pp. 186–256; and Gilles Kepel, *Muslim Extremism in Egypt*.

appeal did not outlast the destruction of his material base of power. He never was the hero of Islamic populists, even though he employed their symbols. Many Islamic fundamentalists saw him as guilty; he murdered the Islamic elite in Iraq and brought the wrath of imperialism down on the heads of his people for the sake of his own personal ambition. In their view, Saddam's megalomania cost the *umma* dearly and was surpassed in its iniquity only by the brutality of the American military punishment.

The war gave Iranian leaders an opportunity to strengthen Tehran's association with anti-imperialist Islamic symbols, while at the same time seeing the Iraqi threat eliminated.[69] The perceived threat posed by American forces in the Gulf, however, dominated Iranian calculations. Iranian leaders described the U.S. attack on Iraq as designed to secure American control over Gulf oil. Some even attributed it to an American desire to control oil as a lever against its new economic competitors in Japan and the unified European market. Ayatollah Khamene'i directed attention away from Rafsanjani's economic agenda and emphasized issues of security and anti-imperial Islamic solidarity.[70] Rafsanjani closed ranks with the *Faqih* (Ayatollah Khamene'i's supreme religious position, inherited from Khomeini), and Iran took the lead in offering an anti-Saddam and anti-American message for Islamic populists across the Near East.

Iran's tactical purpose may have been to bring Saddam down, but its strategic objective was to be sure that the American threat was removed from the Persian Gulf after the war. It did not mind whether there was a Ba'athist, Shi'a, or coalition regime in Iraq and had no intention of confronting the U.S. militarily, having had a glimpse of the power of Desert Storm. Iran moved quickly to develop a regional coalition with Pakistan and Turkey, which would also include Syria, and to advance the conception of a regional security system. Emphasizing the dangers of the American role in the Gulf, Rafsanjani worked to repair Iran's relations with the West European powers and repeatedly proposed a regional approach to security that would rule out the participation of non-regional states.[71] The point was not to force an

---

69. For examples of Iranian editorial opinion see *FBIS-NES*, January 17, 1991, pp. 51–57; *FBIS-NES*, January 22, 1991, pp. 124–130; *FBIS-NES*, February 8, 1991, pp. 60–70; and *FBIS-NES*, February 25, 1991, pp. 95–98.
70. See Ayatollah Khamene'i, "Speech in Qom," January 24, 1991, *FBIS-NES*, January 25, 1991, pp. 44–46.
71. For a good example of Rafsanjani's view, see Hashemi-Rafsanjani, "Friday Sermon," March 8, 1991, *FBIS-NES*, March 12, 1991, pp. 41–45.

American exit—this was far beyond Iran's capability—but to strengthen Iran economically and discredit in populist eyes Washington's participation in regional affairs. By holding out a regional and Islamic vision, Iran aimed to delegitimate the Saudi and Egyptian dependence on American protection. It moved to reopen relations with Riyadh, thereby lessening the appearance of external threat to the Saudi kingdom that Iran might pose. This would further reduce the royal family's ability to claim Islamic legitimacy if it continued to host western forces. King Husayn of Jordan could contribute to the pressure on the House of Saud by advertising the Saudi conquest of Mohammed's direct descendants, Husayn's ancestors the Hashemites, in the Hijaz.[72]

King Husayn paid the price of democracy during the Gulf War. His position reflected the sentiments of Jordan's peoples rather than his interests in warm relations with the Gulf monarchs and the United States.[73] Jordan paid a terrible price economically, but King Husayn's legitimacy was enhanced. The king, however, is neither Palestinian nor Moslem Brother; he does not lead these communities but is constrained by them. Neither the *Ikhwan* (the Moslem Brotherhood) nor Iran is likely to see in the king a long-term ally in Jordan. He is acceptable to them as long as he allows the populist forces for change to prevail. But as long as he adheres to democracy, his relationships with the kingdoms and sheikdoms on the Gulf will remain tense. They will not forgive his temporizing while Saddam called for their heads, and he cannot renounce the desires of the peoples in Jordan. Ultimately, given Jordan's Palestinian population, its future will be determined in the Levant, not the Gulf. It will depend on the course taken by Syria and Egypt.

Although many Sunni Arab nationalists in Syria identified with the message of Saddam, Hafiz Asad could not. Saddam was his bitter rival for nationalist leadership in the eastern Arab world. Asad choose to repress popular pro-Iraqi outbursts in Syria and bide his time. He argued that the true Arab nationalist interest was to protect Syrian resources and work to

---

72. In the Hijaz, site of the holy cities of Mecca and Medina, the British after World War I protected King Husayn's Hashemite ancestor, Sharif Husayn of Mecca, the direct descendant of Mohammed. But the Saudi family, rejecting the British involvement in intra-Arab politics, drove the Hashemite king into exile. In 1932, Abdel Aziz Ibn Saud crowned himself king of a united Saudi Arabia. See Fred Halliday, *Arabia Without Sultans* (Middlesex: Penguin, 1974), pp. 48–49; and David Holden and Richard Jones, *The House of Saud* (London: Sidgwick and Jackson, 1981), pp. 63–86.
73. See King Husayn, "Speech to the Arab and Islamic Nation," February 6, 1991, *FBIS-NES*, February 7, 1991, pp. 27–29; and King Husayn, "News Conference," January 19, 1991, *FBIS-NES*, January 22, 1991, pp. 92–5.

remove the pretext—Saddam's occupation of Kuwait—that evoked imperialist intervention. At the same time, he consolidated a process in Lebanon that protected Syrian interests. Asad's security network was strong enough to contain whatever success Saddam had in generating Syrian sympathy. His control system, however, is heavy with coercive means.[74] Syria's economy is weak and Asad's use of populist symbols of the Arab Nation and Islam are suspect. In the late 1980s his secular bent complicated Syria's alliance with fundamentalist Iran. Rafsanjani might have been willing to secure the state-to-state relationship at the expense of Iran's relationship with the Shi'a fundamentalists represented by Hizbollah in Lebanon, and Sunni fundamentalists in Syria, but Mohtashami, Montarezi, and other important Iranians were not. It is not coincidental that Rafsanjani's first trip abroad after the Gulf War was to Syria and that the question of Hizbollah's autonomy in the south of Lebanon was high on the agenda. If Asad concludes that he cannot survive in a populist Islamic environment, he will have to look to the Arab symbols to secure a viable coalition in Damascus. Here he faces a dilemma. Saddam's defeat removes the traditional rival, but it also calls into doubt the viability of a "peace through strength" confrontational strategy. Asad can pick up the mantle of radical rhetoric, but can he succeed with its agenda?

Asad's most likely turn is toward the Egyptian-Saudi alliance, at least in the short run.[75] Syria did not take active measures to defeat the Baker Plan in 1989–90, and will probably go further toward compromise in 1991, including a willingness to engage in talks with Israel as long as they are linked directly to Israeli-Palestinian talks. From weakness, Asad may let the Baker-Mubarak effort go another round. He is likely to remain skeptical, however, and to secure an internal coalition by hanging tough on territorial return and Palestinian rights while opposing the American presence in the Gulf.

Asad is unlikely to give any overt support to the "reassurance" strategy. He will not recognize Israel, de facto or otherwise, unless he is sure that it is part of a process that will lead to a land-for-peace tradeoff. He will worry that Washington's primary objective will be to hold a conference at which he can recognize Israel, rather than to construct a process that will produce the land-for-peace tradeoffs. He will look for reassurances that Israel will make concessions on the key points relating to land and Palestinian self-determination. Washington's word will not be enough. Asad will look for an

---

74. See Hinnebusch, *Authoritarian Power and State Formation in Ba'thist Syria.*
75. See the "Damascus Declaration," March 6, 1991, *FBIS-NES*, March 7, 1991, pp. 1–2.

active and continuing UN role that can put pressure on Israel if the United States does not. He will also look for a prior international agreement that Arab-Israeli negotiations will lead to the end of Israel's occupation of the land acquired in 1967 and not the Arab legitimation of the Israeli status quo. Israel's settlement policy is likely to be Asad's litmus test for Washington's intentions. If the United States cannot move Israel on this point, he will probably conclude that its peace process is simply an invitation to surrender to Likud's terms. If Washington demonstrates its commitment to the land-for-peace formula, Asad has said many times that he will participate in the process of making peace with Israel.[76]

In 1989 Asad positioned himself to capitalize on Mubarak's and Arafat's failure, and during the Gulf War he straddled the issues waiting for Saddam's demise. Asad is likely to be cautious in 1991 as well, and go along with the U.S.-led efforts, while holding open his options if they fail in 1992 as Washington turns its attention to presidential elections. He may foresee a new alliance that could incorporate a new Ba'ath regime in Iraq along with Jordan and Iran. Currently this would threaten Saudi King Fahd by creating a new coalition based on populist anti-American and Islamic symbols. The Saudis decided shortly after the end of the war to send the Egyptian and Syrian forces home. Evidently, they are less comfortable with Arab nationalist forces on their territory than they are with relying on American and other non-Arab protection. Asad, having just seen Saddam over-reach, is likely to be cautious about prematurely confirming Saudi insecurities. Asad also needs to work with Mubarak to avoid the isolation he faced in 1989. He can afford to let Egypt make another effort to prove that the American-based strategy can work. In 1992, if the next round of talks fail, then in 1992 or early 1993, if the new U.S. administration does not press for progress in the talks, the situation may be more propitious for Asad to strengthen Arab nationalist leverage and press for a new regional coalition. Mubarak and Fahd will be more exposed and vulnerable to competitive symbol manipulation by Asad. The Egyptian regime may even be inclined to join the Arab nationalist–Islamic marriage. This is a marriage with which neither Mubarak nor Asad have

---

76. Asad's intentions and what he will accept as a settlement are controversial and still not tested. For the argument that he will settle for a balance between an Arab Levant centered on Damascus, and Israel in its pre-1967 borders, see Seale, *Asad*. For the argument that he has Greater Syrian ambitions that are inconsistent with Israel's survival, see Daniel Pipes, *Greater Syria: The History of an Ambition* (New York: Oxford University Press, 1990).

been comfortable before, but it is consistent with the evolving populist identity in both communities.

In the midst of the Gulf War, Hosni Mubarak called a special session of the Egyptian Parliament to explain why his course was the true Arab Nationalist path and to tell his countrymen that President Bush had pledged to solve the Palestinian problem when the war was done.[77] President Mubarak's bureaucratic control system was in place, and the November 1990 election (like the previous elections the Supreme Court had over-ruled as rigged) had gone his way.[78] His speech, however, suggested that he felt he needed more. He needed the Arab Nationalist symbol and he needed to claim that his strategy of cooperation with the United States would fulfill the Palestinian aspiration, not abandon it. Material aid and debt forgiveness by the United States surely contribute to Mubarak's utilitarian control, but they will not repair the Egyptian economy.[79] Moreover, they might weaken the regime's legitimacy if they are seen by Arabs as payment for treason against either the Arab Nation or Islam.

Mubarak has a cushion in that many Egyptians identity more strongly with Egypt than they do with the Arab Nation or the *umma*. The Islamic establishment has benefited from the Sadat-Mubarak tenure, and also from Saudi financial support. Mubarak has included them in his coalition. Whether he has the "Zia" option, an alliance of the military with populist Islamic fundamentalism, is doubtful. Although parts of the Moslem Brotherhood have been co-opted, it was a fundamentalist cell in the military that murdered Sadat. Other Islamic movements continue to elicit governmental repression. Egypt could evolve, as Pakistan has, in the direction of a tougher nationalist and Islamic regime, but Mubarak probably cannot. He has used the Ministry of the Interior to repress Islamic populist outbursts with vigor, and he may not be able to reach out and attract credible fundamentalist leaders. If he can make the reassurance strategy related to Israel and the connection to Washington pay off in the nationalist currency that populist forces understand, he can hope to stabilize the Saudi-Syrian axis and draw Jordan and an Iraq after Saddam into the fold.

---

77. Hosni Mubarak, "Speech to Joint Session of People's Assembly," January 24, 1991, *FBIS-NES*, January 25, 1991, pp. 5–9, 7.
78. Low voter turnout and a substantial boycott along with some violence marred the November elections, but they did sustain Mubarak's control. Alan Cowell, "Turnout Appears Low In Egyptian Elections Boycotted by Opposition," *New York Times*, November 30, 1990, p. 12.
79. See William Quandt, *The United States and Egypt* (Washington, D.C.: Brookings, 1990).

The United States, of course, is a critical player in the reassurance strategy. Its policy will not determine Mubarak's future but it will have a important impact on it. Washington seems to vacillate between two beliefs: on the one hand, that its behavior has little effect on the complicated domestic politics of the Near East, and on the other that it can control events, protect regimes, and stop undesired changes. Arguments against change in U.S. policy often take the pessimistic view that hostile populist attitudes in the Islamic world are immutable. Unable to change them, it is argued, Washington should concentrate on deterring them and on slowing down the social and political processes of change that bring populist attitudes to power. Many regional specialists make the opposite argument, suggesting that changing the hostile attitudes would be easier than trying to stop the inevitable consequences of modernization. Opposing change, they fear, will only reinforce the hostile attitudes and create a self-fulfilling prophecy about the antagonism of the region to the United States. What is necessary is a strategy that is not biased in either direction by a strong assumption about what is possible, but that protects U.S. intrinsic interests while pragmatically testing to see how much change in populist attitudes is possible and at what cost.

The Road From Here: Deterrence, Multinationalization, and Democratization

Superior military power may protect U.S. interests, but regional security that is based simply on Washington's ability to intimidate and project coercive influence will be politically vulnerable. It will reinforce local perceptions of the United States as an imperial power and last only as long as the United States can afford and is willing to sustain the power asymmetry. If Washington is to avoid a future war, it will need to build relationships that enjoy the popular support of the national communities in the Near East. It will need to plan for change, design strategy to effect change, and protect its interests and commitments in a period of transition.[80] The strategic design may begin with deterrence, but it should not end there.

In the past, the U.S. deterrence strategy had three parts. First, it provided security assistance to allied governments, helping them to deter internal revolt and revolutionary change. Second, it provided advanced weapons to

---

80. See Robert Pastor, "Preempting Revolutions: The Boundaries of U.S. Influence," *International Security*, Vol. 15, No. 4 (Spring 1991), pp. 54–86.

Gulf allies and a U.S. military force that could shield these allies from external attack. This American force has traditionally been on station at sea and available through air reinforcement, a condition that will probably also obtain in the future. Finally, the strategy also involved an economic and political dimension. Commercial prosperity was encouraged by aid, trade, and direct investment, in the hopes of reducing economic distress and urban deprivation. Economic efforts were aimed at ameliorating the socio-economic propensity for radicalism, while new channels of participation were encouraged.

Hundreds of programs provide the operational substance of the three-part strategy. The general design has been applied many times in the Third World. It failed in Iran, back-fired in Iraq, and is being tested in Egypt. It certainly will be the bedrock of Washington's near-term efforts in the Middle East. It will not be sufficient, however, to affect the political trends that threaten Washington's interests. There are several problems. First, the political economy of *infitah* (opening the local economy to the international economy) creates as many social pressures as it reduces.[81] Secondly, deterring change, the first object, and promoting it, the third, are hard to balance. There rarely is consensus in Washington on which dimension to stress. Should allied regimes meet opposition with unbending force, hoping for eventual capitulation to the realities of power, or should they modify the avenues to power in a way that defuses the hostility? It is possible that either approach could succeed, but the lack of agreement over which way to go typically undermines the coherent pursuit of either tactic and allows each side to argue that its approach was never really tried. Beyond this debate there is a third, more fundamental problem. The three-part strategy rests on active American involvement. It deepens the association between Washington and the regimes with which it is allied. In an era of rising mass politics this can undermine the legitimacy of these allied regimes and become a source of instability in its own right. The best way to minimize this danger is to move toward multinationalization, by which I mean the reduction of unilateral American assistance to individual regimes and the increase in American support for international and regional institutions.

---

81. See Richards and Waterbury, *A Political Economy of the Middle East*, pp. 238–262; John Waterbury, *The Egypt of Nasser and Sadat: The Political Economy of Two Regimes* (Princeton: Princeton University Press, 1983), pp. 123–157; Mohamed Heikal, *Autumn of Fury: The Assassination of Sadat* (New York: Random House, 1983), pp. 84–89.

MULTINATIONALIZATION

The Gulf War crystallized a multinational approach to Gulf security that was unthinkable even a year earlier. After decades of trying to keep Moscow out of the Gulf, Washington through the UN invited it in. Saudi Arabia reestablished relations with the Soviet Union, while the UN sanctioned the use of multilateral naval and ground forces. The allied fighting coalition was heavily American, but even so, the experience established a precedent for collective action that should be built upon. One way to do this would be a UN Conference on Security and Cooperation in the Gulf (CSCG). Introducing the principles familiar to the Conference on Security and Cooperation in Europe (CSCE) will not provide security in the short run, but it may establish parameters for collective sanctions and identify mechanisms for change. The CSCE's opposition to the use of force and its defense of the inviolability of established borders in Europe did not prevent the reunification of Germany, nor would CSCG preclude Arab or Islamic cooperation or even unification. It could accommodate American and European concerns by involving non-regional actors like the United States and the Soviets in Gulf security while, at the same time, calling for the norms of behavior that Iran and other local actors who want only regional participation declare to be their goal.

It may not be possible to expand the acceptance of non-regional forces in Gulf security beyond the GCC States and Egypt. A CSCG effort is likely to be rejected in Tehran and Damascus. Security in the Gulf will still be based primarily on bilateral arrangements. But this effort is still worth pursuing. It would not undermine the other dimensions of a deterrent strategy and it could reduce regional suspicions about American unilateral intentions, although it surely would not erase them. Moreover, the CSCG could contribute to a multilateral regime to constrict the flow of advanced weaponry and unconventional weapons technology to the region. In contrast, unilateral U.S. arms sales to its clients would boost, not reduce, the incentives of other players in the area to seek advanced military power. A multilateral regime that began to relax perceived threats and promised collective defense, and also worked to limit and regulate through arms control the pace and type of military development, might be worth the costs to the United States of accepting negotiated limits on its arms sales.

Unilateral American security assistance contributes to the deterrence function and can bolster the stability of allied Arab regimes, but a highly visible U.S. military presence is often a lightning rod for populist opposition. This is an old problem for the United States in the Gulf and it is a dilemma that the Gulf War did not solve. If the battle over populist legitimacy continues, the multilateral option will not be naive idealism but pragmatic realism. It will pose new technical-military problems but provide the most politically viable avenue for allied involvement in the region. If the United States is to shape change rather than simply try to stop it, it will need to encourage the advancement of multilateral options that have as much regional legitimacy as the alternative conceptions advanced by Iran and Arab populist circles. This will be crucial if genuine progress on the Arab-Israeli front continues to be elusive.

A multilateral approach makes sense in a reassurance strategy for the Arab-Israeli conflict, but Israelis who, for more ideological reasons, are committed to holding land will strongly object. In their eyes, expanding the forum to include the Soviets and Europeans only adds leverage to Palestinian resistance. Conservative Israelis would prefer a bold compellence strategy that from strength seeks lasting Arab concessions on land, Jerusalem, and Palestinian self-determination. This outcome might be possible if the power relationships that underpin it can be sustained. But there is no international consensus for this option, and regional economic and military trends as well as populist domestic trends seem to work against it. On the other hand, the Soviet *aliyah* ("going up" or immigration of Jews to Israel), Israel's military success, and the continuing disharmony in the Arab and Islamic world encourage powerful voices in Israel. No one can be certain about the future power relationships, but a multinational approach to Arab-Israeli issues will better serve U.S. interests than the continuation of a unilateral U.S. role.

During the Camp David decade, Washington was not successful in reassuring Israel, nor did it succeed in inducing major Israeli concessions on the West Bank, Gaza, and other Palestinian issues. The United States could not reassure the Israeli polity by strengthening Israel's leverage without, at the same time, strengthening Likud's argument that no concessions were necessary. Washington lost its credibility in Israel on two counts. It could not defuse Arab hostility toward Israel or the threats that Saddam's popularity exemplified, nor could it convince Israelis that the United States was serious about land-for-peace, its opposition to settlements in Occupied Territories, and its view that Palestinian national aspirations had to be addressed. Too few Israelis were confident of Washington's protection and too many were convinced that they could ignore with impunity Washington's approach to the peace process.

A multinational forum will not force Israel to concede territory, nor will it fundamentally change the power relationships that have emerged from the Gulf War, which heavily favor Israel. It could, however, change the mix of incentives for pursuing security through settlement and reassurance that affect Israeli, Palestinian, and Arab calculations. It would engage new disincentives that Washington by itself cannot apply, such as multilateral economic sanctions or restrictions on aid and trade, should local parties refuse to test the ground for mutual gain. This would apply to Arab states as well as to Israel. For instance, Soviet and European commitment to a process of reassurance would limit Syrian, Jordanian, and Palestinian options. At the same time, Washington's commitment to an international process would imply a comparable limit on Israel's ability to continue settlements without facing sanctions.

Washington's decision to broaden the Camp David process to include direct Soviet joint sponsorship and a peripheral U.N. observer role partially reassures Palestinians and Arab participants without undermining Washington's bilateral obligations to protect Israeli security. As the process moves forward, the United States should strengthen the multilateral dimensions of the international mediation. The Likud leadership will oppose the diminution of Washington's special role as Israel's primary ally and the predominant broker in peace process talks. This evolution will also frustrate Israelis committed to a vision of Greater Israel. Israeli resistance, however, is inevitable if Washington is to pursue its long-standing interests in settlement of the Arab-Israeli conflict based on UN 242 and UN 338. A multinational option will not erase the rock-bottom problems that excite emotions. Neither Arabs nor Israelis will lose sight of the issues of East Jerusalem, Palestinian self-determination, the Right of Return, the PLO, the West Bank, Gaza, and the Golan Heights, regardless of diplomatic disguise, transitional processes, or conference details. Likud leaders, Arab leaders, and Palestinian leaders will continue to be far apart on these questions regardless of which international venue covers a two-track process. Washington alone does not have the ability to bridge the gap. Israelis will resist its pressure and Arabs will doubt U.S. intentions and reliability, given its previous failure to take concrete action to implement its verbal support for various settlement terms. A multinational venue would relax some of the pressure on Washington to "deliver Israel," and at the same time limit Likud's options to evade testing a land-for-peace process. It might align a new mix of forces that will enhance the pressures for seeking compromise rather than reinforcing the determination to prepare for war.

DEMOCRATIZATION

The United States of America is not the enemy of Islam, democratization, or Arab self-determination. Too many Arabs and Moslems believe that it is. Changing this perception should be a major goal of U.S. political strategy. This does not call for appeasement but it does require a strategy that goes beyond reinforcing the credibility of Washington's will and superior power. Washington has to make clear what the purposes of its power are and how these relate to basic American values.

Identifying the forces for democracy has not been easy. The Cold War colored perceptions and led Washington to oppose leaders like Mossadegh in Iran and Nabulsi in Jordan. Today, some Islamic fundamentalists espouse democratic elections and civil freedoms, as in Tunisia, Egypt, and Algeria where they want a chance at power, while other fundamentalists do not protect these principles in countries where they rule, such as the Sudan and Iran. Perhaps it is true that the West's perceptions are imperial and that it treats Moslems as immature and not ready for civilized institutions. Maybe these views do reflect a mind-set that justifies the protection of Western interests through repression and authoritarianism.[82] On the other hand, Islamic liberalism might be a romantic hope of Western academics and Moslem advocates.[83] Maybe there is nothing beyond the demagoguery that would support the institutionalization of democratic process and civil liberties. This debate cannot be settled here. Nor can it be settled without being put to the test by the populist forces that, liberal or not, are achieving empowerment.

If Washington continues its support for individual governments rather than democratic principles, this may push the trend toward repression and revolution, and so might its careless embrace of radical movements. Its influence should be aimed at the institutionalization of democratic processes and the establishment of popular sovereignty. The long-term U.S. relationship with Middle Eastern countries requires a stable *modus vivendi* not only with regimes but also with local populations. Defending U.S. economic concerns by working against popular sovereignty in regional states is not in the long-term interest of the United States. Instead, the institutionalization of electoral processes and judicial procedures that are perceived as fair and efficacious is the policy goal that the United States should pursue. This has been the

---

82. See Edward Said, *Orientalism* (New York: Vintage Books, 1979).
83. See Leonard Binder, *Islamic Liberalism: A Critique of Development Ideologies* (Chicago: University of Chicago Press, 1988).

Why the Third World Still Matters

Steven R. David

$\mathbf{T}$he end of the Cold War and the disintegration of the Soviet Union have not ended the importance of the Third World to American interests and worldwide stability, nor have they ushered in a new era of peace.[1] Because war will not become obsolete in the Third World, and because many Third World states are becoming increasingly powerful, the threat that Third World states pose to themselves and non–Third World countries will persist. Preparing to address these threats must be a central component of American foreign policy in the post–Cold War world.

During the Cold War, a near consensus of scholarly opinion emerged arguing that the United States vastly exaggerated the threats posed by the Soviet Union in the Third World. The Soviets were seen as uninterested in dominating the Third World, incapable of doing so if they tried, and unable to significantly improve their ability to threaten the United States even if their efforts succeeded. Adherents of this view asserted that inasmuch as the Third World—whether under Soviet control or not—posed no threat to the United States, the United States should avoid wasting scarce resources on secondary concerns, especially while truly vital interests (e.g., preventing a

Steven R. David is Professor of Political Science at the Johns Hopkins University.

I would like to thank Stephen Van Evera, Sean Lynn-Jones, Aaron Friedberg and the members of the Johns Hopkins University seminar, "The United States and the Third World," for their suggestions. I would also like to thank the Bradley Foundation for its financial support. The views expressed are my own.

1. Drawing upon the United Nations categorization, I include in the "Third World" all countries *except* the United States, the European republics of the former Soviet Union, Canada, Japan, Australia, New Zealand, South Africa, the European states, and the People's Republic of China. I recognize that the term "Third World" is becoming increasingly problematic with the demise of bipolarity, the end of the "Second World," political fragmentation among the nonaligned, and the high growth rates of some Third World states. Nevertheless, I maintain that states traditionally characterized as "Third World" maintain enough similarities (e.g., young states created by colonial powers) to justify considering them together. For more on this point, see Christopher Clapham, *Third World Politics* (Madison: University of Wisconsin Press, 1985), especially ch. 1; and Steven R. David, "Explaining Third World Alignment," *World Politics*, Vol. 43, No. 2 (January 1991), especially pp. 238–242.

International Security, Winter 1992/93 (Vol. 17, No. 3)
© 1992 by the President and Fellows of Harvard College and of the Massachusetts Institute of Technology.

Soviet attack on Western Europe, deterring superpower nuclear war) required America's full attention.[2]

With the Cold War over, a new set of arguments has emerged reemphasizing the irrelevance of the Third World to American interests. Whatever value the Third World may have held for the United States during the Cold War has, it is now claimed, been lost once the superpower competition for influence ended. Because the Cold War played such a central (if misguided) role in defining the importance of the Third World to the United States and provoking American involvement there, the end of the Cold War will remove all but the most peripheral of U.S. concerns with Third World developments. Moreover, in the post–Cold War era, it is asserted, most Third World countries cannot threaten the United States and the few that can do so will not, because it would not be in their interests. The removal of the superpower competition in the Third World is also seen as eliminating one of the principal causes of conflict among the developing countries. Without American and Soviet involvement, according to this view, Third World states will not be driven to attack one another, nor will they be given the sophisticated weaponry to prosecute the wars that nevertheless may break out. The United States thus confronts Third World states that are less important to its interests and less likely to threaten those interests through war. While disagreements persist regarding the level of involvement the United States should seek to retain in Europe (though virtually all agree that the United States should remain engaged), there is a remarkable unanimity of views that because the Third World poses little threat to American interests, it can be safely ignored.[3]

---

2. For views that the United States exaggerated its interests in the Third World, see Robert H. Johnson, "Exaggerating America's Stakes in Third World Conflicts," *International Security,* Vol. 10, No. 3 (Winter 1984/85), pp. 32–68; Richard E. Feinberg and Kenneth A. Oye, "After the Fall: U.S. Policy Toward Radical Regimes," *World Policy Journal,* Vol. 1, No. 1 (Fall 1983), pp. 201–215; Jerome Slater, "Dominos in Central America: Will They Fall? Does it Matter?" *International Security,* Vol. 12, No. 2 (Fall 1987), pp. 105–134; Barry R. Posen and Stephen W. Van Evera, "Reagan Administration Defense Policy: Departure From Containment," in Kenneth A. Oye, Robert J. Lieber, and Donald Rothchild, eds., *Eagle Resurgent? The Reagan Era in American Foreign Policy* (Boston: Little, Brown, 1987) pp. 75–114; Stephen M. Walt, *The Origins of Alliances* (Ithaca: Cornell University Press, 1987). For a dissenting view, see Steven R. David, "Why the Third World Matters," *International Security,* Vol. 14, No. 1 (Summer 1989), pp. 50–85.
3. This view is shared by many across the political spectrum. See, for example, Patrick J. Buchanan, "America First—and Second, and Third," *The National Interest,* No. 19 (Spring 1990), pp. 77–82; Charles William Maynes, "America Without the Cold War," *Foreign Policy,* (Spring 1990), pp. 3–26; Stephen Van Evera, "Why Europe Matters, Why the Third World Doesn't: America's Grand Strategy After the Cold War," *Journal of Strategic Studies,* Vol. 13, No. 2 (June

Proponents of these views raise cogent points. The threat posed by Soviet expansion in the Third World during the Cold war was exaggerated at times. American involvement in the Third World was indeed largely prompted by fears of Soviet expansion. Most Third World states cannot threaten important American interests and those that can would likely suffer if they attempted to do so. Wars in the Third World have at times been made possible and exacerbated by the superpower competition that has now come to an end.

None of this means, however, that the Third World will no longer pose a significant threat to American interests or that it will gain the peace and stability that has characterized Western Europe since 1945. Although the aggregate threat to the United States from the Third World may be less than it was when the Soviet Union existed, it still is far greater than asserted by those who dismiss the Third World as inconsequential. It is true that the collapse of the USSR has eliminated concerns that Soviet control of Third World states posed a threat to American security. But the United States continues to face threats from Third World states without Soviet backing. Leaders of these states may be unable or unwilling to follow "rational" policies that would safeguard American interests. The growing likelihood that Third World states will act in ways inimical to American interests, due to the persistence of instability often leading to war, combined with the increasing capability of many Third World states to threaten American interests, particularly in the areas of nuclear proliferation and supply of oil, makes the Third World of continuing concern to the United States in the post–Cold War era.

My argument is presented in five parts. I first briefly consider the impact of the superpower competition and its demise in defining the importance of the Third World to the United States. I then examine why the characteristics of many Third World countries (shared by some of the newly emerging countries of Eastern Europe and the former Soviet Union) make them more likely to be beset by instability and war than other states. Third, I discuss the increasing capability of Third World states to threaten American interests and world peace. I then consider specific ways that the instability of Third World states combined with their growing strength poses a threat to American interests. I conclude with some broad suggestions for American policy.

1990), pp. 1–51; and David Hendrickson, "The Renovation of American Foreign Policy," *Foreign Affairs*, Vol. 71, No. 2 (Spring 1992), pp. 48–63.

The United States, the Third World, and the Ending of the Cold War

There is no question that the greatest determinant of American involvement in the Third World since 1945 has been its competition with the Soviet Union. Virtually every American intervention or significant involvement in the Third World was undertaken to counter the perceived spread of Soviet (or Communist) influence. While arguments persist concerning whether it was in American interests to attempt to contain Soviet influence, there is no dispute that the superpower competition limited American freedom of action in the Third World. Because of fears of provoking World War III, triggering direct Soviet intervention, pushing the Soviets to increase military assistance to a client, damaging détente, or provoking Soviet moves against other areas of critical interest to the United States, Washington chose not to act as forcefully as it might have in the Third World.[4] Moreover, by virtue of its very existence as a rival superpower, the USSR weakened American influence by allowing the Third World states to play the superpowers against each other.

The centrality of the Soviet Union in determining American actions in the Third World is especially noteworthy now that the superpower competition is over. The implications of Soviet withdrawal from the Third World have already become apparent. In one respect, the end of the superpower competition has produced increased freedom of action for the United States. In the 1991 war with Iraq, the United States massively attacked a nominal ally of the Soviet Union without fear of provoking a wider conflict, superpower confrontation, increased Soviet aid, or pushing Iraq into the Soviet embrace. Instead of rendering the United Nations paralyzed by a Soviet veto, Moscow cooperated with the United States to bring about some dozen Security Council resolutions condemning Iraq and justifying the use of force against it. Similarly, the United States welcomed the USSR (now Russia) as co-chair of the Middle East Peace Conference after years of trying to restrict Soviet influence. Instead of complicating matters for the United States, the presence of the USSR made it easier for radical states (such as Syria) to participate, while lessening the perception that the process was entirely an American affair. The end of the superpower competition has also brought about a diminished American concern over at least some developments in the Third World, as seen in Washington's agreement to withdraw from bases in the

---

4. Stephen T. Hosmer, *Constraints on U.S. Strategy in Third World Conflicts* (New York: Crane Russak and Company, 1987), ch. I.

Philippines and with its lack of interest in a civil war in Somalia (once a key country in American Third World policy).

In sum, the post–Cold War era is one in which the United States is far freer to act in the Third World, but in which the absence of the Soviet Union makes the reasons to do so appear to be less compelling than ever. This situation raises a key question: Without the prospect of Soviet involvement, why should the United States care about what happens in the Third World?

The Prevalence of Instability in the Third World

Washington needs to be concerned about Third World developments because war is more likely to occur in the Third World than anywhere else. Some of these wars are likely to be fought in areas that are essential for the Western economies (e.g., the Persian Gulf), or with weapons of mass destruction that may inflict terrible damage on the combatants, their neighbors, American allies, or the United States itself. The likelihood of war is so high because Third World states are characterized by domestic instability that leads to internal war and can bring about international war as well. War is also more likely in the Third World than elsewhere because many of the reasons put forth for why war has become obsolete among the developed states simply do not apply to much of the Third World.

The belief that states in the Third World are more war-prone stems, first, from their recent history. From 1945 to 1990 there have been over 100 wars (both internal and interstate) in the Third World. Since 1945 nearly 20 million people have lost their lives in wars. Of this number, about 200,000 deaths occurred in Europe during the Greek civil war and Soviet intervention in Hungary. The rest, over 19 million people, died as a result of wars in the Third World. All of the wars and armed conflicts involving the United States have been in the Third World. It is not an exaggeration to say that war since 1945 has been essentially a Third World affair.[5]

Third World conflict is so prevalent because of the characteristics of many Third World states. A key factor is the relative youth of the states. Western Europe and the Third World both confronted similar problems in forging

---

5. For casualties in Third World wars, see Ruth Leger Sivard, *World Military and Social Expenditures: 1987–88* (Washington, D.C.: World Priorities, 1987) pp. 28–31. For a brief summary of wars in the Third World, see Guy Arnold, *Wars in the Third World since 1945* (London: Cassell Publishers, 1991).

cohesive states. Inculcating a state identity among disparate groups and establishing borders are just some of the fundamental obstacles that had to be overcome. The difference in the Third World is that while it took Western Europe three to four centuries to develop a state, Third World leaders have had only three to four *decades* to accomplish the same task.[6] Even in Latin America, where states have existed for over a century, the time available for state formation has been much less than in Western Europe.[7] It should not, therefore, be surprising that most Third World states lack the cohesion and stability of their West European counterparts.[8]

A second characteristic of the Third World that promotes instability is the legacy of colonialism. Most Third World states are ex-colonies. Outside powers created states where none had existed. Although the degree of correlation with existing ethnic groups varied (high in Southeast Asia, low in Africa and the Middle East), in nearly all cases imposed borders replaced flexible demarcations.[9] Colonial powers further divided ethnic groups by assigning them different tasks based on ethnicity and also by playing them off against one another.[10] Because of the arbitrariness of their borders, many Third World states began and remain more as artificial constructs than as cohesive units.

The consequences of ethnic divisions in the Third World (and elsewhere) are enormous. Unlike Western states, which were built up around an ethnic core that attracted and dominated other ethnic groups, in much of the Third World (especially Africa) there is no ethnic core to give identity to the state.

---

6. One of the best examinations of the European experience in state building is Charles Tilly, "Reflections on the History of European State-Making," in Charles Tilly, ed., *The Formation of National States in Western Europe* (Princeton, N.J.: Princeton University Press, 1975) pp. 3–83. See also Mohammed Ayoob, "The Security Problematic of the Third World," *World Politics*, Vol. 43, No. 2 (January 1991), pp. 265–266.
7. That Latin America imported the political culture of pre-industrial Iberia also explains why its political development has not reached the level of Western Europe. For more on why Latin American states did not develop along European lines, see Joel S. Migdal, *Strong Societies and Weak States: State-Society Relations and State Capabilities in the Third World* (Princeton, N.J.: Princeton University Press, 1988), p. 262; Ayoob, "Security Problematic of the Third World," p. 268; Lawrence E. Harrison, *Underdevelopment is a State of Mind: The Latin American Case* (Lanham, Md.: University Press of America, 1985).
8. There are, of course, exceptions to this overall lack of development. Taiwan, Cuba, North and South Korea, and Israel all developed modern, cohesive states in relatively short times. These exceptions should not obscure the fact that most of the countries in the Third World have not been able to develop into strong states and (as will be discussed below) show few signs of doing so.
9. Clapham, *Third World Politics*, p. 18.
10. Anthony D. Smith, "State-Making and Nation-Building," in John A. Hall, ed., *States in History* (New York: Basil Blackwell, 1986), pp. 252–253.

Rather than facing the difficult (although feasible) task of imposing one group's identity on subordinate groups, many Third World states confront the far more problematic challenge of creating an identity in the first place. Such an undertaking is complicated by the presence of ethnic groups fighting for the control of the state or for the right to secede and establish their own state. Building a united state is also hampered by the lack of a common past among differing ethnic groups. Without a common history and culture to build upon, it is difficult to reach a consensus on present and future policies. How do you appeal to the needs of the "people" when there is no "people" to begin with?[11]

Ethnic fragmentation creates problems among states as well as within them. In some cases, colonial borders divided a single ethnic group among many states (e.g., Ogaden Somalis inhabit Somalia, Ethiopia, Kenya, and Djibouti). Since many in the ethnic group owe allegiance to their group over the state, and since some states will seek to exploit that allegiance to bring members of the group under its jurisdiction, the outcome is often continued tension, at times erupting into war.[12] The denial of statehood to certain ethnic groups (e.g., the Kurds in the Middle East) has also created conflict and instability as these groups seek to rule themselves, while existing states act to suppress their moves towards self-determination. Whether it is a drive towards statehood, secession, or autonomy, colonialism's inattention to the needs of ethnic groups has created instability throughout the Third World, and laid the basis for perpetual conflict and outside intervention.[13]

The timing of gaining independence by Third World states has also contributed to their instability. In Western Europe, state building took place before the view had taken hold that each ethnic group deserved its own state. In the Third World, states were created at a time when ethnic nationalism had gained wide acceptance.[14] Western European state makers had the

---

11. On these points, see Smith, "State-Making and Nation-Building," pp. 241–244, 253, 256, 262. On the more general question of ethnic conflict, see Donald L. Horowitz, *Ethnic Groups in Conflict* (Berkeley: University of California Press, 1985).

12. On the role of ethnicity in conflict on the Horn, see I.M. Lewis, *A Modern History of Somalia* (London: Longman, 1980), esp. pp. 221–222; see also Christopher Clapham, *Transformation and Continuity in Revolutionary Ethiopia* (Cambridge: Cambridge University Press, 1987); Bereket Habte Selassie, *Conflict and Intervention in the Horn of Africa* (New York: Monthly Review Press, 1980).

13. Ayoob, "Security Problematic of the Third World," pp. 271–272. On the problems of ethnicity and secession, see Alexis Heraclides, "Secessionist Minorities and External Involvement," *International Organization*, Vol. 44, No. 3 (Summer 1990); Crawford Young, "The Temple of Ethnicity," *World Politics*, Vol. 35 (July 1983), pp. 652–662.

14. Smith, "State-Making and Nation-Building," pp. 253, 257.

luxury of forging their countries before the emergence of mass political participation. Third World state makers, on the other hand, need to build a state with a relatively well-educated citizenry who seek involvement in the affairs of the state.[15] That many Third World states lack the institutions to channel mass participation and mediate disputes further exacerbates the problems confronting Third World governments.[16] Moreover, Third World leaders, like all leaders, need effective social control to build a strong state. During the era of colonialism, however, many of the outside powers deliberately destroyed the indigenous bonds of social control in order better to rule over their territories. This weakened social control became embedded in many Third World societies, creating a fragility that persists today.[17]

The inability to form strong states has led to internal warfare throughout the Third World. Although obscured by the events of the recent Gulf War, most of the wars and threats to governments in the Third World are internal. Coups d'état, revolutions, insurgencies, and civil conflicts dominate the landscape of the Third World.[18] Recent or continuing internal conflicts have taken place in Afghanistan, India, Sri Lanka, Cambodia, Somalia, Ethiopia, Angola, Sudan, Chad, El Salvador, Guatemala, Peru, Nicaragua, Iraq, and many other Third World states. There is no indication that this prevalence of internal warfare will abate in the near future.

Interstate Warfare in the Third World

The persistence of internal warfare is especially worrisome since it has been a major cause of the interstate warfare that has been all too common throughout the Third World. Internal disorder provokes international conflict as neighboring states act to prevent instability from spreading to them, as India

---

15. Stein Rokkan, "Dimensions of State Formation and Nation-Building: A Possible Paradigm for Research on Variations within Europe," in Tilly, ed., *The Formation of National States in Western Europe*, p. 598.
16. The lack of effective political institutions among the developing countries is a principal theme of Samuel Huntington's landmark work, *Political Order in Changing Societies* (New Haven: Yale University Press, 1968).
17. Migdal, *Strong Societies and Weak States*, pp. 271–273.
18. J. David Singer and Melvin Small, *Resort to Arms: International and Civil Wars, 1816–1980* (Beverly Hills, Calif.: Sage, 1982), pp. 92–95, 98–99, 229–232. For additional treatment of this point, see Steven R. David, *Choosing Sides: Alignment and Realignment in the Third World* (Baltimore: Johns Hopkins University Press, 1991) p. 12; and John Lewis Gaddis, "The Long Peace: Elements of Stability in the Postwar International System," *International Security*, Vol. 10, No. 4 (Spring 1986), p. 112.

did when it supported the efforts of Bangladesh to secede in 1971. Leaders will be inclined to go to war to divert attention from domestic difficulties, as occurred when Argentina invaded the Falklands in 1982. Domestic instability might leave a country too weak to suppress sub-national groups who are left free to provoke attacks from bordering states, with such results as the Israeli invasion of Lebanon in 1982. Internal instability can create the impression that a foe has been so weakened that a "window of opportunity" for invasion has been opened, as seen in Somalia's 1977 assault on Ethiopia.[19]

Interstate warfare is also likely to be an ever-present feature of the Third World because its causes are firmly rooted in the politics and behavior of many Third World states. Third World leaders make war because they rationally conclude that war is in their interests. This is in marked contrast with Western Europe, where war has become virtually obsolete for two main reasons. First, the benefits of conquest have dramatically declined over time. Increasingly, a country's wealth is dependent on knowledge-based forms of production, which in turn are dependent upon a skilled, free population with access to many sources of information. The link between territory and power has thus been broken.[20] The cost of conquering other states has also risen. The development of new weapons has made conquest less attractive because leaders recognize the catastrophic costs that war might entail. Nuclear weapons are especially good at deterring aggression by states since any country with an invulnerable second-strike force can protect itself from more powerful adversaries by threatening them with total destruction.[21]

19. On the relationship between domestic instability and interstate war, see Jack S. Levy, "Domestic Politics and War," in Robert I. Rotberg and Theodore K. Rabb, eds., *The Origin and Prevention of Major Wars* (Cambridge: University of Cambridge Press, 1988), especially pp. 94, 98–99; Richard Ned Lebow, *Between Peace and War: The Nature of International Crisis* (Baltimore: Johns Hopkins University Press, 1981) esp. pp. 66–71; and Jonathan Wilkenfeld, "Domestic and Foreign Conflict Behavior of Nations," *Journal of Peace Research*, Vol. 5 (1968), pp. 56–69. For an argument that the primary cause of international peace in Europe from 1740 to 1960 was internal stability, see Richard Rosecrance, *Action and Reaction in World Politics* (Boston: Little, Brown and Company, 1963).
20. Stephen Van Evera, "Primed for Peace: Europe After the Cold War," *International Security*, Vol. 15, No. 3 (Winter 1990/91), p. 14; Carl Kaysen, "Is War Obsolete?" *International Security*, Vol. 14, No. 4 (Spring 1990), pp. 49, 50, 53. On knowledge as a basis for production, see Lynn Krieger Mytelka, "Knowledge-Intensive Production and the Changing Internationalization Strategies of Multinational Firms," in James A. Caporaso, ed., *A Changing International Division of Labor* (Boulder, Colo.: Lynne Rienner, 1987).
21. The best account of the ways in which nuclear weapons inhibit war is Kenneth Waltz, *The Spread of Nuclear Weapons: More May be Better*, Adelphi Paper No. 171 (London: International Institute of Strategic Studies [IISS], 1981). On this point, see also John J. Mearsheimer, "Back to the Future: Instability in Europe After the Cold War," *International Security*, Vol. 15, No. 1 (Summer 1990), pp. 19–20; Van Evera, "Primed for Peace," pp. 12–14.

These conditions promoting peace do not apply to the Third World. With some notable exceptions (especially in East Asia), the skills of the workforce are not a major component of most Third World countries' strength. As the Arab-Israeli dispute demonstrates, land is still viewed as critical for security because it is a potential staging area for invasion, a possible site for the deployment of threatening weaponry, and because it is needed to control such vital resources as water. In some areas of the world, land might not be a direct contributor to wealth and power, but as shown by the Iraqi invasion of Kuwait, seizing another country's territory (and oil) is still seen as a way to quick enrichment. Nuclear weapons also cannot be counted upon to pacify the Third World. Most Third World states do not have nuclear weapons and are thus denied the deterrent effect they carry. More important, as discussed below, the possession of nuclear weapons is less likely to deter war among Third World states than states outside of the Third World.

Third World states are more likely to go to war, in part because public support for war is likely to be greater in the Third World than elsewhere. Militarism and hyper-nationalism have both declined markedly in Western Europe.[22] Because West European states are democratic, West European leaders would need the support of their people to go to war. With the decline of hyper-nationalism and militarism, and the realization that war would not benefit them, the West European people are less likely to provide that support.[23] In the Third World, however, militarism and hyper-nationalism are still very much alive. Enemies are vilified and dehumanized in the press and textbooks; class differences within states are great, raising the possibility of going to war to justify the privileged position of the elite; and the glories of military struggle are celebrated. Because of the persistence of hyper-nationalism and militarism fed by nationalist, ethnic, and religious fervor, it is far easier to mobilize armies for war in the Third World than elsewhere.[24]

The religious beliefs of many Third World states may also make them less resistant to going to war. The chief concern of the United States and the West lies with fundamentalist Islamic regimes. This is not because Islam is any more warlike than other religions such as Judaism or Christianity. Rather, the concern is that fundamentalists of any religion might pursue extreme

---

22. Van Evera, "Primed for Peace," pp. 18–24, 26–27; Kaysen, "Is War Obsolete?" p. 58.
23. Kaysen, "Is War Obsolete?" p. 57.
24. Eliot A. Cohen, "Distant Battles: Modern War in the Third World," *International Security,* Vol. 10, No. 4 (Spring 1986), pp. 168–169.

policies leading to war. Islamic fundamentalists are a particular worry because they have already come to power in two states (Iran and the Sudan), nearly came to power in a third (Algeria), and potentially can come to power in many more. That Islamic fundamentalism is most likely to attain power in the Middle East, a region where the stakes for the West are so high, enhances the threat to American interests. Since Islamic fundamentalists share a belief that the West is immoral and corrupt, and are prepared to act to spread their beliefs, their gaining control of states raises legitimate concerns that Islam will be selectively interpreted by some Third World leaders to mobilize their populations for war.[25]

Because Third World cultures differ from those of the West, deterring Third World states from engaging in war may be more difficult. Successful deterrence requires convincing adversaries not to undertake actions because their costs would be greater than their benefits. Deterrence will only work if one side can successfully signal to an adversary what the costs of its behavior will be, and if it correctly judged those costs to be unacceptable to its adversary. Culture includes a learned set of attitudes, beliefs, and sentiments, and thus when dealing with different cultures misunderstandings in signalling intentions are more likely.[26] Moreover, it will be far more difficult to determine just what constitutes an unacceptable cost for a different culture. The lack of experience in dealing with a specific adversary, as opposed to the learning that comes with long-term dealings with a country, as was the case with the U.S.-Soviet relationship, further complicates understanding another's culture and achieving successful deterrence. For precisely these reasons, American deterrence failures in Vietnam have been blamed on the misunderstandings that arise when different cultures interact.[27]

The ideologies of many Third World states are more supportive of war than ideological beliefs held elsewhere. Even during the Cold War, neither

25. For a general study of Western and Islamic attitudes towards war, see James Turner Johnson and John Kelsay, eds., *Cross, Crescent and Sword: The Justification and Limitation of War in Western and Islamic Traditions* (New York: Greenwood Press, 1990). For a discussion of Jewish attitudes toward war as seen in religious writings, see Efraim Inbar, "War in the Jewish Tradition," *The Jerusalem Journal of International Relations*, Vol. 9, No. 2 (June 1987), pp. 83–99. For a recent account of the prospects for Islamic fundamentalism spreading throughout the Middle East and the Central Asian republics of the former Soviet Union, see *The Economist*, April 4–10, 1992, pp. 47–49.

26. See, for example, Robert Jervis, Richard Ned Lebow, and Janice Gross Stein, eds., *Psychology and Deterrence* (Baltimore: Johns Hopkins University Press, 1985), pp. 10, 28–29, 210–211.

27. On imposing American values and thinking on Vietnam, see for example Stanley Karnow, *Vietnam: A History* (New York: Viking Press, 1983) pp. 18, 482.

of the superpowers sought war, nor did either seek the destruction of the other side. The United States and the Soviet Union successfully subordinated their ideological differences to the common goal of maintaining order.[28] More broadly, West European countries have assimilated the social ideas and attitudes of peace.[29] In the Third World, however, ideologically driven religious, ethnic, and political hatreds persist. Third World states openly seek the destruction of their neighbors, as seen in Arab calls for the elimination of Israel, Indonesia's brutal suppression of East Timor, and Iraq's attempted incorporation of Kuwait. There have been no fundamental changes in ideas and attitudes in much of the Third World that would make war obsolete.

The prevalence of revolutionary states in the Third World also enhances the prospects for war. All of the self-proclaimed revolutionary states are in the Third World. They are more prone to conflict because they are more likely to seek to impose their ideological beliefs on other countries. This can lead to war, as neighboring states either resist their expansion or preemptively attack out of fear that such expansion is imminent. Iraq's invasion of Iran is a clear example of a country seeking to prevent the spread of revolutionary zeal by attempting to topple its adversary's regime. In addition, revolutionary regimes often fear counter-revolution, leading them to attack countries they believe are supporting their opponents. Nicaragua's actions against Honduras, North Vietnam's war with South Vietnam, and Libya's invasion of Chad were all efforts to prevent foreign-backed counter-revolutionaries from overthrowing a revolutionary regime.[30] It is not surprising that revolutionary Third World states such as Libya, Cuba, Nicaragua, and Vietnam have all been involved in a large number of wars and conflicts.

The absence of democracy in the Third World also contributes to war. As Michael Doyle persuasively argues, democratic states are less likely to go to war with one another.[31] The belief that one's own republic is just leads one to respect other democratic states and not interfere in their policies. Democracies do not generally assert claims to rule over other democracies; their checks and balances make it more difficult to make the decision to go to war;

---

28. Gaddis, "The Long Peace," pp. 126–131.
29. For a persuasive argument that changes in the values of the developed states are an important contributor to peace, see John Mueller, *Retreat from Doomsday: The Obsolescence of Major War* (New York: Basic Books, 1989).
30. Van Evera, "Primed for Peace," p. 30.
31. One of the best arguments for why democracy helps produce peace is by Michael Doyle, "Kant, Liberal Legacies, and Foreign Affairs," parts 1 and 2, *Philosophy and Public Affairs*, Vol. 12, No. 3 and No. 4 (Summer and Fall 1983), pp. 205–235 and 325–353.

they encourage free speech, thus dampening hyper-nationalism; and they emphasize the non-violent resolution of conflict. While it is premature to conclude that democratic states will never go to war with one another, the absence of such wars is a strong indication that democracy does inhibit conflict when other democracies are concerned. Because most Third World governments are not democratic, the peace inducing-effects of democracy are largely unavailable.[32]

Western Europe and the United States have been fortunate that since World War II there have been few domestic groups pushing for war.[33] This is in marked contrast to the time preceding World War I when, for example, the German Junkers pushed for aggression to justify their privileged position, or before World War II when Japanese militarists brought Tokyo into war. Some Third World states, however, continue to have domestic constituencies who benefit from continued conflict. Syria's Haffez Assad benefits from continued war in the Middle East to justify rule in a country where his religious group, the Alawites, are a small minority.[34] Somalia's Siad Barre invaded Ethiopia in part to gain the support of ethnic Somalis living near Somalia's border with Ethiopia.[35]

Third World leaders are not restrained from going to war even when public support for war is weak. Since most Third World countries are not democracies, the leadership does not depend on the people's support for war. Equally important, Third World leaders no longer need to fear that a loss in war will inevitably mean a loss of power. Improved capabilities for suppression have made Third World leaders less vulnerable to the uprisings, coups, or revolutions that often follow military setbacks. Whereas defeat in the 1967 Middle East war helped bring about the downfall of the leader of Syria, defeat in the 1973 war did little to threaten Assad's rule. Saddam Hussein is vivid proof that a ruthless leader can survive eight years of ruinous stalemate with one adversary and a crushing defeat by another. Somalia's Siad Barre, Egypt's

32. For a list of countries that are not democratic, see Raymond D. Gastil, *Freedom in the World: Political Rights and Civil Liberties, 1988–1989* (New York, Freedom House, 1989), pp. 70–71.
33. On how domestic influences helped keep the peace during the Cold War, see Gaddis, "The Long Peace," pp. 114–119.
34. Daniel Pipes, "Is Damascus Ready for Peace?" *Foreign Affairs*, Vol. 70, No. 4 (Fall 1991), p. 38.
35. Lewis, *A Modern History of Somalia*, pp. 221–2; Marina Ottaway, *Soviet and American Influence in the Horn of Africa* (New York: Praeger, 1982), pp. 82, 173.

Anwar Sadat, and Iran's Ayatollah Khomeini are further examples of Third World leaders whose military losses did little to shake their hold on power.[36]

The absence of constraints on going to war for Third World leaders is critical because most Third World countries are led by a narrow elite. This elite tends to be alienated from the population at large and focused on meeting its own narrow interests, the most important of which is remaining in power. If a Third World leadership judges that going to war will enhance its prospects of remaining in power (by, for example, increasing the wealth available for distribution to key domestic groups), it is likely that it will choose war.[37] This will be so even if war might not be in the broader national interest. Since it is more likely that war will serve some narrow group than the society at large, basing the decision to go to war on the interests of a small elite makes that decision more likely. That power is concentrated in the Third World also facilitates the decision for war by removing potential dissenters.[38]

The Bleak Future of the Third World

For the foreseeable future, the end of the Cold War will do little to improve the lot of Third World states and in one crucial aspect—interstate warfare— the condition of the Third World is likely to get much worse. Those who see hope for a more stable Third World often look to economic growth. After all, if the newly industrializing countries (NICs) such as Taiwan, Singapore, Hong Kong, and South Korea have gained an appreciable amount of stability from their export-driven economic prowess, why cannot others follow their example? Putting aside for the moment the uncertain future of at least some of the NIC success stories (Hong Kong is scheduled to be absorbed by the People's Republic of China in 1997, and South Korea faces a major military threat from a potentially nuclear-armed North Korea), the prospect that many Third World countries will emulate the NICs is low. Generating wealth by exporting to the developed states is extremely difficult due to a slackening

---

36. Cohen, "Distant Battles," pp. 166–167 makes a similar point.
37. On how concerns for his political survival helped lead Saddam Hussein to invade Kuwait, see Efraim Karsh and Inari Rautsi, *Saddam Hussein: A Political Biography* (New York: Free Press, 1991), ch. 9.
38. On the importance of focusing on Third World leaders to understand Third World foreign policy, see David, *Choosing Sides: Alignment and Realignment in the Third World*, esp. ch. 1.

of global demand for goods produced in the Third World and increased protectionism in economic sectors where the Third World does well (e.g., textiles). Developing high technology industries is also problematic given the lack of an educational base in most Third World countries. The declining costs of raw materials, especially when compared with manufactured goods, and the diminishing role played by labor in the cost of goods further impedes Third World economic development. Moreover, it is now argued that the success of Asian NICs has much to do with the fact that they are all strong states—a missing ingredient throughout much of the Third World. It is not surprising that few if any Third World countries have duplicated the performance of the NICs, or are expected to do so in the near future.[39]

Nor can democracy be looked upon as a savior for the Third World. Despite some impressive (but possibly short-lived) gains in Latin America, democracy shows few signs of sweeping the Third World. Before democracy can take root, certain conditions are usually necessary. They include reasonably equitable divisions of wealth and land, high levels of education, cultural norms supportive of democratic rule, and the absence of significant internal strife and ethnic conflict.[40] These conditions are not met in the vast majority of Third World states and show few signs of developing.

The exploding population of the Third World further complicates the attainment of political stability. In the Third World of today, the population pressures forecast by Malthus are coming true, but the remedies that precluded disaster elsewhere are not available. Almost all projections predict much greater population growth in the Third World than in the developed world. Most of the world's people already live in the Third World and the

---

39. Robin Broad and John Cavanagh, "No More NICs," *Foreign Policy*, No. 72 (Fall 1988), pp. 81–101. For another pessimistic assessment of Third World development prospects, see Peter Drucker, "The Changed World Economy," *Foreign Affairs*, Vol. 64, No. 4 (Spring 1986), pp. 768–791.

40. For more on the problems and preconditions of establishing democracy, see Samuel P. Huntington, *The Third Wave: Democratization in the Late Twentieth Century* (Norman, Okla.: University of Oklahoma Press, 1991); Robert A. Dahl, *Polyarchy: Participation and Opposition* (New Haven: Yale University Press, 1971), pp. 48–188; and Seymour Martin Lipset, *Political Man: The Social Bases of Politics* (Baltimore: Johns Hopkins University Press, 1981), pp. 27–63. For why the United States cannot and should not attempt to impose democracy in the Third World, see Stephen Van Evera, "The United States and the Third World: When to Intervene?" in Kenneth Oye, Robert Lieber, and Donald Rothchild, eds., *Eagle in a New World: American Grand Strategy in the Post–Cold War World* (New York: HarperCollins, 1992), pp. 117–122. For a more optimistic view on the spread of democracy (but one which acknowledges that it may take a long time), see Francis Fukuyama, *The End of History and the Last Man* (New York: Basic Books, 1992).

population of the Third World is doubling every 25 years.[41] There are few signs that the Third World will be able to cope with this explosive growth.

Environmental changes such as global warming, deforestation, and topsoil erosion are also likely to complicate Third World efforts to achieve stability. Such changes are likely to lead to reduced food production and economic decline. Poor countries will be especially hard-hit because they lack the resources to deal with environmentally related problems (for example, by building better dikes and dams to prevent floods), and their political institutions are more likely to be too weak to cope with the disruptions they cause. As a result, any growth in GNP will probably be absorbed by increased problems caused by a changing environment. Internal instability will increase as Third World governments lack the ability to deal with mounting difficulties; resort to dictatorial control and increased repression may result. Externally, increased warfare among Third World states can be expected due to conflicts over resources such as clean water and productive land. Conflicts may also increase between Third World and non–Third World countries as the Third World attempts to redress the growing gap in living standards exacerbated by the impact of the environment.[42] Far from getting better, conditions in the Third World—and the prospects for peace—are likely to worsen over time.[43]

The End of the Superpower Competition and Third World Conflict

Despite the initial benefits of the end of the Cold War, the withdrawal of the United States and the former Soviet Union from the Third World is likely to

---

41. By 2025, it is estimated that 84 percent of the earth's population will reside in the developing states. While in the early 1990s many of the industrialized democracies are among the most populous of countries, by 2025, only the United States and Japan will be in the top twenty countries by population. Of special interest to the United States, from 1940 to 1980 Mexico's population tripled from 20 million to 67 million. At present, it is 88 million and climbing rapidly. See Nicholas Eberstadt, "Population Change and National Security," *Foreign Affairs*, Vol. 70, No. 3 (Summer 1991), pp. 117–118; and Kimberly A. Hamilton and Kate Holder, "International Migration and Foreign Policy: A Survey of the Literature," *The Washington Quarterly*, Vol. 14, No. 2 (Spring 1991), p. 195.

42. These points are persuasively made in Thomas Homer-Dixon, "On the Threshold: Environmental Changes as Causes of Acute Conflict," *International Security*, Vol. 16, No. 2 (Fall 1991), especially pp. 78, 88, 106. See also Jessica Tuchman Mathews, "Redefining Security," *Foreign Affairs*, Vol. 68, No. 2 (Spring 1989), pp. 162–177.

43. For a similar view that, because of the capability and behavior of Third World governments, the prospects of the Third World will not appreciably improve in the near future, see Robert H. Jackson, *Quasi-States: Sovereignty, International Relations, and the Third World* (Cambridge: Cambridge University Press, 1990), especially pp. 189–190.

produce *greater* conflict among Third World states. It is true that the end of the superpower competition might help end some wars in the Third World. Movements towards peace in regional conflicts in the Middle East, Southeast Asia, and Southern Africa give cause for hope. But most conflicts in the Third World have had indigenous sources. The superpowers may have exacerbated tensions, but those tensions existed before superpower involvement and will persist after their departure. The continuing conflicts in Afghanistan, Somalia, and the Sudan attest to the resilience and indigenous roots of Third World conflict.[44]

More important, the lessening of American and Soviet influence in the Third World will weaken an important constraint on interstate war. The United States and the Soviet Union frequently acted to prevent the outbreak of war to avoid a client being defeated, a superpower confrontation, or being dragged into a conflict.[45] Perhaps if the Soviet Union had maintained influence over Iraq, Baghdad's 1990 invasion of Kuwait would never have happened. With the Cold War over, leaders desirous of enriching themselves will be able to prey on wealthier neighbors free from the concern that those neighbors are protected by the United States or the Soviet Union. Ethnic, religious, and border disputes will be likely more than ever lead to conflict.

The superpowers also often acted as a restraining influence once wars had broken out, mitigating the anarchy of the Third World. The superpowers played a major role in ending wars in the Middle East, between India and Pakistan, and in Angola, Ethiopia, and Cambodia. The role of the superpowers was especially pronounced when the existence of a state was threatened. Previously, especially in the Middle East, one or both of the superpowers would intervene to preserve the territorial integrity of the countries. Now, except for extreme cases such as Kuwait, whose oil derived–importance is not linked to the old superpower competition, great power interventions to

44. For a similar argument, see Ayoob, "The Security Problematic of the Third World," pp. 281–283.
45. For example, the Soviet Union attempted to restrain Sadat from going to war in the early 1970s, and the United States was largely successful in the late 1970s and early 1980s in dissuading Somalia from attacking Ethiopia. On the Soviet Union, see Anwar Sadat, *In Search of Identity: An Autobiography* (New York: Harper and Row, 1978); and George Breslauer, "Soviet Policy in the Middle East, 1967–1972: Unalterable Antagonism or Collaborative Competition?" in Alexander L. George, ed., *Managing U.S.–Soviet Rivalry: Problems of Crisis Prevention* (Boulder, Colo.: Westview Press, 1983), pp. 65–106. On the United States and Somalia, see David Korn, *Ethiopia, the United States, and the Soviet Union* (Carbondale: Southern Illinois University Press, 1986), pp. 74, 75; Cyrus Vance, *Hard Choices: Critical Years in America's Foreign Policy* (New York: Simon and Schuster, 1983), p. 88.

preserve the existence of Third World states may become a relic of the past. Wars in the Third World will continue, only there will be less chance that other states will intervene to stop them.

The Increasing Capability of the Third World to Threaten American Interests

Even a Third World prone to instability and conflict is not necessarily of concern to the United States. However, many Third World states, predisposed to war, are also increasingly capable of threatening the United States and its allies. After a discussion of how the Third World can damage American interests, specific ways in which they are likely to do so are considered in this section.

First, American import dependence on foreign oil has steadily increased to the point where for the first time in history foreign suppliers now meet over half of U.S. petroleum needs. American allies are even worse off, with foreign oil accounting for more than 60 percent of West European requirements and almost all of Japan's needs.[46] The demand for oil will in all probability rise due to the emergence of newly industrialized states (especially in Asia) and the decrease in energy efficiency after a decade of low oil prices. Meanwhile, the supply of oil to meet this rising demand will almost surely decrease over time; no new big oil fields are waiting to be exploited, and former major oil producers such as the United States and the former Soviet Union have experienced major declines in production. Foreign investment in the former Soviet Union may result in increases of production, but no one knows if major deposits exist to be exploited or, if such deposits exist, whether the necessary actions will be undertaken to do so.[47] A major

46. Senate Committee on Finance, Subcommittee on Energy and Agricultural Taxation, *Dependence on Foreign Oil*, 101st Cong., 2d sess., July 27, 1990 (Washington, D.C.: U.S. Government Printing Office [U.S. GPO], 1990), p. 2; Department of Energy, *Energy Security: A Report to the President of the United States* (Washington, D.C.: U.S. GPO, March 1987). For more detailed statistics on American imports of foreign oil, see Energy Information Administration, *Petroleum Supply Annual, 1987*, Vol. 2 (Washington, D.C.: U.S. GPO, June 2, 1988), esp. pp. 172–230 (table 15).

47. Edward Morse, "The Coming Oil Revolution," *Foreign Affairs*, Vol. 69, No. 5. (Winter 1990/1991), pp. 39, 43, 44. See also Matthew L. Wald, "U.S. Oil Output Drops: Consumption Also Falls," *New York Times*, January 16, 1992 p. D1. Edward H. Murphy of the American Petroleum Institute is quoted as stating, "It's quite possible that the age of major domestic production is coming to an end." On the Soviet side, it is reported that by the end of 1993, there will be a production drop of 20 percent as compared to 1991. See Celestine Bohlen, "Russians Take a

portion of the shortfall will have to be made up by the Persian Gulf states that possess nearly 70 percent of the world's excess production capacity and are the likely locale of any new major oil finds.[48]

Even if the United States somehow reduces its dependence on Persian Gulf oil, a disruption in supply would severely hurt American interests. The United States is obligated to share its oil with its Western allies as part of the International Energy Agency agreement, and a cutoff in the Gulf would surely spur competition for remaining sources of oil, producing major price increases. For the global market, what is critical is not so much where the oil comes from but how much is available for purchase. Oil is a fungible commodity. If Persian Gulf oil is kept from going to market, the worldwide supply would dramatically decrease and the price of all oil would rise markedly. Although efforts to reduce reliance on foreign oil (e.g., establishment of petroleum reserves, conservation) have helped some, it appears increasingly certain that the economies of the United States and the West will remain dependent on the Persian Gulf states for the foreseeable future.[49]

The second way in which Third World states can endanger American interests is in their ability to threaten the United States and other countries militarily. Approximately a dozen Third World countries have or are attempting to develop nuclear weapons. This group includes Libya, Iraq, Iran, and North Korea, who are avowed enemies of the United States and its allies.[50] As the near development of nuclear weapons by Iraq demonstrated, international inspection in a country and formal adherence to the Non-Proliferation Treaty is not enough to prevent it from acquiring nuclear arms. The Iraqi episode is further evidence of how little the United States knows about the developing nuclear capabilities of Third World states, including those

---

Flier on Oil in Capitalism for the Masses," *New York Times*, January 19, 1992, p. A1. For a dissenting view that challenges the notion that oil (or any other commodity) will become increasingly scarce, see Julian L. Simon, *The Ultimate Resource* (Princeton: Princeton University Press, 1981), especially pp. 42–50.

48. American imports of Persian Gulf oil have already increased 450 percent from 1985, and have reached a point where the Arab OPEC countries supply the United States with approximately 25 percent of its import needs (about 13 percent of total petroleum requirements). Energy Information Administration, *Monthly Energy Review, October 1991* (Washington, D.C.: U.S. GPO, 1991), Table 1.8, "U.S. Dependence on Petroleum Net Imports," p. 13. Senate Committee on Finance, *Dependence on Foreign Oil*, p. 2; Department of Energy, *Energy Security*, p. 50.

49. Senate Committee on Finance, *Dependence on Foreign Oil*, p. 2; Department of Energy, *Energy Security*, pp. 2, 10, 35, 27, 36.

50. For a comprehensive assessment of proliferation prospects, see Leonard S. Spector with Jacqueline R. Smith, *Nuclear Ambitions* (Boulder, Colo.: Westview Press, 1990).

that are its adversaries. A small number of nuclear weapons directed against the United States or an ally would do catastrophic damage, and an effective defense against nuclear attack has not been devised. Far from allaying U.S. fears, the disintegration of the USSR has exacerbated concerns about nuclear proliferation. Not only has the restraining influence of the USSR on global proliferation been lost, there are also thousands of Soviet nuclear scientists now out of work who may be tempted to offer their services to Third World bidders. Several of the countries who are most likely to take advantage of the expertise of emigrating Soviet scientists, such as Cuba and Syria, are of special concern to the United States because of their support of terrorism and anti-American actions.[51] Moreover, the breakup of the Soviet Union has raised fears that nuclear weapons will be—or may already have been—transferred to Third World countries.[52]

The spread of chemical and biological weapons is also cause for alarm. As many as twenty-four countries (most in the Third World) either have or are actively seeking to acquire chemical weapons.[53] Chemical arms are relatively easy to develop and can be delivered by weapons already in virtually every Third World arsenal, such as aircraft and artillery. When used effectively, chemical weapons can kill 40 to 700 times as many people (depending on weather and other conditions) as a comparable conventional weapon. Biological weapons—living organisms that spread such as anthrax—are probably in the arsenals of four Third World countries (Iraq, Syria, North Korea, and Taiwan). They are exceedingly difficult to defend against, requiring the inoculation of the population before an attack, and even then the effectiveness of such a measure is in doubt. Biological weapons are very lethal; an effective attack could kill as many people as a small nuclear weapon.[54]

---

51. For an account of how the USSR helped the cause of non-proliferation, see Joseph Pilat, "The Major Suppliers: A Baseline for Comparison," in William C. Potter, ed., *International Nuclear Trade and Non-Proliferation: The Challenge of the Emerging Suppliers* (Lexington, Mass,: Lexington Books, 1990), p. 53. On concerns that Soviet scientists will sell their expertise in the Third World, see, for example, Eric Schmitt, "U.S. Aides Worry About Spread of Arms From Sales by the Soviets," *New York Times*, November 16, 1991, p. 5; and Elaine Sciolino, "Iraqis Could Pose a Threat Soon, CIA Chief Says," *New York Times*, January 16, 1992, p. A9.
52. See, for example, Philip J. Hilts, "Tally of Ex-Soviets' A-Arms Stirs Worry," *New York Times*, March 16, 1992, p. A3, noting unconfirmed reports that two or three tactical nuclear weapons missing from Kazakhstan may have wound up in neighboring Iran.
53. Elisa D. Harris, "Chemical Weapons Proliferation: Current Capabilities and Prospects for Control," in Aspen Strategy Group, *New Threats: Responding to the Proliferation of Nuclear, Chemical and Delivery Capabilities in the Third World* (Lanham, Md.: University Press of America, 1990); Steve Fetter, "Ballistic Missiles and Weapons of Mass Destruction: What is the Threat? What Should be Done?" *International Security*, Vol. 16, No. 1 (Summer 1991), p. 14.
54. Fetter, "Ballistic Missiles and Weapons of Mass Destruction," pp. 14, 22, 24–28. For addi-

Nuclear, chemical, and biological weapons are even more threatening when mounted on ballistic missiles. According to the Stockholm International Peace Research Institute (SIPRI), approximately twenty-five countries (most in the Third World), have or are developing ballistic missiles.[55] All of the Third World countries that have or are developing nuclear, chemical, and biological weapons also either have or are developing ballistic missiles.[56] These weapons are especially destabilizing because defense against them is virtually impossible, which increases the motivation to preempt in a crisis.[57] Even against the antiquated Scuds of Iraq, Patriot defensive missiles were not nearly as successful as initially believed.[58] As the ranges of ballistic missiles increase, American allies and the United States itself can become targets. [59] Moreover, for Third World states that are unable to develop or acquire ballistic missiles, cruise missiles (essentially flying torpedoes) may be the weapon of choice. Cruise missiles are relatively easy to develop and are fully capable of delivering weapons of mass destruction to targets on America's coasts from off-shore ships with devastating accuracy.

The increasing ability of Third World countries to strike out at the United States and its allies is also seen in the conventional arena. Third World countries are busily acquiring huge amounts of arms, some of which are equal to the best in the arsenals of the great powers. This reflects the willingness of arms sellers such as the United States, the former Soviet Union, Britain, France, and China to sell their most modern weaponry and technology.[60] The collapse of the Soviet Union could well increase the spread of arms as the former Soviet republics sell advanced weaponry to gain hard

---

tional lists of countries suspected of having nuclear, chemical, or biological weapons, see Geoffrey Kemp, "Regional Security, Arms Control, and the End of the Cold War," *Washington Quarterly*, Vol. 13, No. 4 (Autumn 1990), p. 38.

55. Aaron Karp, "Ballistic Missile Proliferation," in Stockholm International Peace Research Institute (SIPRI), *SIPRI Yearbook 1990* (Oxford: Oxford University Press, 1990).

56. Fetter, "Ballistic Missiles and Weapons of Mass Destruction," p. 14.

57. On the dangers of ballistic missiles, see Mark A. Heller, "Coping with Missile Proliferation in the Middle East," *Orbis*, Vol. 35, No. 1 (Winter 1991) pp. 15–28. For an argument that missile proliferation is not that significant (because of their lack of range, and the ability of aircraft to perform the same functions), see Uzi Rubin, "How Much Does Proliferation Matter?" *Orbis*, Vol. 35, No. 1 (Winter 1991), pp. 29–39.

58. Theodore A. Postol, "Lessons from the Gulf War Patriot Experience," *International Security*, Vol. 16, No. 3 (Fall 1991), pp. 119–171.

59. For a view that Iraq was well on its way to building a ballistic missile that could reach New York, see Kathleen C. Bailey, "Can Missile Proliferation Be Reversed?" *Orbis*, Vol. 35, No. 1 (Winter 1991), p. 5.

60. Geoffrey Kemp, "Regional Security, Arms Control, and the End of the Cold War," p. 37.

currency and keep their weapons industry alive.[61] With both the United States and the former Soviet Union reducing their own arsenals, pressures to sell in the Third World are likely to increase. Many Third World countries also produce their own weapons. Argentina, Brazil, India, Israel, and South Korea each manufactures the four major types of arms—aircraft, armor, missiles, and naval vessels.[62] Equally important is the growing number of Third World countries that produce basic ammunition and weapons, such as Egypt, Pakistan, China, and Singapore.[63] These arms lack the high profile of technologically advanced weapons, but do much of the killing and cause much of the destruction in wars in the Third World.

While there is debate as to just how much these developments free the Third World from dependence for arms on the great powers, it is clear that the growth in the number of weapons suppliers combined with indigenous production has decreased America's ability to control Third World conflicts.[64] The availability of arms from many sources makes it easier for Third World countries to initiate wars to resolve disputes and will allow Third World countries to persist in wars that the United States and its allies may wish stopped. The days when the United States or the Soviet Union could end a conflict simply by withholding arms are clearly at an end.[65]

How Third World Instability Combined With Growing Power Threatens American Interests

Even if it is accepted that Third World states are likely to remain unstable and conflict-ridden, that American dependence on Persian Gulf oil will grow,

---

61. Steven Greenhouse, "Post-Soviet Arms Industry is Collapsing," *New York Times*, June 9, 1992, p. A3.
62. Andrew L. Ross, "Arms Acquisition and National Security: The Irony of Military Strength," in Edward E. Azar and Chung-in Moon, eds., *National Security in the Third World: The Management of International and External Threats* (College Park, Md.: Center for International Development and Conflict Management, University of Maryland, 1988), p. 167.
63. Cohen, "Distant Battles: Modern War in the Third World," p. 160.
64. For an argument that the Third World remains dependent on the superpowers for arms (because of their ability to supply large numbers of advanced weapons quickly), see Stephanie Neuman, "Arms and Superpower Influence: Lessons From Recent Wars," *Orbis*, Vol. 30, No. 4 (Winter 1987), pp. 711–729. For an argument that superpower control has diminished (because of Third World production and an increase in the number of suppliers), see Michael T. Klare, "The Arms Trade: Changing Patterns in the 1980s," *Third World Quarterly*, Vol. 9, No. 4 (October 1987), pp. 1257–1278. For a view that takes into account both arguments, see Ross, "Arms Acquisition and National Security."
65. Michael Klare makes a similar point. See Klare, "The Arms Trade," p. 1278.

and that the proliferation of weapons of mass destruction will continue throughout the Third World, the case for American engagement among the developing states has still not been made. The justification for American concern about the Third World rests on showing how the combination of instability and power within the Third World threatens the United States. That in turn requires demonstrating why there is a real risk that Third World states with a capability to harm the United States might actually do so.

Those who assert that American interests are not threatened by growing dependence on Persian Gulf oil emphasize that whoever owns the petroleum must sell it to reap any benefits. Moreover, they argue, suppliers can no longer exclude certain countries from purchasing the oil. With most of the major oil importers committed to share any petroleum that reaches the market, selective embargoes have become impossible. Adherents of this view acknowledge that large price increases are a possibility, but discount their impact, arguing that any precipitous price rise would cause additional non-OPEC production, accelerate efforts for energy alternatives, and increase conservation among the industrialized states to the detriment of producers. This logic explains both Saudi Arabia's efforts to moderate any price increases in oil and Japan's relative lack of concern over Saddam Hussein's invasion of Kuwait, despite Tokyo's extreme dependence on Persian Gulf oil. In sum, goes the argument, because the Persian Gulf states cannot threaten the West's supply of oil without damaging their own interests even more, the West need not fear that its vital interests would be endangered by developments in the Gulf.[66]

However, the nature of Third World states, and of the Persian Gulf countries in particular, refutes this view for two fundamental reasons. First, conflict within and among Persian Gulf states may prevent the production of oil regardless of the economic costs. There have been sixteen disruptions in the Middle East since 1950, and as the 1991 Gulf War so vividly demonstrates, interruptions in supply are not dependent on the Cold War.[67] The instability that characterizes much of the Third World is very much in evidence in the Gulf. Saudi Arabia, which possesses the world's largest oil reserves, faces a multiplicity of domestic threats, any one of which could disrupt production for long periods of time, including a potential revolt by

66. For a succinct expression of this view, see Van Evera, "The United States and the Third World: When to Intervene?" p. 128.
67. Department of Energy, *Energy Security,* p. 10.

the 400,000 Saudi Shi'ites, who have already engaged in major riots in 1979; a takeover of the government by Muslim zealots similar to the 1979 effort that resulted in the seizure of the Grand Mosque of Mecca (Islam's holiest shrine); or a civil war between rival Saudi clans.[68] Similar vulnerabilities exist within the other Gulf states as well. Insofar as external war is concerned, the Iraqi invasions of Iran and Kuwait are stark illustration of the role played by interstate conflict within the region. Another Arab-Israeli war or renewed efforts by Iran to establish its hegemony could also threaten the stability of this vital region, and might remove Persian Gulf oil from the world market for long periods of time. A protracted war within or among states could destroy pumping stations, pipelines, and refineries.

The second reason why economic logic might not work in the Persian Gulf is the impact of culture and religion. Those who minimize the threat posed by American dependence on Persian Gulf oil assume that whoever controls the oil will behave in an economically rational (i.e., profit maximizing) manner. But what rationality or desire for economic gain underlay Saddam Hussein's torching of the Kuwaiti oil fields when defeat for the Iraqi forces was imminent? In Saudi Arabia, the religious extremists who took over the Grand Mosque emphasized the need to prevent Saudi Arabia's moral collapse by removing the corrupting influences of the West. Although several hundred rebels were eventually defeated, it took the Saudi government two weeks and 578 casualties (including 127 deaths) to do so.[69] If similar insurgents were to gain power, they might seek to recreate a state along the lines of the society idealized by the Prophet Muhammad in the seventh century and might attempt to eliminate all of the corrupting influences of the West, including those involved with the production and sale of oil. Fundamentalist leaders, of course, might behave according to Western precepts with regards to the sale of oil if they seized power, but then again they might not. To assume that their cultural and religious beliefs would have no effect on economic behavior is as dangerous as it is foolhardy.

Even more critical is the impact of the proliferation of weapons of mass destruction—especially nuclear arms—to the Third World on American in-

68. For threats to Saudi security, see Nadav Safran, *Saudi Arabia: The Ceaseless Quest for Security* (Cambridge, Mass.: Belknap Press and Harvard University Press, 1985), pp. 357–364; Samuel P. Huntington, "The Renewal of Strategy," in Samuel P. Huntington, ed., *The Strategic Imperative: New Policies for American Security* (Cambridge, Mass.: Ballinger, 1983) p. 46.
69. Safran, *Saudi Arabia*, p. 444. See also Gary Samore, "Royal Family Politics in Saudi Arabia (1953–1982)," Ph.D. diss., Harvard University, 1983, pp. 442–459.

terests. The key question is not whether Third World countries will be able to threaten the United Sates in the post–Cold War era with such weapons—they will—but rather whether they will be inclined to do so. Those who argue that proliferation should not be a major concern of the United States (most notably, Kenneth Waltz) assume that Third World states will behave essentially like the existing nuclear powers in their use or non-use of nuclear weapons. Since nuclear weapons have induced caution and reduced the margin for miscalculation among the great powers, there is no reason to believe it will be different for the minor powers. Radical and revolutionary states, they say, would not use nuclear weapons recklessly because their leaders would recognize the price of doing so. Even leaders assumed to be irrational (at least by Western standards) are still sensitive to costs. Accidents, unauthorized launchings, or theft of nuclear weapons would not be more likely in the Third World, it is asserted, since the leaders of the countries would have every incentive not to allow their nuclear arms to fall out of their control. Third World conflicts are seen as being no more intense than conflicts elsewhere, and even if an interstate nuclear war broke out, for example between India and Pakistan, or Israel and Iraq, they argue that American interests might be best served by remaining aloof. In sum, this view asserts, Third World states are no more likely to use nuclear weapons than the major powers, and if they do the result would not threaten American interests.[70]

These are all cogent points, but precisely because Third World states are more likely to engage in internal and external warfare, nuclear weapons are more likely to be used and American interests are more likely to be endangered than if such weapons were deployed by more stable states. Internal conflict in the Third World heightens the likelihood of nuclear use in several ways. Widespread domestic turmoil may prevent a state from exercising control over its nuclear weapons despite its best efforts to do so, and nuclear weapons could thus fall into the hands of terrorists, particularly in the Middle East where terrorist groups are so prevalent and powerful. Terrorist groups are likely to have fewer inhibitions about launching nuclear strikes. Nuclear weapons might fall into the hands of insurgents in a civil conflict; because civil wars are often more brutal and destructive than inter-state wars, the intensity of feelings could overcome any inhibitions that threats of retaliation

---

70. These points are most persuasively made by Kenneth Waltz in *The Spread of Nuclear Weapons: More May Be Better*; and Shai Feldman, *Israeli Nuclear Deterrence: A Strategy for the 1980s* (New York: Columbia University Press, 1982).

would engender. For example, it is doubtful that nuclear deterrence could have been relied upon to keep the peace if a Lebanese faction had gained control of nuclear arms during that country's civil war, or if Peru's Shining Path movement possessed nuclear weapons today.

The greater propensity of many Third World states to engage in interstate war also undermines the arguments of those who dismiss the consequences of nuclear proliferation. For deterrence to work, a state needs to be able to identify its adversary. But in a Third World filled with conflict, this will be problematic for several reasons. First, the number of Third World states acquiring nuclear weapons is likely to increase in the near future. Equally important, in a Third World where the threat of war is always present, many Third World states have multiple enemies. The United States and the Soviet Union had the luxury of being able to focus on each other in establishing their deterrent relationship. The emergence of medium nuclear powers complicated the superpower balance, but did not alter it. But in the Third World there may be many small nuclear powers, most of which face many adversaries. With nuclear weapons able to be launched from sea, air, and even from trucks, it might be difficult if not impossible to determine the origin of a nuclear strike. If Israel is attacked in a Middle East where Iran, Iraq, Libya, Syria, and Saudi Arabia all maintain nuclear weapons, against whom should it retaliate? Countries might also use terrorist groups to launch nuclear strikes in an effort to avoid responsibility and thus retaliation.

The intensity of the conflict faced by many Third World states also makes nuclear war more likely than among the great powers. It is true that the United States and the Soviet Union have had tense relations, and that the Soviet Union and China even engaged in brief armed clashes in 1969. Nevertheless, these countries have never experienced the degree of hostility that characterizes many Third World countries (e.g., Israel and most of the Arab states, or North and South Korea). Moreover, because the very existence of some Third World states is threatened, their resort to nuclear weapons becomes all the more probable. Israel, for example, was reported to consider the use of nuclear weapons against invading Arab forces during the October 1973 War on at least two occasions.[71] In addition, the problems of preempting another state's nuclear capability did not prevent Israel from attacking Iraq's nuclear reactor in 1981. As more states seek nuclear weapons, attacks of this kind and retaliations, some of which might be nuclear, cannot be ruled out.

---

71. Safran, *Israel: The Embattled Ally*, p. 489.

Because the threat of war is so high, the possibilities of accidental or unauthorized launchings will also be greater in the Third World than elsewhere. The need to prevent preemption of small nuclear forces could force new nuclear states to adopt a "hair-trigger" response to conventional or nuclear attacks. Such a response combined with primitive radar and command and control capabilities might lead to inadvertent nuclear strikes. In addition, it is likely that Third World regimes would disperse nuclear weapons and move them from place to place to enhance their protection from attack. These steps might also increase the chances that lower-ranking officers could launch nuclear weapons without authority from the government, and that the nuclear weapons themselves would be more vulnerable to subnational or terrorist groups.

Finally, it is true that Third World states might be able to duplicate the mutual assured destruction relationship of the superpowers. But deterrence is essentially a psychological concept in which one side attempts to persuade the other not to do something it is fully capable of doing, by threatening it with unacceptable costs. The culture and psychology of the leadership necessarily play a role in determining when costs outweigh benefits. Risking the destruction of several cities for some political gain would be unthinkable for most leaders, but not necessarily for all. Western concepts of nuclear deterrence may not obtain everywhere.

This spread of nuclear weapons to a Third World beset with internal and international instabilities threatens American interests in many ways. Internal war in an economically critical area (such as the Persian Gulf) could cause catastrophic damage to the economies of the United States and its allies. Nuclear war within a Third World country could make subsequent nuclear use more likely, while encouraging the proliferation of nuclear weapons to still more countries. The use of nuclear weapons in a domestic conflict might also spread beyond the borders of the country involved, threatening American allies. The environmental effects of nuclear war, even an internal one, cannot be dismissed, especially if many weapons are employed.

The greater likelihood that Third World states will use nuclear weapons against other states is even more threatening to American interests than their use in a domestic conflict. The possession of nuclear arms by an enemy of the United States could deter the United States from acting to defend its interests. It is difficult to believe that the United States would have intervened against Saddam Hussein by placing some half a million troops in a relatively small area if Washington had believed that Iraq had nuclear weapons. Indeed, a major lesson of the U.S.–Iraqi war for would-be Third World hegemons is not to refrain from attacking American interests, but to wait to acquire a nuclear weapons capability before doing so. The United States might also be deterred from taking actions against states engaged in terrorist activities. As Libyan Leader Muammar Qadhafi remarked, "If at the time of the U.S. raid on Tripoli [1986] we had possessed a deterrent-missile that could reach New York, we could have hit it at the same moment."[72] Nuclear war between Third World states, for example in East Asia, could interrupt international trade, badly hurting the Western economies. Interference with American commerce propelled the United States into war in the past (for example, the War of 1812 and World War I), and could do so again, especially given the far greater damage a nuclear conflict would produce.[73]

American allies are also threatened by the prospect of nuclear-armed Third World states. Any close friend of the United States, including states in Western Europe (which are geographically closer to likely proliferators), could be threatened with nuclear attack by countries seeking to influence American policy. U.S. resupply of Israel during a Middle Eastern war, for example, might be undermined by threats to strike at America's European allies. More generally, regional conflicts endanger U.S. allies and friends throughout the Third World. South Korea, Taiwan, Israel, India, and Pakistan are all threatened by nuclear armed adversaries.

Most alarmingly, nuclear weapons might be directed against the United States itself. Motives for attacking the United States are as wide-ranging as the groups and countries of the Third World who hate the United States, its actions, and its policies. At least six Third World states are expected to have intercontinental ballistic missiles by the end of this decade, making them capable of instant destruction of American cities. Many others, no doubt, will follow in their footsteps. Moreover, Third World states and other actors without ballistic missiles could still deliver nuclear weapons against the United States by using aircraft, cruise missiles, ships, and conceivably even suitcases. Aside from the obvious catastrophic damage done to American

---

72. Libyan Television, April 19, 1990, address by Muammar Qadhafi to the students of the Higher Institute of Applied Social Sciences at the Great Faith University; in Foreign Broadcast Information Service, *Daily Report: Middle East and Africa*, April 23, 1990; cited by Uzi Rubin, "How Much Does Missile Proliferation Matter?" p. 38.
73. I am grateful to Stephen Van Evera for drawing my attention to this point.

interests should one of these arms actually be detonated, efforts to prevent threatened attacks could result in suspension or compromise of civil liberties.[74]

For the same reasons that Third World countries and groups armed with nuclear weapons threaten the interests of the United States, these same countries and groups threaten American interests when they deploy other weapons of mass destruction, namely chemical and biological arms (and in some cases even conventional arms). The lesser damage caused by these weapons is more than made up by the greater ease with which they can be manufactured and used. One can expect that countries hostile to American interests that are unable to acquire nuclear weapons will seek to rely on chemical or biological arms to threaten the United States and its allies. It is of some comfort that Iraq did not use such weapons in its war against the United States. Nevertheless, it did employ them to great effect against the Iranians, and Washington cannot count on being as fortunate the next time it confronts a chemically-armed Third World adversary.

Conclusions and Policy Recommendations

The Third World is and will for the foreseeable future be characterized by a great number of states whose instability is likely to lead to internal and external conflict. The youth of Third World countries, the legacy of colonialism, and ethnic divisions both within and among countries have prevented the formation of strong stable states such as in Western Europe. Those factors that have contributed to the "long peace" among the developed countries are largely absent in the Third World. The resulting turmoil, when combined with the growing power of many Third World states, threatens the United States and global peace.

This does not mean that all Third World states will behave irresponsibly or threaten American interests. Many Third World states (especially in Africa) will be too weak to pose much of a threat to the United States. Other Third World states (e.g., the newly industrializing countries of East Asia) may develop to the point that instability ceases to be a problem. Nevertheless, as

---

74. Lewis Dunn, "What Difference Will it Make?" in Kenneth Waltz and Robert Art, eds., *The Use of Force*, 2nd ed. (Lanham, Md.: University Press of America, 1983), p. 613. Dunn does an excellent job of detailing the dangers of nuclear proliferation.

the United States increases its dependence on Third World oil and as weapons of mass destruction continue to proliferate, a substantial number of Third World countries will gain the capability to threaten the United States, while lacking the stability and political development that would make them less likely to do so.

Much of the focus on threats to the United States has been on the Middle East, because of the area's oil wealth and the number of potential proliferators. But other Third World states such as Mexico, Venezuela, and Nigeria can also damage American interests should their supplies be removed from the market. More important, nuclear arms and other weapons of mass destruction will increasingly come within the reach of countries throughout the Third World, including those in Latin America, Africa, and Asia. Other interests maintained by the United States in the Third World also widen America's concerns beyond the states of the Middle East. These interests include growing economic ties, humanitarian concerns, problems posed by Third World immigration, combatting terrorism, protecting American citizens abroad, safeguarding the environment, lessening the traffic in illegal drugs, and the desire of any great power to expand its influence.[75] These challenges are likely to become more acute over time and in themselves warrant serious and sustained American attention to the Third World.

Nor does the increasing Third World threat mean that states outside the Third World are not worrisome. Many of the same characteristics that should cause the United States to worry about the Third World also apply to the newly emerging states in Europe. Young states confronting border disputes, ethnic hatreds, and religious fanaticism can just as well describe the republics of the former Soviet Union and some of the countries in Eastern Europe as it does many of the states in the Third World. Insofar as these characteristics promote instability and conflict in the Third World, so will they in Europe.

What does this mean for American policy? First, the United States must redouble its efforts to free itself from dependence on Persian Gulf oil. American moves towards greater energy independence must not evaporate as soon as a crisis ends or the price of gasoline falls. The security of American and Western oil supplies cannot depend on the Gulf states' desire for economic profit when prolonged warfare may eliminate their very ability to

---

75. For a broad overview of the interests the United States maintains in the Third World, see David, "Why the Third World Matters," pp. 50–85.

extract petroleum. Increased efforts at conservation, discovering new oil fields, and developing alternative energy sources are certainly steps in the right direction.

Militarily, the United States must retain the option of massive intervention in the Persian Gulf both to protect countries from interstate aggression (as was the case with Iraq's invasion of Kuwait), and to suppress a major civil conflict. The 1991 Gulf War deployment included over nine U.S. ground divisions and six aircraft carriers. The United States must sustain the ability to intervene on this scale, including the maintenance of adequate air and sealift and supporting air power.[76]

The United States must also be prepared to deny control over nuclear weapons to regimes, groups, and individuals who are likely to threaten American interests. The United States must continue its efforts to enhance international norms against the spread of nuclear weapons such as the Non-Proliferation Treaty, improve international safeguards, and reassure friendly states (at times with treaty guarantees) that they will not need nuclear weapons to ensure their security. Should these efforts fail, the United States needs to be prepared to use military action to preempt the developing nuclear capabilities of countries and groups who are likely to use those weapons against American allies or the United States itself.

Assuming that an anti-proliferation policy will never be foolproof, the United States must develop systems to protect itself from nuclear attacks from the Third World. A defensive system designed to deal with the Third World ballistic missile threat need not be on the scale of the space-based Reagan-Bush Strategic Defense Initiative or even the increasingly ambitious "Global Protection Against Limited Strikes" (GPALS) program. Instead, a more modest ground-based system of far less cost that is consistent with the ABM treaty (or a reasonable modification of it) would be preferable. For non–ballistic missile nuclear threats, the United States needs to improve air and coastal defenses and develop better means to prevent nuclear materials from being smuggled into the country.

The United States should act under the general principle that it will seek to lessen the frequency of wars in the Third World. In practice, American military intervention would be limited to those rare conflicts that threaten American vital interests. For the great majority of Third World conflicts that

---

76. Van Evera, "The United States and the Third World: When to Intervene?" p. 132.

do not engage core American concerns, the United States should work through the United Nations. The post–Cold War world has provided the UN with the opportunity to be truly a force for peace. As demonstrated by the 1991 Iraqi War, and (in a very different way) efforts to bring about peace settlements in Cambodia and Namibia, the United Nations can play an important role in settling Third World conflicts. The UN, with American support, can deter and restrain Third World conflicts by threatening would-be aggressors with economic sanctions, diplomatic isolation, and even international intervention. These sanctions could be applied to both civil and international war.

Equally important, the United States should address the root causes of instability in the Third World. While the prospects for fundamental change are not bright, American assistance can make a difference in certain countries. The United States has to be especially careful not to allow understandable concerns over developments in Europe to force out equally pressing needs in the Third World. The United States should do more to promote democracy and human rights in the Third World. Funding of democratic groups, increased assistance to countries embracing democracy, and the punishment (through diplomatic and trade sanctions) of states that violate the basic rights of their people should be pursued with renewed vigor. In addition, the United States should redouble its efforts to promote economic development and modernization in the Third World. These policies are not only the right things to do because they hold out the hope of improving the quality of life in the Third World, they are also in America's interests because they will help defuse some of the tensions and resentments that threaten global peace.

An engaged policy in the Third World need not be expensive. With over half of the defense spending geared to Europe, there is ample opportunity to redirect resources to the Third World. American policy makers must not allow recognition of the Third World threat to be used as an excuse to justify military expenditures that are no longer needed as a result of the collapse of the Soviet Union. Indeed, none of the security recommendations discussed above would preclude a substantial reduction in American military spending. The United States presently spends only about one percent (approximately $16 billion) of its budget on foreign aid. Increasing or at least maintaining that sum could do much to sustain U.S. leadership in the world without posing any threat to America's overall economic health.

The United States must not allow its understandable joy over the ending of the Cold War become an excuse for isolationist complacency. The growing power and instability of some Third World states threatens American interests in ways whose implications are still unknown. The threats may not be as catastrophic as those presented by the former Soviet Union, but they are far more likely to arise. Just as the United States had to confront the challenge presented by the USSR, so too will it have to address the new threats posed by less powerful but potentially more dangerous adversaries.

Ballistic Missiles and Weapons of Mass Destruction

Steve Fetter

What Is the Threat?
What Should be Done?

$\mathbf{I}$raqi missile attacks against cities in Israel and Saudi Arabia have focused attention on the continuing proliferation of ballistic missile technology throughout the third world.[1] According to the Stockholm International Peace Research Institute, 25 countries have acquired or are trying to acquire ballistic missiles, either through purchase or indigenous production.[2] All but a few are developing countries, and the list encompasses some of the most volatile regions of the world. The greatest concentration is in the Middle East, where nine nations have missile programs. Missiles have also spread to other hot spots, including India and Pakistan, North and South Korea, Brazil and Argentina, Taiwan, and South Africa.

What are these missiles for, and why do countries want them? In particular, what types of warheads are emerging missile forces likely to be armed with? What capabilities will these missiles provide to their possessors, and what threats to international security will they pose? How should the United States and its allies respond to minimize these threats?

Since their invention in the 1930s, guided ballistic missiles have been used extensively in war only four times: the Germans launched over 2000 V-2

Steve Fetter is an Assistant Professor in the School of Public Affairs at the University of Maryland, College Park.

I would like to thank Elisa Harris, Milton Leitenberg, Janne Nolan, Julian Perry Robinson, and Stephen Van Evera for their helpful comments, and the Federation of American Scientists for its generous support.

1. The proliferation of ballistic missile technology is well chronicled. See, for example, Janne E. Nolan, *Trappings of Power: Ballistic Missiles in the Third World* (Washington, D.C.: Brookings, 1991); Aaron Karp, "Ballistic Missile Proliferation," in Stockholm International Peace Research Institute (SIPRI), *SIPRI Yearbook 1990: World Armaments and Disarmament* (Oxford: Oxford University Press, 1990); Robert D. Shuey, Warren W. Lenhart, Rodney A. Snyder, Warren H. Donnelly, James E. Mielke, and John D. Moteff, *Missile Proliferation: Survey of Emerging Missile Forces* (Washington, D.C.: Congressional Research Service, February 9, 1989); and Martin S. Navias, "Ballistic Missile Proliferation in the Middle East," *Survival*, Vol. 31, No. 3 (May/June 1989), pp. 225–239.
2. Karp, "Ballistic Missile Proliferation," pp. 382–390. See Table 2 for a list of countries with missile programs.

International Security, Summer 1991 (Vol. 16, No. 1)
© 1991 by the President and Fellows of Harvard College and of the Massachusetts Institute of Technology.

missiles against urban British and European targets during World War II; Iraq and Iran together launched nearly 1000 missiles against each other's cities during the 1980–88 Iran-Iraq war; the Kabul government fired over 1000 Soviet-made Scud missiles against *Mujahideen* guerrillas in the Afghanistan civil war; and Iraq launched about 80 modified Scud missiles against cities in Israel and Saudi Arabia in the 1991 Persian Gulf war. Three of these four cases occurred in the last decade, and in all four cases the missiles were armed solely with conventional (i.e., high-explosive) warheads. Moreover, these missiles were used mainly for strategic attacks against cities, perhaps because they lacked the accuracy necessary to strike even soft military targets such as airfields.

Ballistic missiles with ranges greater than a few hundred kilometers are, however, an exceptionally inefficient vehicle for the delivery of conventional munitions. This has long been recognized by the nuclear powers, which rely on ballistic missiles almost exclusively for the delivery of nuclear warheads. The inefficiency of conventionally armed missiles seems to be well understood by the new missile states as well, since most of them are also actively seeking nuclear, chemical, and biological weapons. A missile armed with a Hiroshima-sized nuclear weapon is roughly 10,000 times more deadly than the same missile armed with high explosives. Fortunately, the development of nuclear weapons is expensive, easy to detect, and relatively easy to thwart with export controls. Chemical warheads, on the other hand, are far easier to acquire, and while they may be far less deadly than nuclear warheads, they could kill as many people as dozens or even hundreds of conventionally armed missiles. Even worse, biological warheads that disperse anthrax spores offer the possibility of inflicting casualties on the scale of small nuclear weapons.

As missile ranges increase, the civilian populations of U.S. allies (and eventually the United States itself) will become increasing vulnerable to weapons of mass destruction. Responding to this threat should be a major preoccupation of the United States, just as ameliorating the Soviet nuclear threat has been a major policy goal for more than four decades. In fact, emerging missile arsenals may be an even greater menace, since the probability of inadvertent or accidental use is likely to be much higher, crisis instabilities are likely to be more severe, and several of these states are less politically stable than the Soviet Union has been.

Policy responses might include carrots (security guarantees and arms control), sticks (export controls, deterrence, or preventive war), and defenses (missile, aircraft, and civil defenses). The United States has tried each of these in a somewhat haphazard manner, with mixed success. Security guarantees cannot be extended to every state, and arms control is often unappealing to rogue states or their neighbors. Export controls are notoriously difficult to enforce, and are undercut by Third World suppliers and by the similarity of military and peaceful activities. Preventive war can be highly effective, but the risks and costs it entails (combined with the international environment it fosters) make it of very limited use as an instrument of national policy. Defenses are unlikely to be effective for a variety of reasons, and deterrence may not work in many situations. Nonetheless it is imperative, despite these shortcomings, that we weave these policy threads into a coherent and self-consistent fabric to protect civilians from weapons of mass destruction.

Missiles in the Middle East and Asia: Who's Got What?

To illustrate the missile capabilities that have become available to Third World countries, Table 1 gives the characteristics of missiles deployed in the Middle East and Asia. Israel has the most sophisticated missile capability, having orbited two satellites with its Shavit space launch vehicle. If the Shavit was used as a ballistic missile, it would be capable of delivering a half-tonne[3] payload at intercontinental ranges.[4] The Jericho 2, which is based on the same technology, can probably deliver at least two tonnes on any Arab country. India also has an ambitious program to develop satellite launchers and long-range ballistic missiles; its Agni missile is roughly comparable to the Jericho 2. In contrast to the indigenous Israeli and Indian development, Saudi Arabia purchased its missiles from China. The 68-tonne single-stage DF-3, which is limited to ranges of less than 3500 kilometers with a 1-tonne payload,[5] is the largest missile deployed outside of the five nuclear powers.[6]

---

3. One tonne (te) = 1 metric ton = 1,000 kilograms = 2,200 pounds = 1 long ton = 1.1 short tons.

4. The estimates of throwweight versus range given here are the result of calculations based on the known or inferred characteristics of these missiles. For the characteristics of the Shavit, see Steve Fetter, "Israeli Ballistic Missile Capabilities," *Physics and Society*, Vol. 19, No. 3 (July 1990), pp. 3–4. I assume that the Jericho 2 is composed of the first two stages of the Shavit.

5. For the characteristics of the DF-3, see Zuwei Huang and Xinmin Ren, "Long March Launch Vehicle Family—Current Status and Future Development," *Space Technology*, Vol. 8, No. 4 (1988), pp. 371–375.

6. For comparison, the U.S. Minuteman III ICBM weighs 35 tonnes, the Trident II SLBM weighs 57 tonnes, and the MX missile weighs 88 tonnes. It should be noted the United States has

Table 1. Ballistic missiles deployed in Asia and the Middle East.

Missile	Country	Missile Mass (te)	Fuel/ Stages[a]	Throw- weight[b] (te)	Range[b] (km)	Supplier
Scud-B	Afghanistan, Egypt, Iran, Iraq, Libya, North Korea, Syria, Yemen	6	L/1	1	300	USSR
al-Abbas	Iraq	8	L/1	1	450	USSR (modified by Iraq)
DF-3	Saudi Arabia	68	L/1	2	2800	China
Jericho 1	Israel		S/2	1	500	
Jericho 2	Israel, South Africa?	≈16	S/2	2	2000	Israel?
Prithvi	India	4	L/1	1	240	
Agni	India	14	S/L/2	1	2500	

NOTES: Includes all missiles with a payload of at least 500 kilograms at a range of 300 kilometers, which is the threshold for export restrictions under the Missile Technology Control Regime.

a. "L" = liquid; "S" = solid.
b. Typical payload/range combinations.

At the other end of the spectrum is the ubiquitous Soviet Scud-B missile, capable of delivering a 1-tonne payload at a range of only 300 kilometers.[7] The Scud-B was modified by Iraq to carry a much smaller payload at ranges of up to 600 kilometers, enabling its use in attacks on Teheran, Riyadh, and Tel Aviv during the 1980–88 and 1991 Persian Gulf wars. A more extensive modification, called the al-Abbas, may be capable of delivering a half-tonne warhead at such ranges.[8]

---

struggled for nearly two decades to develop a mobile basing mode for the MX, in part because of the large size of the missile.

7. For the characteristics of the Scud-B, see Steven Zaloga, "Ballistic Missiles in the Third World: Scud and Beyond," *International Defense Review*, Vol. 21 (November 1988), p. 1427.

8. For the characteristics of the modified Scuds, see W. Seth Carus and Joseph S. Bermudez, Jr., "Iraq's Al-Husayn Missile Programme," *Jane's Soviet Intelligence Review*, May 1990, pp. 205.

WHY BUY MISSILES?

Why use ballistic missiles rather than aircraft? After all, aircraft are reusable, more versatile, and are capable of much better accuracy than first-generation missiles. The most common answer is that it is much easier to defend against an attack by aircraft. Even though British air defenses were very good late in World War II, Britain was utterly defenseless against the V-2, which reentered the lower atmosphere at speeds in excess of Mach 3. Not until the United States deployment of the Patriot anti-tactical missile system in Saudi Arabia and Israel has a country demonstrated a capability to defend itself against attack by even short-range missiles. Although the Patriot system was apparently very effective,[9] it was far from perfect and, in the face of U.S. air supremacy, missile attack was Iraq's only means to carry out strategic attacks on U.S. allies.

A comparison of costs shows, furthermore, that missiles are rarely a cost-effective means for delivering conventional explosives. Although aircraft are about three times as expensive as missiles per unit takeoff or launch weight,[10] aircraft can carry up to ten times more payload per unit takeoff weight to intermediate ranges.[11] Moreover, aircraft can be reused until they are shot down. Figure 1 shows that missiles are only cost-effective for very short ranges or if aircraft attrition rates are very high. For example, at a range of 500 kilometers, a single-stage missile is only cost-effective if aircraft attrition rates are greater than 35 percent per sortie. Even modern, solid-fuel, two-stage missiles are not cost-effective at such ranges unless aircraft attrition rates are greater than 25 percent per sortie. Attrition rates greater than 10 percent are rare, and only occur when a combatant is greatly overmatched or when targets are especially well-defended.[12]

---

9. The actual effectiveness of Patriot interceptors in destroying Scud warheads is subject to intense debate. See footnote 61.
10. Based on unit flyaway costs and maximum takeoff/launch weights of seven U.S. missiles and seven U.S. aircraft given in Thomas B. Cochran, William M. Arkin, and Milton M. Hoenig, *Nuclear Weapons Databook*, Vol. I: *U.S. Nuclear Forces and Capabilities* (Cambridge, Mass.: Ballinger, 1984).
11. For example, 30–35 percent of the takeoff weight of U.S. aircraft is payload at unrefueled ranges of up to 1500 kilometers. International Institute for Strategic Studies (IISS), *The Military Balance 1988–89* (London: IISS, 1988). For comparison, the throwweight of the Scud-B missile is 17 percent of its launch weight at a range of only 300 kilometers, and the throwweight of the modified Scuds used against Teheran and Tel Aviv was less than 3 percent of the launch weight.
12. The overall attrition rate for American aircraft in the European theatre from August 1942 to May 1945 was 2 percent per sortie, although the loss rate in a single raid on a particularly well-defended target (the Schweinfurt ball-bearing plant) reached 20 percent. Robert Futrell, *Ideas, Concepts, Doctrine: A History of Basic Thinking in the United States Air Force 1907–1964* (Maxwell

Figure 1. **The relative cost-effectiveness of missiles and aircraft as a function of their range and the aircraft attrition rate per sortie.**

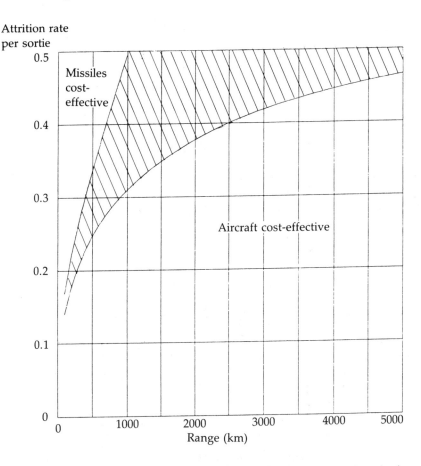

NOTES: Lines give the attrition rate at which missile and aircraft costs per unit payload delivered to a given range are equal, assuming that aircraft cost three times as much as missiles per unit mass; that the aircraft mass is equal to $(r/900 + 2)$ times the payload mass, where r is the combat radius in kilometers (from a best-fit to U.S. aircraft); and that missiles have a specific impulse of 250 seconds. The top curve is for a single-stage missile with a booster-to-fuel mass ratio of 1.15; the bottom curve is for a two-stage missile with a ratio of 1.05. The attrition rate per sortie is equal to $(1 + s)^{-1}$, where s is the average number of sorties; the break-even point occurs when $s = CR(M_a/M_m)$, where CR is the cost ratio per unit mass $(CR = 3)$ and M_a and M_m are the aircraft and missile mass per unit payload mass at a given range.

The loss of highly trained pilots when aircraft are shot down is undoubt-edly an important reason for preferring to use missiles when attrition rates are higher than, say, ten percent. This consideration points to another pos-sibility, however: remove the pilots. Pilotless aircraft or cruise missiles gen-erally are not reusable,[13] but they could be much cheaper than piloted craft. The current U.S. sea-launched cruise missile (SLCM), with a flyaway cost of about $1.5 million and a payload of less than 500 kilograms at a range of 1,300 kilometers, is not a bargain. But with the advent of low-cost satellite navigation receivers in the near future, high accuracy will be possible without the sophisticated radar and optical digital-scene-matching technology em-ployed in the SLCM. It should then be possible to build a simple, low-flying cruise missile with the same payload and range as the SLCM for less than $250,000.[14] Even at this price, cruise missiles would not be cost-effective unless the attrition rate for piloted aircraft were very high (e.g., greater than 15 percent per sortie).[15]

Air Force Base, Ala.: Air University, 1974), p. 80; R.V. Jones, *Most Secret War* (Sevenoaks, England: Coronet, 1979). The North Vietnamese inflicted attrition rates of 3 percent per sortie on U.S. B-52s over Hanoi in 1972 using Soviet SA-2 surface-to-air missiles (SAMs). During the 1973 war, Israeli A-4 aircraft suffered attrition rates of 1 to 1.5 percent from Soviet SA-6 SAMs. Even against the Soviet Union, which has the most extensive air defense network in the world, the U.S. Air Force estimated (in the mid-1970s) that its bombers would suffer attrition rates of no more than 15 percent. Alton H. Quanbeck and Archie L. Wood, *Modernizing the Strategic Bomber Force: Why and How* (Washington, D.C.: Brookings, 1976), pp. 64–65.

13. Cruise missiles might eventually be designed to release bombs and return to landing strips, but this would result in at least a factor of two decrease in their range and would add consid-erably to their cost.

14. Beech Aircraft Corporation makes a turbojet-powered drone (the MQM-107) with a maxi-mum payload of about 200 kilograms and a range of about 800 kilometers that sells for about $160,000; a similar vehicle with a payload of 500 kilograms and range a range of 1300 kilometers could probably be built for about $250,000 (i.e., six times less than the SLCM). Northrup and Teledyne Ryan also make unpiloted aircraft for targets and reconnaissance, although at some-what higher prices. Teledyne can equip its drones with light-weight Global Positioning System (GPS) receivers, resulting in accuracies of about 30 meters for commercial users. Teledyne has also developed a radar altimeter that allows its drone to fly over water just 10 feet above the wave tops. By using propellers instead of turbojet engines, the cost to deliver 500 kilograms to 1300 kilometers would be less than $100,000, but the speed would be much lower. (Based on author's communications with Beech Aircraft, Northrup, and Teledyne engineers, March 27, 1991.)

15. For example, the U.S. A-6 and F-15 can deliver 8100 and 9000 kilograms of payload at a distance of 1250 and 1440 kilometers for a flyaway cost of $19 and $22 million, respectively. Sixteen to 18 cruise missiles each carrying 500 kilograms would be required to deliver an equal payload, which, at $250,000 per missile, would cost about $4 million—about five time less than the cost of aircraft. Therefore, ignoring the loss of pilots, attrition rates greater than 15 percent are necessary to make cruise missiles cost-effective compared to piloted aircraft, even if the cruise missiles themselves suffer no attrition.

Apart from air defenses, there are other, perhaps more powerful incentives to buy missiles rather than aircraft. First, missile attack appears to have a greater psychological impact than bombing. The suddenness of missile attack, combined with feelings of defenselessness, terrorized the populations of London and Teheran. Even in Tel Aviv, missile attacks had a psychological and political impact far out of proportion to the physical damage they caused (only one death was caused by some 38 missiles launched at Israel, apart from heart attacks, asphyxiations, and car accidents caused by anxiety over the attacks). Such effects can far outweigh the military significance of missile attacks. For example, by threatening to provoke Israeli retaliation, and thereby possibly break up the Arab coalition arrayed against Iraq, the "militarily insignificant" Scud played a central political role early in the 1991 Persian Gulf war.

There are also domestic and international political reasons for buying missiles instead of aircraft. Programs to develop missiles can be justified as civilian space programs, just as a nuclear weapons program can be aided and masked by a civilian nuclear program. Missiles are important symbols of prestige and technological achievement. Once a nation has acquired missiles, its rivals may feel impelled to follow suit. Nations may also feel that it is easier to deter missile attack by deploying a missile force of their own rather than simply augmenting some other capability. This may explain why Saudi Arabia purchased the Chinese DF-3 missile,[16] which is an exceedingly inefficient vehicle for the delivery of conventional munitions. Further, because missiles do not require pilots, better control can be maintained over their use. Missiles do not defect.

Warheads for Ballistic Missiles

Political considerations aside, nations will choose to acquire ballistic missiles rather than aircraft if the weapons they carry are so destructive that the reusability of aircraft is unimportant, or if speed of delivery is of primary importance. (This is, after all, why all five nuclear powers rely primarily on ballistic missiles.) The destructiveness and speed of delivery of nuclear-armed

---

16. In March 1988 Saudi Arabia announced that it had purchased DF-3 missiles (known in the west as the CSS-2) from China. Neither the price nor the number of missiles was disclosed, but 60 to 120 missiles are generally believed to have been purchased at a total cost of several billion dollars.

ballistic missiles creates the possibility of a damage-limiting preemptive attack; the lack of defenses against intercontinental ballistic missiles makes an attack virtually unstoppable. It is also much less expensive to keep a missile force on continuous alert. Thus, the desire to be able to deliver nuclear weapons quickly and surely may explain why a few states, most notably Israel and India, are developing ballistic missiles. But what about countries that have no nuclear program, or whose nuclear programs are only in their infancy? Will their ballistic missiles continue to carry conventional warheads, or will they turn to chemical or biological warheads?

CONVENTIONAL WARHEADS

Missile attacks have so far been limited to conventional warheads, but even the largest such warheads cannot do much damage. For example, the average V-2 missile landing in London killed five people, injured 13, and damaged 40 buildings with its 1-tonne warhead.[17] The Scud-B, which also carries a 1-tonne warhead, would cause similar numbers of casualties in cities of comparable population density. Such missiles would only be useful in strategic attacks against cities, but a truly strategic threat (or a strategic deterrent) would require a capability to launch tens of thousands of such missiles. Conventionally armed missiles cannot be decisive militarily, and a nation certainly could not hope to deter nuclear attack by fielding a force of conventionally armed missiles.

Not surprisingly, then, as Table 2 shows, most of the nations with ballistic missile programs are also pursuing unconventional weapons. Because con-

---

17. The 518 V-2 missiles that landed in London killed 2754 and seriously injured 6523 people, for an average of 5.3 deaths and 12.6 injuries per missile impact. Although the energy released by the V-1 cruise-missile warhead was similar to that released by the impact of the V-2 (equivalent to 1 ton of TNT), only 2.2 deaths and 6.3 serious injuries resulted per V-1 attack, mostly because warning of the approach of the subsonic cruise missile allowed residents to take protective actions. This suggests that civil defense can reduce casualties from conventional attacks by a factor of two. U.S. Strategic Bombing Survey, Physical Damage Division, "V-Weapons in London," Report No. 152, January 1947. The effective lethal area of the V-2 warhead was about 1,500 square meters (0.15 hectares); the population density of London during the attacks was about 35 per hectare. Based on the V-2 experience, the number of deaths without warning is equal to $0.15pY^{2/3}$, where p is the population density per hectare and Y is the yield of the warhead (including its kinetic energy on impact) in tons of TNT equivalent. The modified Scuds used against Tel Aviv reportedly carried 200-kilogram warheads; since the population density of Tel Aviv is about 35 per hectare, and since warning of attack was available, one would have expected an average of about 0.7 deaths per missile impact. That the actual number of deaths in Israel was far less (one death from 11 missile impacts, six of which occurred within Tel Aviv) merely emphasizes the probabilistic nature of such attacks, as does the attack on a U.S. barracks that killed dozens of soldiers.

Table 2. Third-world ballistic missiles, nuclear weapons, chemical weapons, and biological weapons.

	Acquiring or trying to acquire:			
Country	Ballistic Missiles?[a]	Nuclear Weapons?[b]	Chemical Weapons?[c]	Biological Weapons?[d]
Afghanistan	Yes			
Algeria	Yes[e]			
Argentina	Yes	Possible	Possible	
Brazil	Yes	Possible		
Burma			Likely	
Cuba	Yes[e]		Possible	
Egypt	Yes		Likely	
Ethiopia			Likely	
India	Yes	Yes	Likely	
Indonesia	Planned		Possible	
Iran	Yes	Possible	Likely	
Iraq	Yes	Possible	Yes	Likely
Israel	Yes	Yes	Likely	
Korea, North	Yes	Possible	Likely	Likely
Korea, South	Yes		Likely	
Kuwait	Yes[e]			
Libya	Yes	Possible	Likely	
Pakistan	Yes	Likely	Likely	
Saudi Arabia	Yes		Possible	
South Africa	Yes	Likely	Possible	
Syria	Yes		Likely	Likely
Taiwan	Yes		Likely	Likely
Thailand	Possible		Possible	
Vietnam	Possible		Likely	
Yemen	Yes			

SOURCES:
a. Aaron Karp, "Ballistic Missile Proliferation," in Stockholm International Peace Research Institute [SIPRI], *SIPRI Yearbook 1990* (Oxford: Oxford University Press, 1990); and Statement of Rear Admiral Thomas A. Brooks, Director of Naval Intelligence, before the Seapower, Strategic, and Critical Materials Subcommittee of the House Armed Services Committee, March 7, 1991.
b. Leonard S. Spector, *Nuclear Ambitions: The Spread of Nuclear Weapons, 1989–90* (Boulder, Colo.: Westview Press, 1990).
c. Elisa D. Harris, "Chemical Weapons Proliferation: Current Capabilities and Prospects for Control," in Aspen Strategy Group, *New Threats: Responding to the Proliferation of Nuclear, Chemical, and Delivery Capabilities in the Third World* (Washington, D.C.: University Press of America, 1990); and Statement of Rear Admiral Brooks.
d. Statement of Rear Admiral Brooks; and Statement of Admiral William O. Studeman before the Seapower, Strategic, and Critical Materials Subcommittee of the House Armed Services Committee, March 1, 1988.
e. Short-range (less than 100 kilometers) missiles only.

ventional weapons lack destructive power and nuclear weapons are difficult to develop, many believe that chemical or biological weapons will soon be the warhead of choice for emerging ballistic missile arsenals.

CHEMICAL WARHEADS

Chemical weapons have been used in war since ancient times, but they have never been delivered by modern ballistic missiles. Over 100,000 tons of chemical agents were released by artillery shells, mortars, bombs, grenades, and gas cylinders in World War I, producing about 100,000 fatalities and over 1,000,000 total casualties.[18] More potent chemical weapons were developed and stockpiled by Germany, the United States, the United Kingdom, and other combatants in World War II, but their uncertain military utility, combined with the deterrent effect of opposing chemical arsenals, prevented their use. Nazi Germany examined the possibility of arming the V-2 missile with chemical agents, but decided to use high explosives because their effects were more predictable and reliable, and because they feared allied chemical retaliation against German cities.

It is not clear how nations will choose in the future. The most deadly use of chemical weapons since World War I occurred during the Iran-Iraq war.[19] Even though both nations were armed with ballistic missiles, they used aircraft and artillery, not ballistic missiles, to deliver chemical agents.[20]

---

18. For a review of the development, use, and alleged use of chemical weapons, see SIPRI, *The Problem of Chemical and Biological Warfare,* Vol. I: *The Rise of CB Weapons* (New York: Humanities Press, 1971); and Victor A. Utgoff, *The Challenge of Chemical Weapons: An American Perspective* (London: Macmillan, 1990).

19. Other large-scale uses of chemical agents since World War I include the use of lethal agents by Italy in its 1935–36 invasion of Ethiopia, by Japan during its occupation of Manchuria from 1937–45, and by Egypt during its intervention in the civil war in Yemen during the mid-1960s. Several unsubstantiated claims of large-scale uses of lethal agents have also been recorded, including alleged uses of chemicals by the United States against North Korea, by Vietnam against Laos and Kampuchea, and by the Soviet Union in Afghanistan. In terms of tonnage, the largest use of chemical agents since World War I was the use of herbicides and non-lethal agents by the United States in Vietnam, but the United States maintains that such agents are not covered by the Geneva protocol.

20. Most analysts believe that neither country had the technical capability to mount chemical weapons on ballistic missiles during the war, and there is much debate about whether Iraq had acquired this capability before the 1991 Persian Gulf War. It is unclear, however, why nations that could manufacture chemical artillery shells would find it especially difficult to arm missiles with chemical warheads. See Thomas L. McNaugher, "Ballistic Missiles and Chemical Weapons in the Iran-Iraq War," *International Security,* Vol. 15, No. 2 (Fall 1990), pp. 5–34, for a description and evaluation of the use of chemical agents and ballistic missiles in the Iran-Iraq War.

It is often claimed that one to two dozen countries stockpile or are actively seeking chemical weapons (see Table 2), but only the United States, the Soviet Union, and Iraq openly admit to stockpiling (and Iraq, to using) such weapons. Of those nations with ballistic missiles, Egypt, India, Iran, Israel, North and South Korea, Libya, Pakistan, Syria, and Taiwan are strongly suspected of stockpiling or producing chemical weapons.[21] While the United States and the Soviet Union are the only countries known to have outfitted missiles with chemical warheads, there are strong suspicions that Syria and Iraq have attempted to do so.[22]

CHEMICAL AGENTS. A variety of chemical agents have been developed that can kill and incapacitate. Choking agents, of which phosgene is the most lethal example, attack the respiratory system, causing irritation and inflammation of the bronchial tubes and lungs.[23] At lethal concentrations the lungs become so full of fluid that the victim dies of anoxia. Blood agents, such as hydrogen cyanide, act by preventing the utilization of oxygen in the blood.[24] Choking and blood gases are respiratory agents, and are therefore readily defeated by gas masks. Blister agents, of which mustard is the best known, can injure and kill by absorption through the skin as well by inhalation of vapors or aerosols.[25] Because they are liquids at normal temperatures, their dissemination is easier to control than a gas. These properties made blister agents the most effective chemical agents at the end of World War I.

Nerve agents, first discovered in Germany shortly before World War II, are far more deadly than the choking, blood, and blister agents used in World War I. Nerve agents work by interfering with cholinesterase, an enzyme involved in nerve transmission. Symptoms of nerve-agent poisoning include sweating, nausea, vomiting, staggering, coma, and convulsion, followed by cessation of breathing and death. When inhaled, nerve agents are lethal in concentrations over ten times smaller than choking, blood, or blister agents; like mustard, nerve agents are readily absorbed through the skin.

---

21. Statement of Rear Admiral Thomas A. Brooks, Director of Naval Intelligence, before the Seapower, Strategic, and Critical Materials Subcommittee of the House Armed Services Committee, March 7, 1991.
22. Iraq recently revealed that it possesses 30 chemical warheads for its modified Scud missiles, but details about the design of the warheads is not available. Iraq also disclosed supplies of 75 tons of Sarin and 500 tons of Tabun. See Don Oberdorfer and Ann Devroy, "State Department Calls Iraq's Figures on Weapons 'Short of Reality'," *Washington Post*, April 20, 1991, p. A15.
23. Other common chokings agents include chlorine, chloropicrin, and diphosgene.
24. Other common blood agents include cyanogen chloride and arsine.
25. Other common blister agents include lewisite and various nitrogen mustard compounds.

They vary in consistency from sarin, which is watery and volatile, to VX, which has the viscosity of motor oil. Production costs are low—as little as $10–20 per kilogram of agent.[26]

The lethality of chemical agents is typically stated in terms of the LCt_{50}, which is the product of the concentration of the agent in air in milligrams per cubic meter (mg/m^3), multiplied by the length of the exposure in minutes that would result in death to 50 percent of the adults exposed.[27] The ICt_{50} is the dose that would result in militarily significant incapacitation to half of the exposed population. The estimated LCt_{50} and ICt_{50} for various chemical agents are given in Table 3.

CHEMICAL WARHEAD DESIGN. The United States and the Soviet Union are the only two countries known to have developed chemical warheads for ballistic missiles. The chemical warheads developed by the United States for the Little John, Honest John, and Sergeant missiles carry a large number of bomblets, each filled with a small amount of agent (about 600 grams of sarin or VX). The height at which the bomblets are released determines the diameter of the impact pattern on the ground. A burster charge containing a few hundred grams of high explosive detonates when the bomblets strike the ground, creating a small cloud of agent. Agent comprises 30–40 percent of the total weight of these warheads.[28]

Soviet chemical warheads are designed quite differently. Diagrams of the FROG and Scud-B warheads displayed at the Soviet Shikhany Central Proving Ground in October 1987 show a small, cylindrical burster charge surrounded by a large amount of liquid agent. According to the diagram, the 985-kilogram Scud warhead contains 555 kilograms of thickened VX; the burster charge appears to contain only about 20 kilograms of high explosive.[29]

---

26. The United States produced sarin for about $3/kilogram during 1954–56 and VX for about $5/kilogram during 1961–67, which is equivalent to $12/kilogram and $18/kilogram at today's prices. SIPRI, *The Problem of Chemical and Biological Warfare*, Vol. II: *CB Weapons Today* (New York: Humanities Press, 1973), pp. 53. Producing the agent would therefore cost a few thousand dollars per missile, assuming that a 1-tonne missile warhead would contain 300 kilograms of agent.
27. For example, the LCt_{50} of sarin is 100 mg·min/m^3, meaning that exposure to a concentration of 10 mg/m^3 for 10 minutes or 100 mg/m^3 for 1 minute would be fatal to half those exposed.
28. The 110-kilogram M206 warhead for the Little John contained 31 kilograms of GB; the 560-kilogram M79 and M190 warheads for the Honest John contained 177 and 217 kilograms of GB; the 680-kilogram M213 warhead for the Sergeant contained 195 kilograms of GB. Agent masses from SIPRI, *CB Weapons Today*, p. 84; warhead masses from Cochran, *U.S. Nuclear Forces and Capabilities*.
29. S.J. Lundin, J.P. Perry-Robinson, and Ralph Trapp, "Chemical and Biological Warfare: Developments in 1987," SIPRI, *SIPRI Yearbook 1988: World Armaments and Disarmament* (Oxford:

Table 3. The properties of various chemical agents.

Agent	Volatility (mg/m³)[a]	Respiratory[b] Lethal Dose LCt50 (mg · min/m³)	Respiratory[b] Incap. Dose ICt50 (mg · min/m³)	Percutaneous[c] Lethal Dose LCt50 (mg · min/m³)
Tabun (GA)	610	400	300	40,000
Sarin (GB)	22,000	100	75	15,000
Soman (GD)	3,900	100	75	10,000[d]
VX	10	100	50	1,000[d]
Mustard (HD)	920	1500	200	10,000
Phosgene (CG)	4,000,000	3200	1600	n.a.
Hydrogen Cyanide	1,100,000	5000[e]	2000[e]	n.a.

SOURCE: FM 3-9, *Military Chemistry and Chemical Compounds* (Washington, D.C.: Department of the Army, October 1975).

NOTES: These estimates are for resting, unprotected adults; for highly active adults (e.g., soldiers in heavy combat or civilians running for cover after a missile attack) or for children, the LCt50 and ICt50 could be three to four times lower.

a. Mass of vapor per cubic meter of air at 25° C. For comparison, the volatility of water at 25° C is 23,000 mg/m³.
b. Median lethal and incapacitating dosage for unprotected men breathing at a rate of 10 liters per minute.
c. Median lethal dosage for men in ordinary combat clothing.
d. Stockholm International Peace Research Institute, *The Problem of Chemical and Biological Warfare*, Vol. II: *CB Weapons Today* (New York: Humanities Press, 1973), pp. 42–43.
e. Depends on concentration; values given here are for a concentration of 100 mg/m³. LCt50 = 2000 mg·min/m³ at a concentration of 200 mg/m³.

Apparently the warhead shell is fragmented by the burster charge hundreds of meters above the ground, and wind-shear forces break the exposed liquid into droplets, which rain onto the ground below.

The effects of chemical agents depend largely on the size of the aerosol particles. Particles with diameters greater than 10 microns pose a hazard via direct absorption through the skin or, in warm weather, by the evaporation and subsequent inhalation of the vapors. Aerosols larger than 10 microns pose relatively little inhalation hazard since such particles are trapped by the upper respiratory tract, where absorption into the bloodstream is slow. Al-

Oxford University Press, 1988), p. 111; *Soviet Military Power: An Assessment of the Threat 1988* (Washington, D.C.: U.S. Department of Defense, 1988), p. 77.

though spray tanks can efficiently distribute agent as a fine aerosol, missile warheads using explosive charges probably cannot disperse more than one-half of the agent as particles with diameters of less than 5 microns, the particle sizes that maximize retention in the lung and absorption into the bloodstream.

Large particles settle quickly onto the target below, heavily contaminating a relatively small area; aerosols, on the other hand, drift with the wind, posing an inhalation hazard over a much larger area. Since large particles are not readily inhaled and do not stay airborne for long, the primary hazard is skin contact with the agent. For this reason, persistent agents are usually made into coarse aerosols, so that a particular target (e.g., an airstrip) can be made unusable, except by protected personnel, for an extended period of time. For strategic attacks against unprotected civilians, an agent capable of forming a fine (less than 5-micron–diameter) aerosol would have the greatest potential for causing deaths over a large area. The U.S. Army recommends using the more volatile agent sarin (rather than VX) against troops that are unprotected or who are carrying, but not wearing, masks.[30] Fine aerosols are carried along by the wind, gradually diluted by atmospheric turbulence and removed by deposition onto the ground, forming cigar-shaped dose contours.

The concentration of agent downwind from a chemical attack depends on the mass of agent released, the size of the particles, the height of burst, and the initial size of the aerosol cloud, as well as the atmospheric stability, wind speed, mixing height, and temperature. Since the United States has undoubtedly conducted extensive tests, it is reasonable to assume that current U.S. warheads can disseminate sarin as a fine aerosol with reasonable efficiency. While it should not be too difficult for Third World countries to develop the chemical-bomblet warhead technology that the United States had in the 1950s, it would be far easier and more efficient to spray chemical agents from aircraft or cruise missiles. Indeed, Iraq primarily used helicopters, which it bought from the United States for crop dusting, to spray lethal chemical agents on Kurdish civilians in 1988.[31]

To explore the range of casualties that might result from chemical attacks on unprotected civilians, a dispersion model was developed to predict the

---

30. FM 3-10, *Employment of Chemical Agents* (Washington, D.C.: Department of the Army, March 1966), p. 19.
31. Stuart Auerbach, "$1.5 Billion in U.S. Sales to Iraq," *Washington Post*, March 11, 1991, p. A1, A16.

areas that would receive lethal or incapacitating doses under a variety of conditions and assumptions.[32] Calculations were done for ground-level releases of 100 to 1000 kilograms of agent on urban targets under three sets of weather conditions: a clear, sunny day with a light breeze; an overcast and windy day or night; and a clear, calm night.[33] The agent was assumed to be released by the missile warhead in three different forms: as vapor over a period of hours, instantaneously as a fine aerosol, or half as vapor and half as fine aerosol, with an initial cloud diameter of 50 to 150 meters. The results, given as the area covered by doses greater than the lethal or incapacitating dose to mildly active, unprotected adults per tonne of agent released, are given in Table 4. In general, elevated releases, coarser aerosols, and larger initial cloud sizes lead to smaller lethal areas than small, ground-level clouds of fine aerosol.

Assuming that about half of the agent is disseminated as a fine aerosol (with most of the remainder evaporating within a few hours in warm weather), the lethal area ranges from about 20 to 40 hectares per tonne[34] (ha/te) of agent released under the least favorable weather conditions explored, to 250 to 400 ha/te under the most favorable conditions for an attacker. The corresponding areas for incapacitating effects are an additional 20 to 50 ha/te for unfavorable conditions and 300 to 400 ha/te for favorable conditions.

It should be noted that the least favorable conditions explored here are relatively unfavorable (from the attacker's point of view) but reasonably likely conditions; much higher wind speeds or larger aerosol particles would decrease these areas substantially. On the other hand, the most favorable

---

32. The model was verified by comparing its results with U.S. Army estimates of the number of sarin-filled 105-millimeter, 155-millimeter, and 8-inch artillery shells required to produce 50 percent casualties among mildly active, unprotected troops over an area of one hectare. Good agreement was obtained over a variety of stability conditions and wind speeds by assuming that 50 percent of the agent is released in a small cloud of fine aerosol at ground level over rural terrain, and that at high temperatures the remaining 50 percent evaporates in a matter of hours. See FM 3-10, *Employment of Chemical Agents*, pp. 97–99. Under a reasonable set of assumptions, the model also showed good agreement with estimates presented by IISS, *The Military Balance 1988–89*, p. 248, for the effects of chemical attacks with Soviet Scud and FROG missiles. A detailed description of the model (and the computer model itself) is available upon request to the author.

33. Stability is a measure of the tendency of air near the ground to mix vertically. During unstable conditions mixing is rapid; during stable conditions air is trapped near the ground. In general, unstable conditions occur during clear, calm days; stable conditions occur during clear, calm nights. Extensive cloud cover or high wind speeds create neutral conditions (i.e., air near the ground tends neither to rise or sink).

34. One hectare (ha) = 10,000 square meters = 0.01 square kilometers = 2.5 acres. An average city block covers an area of about two hectares.

Table 4. The areas over which unprotected adults would receive lethal and incapacitating doses of sarin, per tonne of agent released.

Weather Conditions[a]	Agent Form[b]	Area Affected (hectares/tonne)	
		Lethal Dose	Incapacitating Dose
Clear, sunny day, light breeze	vapor	10–18	26–37
	a/v	17–32	47–64
	aerosol	29–48	73–94
Overcast with moderate wind, day or night	vapor	9–16	13–34
	a/v	19–37	27–83
	aerosol	37–63	54–150
Clear, calm night	vapor	150–460	420–1300
	a/v	260–400	590–820
	aerosol	240–430	380–900

NOTES: Assumes LCt_{50} of 70 mg·min/m^3 and ICt_{50} of 35 mg·min/m^3 (appropriate for mildly active, unprotected men), for releases of 100 to 1,000 kilograms of sarin on an urban target.

a. "Clear, sunny day, light breeze" corresponds to Pasquill class "A" stability for residential urban areas, a mixing height of 2,000 meters, and a wind speed of 2 meters per second; "overcast" corresponds to class "D" stability, a mixing height of 1,000 meters, and a wind speed of 5 meters per second; "clear, calm night" corresponds to class "F" stability, a mixing height of 250 meters, and a wind speed of 1 meter per second.

b. a/v = 50 percent fine aerosol, 50 percent vapor. The deposition velocity is assumed to be 0.01 meters per second for a fine aerosol, 0 meters per second for vapor.

weather conditions explored here are not uncommon—at one desert location in the southwestern United States, such conditions occur about one-third of the time.[35] Because the attacker chooses the time and place of an attack, it can therefore control to some extent the weather conditions during an attack.[36]

If we assume that the average chemical warhead is 30 percent agent by weight, and that about half of the agent is released as respirable aerosol, then under even relatively unfavorable conditions a sarin-armed missile with

35. *Reactor Safety Study*, WASH-1400 (Washington, D.C.: U.S. Nuclear Regulatory Agency, 1975), Appendix VI, p. 5-3.

36. Although Third World countries may not have weather satellites, they could use commercial weather forecasts, news broadcasts, or even spies to determine weather conditions in remote cities, even during war.

a throwweight of 1 tonne could kill unprotected people over an area of 6 to 10 hectares and incapacitate over another 8 to 11 hectares. Under favorable conditions for an attacker, unprotected people would be killed over an area of 100 hectares and incapacitated over an additional 120 hectares. If used against an unprepared city with a population density of 35 per hectare (e.g., Tel Aviv or Riyadh), 200 to 3,000 people would be killed and a somewhat greater number seriously injured, depending on the weather conditions. This is 40 to 700 times as many deaths, and 20 to 300 times as many injuries, as would result from the same missile armed with a conventional warhead.[37] Since many cities in the Middle East and Asia have much greater population densities (e.g., 100 to 300 per hectare),[38] the potential exists for huge numbers of deaths in unprotected civilian populations.

DEFENSE AGAINST CHEMICAL AGENTS. While it is possible to protect civilians against chemical attack, protection is never perfect. It is commonly assumed that by remaining indoors and closing all doors and windows the dose can be greatly reduced, but in fact agent will still leak in. Even tightly sealed dwellings will not afford much protection unless they are thoroughly ventilated as soon as the cloud passes, for otherwise the occupants will receive about the same dose as unprotected individuals, but at a slower rate.[39] Gas masks provide protection against all but very high concentrations of nerve agent, but they must be applied immediately and they must fit properly. Even among soldiers carrying masks and trained for chemical combat, the U.S. Army estimates that 4 to 8 percent of troops that would have died

---

37. See footnote 17.

38. Average population densities of major cities range from 25 (Miami) to 1,000 (Hong Kong) per hectare. Most cities have 30 to 300 people per hectare, with western cities at the lower end and older Asian cities at the upper end of this range. The average population densities of selected Asian and Middle Eastern cities are as follows: Bombay, 41; Haifa, 100; Baghdad, Istanbul, and Karachi, 130; Ankara and Kiev, 160; Calcutta, 190; Delhi, 200; Teheran and Lahore, 240; Alexandria, 290; Cairo, 320. *The World Almanac* (New York: Pharos, 1989), pp. 738–739.

39. If people remain inside buildings for several hours, the dose inside will be nearly equal to the dose outside. To see this, consider a house of volume V in which the residence time of air is τ; air will flow into the house at a rate of V/τ. If the concentration of agent in the outside air is C for the time of the cloud passage t, then amount of agent flowing into the house is $C(V/\tau)t$, and the concentration of agent inside the house, c, is equal to Ct/τ. Therefore, the time-integrated dose inside the house $(c\tau)$ is equal to the dose outside (Ct). If the building is tightly sealed, τ will be large (e.g., 10 hours) and c will be much smaller than C, and occupants can greatly decrease their total dosage by ventilating the house after the cloud passes. To do this, however, the occupants must be told when it is safe to go outside. A series of chemical attacks, or fears of additional attacks, could keep people in their houses for many hours (comparable to the residence times of air in western dwellings). In fact, residents of Tel Aviv were kept in their houses for hours at a time merely in anticipation of such attacks.

without masks will die nevertheless because of delayed masking, mask leak-age, defective or missing masks, or early unmasking.[40] The percentage of masking errors among civilians would undoubtedly be much higher; it seems unlikely that even the best civil defense program could reduce fatalities to much less than 10 percent of the number that would die without protection.

Depending on the circumstances, chemical weapons can be a minor nuis-ance or weapons of mass destruction. Based on the example given above, chemical warheads are likely to be more deadly than conventional munitions even if used against a well-prepared population under unfavorable weather conditions;[41] they may be 50 times more deadly if civil defense is ineffective *or* weather conditions are favorable, and 500 times more deadly than con-ventional warheads when used against unprepared populations under fa-vorable weather conditions. (Compared to a Hiroshima-sized nuclear weapon, chemical warheads would result in $1/10$ to $1/2000$ of the number of deaths.)[42] In view of these estimates, it is not hard to see why a Third World military planner with a limited number of inaccurate but expensive missiles might prefer chemical over conventional warheads.

Although they are capable of causing widespread death and suffering, chemical warheads do not constitute a "poor's man atom bomb," especially if used against a well-prepared adversary. Biological weapons, in contrast, could approach nuclear weapons in lethality.

BIOLOGICAL WARHEADS

No nation is known to possess biological weapons today, but the United States, the United Kingdom, and Japan are known to have developed several types of biological weapons in the past (such stocks have since been de-stroyed), and Iraq and Syria are strongly suspected of stockpiling such weap-ons today.[43]

---

40. FM 3-10, *Employment of Chemical Agents*, p. 36.
41. If chemically armed missiles are to be no more deadly than similar missiles armed with high explosives, civil defenses would have to limit deaths to no more than 1 percent of the number that would die without protection. Such a high degree of protection seems extremely unlikely.
42. Based on the bombings of Hiroshima and Nagasaki, the lethal area of a 20-kiloton nuclear weapon is about 10 square kilometers (1,000 hectares). Samuel Glasstone and Philip J. Dolan, *The Effects of Nuclear Weapons* (Washington, D.C.: U.S. Department of Defense, 1977), p. 544.
43. The United States believes that Iraq has anthrax as well as botulism warheads. Statement of Rear Admiral Brooks, March 7, 1991.

Biological agents can be divided into two distinct categories: toxins (toxic chemicals produced by living organisms)[44] and pathogens (living organisms that produce disease). One of the most studied toxins is botulinal toxin, which is lethal at concentrations a thousand times smaller than sarin. Botulinal toxin is not suited to air delivery (especially by ballistic missile) because it decays rapidly upon exposure to air. Experiments in which clouds of botulinal toxin were released over lines of tethered animals showed that the number of deaths caused would not be much greater than that from an equal quantity of nerve agent.[45] Other toxins have been studied, but none seems to have convincing advantages over nerve agents for strategic missile attacks.

Pathogens, on the other hand, may have significant advantages over nerve agents in their ability to kill large numbers of civilians. In particular, *bacillus anthracis*, the bacteria that causes anthrax, seems especially well suited for dissemination by missiles or bombs because of its ability to form spores that can survive violent dissemination methods and exposure to sun, air, and rain. Because anthrax is not an infectious disease, it can be used as discriminately as chemical agents. Anthrax bacteria are deadly in concentrations a thousand times smaller than nerve agents, with an estimated ECt_{50} (the dose at which 50 percent of the exposed population would contract the disease) of only 0.1 mg·min/m^3. Left untreated, anthrax kills nearly all who contract it within a few days. Although vaccines are available, they must be administered before exposure and their effectiveness against massive doses is uncertain. Mass vaccination programs are unlikely to be popular unless the situation is obviously dire. Treatments with antibiotics have been developed, but patients must be treated early, before symptoms of the disease are apparent. It is doubtful whether sufficient stocks of antibiotics would exist to treat the hundreds of thousands of people who might fear that they were infected during an attack on a large city, let alone enough medical personnel to administer the injections in the short time available (a day or two).

Table 5 gives the ECt_{50}, incubation period, and mortality rate for *bacillus anthracis* and several other pathogens. Some pathogens have an ECt_{50} that is much lower than that of anthrax, but their mortality rates are usually lower, the incubation times are longer, the pathogens are more difficult to dissem-

---

44. Toxins have been produced synthetically, which blurs the distinction between toxin and chemical agents. The classification of toxins as biological rather than chemical agents dates back to a time when synthetic production was not possible.
45. SIPRI, *CB Weapons Today*, p. 60.

Table 5. Pathogens considered for use as biological weapons.

Pathogen	Disease	Respiratory ECt_{50}[a] $(mg \cdot min/m^3)$	Time to Effect (days)	Mortality Rate (percent)
F. tularensis	Tularemia	0.001	2–5	0–60
B. anthracis	Anthrax	0.1	1–4	95–100
P. pestis	Plague	[b]	3–4	90–100
C. burnetii	Q fever	0.001	18–21	1–4
VEE virus	VEE	0.001	2–5	0–2

SOURCE: Stockholm International Peace Research Institute, *The Problem of Chemical and Biological Warfare,* Vol. II: *CB Weapons Today* (New York: Humanities Press, 1973), pp. 42–43.

NOTES:
a. Median pathogen dosage that would produce the disease in resting, unprotected men, assuming agent-infested particles with diameters of 1 to 5 microns, and assuming that a fraction of the organisms die during dissemination (95 percent for tularemia, 50 percent for anthrax, 90 percent for Q fever, and 80 percent for VEE).
b. Plague is highly contagious; the number of people exposed to a given concentration of the *pasteurella pestis* bacteria would not be an accurate indication of how many people would eventually contract the disease. A dose of about 3,000 bacteria per man would result in a 50 percent probability of contracting the disease.

inate and less hardy when airborne, or the diseases are contagious, making these agents less useful than *bacillus anthracis* for strategic missile attacks. The possibility that suitable pathogens remain to be discovered that are a hundred times more lethal than *bacillus anthracis* cannot be ruled out, however.

As above, a dispersion model was used to estimate the areas that would receive a given concentration of pathogen for attacks with 10 to 100 kilograms of agent distributed as a fine aerosol.[46] Doses greater than 0.1 mg·min/m^3 (the estimated ECt_{50} for anthrax) can be produced over 20 to 40 hectares per kilogram of bacteria released on a calm, sunny day; 65–100 ha/kg for a windy,

46. The range of delivered biological agent masses is assumed to be ten times smaller than the range of delivered chemical agent masses because biological agents are more difficult and fragile to disperse and more expensive to produce, and because more casualties could be reliably produced by distributing the available agent among many missiles. See, for example, Matthew Meselson, Martin M. Kaplan, and Mark A. Mokulsky, "Verification of Biological and Toxin Weapons Disarmament," in Francesco Calogero, Marvin L. Goldberger, and Sergei P. Kapitza, eds., *Verification: Monitoring Disarmament* (Boulder, Colo.: Westview, 1991), p. 152.

overcast day; and 30–260 ha/kg for a calm, clear night. Kilogram for kilogram, anthrax produces lethal concentrations over an area about one thousand times larger than does sarin; warhead for warhead, roughly one hundred times larger.

To illustrate the magnitude of the casualties that could be produced by biological weapons, consider a missile armed with 30 kilograms of anthrax spores. Lethal doses to unprotected adults would result over an area of 6 to 80 square kilometers, depending on the weather conditions and assumptions about the release; since the cigar-shaped lethal area would extend 10 to 30 kilometers downwind, only 5 to 25 square kilometers of the lethal area might lie within the targeted city.[47] Even with civil defense, the effective lethal area might be 0.5 to 2 square kilometers. (For comparison, the lethal area of a Hiroshima-type fission bomb is about 10 square kilometers.) Thus, even when used against a prepared population, anthrax warheads could rival small nuclear weapons in their ability to kill people, although the outcome would be highly unpredictable due to uncertainties in the weather and the effectiveness of dissemination, civil defense, and medical treatment.

Unlike chemical agents, the most persistent of which might pose a continuing hazard to large numbers of humans for up to a few weeks, anthrax spores could survive for decades in soil. Unless extensive decontamination measures are taken, spores in resuspended dust could continue to infect people long after an attack. During World War II, Britain, Canada, and the United States detonated experimental anthrax bombs on Gruinard Island; the island was only declared safe again in 1988 after burning the heather and treating the ground with formaldehyde.[48] It is difficult to make quantitative estimates of the number of people that might be exposed in this way because of uncertainties in evacuation and decontamination procedures, the lifetime of the spores, the concentration of resuspended spores as a function of time, and the time dependence of the dose-response relationship.[49] The persistency of agents such as anthrax would limit the usefulness of such weapons in

---

47. A city of one million inhabitants with an average population density of 35 per hectare would have a diameter of roughly 10 kilometers. If warheads are detonated in the optimal location (on the edge of the city on its windward side), then at most only the first 20 kilometers of the lethal area would lie within the city.
48. L.M. Astra, "Germs and Ideas: What the Public Record Says About Chemical and Biological Warfare, Both Here and Abroad," *City Paper* (Washington, D.C.), February 22, 1991, p. 11.
49. For example, inhaling a thousand spores a day for a thousand days will not result in the same effects as inhaling a million spores in a single day.

taking and holding territory, but it would not necessarily make the threat to use such weapons less credible than the threat to use nuclear weapons.

Table 6 gives rough estimates of the number of people that might be killed in a large, sparsely populated city by a missile armed with a conventional, chemical, biological, or nuclear warhead, with and without effective civil defenses. Up to ten times as many casualties would result if these weapons were used in a densely populated city such as Cairo, Teheran, or Lahore. In very rough terms, a relatively small (20-kiloton) nuclear warhead is 10,000 times as destructive as a 1-ton conventional explosive, 10 to 100 times as deadly as a nerve-agent warhead, but no more deadly than an anthrax warhead used against an unprotected population. Used against a well-protected population, nuclear weapons are 100 to 1,000 times more deadly than chemical weapons and about 10 times as deadly as an anthrax warhead.

Do chemical and biological weapons qualify as "weapons of mass destruction," and should we think about these weapons in the same way that we have come to think about nuclear weapons? Anthrax weapons (or weapons using similarly lethal pathogens) certainly are able to kill enough people to qualify for this dubious distinction, even if they cannot knock over buildings.

Table 6. A comparison of the casualties produced by nuclear, chemical, biological, and high-explosive warheads.

Type of Warhead	Without Civil Defense		With Civil Defense[a]	
	Dead	Injured	Dead	Injured
Conventional (1 tonne of high explosive)	5	13	2	6
Chemical (300 kilograms of sarin)	200–3,000	200–3,000	20–300	20–300
Biological (30 kilograms of anthrax spores)	20,000–80,000		2,000–8,000	
Nuclear (20 kilotons)	40,000	40,000	20,000	20,000

NOTES: Assumes a missile with a throwweight of 1 tonne aimed at a large city with an average population density of 30 per hectare. Assumes that civil defenses reduce casualties from conventional and nuclear explosions by a factor of two, and casualties from chemical and biological weapons by a factor of ten.

Whether or not chemical warheads should be classified as massively destructive appears to depend on the willingness and the capacity of civilian populations to prepare for such attacks. While civil defense is relatively straightforward, one should bear in mind that the capacity of many Third World nations to prepare and train for chemical attacks is limited; many western nations, while possessing the capacity, lack the willingness to prepare.[50] In the final analysis, however, it depends on the threshold of pain in a particular country or region. Western nations often react violently to events that involve even a handful of civilian deaths. Thus, while chemical weapons may be hundreds or thousands of times less deadly than nuclear weapons, chemical attacks on western nations may well trigger political and military responses similar to those that would be provoked by nuclear or anthrax attacks.

Why Should We Care About Proliferation?

There are five reasons that we should be at least as concerned about the proliferation of weapons of mass destruction in the future as we have been about nuclear proliferation in the past: (1) proliferation complicates U.S. foreign policy; (2) crisis instabilities are likely to more severe; (3) the probability of inadvertent or accidental use is likely to be greater; (4) transfers to terrorist or sub-national groups are more likely; and (5) at least some of the future possessor nations are likely to be politically unstable, aggressive, and difficult to deter.

To see how missile proliferation, coupled with unconventional warheads, might complicate foreign policy, consider how the response to the Iraqi invasion of Kuwait might have been different if Iraq had possessed the capability to launch chemical, biological, or nuclear weapons against Paris or London. In the face of such a threat, would France and the United Kingdom have joined the United States in attacking Iraq? Indeed, if Iraq threatened to hold European cities "hostage," would even the United States have risked an attack? And if Iraq carried out threats to launch such weapons at the first notice of an allied attack, how would the United States and its allies have

---

50. The dismal history of civil defense precautions against nuclear attack in the United States should give pause to anyone contemplating a similar program to guard against chemical or biological attack. See, for example, Robert Scheer, *With Enough Shovels: Reagan, Bush, and Nuclear War* (New York: Vintage, 1983).

responded? The result would not necessarily be total paralysis; in the case of Iraq, for example, the United States could have preemptively destroyed the missile sites, as it did in the war. If weapons were launched nevertheless, massive conventional attacks would have been adequate to punish and defeat Iraq.

With regard to crisis instability, Third World weapons are more vulnerable to preemptive attack than are the forces of the nuclear powers, whether based on missiles or aircraft. The short distances separating nations in the Middle East make airbases and missile launch sites tempting targets for preemptive strikes; ballistic missiles, either with more accurate or with more powerful warheads, make it possible to attack such targets in just a few minutes. While light-weight missiles such as the Scud are readily mobile and thus can be difficult to destroy if dispersed throughout the countryside, longer-range missiles weighing more than ten or twenty tonnes are too heavy to be truly mobile and probably would be launched from a few (perhaps hardened) fixed sites. Missiles have the advantage of not requiring visible facilities such as airstrips, but, unlike aircraft, missiles cannot escape attack without being used offensively.

Although missiles themselves might not significantly worsen the vulnerability problem, weapons of mass destruction might, because the benefits that could be derived from a successful first strike would be much greater. Just as the early U.S. and Soviet nuclear forces were vulnerable to preemptive attack, so may emerging arsenals of mass destruction in the Third World create instability. If, during a crisis, one side believes that war is inevitable, it may try to preemptively destroy the other side's vulnerable but valuable weapons of mass destruction. Even if both sides prefer not to preempt, each may fear that the other side will; consequently, both may decide to launch at the first (perhaps false) indication of an attack. This crisis-stability problem is even worse than the one faced by the superpowers,[51] because warning of an attack will be shorter, because of the shorter range, and much less reliable, because of the primitive intelligence-gathering capabilities of most Third World nations. The United States and the Soviet Union have managed to keep their nuclear forces on constant alert for three decades without an accidental launch. It is open to question whether the new missile states,

---

51. For a discussion of crisis stability in the superpower context, see Desmond Ball, et al., *Crisis Stability and Nuclear War* (Ithaca, N.Y.: Cornell University, 1987).

lacking the wealth, technology, and political stability of the superpowers, can be expected to compile as good a record.

The possibility of unauthorized use or accident also creates dangers. Although political control over weapon systems may be very strong in authoritarian states, unauthorized use and accidental launches are not physically prevented by sophisticated permissive action links and environmental sensing devices, such as those used in U.S. nuclear weapons. A group of military officers might use or threaten to use such weapons on their own authority, either to satisfy an overzealous hatred of the enemy or to blackmail their own civilian government.

The probability of large-scale attacks by sub-national or terrorist organizations will become far more worrisome as weapons of mass destruction spread to Third World countries that sponsor acts of terrorism, such as Iran, Iraq, Libya, North Korea, and Syria. If the supplier of such weapons is known, victim nations could respond by retaliating against the supplier nation; but if the supplier cannot be positively identified, a forceful response to an anonymous attack could trigger widespread resentment, especially if the suspected supplier can plausibly deny its involvement. Terrorist attacks might also be calculated to catalyze war between two states.

With the possible exception of the Soviet Union in recent times, the nuclear powers exhibit an exceptional degree of internal political stability. Many of the potential proliferators listed in Table 2 do not enjoy the same degree of stability. Some states, such as Afghanistan, Iraq, and South Africa, have deep internal divisions. Other pairs of states, such as India and Pakistan, North and South Korea, and Israel and various Arab states, have deep religious, ideological, or cultural animosities, often combined with active border disputes, that weaken deterrence. Some authoritarian states are ruled by aggressive dictators, such as Libya's Muammar Qaddafi or Iraq's Saddam Hussein, who have little regard for international norms of behavior. Many of the new missile states are not happy with the status quo, and may look upon their newly acquired capabilities for mass destruction as instruments of intimidation and change. The probability of conflict within and among the new missile states will be substantially higher than has been the case with the present nuclear powers, which increases the probability that weapons of mass destruction will be used. Even if the United States or it allies would not be directly threatened, we should still be concerned because of the human suffering that would result from the use of such weapons.

What Can We Do About Proliferation?

The United States has a declaratory policy of preventing the proliferation of weapons of mass destruction, but this policy has been applied rather unevenly over time and among nations. Many of these inconsistencies have resulted from balancing the goal of nonproliferation against other goals of U.S. policy, such as containing the Soviet Union, supporting the state of Israel, or balancing the trade deficit. In most cases nonproliferation has taken a back seat to these other goals. It is time to give nonproliferation higher priority.

Possible policy responses fall into four broad categories: carrots, sticks, defenses, and management. *Carrots* include security guarantees and arms control arrangements designed to reassure states that are worried that they might need missiles or unconventional weapons for their defense. *Sticks* include export controls, deterrence through the threat of retaliation, economic sanctions, and the threat of preventive war, all of which are intended to thwart or deter proliferation. *Defenses,* both active and passive, seek to insulate the United States (and possibly its allies) from the effects of proliferation. *Management* refers to measures designed to cope with proliferation in a cooperative fashion by, for example, transferring technology or information that decreases the probability of accident, misuse, or instability.

SECURITY GUARANTEES

Promising to defend a country if it is attacked can alleviate its desires for advanced weaponry, but this strategy has obvious limitations. The U.S. commitment to defend South Korea and Taiwan, not to mention Germany and Japan, may have averted the development of nuclear weapons by each of these nations. It is extremely difficult, however, to identify additional nations among those listed in Table 2 to which the United States could extend security guarantees. Even in the case of moderate Arab states such as Egypt and Saudi Arabia, guarantees would encounter strong opposition from supporters of Israel. Collective security guarantees, in which large groups of nations (e.g., the United Nations) agree to come to the aid of any member under attack, are more appealing, but for most nations collective security does not seem sufficiently reliable to forestall the desire to acquire advanced weapons.

ARMS CONTROL

Chemical, biological, and nuclear weapons have been the subject of multi-lateral arms control treaties; missiles have not. Although arms control treaties cannot prevent proliferation, they can provide a mechanism whereby nations that prefer not to develop certain types of weapons can be reassured that their rivals are also not developing them. If a nation believes that it would be better off if both it *and* its rivals refrained from acquiring certain weapons, then arms control should be an attractive solution. Unfortunately, it is not always so simple. For example, although India might be worse off if both it and Pakistan had ballistic missiles or nuclear weapons, India also faces an-other rival—China—which already has both and shows no interest in giving them up. Moreover, some nations (e.g., Israel) probably believe that they are better off if they possess weapons of mass destruction, even if it means that their rivals are free to develop the same weapons, for otherwise inferi-orities in conventional weaponry or manpower could threaten their survival.

The 1925 Geneva Protocol prohibits the use (or, as interpreted by some countries, the first use) of chemical and biological weapons in war, but not the production or stockpiling of such weapons.[52] Virtually all nations support a verified worldwide ban on chemical weapons, and negotiations on a Chem-ical Weapons Convention (CWC) are continuing in the multilateral Confer-ence on Disarmament in Geneva.[53] Although the widespread commercial uses of chemicals makes a ban notoriously difficult to verify, the verification procedures under consideration are impressive, and it appears that, through a combination of continuous monitoring and on-site inspection, nonprod-uction by parties to a treaty can be adequately verified.[54]

Although the Bush administration strongly supports the goals of the CWC, it has argued that the United States must retain a small stockpile of chemical weapons for deterrent purposes until all other states capable of manufactur-ing chemical weapons have joined the treaty. As might be expected, this

---

52. See Utgoff, *The Challenge of Chemical Weapons*, for a review of the history of chemical arms control.
53. On January 11, 1989, 149 countries reaffirmed their commitment to the Geneva Protocol and to a global ban on chemical weapons in the Paris Conference on the Prohibition of Chemical Weapons. Although this may appear to justify some optimism about the near-term prospects for a ban on chemical weapons, one should remember that negotiations to ban chemicals have been continuing off and on for nearly a century, and that the current set of talks began two decades ago.
54. For a review of the verification problem, see Karlheinz Lohs, Julian P. Perry Robinson, and Nikita P. Smidovich, "Verification and Chemical-Warfare Weapons," in Calogero, Goldberger, and Kapitza, *Verification: Monitoring Disarmament*, pp. 123–148.

position has come under heavy criticism by those who claim that it smacks of the division between the "haves" and the "have nots" that undermined adherence to the nuclear Non-Proliferation Treaty (NPT). The administration claims that this clause will be an incentive for potential holdouts to join the treaty. The administration's argument highlights the main problem with all multilateral arms control: what about states that will not sign the treaty? Since chemical weapons appear to be the main instrument by which some Arab states (e.g., Syria and Iraq) hope to offset the Israeli nuclear arsenal, it is unlikely that chemical weapons will disappear completely any time soon.[55] Other states with powerfully armed neighbors may draw similar conclusions. There is always the hope that nonsignatories will heed world opinion and observe the taboo on the use of chemicals, but it is wise not to put too much faith in the power of international norms, especially those that have been broken in the recent past. The CWC will not prevent proliferation, but that is too high a standard to set for arms control. The appropriate question is whether the world will be a better place with a treaty than without one; in the case of the CWC, the answer is clearly "yes."

The development, production, stockpiling, and transfer of biological weapons is banned by the Biological Weapons Convention (BWC) of 1972, but the verification provisions of the BWC are limited. Parties to the BWC agree to cooperate with UN investigations, but such investigations must be approved by the Security Council, subject to the veto power of its permanent members. Various confidence-building measures have been adopted at the BWC review conferences, but these measures fall far short of the continuous monitoring and on-site inspections contemplated for the CWC. Since chemical agents are more likely to proliferate, because they are easier to produce and disseminate and their effects are more predictable, the lack of stringent BWC verification may not be worrisome now. But if the CWC makes chemical weapons far more difficult to acquire, then biological weapons may come to be seen as an attractive alternative, and their proliferation may become more of a problem.

In a recent trip to the Middle East, U.S. Secretary of State James Baker reportedly found "a lot of sympathy" among Persian Gulf states for a regional

---

55. The link between Israeli nuclear weapons and Arab development of chemical weapons has been made explicit by Arab leaders on several occasions, including during the Paris Conference on the Prohibition of Chemical Weapons. See, for example, Harry Anderson, "Showdown With Libya," *Newsweek*, January 16, 1989, p. 16.

ban on weapons of mass destruction, and even found "considerable interest" in the idea in Israel.[56] Although these discussions are commendable, there is little reason to believe that such an agreement could be achieved without solving the larger political problems in the Middle East, especially the Palestinian problem and the question of the occupied territories. If progress is not made along this front, the connection between Israeli nuclear weapons and Arab chemical (and possibly biological) weapons may create difficulties for the NPT as well as for the CWC. The final NPT review conference is scheduled for 1995, at which time the duration of the NPT will be decided. At least seven potential adversaries of Israel are signatories of the NPT: Egypt, Iran, Iraq, Libya, Saudi Arabia, Syria, and Yemen. Israel is not. All except Saudi Arabia and Yemen are strongly suspected of stockpiling chemical weapons; all but Yemen have acquired or are trying to acquire missiles capable of striking Israel. It is likely that the final NPT review conference will be used as a forum in which this group of countries, perhaps joined by other non-aligned nations, will insist that Israel join the NPT. Indeed, it is not inconceivable that these countries may tie their continued adherence to the NPT, as well as their support for the CWC, to Israeli accession to the NPT (or other equivalent steps). This situation would present the United States with a difficult management problem for which it should be prepared.

EXPORT CONTROLS

Controls on the export of key technologies and materials can slow proliferation, but such controls work much better and engender less resentment if they are coupled with a comprehensive arms control regime. In the NPT, for example, exports to signatories are accompanied by "safeguards" to verify that the exports (e.g., nuclear reactors) are not being used for military purposes. Supplier nations that are party to the NPT must require safeguards on all such exports, even to nations that are not parties to the Treaty.[57] This coupling between arms control and export controls may be an important reason for the relatively slow pace of nuclear proliferation. Unfortunately,

---

56. Don Oberdorfer, "Mideast Arms Sale Curb Favored; Israel, Arabs Study Regional Ban on Weapons of Mass Destruction," *Washington Post*, March 23, 1991, p. A15.
57. NPT signatories can, however, supply technology to nations that have unsafeguarded facilities that were developed indigenously or that were supplied by a nonsignatory. This loophole has allowed several nonsignatories to use the knowledge and experience gained from imports of foreign nuclear technologies to pursue weapon development in indigenously developed facilities. Under domestic laws, however, the United States, Canada, and Sweden require safeguards on all facilities in a country to which nuclear technologies are exported.

no comparable arrangements yet exist for the control of exports of chemical, biological, and ballistic-missile technology or materials. In general, export controls in these areas have been adopted only after proliferation problems were widely recognized. Even after controls are adopted, competition among suppliers and illegal exports often undermine their effectiveness.

Multilateral export controls were recently extended to missile technology through the Missile Technology Control Regime (MTCR).[58] Although the MTCR has slowed missile programs in several countries, the regime is "too little, too late." One important flaw in the MTCR is that several current and potential future exporters of missile technology are not part of the regime, including China, India, Israel, North and South Korea, Taiwan, Brazil, and Argentina. Without the cooperation of all important suppliers, export controls can slow, but cannot stop, proliferation. Another major flaw is that the MTCR allows exports of missile technology for use in civilian applications such as space launch vehicles, even though the same technologies can be used in weapons. Even if the MTCR required safeguards to verify that exports were only being used in civilian applications (which it does not), the knowledge and experienced gained would alone be sufficient in many cases to greatly aid military programs. And even if missile technologies were only exported to nations without military programs, sounding rockets and space launch vehicles developed for peaceful uses could quickly and easily be converted into ballistic missiles.

The prospects for export controls on chemical and biological warfare capabilities are not much brighter. The Australia Group, a loosely knit group of 23 countries including the United States, has for some time limited the export to certain countries of selected equipment and chemicals that can be used in the production of chemical agents, and yet chemical weapons have spread, with key technologies often slipping through the export controls of U.S. allies. The United States recently expanded its export restrictions,[59] but this will be of little help unless most other supplier nations follow suit. Once

---

58. The MTCR was initially an agreement between the Canada, France, Germany, Italy, Japan, United Kingdom, and the United States to limit the export of missiles capable of delivering a payload of at least 500 kilograms over a range of 300 kilometers, as well as missile systems, subsystems, and technologies that would be required to assemble such weapons. Spain, Belgium, the Netherlands, and Luxembourg have since joined the agreement; Sweden, Norway, and the Soviet Union have approved the MTCR restrictions but have not officially subscribed to the agreement.

59. "Fact Sheet on Enhanced Proliferation Control Initiative," Office of the Press Secretary, The White House, December 13, 1990.

again, a large part of the problem is that many of the chemicals and production techniques required for chemical and biological weapons have legitimate civilian uses.[60] Many of the items whose export the United States limits are used to make plastics, pharmaceuticals, and fertilizers. Nerve agents, for example, are chemically similar to common organophosphate pesticides. Fermenters can be used to produce antibiotics as well as pathogens. Industrialized nations will find it difficult to deny technologies essential for the production of goods such as pesticides and antibiotics, even to the growing list of countries with a suspected interest in developing chemical or biological weapons; yet it is difficult, if not impossible, to ensure that such exports would not or could not be used for military purposes.

The power of export controls by the industrialized nations is waning. Several Third World countries, such as India and Brazil, have thriving chemical industries of their own, and they are highly unlikely ever to join the Australia Group or similar supplier groups. The only hope of enlisting the cooperation of such states is to embed export restrictions in an arms control framework that makes no distinctions between western and eastern, nuclear and non-nuclear, or industrialized and developing nations. In the case of nuclear weapons, chemical weapons, and ballistic missiles, the United States has been unwilling to go this far.

DETERRENCE, SANCTIONS, AND PREVENTIVE WAR
Deterrence and preventive war represent the dark side of nonproliferation policy. Deterrence through threat of retaliation in kind is widely credited with preventing the use of chemical weapons in World War II, as well as the non-use of nuclear weapons since the end of World War II. Some claim that during the 1991 Gulf war, it was the possession of chemical weapons by the United States and the implicit threat to use these weapons that deterred Iraq from using its chemical weapons against allied ground troops, but this is far from obvious. First, Iraq apparently did not stockpile chemical weapons in Kuwait, and could not do so once the air war began destroying its supply lines. Iraqi forces might have used chemicals if they were available. Second, although most high-level officials were careful to say that the United States would consider all options if U.S. troops were attacked with chemical agents,

---

60. Stuart Auerbach, "U.S. to Curb Export of Ingredients in Chemical Weapons," *Washington Post*, February 27, 1991, p. G1, G3.

others made it clear that the United States would not respond in kind. Indeed, the United States did not even have chemical weapons available for use in the Middle East.

It is theoretically impossible to prove that deterrence works, since it is always possible that the other side had no intention of using that which they were supposedly deterred from using. Only failures of deterrence can be verified. If one has faith in the power of the threat of retaliation in kind, then maintaining chemical arsenals might be better than a CWC that does not enjoy universal adherence. Some states or some leaders may not be deterrable, however. Moreover, the United States can deal militarily with most of the emerging unconventional threats by means of overwhelming conventional force, thus obviating the need for "in kind" retaliation.

The war against Iraq was a preventive war in the minds of many Americans. A primary goal of the war was to destroy Iraq's potential to make and deliver nuclear, chemical, and biological weapons—to make war now, rather than later when Iraq might be armed with long-range weapons of mass destruction. The destruction of the Iraqi Osiraq reactor by Israel is another example of a preventive use of force. The use of force, especially on the scale of U.S. actions in Iraq, will generally be limited to the most exceptional circumstances and the most obviously aggressive and nefarious governments. The use of economic sanctions is far more palatable, but sanctions by the United States alone are insufficient. However, the United Nations may be able to make more widespread use of sanctions to punish nations that use or threaten to use weapons of mass destruction, thereby deterring others from following the same path.

DEFENSE

Even if arms control and export controls are reasonably effective, weapons of mass destruction will likely be acquired by a handful of determined states. Should the United States and its allies rely on the threat of retaliation to deter the use of such weapons, or should they pursue the development of defensive systems that could render such weapons "impotent and obsolete"? When this question was raised by President Reagan in 1983 in the context of the Soviet nuclear threat, general agreement emerged among defense analysts that the goal of a perfect defense was unattainable, and that the benefits of less-than-perfect defenses were unclear, and might well be negative. The use of Scud missiles in the Persian Gulf War and the apparent success of the

Patriot system in shooting them down[61] has rekindled the debate about the desirability of ballistic missile defenses.[62] Now that perceptions of a Soviet threat have dimmed, should the United States develop defensive systems capable of shooting down missiles launched by Third World countries? I do not think so.

The Patriot is a ground-launched interceptor initially designed to shoot down aircraft, which has some capability to intercept short-range ballistic missiles (which travel at relatively low speeds) in their terminal or reentry phase. Although intercepting faster, longer-range missile warheads is far more challenging (especially at ranges of several thousand kilometers), it should be possible to build a system capable of destroying long-range missile warheads with non-nuclear interceptors in the near future. But a major problem with terminal systems is that they can only defend a limited area ("footprint" or area of coverage). The Patriot system, which has a small footprint, could be successful because the number of targets within range of Iraqi missiles was small. Defending cities from longer-range missiles would not only require a more sophisticated interceptor, but would require far more interceptor sites to defend all possible targets within range of the missile.

In designing terminal defenses against chemically armed missiles, care must be taken that warhead destruction will be high in the atmosphere. If the agent is released as a fine aerosol at altitudes of a few hundred meters or more, it will be sufficiently diluted by the time the cloud reaches the ground that doses will be inconsequential. If, on the other hand, the high explosive in the chemical warhead is not detonated, the agent may be released as relatively large droplets which rain quickly onto the ground (similar to the way in which agent is released from Soviet chemical warheads).[63] The lethal area formed by such a release would, however, be much smaller than that resulting from a successful missile attack.

---

61. It is not yet clear how successful the Patriot really was in destroying incoming Scud warheads. Some analysts claim that while the Patriot's fragmentation warhead many have destroyed the Scud missile body, in many cases it did not detonate the high explosives in the Scud warhead. Casualties were minimized nevertheless, because live warheads were knocked off course. See William Safire, "The Great Scud-Patriot Mystery," *New York Times*, March 7, 1991, p. A25; and R. Jeffrey Smith, "Patriot Missiles Less Effective in Israel," *Washington Post*, April 26, 1991, p. A41.
62. See, for example, Harold Brown, "Yes on Patriot, No on SDI," *Washington Post*, March 27, 1991, p. A23.
63. Theodore A. Postol, "The Prospects for Successful Air Defense Against Chemically-armed Tactical Ballistic Missile Attacks on Urban Areas," March 7, 1991 (unpublished).

Even a highly effective terminal defense is unlikely to destroy more than 90 percent of incoming targets, but if only one nuclear or biological warhead penetrates the defenses of a city, thousands of people will die. Even the penetration of a single chemical warhead could result in hundreds of deaths and generate widespread panic in an unprepared population. Military planners are not likely to be satisfied with a 10 percent probability of penetration, however. Rather, it is probable that the deployment of defenses will prompt the search for offensive countermeasures (e.g., decoys, chaff, multiple warheads, maneuvering warheads, etc.), triggering an offense-defense arms race that leaves both sides less secure. It was the avoidance of just this sort of situation that lead the United States and the Soviet Union to limit strategic missile defenses in the Anti–Ballistic Missile (ABM) Treaty.

Only intercontinental-range missiles could threaten the U.S. homeland (except, possibly, from Cuba). Outside of the five declared nuclear powers, only Israel and India could strike the United States in the near future. However, important U.S. allies, such as the United Kingdom, France, Germany, and Japan, may soon be within range of the missile forces of several countries, and the United States might wish to protect its allies from attack. But space-based systems intended to intercept missiles in their boost phase, such as the SDI "brilliant pebbles" proposal, will not be able to engage short-range missiles or intermediate-range ballistic missiles that fly slightly depressed trajectories.[64] Such systems might be able to destroy ICBMs, but their benefits are unclear, given how few countries will possess ICBMs, and given that any country sophisticated enough to develop ICBMs could certainly find other ways to deliver nuclear, chemical, and biological weapons if faced with an effective missile defense. Indeed, cruise missiles—about which SDI-type systems can do very little—may in the not-too-distant future prove to be far more effective delivery systems for emerging nuclear, chemical, and biological arsenals than ballistic missiles. Cruise missiles are extremely difficult to defend against.

Deployment of almost any type of defense against long-range missiles or the transfer of relevant technologies to U.S. allies would violate provisions of the ABM Treaty. Under the ABM Treaty, the United States and the Soviet Union are permitted to deploy no more than 100 ground-launched missiles,

---

64. David C. Wright and Lisbeth Gronlund, "Underflying Brilliant Pebbles," *Arms Control Today*, Vol. 21, No. 4 (May 1991), p. 16.

all at a single, fixed site. Mobile or space-based systems are prohibited, and neither country may transfer ABM technologies to third parties. Any system capable of efficiently destroying intermediate-range missiles would have some capability against strategic missiles, which may violate the Treaty. In contemplating defenses against longer-range Third World missiles, the United States must judge whether the benefits afforded by such a defense would be worth jeopardizing the ABM Treaty and the two decades of U.S.-Soviet arms control efforts that are based upon it. The United States and the Soviet Union could agree to deploy defenses in a cooperative fashion to defend against third-party missiles, but this is highly unlikely in the foreseeable future.

MANAGEMENT

As noted above, Third World missiles and weapons of mass destruction are likely to be far more vulnerable to crisis instability, accidents, and intentional misuse than U.S. and Soviet nuclear arsenals have been. While this is undoubtedly a good reason to avoid proliferation in the first place, additional nations will acquire such weapons despite our best efforts at dissuasion. Should the United States quietly offer to help improve the safety and stability of their weapons? It seems illogical to spend billions of dollars ensuring the safety and security of our own weapons, while doing nothing to ensure the safety and security of weapons that may be pointed at us or our allies. If crisis stability becomes a major problem, the United States could extend warnings or assurances as to missile attack, in hopes of preventing inadvertent launches and deterring preemptive strikes. Such measures might be in the best interest of the United States and the world community in general, but it is extremely difficult for a government to command this degree of flexibility in foreign policy. Moreover, such behavior on our part would be interpreted by other Third World nations as a "wink and a nod" to successful proliferators, and this would inevitably undermine the even more important task of preventing the spread of such weapons to additional states.

Conclusions

Ballistic missile proliferation continues, with several nations seeking ever-longer ranges. It is only a matter of time before cruise-missile technology proliferates in similar fashion. Long-range ballistic missiles armed with conventional warheads do not make military sense. This simple fact seems to be well understood, since many of these same nations are also actively pursuing nuclear, chemical, and biological weapons. Nuclear weapons are by far the most difficult to acquire; the requisite technologies to produce nuclear materials are expensive and export controls are relatively effective. Chemical weapons are much easier to acquire, and a missile armed with a chemical warhead could kill as many people as dozens or even hundreds of conventionally armed missiles. Biological weapons are more difficult to produce and more unpredictable in their effects, but could inflict casualties on the scale of small nuclear weapons. Therefore, it should not be surprising if the future of missile proliferation points in the direction of chemical and biological weaponry, since for many states these are the only weapons that could constitute a strategic threat or a strategic deterrent.

In dealing with this emerging threat, the United States and its allies should resist calls to develop ballistic missile defenses or to rely on deterrence or threat of military force. Defenses would be costly and imperfect; they would trigger offensive countermeasures and endanger superpower arms control; and they would address only one of the ways in which weapons of mass destruction could be delivered (and probably the least likely way they would be delivered to the United States). While deterrence may work among the nuclear powers, it is an unreliable foundation for Third World security, due to the increased probability of accidents, unauthorized use, crisis instability, political instability, and transfers to terrorist or sub-national groups.

The best approach lies in the creation of a comprehensive arms control regime that covers all of these weapons, and which incorporates safeguards to ensure that exports—even to nonsignatories—are used only for peaceful purposes, coupled with the expanded use of the United Nations to foster collective security in the longer term. Comprehensive arms control regimes are unlikely to be created, however, if the superpowers continue to viewed by Third World nations as "advocating water, but drinking wine." The superpowers are unlikely to command much authority in their efforts to limit nuclear weapons or ballistic missiles if they continue to develop, test, and deploy new types of nuclear weapons and missiles that they claim are essential for their security. Nor are they likely to muster much support for a "ban" on chemical weapons that permits the superpowers to retain small stockpiles for their own security. Nor are Third World countries likely to support treaties that permit their enemies to possess (or even use) weapons of mass destruction with impunity. The United States should promote the United Nations as the appropriate forum for addressing security and proliferation concerns. In particular, more use should be made of global economic sanctions to punish nations that violate agreed international norms, such as using or threatening to use weapons of mass destruction.

During the Cold War, efforts to stem proliferation often took a back seat to superpower confrontation, as illustrated by the U.S. decision to extend aid to Pakistan in support of *Mujahideen* guerrillas in Afghanistan, rather than cut it off in response to Pakistan's nuclear developments. Perhaps with the end of the Cold War and the Persian Gulf War, the United States and its allies can focus their attention firmly on the proliferation problem. A coherent, self-consistent, and high-priority effort is urgently needed if the United States and it allies are to avert the growing vulnerability of civilian populations to attacks with weapons of mass destruction.